McGraw-Hill | Reading

Wonders

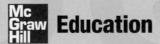 Education

Bothell, WA • Chicago, IL • Columbus, OH • New York, NY

 TextEvaluator.

ETS and the ETS logo are registered trademarks of Educational Testing Service (ETS).
TextEvaluator is a trademark of Educational Testing Service.

Cover and Title Pages: Nathan Love

www.mheonline.com/readingwonders

C

The McGraw·Hill Companies

 Education

Send all inquiries to:
McGraw-Hill Education
Two Penn Plaza
New York, New York 10121

Printed in China

7 8 9 DSS 17 16 15 14

McGraw-Hill Reading

Wonders

CCSS Reading/Language Arts Program

Program Authors

Dr. Diane August
Managing Director,
American Institutes for Research
Washington, D.C.

Dr. Donald Bear
Iowa State University
Ames, Iowa

Dr. Janice A. Dole
University of Utah
Salt Lake City, Utah

Dr. Jana Echevarria
California State University, Long Beach
Long Beach, California

Dr. Douglas Fisher
San Diego State University
San Diego, California

Dr. David J. Francis
University of Houston
Houston, Texas

Dr. Vicki Gibson
Educational Consultant
Gibson Hasbrouck and Associates
Wellesley, Massachusetts

Dr. Jan Hasbrouck
Educational Consultant
and Researcher
J.H. Consulting
Vancouver, Washington
Gibson Hasbrouck and Associates
Wellesley, Massachusetts

Margaret Kilgo
Educational Consultant
Kilgo Consulting, Inc.
Austin, Texas

Dr. Jay McTighe
Educational Consultant
Jay McTighe and Associates
Columbia, Maryland

Dr. Scott G. Paris
Vice President, Research
Educational Testing Service
Princeton, New Jersey

Dr. Timothy Shanahan
University of Illinois at Chicago
Chicago, Illinois

Dr. Josefina V. Tinajero
University of Texas at El Paso
El Paso, Texas

McGraw Hill Education

Bothell, WA • Chicago, IL • Columbus, OH • New York, NY

PROGRAM AUTHORS

Dr. Diane August

American Institutes for Research, Washington, D.C.

Managing Director focused on literacy and science for ELLs for the Education, Human Development and the Workforce Division

Dr. Donald R. Bear

Iowa State University

Professor, Iowa State University

Author of *Words Their Way, Words Their Way with English Learners, Vocabulary Their Way,* and *Words Their Way with Struggling Readers, 4–12*

Dr. Janice A. Dole

University of Utah

Professor, University of Utah

Director, Utah Center for Reading and Literacy

Content Facilitator, National Assessment of Educational Progress (NAEP)

CCSS Consultant to Literacy Coaches, Salt Lake City School District, Utah

Dr. Jana Echevarria

California State University, Long Beach

Professor Emerita of Education, California State University

Author of *Making Content Comprehensible for English Learners: The SIOP Model*

Dr. Douglas Fisher

San Diego State University

Co-Director, Center for the Advancement of Reading, California State University

Author of *Language Arts Workshop: Purposeful Reading and Writing Instruction* and *Reading for Information in Elementary School*

Dr. David J. Francis

University of Houston

Director of the Center for Research on Educational Achievement and Teaching of English Language Learners (CREATE)

Dr. Vicki Gibson

Educational Consultant Gibson Hasbrouck and Associates

Author of *Differentiated Instruction: Grouping for Success, Differentiated Instruction: Guidelines for Implementation,* and *Managing Behaviors to Support Differentiated Instruction*

Dr. Jan Hasbrouck

J.H. Consulting Gibson Hasbrouck and Associates

Developed Oral Reading Fluency Norms for Grades 1–8

Author of *The Reading Coach: A How-to Manual for Success* and *Educators as Physicians: Using RTI Assessments for Effective Decision-Making*

Margaret Kilgo

Educational Consultant Kilgo Consulting, Inc., Austin, TX

Developed Data-Driven Decisions process for evaluating student performance by standard

Member of Common Core State Standards Anchor Standards Committee for Reading and Writing

Dr. Scott G. Paris

Educational Testing Service,
Vice President, Research

Professor, Nanyang Technological
University, Singapore, 2008–2011

Professor of Education and Psychology,
University of Michigan, 1978–2008

Dr. Timothy Shanahan

University of Illinois at Chicago

Distinguished Professor, Urban Education

Director, UIC Center for Literacy

Chair, Department of Curriculum &
Instruction

Member, English Language Arts Work
Team and Writer of the Common Core
State Standards

President, International Reading
Association, 2006

Dr. Josefina V. Tinajero

University of Texas at El Paso

Dean of College of Education

President of TABE

Board of Directors for the American
Association of Colleges for Teacher
Education (AACTE)

Governing Board of the National Network
for Educational Renewal (NNER)

Consulting Authors

Kathy R. Bumgardner

National Literacy Consultant

Strategies Unlimited, Inc.
Gastonia, NC

Jay McTighe

Jay McTighe and Associates

Author of *The Understanding by Design
Guide to Creating High Quality Units* with
G. Wiggins; *Schooling by Design: Mission,
Action, Achievement* with G. Wiggins;
and *Differentiated Instruction and
Understanding By Design* with C. Tomlinson

Dr. Doris Walker-Dalhouse

Marquette University

Associate Professor, Department
of Educational Policy & Leadership

Author of articles on multicultural
literature, struggling readers, and
reading instruction in urban schools

Dinah Zike

Educational Consultant

Dinah-Might Activities, Inc.
San Antonio, TX

Program Reviewers

Kelly Aeppli-Campbell
Escambia County School District
Pensacola, FL

Marjorie J. Archer
Broward County Public Schools
Davie, FL

Whitney Augustine
Brevard Public Schools
Melbourne, FL

Antonio C. Campbell
Washington County School District
Saint George, UT

Helen Dunne
Gilbert Public School District
Gilbert, AZ

David P. Frydman
Clark County School District
Las Vegas, NV

Fran Gregory
Metropolitan Nashville Public Schools
Nashville, TN

Veronica Allen Hunt
Clark County School District
Las Vegas, NV

Michele Jacobs
Dee-Mack CUSD #701
Mackinaw, IL

LaVita Johnson Spears
Broward County Public Schools
Pembroke Pines, FL

Randall B. Kincaid
Sevier County Schools
Sevierville, TN

Matt Melamed
Community Consolidated School
   District 46
Grayslake, IL

Angela L. Reese,
Bay District Schools
Panama City, FL

Eddie Thompson
Fairfield City School District
Fairfield Township, OH

Patricia Vasseur Sosa
Miami-Dade County Public Schools
Miami, FL

Dr. Elizabeth Watson
Hazelwood School District
Hazelwood, MO

TEACHING WITH

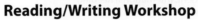

McGraw-Hill Reading

Wonders

Reading/Writing Workshop

- **Videos**
- **Photographs**
- **Interactive Graphic Organizers**

TEACH

Close Reading
Short Complex Texts

Minilessons
Comprehension
Strategies and Skills
Genre
Vocabulary Strategies
Writing Traits

Grammar Handbook

Reading/Writing Workshop

- **Visual Glossary**
- **Interactive Minilessons**
- **Interactive Graphic Organizers**

APPLY

Close Reading
Anchor Texts
Extended Complex Texts
Application of
Strategies and Skills

Literature Anthology

- **e Books**
- **Interactive Texts**
- **Listening Library**
- **English/Spanish Summaries**

Master the Common Core State Standards!

Leveled Readers

- e Books
- Interactive Texts
- Leveled Reader Search
- Listening Library
- Interactive Activities

DIFFERENTIATE

Leveled Readers
Small Group Instruction
with Differentiated Texts

Collection of Texts

- Online Research
- Writer's Workspace
- Interactive Group Projects

INTEGRATE

Research and Inquiry
Short and Sustained Research Projects

Text Connections
Reading Across Texts

 Write About Reading
Analytical Writing

 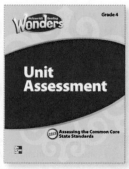  

Weekly Assessment **Unit Assessment** **Benchmark Assessment**

- Online Assessment
- Test Generator
- Reports

ASSESS

Weekly Assessment

Unit Assessment

Benchmark Assessment

PROGRAM COMPONENTS

Reading/Writing Workshop

Literature Anthology

Teacher Editions

Leveled Readers

Classroom Library Tradebooks

Your Turn Practice Book

Visual Vocabulary Cards

Leveled Workstation Activity Cards

CCSS Assessing the Common Core State Standards

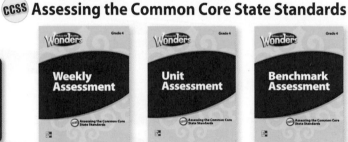

Sound-Spelling Cards

High-Frequency Word Cards

Response Board

Weekly Assessment

Unit Assessment

Benchmark Assessment

 Go Digital

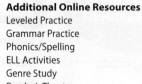

For the Teacher

For the Students

 Plan
Customizable Lesson Plans

 Assess
Online Assessments Reports and Scoring

 Professional Development
Lesson and CCSS Videos

 My To Do List
Assignments Assessment

 Words to Know
Build Vocabulary

 Teach
Classroom Presentation Tools Instructional Lessons

 Collaborate
Online Class Conversations Interactive Group Projects

Additional Online Resources
Leveled Practice
Grammar Practice
Phonics/Spelling
ELL Activities
Genre Study
Reader's Theater
Tier 2 Intervention

 Read
e Books
Interactive Texts

Play
Interactive Games

 Manage and Assign
Student Grouping and Assignments

 School to Home
Digital Open House Activities and Messages

Write
Interactive Writing

School to Home
Activities for Home
Messages from the Teacher
Class Wall of Student Work

www.connected.mcgraw-hill.com

viii

UNIT 1 CONTENTS

Unit Planning

Weekly Lessons

Writing Process — Genre Writing: Narrative Text

Model Lesson — Extended Complex Text

Close Reading Routine

Program Information

(t to b) Tim Macpherson/Stone+/Getty Images; Masterfile; Masterfile; Gunter Marx/Alamy; Echo/Cultura/Getty Images

UNIT OVERVIEW
Think It Through

Week 1	Week 2	Week 3
CLEVER IDEAS	**THINK OF OTHERS**	**TAKE ACTION**

READING

Week 1 — CLEVER IDEAS

ESSENTIAL QUESTION
Where do good ideas come from?

Build Background

CCSS Vocabulary
L.4.6 *brainstorm, flattened, frantically, gracious, muttered, official, original, stale*
Context Clues: Synonyms

CCSS Comprehension
RL.4.3 Strategy: Make Predictions
Skill: Sequence
Genre: Fairy Tale
Analytical Writing  Write About Reading

CCSS Phonics
RF.4.3a Short Vowels, Inflectional Endings

CCSS Fluency
RF.4.4b Intonation

Week 2 — THINK OF OTHERS

ESSENTIAL QUESTION
How do your actions affect others?

Build Background

CCSS Vocabulary
L.4.6 *accountable, advise, desperately, hesitated, humiliated, inspiration, self-esteem, uncomfortably*
Idioms

CCSS Comprehension
RL.4.3 Strategy: Make Predictions
Skill: Problem and Solution
Genre: Realistic Fiction
Analytical Writing Write About Reading

CCSS Phonics
RF.4.3a Long *a*, Inflectional Endings

CCSS Fluency
RF.4.4b Expression and Rate

Week 3 — TAKE ACTION

ESSENTIAL QUESTION
How do people respond to natural disasters?

Build Background

CCSS Vocabulary
L.4.6 *alter, collapse, crisis, destruction, hazard, severe, substantial, unpredictable*
Context Clues: Multiple-Meaning Words

CCSS Comprehension
RI.4.5 Strategy: Reread
Skill: Compare and Contrast
Genre: Expository Text
Analytical Writing Write About Reading

CCSS Phonics
RF.4.3a Long *e*, Plurals

CCSS Fluency
RF.4.4c Accuracy

LANGUAGE ARTS

Week 1

CCSS Writing
W.4.10 Trait: Ideas

CCSS Grammar
L.4.1f Sentences

CCSS Spelling
L.4.2d Short Vowels

CCSS Vocabulary
L.4.4a Build Vocabulary

Week 2

CCSS Writing
W.4.10 Trait: Ideas

CCSS Grammar
L.4.1f Subjects and Predicates

CCSS Spelling
L.4.2d Long *a*

CCSS Vocabulary
L.4.5b Build Vocabulary

Week 3

CCSS Writing
W.4.10 Trait: Ideas

CCSS Grammar
L.4.2c Compound Sentences

CCSS Spelling
L.4.2d Long *e*

CCSS Vocabulary
L.4.5b Build Vocabulary

 Writing Process **Genre Writing: Narrative** Friendly Letter T344–T349

Review and Assess

Week 4	Week 5	Week 6
IDEAS IN MOTION	**PUTTING IDEAS TO WORK**	

Week 4 — IDEAS IN MOTION

ESSENTIAL QUESTION
How can science help you understand how things work?

Build Background

CCSS Vocabulary
L.4.6 *accelerate, advantage, capabilities, friction, gravity, identity, inquiry, thrilling*
Context Clues: Definitions and Restatements

CCSS Comprehension
RI.4.5 Strategy: Reread
Skill: Cause and Effect
Genre: Narrative Nonfiction
Analytical Writing Write About Reading

CCSS Phonics
RF.4.3a Long *i*, Inflectional Endings

CCSS Fluency
RF.4.4b Phrasing and Rate

CCSS Writing
W.4.10 Trait: Organization

CCSS Grammar
L.4.1a Clauses and Complex Sentences

CCSS Spelling
L.4.2d Long *i*

CCSS Vocabulary
L.4.4a Build Vocabulary

Week 5 — PUTTING IDEAS TO WORK

ESSENTIAL QUESTION
How can starting a business help others?

Build Background

CCSS Vocabulary
L.4.6 *compassionate, enterprise, exceptional, funds, innovative, process, routine, undertaking*
Suffixes

CCSS Comprehension
RI.4.2 Strategy: Reread
Skill: Main Idea and Key Details
Genre: Persuasive Article
Analytical Writing Write About Reading

CCSS Phonics
RF.4.3a Long *o*, Compound Words

CCSS Fluency
RF.4.4b Phrasing and Rate

CCSS Writing
W.4.10 Trait: Sentence Fluency

CCSS Grammar
L.4.1f Run-On Sentences

CCSS Spelling
L.4.2d Long *o*

CCSS Vocabulary
L.4.4a Build Vocabulary

Week 6

CCSS Reader's Theater
RF.4.4a Focus on Vocabulary
Fluency: Intonation, Phrasing, Accuracy

CCSS Reading Digitally
SL.4.2 Notetaking
Skimming and Scanning
Navigating Links

CCSS Research and Inquiry
W.4.7 Parts of a Library
Unit Projects
Presentation of Ideas

Unit 1 Assessment

Unit Assessment
pages 1–27

Fluency Assessment
pages 182–191

CCSS Writing
SL.4.4 Publishing Celebrations
Portfolio Choice

Writing Process **Genre Writing: Narrative** Personal Narrative T350–T355

UNIT OPENER

Unit 1

Think It Through

The BIG Idea
How can a challenge bring out our best?

16

The Crow and the Pitcher

A thirsty crow was flying high above the hot, dry desert when she spied a broken pitcher. The top was sharp and jagged, but she saw that there was water in the bottom. She poked her beak into the pitcher but could not reach the water so she picked up a pebble and threw it at the pitcher hoping to smash it. The pebble fell into the pitcher, hitting the water with a plop.

The angry crow picked up another pebble and was about to throw it when she stopped. She flew to the pitcher and dropped the pebble inside.

Plop!

She dropped another pebble, and another, and another.

Plop! Plop! Plop!

With each pebble the water rose closer to the top. Soon the crow was able to drink the water.

17

READING/WRITING WORKSHOP, pp. 16–17

Reading/Writing Workshop

The Big Idea *How can a challenge bring out our best?*

Talk About It

Have students read the Big Idea aloud. Ask students to identify a time when they were challenged to solve a problem. Students may list small challenges at home and at school.

Ask: *How can a challenge help you learn new things?*

Have students discuss in partners or in groups, and then share their ideas with the class.

Music Links Introduce a song at the start of the unit. Go to www.connected. mcgraw-hill.com
Resources Media: Music to find audio recordings, song lyrics, and activities.

Read the Folktale: "The Crow and the Pitcher"

Read aloud "The Crow and the Pitcher." Ask students questions to explore the theme.

→ What is the crow's challenge?

→ Why does she keep dropping pebbles inside the pitcher?

→ What do the crow's actions say about her character?

Onomatopoeia Review that onomatopoeia, or sound words, emphasize the sound that something makes. Ask students to identify onomatopoeia in "The Crow and the Pitcher."

Moral Review that a moral is a lesson. Have students identify the moral of "The Crow and the Pitcher" and cite evidence to support it.

RESEARCH AND INQUIRY

Weekly Projects Each week students will produce a project related to the Essential Question. They will then develop one of these projects more fully for the Unit Research Project. Through their research, students will focus their attention on:

→ parts of a library and using a card catalog.

→ summarizing and categorizing information.

Shared Research Board You may wish to develop a Shared Research Board. Students can post questions, ideas, and information that they research about the unit theme. Students can post articles, illustrations, or information they gather as they do their research. They can also post notes with questions they have as they read the text.

> **WEEKLY PROJECTS**
> Students work in pairs or small groups.
> **Week 1** Interview a Classmate, T28
> **Week 2** Research the Effects of Human Actions, T92
> **Week 3** Make a Poster, T156
> **Week 4** Research a Topic, T220
> **Week 5** Research a Famous Business Owner, T284
>
> **WEEK 6**
> Students work in small groups to complete and present one of the following projects.
> → Give a Presentation
> → Create a Multimedia Presentation
> → Create a Newscast
> → Do an Experiment
> → Research a Business

 **Go Digital**

COLLABORATE
Post student questions and monitor student online discussions. Create a Shared Research Board.

Go Digital! www.connected.mcgraw-hill.com

WRITING

Analytical Writing

Write About Reading As students read and reread each week for close reading of text, students will take notes, cite evidence to support their ideas and opinions, write summaries of text, or develop character sketches.

Writing Every Day: Focus on Writing Traits

Each week, students will focus on a writing trait. After analyzing an expert and student model, students will draft and revise shorter writing entries in their Writer's Notebook, applying the trait to their writing.

Writing Process: Focus on Narrative Writing

Over the course of the unit, students will develop 1 to 2 longer narrative texts. Students will work through the various stages of the writing process, allowing them time to continue revising their writing and conferencing with peers and teacher.

> **WEEKLY WRITING TRAITS**
> **Week 1** Descriptive Details, T30
> **Week 2** Focus on an Event, T94
> **Week 3** Supporting Details, T158
> **Week 4** Sequence, T222
> **Week 5** Sentence Length, T286
>
> **GENRE WRITING: NARRATIVE TEXT**
> Choose one or complete both 2- to 3-week writing process lessons over the course of the unit.
> Friendly Letter, T344–T349
> Personal Narrative, T350–T355

  **Go Digital**

WRITER'S WORKSPACE
Ask students to work through their genre writing using the online tools for support.

Start Smart

Help your students to grow into critical readers, writers, and thinkers.

The Start Smart lessons provide an introduction to the key instructional routines and procedures that you will use throughout the year.

Use the first one to two weeks of school to model with students the key instructional routines and procedures for

- **Collaborative Conversations**
- **Vocabulary**
- **Accessing Complex Text**
- **Close Reading of Text**
- **Citing Text Evidence**
- **Decoding Multisyllabic Words**
- **Fluency**
- **Writing**
- **Writing About Reading**
- **Research and Inquiry**

During this time, use the Placement and Diagnostic Assessments to determine instructional and grouping needs for your students.

START SMART →

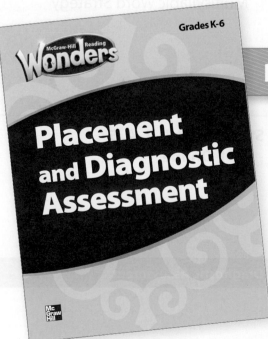

Start Smart 1–2 PDF Online

Close Reading of Literature

Where Have All the Fish Gone?
Use Text Evidence to understand:

- Genre: Folktale
- Story Structure
- Theme
- Point of View
- Cross-Text Comparisons

Close Reading of Informational Text

A Strange Disappearance
Use Text Evidence to understand:

- Genre: Informational Text
- Text Structure
- Main Idea and Key Details
- Author's Point of View
- Cross-Text Comparisons

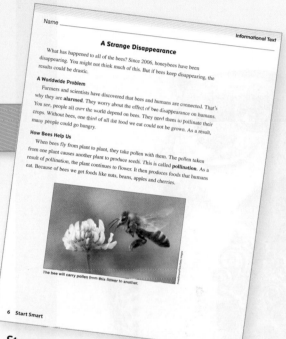

Start Smart 6–7 PDF Online

Placement and Diagnostic Assessment

Grades K-6

Wonders

Placement and Diagnostic Assessment

McGraw Hill

Assessment

- Fluency
- Comprehension
- Phonics
- Vocabulary
- Spelling
- Writing

Go Digital

www.connected.mcgraw-hill.com
all materials provided online

Suggested Lesson Plan

- **Introduce key instructional routines**
- **Establish classroom procedures**

DAYS 1–2	DAYS 3–4
Collaborative Conversations Procedures for participating in class discussions - Take Turns Talking - Listen Carefully - Add New Ideas **Vocabulary** Define/Example/Ask Routine Word Walls **Close Reading of Literature** Shared Reading of "Where Have All the Fish Gone?" **Genre:** Folktale	**Close Reading of Literature** Reread "Where Have All the Fish Gone?" Use Text Evidence to Understand - Genre - Story Structure - Theme - Point of View - Cross-Text Comparisons _Analytical Writing_ Write About Reading **Vocabulary** Context Clues Using a Thesaurus **Phonics and Decoding** Multisyllabic Word Strategy
Start Smart 1–3 PDF Online 	**Start Smart 1–2, 4, 5 PDF Online** 

Administer Placement and Diagnostic Assessment

☞ **Go** Digital

www.connected.mcgraw-hill.com

all materials provided online

DAYS 5–6	DAYS 7–8	DAYS 9–10

DAYS 5–6

Collaborative Conversations

Procedures for participating in class discussions

- Prepare for Discussions
- Ask and Answer Questions
- Take on Discussion Roles
- Be Open to All Ideas

Close Reading of Informational Text

Shared Reading of "A Strange Disappearance"

Genre: Expository Text

DAYS 7–8

Close Reading of Informational Text

Reread "A Strange Disappearance"

Use Text Evidence to Understand

- Main Idea and Key Details
- Text Structure
- Author's Point of View
- Cross-Text Comparisons

Analytical Writing Write About Reading

Vocabulary

Using a Dictionary or Glossary

Morphology

Phonics and Decoding

6 Syllable Types

Link to Spelling

Fluency

Fluency Routines

DAYS 9–10

Independent Reading

Independent Reading Routines

Writing

Analyze a writing model

Focus on revision assignments

Set up Writer's Notebooks

Integrate Ideas *Analytical Writing*

Research and Inquiry

Text Connections

Write About Reading

Start Smart 3, 6–7 PDF Online

Start Smart 4–8 PDF Online

Start Smart 6 PDF Online

Administer Placement and Diagnostic Assessment →

Introduce the Concept

 MINILESSON **10** Mins

Build Background

OBJECTIVES

 CCSS Come to discussions prepared, having read or studied required material; explicitly draw on that preparation and other information known about the topic to explore ideas under discussion. **SL.4.1a**

ACADEMIC LANGUAGE

• *cooperate, harmony*
• Cognates: *cooperar, armonía*

ESSENTIAL QUESTION

What discoveries can people make when they cooperate with others?

Tell students that throughout the year you will introduce them to new **weekly concepts** that they will discuss and read about. Explain that the weekly concept will be presented in the form of an Essential Question at the beginning of each week. Each selection they read during the week will help them gain a deeper understanding of the weekly concept so they can answer the essential question.

Write the **Essential Question** on the board and read it aloud. Show a picture from a textbook or magazine that shows people or animals working together. Explain that when people **cooperate**, they work together toward the same goal. They live together in **harmony,** or in friendly agreement. Discuss the topic of discoveries. Focus on what people discover about themselves and others when they work together.

→ When people live in harmony, they live side-by-side peacefully.

→ To live together peacefully, people must cooperate and do their part.

→ When people act greedy or do not do their share, harmony can be disrupted, or broken.

Talk About It

Explain that after students discuss the Essential Question, they will have the chance to Talk About It. In these activities, they will use **concept words**, words such as *cooperate* and *harmony* that are related to the topic of the selection, to discuss the Essential Question in pairs or groups. They will use the Concept Web on the **Graphic Organizer 61 Online PDF** to generate words and phrases related to the Essential Question. This is an opportunity to introduce students to academic language including domain-specific words or words related to the Essential Question of the week.

Ask: *What have you discovered about yourself by cooperating with someone? How can working together help you maintain harmony at home or in your community?* Have students discuss in pairs or groups.

→ Provide copies of **Graphic Organizer 61 Online PDF**. Model using the Concept Web to generate words and phrases related to teamwork, including *cooperate* and *harmony*. Add students' contributions.

COLLABORATE

Have partners continue the discussion by sharing what they have learned about teamwork. They can complete the Concept Webs, generating additional related words and phrases.

Collaborative Conversations

Distribute the **Speaking and Listening Checklists** from the **Teacher's Resource 97–98 Online PDF**. Explain that there are certain discussion guidelines students should follow to make sure they are being a respectful and active participant and listener.

Take Turns Talking Remind students to take turns speaking. As they engage in partner, small-group, and whole-class discussions, encourage them to follow these discussion rules. They should

→ wait for a speaker to finish before they speak. They should not speak over others.

→ quietly raise their hand to let others know they would like to speak.

→ ask others to tell their opinions so that all have a chance to share.

Listen Carefully Remind students to listen carefully to speakers. They should

→ always look at the person who is speaking.

→ respect others by not interrupting them.

→ repeat key ideas expressed to check understanding.

Add New Ideas Encourage students to add new ideas to their conversations. They should

→ stay on topic.

→ connect their own ideas to what their peers have said.

→ look for ways to connect their personal experiences or prior knowledge to the conversation.

Circulate and monitor students' conversations. Ask students to evaluate their discussions. Is their conversation staying on topic?

GRAPHIC ORGANIZER 61 Online PDF

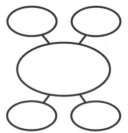

→ Vocabulary

Vocabulary Routine

MINILESSON 10 Mins

Explain that each week you will introduce words that students will find in many texts. Knowing these words will help them become better readers. When introducing conversational and academic Tier 2 and Tier 3 words, use the **Define/Example/Ask** routine. Describe the routine to students.

Define You will tell them the meaning of the word using student-friendly language—words they already know. (Example: The word *enormous* means "very big.")

Example You will give them an example of how the word is used, using their own common experiences. (Example: *Our school has an enormous gym. It is bigger than any other room in the school.*)

Ask You will ask them a question that helps them connect the word to known words and use the word in speaking. (Example: *What have you seen that is enormous? What words mean the same, or nearly the same, as* enormous? *What words mean the opposite of* enormous?) Through questions, you can observe if students understand a word's meaning.

Always have students pronounce the words multiple times throughout the instruction. They will also discuss meanings with a partner, which will give them opportunities to use words in speaking and listening.

Compare words that sound almost the same to help students avoid confusion. For example, when teaching *carnivore*, write *carnivore* and *carnival* on the board. Say each slowly. Have students repeat. Compare the spellings. Ask: *What's the same in both words? What's different?*

OBJECTIVES

CCSS Acquire and use accurately grade-appropriate general academic and domain-specific words and phrases, including those that signal precise actions, emotions, or states of being (e.g., *quizzed, whined, stammered*) and that are basic to a particular topic (e.g., *wildlife, conversation,* and *endangered* when discussing animal preservation). **L.4.6**

Go Digital

Where Have All the Fish Gone?
A Retelling of a Hawaiian Folktale

Hawaii there was a shark named Mano. Like n
the form of a human. He enjoyed life as a sha
He wanted to see a human village and find a hu
be a wise idea," warned his mother. "Humans r
ill, Mano wanted badly to see how humans lives
il.

Where Have All the Fish Gone?

Vocabulary Routine

Define: To **adapt** means to change.

Example: We had to adapt to our new class schedule when reading class was moved to the afternoon.

Ask: What have you had to adapt to? What words mean the same as *adapt*?

Define: To **succeed** means to achieve a goal.

Example: We all succeeded in passing this week's spelling test.

Ask: What is the opposite of succeeding?

MINILESSON
10 Mins

Building Vocabulary

Word Walls Word walls are an interactive tool for teaching vocabulary, spelling, and reading. Word walls can be used to help students

→ learn about words and how they work.

→ understand and use words in their reading, writing, and speaking.

→ recognize connections between words and identify common characteristics, such as words that are synonyms, words that have prefixes or suffixes, and words that share Greek or Latin roots.

→ expand their vocabularies and word usage.

How to Set Up a Word Wall To set up word walls, use a bulletin board or chart or even the side of a file cabinet to set up a main word wall and/or two or three smaller word walls.

→ Choose words from students' reading, including vocabulary, science, and social studies words. As you read "Where Have All the Fish Gone?" on **Start Smart 1–2 Online PDF**, pick six words for this week.

→ Handwrite or type each word on a separate piece of paper and place it on the word wall.

→ Introduce between five and ten new words each week. Try to include useful words that students might use in writing and speaking. Words can also be added to the wall as they are encountered.

→ Point out the new words, read them, and then have students spell them letter by letter.

→ As words become part of the students' active vocabulary, move them to a review board. Every few weeks, remove mastered words but retain ones that still need to be practiced.

→ Provide enough practice so that words are read and spelled automatically. Make sure that word-wall words are always spelled correctly in the student's daily writing.

Special word walls with a particular focus are also useful. Words can be grouped as high-frequency words, vivid verbs, colorful adjectives, homonyms, contractions, synonyms and antonyms, science and social studies words, or words with Greek and Latin roots.

Use the word wall daily to practice words, incorporating a variety of activities, such as identifying related words, playing the guessing game "What word am I?" or using domain-specific words to generate semantic maps.

Why It Matters

Three Tiers of Words

Tier 1 words are those commonly used in speech, such as *mom, table,* and *book.* At Grades 3–6, these words mainly appear in the high-frequency word review in Approaching Level Small Group instruction.

Tier 2 words are words found in many sources that have wide applicability, such as *compare, enormous,* and *vital.* A lack of knowledge of these words can severely hinder comprehension of text. Most vocabulary words are Tier 2 words.

Tier 3 words are those content-specific words that do not appear in many sources and can be taught at point of use, such as *lava, bipartisan,* and *Louisiana Purchase.* Tier 3 words are covered mainly through Access Complex Text features on domain-specific vocabulary.

Routine

Periodic Vocabulary Review

Repeated exposures are critical for learning new vocabulary. When vocabulary words are introduced, students encounter the words in multiple contexts. The words are always reviewed the next week in Build Vocabulary. In addition, you should do a periodic review of vocabulary words about twice per unit.

1. For a complete list of words introduced in each week, see the **Word Lists online PDF.**

2. Have students choose five to ten words and write sentences using the words. Then have partners discuss each other's work.

3. As needed, students can check the meanings or pronunciations of words using the online **Glossary**.

→ Shared Reading

Reading Literature: "Where Have All the Fish Gone?"

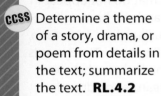

Where Have All the Fish Gone?
A Retelling of a Hawaiian Folktale

Many years ago in Hawaii there was a shark named Mano. Like many sharks back then, Mano could take the form of a human. He enjoyed life as a shark, but he wanted to experience more. He wanted to see a human village and find a human friend.

"Son, that may not be a wise idea," warned his mother. "Humans might not care for your shark habits." Still, Mano wanted badly to see how humans lived. He would just have to be very careful.

One day, while he swam near the shore, he heard a cry for help. It was a young woman named Makana. Makana swam in the ocean each morning. That particular day, the waves were rough. She could not get back to shore. Mano saw his chance! He took his human form and carefully rescued Makana from the rough water.

On the shore, Makana said, "Please tell me your name, kind stranger. How can I ever repay you?"

"I am Mano. I ask for no repayment other than a visit to your village."

"Of course! My friends and family will be grateful for the help you gave me."

That night, the caring villagers made a feast to celebrate Makana's rescue. There were plates piled with sweet fruit, boiled taro root, and fresh fish. Mano ate several helpings of fish. He was, after all, as hungry as a shark.

Online PDF

OBJECTIVES

CCSS Determine a theme of a story, drama, or poem from details in the text; summarize the text. **RL.4.2**

CCSS By the end of the year, read and comprehend literature, including stories, dramas, and poetry, in the grades 4–5 text complexity band proficiently, with scaffolding as needed at the high end of the range. **RL.4.10**

ACADEMIC LANGUAGE

complex text, genre

MINILESSON
10 Mins

Each week students will read a short literature or informational text. First you will read it together to understand what the author has to say. During the first reading, students can take notes on words they do not know or ideas or plot points that are not clear.

Distribute the folktale "Where Have All the Fish Gone?" on **Start Smart 1–2 Online PDF**. Read the story with students. Discuss the purpose and genre of the selection, and use these literature elements to analyze the text.

A C T Access Complex Text

► Purpose and Genre

Explain that folktales are tales passed down from one generation to the next. They often help readers understand the teller's culture. Tell students that the purpose of folktales is often to teach a lesson or explain something in nature. The lesson, or what the characters learn, and the explanation are sometimes stated at the end of the story. Discuss with students how the purpose of this folktale is to teach a lesson about how greediness can destroy a friendship. Readers can identify important details in the story that support the theme.

→ *How does Mano help Makana?* (He rescues her from rough water.)

→ *Why does Mano want to go to Makana's village?* (He wants to experience life as a human.)

→ *How does Mano take advantage of the villagers' friendship?* (After the villagers show Mano the best places to find fish, he takes the form of a shark and eats all the fish.)

→ *What happens as a result of Mano's greediness?* (The villagers do not have enough fish to eat.)

→ *What does Mano learn?* (He learns that greediness will destroy friendships.)

Go Digital

Where Have All the Fish Gone?
A Retelling of a Hawaiian Folktale

n Hawaii there was a shark named Mano. Like m ke the form of a human. He enjoyed life as a shar He wanted to see a human village and find a hur nt be a wise idea," warned his mother. "Humans till, Mano wanted badly to see how humans lives d.

Where Have All the Fish Gone?

A C T Access Complex Text

▶ Introduce Types of Complex Text

Tell students that this year they will encounter complex texts in a variety of genres that require them to read carefully and think deeply about what they are reading. They will need to read paragraph by paragraph, determine the meaning of unfamiliar words, and connect and make inferences about information and ideas as they go. To help students understand these complex texts, you may need to provide additional scaffolding.

Purpose The purpose of a text may be more complicated than simply to inform, entertain, or persuade. Students will need to determine where to focus their attention at any given time—on the characters, the setting, or the plot. They will need to recognize that the author has a perspective, or point of view, and may be more sympathetic to some characters than others.

Genre Different genres incorporate different literary elements and devices. Readers need to attend to these to comprehend the text fully. Students need to understand the "rules" for fictional genres. For example, they should recognize that folktales have a message and the characters' actions reveal that message.

Organization Students may need to understand how a text is organized in order to find evidence within the text. In narratives, students may find that stories do not follow a linear sequence. Stories may include literary devices such as foreshadowing and flashbacks that interrupt the sequence.

Connection of Ideas When reading complex fictional texts, students need to make inferences and synthesize information throughout the text. They must recognize that the characters' actions and motivations may be implied rather than explicit.

Sentence Structure Complex sentence structures, such as dialogue or formal and informal language, may be challenging for students and require close reading.

Specific Vocabulary Fiction texts may include idioms, similes, metaphors, regionalisms, and concept words that require students to use a dictionary, context clues, or knowledge of word parts.

Prior Knowledge Complex fiction texts may assume a level of prior knowledge that students may not have. Students may need more cultural/historical background, as well as an understanding of human emotions, to comprehend characters' feelings and actions.

Routine

Close Reading

1. Students read the story once carefully, paying attention to what happens in the plot. They should take notes about anything they don't understand.

2. Students reread and discuss important shorter passages from the story. They should generate questions about character traits and how the traits affect the events in the story. Then they should work with partners or small groups to answer the questions using text evidence.

3. Students write about what they have read. They may analyze how the characters' actions affect the plot or write an opinion about some aspect of the story. Remind them that they need to support their ideas with text evidence.

START SMART 1–2 Online PDF

Where Have All the Fish Gone?

A Retelling of a Hawaiian Folktale

Many years ago in Hawaii there was a shark named Mano. Like many sharks back then, Mano could take the form of a human. He enjoyed life as a shark, but he wanted to experience more. He wanted to see a human village and find a human friend.

"Son, that may not be a wise idea," warned his mother. "Humans might not care for your shark habits." Still, Mano wanted badly to see how humans lived. He would just have to be very careful.

One day, while he swam near the shore, he heard a cry for help. It was a young woman named Makana. Makana swam in the ocean each morning. That particular day, the waves were rough. She could not get back to shore. Mano saw his chance! He took his human form and carefully rescued Makana from the rough water.

On the shore, Makana said, "Please tell me your name, kind stranger. How can I ever repay you?"

"I am Mano. I ask for no repayment other than a visit to your village."

"Of course! My friends and family will be grateful for the help you gave me."

That night, the caring villagers made a feast to celebrate Makana's rescue. There were plates piled with sweet fruit, boiled taro root, and fresh fish. Mano ate several helpings of fish. He was, after all, as hungry as a shark.

Comprehension

Genre and Story Structure

Where Have All the Fish Gone?
A Retelling of a Hawaiian Folktale

Many years ago in Hawaii there was a shark named Mano. Like many sharks back then, Mano could take the form of a human. He enjoyed life as a shark, but he wanted to experience more. He wanted to see a human village and find a human friend.

"Son, that may not be a wise idea," warned his mother. "Humans might not care for your shark habits." Still, Mano wanted badly to see how humans lived. He would just have to be very careful.

One day, while he swam near the shore, he heard a cry for help. It was a young woman named Makana. Makana swam in the ocean each morning. That particular day, the waves were rough. She could not get back to shore. Mano saw his chance! He took his human form and carefully rescued Makana from the rough water.

On the shore, Makana said, "Please tell me your name, kind stranger. How can I ever repay you?"

"I am Mano. I ask for repayment other than a visit to your village."

"Of course! My friends and family will be grateful for the help you gave me."

That night, the caring villagers made a feast to celebrate Makana's rescue. There were plates piled with sweet fruit, boiled taro root, and fresh fish. Mano ate several helpings of fish. He was, after all, as hungry as a shark.

Online PDF

OBJECTIVES

CCSS Refer to details and examples in a text when explaining what the text says explicitly and when drawing inferences from the text. **RL.4.1**

CCSS Describe in depth a character, setting, or event in a story or drama, drawing on specific details in the text (e.g., a character's thoughts, words, or actions). **RL.4.3**

CCSS Explain major differences between poems, drama, and prose, and refer to structural elements of poems (e.g., verse, rhythm, meter) and drama (e.g., casts of characters, settings, descriptions, dialogue, stage directions) when writing or speaking about a text. **RL.4.5**

ACADEMIC LANGUAGE
character, setting, plot

1 Explain

Genre Tell students that throughout the year they will be learning more about different fiction **genres**. Knowing the characteristics of a genre will help them predict the kinds of information the author will provide as they read. This year fourth graders will learn the structural elements of fairy tales, folktales, fantasies, historical fiction, and tall tales, as well as realistic fiction. Students will also compare and contrast the themes, topics, and patterns of events in stories, myths, and traditional literature from different cultures.

Distribute the Genres chart on **Start Smart 3 Online PDF**. Review the names of the fiction genres; then help students list key characteristics for each. Tell students that as they read new stories, they will be recording examples of each genre type and adding to the list of characteristics.

Story Structure Tell students that story structure refers to the way the author has organized the events in the plot using three basic story elements: character, setting, and plot. When analyzing story structure, readers focus on those elements.

→ **Character** A character is a person or animal in a story. To understand a character, readers must pay attention to what the author directly states about the character; what the character does, says, and thinks; and how the character reacts to other characters. Tell students that this year they will pay special attention to describing characters based on the characters' thoughts, words, or actions.

→ **Setting** The setting is where and when the story takes place. Readers analyze the setting to see how it affects the way characters behave and how it can influence or limit plot events. This year, students will describe the setting in depth, using specific details in the text.

→ **Plot** The plot is the series of events that take place in a story. Readers study plot to better understand what happens and why it happens. Tell students that they will be identifying plot events in the stories and identifying how characters' actions contribute to those events. They will also compare plots and patterns of events in stories, myths, and traditional literature.

2 Model Close Reading: Text Evidence

Explain that close reading is reading carefully and paying attention to the details. The purpose of close reading is not just to summarize or find the main idea. Close reading requires readers to analyze and evaluate what they read to make decisions about the genre and the story's structure.

Make Inferences Explain that authors do not always tell readers everything that takes place in a story, so readers must put together details to figure out what is happening. Using the details as clues, readers must make inferences about what is not stated in the text.

Cite Text Evidence Tell students that citing text evidence is using evidence or examples from the text to support answers and inferences. Explain that as students answer questions, they will be asked to directly quote the section of the text that they used to answer the question or to make an inference. In a fiction text, they might use a character's words or actions or an author's description as text evidence. Point out that students must do close reading to cite evidence directly from the text.

Genre Reread "Where Have All the Fish Gone?" on **Start Smart 1–2 Online PDF**. Have students identify two characteristics that show "Where Have All the Fish Gone?" is a folktale.

Character, Setting, Plot Reread paragraph 1. Ask: *What problem does Mano have?* Model close reading and citing text evidence.

Think Aloud To answer this question, I read closely and pay attention to details about Mano. Mano's problem is that he's curious about human life and wants to find a human friend. Here is the evidence that shows me the problem: "He enjoyed life as a shark, but he wanted to experience more. He wanted to see a human village and find a human friend." This evidence shows that Mano's problem is that he wants to experience life as a human and find a human friend.

3 Guided Practice of Close Reading

Reread Reread paragraphs 2 and 3 with students. Ask: *What do Mano's actions tell you about his character? Make an inference.* (Mano is determined and doesn't listen to advice. Mano's mother warns him about befriending humans. "Still, Mano wanted badly to see how humans lived. He would just have to be very careful." When Makana could not get back to shore, "Mano saw his chance!")

Continue close reading of the story; help students identify more character actions and key events. Guide students to read closely to make inferences about characters and events using text evidence.

Why It Matters

Text Evidence

Students will be expected to read more closely in order to accurately comprehend and gain knowledge from text. Asking and answering text-dependent questions focuses students on the details in the text. Close reading of text requires that students reread to find evidence in the text to support any inferences or predictions the students make while reading and to evaluate arguments made in the text.

Students must be taught and have many opportunities to practice the thinking required for locating relevant and accurate text evidence to support their answers in both discussions and writing tasks. Students need to be able to show that they can find the details of what is explicitly stated and can make logical inferences beyond what is explicitly stated in the text.

START SMART 3 Online PDF

Genres

Type	Key Characteristics	Examples
Adventure		
Drama (Play)		
Fable		
Fairy Tale		
Fantasy		
Folktale		
Historical Fiction		
Legend		
Myth		
Poetry		
Realistic Fiction		
Science Fiction		
Autobiography		
Biography		
Expository		
Narrative Nonfiction		
Technical/Procedural		

→ Comprehension

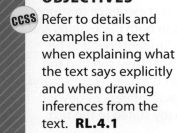
Online PDF

OBJECTIVES

CCSS Refer to details and examples in a text when explaining what the text says explicitly and when drawing inferences from the text. **RL.4.1**

CCSS Determine a theme of a story, drama, or poem from details in the text; summarize the text. **RL.4.2**

CCSS Compare and contrast the point of view from which different stories are narrated, including the difference between first- and third-person narrations. **RL.4.6**

ACADEMIC LANGUAGE

• *point of view, theme*
• Cognates: *punto de vista, tema*

MINILESSON
10 Mins

Theme and Point of View

1 Explain

Tell students that as good readers read narrative texts, they go beyond character, setting, and plot to analyze theme and point of view. Focusing on these elements and making inferences will help students read more closely and will deepen their understanding.

→ **Theme** The theme is the overall lesson or message an author wants to express through the story. Usually readers will need to **make inferences** to determine the theme. They will put together the important details of a story, decide what the message is, and use the details to paraphrase the theme. Readers should read the entire story before determining the theme.

→ **Point of View** In fiction, point of view refers to who is telling the story and how he or she presents events. In a first-person narrative, the reader sees events from one character's perspective. In a third-person narrative, the narrator may present the feelings of one or all the characters. In Grade 4, students will distinguish between first- and third-person narratives and will identify specific details about point of view.

→ **Make Inferences** As students determine the theme and point of view, they will need to make inferences. To make an inference, they will use important details in the text to determine information that the author does not state in the story.

2 Model Close Reading: Text Evidence

Reread Reread the dialogue between Makana and Mano on PDF page 1. Tell students to focus on how the dialogue shows the turning point of the story—Mano is about to get to experience human life. Model how to do a close reading of a literature text.

Paraphrase During the year students may be asked to answer a question by paraphrasing part of the text. Explain that paraphrasing means to restate text in your own words. It helps you make sure you understand what you read. Model paraphrasing the dialogue.

Think Aloud I might paraphrase this way: When Makana got to shore, she asked "What can I do to return your favor?" Mano said, "I am Mano. All I want is to visit your village." Makana replied, "Sure! My friends and family will be thankful to you for saving me."

3 Guided Practice of Close Reading

Theme Review Mano's actions in paragraph eight on top of PDF page 2. Model citing text evidence to make an inference about theme.

Think Aloud Mano goes to the secret place and carelessly gobbles up fish. I can make the inference that the theme of this story is going to be about the effects of greediness. I can support this inference with evidence from the text. The text says, "He knew it was greedy, but he could not help himself!" This hints that Mano knows he is doing something wrong and will probably learn a lesson from it.

Reread Reread the final paragraphs. Ask: *What is the theme of this story? Make an inference. Cite text evidence to support your inference.* (*Answer* I infer that the theme of this story is this: Greed can destroy a friendship. *Evidence* Mano says, "If I had not been so greedy, Makana would still be my friend." The text also says, "To this day, sharks know that it is their greedy habits that cost them friendship with humans.")

Point of View Reread paragraph 1 on PDF page 1. Ask: *From what point of view is this story being told? How do you know?* Model how to cite text evidence to determine the point of view.

Think Aloud This story is told by a third-person narrator. The text says, "Mano could take the form of a human. He enjoyed life as a shark, but he wanted to experience more." Mano is not the narrator. The narrator is someone outside of the story who knows how Mano feels.

Reread Reread paragraph 2: Ask: *What is Mano's mother's point of view about his idea?* (*Answer* Mano's mother does not think it is a good idea for Mano to become friends with humans. *Evidence* Mano's mother says, "Son, that may not be a wise idea…. Humans might not care for your shark habits.") Discuss how the story might differ if Mano told it.

Write About Reading: Summarize Ask pairs of students to work together to write a summary of "Where Have All the Fish Gone?" Select pairs to share their summaries with the class.

Compare Across Texts Explain that when students compare across texts, they look for similarities and differences in the way that themes, topics, and patterns of events are treated. In Grade 4, students will compare stories, myths, and traditional literature from different cultures.

Ask students to compare the passage with a classic folktale from another culture that has a similar theme. Have students summarize the plots of each story. Then help them state the theme of each story. Guide students to identify similarities and differences in how the shared theme is expressed.

→ Vocabulary Strategy

Where Have All the Fish Gone?
A Retelling of a Hawaiian Folktale

Many years ago in Hawaii there was a shark named Mano. Like many sharks back then, Mano could take the form of a human. He enjoyed life as a shark, but he wanted to experience more. He wanted to see a human village and find a human friend.

"Son, that may not be a wise idea," warned his mother. "Humans might not care for your shark habits." Still, Mano wanted badly to see how humans lived. He would just have to be very careful.

One day, while he swam near the shore, he heard a cry for help. It was a young woman named Makana. Makana swam in the ocean each morning. That particular day, the waves were rough. She could not get back to shore. Mano saw his chance! He took his human form and carefully rescued Makana from the rough water.

On the shore, Makana said, "Please tell me your name, kind stranger. How can I ever repay you?"

"I am Mano. I ask for no repayment other than a visit to your village."

"Of course! My friends and family will be grateful for the help you gave me."

That night, the caring villagers made a feast to celebrate Makana's rescue. There were plates piled with sweet fruit, boiled taro root, and fresh fish. Mano ate several helpings of fish. He was, after all, as hungry as a shark.

Online PDF

OBJECTIVES

CCSS Determine or clarify the meaning of unknown and multiple-meaning words and phrases based on grade 4 reading and content, choosing flexibly from a range of strategies. Use context (e.g., definitions, examples, or restatements in text) as a clue to the meaning of a word or phrase. **L.4.4a**

CCSS Determine or clarify the meaning of unknown and multiple-meaning words and phrases based on grade 4 reading and content, choosing flexibly from a range of strategies. Consult reference materials (e.g., dictionaries, glossaries, thesauruses), both print and digital, to find the pronunciation and determine or clarify the precise meaning of key words and phrases. **L.4.4c**

Context Clues

1 Explain

Students can sometimes use the words surrounding a new, unfamiliar word to figure out its meaning. This is a good strategy to use when reading alone, especially when a dictionary or glossary is not readily available. Emphasize that students will not always find context clues for an unknown word. Also point out that words or phrases that seem to be clues can sometimes be misleading.

2 Model

Explain the following types of context clues.

→ **Definition** The author provides a direct definition of an unfamiliar word, right in the sentence. The signal words *is, are, means,* and *refers to* are used.

→ **Appositive or Restatement** An appositive or restatement is a word or phrase that comes right after an unfamiliar word and that defines or explains the unfamiliar word. It is set off by commas and often begins with the signal word *or*.

→ **Synonym** The author uses another word or phrase that is similar in meaning or can be compared to the unfamiliar word. The signal words *also, as, identical, like, likewise, resembling, same, similarly,* and *too* may be used.

→ **Antonym** The author uses another word or phrase that means the opposite of, or is in contrast to, an unfamiliar word. The signal words *but, however, in contrast, instead of, on the other hand, though,* and *unlike* may be used.

→ **Example** The author gives several words or ideas that are examples of the unfamiliar word. The signal words *for example, for instance, including, like,* and *such as* may be used.

→ **Sentence and Paragraph** The author provides clues to the word's meaning in the surrounding words and sentences.

Model using paragraph clues to figure out the meaning of *lagoon* in the eighth paragraph on the top of **Start Smart 2 Online PDF**.

3 Guided Practice

Write the Example Sentences in the Context Clues box. Help students use context clues to figure out the meaning of the word in italics.

Go Digital

Where Have All the Fish Gone?
A Retelling of a Hawaiian Folktale

Where Have All the Fish Gone?

Dictionary Entry

Thesaurus Entry

Thesaurus

MINILESSON
10 Mins

Using a Thesaurus

1 Explain

Tell students the following:

→ A **thesaurus** is a print or digital reference source that lists words and their **synonyms**, or words with similar meanings, and **antonyms**, or words with opposite meanings.

→ The word that you look up in a thesaurus is called the **entry word**. Entry words are usually listed in alphabetical order. Some thesauruses are organized by concept or category.

→ **Guide words** show the first and last entries on each page.

→ Some entries include a **cross-reference** that will guide you to other words with similar or opposite meanings.

→ Students can use synonyms and antonyms to make their writing more vivid, precise, and interesting.

2 Model

Use **Thesaurus Entry** on **Start Smart 4 Online PDF** to identify parts of a thesaurus. Model how to use a thesaurus, such as how to look up a synonym for a word and use it to revise your writing. Point out how readers can also use a thesaurus to expand their understanding of related words. Explain that a thesaurus lists words with similar meanings. However, the words in one entry represent **shades of meaning**. Display the word pairs *depressed/sad* and *happy/ecstatic*. Point out that *depressed* is an extreme form of *sad* and *ecstatic* is an extreme form of *happy*. When using a thesaurus, remind students to choose the word that best represents the shade of meaning they want to express.

3 Guided Practice

Have students use a grade-appropriate print or online thesaurus to look up *greedy*. Have them list the related words and discuss how the meanings differ. Then have students use the words in sentences to show the shades of meaning.

Context Clues

Example Sentences

1. A *predator* is an animal that hunts other animals for food.

2. The bones of the *enormous*, or very large, dinosaur are being moved to the museum.

3. The *cougar*, like other big cats, eats mostly small animals.

4. Unlike most animals that hunt during the day, *nocturnal* animals hunt only at night.

5. We are reading about *mammals*, such as apes, cows, horses, and whales.

6. The parrots had to *adapt* to their changing environment. They moved to a deeper part of the forest, where trees were not being cut down. They also began eating different plants and insects.

START SMART 4 Online PDF

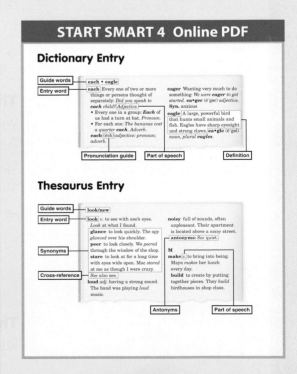

Phonics/Word Study

MINILESSON 10 Mins

Multisyllabic Word Strategy

Go Digital

Decoding

OBJECTIVES

CCSS Know and apply grade-level phonics and word analysis skills in decoding words. Use combined knowledge of all letter-sound correspondences, syllabication patterns, and morphology (e.g., roots and affixes) to read accurately unfamiliar multisyllabic words in context and out of context. **RF.4.3a**

ACADEMIC LANGUAGE

- *prefix, suffix, multisyllabic*
- Cognates: *prefijo, sufijo*

1 Explain

Explain to students that they will be reading many unfamiliar words this year. You will be helping them decode, or sound out, these words in context and use word parts to determine each word's meaning. To help them, you will use a consistent Decoding Strategy that will make reading these unfamiliar multisyllabic words easier.

2 Model

Distribute copies of the **Decoding Strategy Chart** on **Start Smart 5 Online PDF**. Then do the following:

→ Write the word *rebuilding* on the board in a sentence. Do not pronounce the word.

→ Have students read aloud Step 1 of the Decoding Strategy: *Look for word parts (prefixes) at the beginning of the word.*

Think Aloud Let's look at this word. It is spelled *r-e-b-u-i-l-d-i-n-g*. This is a long word. To help me read it, I will look for parts of the word that I know. I start by looking at the beginning. In this word I see the prefix *re-*. A **prefix** is a word part that always appears at the beginning of a word. It changes the meaning of the word. The prefix *re-* means "again." Let's underline the prefix *re-*. I have seen this prefix in many words, such as *remake* and *reheat*.

→ Have students read aloud Step 2 of the Decoding Strategy: *Look for word parts (suffixes) at the end of the word.*

Think Aloud Then I look at the end of the word. Many common word parts appear at the end of a word. These are called suffixes. A **suffix** can change the meaning of a word and often its part of speech. For example, it can change a noun, such as *boat*, into a verb, such as *boating*. I see the common suffix *-ing* at the end of this word.

→ Have students read aloud Step 3 of the Decoding Strategy: *In the base word, look for familiar spelling patterns.* Have students think about what they know about syllables, and point out you will be reviewing the six syllable types later in Start Smart. Use the Decoding Multisyllable Words Routine on page S18 as necessary.

Think Aloud All that's left in this word are the letters *b-u-i-l-d*. These letters form the word *build*. That's a word I already know how to read.

→ Have students read aloud Step 4 of the Decoding Strategy: *Sound out and blend together the word parts.*

Think Aloud Let's put the word parts together: re-build-ing.

→ Have students read aloud Step 5 of the Decoding Strategy: *Say the word parts fast. Adjust your pronunciation as needed. Ask yourself: "Is this a word I've heard before?" Then read the word in the sentence and ask: "Does it make sense in this sentence?"*

Think Aloud Now I will say the word parts quickly: *rebuilding*. That's a word I have heard before. I know they were rebuilding the homes destroyed by the earthquake. Using the word parts, I can also figure out what the word means. Since *re-* means "again," I can figure out that *rebuilding* means "building again."

3 Guided Practice

Students can use the decoding strategy to help them monitor accuracy in their decoding as they read words with prefixes and suffixes in context. Guide students in using the Decoding Strategy Chart on **Start Smart 5 Online PDF** to read these and other words: *uncooked, rewinding, disappeared, preordered, undercooked.*

Word Building

Tell students that they will have an opportunity to work with word parts to see how many words they can form. Display the following **Word-Building Cards**: *un, re, ed, ing, ful, chain, block, fill, call, color.*

Ask students to do the following:

→ Read each syllable.

→ Ask yourself: *Does this syllable normally appear at the beginning of a word, at the end, or somewhere in the middle?*

→ Then use the word parts to form words. Once you make a real word—a word you have heard before—record it on your paper. See how many words you can make.

Routine

Decoding Multisyllable Words
Use this routine to help students decode multisyllable words using syllable patterns.

1. Explain that every syllable has a vowel sound. Introduce a syllable pattern. Model decoding a sample word with the pattern.

2. Have students practice reading syllables and simple words with the syllable pattern. Review previously taught syllable types.

3. Write more syllables and words containing the syllables on the board. For example, *can* and *candle*. Help students blend the word parts and the whole words.

4. Have students build words using the new syllable type using Word Building Cards.

5. Have students use the Decoding Strategy Chart to help them decode longer, more complex multisyllabic words.

START SMART 5 Online PDF

Decoding Strategy Chart

Step 1	Look for word parts (prefixes) at the beginning of the word.
Step 2	Look for word parts (suffixes) at the end of the word.
Step 3	In the base word, look for familiar spelling patterns. Think about the six syllable-spelling patterns you have learned.
Step 4	Sound out and blend together the word parts.
Step 5	Say the word parts fast. Adjust your pronunciation as needed. Ask yourself: "Is this a word I have heard before?" Then read the word in the sentence and ask: "Does it make sense in this sentence?"

Introduce the Concept

10 Mins
MINILESSON

Build Background

OBJECTIVES

 CCSS Come to discussions prepared, having read or studied required material; explicitly draw on that preparation and other information known about the topic to explore ideas under discussion. **SL.4.1a**

 CCSS Review the key ideas expressed and explain their own ideas and understanding in light of the discussion. **SL.4.1d**

ACADEMIC LANGUAGE

• *observing, interdependence*

• Cognate: *observando*

ESSENTIAL QUESTION

What can you discover by observing nature?

Write the **Essential Question** on the board and read it aloud. Show a picture from a textbook or magazine that shows an animal's home. Tell students that **observing** is watching someone or something closely. Discuss the topic of **interdependence**. Focus on the way that plants, animals, and humans depend on one another.

→ Plants and animals in an ecosystem are connected. They depend on one another for survival.

→ Human actions can affect the environment. Pollution, building, hunting, and fishing can all impact plants and animals.

→ If one plant or animal disappears or dies out, it affects other plants and animals.

→ Closely observing nature can help us discover how our actions are affecting the environment and what we can do to help.

Talk About It

COLLABORATE

Tell students that after they discuss the Essential Question, they will have the chance to Talk About It. In these activities, they will use concept words, which are words related to the topic of the selection, to discuss the Essential Question in pairs or groups. They will use the Concept Web on the **Graphic Organizer 61 Online PDF** to generate words and phrases related to the Essential Question. Review the words *observing* and *interdependence* and use this opportunity to introduce students to academic language including domain-specific words or words related to the Essential Question of the week.

Ask: *What are some examples of interdependence you have discovered by observing your environment?* Have students discuss this question in pairs or groups.

Go Digital

Use Graphic Organizer

→ Distribute copies of the Concept Web on **Graphic Organizer 61 Online PDF**. Model using the Concept Web to generate words related to discoveries in nature. Add students' contributions.

Have partners continue the discussion by sharing what they have learned about discoveries they can make in nature. They can complete the Concept Webs, generating additional words and phrases.

Collaborative Conversations

Review the Speaking and Listening Checklists from the **Teacher's Resource 97–98 Online PDF**. Remind students that, during partner, small-group, and whole-class discussions, they should follow guidelines to make sure they are prepared to participate actively.

Prepare for Discussions Before they come to a discussion, students should make sure they are prepared. They should

→ read or study the material being discussed before coming.

→ use preparation and knowledge about the topic to explore discussion ideas.

Ask and Answer Questions As students engage in discussions, encourage them to ask and answer questions. They should

→ ask questions to clarify ideas or follow up on information.

→ wait after asking a question to give others a chance to respond.

→ answer questions with complete ideas.

Take on Discussion Roles Encourage students to take on roles to help keep the discussion on track. Assigned roles can include

→ a questioner who asks questions that keep the discussion moving and makes sure everyone gets a turn.

→ a recorder who takes notes and reports to the class.

Be Open to All Ideas Remind students to be open to all ideas. They should

→ understand that all ideas and questions are important and should be heard.

→ respect others' opinions yet not hesitate to offer a different opinion.

→ explain their own ideas and insights in light of the discussion.

Circulate and monitor students' conversations. Ask students to evaluate their conversations. Had they prepared sufficiently? Were they accepting of others' ideas?

Why It Matters

Collaborative Conversations

Students need many opportunities to engage in a variety of structured conversations about text and topics they are learning about. These discussions should take place in various settings, including whole class, small group and partner conversations. The discussions should engage students in meaningful dialogue that allows them to use their academic and domain-specific language and concepts as well as learn more about the topic being explored.

Participation in these conversations requires specific expectations on the part of the student as both speaker and listener. Students must learn to contribute relevant and accurate new information by staying on topic, respond to and develop ideas that others have contributed, and summarize and synthesize various ideas. At times, participating in a specific conversation requires that students prepare for the discussion by reading ahead of time or gathering specific information.

GRAPHIC ORGANIZER 61 Online PDF

→ # Shared Reading

The bee will carry pollen from this flower to another.

Online PDF

OBJECTIVES

CCSS Describe the overall structure (e.g., chronology, comparison, cause/effect, problem/solution) of events, ideas, concepts, or information in a text or part of a text. **RI.4.5**

CCSS By the end of year, read and comprehend informational texts, including history/social studies, science, and technical texts, in the grades 4–5 text complexity band proficiently, with scaffolding as needed at the high end of the range. **RI.4.10**

ACADEMIC LANGUAGE

organization, sentence structure, cause and effect

Reading Informational Text: "A Strange Disappearance"

MINILESSON 10 Mins

Distribute the expository text "A Strange Disappearance" on **Start Smart 6–7 Online PDF**. Read the text with students. Discuss the organization and sentence structure in the selection and use these elements to analyze the text.

A C T **A**ccess **C**omplex **T**ext

▶ **Organization and Sentence Structure**

Explain that identifying a text structure helps students know what to look for as they read. If they see cause-and-effect signal words as they read, they can expect that information will be presented as causes and effects. In "A Strange Disappearance," the author uses causes and effects to show readers the effects of the bees disappearing.

→ In "A Worldwide Problem" what might be the effect of bees disappearing? (People could go hungry.) What phrase helps you recognize the cause-and-effect text structure? *(As a result)*

→ The text says that as a result of pollination, plants continue to flower. Is pollination the cause or the effect of plants continuing to flower? (the cause)

Explain that when sentences in expository text are not clear or have unfamiliar structures, such as rhetorical questions, students will need to read carefully and think about what the author is saying. Read aloud the first sentence of the passage. Ask: *Is this the reader's question or the narrator's question?* (the narrator's) Explain that the narrator does not expect readers to answer the question. Instead, he or she is using the question to focus readers' attention on the information that follows.

Point out the second paragraph. Have a student read the fifth sentence aloud. Ask:

→ When the author writes, "They need them to pollinate their crops. . .," does *they* refer to the people or the bees? (the people)

Go Digital

A Strange Disappearance

d to all of the bees? Since 2006, honeybees have ight not think much of this. But if bees keep disappear ic.

m

tists have discovered that bees and humans are c d. They worry about the effect of bee disappear

A Strange Disappearance

A C T Access Complex Text

▶ Discuss Types of Complex Text

Explain that this year students will encounter complex nonfiction texts that require them to read carefully and think deeply about what they are reading. They will need to read paragraph by paragraph, determine the meaning of unfamiliar words, and connect and make inferences about ideas as they go. You may need to provide additional scaffolding to help students.

Purpose In narrative nonfiction, students may be unsure whether to focus on a real person's feelings and actions or on factual information. This ACT can help clarify students' focus. It can also help students explore and make inferences about the author's purpose in an informational text when it is not clearly stated.

Genre Informational text, especially in science and social studies/history, requires students to recognize text features, signal words, and text structure. This ACT can help students recognize specific features in informational texts and how to use them to comprehend what they are reading better. It can help them understand how to read complex science and social studies texts.

Organization When an informational text lacks signal words or uses more than one text structure, students may need support in determining the organization in order to find text evidence. This ACT supports students by pointing out text structures and how they are used to give information.

Connection of Ideas Informational text usually includes several important ideas and details. This ACT shows students how to link specific information together to find the essential idea.

Sentence Structure Nonfiction texts often include long, dense sentences. This ACT may show students how to interpret difficult sentences or how to break them into more understandable forms.

Specific Vocabulary Nonfiction texts may be filled with sophisticated academic language and domain-specific words and jargon that students do not know. There may not be adequate context for them to infer the meaning. This ACT will support students by showing them how to use other vocabulary strategies, such as identifying word parts or using a dictionary.

Prior Knowledge Informational texts may contain domain-specific information that students lack the prior knowledge to comprehend. This ACT will provide background information that provides support for domain-specific ideas and details in the text.

START SMART 6–7 Online PDF

A Strange Disappearance

What has happened to all of the bees? Since 2006, honeybees have been disappearing. You might not think much of this. But if bees keep disappearing, the results could be drastic.

A Worldwide Problem

Farmers and scientists have discovered that bees and humans are connected. That's why they are **alarmed**. They worry about the effect of bee disappearance on humans. You see, people all over the world depend on bees. They need them to pollinate their crops. Without bees, one third of all the food we eat could not be grown. As a result, many people could go hungry.

How Bees Help Us

When bees fly from plant to plant, they take pollen with them. The pollen taken from one plant causes another plant to produce seeds. This is called **pollination**. As a result of pollination, the plant continues to flower. It then produces foods that humans eat. Because of bees we get foods like nuts, beans, apples and cherries.

The bee will carry pollen from this flower to another.

→ Comprehension

A Strange Disappearance

What has happened to all of the bees? Since 2006, honeybees have been disappearing. You might not think much of this. But if bees keep disappearing, the results could be drastic.

A Worldwide Problem

Farmers and scientists have discovered that bees and humans are connected. That's why they are **alarmed**. They worry about the effect of bee disappearance on humans. You see, people all over the world depend on bees. They need them to pollinate their crops. Without bees, one third of all the food we eat could not be grown. As a result, many people could go hungry.

How Bees Help Us

When bees fly from plant to plant, they take pollen with them. The pollen taken from one plant causes another plant to produce seeds. This is called **pollination**. As a result of pollination, the plant continues to flower. It then produces foods that humans eat. Because of bees we get foods like nuts, beans, apples and cherries.

The bee will carry pollen from this flower to another.

Online PDF

MINILESSON 10 Mins

Main Idea and Text Structure

1 Explain

Genre Tell students that they will learn about informational genres, including nonfiction narratives, such as biographies or autobiographies, and expository text. Point out that informational text often contains text features, such as headings and boldface key words, and illustrations, such as photographs and captions, maps, charts, diagrams, time lines. Discuss nonfiction genres using **Start Smart 3 Online PDF**.

As students read informational text, they will learn to identify main ideas and key details and different kinds of text structures.

Main Idea and Key Details The main idea is the most important point an author makes about a topic. To find the main idea, readers sort the details into important and less important. Then they decide what the key details have in common to determine the main idea.

Text Structure Explain that text structure is the organizational pattern a nonfiction writer uses to present information. Identifying text structure can help students understand key events and information. Students will learn to identify these text structures:

→ **Sequence** Ideas, events, or the steps in a process are presented in time order. Signal words such as *first, next, after,* and *when* help readers recognize the sequence text structure. Sequence often appears in history and procedural texts and biographies.

→ **Cause and Effect** The writer analyzes and explains why events happen and tells what causes them to happen. Signal words such as *because, therefore, so, due to,* and *as a result* can all signal the cause-and-effect text structure. Cause-and-effect relationships often appear in science and history texts.

→ **Compare and Contrast** The writer presents similarities or differences of two or more people, places, objects, events, or ideas. Signal words such as *however, unlike, although, like, similarly,* and *on the other hand* can help readers recognize the compare-and-contrast text structure.

→ **Problem and Solution** The writer presents a problem and then presents possible solutions. Tell students that in this text structure, problems may be stated as a question. Problems and solutions appear in both science and history texts.

Go Digital

A Strange Disappearance

xd to all of the bees? Since 2006, honeybees have ught not think much of this. But if bees keep disa ic.

m tists have discovered that bees and humans are c d. They worry about the effect of bee disappeari

A Strange Disappearance

Genre

Genre

OBJECTIVES

CCSS Refer to details and examples in a text when explaining what the text says explicitly and when drawing inferences from the text. **RI.4.1**

CCSS Determine the main idea of a text and explain how it is supported by key details; summarize the text. **RI.4.2**

CCSS Describe the overall structure (e.g., chronology, comparison, cause/effect, problem/solution) of events, ideas, concepts, or information in a text or part of a text. **RI.4.5**

ACADEMIC LANGUAGE

• *main idea, key details, text structure*

• Cognate: *detalles*

2 Model Close Reading: Text Evidence

Remind students that close reading is reading carefully and paying attention to details. The purpose is to evaluate what they read to identify main ideas and text structures.

Tell students that **citing text evidence** is using evidence from the text to support answers. When answering questions, they will be asked to point out the exact text they used to answer the question or make an inference. Students must do close reading in order to cite text evidence.

Main Idea and Key Details Reread the section "A Worldwide Problem" in "A Strange Disappearance" on **Start Smart 6–7 Online PDF**. Ask: *What is the main idea of this section?* Model close reading and citing text evidence.

Think Aloud I will sort the details to find the main idea. In this paragraph most of the details seem important. I will see what they have in common to figure out the main idea. The first sentence, "Farmers and scientists have discovered that bees and humans are connected," tells that humans and bees affect one another. The other details tell how people depend on bees. From these key details, I think the main idea is this: If bees disappear, it will cause problems for humans.

3 Guided Practice of Close Reading

Genre Reread the rest of the article with students. Have them identify details that show the article is informational text.

Reread Paragraph 3 Ask: *What is the main idea? Cite text evidence to support your answer.* (*Answer* Bees help humans by pollinating plants. *Evidence* As a result of pollination, the plant continues to flower. It then produces foods that humans eat.)

Text Structure Model how to identify causes and effects in "How Bees Help Us." Point out the cause-and-effect signal words *as a result* and *because*. Have students reread "Helping Bees, Helping Ourselves." Ask: *What is the text structure here? What signal word gives you a clue?* (*Answer* "Helping Bees, Helping Ourselves" has a cause-and-effect text structure. *Evidence* The signal word *caused* in "Still, the discovery of disappearing bees has caused people to take action.")

Write About Reading: Summarize Model how to write a summary of the first section of the article. Then have students complete the summary, drawing on the main ideas of each section.

Routine

Notetaking on Graphic Organizers

One clear, organized way to take notes is on a graphic organizer. Taking notes on an organizer will also help students determine important ideas or key details or see how the author has organized information using a text structure. Taking notes will also help them remember what they read.

1. When students begin reading a new informational text, display the organizer and discuss what kind of information goes in each section.

2. As students begin reading, model how to take notes on the organizer.

3. As students use their organizers, give them feedback.

4. Model using informational-text graphic organizers at least once a week until students are comfortable using them.

START SMART 3 Online PDF

Genres

Type	Key Characteristics	Examples
Adventure		
Drama (Play)		
Fable		
Fairy Tale		
Fantasy		
Folktale		
Historical Fiction		
Legend		
Myth		
Poetry		
Realistic Fiction		
Science Fiction		
Autobiography		
Biography		
Expository		
Narrative Nonfiction		
Technical/Procedural		

→ Comprehension

Author's Point of View

MINILESSON **10** Mins

Sidebar (left column)

A Strange Disappearance

What has happened to all of the bees? Since 2006, honeybees have been disappearing. You might not think much of this. But if bees keep disappearing, the results could be drastic.

A Worldwide Problem

Farmers and scientists have discovered that bees and humans are connected. That's why they are **alarmed**. They worry about the effect of bee disappearance on humans. You see, people all over the world depend on bees. They need them to pollinate their crops. Without bees, one third of all the food we eat could not be grown. As a result, many people could go hungry.

How Bees Help Us

When bees fly from plant to plant, they take pollen with them. The pollen taken from one plant causes another plant to produce seeds. This is called **pollination**. As a result of pollination, the plant continues to flower. It then produces foods that humans eat. Because of bees we get foods like nuts, beans, apples and cherries.

The bee will carry pollen from this flower to another.

Online PDF

OBJECTIVES

 Compare and contrast a firsthand and secondhand account of the same event or topic; describe the differences in focus and the information provided. **RI.4.6**

 Explain how an author uses reasons and evidence to support particular points in a text. **RI.4.8**

 Integrate information from two texts on the same topic in order to write or speak about the subject knowledgeably. **RI.4.9**

ACADEMIC LANGUAGE

• *author's point of view, compare*

• Cognate: *comparar*

S25

Main column

1 Explain

Tell students that when they read informational texts, they may need to make inferences to identify the author's point of view. Students may also need to compare and contrast texts on the same topic. Explain that focusing on these skills will help them read more closely and with greater understanding.

Point out that the **author's point of view** is the author's position or attitude about a topic. In fourth grade, readers will identify firsthand and secondhand accounts of the same event or topic and describe the differences in the focus or information.

→ Readers should analyze the kinds of details an author presents to help them figure out the author's point of view.

→ Positive and negative words, such as *wonderful* or *awful,* can also help readers figure out how the author feels about the topic.

→ As students read, they should evaluate how the author uses reasons and evidence to support particular points in a text.

Make Inferences Authors may not state their point of view. The details authors include and words they use can help readers infer it.

Compare Across Texts Good readers connect what they read in informational texts to related texts they have read. Point out that this year students will often compare and contrast the most important points presented in two informational texts on the same topic.

2 Model Close Reading: Text Evidence

Reread Reread paragraph 2 on PDF page 6. Have students focus on the author's point of view, or attitude about the disappearance of bees.

Author's Point of View Identify details about bees disappearing in the section "A Worldwide Problem." Then model using text evidence to make an inference about the author's point of view.

Think Aloud The author says farmers and scientists are "alarmed" by bees disappearing. "They worry about the effect of bee disappearance on humans." The author also says, "Many people could go hungry." These details help me infer the author is worried about bees disappearing and wants readers to worry too. *Alarmed* is a strong negative word that shows just how concerned the author is.

Right column

Go Digital

A Strange Disappearance

3 Guided Practice of Close Reading

Reread Reread "A Beekeeper's Perspective" with students. Ask: *What is Dave Hackenberg's perspective about bees disappearing? Is it the same as the author's? Cite evidence to support your answer. (Answer Dave Hackenberg and the author are both concerned about bees disappearing. However, they are worried for different reasons. Dave Hackenberg depends on bees to make his living. The author is worried that people will go hungry. Evidence Dave Hackenberg says, "If many more bees die, I'll probably be out of business." The author says, "Without bees, one third of all the food we eat could not be grown. As a result, many people could go hungry.")*

Compare Across Texts Explain that the topic of "A Strange Disappearance" is about animals and our environment. Share another short informational text about this topic, such as one about monarch butterflies. Explain that you will make inferences to compare and contrast information in the two articles.

Think Aloud This week I read two informational texts about the same topic—animals that are disappearing. The first was about disappearing bees, and the second was about the declining number of female monarch butterflies. To understand more about the topic of animals and the environment, I will make inferences to decide how the two articles are alike and different. I can infer the articles are alike because both are about animals that are mysteriously disappearing or declining in number. I can make inferences about how they are different, too. Bees disappearing directly impacts humans because it affects food production and beekeepers' jobs. The decline of female monarchs does not have quite as direct an impact on humans. By comparing key details, I can make inferences about these two kinds of animals and the problems facing them.

Ask: *How is "A Strange Disappearance" similar to another nonfiction text about animals you have read? How is it different? Cite text evidence to support your answer. (Sample Answer I read a nonfiction book about vanishing amphibians. It described a fungus that is causing mass extinction to amphibians. "A fungus is killing many amphibians that have already been affected by loss of habitat, pollution, and climate change." This is like the article about bees because both tell how animals are disappearing due to environmental changes. The texts are different in that scientists know what is causing the amphibians to disappear but the bee disappearance is a mystery.)*

Comparing Sources

First- and Secondhand Accounts

Explain that this year students will often compare information in two different texts on the same topic. Sometimes they will read both firsthand and secondhand accounts.

- A **firsthand account** (or primary source) is written by someone who saw or took part in the events he or she describes.

- A **secondhand account** (or secondary source) is written by someone who was not present at the events he or she describes.

Point out that letters, diary entries, and autobiographies are firsthand accounts, while expository articles, textbooks, and encyclopedias are examples of secondhand accounts.

→ # Vocabulary Strategy

Online PDF

OBJECTIVES

CCSS Determine or clarify the meaning of unknown and multiple-meaning words and phrases based on grade 4 reading and content, choosing flexibly from a range of strategies. Use common, grade-appropriate Greek and Latin affixes and roots as clues to the meaning of a word (e.g., *telegraph, photograph, autograph*). **L.4.4b**

CCSS Determine or clarify the meaning of unknown and multiple-meaning words and phrases based on grade 4 reading and content, choosing flexibly from a range of strategies. Consult reference materials (e.g., dictionaries, glossaries, thesauruses), both print and digital, to find the pronunciation and determine or clarify the precise meaning of key words and phrases. **L.4.4c**

ACADEMIC LANGUAGE
prefix, suffix

MINILESSON
10 Mins

Using a Dictionary or Glossary

1 Explain

Display the Dictionary Entry on **Start Smart 4 Online PDF.** Explain:

→ A **dictionary,** or a **glossary** in a nonfiction book, lists words in alphabetical order. Dictionaries and glossaries may be found online as well as in print.

→ **Entry words** show the spelling and syllabication, or how many syllables a word has.

→ **Guide words** show the first and last words on the page. Words on the page come between the guide words alphabetically.

→ The **pronunciation** of each word is shown in parentheses, and the **part of speech** is shown after the pronunciation.

→ You use a dictionary or glossary to look up an unfamiliar word or to confirm a word's **meaning** to make sure you use it correctly.

2 Model

Model using a dictionary, including the **pronunciation key**. Explain how to look up a word's meaning and choose the definition that best fits the context of the sentence. The first entry for a word may not be the one that students are looking for. They should read all the entries to see which meaning makes sense in the sentence. Display: *She will pitch the tent at the campsite before it gets dark.*

Think Aloud I know that *pitch* can mean "throw a ball." That doesn't make sense here, so *pitch* must have more than one meaning. When I look in a dictionary, I see that *pitch* also means "set up firmly in the ground." That meaning makes sense in the sentence. You have to set up a tent by putting the tent poles firmly in the ground.

Point out that a dictionary can help students confirm meanings of unfamiliar words.

3 Guided Practice

Point out the word *produce* in paragraph 3 of "A Strange Disappearance" on **Start Smart 6–7 Online PDF**. Have partners find the relevant meaning and pronunciation of *produce* in a dictionary and explain how they decided which meaning was correct.

Go Digital

A Strange Disappearance

Dictionary

MINILESSON 10 Mins

Morphology

1 Explain

Greek and Latin Roots Point out words in English come from many languages. About 60 percent of English words come from the Greek and Latin languages. Words with Greek roots are common in science and social studies. Words with Latin roots are common in literature.

→ A root word, such as *jump*, can stand alone as a word in English. A root, such as *tele*, is not a word in English. It must be combined with other word parts, such as **prefixes, suffixes,** and other **roots.**

→ Learning the meaning of common roots can help students gain access to many words. For example, by knowing that *tri* means "three," they can figure out the meanings of the words *tricycle*, *triple*, and *triplet*.

Prefixes and Suffixes A **prefix** is a word part that is added to the beginning of a word and changes its meaning. A **suffix** is a word part that is added to the end of a word, changing the word's meaning, and often its part of speech.

→ Common prefixes include *un-, re-, dis-, in-, non-, over-, mis-, sub-*.

→ Common suffixes include *-s, -es, -ed, -ing, -ly, -y, -able,* and *-ful*. Some common suffixes, such as *-y* and *-able*, come from Latin.

→ Students can use the meaning of a prefix or suffix to help them determine the meaning of the whole word.

2 Model

→ Write the following roots on the board: *uni* and *bi*. Pronounce each root. Explain that *uni* means "one" and *bi* means "two."

→ Point out that roots must be combined with other roots or word parts to form a word: *unity*, *biannual*.

3 Guided Practice

→ Write these words on the board: *unicycle, bicycle, union, university, bicentennial, bisect*. Guide students to identify the root in each and then use the root's meaning to define the whole word. Have students work with a partner to generate a list of common Greek and Latin roots, their meanings, and sample words.

Routine

Unfamiliar Word Routine

Students should use vocabulary strategies flexibly and in tandem. Suggest the following routine for when students encounter an unfamiliar word.

1. First, look for **familiar parts** within the word. Does the word contain a prefix, suffix, or root that you already know?

2. Next, look at the surrounding sentences for **context clues**. Are there other words nearby that help explain or describe the word or give examples?

3. Finally, decide how important the word is for understanding the selection. If the word seems important, **use a dictionary**. If it does not seem important, keep reading.

Caution students to be careful when using context clues. Often no helpful clues appear near a word. Sometimes, even, the surrounding words can give misleading clues.

START SMART 4 Online PDF

Dictionary Entry

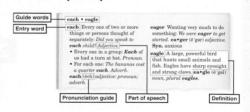

Thesaurus Entry

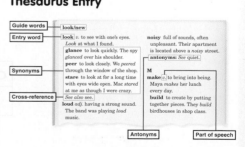

Phonics

MINILESSON
20 Mins

6 Syllable Types

OBJECTIVES

CCSS Use combined knowledge of all letter-sound correspondences, syllabication patterns, and morphology (e.g., roots and affixes) to read accurately unfamiliar multisyllabic words in context and out of context. **RF.4.3a**

Know and apply grade-level phonics and word analysis skills in decoding words.

ACADEMIC LANGUAGE
syllables

1 Explain

Students will work with the six syllable types this year. Knowing these syllable types will help them read long, unfamiliar words. Display the name of each syllable type and examples for students to record in their writer's notebooks.

❶ Closed These syllables end in a consonant. The vowel sound is generally short. The vowel is enclosed (or closed in) by the consonants. (rab/bit, nap/kin)

❷ Open These syllables end in a vowel. The vowel sound is generally long. The vowel is open and free to say its name. (ti/ger, pi/lot)

❸ Final Stable Usually when *le* or *ion* appears at the end of a word and a consonant comes before it, the consonant + *le* or + *ion* form the final stable syllable. (ta/ble, lit/tle, ac/tion, ten/sion)

❹ Vowel Team Many vowel sounds are spelled with vowel digraphs, or teams, such as *ai, ay, ee, ea, oa, ow, oo, oy, oi, ie,* and *ei.* The vowel teams must stay together and appear in the same syllable. (ex/plain/ing, team/mate)

❺ r-Controlled When a vowel is followed by the letter *r*, the vowel and the *r* must appear in the same syllable. Therefore, they act as a team that cannot be broken up. (tur/tle, mar/ket)

❻ Final (Silent) e (VCe) When a word has a vowel-consonant-*e* spelling pattern, the vowel and the final silent *e* must stay in the same syllable. (com/pete, de/cide)

2 Model/Guided Practice

Write these syllables on the board: *pub, ble, pro, cade, ver, mar, ount, tle, vise, aim, cab, ite, co, ate, ple, ma, eed, irt, ran, mid, cle, tion, ta, ide, den, gle, ore, oach, sion, ba, oon.* Draw a Syllable Sort Chart. Model how to sort each kind of syllable, writing it on the chart under the correct heading. Help students sort the remaining syllables.

closed	open	final stable	vowel team	*r*-controlled	final *e*

Go Digital

Decoding

Decoding Words

Review the Decoding Strategy Chart on **Start Smart 5 Online PDF**. Write these word lists on the board. These lists contain real and nonsense words. Use the word lists to assess students' decoding abilities. To give students practice reading the words in context, write sentences using real words for the six syllable types from the word lists below.

Word Lists

List 1: (real) *tab, peg, give, gob, hub, fuss, cell, puff, fizz, hog* (nonsense) *gat, ved, hib, mog, lun, quat, lem, fid, mog, sug*

List 2: (real) *clamp, wreck, chick, brisk, stomp, help, shrub, think, when, grand* (nonsense) *shuzz, chend, stiss, threg, phum, whep, flod, belp, slamp, crint*

List 3: (real) *space, preach, dries, boast, train, spray, knight, squeeze, ply, whole, huge* (nonsense) *sote, feam, boap, glay, cright, deest, sny, flain, shabe, pabe*

List 4: (real) *flair, shook, scorch, term, vault, quirk, churn, barge, halt, broil* (nonsense) *boit, stoud, plar, loy, mern, noof, gurst, torth, blirch, stook*

List 5: (real) *absent, bonus, reptile, exclaim, poodle, pumpkin, mutate, compete, appoint, scribble, fiction, region* (nonsense) *rigfap, churnit, bapnate, deatloid, foutnay, moku, wolide, lobam, nagbo, flizzle*

Link to Spelling

Dictation Dictate the following words for students to spell: *smell, queen, running, babies, pair, pear, trick, shrub, blaze, grain, cheat, flight, throat, germ, fault, pork, point, mouth, bloom, problem, frozen, crisis, deleted, stampede, complaining, unclear, formal, border, gentle, bridle, puzzle, contraction*. Provide context sentences for the homophones *pear* and *pair*.

→ Pronounce one word at a time. Have students clearly say the word. Then repeat the word and use it in a sentence. Prompt students to write one syllable at a time for multisyllabic words.

→ After dictation is completed, write the words on the board. Ask students to proofread their spellings and correct any errors by writing the correct spelling beside the incorrect spelling. Analyze each student's spelling errors. Tell students as they learn to spell words this year, they will use spelling patterns, word families, syllable patterns, ending rules, and word parts to help them spell words correctly.

Why It Matters

Syllable Types

As students read increasingly complex texts, they will encounter many multisyllabic words. To decode multisyllabic words, students must be able to divide the words into recognizable chunks.

There are six syllable patterns that comprise most of the syllables in English words. Providing instruction and ample practice in dividing words into syllables will help students decode longer, unfamiliar words. Students can use this strategy as needed to help them to read more complex text.

START SMART 5 Online PDF

Decoding Strategy Chart

Step 1	Look for word parts (prefixes) at the beginning of the word.
Step 2	Look for word parts (suffixes) at the end of the word.
Step 3	In the base word, look for familiar spelling patterns. Think about the six syllable-spelling patterns you have learned.
Step 4	Sound out and blend together the word parts.
Step 5	Say the word parts fast. Adjust your pronunciation as needed. Ask yourself: "Is this a word I have heard before?" Then read the word in the sentence and ask: "Does it make sense in this sentence?"

Reading Every Day

A Strange Disappearance

What has happened to all of the bees? Since 2006, honeybees have been disappearing. You might not think much of this. But if bees keep disappearing, the results could be drastic.

A Worldwide Problem

Farmers and scientists have discovered that bees and humans are connected. That's why they are **alarmed**. They worry about the effect of bee disappearance on humans. You see, people all over the world depend on bees. They need them to pollinate their crops. Without bees, one third of all the food we eat could not be grown. As a result, many people could go hungry.

How Bees Help Us

When bees fly from plant to plant, they take pollen with them. The pollen taken from one plant causes another plant to produce seeds. This is called **pollination**. As a result of pollination, the plant continues to flower. It then produces foods that humans eat. Because of bees we get foods like nuts, beans, apples and cherries.

The bee will carry pollen from this flower to another.

Online PDF

OBJECTIVES

CCSS Read with sufficient accuracy and fluency to support comprehension. Read grade-level text with purpose and understanding. **RF.4.4a**

CCSS Read with sufficient accuracy and fluency to support comprehension. Read grade-level prose and poetry orally with accuracy, appropriate rate, and expression on successive readings. **RF.4.4b**

CCSS Read with sufficient accuracy and fluency to support comprehension. Use context to confirm or self-correct word recognition and understanding, rereading as necessary. **RF.4.4c**

ACADEMIC LANGUAGE

rate, accuracy, expression

MINILESSON
10 Mins

Fluency

Establish Yearly Goals

Explain the three key aspects of fluency: rate, accuracy, and expression.

→ **Rate** The rate at which students read is important. Students need to read at a pace appropriate for the level of text difficulty. In Grade 4, the goal by the end of the year is to read 123 words correct per minute (WCPM). Explain to students that you will be testing them on their rate throughout the year to meet this goal. Rereading previously read passages and stories is one way they will increase their rate.

→ **Accuracy** Correctly identifying words is key to skilled, fluent reading. Explain to students that the work they do in phonics and word study will help them read longer and harder words. They will also use the **Syllable Speed Drill** on **Start Smart 8 Online PDF** to help them become automatic at reading those words with more complex spelling patterns or words that have irregular spellings. Also remind students to use context to confirm or self-correct word recognition and understanding and to reread as necessary.

→ **Expression** Fluent readers read with proper phrasing and intonation, or prosody. They read dialogue the way characters would say it. They speed up when the action gets exciting and slow down for difficult parts of text. This means the reader is decoding and comprehending the text at the same time—the hallmark of a skilled, fluent reader.

Daily Fluency

Students will practice fluency by **echo reading** (repeating a sentence after you) and **choral reading** (reading along with you). Resources for daily practice include:

→ fluency **Workstation Activity Cards**

→ weekly comprehension/fluency passages in **Your Turn Practice Book**

→ weekly differentiated passages on **Approaching** and **Beyond Level Reproducibles**

→ **Leveled Readers**

→ **Reader's Theater** plays for each unit, available online

Model reading the first two paragraphs of "A Strange Disappearance" on **Start Smart 6 Online PDF** fluently. Then reread the passage a sentence at a time and have students echo read. Provide constructive feedback.

Go Digital

A Strange Disappearance

ed to all of the bees? Since 2006, honeybees have ight not think much of this. But if bees keep disa ic.

m
tists have discovered that bees and humans are c
d. They worry about the effect of bee disappearan

A Strange Disappearance

Syllable Speed Drill

Fluency

MINILESSON
20 Mins

Independent Reading

Daily Sustained Silent Reading

Students should read independently from text they self-select for information and for enjoyment. Independent reading is based on the principle that if students read more, their reading skills will improve and their enjoyment will increase. Students can read independently during sustained silent reading time, as well as during Small Group when they do reading activities using their **Workstation Activity Cards**.

Sustained silent reading should last from 15 minutes to 30 minutes, depending on the grade level. During this time, students can read material that interests them at their own reading level. Set aside a block of time each day.

Selecting a Book Some students may need to learn how to select a book.

→ Make a suggestion based upon a student's special interest.

→ If a student shows interest in an author, genre, or topic from the selections read that week, recommend a title from the online **Unit Bibliography**.

→ Begin a book-sharing session in the classroom. Set aside a few minutes each week for a class discussion on books students have read.

Setting Up a Reading Log To help monitor students' independent reading, have them create a reading log, or response journal, where they record reactions and feelings about what they are reading. As you review the logs, you may want to write specific prompts to guide students, such as, *How does the story make you feel? What information is new to you? What information is confusing? What new words did you learn? Are you enjoying what you read? Why or why not?*

Literature Circles When groups of students are reading the same book, they can come together and discuss what they have read so far in a Literature Circle. Reading might include leveled readers, classroom library books, or books students choose themselves Once groups are formed and a book is chosen, students can work together to plan how they will read the book: How long will it take? How many pages will be read each day/week? Encourage everyone to participate. Assign roles that rotate each week including facilitator, one who reads, and recorder of comments. Literature circles should end with a few minutes for students to record their thoughts in their reading logs.

Routine

Fluency Practice

Each day students will practice fluency.

1. Model reading the week's fluency passage at the beginning of the week.

2. Pair a more fluent reader with a slightly less fluent one.

3. Provide text to partners. They should take turns reading the passage to each other.

4. After each turn, encourage them to discuss the speed with which the reader read the passage, the phrasing, the expression. Partners should provide constructive feedback. Have students repeat the reading several times.

5. At the week's end, have partners take turns doing a timed read for a minute. One partner times the other and marks miscues and the last word read. Then students can count miscues and total number of words. Encourage them to reread and try for a better score.

START SMART 8 Online PDF

Syllable Speed Drill

ing	un	ture	dis	com
im	ter	ment	er	der
ver	ble	tion	num	re
est	ple	de	ex	en
bout	per	tle	pro	dif
fore	fa	el	ful	pic
por	tween	hap	nev	ness
non	mis	ly	ic	less
lect	heav	sub	rep	semi
ma	mid	tend	pre	cial

Writing Every Day

OBJECTIVES

 Produce clear and coherent writing in which the development and organization are appropriate to task, purpose, and audience. W.4.4

 Write routinely over extended time frames (time for research, reflection, and revision) and shorter time frames (a single sitting or a day or two) for a range of discipline-specific tasks, purposes, and audiences. W.4.10

ACADEMIC LANGUAGE

- *writing traits, ideas, details, topic, rubric*
- Cognate: *detalles*

MINILESSON 10 Mins

Writing Traits: Ideas

Details

Tell students that this year you will help students understand and apply the **six traits** that underlie effective writing: **Ideas, Organization, Word Choice, Voice, Sentence Fluency,** and **Conventions**. You will teach them specific skills related to each trait, and you will also guide students in how to **present** their writing at appropriate times.

Explain that one writing habit they will be using all year is analyzing both expert models from the literature they read and student models showing revisions. You will focus on one writing trait each week, such as Ideas, and they will revise short pieces of writing to practice using the trait.

Expert Model Reread the first two paragraphs of "A Strange Disappearance" on **Start Smart 6 Online PDF**. Point out that the paragraphs offer an excellent example of the writing trait Ideas and the skill Details. Discuss how the author develops ideas by using details to

→ give more information about the main topic, disappearing bees.

→ give examples and facts that support and explain the ideas.

Draft Have students write a short paragraph about a place that is important to them. They should include descriptive details.

Revise Tell students that another writing habit they will be using is carefully rereading and revising their work. This will help them check for errors and strengthen their writing based on feedback. Have partners read the descriptive paragraphs they wrote. Have them discuss revisions that would make each piece of writing stronger. For example, are there more reasons and examples they can add?

Set Up Writer's Notebooks

Tell students they will be writing every day in writer's notebooks. These notebooks will be used for the following activities:

→ Students will be writing to a prompt every week. They will check their writing during independent time and make any necessary revisions. Then, during conferences, you will analyze their writing to see if any additional errors were made that they did not correct or notice. This is one way you will help them become better writers and individualize writing instruction.

→ They will complete revision assignments based on writing needs.

→ They will write responses to reading to deepen their understanding.

Have students write their name on the front of their writer's notebook. Remind them to write the date at the beginning of each new piece.

Then have students turn to the back of their writer's notebooks. Have them write these headings on separate pages: *synonyms, antonyms, idioms, prefixes, suffixes, multiple-meaning words, related words, syllable types*. Students will use these pages to record words they learn for each heading.

Writing Process

Focus on Genre Writing

Explain that over the course of each unit students will develop one or two longer pieces of writing related to a specific genre: narrative text, informative text, or opinion writing. For these longer pieces students will work through all of the stages of the writing process: Prewrite, Draft, Revise, Proofread/Edit, and Publish. They will also have the opportunity to present their writing.

As they write, students will apply what they learned in their weekly lessons on writing traits. Because good writers continually revise their work, students will have various opportunities to improve their longer pieces through revision. Students will regularly conference with peers and the teacher to gain feedback. These conferences will always involve three steps:

→ talking about the strengths of the writing

→ focusing on how the writer uses the targeted writing traits

→ making concrete suggestions for revisions

Emphasize the importance of revision. You will guide students to reread and revise their longer pieces repeatedly, focusing on different writing traits. For example, they may revise their writing first to clarify the **organization**, next to add details to support their **ideas**, then exercise **word choice** by replacing vague words with vivid, specific words and incorporate opinions through **voice**. They may revise again to improve their **sentence fluency** by using different types of sentences. They may reread their work a final time to check for grammar and spelling **conventions**.

Tell students they will also be using rubrics as they write and revise this year. You will give them rubrics before they begin writing to help them understand what to do to create a good piece of writing.

Why It Matters

Grammar and Writing

Grammar instruction is most effective when it is integrated into writing instruction. Rather than providing isolated exercises in which students memorize parts of speech or label parts of a sentence, grammar instruction should focus on how language functions in writing and speaking. The point of learning grammar is to help students express their ideas. As students learn to write, they need to be able to use grammar nimbly to communicate in a variety of print and digital formats.

Incorporate grammar instruction as students write short informal pieces and formal genre writing. After students write a draft, analyze the piece together and look for common grammatical errors. When students become more confident with their grammar skills, they can analyze their writing independently.

Wrap Up the Week
Integrate Ideas

OBJECTIVES

CCSS Conduct short research projects that build knowledge through investigation of different aspects of a topic. **W.4.7**

CCSS Engage effectively in a range of collaborative discussions (one-on-one, in groups, and teacher-led) with diverse partners on *grade 4 topics and texts*, building on others' ideas and expressing their own clearly. Review the key ideas expressed and explain their own ideas and understanding in light of the discussion. **SL.4.1d**

CCSS Integrate information from two texts on the same topic in order to write or speak about the subject knowledgeably. **RI.4.9**

ACADEMIC LANGUAGE
research, resources, reliable

RESEARCH AND INQUIRY

Explain that students will work in pairs or groups to complete a short research project that explores what beekeepers do. They will use their research to create a mock interview with a beekeeper. Discuss the following steps.

COLLABORATE

❶ **Share What You Know** Have students review what they learned about bees and beekeeping from "A Strange Disappearance." Have them brainstorm questions they would like to ask a beekeeper, such as "How do you avoid getting stung?" Ask them to choose five questions on which to focus their research. Have students use the online Interview Form for help.

❷ **Find Resources** Review how to locate and use reliable print and online resources. Have students find facts about beekeeping as well as quotes or descriptions from actual beekeepers.

❸ **Guided Practice** Review with students how to cite and record the sources they use.

❹ **Create the Project: Mock Interview** Have the students use their research to create a mock interview with a beekeeper. They should write the answers to their questions from the point of view of a beekeeper.

Present the Interview

Have students present their interview to another pair or group. Remind them to speak clearly at an understandable pace. Discuss whether students should use formal or informal language. Have students use online Presentation Checklist 1 to evaluate their presentations.

Go Digital

Collaborate

TEXT CONNECTIONS

Text to Text

At the end of each week students will have the opportunity to gain a deeper understanding of the texts they have read by analyzing information while comparing different texts.

Cite Evidence Explain that students will work together to review and discuss what they have learned about the weekly theme by looking carefully at the texts they have read. In groups, they will use their notes to record and compare information about the Essential Question on Foldables®. Have groups compare information they have learned about animals in their world.

Model Comparing Information In both "Where Have All the Fish Gone?" and "A Strange Disappearance," the text is about animals in our world. We can place that on our Three-Panel Foldables® under **Alike**. Also, under **Alike**, we can add that both passages try to explain something about animals. Under **Different**, we can write that the folktale explains why sharks and people aren't friends and "A Strange Disappearance" explores why bees are disappearing.

Present Information Ask groups to present their findings and compare information on the charts that is similar and different.

WRITE ABOUT READING

Each week students will write a short analysis or opinion on how the author used the key skills they have been applying. Students will analyze *how the author's use of the skill brings meaning to the text*. They will also practice key skills used in writing explanatory or opinion pieces. Below is an example using "Where Have All the Fish Gone?"

Write an Analysis

Cite Evidence Using text evidence, students will analyze how the author uses character and setting. Ask how and why questions such as *Why is the setting an important part of this folktale?* and *How did the author show what Mano is like?*

Have students write an analysis that explains how the author uses character and setting.

Present Your Ideas Ask partners to share their paragraphs and discuss the evidence they cited from the text to support their ideas.

Why It Matters

Writing About Reading

Writing about texts is an important way in which students will be asked to explore and develop deep comprehension of text. Students will be provided many opportunities to write to

- summarize central ideas/themes and the key supporting details and ideas.
- analyze how the author develops ideas or provides information in a text.
- reflect on various aspects of a text, for example, the point of view of a text.
- support or defend a claim or argument about a text, citing text evidence.
- research topics by gathering and synthesizing evidence from text and other sources.

Alike	Different	What I Discovered

Three-Panel

Placement and Diagnostic Assessment

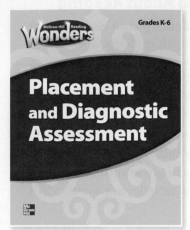

Grades K-6

McGraw-Hill Reading
Wonders

Placement
and Diagnostic
Assessment

PDFs Online

Observe students throughout the Start Smart instruction as they complete assignments, respond orally in class, and read aloud. Take note of individual students' skill needs.

Fluency Benchmark Assess each student's fluency level. This test will show which students are below grade level, on level, and above grade level based on national fluency norms.

For students below level, use the Placement Decisions chart in **Placement and Diagnostic Assessment** to determine which tests need to be administered to figure out each student's specific skill needs. The results of these tests will assist you in determining which students need intervention and help you provide appropriate small group lessons to fill in skill gaps and get all struggling readers on level.

DIAGNOSTIC ASSESSMENT INCLUDES . . .

→ **Foundational Skills Assessments**

- **Basic Assessments** (determine lower-level skill deficiencies, when applicable; include phonemic awareness, Sight Word Fluency/high-frequency words, and alphabet recognition using Letter Naming Fluency)

- **Phonics Survey** (determines decoding abilities and skill deficiencies; developed by program author Jan Hasbrouck)

→ **Fluency Passages** (determine Oral Reading Fluency Rate, Oral Reading Accuracy, and Prosody level; WCPM scores correlated to national norms developed by program author Jan Hasbrouck)

→ **Leveled Passages** (determine reading level and comprehension abilities)

→ **Vocabulary** (determines speaking and reading vocabulary proficiency)

→ **Inventory of Developmental Spelling** (determines encoding abilities; developed by program author Donald Bear)

☞ **Go**
Digital

www.connected.mcgraw-hill.com

Diagnose and Prescribe

Use the results of the Placement and Diagnostic Assessments to provide appropriate Small Group instruction in Unit 1. Focus on rebuilding lower-level skills needed to accelerate students' progress.

✓ TESTED SKILLS	If ...	Then ...
FLUENCY Oral Reading Fluency Passages	Students' WCPM scores are below the 50th percentile ...	Assess comprehension abilities using the Leveled Passages and decoding abilities using the Phonics Survey.
COMPREHENSION Leveled Passages	Students score below 80% on the passages ...	Consider students' reading levels when providing preteach and reteach lessons to support students while reading the Core selections.
PHONICS Phonics Tasks	Students score below 80% on a skill subset that correlates to their grade level ...	Assess basic skills, such as letter names and sounds, featured in tasks correlated to lower grade levels to identify issues in phonics skills development.
VOCABULARY Verbal Language Scales	Students' results are below grade level ...	Provide direct instruction in specific vocabulary necessary for school success, and test fluency and phonemic awareness ability to identify lack of underlying skills.
SPELLING Inventory of Developmental Spelling	Students score below grade level ...	Provide practice in the spelling patterns with which students are struggling.
WRITING Writing Prompt	Students score below grade level ...	Focus modeling and conferencing revision suggestions on those areas in which students need more scaffolding and practice.

Response to Intervention

Use the appropriate sections of the ***Placement and Diagnostic Assessment*** as well as students' assessment results to designate students requiring:

 Intervention Online PDFs

 WonderWorks Intervention Program

WEEKLY OVERVIEW

McGraw-Hill Reading
Wonders

Reading/Writing Workshop

Mc Graw Hill

TEACH AND MODEL

CCSS Shared Read | Genre • Fairy Tale

The Dragon Problem

Essential Question
Where do good ideas come from?
Read how Liang gets a good idea.

22

Once upon a time, long before computers, baseball, or pizza, there lived a young man named Liang. During the day, Liang helped his father build furniture. At night, he made unique, **original** toys for the children in the village. He made birds with flapping wings. He carved dragons with rippling, moving scales, sharp claws, and red eyes. Every child in the village had one of Liang's dragons.

Liang knew a lot about dragons because one lived nearby on a mountain. A few times a year, the dragon would swoop down on the village. He ate water buffalo, pigs, and any people unlucky enough to be around. The Emperor had done nothing to get rid of the dragon even though his summer palace was near Liang's village.

One day in May, the Emperor and his family arrived to take up residence at his summer palace. As the procession passed through the village, the **gracious** Princess Peng smiled kindly at Liang. He fell instantly in love.

At dinner that night, Liang told his father that he wanted to marry Princess Peng. His father almost choked on the **stale**, hard rice ball he was eating.

"You're joking," his father said when he finally could speak.

"I'm serious!" insisted Liang.

His father began laughing so hard that the old chair he was sitting on broke. He lay on top of the **flattened** chair still laughing.

23

✔ Vocabulary

brainstorm
flattened
frantically
gracious
muttered
official
original
stale

🔍 Close Reading of Complex Text

Shared Read "The Dragon Problem," 22–25

Genre Fairy Tale

Lexile 740

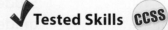 *TextEvaluator™* 26

Minilessons

✔ Tested Skills CCSS

✔ **Comprehension Strategy**	Make Predictions, T18–T19
✔ **Comprehension Skill**	Sequence, T20–T21
✔ **Genre**	Fairy Tale, T22–T23
✔ **Vocabulary Strategy**	Context Clues: Synonyms, T24–T25
✔ **Writing Traits**	Ideas, T30–T31
Grammar	Sentences, T34–T35

 Go Digital

www.connected.mcgraw-hill.com

CLEVER IDEAS
Essential Question
Where do good ideas come from?

WEEK 1

APPLY WITH CLOSE READING

Complex Text

Literature Anthology

PAIRED READ

The Princess and the Pizza, 10–27
Genre Fairy Tale
Lexile 780
(ETS) *TextEvaluator*™ 36

"Tomás and His Sons," 28–31
Genre Fable
Lexile 650
(ETS) *TextEvaluator*™ 31

Differentiated Text

Leveled Readers   *Include Paired Reads*

APPROACHING
Lexile 530
(ETS) *TextEvaluator*™ 28

ON LEVEL
Lexile 750
(ETS) *TextEvaluator*™ 32

BEYOND
Lexile 860
(ETS) *TextEvaluator*™ 41

ELL
Lexile 430
(ETS) *TextEvaluator*™ 11

Extended Complex Text

The Skirt
Genre Realistic Fiction
Lexile 540
(ETS) *TextEvaluator*™ 27

Accidental Hero
Genre Fiction
Lexile 780
(ETS) *TextEvaluator*™ 50

Classroom Library

Classroom Library lessons available online.

TEACH AND MANAGE

How You Teach

INTRODUCE

Weekly Concept
Clever Ideas

Reading/Writing Workshop
18–19

TEACH

Close Reading
"The Dragon Problem"

Minilessons
Make Predictions, Sequence, Fairy Tale,
Synonyms, Writing Traits

**Reading/Writing
Workshop
22–25**

APPLY

Close Reading
The Princess and the Pizza
"Tomás and His Sons"

**Literature
Anthology
10–31**

👉 **Go** Digital

Interactive Whiteboard

Interactive Whiteboard

Mobile

How Students Practice

WEEKLY CONTRACT

PDF Online

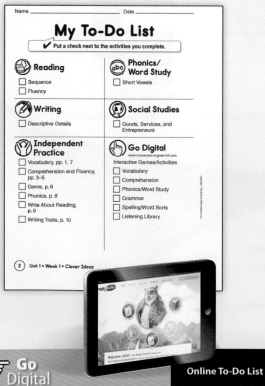

Name _____ Date _____

My To-Do List
✔ Put a check next to the activities you complete.

📖 **Reading**
☐ Sequence
☐ Fluency

🔤 **Phonics/ Word Study**
☐ Short Vowels

✏️ **Writing**
☐ Descriptive Details

🌐 **Social Studies**
☐ Goods, Services, and Entrepreneurs

✋ **Independent Practice**
☐ Vocabulary, pp. 1, 7
☐ Comprehension and Fluency, pp. 3–5
☐ Genre, p. 6
☐ Phonics, p. 8
☐ Write About Reading, p. 9
☐ Writing Traits, p. 10

👆 **Go Digital**
www.connected.mcgraw-hill.com
Interactive Games/Activities
☐ Vocabulary
☐ Comprehension
☐ Phonics/Word Study
☐ Grammar
☐ Spelling/Word Sorts
☐ Listening Library

② Unit 1 • Week 1 • Clever Ideas

LEVELED PRACTICE AND ONLINE ACTIVITIES

Your Turn Practice Book
2–10

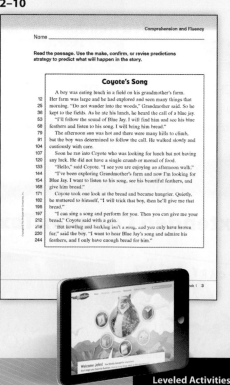

Name _____

Comprehension and Fluency

Read the passage. Use the make, confirm, or revise predictions strategy to predict what will happen in the story.

Coyote's Song

A boy was eating lunch in a field on his grandmother's farm. Her farm was large and he had explored and seen many things that morning. "Do not wander into the woods," Grandmother said. So he kept to the fields. As he ate his lunch, he heard the call of a blue jay.

"I'll follow the sound of Blue Jay. I will find him and see his blue feathers and listen to his song. I will bring him bread."

The afternoon sun was hot and there were many hills to climb, but the boy was determined to follow the call. He walked slowly and cautiously with care.

Soon he ran into Coyote who was looking for lunch but not having any luck. He did not have a single crumb or morsel of food.

"Hello," said Coyote. "I see you are enjoying an afternoon walk."

"I've been exploring Grandmother's farm and now I'm looking for Blue Jay. I want to listen to his song, see his beautiful feathers, and give him bread."

Coyote took one look at the bread and became hungrier. Quietly, he muttered to himself, "I will trick that boy, then he'll give me that bread."

"I can sing a song and perform for you. Then you can give me your bread," Coyote said with a grin.

"But howling and barking isn't a song, and you only have brown fur," said the boy. "I want to hear Blue Jay's song and admire his feathers, and I only have enough bread for him."

Leveled Readers

👉 **Go** Digital

Online To-Do List

Leveled Activities

Writer's Workspace

DIFFERENTIATE

SMALL GROUP INSTRUCTION
Leveled Readers

Mobile

INTEGRATE

Research and Inquiry
List, T28

Text Connections
Compare Sources of Clever
Ideas, T29

Analytical Writing **Write About Reading**
Write an Analysis, T29

Online Research
and Writing

ASSESS

Weekly Assessment
1–12

Online
Assessment

LEVELED WORKSTATION CARDS

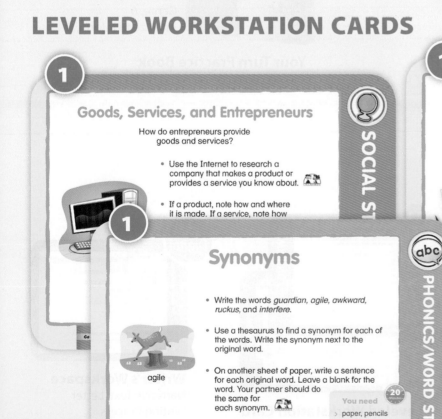

1

Goods, Services, and Entrepreneurs

SOCIAL ST

How do entrepreneurs provide
goods and services?

• Use the Internet to research a
company that makes a product or
provides a service you know about.

• If a product, note how and where
it is made. If a service, note how

1

Synonyms

PHONICS/WORD STUDY

• Write the words *guardian, agile, awkward,
ruckus,* and *interfere.*

• Use a thesaurus to find a synonym for each of
the words. Write the synonym next to the
original word.

agile

• On another sheet of paper, write a sentence
for each original word. Leave a blank for the
word. Your partner should do
the same for
each synonym.

You need
› paper, pencils
› dictionary or
thesaurus

20

• Exchange papers and use
one of the ten words to
complete each sentence.

Go Digital! www.connected.mcgraw-hill.com • Interactive Games and Activities • Grade 4

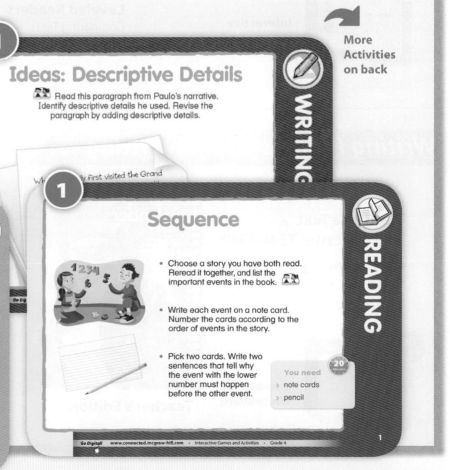

**More
Activities
on back**

1

Ideas: Descriptive Details

WRITING

Read this paragraph from Paulo's narrative.
Identify descriptive details he used. Revise the
paragraph by adding descriptive details.

When ___ly first visited the Grand

1

Sequence

READING

• Choose a story you have both read.
Reread it together, and list the
important events in the book.

• Write each event on a note card.
Number the cards according to the
order of events in the story.

• Pick two cards. Write two
sentences that tell why
the event with the lower
number must happen
before the other event.

You need
› note cards
› pencil

20

Go Digital! www.connected.mcgraw-hill.com • Interactive Games and Activities • Grade 4

TEACH AND MANAGE **T5**

DEVELOPING READERS AND WRITERS

Write to Sources and Research

Retell, T20–T21

Note Taking, T25B, T25T

Summarize, T25R

Sequence, T25R

Make Connections: Essential Question, T25R, T25V, T29

Key Details, T25T, T25U

Research and Inquiry, T28

Analyze to Inform/Explain, T29

Comparing Texts, T41, T49, T53, T59

Predictive Writing, T25B

Teacher's Edition

Literature Anthology

Summarize, 27
Sequence, 27

Leveled Readers
Comparing Texts
Sequence

Your Turn Practice Book

Sequence, 3–5
Genre, 6
Analyze to Inform, 9

Interactive Whiteboard

Narrative Text
Friendly Letter, T344–T349

Conferencing Routines
Teacher Conferences, T346
Peer Conferences, T347

Interactive Whiteboard

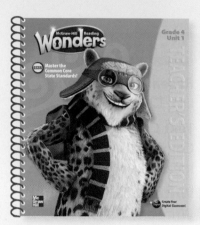

Teacher's Edition

Leveled Workstation Card
Letter, Card 24

Writer's Workspace
Narrative Text: Letter
Writing Process
Multimedia Presentations

Writing Traits • Write Every Day

Writing Trait: Ideas
Descriptive Details, T30–T31

Conferencing Routines
Teacher Conferences, T32
Peer Conferences, T33

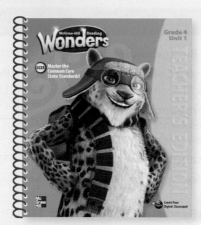

Teacher's Edition

Ideas: Details,
30–31

Reading/Writing Workshop

**Interactive
Whiteboard**

Ideas:
Details, 1

Leveled Workstation Card

Ideas: Details, 10

Your Turn Practice Book

Grammar and Spelling

Grammar
Sentences, T34–T35

Spelling
Short Vowels, T36–T37

**Interactive
Whiteboard**

Teacher's Edition

Sentences

Short Vowels
Word Sorts

Online Spelling and Grammar Games

SUGGESTED LESSON PLAN

	DAY 1	**DAY 2**

Whole Group — Teach, Model and Apply

Reading/Writing Workshop

READING

DAY 1

Build Background Clever Ideas, T10–T11

Listening Comprehension Interactive Read Aloud: "The Princess and the Pea," T12–T13

Comprehension
• Preview Genre: Fairy Tale
• Preview Strategy: Make Predictions

✓**Vocabulary** Words in Context, T14–T15

Practice *Your Turn,* 1

Close Reading of Complex Text "The Dragon Problem," 22–25

DAY 2

✓**Comprehension**
• Strategy: Make Predictions, T18–T19
• Skill: Sequence, T20–T21
• Write About Reading ● *Analytical Writing*
• Genre: Fairy Tale, T22–T23

✓**Vocabulary** Strategy: Synonyms, T24–T25

Practice *Your Turn,* 2–7

DIFFERENTIATED INSTRUCTION   Choose across the week to meet your students' needs.

Small Group

Approaching Level

DAY 1

Leveled Reader *Clever Puss,* T40–T41

Phonics/Decoding Decode Words with Short *e,* T42 TIER 2

Vocabulary
• Review High-Frequency Words, T44 TIER 2
• Answer Choice Questions, T45

DAY 2

Leveled Reader *Clever Puss,* T40–T41

Vocabulary Review Vocabulary Words, T44 TIER 2

Comprehension
• Identify Important Events, T46 TIER 2
• Review Sequence, T47

On Level

DAY 1

Leveled Reader *Jack and the Extreme Stalk,* T48–T49

Vocabulary Review Vocabulary Words, T50

DAY 2

Leveled Reader *Jack and the Extreme Stalk,* T48–T49

Comprehension Review Sequence, T51

Beyond Level

DAY 1

Leveled Reader *Charming Ella,* T52–T53

Vocabulary Review Domain–Specific Words, T54

DAY 2

Leveled Reader *Charming Ella,* T52–T53

Comprehension Review Sequence, T55

English Language Learners

DAY 1

Shared Read "The Dragon Problem," T56–T57

Phonics/Decoding Decode Words with Short *e,* T42

Vocabulary
• Preteach Vocabulary, T60
• Review High-Frequency Words, T44

DAY 2

Leveled Reader *Jack and the Extreme Stalk,* T58–T59

Vocabulary Review Vocabulary, T60

Writing Writing Trait: Ideas, T62

Grammar Sentences, T63

LANGUAGE ARTS   Writing Process: Friendly Letter T344–T349   Use with Weeks 1–3

Whole Group — Writing, Grammar, Spelling, Build Vocabulary

DAY 1

✓**Readers to Writers**
• Writing Traits: Ideas/Descriptive Details, T30–T31
• Writing Entry: Prewrite and Draft, T32

Grammar Sentences, T34

Spelling Short Vowels, T36

Build Vocabulary
• Connect to Words, T38
• Academic Vocabulary, T38

DAY 2

Readers to Writers
• Writing Entry: Revise, T32

Grammar Sentences, T34

Spelling Short Vowels, T36

Build Vocabulary
• Expand Vocabulary, T38
• Review Synonyms, T38

☞ **Go**
Digital

CUSTOMIZE YOUR OWN
LESSON PLANS

www.connected.mcgraw-hill.com

DAY 3	DAY 4	DAY 5 Review and Assess

READING

Phonics/Decoding • Short Vowels, T26 • Inflectional Endings, T27 **Practice** *Your Turn,* 8 **Close Reading** *The Princess and the Pizza,* 10–27 *Analytical Writing* Literature Anthology	**Fluency** Intonation, T27 **Integrate Ideas** *Analytical Writing* • Research and Inquiry, T28 **Practice** *Your Turn,* 3–5 **Close Reading** "Tomás and His Sons," 28–31 *Analytical Writing*	**Integrate Ideas** *Analytical Writing* • Research and Inquiry, T28 • Text Connections, T29 • Write About Reading, T29 **Practice** *Your Turn,* 9

DIFFERENTIATED INSTRUCTION

Leveled Reader *Clever Puss,* T40–T41 **Phonics/Decoding** Review Short Vowels, T42 TIER 2 **Fluency** Intonation, T46 TIER 2 **Vocabulary** Context Clues: Synonyms, T45	**Leveled Reader** Paired Read: "Rabbit and the Well," T41 *Analytical Writing* **Phonics/Decoding** Practice Short Vowels, T43	**Leveled Reader** Literature Circles, T41 **Comprehension** Self-Selected Reading, T47 **Phonics/Decoding** Inflectional Endings, T43
Leveled Reader *Jack and the Extreme Stalk,* T48–T49 **Vocabulary** Context Clues: Synonyms, T50	**Leveled Reader** Paired Read: "Stone Soup," T49 *Analytical Writing*	**Leveled Reader** Literature Circles, T49 **Comprehension** Self-Selected Reading, T51
Leveled Reader *Charming Ella,* T52–T53 **Vocabulary** • Context Clues: Synonyms, T54 • Synthesize, T54 *Gifted and Talented*	**Leveled Reader** Paired Read: "Ivana and the Ogre," T53 *Analytical Writing*	**Leveled Reader** Literature Circles, T53 **Comprehension** • Self-Selected Reading, T55 • Independent Study: Clever Ideas, T55 *Gifted and Talented*
Leveled Reader *Jack and the Extreme Stalk,* T58–T59 **Phonics/Decoding** Review Short Vowels, T42 **Vocabulary** Context Clues: Synonyms, T61 **Spelling** Words with Short Vowels, T62	**Leveled Reader** Paired Read: "Stone Soup," T59 *Analytical Writing* **Vocabulary** Additional Vocabulary, T61 **Phonics/Decoding** Practice Short Vowels, T43	**Leveled Reader** Literature Circles, T59 **Phonics/Decoding** Inflectional Endings, T43

LANGUAGE ARTS

Readers to Writers • Writing Entry: Prewrite and Draft, T33 **Grammar** Mechanics and Usage, T35 **Spelling** Short Vowels, T37 **Build Vocabulary** • Reinforce the Words, T39 • Synonyms, T39	**Readers to Writers** • Writing Entry: Revise, T33 **Grammar** Sentences, T35 **Spelling** Short Vowels, T37 **Build Vocabulary** • Connect to Writing, T39 • Shades of Meaning, T39	**Readers to Writers** • Writing Entry: Share and Reflect, T33 **Grammar** Sentences, T35 **Spelling** Short Vowels, T37 **Build Vocabulary** • Word Squares, T39 • Morphology, T39

DIFFERENTIATE TO ACCELERATE

  Scaffold to Access Complex Text

IF	the text complexity of a particular selection is too difficult for students
THEN	see the references noted in the chart below for scaffolded instruction to help students Access Complex Text.

Qualitative   Quantitative

Reader and Task

TEXT COMPLEXITY

Reading/Writing Workshop	**Literature Anthology**	**Leveled Readers**		**Classroom Library**

Quantitative

Reading/Writing Workshop	**Literature Anthology**	**Leveled Readers**		**Classroom Library**
"The Dragon Problem" Lexile 740 *TextEvaluator*™ 26	*The Princess and the Pizza* Lexile 780 *TextEvaluator*™ 36 "Tomás and His Sons" Lexile 650 *TextEvaluator*™ 31	**Approaching Level** Lexile 530 *TextEvaluator*™ 28 **Beyond Level** Lexile 860 *TextEvaluator*™ 41	**On Level** Lexile 750 *TextEvaluator*™ 32 **ELL** Lexile 430 *TextEvaluator*™ 11	*The Skirt* Lexile 540 *TextEvaluator*™ 27 *The Accidental Hero* Lexile 780 *TextEvaluator*™ 50

Qualitative

What Makes the Text Complex?

- **Connection of Ideas** Character Motivation T17
- **Specific Vocabulary** Context T19

 See Scaffolded Instruction in Teacher's Edition T17 and T19.

What Makes the Text Complex?

- **Purpose** Illustrations T25A; Entertain T25M
- **Specific Vocabulary** Context T25C, T25E
- **Prior Knowledge** Fairy Tales T25F
- **Sentence Structure** T25L
- **Organization** Dialogue T25I; Devices T25S
- **Connection of Ideas** Details T25K, T25O
- **Genre** Fairy Tales T25G; Fables T25U

 See Scaffolded Instruction in Teacher's Edition T25A–T25V.

What Makes the Text Complex?

- **Specific Vocabulary**
- **Sentence Structure**
- **Connection of Ideas**
- **Genre**

 See Level Up lessons online for Leveled Readers.

What Makes the Text Complex?

- **Genre**
- **Specific Vocabulary**
- **Prior Knowledge**
- **Sentence Structure**
- **Organization**
- **Purpose**
- **Connection of Ideas**

 See Scaffolded Instruction in Teacher's Edition T360–T361.

Reader and Task

The Introduce the Concept lesson on pages T10–T11 will help determine the reader's knowledge and engagement in the weekly concept. See pages T16–T25 and T28–T29 for questions and tasks for this text.

The Introduce the Concept lesson on pages T10–T11 will help determine the reader's knowledge and engagement in the weekly concept. See pages T25A–T25V and T28–T29 for questions and tasks for this text.

The Introduce the Concept lesson on pages T10–T11 will help determine the reader's knowledge and engagement in the weekly concept. See pages T40–T41, T48–T49, T52–T53, T58–T59, and T28–T29 for questions and tasks for this text.

The Introduce the Concept lesson on pages T10–T11 will help determine the reader's knowledge and engagement in the weekly concept. See pages T360–T361 for questions and tasks for this text.

Go Digital! www.connected.mcgraw-hill.com

Monitor and *Differentiate*

IF ▶ you need to differentiate instruction

THEN ▶ use the Quick Checks to assess students' needs and select the appropriate small group instruction focus.

✓ Quick Check

Comprehension Strategy Make, Confirm, or Revise Predictions T19

Comprehension Skill Character, Setting, Plot: Sequence T21

Genre Fairy Tale T23

Vocabulary Strategy Synonyms T25

Phonics/Fluency Short Vowels T27

If No → | Approaching Level | **Reteach** T40–T47
| ELL | **Develop** T56–T63

If Yes → | On Level | **Review** T48–T51
| Beyond Level | **Extend** T52–T55

Level Up with Leveled Readers

IF ▶ students can read their leveled text fluently and answer comprehension questions

THEN ▶ work with the next level up to accelerate students' reading with more complex text.

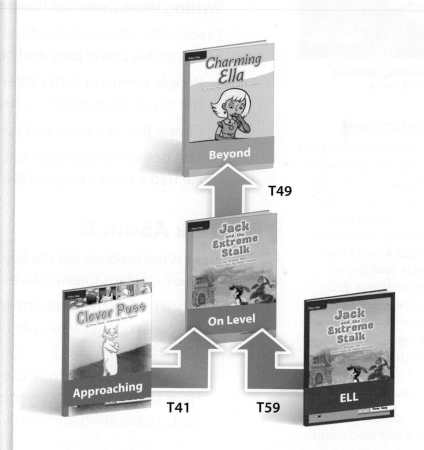

T49

T41   T59

ENGLISH LANGUAGE LEARNERS
SCAFFOLD

IF ELL students need additional support **THEN** ▶ scaffold instruction using the small group suggestions.

| Reading/Writing Workshop "The Dragon Problem" T56–T57 | Leveled Reader *Jack and the Extreme Stalk* T58–T59 "Stone Soup" T59 | Additional Vocabulary T61 around different once soon | live materials problem | Using Context Clues: Synonyms T61 | Writing Ideas T62 | Spelling Words with Short Vowels T62 | Grammar Sentences T63 |

Note: Include ELL Students in all small groups based on their needs.

→ Introduce the Concept

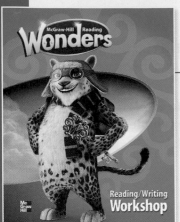

Reading/Writing Workshop

OBJECTIVES

CCSS Engage effectively in a range of collaborative discussions (one-on-one, in groups, and teacher led) with diverse partners on *grade 4 topics and texts,* building on others' ideas and expressing their own clearly. Follow agreed-upon rules for discussions and carry out assigned roles. **SL.4.1b**

CCSS Paraphrase portions of a text read aloud or information presented in diverse media formats, including visually, quantitatively, and orally. **SL.4.2**

Build background on clever ideas.

 MINILESSON 10 Mins

Build Background

ESSENTIAL QUESTION
Where do good ideas come from?

Have students read the Essential Question on page 18 of the **Reading/Writing Workshop**. Tell them that *original* means new.

Discuss the photograph of the boy on the motorcycle with students. Focus on his clever idea and how it led to an original invention.

→ People come up with clever and original ideas every day. They can be the result of an accident, **brainstorming,** or observation.

→ Characters in a story can have clever ideas.

→ The boy in this picture built a motorcycle out of objects in his room. He had a clever, original idea.

Talk About It

Ask: *What problem did the boy solve with his idea? What other problems have clever ideas solved?* Have students discuss in pairs or groups.

→ Model using the Concept Web to generate words and phrases that describe how people think up clever ideas. Add students' contributions.

→ Have partners continue the discussion by paraphrasing what they have learned about clever ideas. They can complete the Concept Web, generating additional related words and phrases.

Collaborative Conversations

Take Turns Talking As students engage in partner, small-group, and whole-class discussions, encourage them to

→ wait for a person to finish before they speak. They should not speak over others.

→ quietly raise their hand to let others know they would like a turn to speak.

→ ask others in the groups to share their opinions so that all students have a chance to share.

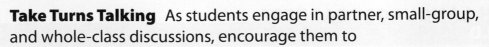

Discuss the Concept

Watch Video

Use Graphic Organizer

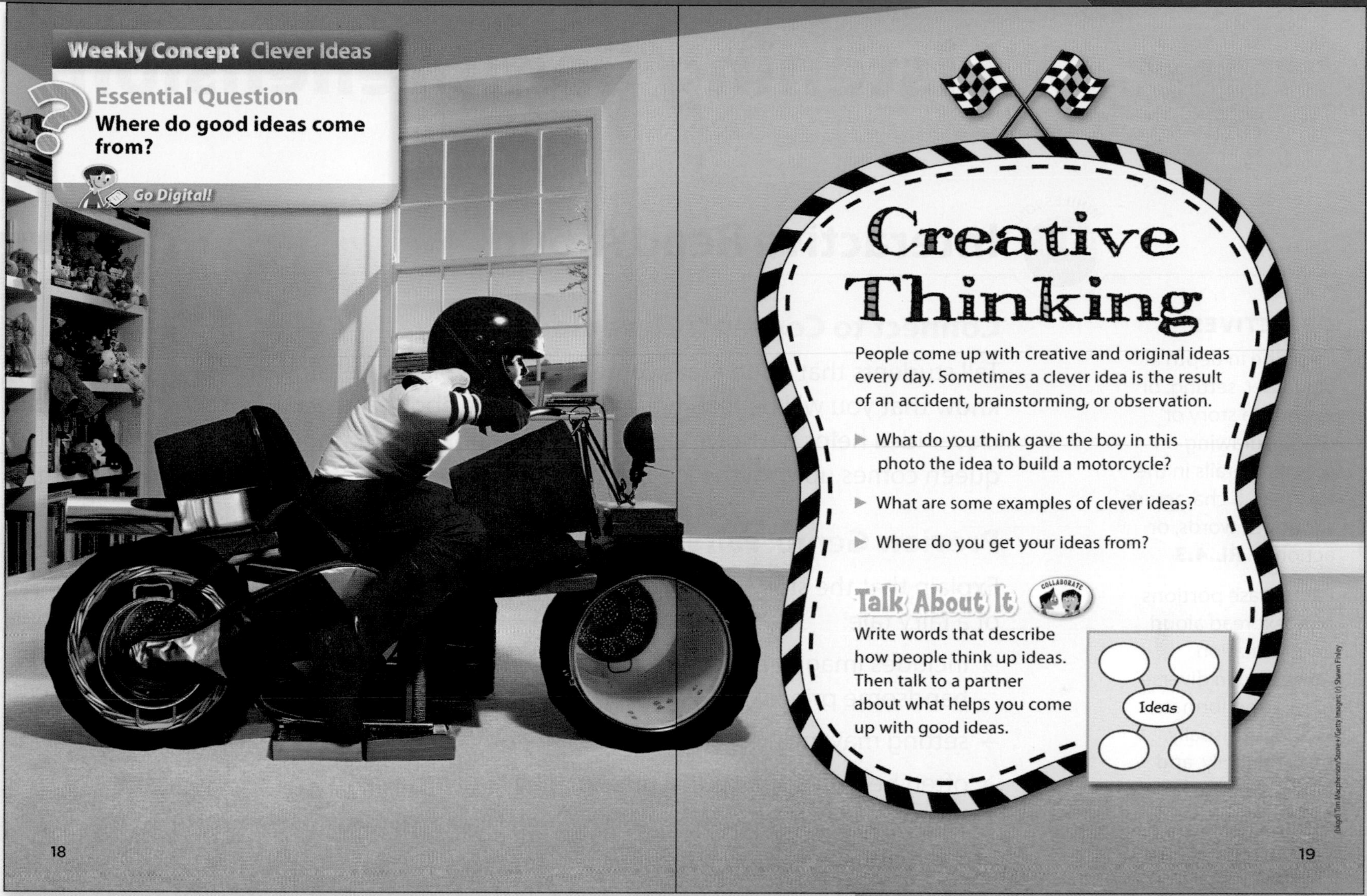

Weekly Concept Clever Ideas

Essential Question

Where do good ideas come from?

Go Digital!

Creative Thinking

People come up with creative and original ideas every day. Sometimes a clever idea is the result of an accident, brainstorming, or observation.

- What do you think gave the boy in this photo the idea to build a motorcycle?
- What are some examples of clever ideas?
- Where do you get your ideas from?

Talk About It COLLABORATE

Write words that describe how people think up ideas. Then talk to a partner about what helps you come up with good ideas.

Ideas

18

19

READING/WRITING WORKSHOP, pp. 18–19

GRAPHIC ORGANIZER 62

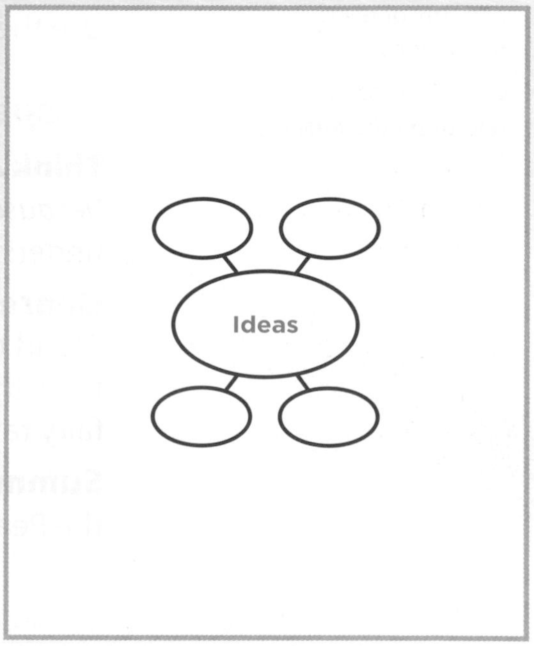

ENGLISH LANGUAGE LEARNERS SCAFFOLD

Beginning	Intermediate	Advanced/High
Use Visuals Tell students about the photograph. *The boy had an idea. His idea was to build a motorcycle. What did the boy do?* Repeat students' responses, correcting grammar and pronunciation as needed.	**Describe** Ask students to describe the photograph. Ask: *Where do you think the boy got his idea? What did the boy use to build the motorcycle?* Elicit details to support students' responses.	**Discuss** Ask students to discuss the concept of clever ideas. Ask: *Can you think of a time when you had a creative or original idea? What did you do?* Ask additional questions to help students elaborate.

Listening Comprehension

MINILESSON
10 Mins

Interactive Read Aloud

Go Digital

Connect to Concept: Clever Ideas

Tell students that good ideas come from many places. Let students know that you will be reading aloud a passage about a queen whose clever idea helps her solve a problem. Ask them to think about how the queen comes up with the idea, and why it works.

View Illustrations

Preview Genre: Fairy Tale

Explain that the story you will read aloud is a fairy tale. Discuss features of a fairy tale:

→ includes imaginary characters, such as a beautiful princess and a handsome prince

→ setting may include kingdoms, castles, or villages

→ often begins "once upon a time" or "in a land far away"

Tell students that as you read, they should listen carefully for examples of the features of a fairy tale.

Preview Comprehension Strategy: Make Predictions

Point out that readers can use clues in the text along with what they already know to make predictions about what might happen. As they continue to read, they may confirm or revise their predictions based on new information.

Use the Think Alouds on page T13 to model the strategy.

Respond to Reading

Think Aloud Clouds Display Think Aloud Master 3: *I predicted ____ because . . .* to reinforce how you used the make predictions strategy to understand content.

Model Think Alouds

Genre Features With students, discuss the elements of the Read Aloud that let them know it is a fairy tale. Ask them to think about other texts that you have read or they have read independently that were fairy tales.

Fill in Genre Chart

Summarize Have students briefly retell the story "The Princess and the Pea" in their own words.

OBJECTIVES

CCSS Describe in depth a character, setting, or event in a story or drama, drawing on specific details in the text (e.g., a character's thoughts, words, or actions). **RL.4.3**

CCSS Paraphrase portions of a text read aloud or information presented in diverse media and formats, including visually, quantitatively, and orally. **SL.4.2**

• Listen for a purpose.
• Identify characteristics of a fairy tale.

ACADEMIC LANGUAGE

• *fairy tale; make, confirm, or revise predictions*
• Cognates: *confirmar, revisar predicciones*

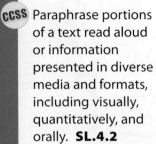

The Princess and the Pea

Once upon a time, there was a prince who wanted to marry a true princess. He had searched the country and found many who claimed to be princesses, but each time he would find that something was not quite right. He wondered if he was doomed to live his life alone. **1**

One rainy night a girl knocked at the castle door. She said that she was a princess, lost from her companions when thunder frightened her horse and he ran away with her into the night.

The queen took pity on the shivering, drenched girl. Could she be a real princess as she claimed? How could they know for sure? At that moment the queen devised a plan.

A room was prepared for the girl in which twenty mattresses were piled high onto a bed. Under the mattresses lay one small pea. A true princess would surely feel the pea beneath the mattresses. **2**

All night the girl tossed and turned, yet she could not find a comfortable position. After no sleep, she rose the next morning to find the queen in the main hall.

"I trust you slept well," said the queen.

"I don't wish to seem ungrateful for the warm bed," said the girl, "but I fear I'm black and blue from something hard in the bed that kept me awake!"

Aha! thought the queen. *She is a true princess.* Just then the prince entered the main hall. He thought he had never seen anyone so beautiful in his life. **3**

"I am Princess Millicent," she said. "Your mother graciously took me in, and yet I've repaid that kindness with nothing but bitter complaints."

"Your complaints are justified," said the queen. She told them about the pea. "Only a real princess would have detected such an object."

Immediately the prince asked for her hand in marriage. Soon the prince and princess wed and lived happily ever after.

1 Think Aloud I wonder if the prince will find a princess. From what I know about fairy tales, I can **make a prediction** that he will. After I read, I can **confirm my prediction.**

2 Think Aloud I don't think anyone could feel a pea under twenty mattresses. I will **make a prediction** that she won't feel it there. But I think that the prince will marry her anyway.

3 Think Aloud My second prediction was incorrect. I read that she felt the pea so she must be a real princess. Since the prince is impressed by her beauty, maybe I can **confirm my prediction** that the prince will marry her.

Stocktrooker/SuperStock

→ Vocabulary

Go Digital

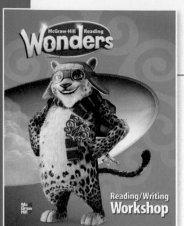

Reading/Writing Workshop

OBJECTIVES

CCSS Acquire and use accurately grade-appropriate general academic and domain-specific words and phrases, including those that signal precise actions, emotions, or states of being (e.g., *quizzed, whined, stammered*) and that are basic to a particular topic (e.g., *wildlife, conservation,* and *endangered* when discussing animal preservation). **L.4.6**

• Learn meanings of new vocabulary words.

• Use new words in sentences.

 MINILESSON 10 Mins

Words in Context

Model the Routine

Introduce each vocabulary word using the Vocabulary Routine found on the Visual Vocabulary Cards.

Visual Vocabulary Cards

Vocabu...
Define:
Example:
Ask:

Vocabulary Routine

Define: To be **gracious** means to show kindness and courtesy.

Example: Justin's mom is gracious and kind when his friend comes over.

Ask: What is an antonym for *gracious*?

gracious

Use Visual Glossary

Definitions

→ **brainstorm**   To **brainstorm** means to solve a problem by having group members all contribute ideas freely.

→ **flattened**   **Flattened** means made flatter, or more level or smooth.

→ **frantically**   To act **frantically** means to act wildly excited due to worry or fear.

→ **muttered**   **Muttered** means spoken in a low, unclear way.

→ **official**   To be **official** means to be properly approved or authorized.
   Cognate: *oficial*

→ **original**   To be **original** means to do, make, or think of something new or different.
   Cognate: *original*

→ **stale**   Something can be called **stale** if it is old or not fresh.

Talk About It

COLLABORATE

Have students work with a partner and look at each picture and discuss the definition of each word. Then ask students to choose three words and write questions for their partner to answer.

CCSS Words to Know

Vocabulary

Use the picture and the sentences to talk with a partner about each word.

brainstorm

The boys began to **brainstorm** ideas for their project.

Describe a time you had to brainstorm some ideas.

flattened

Jess enjoyed rolling out the **flattened** dough.

What is something else that can be flattened?

frantically

The dog was **frantically** digging up sand.

Describe a time when you frantically searched for something.

gracious

Justin's mom is **gracious** and kind when his friend comes over.

What is an antonym for gracious?

muttered

Dan **muttered** to himself as he read my paper.

When might you mutter something instead of saying it loudly?

official

Signing the contract will make the sale **official**.

What is an example of an official document?

original

Maria's artwork was unique and **original**.

What do you think makes something original?

stale

Grandfather and Mia threw the hard, **stale** bread out for the birds to eat.

What other kinds of food get stale?

Your Turn COLLABORATE

Pick three words. Write three questions for your partner to answer.

Go Digital! *Use the online visual glossary*

20

21

READING/WRITING WORKSHOP, pp. 20–21

ELL ENGLISH LANGUAGE LEARNERS SCAFFOLD

Beginning	Intermediate	Advanced/High
Use Visuals *Let's look at the picture for the word* gracious. Act out a gracious gesture, such as handshaking or bowing. Have students repeat a gracious gesture. Ask: *Are gracious people nice to others?* Elaborate on their answers.	**Describe** Have students describe the picture for *gracious*. Help them with the pronunciation. Ask: *How can people be gracious?* Have them turn to a partner and describe ways that people can be gracious. Correct the meaning of students' responses as needed.	**Discuss** Ask students to talk about the picture with a partner and write their own definition for the word *gracious*. Then have them share the definition with the class. Provide more examples or repeat the answer using proper academic language.

ON-LEVEL PRACTICE BOOK p. 1

gracious	flattened	muttered	brainstorm
stale	frantically	official	original

Finish each sentence using the vocabulary word provided.
Possible responses provided.

1. (gracious) The young girl was *gracious* enough to help her brother make gifts for their parents.

2. (stale) After two days the bread was too *stale* to eat.

3. (flattened) He always fixed his hair so that it was *flattened* and combed down.

4. (frantically) After we got separated we *frantically* looked for each other in the crowd.

5. (muttered) I could not hear the answer my brother *muttered*.

6. (official) After she won the cooking contest, she became the *official* chef of the restaurant.

7. (brainstorm) We all decided to *brainstorm* to come up with ideas for a class project.

8. (original) The second book he wrote was even better than the *original* one.

APPROACHING p. 1	BEYOND p. 1	ELL p. 1

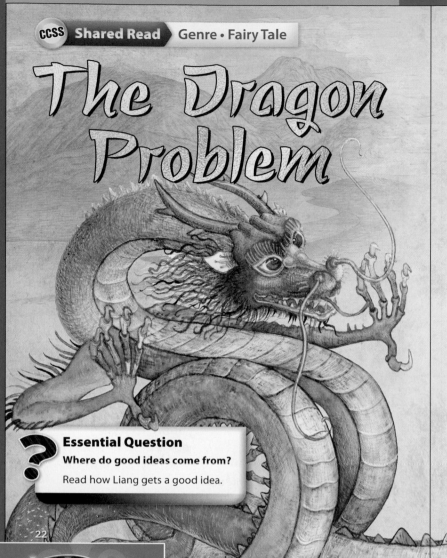

CCSS **Shared Read** Genre • Fairy Tale

The Dragon Problem

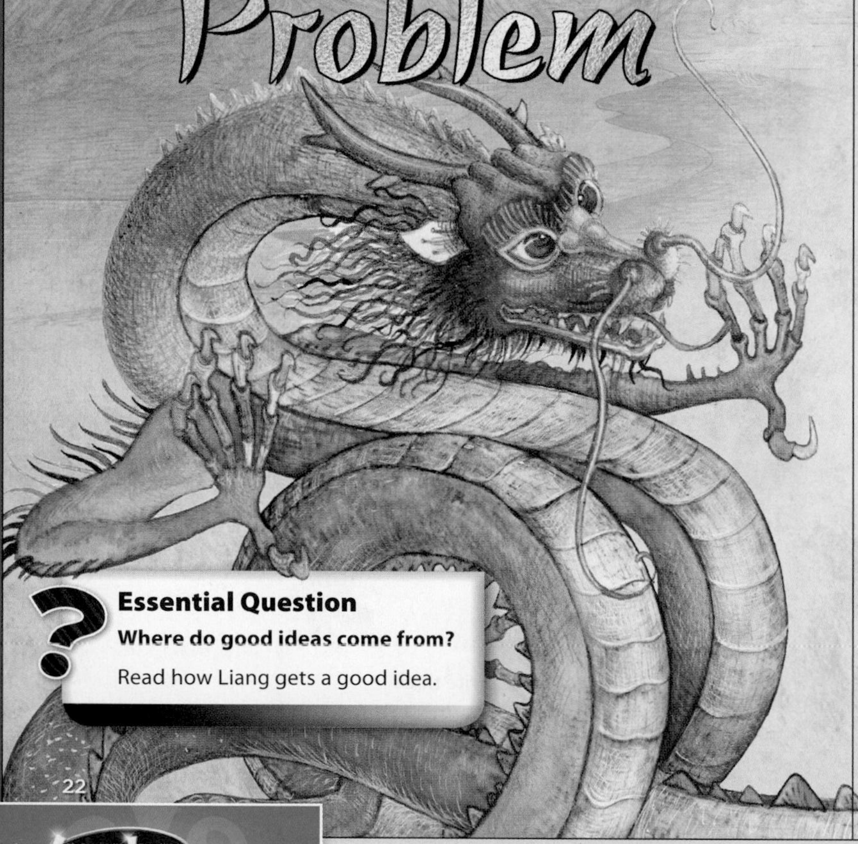

Essential Question

Where do good ideas come from?

Read how Liang gets a good idea.

Once upon a time, long before computers, baseball, or pizza, there lived a young man named Liang. During the day, Liang helped his father build furniture. At night, he made unique, **original** toys for the children in the village. He made birds with flapping wings. He carved dragons with rippling, moving scales, sharp claws, and red eyes. Every child in the village had one of Liang's dragons.

Liang knew a lot about dragons because one lived nearby on a mountain. A few times a year, the dragon would swoop down on the village. He ate water buffalo, pigs, and any people unlucky enough to be around. The Emperor had done nothing to get rid of the dragon even though his summer palace was near Liang's village.

One day in May, the Emperor and his family arrived to take up residence at his summer palace. As the procession passed through the village, the **gracious** Princess Peng smiled kindly at Liang. He fell instantly in love.

At dinner that night, Liang told his father that he wanted to marry Princess Peng. His father almost choked on the **stale**, hard rice ball he was eating.

"You're joking," his father said when he finally could speak.

"I'm serious!" insisted Liang.

His father began laughing so hard that the old chair he was sitting on broke. He lay on top of the **flattened** chair still laughing.

Valerie Sokolova

22 23

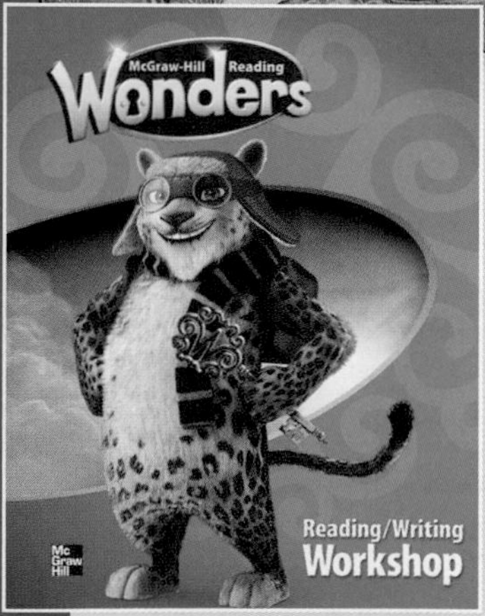

Reading/Writing Workshop

READING/WRITING WORKSHOP, pp. 22–23

Shared Read

Lexile 740L *TextEvaluator*™ 26

Connect to Concept: Clever Ideas

Explain that "The Dragon Problem" is a story about someone who uses a clever idea to solve a problem. Read "The Dragon Problem" with students. Note the vocabulary words previously taught are highlighted in the text.

Close Reading

Reread Paragraph 1: Tell students you are going to take a closer look at the introduction to "The Dragon Problem." Reread the first paragraph together. Ask: *Who is the main character? What does the author want us to know about him?* Model how to cite evidence to answer the question.

The main character is Liang. In the first paragraph, it says that he makes toy dragons for the children in his town. I think Liang's connection to dragons might be important later in the story.

Reread Paragraph 2: Model how to paraphrase the rest of the introduction in the second paragraph. Remind students that paraphrasing or restating the text in your own words helps to ensure that you understand what you are reading.

A dragon lived on a mountain close to Liang's village. He came to the village every few months and ate any animals and people who got in his way. The Emperor had a castle near the village, but had not done anything about the dragon.

"I'll show him," Liang **muttered** angrily as he stomped out of the room.

The next morning, the Emperor's messenger made an **official** announcement.

"His Most Noble Emperor proclaims that whoever gets rid of the dragon will marry his daughter, Princess Peng."

When he heard the announcement, Liang raced to the palace to be the first to sign up. Then he looked for his friend Lee to help him **brainstorm** ideas for getting rid of the dragon. Unfortunately, Lee was away. Liang sat on a bench frowning. Nearby, children were playing with the toy dragons he had made them.

"Liang, what's wrong?" the children asked.

"I have to get rid of the dragon on the mountain," he told them.

"I have an idea," said little Ling Ling. "Why don't you carve a giant dragon and leave it by the cave? It will alarm the real dragon and scare him into flying away."

Liang stared at her. "Perfect!" he shouted and rushed home. He worked **frantically** for days making a huge, scary dragon's head. The night he finished, he loaded it onto a cart and went up the mountain. When he got near the cave, Liang put the wooden head on top of a big rock. From the front, it looked like the rest of the dragon's body was behind the rock.

Liang hid in the bushes and gave a loud roar. "What's that noise?" growled the dragon rushing out of his cave. Then he saw the massive dragon head glaring at him. "Go away, or I'll eat you up," he commanded.

The huge dragon continued to glare at him. "He must be very strong. He's not afraid of me," thought the dragon, who, like all bullies, was a coward. He decided that now was a good time to take a long trip.

"Actually, I'm leaving now. Please make yourself at home in my cave," the dragon called out as he flew away.

A year later, Liang and Princess Peng were married. They opened a toy shop together and lived happily ever after.

Make Connections

Talk about where Liang's idea for scaring the dragon came from. **ESSENTIAL QUESTION**

Tell about a time when a friend helped you think of a good idea. **TEXT TO SELF**

24 25

READING/WRITING WORKSHOP, pp. 24–25

Make Connections

ESSENTIAL QUESTION

Have students review their purpose for reading and tell a partner what they have learned about clever ideas. Students should also discuss where Liang's ideas for scaring the dragon come from.

Continue Close Reading

Use the following lessons for focused rereadings.

→ Make, Confirm, or Revise Predictions, T18–T19

→ Character, Setting, Plot: Sequence, T20–T21

→ Fairy Tale, T22–T23

→ Context Clues, T24–T25

A C T Access Complex Text

▶ Connection of Ideas

Students may have difficulty understanding the dragon's implied motivation for leaving his cave. Read the second and third paragraphs on page 25.

→ *Why does the dragon leave his cave to the wooden dragon?* (The wooden dragon is not scared of the dragon, so the dragon becomes scared of the wooden dragon. He leaves because he is scared.)

→ *The dragon decides to take a long trip. What do we find out about the dragon in this section?* (The dragon is a coward.)

→ Comprehension Strategy

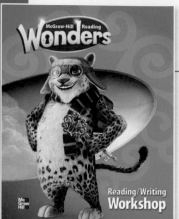

Reading/Writing Workshop

MINILESSON 10 Mins

Make, Confirm, or Revise Predictions

1 Explain

Explain that when they read a story, students may use text clues, illustrations, and other features to predict what will happen next. Remind students that making predictions will help them better understand the characters and plot of a story.

→ Good readers use clues from the story to make a prediction.

→ Students may stop to confirm or revise their predictions if necessary.

→ Often, students may find that making predictions will help them understand why a character speaks and acts in certain ways.

Point out that making predictions will help students follow and remember the events in a story.

2 Model Close Reading: Text Evidence

Model how to use clues from the story to make a prediction about what Liang will do to marry Princess Peng. Confirm the prediction by rereading page 24.

3 Guided Practice of Close Reading

COLLABORATE

Have students work in pairs to make a prediction about whether the dragon will return to his cave. Direct them to the final paragraph of the story. Partners can tell what clues in the text led to their predictions. Have partners discuss other predictions they can make as they read "The Dragon Problem."

Go Digital

View "The Dragon Problem"

OBJECTIVES

CCSS Refer to details and examples in a text when explaining what the text says explicitly and when drawing inferences from the text. **RL.4.1**

• Use text clues, illustrations, and other features to make a prediction about a story.

• Read to confirm predictions.

• Revise predictions as necessary.

ACADEMIC LANGUAGE

• *predict, confirm*

• Cognates: *predecir, confirmar*

Comprehension Strategy

Make Predictions

When you read the story "The Dragon Problem," you can use text clues and illustrations to predict what will happen next.

 Find Text Evidence

As I read, I see that Liang wants to marry Princess Peng. Then the Emperor announces that anyone who gets rid of the dragon will marry his daughter. My prediction that Liang will try to get rid of the dragon was correct.

page 24

I read that Liang is going to the palace to sign up to get rid of the dragon. My prediction was correct.

Your Turn

Make a prediction about whether the dragon will ever return to his cave. Tell what clues in the text led to your prediction. As you read, remember to use the strategy Make Predictions.

26

READING/WRITING WORKSHOP, p. 26

A C T Access Complex Text

▶ Specific Vocabulary

Students may have difficulty contextualizing the inferred actions surrounding the word *brainstorm*. Read page 24.

→ *Why does Liang want to find Lee?* (He needs ideas for how to get rid of the dragon.)

→ *What do the children do after Liang tells them his problem?* (They help him come up with an idea to get rid of the dragon.)

→ *What do these clues tell you about the word* brainstorm? (Brainstorming means working together to come up with ideas.)

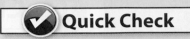

Monitor and *Differentiate*

✓ Quick Check

Do students use clues from the text to make predictions as they read? Do they read to confirm and revise if necessary?

Small Group Instruction

If No → | **Approaching Level** | Reteach p. T40 |
| **ELL** | Develop p. T56 |

If Yes → | **On Level** | Review p. T48 |
| **Beyond Level** | Extend p. T52 |

ON-LEVEL PRACTICE BOOK pp. 3–4

Read the passage. Use the make, confirm, or revise predictions strategy to predict what will happen in the story.

Coyote's Song

A boy was eating lunch in a field on his grandmother's farm.
12 Her farm was large and he had explored and seen many things that
25 morning. "Do not wander into the woods," Grandmother said. So he
36 kept to the fields. As he ate his lunch, he heard the call of a blue jay.
53 "I'll follow the sound of Blue Jay. I will find him and see his blue
68 feathers and listen to his song. I will bring him bread."
79 The afternoon sun was hot and there were many hills to climb,
91 but the boy was determined to follow the call. He walked slowly and
104 cautiously with care.
107 Soon he ran into Coyote who was looking for lunch but not having
120 any luck. He did not have a single crumb or morsel of food.
133 "Hello," said Coyote. "I see you are enjoying an afternoon walk."
144 "I've been exploring Grandmother's farm and now I'm looking for
154 Blue Jay. I want to listen to his song, see his beautiful feathers, and
168 give him bread."
171 Coyote took one look at the bread and became hungrier. Quietly,
182 he muttered to himself, "I will trick that boy, then he'll give me that
196 bread."
197 "I can sing a song and perform for you. Then you can give me your
212 bread," Coyote said with a grin.
218 "But howling and barking isn't a song, and you only have brown
230 fur," said the boy. "I want to hear Blue Jay's song and admire his
244 feathers, and I only have enough bread for him."

| **APPROACHING** pp. 3–4 | **BEYOND** pp. 3–4 | **ELL** pp. 3–4 |

Comprehension Skill

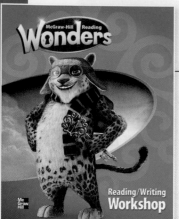

Reading/Writing Workshop

OBJECTIVES

CCSS Describe in depth a character, setting, or event in a story or drama, drawing on specific details in the text (e.g., a character's thoughts, words, or actions). **RL.4.3**

Identify the sequence of events in a story.

ACADEMIC LANGUAGE
- *sequence*
- Cognate: *secuencia*

SKILLS TRACE

CHARACTER, SETTING, PLOT

Introduce Unit 1 Week 1

Review Unit 1 Weeks 2, 6; Unit 2 Week 6; Unit 3 Week 6; Unit 4 Week 6; Unit 5 Weeks 1, 2; Unit 6 Week 6

Assess Units 1, 5

Character, Setting, Plot: Sequence

1 Explain

Explain to students that sequence is the order in which the key events of a story take place.

→ Students can summarize the plot by putting a story's key events in sequence.

→ Remind students that putting key events in order will help them understand the story.

2 Model Close Reading: Text Evidence

Identify the key events in the story "The Dragon Problem" on pages 23 and 24. Then model stating the events written on the graphic organizer in order by using words such as *first* and *next*.

 Write About Reading: Retell Model for students how to use the sequence of events from the graphic organizer to retell the first part of the story.

3 Guided Practice of Close Reading

 Have students complete a graphic organizer for "The Dragon Problem," going back into the text to find important plot events in the middle and end of the story. Students can work in pairs. Discuss the events as students complete the graphic organizer.

 Write About Reading: Retell Ask pairs to work together to write a retelling of "The Dragon Problem." Select pairs of students to share their retellings with the class.

Go Digital

Present the Lesson

Comprehension Skill

Sequence

Sequence is the order in which the key **story events** take place. Putting a story's events in sequence will help you to understand the **setting**, the **characters**, and the **plot**.

Find Text Evidence

When I reread pages 23 and 24 of "The Dragon Problem," I see that Liang wants to marry Princess Peng. The next day, the Emperor's messenger announces that anyone who gets rid of the dragon will marry the princess.

| Character |
| Liang |

| Setting |
| village in ancient China |

| Beginning |
| Liang sees Princess Peng and falls in love. The next day, the Emperor says anyone who gets rid of the dragon will marry the princess. |

| Middle |
| |

| End |
| |

Put key story events in order to help you summarize the plot.

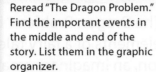

Your Turn COLLABORATE

Reread "The Dragon Problem." Find the important events in the middle and end of the story. List them in the graphic organizer.

Go Digital!
Use the interactive graphic organizer

27

READING/WRITING WORKSHOP, p. 27

Monitor and *Differentiate*

✔ Quick Check

As students complete the graphic organizer, do they successfully identify story events in sequence?

⬇

Small Group Instruction

If No → | Approaching Level | Reteach p. T47
| ELL | Develop p. T56

If Yes → | On Level | Review p. T51
| Beyond Level | Extend p. T55

ENGLISH LANGUAGE LEARNERS SCAFFOLD

Beginning	Intermediate	Advanced/High
Describe Review the definition of *sequence*. Say: *We use the words beginning, middle, and end to show sequence. Beginning is what happens first*. Reread the third paragraph on page 23. Say: *In the beginning, Liang sees Princess Peng and falls in love. This happens first*. Have students repeat.	**Identify** Reread "The Dragon Problem" on pages 23 and 24. Ask: *What happens first in the story? What happens next?* Have partners identify the sequence of events. Then have them fill in the sentence frames. *In the beginning, _____. Then, _____.*	**Discuss** Have students reread "The Dragon Problem" on pages 23 and 24 and identify the sequence of events. Have students fill in the graphic organizer with key events. Then have them work in pairs to discuss the sequence of events.

ON-LEVEL PRACTICE BOOK pp. 3–5

A. Reread the passage and answer the questions.
   Possible responses provided.

1. What are two events that happen after the boy hears Blue Jay?

   He climbs hills. He runs into Coyote.

2. Why is the setting of the woods important to the story?

   The woods are where Coyote tricks the boy.

3. Use the sequence of events to summarize the plot.

   First, the boy hears a blue jay. Then, he follows the sound of Blue Jay.

   Next, he finds Coyote who tricks the boy into giving him bread. Finally

   the boy finds his way home and Grandmother tells him he should have

   stayed on the right path.

B. Work with a partner. Read the passage aloud. Pay attention to intonation. Stop after one minute. Fill out the chart.

	Words Read	–	Number of Errors	=	Words Correct Score
First Read		–		=	
Second Read		–		=	

APPROACHING pp. 3–5	BEYOND pp. 3–5	ELL pp. 3–5

→ Genre: Literature

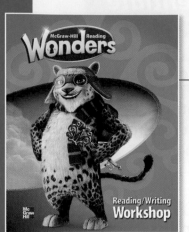

Reading/Writing Workshop

OBJECTIVES

CCSS Make connections between the text of a story or drama and a visual or oral presentation of the text, identifying where each version reflects specific descriptions and directions in the text. **RL.4.7**

CCSS By the end of the year, read and comprehend literature, including stories, dramas, and poetry, in the grades 4–5 text complexity band proficiently, with scaffolding as needed at the high end of the range. **RL.4.10**

Recognize the characteristics of a fairy tale.

ACADEMIC LANGUAGE

• fairy tale, fiction, character
• Cognate: *ficción*

 MINILESSON 10 Mins

Fairy Tale

1 Explain

Share with students the following key characteristics of a **fairy tale**.

→ Fairy tales have a main character who must go on a long journey or complete a difficult task.

→ Fairy tales usually contain imaginary creatures such as dragons.

→ Fairy tales end happily.

2 Model Close Reading: Text Evidence

Model ways to identify that "The Dragon Problem" is a fairy tale. Reread page 24 and identify elements of a fairy tale, such as Liang's task of getting rid of the dragon, an imaginary creature. Then point out the illustration. Ask: *What clue does the illustration give about Liang's plan to get rid of the dragon?*

3 Guided Practice of Close Reading

Have students work with partners to discuss whether the ending of "The Dragon Problem" is surprising for a fairy tale. Partners should discuss their reasoning with each other. Then have them share their work with the class.

Go Digital

Present the Lesson

Genre Literature

Fairy Tale

"The Dragon Problem" is a fairy tale.

Fairy tales:
- Have a main character who must complete a difficult task or journey.
- Usually contain imaginary creatures.
- Include illustrations and have a happy ending.

 Find Text Evidence

"The Dragon Problem" is a fairy tale. The story's main character must complete a difficult task. The story includes an imaginary creature, a dragon.

Use Illustrations Fairy tales are usually illustrated. Illustrations give visual clues about the characters, settings, and events in the story.

 Your Turn

With a partner, discuss whether the ending is surprising for a fairy tale. Explain why or why not.

28

READING/WRITING WORKSHOP, p. 28

Monitor and *Differentiate*

✓ **Quick Check**

Ask students to identify features of a fairy tale in "The Dragon Problem." Can they correctly identify these features?

Small Group Instruction

If No → | Approaching Level | Reteach p. T40
| ELL | Develop p. T56

If Yes → | On Level | Review p. T48
| Beyond Level | Extend p. T52

ELL ENGLISH LANGUAGE LEARNERS SCAFFOLD

Beginning	Intermediate	Advanced/High
Use Visuals Point to the illustration on page 22. Say: *The picture shows a dragon. The dragon is a character in the story.* Remind students that fairy tales include imaginary creatures such as dragons. Ask: *Is "The Dragon Problem" a fairy tale?*	**Explain** Have students identify elements of a fairy tale. Reread page 24. Ask: *What is Liang's challenge or difficult task? What does he decide to do?* Have students work in pairs to explain why "The Dragon Problem" is a fairy tale.	**Discuss** Reread page 24. Have students tell why "The Dragon Problem" is a fairy tale. Then have partners discuss characteristics of fairy tales using academic vocabulary.

ON-LEVEL PRACTICE BOOK p. 6

Before the Ball

I waved my wand. Light flashed, and in a puff of smoke, the pumpkin transformed into a beautiful horse and carriage! I turned to Cinderella and smiled. "Not bad. What do you think?" I asked.

"It's perfect!" Cinderella shouted. "How can I ever repay you for all you have done?"

"You can get into that carriage and get to the ball on time!" I said, and sent her on her way. Finally, Cinderella was off to the ball. My work was done.

Answer the questions about the text.

1. How do you know this story is a fairy tale?

   It has characters and events that could not exist in real life.

2. What events in the text identify it as a fairy tale?

   The main character completes a task; there is a happy ending.

3. What task does the main character have to complete? How does she complete it?

   The main character has to get Cinderella to the ball. She completes the

   task by turning the pumpkin into a carriage.

4. What other text feature does "Before the Ball" include? How does it show that the story is a fairy tale?

   illustration; The illustration shows that the character does not dress the

   way people do in real life; her actions could not happen in real life.

| APPROACHING p. 6 | BEYOND p. 6 | ELL p. 6 |

→ Vocabulary Strategy

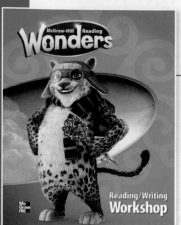

Reading/Writing Workshop

 MINILESSON 10 Mins

Context Clues

1 Explain

Remind students that they can often figure out the meaning of an unknown word by using context clues within the paragraph. Sometimes the author will use **synonyms** as context clues.

→ To find synonyms, students can look for words, separated by commas, that are near the unfamiliar word. These words may have the same meaning as the unknown word.

2 Model Close Reading: Text Evidence

Model using synonyms in the third sentence on page 23 to find the meaning of *unique*. Explain that the word *original* has a similar meaning to *unique*.

3 Guided Practice of Close Reading

Have students work in pairs to figure out the meanings of *rippling*, *alarm,* and *massive* in "The Dragon Problem." Encourage partners to go back into the text and use synonyms to help them determine each word's definition.

CCSS OBJECTIVES
Demonstrate understanding of figurative language, word relationships, and nuances in word meanings. Demonstrate understanding of words by relating them to their opposites (antonyms) and to words with similar but not identical meanings (synonyms). **L.4.5c**

ACADEMIC LANGUAGE
• *context clues, definitions, synonyms*
• Cognates: *definiciones, sinónimos*

SKILLS TRACE

CONTEXT CLUES: SYNONYMS

Introduce Unit 1 Week 1

Review Unit 1 Weeks 1, 2; Unit 4 Weeks 3, 5

Assess Units 1, 4

Use Reference Sources

Thesaurus Have students consult a print or online thesaurus to find other synonyms for the words *ripple, alarm,* and *massive*. Discuss the slight differences in meaning between the various synonyms given. Then have students choose an appropriate synonym to replace each word in the selection.

Review a thesaurus entry for the word *massive*. Discuss each part of the entry, including the definition, part of speech label, and lists of synonyms and antonyms. Then have students identify each of these parts in a thesaurus entry for *alarm*.

Go Digital

Present the Lesson

Vocabulary Strategy CCSS

Synonyms

As you read "The Dragon Problem," you may come across a word that you don't know. Look at the surrounding words and sentences for clues. Sometimes the author uses a synonym, a word that means almost the same thing as the unfamiliar word.

 Find Text Evidence

When I read the third sentence on page 23 in "The Dragon Problem," the word original *helps me to figure out what the word* unique *means.*

At night, he made unique, original toys for the children in the village.

Your Turn

COLLABORATE

Look for synonyms to find the meanings of the following words in "The Dragon Problem."
rippling, *page 23*
alarm, *page 24*
massive, *page 25*

29

READING/WRITING WORKSHOP, p. 29

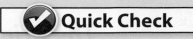

Monitor and *Differentiate*

✓ Quick Check

Can students identify and use context clues to determine the meanings of *rippling, alarm,* and *massive?*

⬇

Small Group Instruction

If No → | **Approaching Level** | Reteach p. T45 |
| **ELL** | Develop p. T61 |

If Yes → | **On Level** | Review p. T50 |
| **Beyond Level** | Extend p. T54 |

 ENGLISH LANGUAGE LEARNERS
SCAFFOLD

Beginning	Intermediate	Advanced/High
Derive Meaning Point out the words *rippling, alarm,* and *massive* in the story. Demonstrate *rippling* by showing the movement of a wave. Act out or pantomime the words *massive* and *alarm* for students. Then help them replace the words with words they know. Point out the cognate for *alarm* is *alarmar.*	**Practice** Point out the words *rippling, alarm,* and *massive.* Define each word. Have students find synonyms in the story and share them with a partner. Elicit from students how cognates helped them understand the text (*dragon, problem, princess, mountain*).	**Know and Use** Point out the words *rippling, alarm,* and *massive.* Ask students to identify synonyms for each word using clues in the story. Have students define the words. Then have partners share their definitions and confirm the meaning of each word using a dictionary.

ON-LEVEL PRACTICE BOOK p. 7

Read the sentences below. Circle the synonym clue in the sentence that helps you understand the meaning of each word in bold. Then, in your own words, write the meaning of the word in bold.

1. It can be fun to **explore** all the rooms of a museum. You can discover things you have never seen.

   to go see, to find something new

2. The pilot told us the plane would **depart** in five minutes. We were glad it would leave on time.

   to leave

3. The camel moved slowly, **burdened** by all packages it carried. People who saw the camel thought it was too loaded down.

   slowed down by something heavy

4. She **stumbled** into the room, tripping over the small step she had not seen in the doorway.

   tripped or fell

5. It was the **howling** that frightened the campers. Never before had they heard such a loud barking sound in the woods.

   a barking or crying sound

6. My cousin got **accustomed** to sleeping late during the summer. It was hard for her to get used to waking up early once school started.

   to be used to something

7. When it came time to **perform** for the judge, the singer was not nervous. He had been singing in contests since he was a child.

   to act or sing for another person or people

| APPROACHING p. 7 | BEYOND p. 7 | ELL p. 7 |

Develop Comprehension

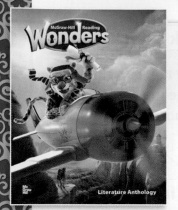

Literature Anthology

The Princess and the Pizza

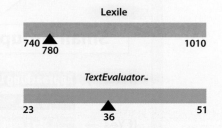

Text Complexity Range

Lexile

740 ▲ 780   1010

TextEvaluator™

23   36 ▲   51

Options for Close Reading

→ Whole Class

→ Small Group

→ Independent

CCSS **Genre · Fairy Tale**

The Princess and the Pizza

by Mary Jane and Herm Auch

1

Essential Question

Where do good ideas come from?

Read to find out how a princess gets out of a difficult situation.

Go Digital!

10

A C T Access Complex Text

What makes this text complex?

▶ **Purpose**

▶ **Specific Vocabulary**

▶ **Genre**

▶ **Organization**

▶ **Connection of Ideas**

▶ **Purpose**

Point out the illustration on pages 10–11. Have students connect the title to the illustration while making predictions about the purpose of the text. Tell students that determining the purpose of a text before reading it will help them understand it.

11

Predictive Writing

Have students read the title, preview the illustrations, and write their predictions about the characters and setting of this fairy tale. Point to the pizzas and encourage them to share how this might be a non-traditional fairy tale.

ESSENTIAL QUESTION

Ask a student to read aloud the Essential Question. Have students discuss how the story might help them answer the question.

Note Taking: Use the Graphic Organizer

As students read the selection, ask them to take notes by filling in the graphic organizer on **Your Turn Practice Book page 2** to record the character, setting, and events.

❶ Text Features: Illustrations

Look at the illustration on pages 10–11. Who do you think the main character is? (the princess in the middle) Why might it be hard to determine what time period it is? (It seems like a long time ago, but the princess is serving pizza.)

→ *Do you think the author wants to inform, entertain, or persuade with this story?* (entertain) *How might this fairy tale be different from others you've read? Explain why.* (Possible answer: This fairy tale might be funnier. Fairy tales do not usually have pizza, and the picture shows a princess in a pizza cart, leading a horse using pizza hanging from a stick.)

Develop Comprehension

② Skill: Sequence

Where does Paulina live? (She lives with her father in a kingdom neighboring the one where he was once king.) Why is Paulina upset on pages 12–13? (She misses doing princess activities.) Add these details to your chart.

Character
Paulina

Setting
a small kingdom

Beginning

↓

Middle

↓

End

Princess Paulina needed a job. Her father had given up his throne to become a wood-carver and moved them to a humble shack in a neighboring kingdom. Since the king was still learning, his carvings didn't sell, and Paulina's garden barely kept enough on the table.

Paulina missed princessing. She missed walking the peacock in the royal garden, surveying the kingdom from the castle tower, and doing the princess wave in royal processions.

12

A C T Access Complex Text

▶ Specific Vocabulary

Tell students that fairy tale writers sometimes insert words that lighten the mood in a humorous way. These words can be difficult to define out of context, but in the text they make sense.

→ Point to the words *princessing* and *princess-waving*. What used to happen when Paulina "princessed"? (She walked the peacock, surveyed the kingdom, and princess-waved.)

→ Tell students to monitor the different ways the author uses the word *princess* in a humorous way.

Paulina tried walking a stray chicken around her shack, but it only pecked at her bare toes. Surveying the kingdom from the shack's leaky roof made even more holes. She tried princess-waving to the townspeople from her father's cart, but nobody bothered to wave back. They just thought she was swatting at flies.

13

③ Strategy: Make Predictions

Teacher Think Aloud I will use the details about Paulina on pages 12 and 13 to make a prediction about what will happen to her in the story. I can see that she likes doing princess activities. Her father has given up his throne in their old kingdom and so she no longer gets to do the things she likes. I can predict that she will end up trying to be a princess again in some way. I will read to find out how she might try to become a princess again.

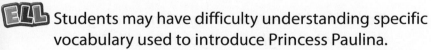

ELL Students may have difficulty understanding specific vocabulary used to introduce Princess Paulina.

→ Have students demonstrate how they wave. Say: *Princess Paulina had a special princess wave. What did Princess Paulina call her walking and her waving?* (princessing)

→ Have students point to Paulina. Ask: *What is she doing?* (princess waving) *What do the people think she is doing?* (swatting flies) *How does this make her feel?* (sad because she misses princessing)

Develop Comprehension

4 Skill: Sequence

Which event from page 14 makes Paulina excited? (Queen Zelda announces that she is running a competition to find a princess to become her son's bride.) Where would this event go on the chart? (It would go in the Beginning box in the plot sequence section.) Add this event to the chart.

Character
Paulina

Setting
a small kingdom

Beginning
Paulina enters a competition to marry a prince and is confident she will win.

↓

Middle

↓

End

One day, a page rode past the shack, announcing that Queen Zelda of Blom was seeking a true princess to become the bride of her son, Prince Drupert.

4 "This is my chance to get back to princessing," Paulina cried. She rummaged through her trunk of ex-princess stuff, brushed the wood shavings from her best ball gown, and blew away the bits of sawdust that clung to her diamond tiara. Then she tucked a piece of garlic into her bodice for good luck, snipped some fragrant herbs to cover up the garlic smell, and headed for the castle.

Paulina didn't expect much competition. There wasn't another princess for hundreds of miles. But when she got to Blom Castle, Paulina found she was only one of twelve princesses hoping to become the royal bride.

STOP AND CHECK

Make Predictions How does Paulina feel about her chances of winning the competition? Use text clues to make a prediction.

14

A C T Access Complex Text

▶ Specific Vocabulary

Some vocabulary used in fairy tales can be difficult for students because the objects exist in an unfamiliar world. Point out the words *gown*, *tiara*, and *bodice* on page 14 and *throne* on page 15.

→ *What context clues help you determine the meaning of* gown*?* (ex-princess stuff, best ball)

→ *If a ball in this sentence means "an extravagant dance," what might a ball gown look like?* (an extravagant dress)

→ Use similar prompts and the illustration on page 14 to review *tiara*, *bodice*, and *throne*.

When she looked into her assigned room, Paulina saw her bed piled with sixteen mattresses. "Oh, for Pete's sake. The old princess-and-the-pea trick. That's so once-upon-a-time." Naturally, Paulina didn't sleep all night because she felt the lumpy pea through all of the mattresses.

When the twelve princesses gathered in the throne room the next morning, the seven who looked bright-eyed were sent home. Now only Paulina and four other sleepy princesses remained.

First, they were made to write essays entitled "Why I Want to Have the **Gracious** and Exquisitely Beautiful Queen Zelda for My Mother-in-Law."

15

LITERATURE ANTHOLOGY, pp. 14–15

STOP AND CHECK

Make Predictions How does Paulina feel about her chances of winning the competition? (Paulina is confident that she will win the competition since she thinks there are no other real princesses near. I think she will probably win because she's confident.)

 Skill: Make Inferences

What is the first activity the contestants must complete? (They have to write an essay.) **What is humorous about the title of the essay?** (It's funny because the queen probably decided what the essay would be about. The title describes the queen as "gracious and exquisitely beautiful," so the queen is complimenting herself while she tests the princesses.) **What does the essay's title tell you about the queen?** (She thinks a lot of herself. The contest is supposed to be about finding somebody for her son, but this first activity is all about her.)

▶ **Prior Knowledge**

Remind students to recall details from other famous fairy tales, such as "The Princess and the Pea," to help them understand this story.

→ *How do you know Paulina is a real princess?* (She doesn't sleep because a pea is placed beneath her sixteen mattresses.)

ELL Help students understand the phrase "rummaged through." Explain that "rummage through" means "to look through something." Demonstrate how to rummage through a box or container. Then have students fill in the frame: *Princess Paulina _____ her trunk.* (rummaged through)

Develop Comprehension

6 Skill: Sequence

How does Paulina react to Queen Zelda's tests? (She thinks they are ridiculous. She offers suggestions for how to make them easier.) How does Queen Zelda react to Paulina's comments? (She becomes angry with her. She says that Paulina has a big mouth.)

A character's personality often moves the plot forward by creating conflict for the main character. How does Paulina's personality make things difficult for her on these pages? (The queen won't help Paulina out when the other princesses take most of the cooking supplies because the queen does not like Paulina.)

Prince Drupert and Queen Zelda finally appeared on the balcony. Queen Zelda did all the talking. "Congratulations, ladies, you have written some lovely essays, which I will keep in my scrapbook. And you have all passed the mattress test. But to make absolutely sure you are of royal blood, there is a second test. Only a true princess can wear these glass slippers."

"For Pete's sake, you never heard of sneakers?" Paulina asked.

Queen Zelda gave Paulina a sharp look. "Nobody said you had to hike in them. Just try them on."

After the royal page made his way around the room with the slippers, two big-footed princesses were sent home. Now only Paulina and two others remained. One was followed around by seven strange little men, and the other had such a long braid dragging behind her, Paulina kept tripping over it.

"For Pete's sake, you never heard of scissors?" Paulina cried.

Queen Zelda glared at Paulina.

16

ACT Access Complex Text

▶ **Genre**

Tell students that this story is a special kind of fairy tale called a fractured fairy tale. Authors of fractured fairy tales make references to familiar fairy tales in their stories. Have students reread page 16 to identify the fairy tale references.

→ *What references to familiar fairy tales does the author make on page 16?* ("glass slippers," *Cinderella*; "One was followed around by seven strange little men," *Snow White*; "the other had such a long braid," *Rapunzel*)

→ *Why does the author include these references?* (They make the story humorous.)

"You all have passed the second princess test. Your final task is to cook a feast that proves you worthy of being my dear Drupert's wife."

This set up a wail among the princesses, especially Paulina. "For Pete's sake. You have no royal chef?"

"Silence!" said the queen. "The table holds the makings for three fine feasts. Choose well, for the winner will become my dear Drupert's bride."

As Paulina started for the table, the long-haired princess tripped her, then loaded up with food. By the time Paulina got there, the seven strange little men had run off with everything but some flour, yeast, water, three overripe tomatoes, and a hunk of **stale** cheese.

"Hey, that's not fair! Queen Zelda, will you help me?"

"No," said the queen. "Because you have a big mouth."

17

LITERATURE ANTHOLOGY, pp. 16–17

7 Author's Craft: Word Choice

Authors choose descriptive words carefully to add rich meaning to text. What adjectives and verbs does the author use on these pages to describe how Queen Zelda feels about Paulina? Turn to a partner and identify specific words. (On page 16, it says that the queen glared at Paulina. The word *glared* tells us that the queen is annoyed.)

ELL Help students understand idioms and expressions on pages 16–17. Say the expression "for Pete's sake." Explain that it is used to show when someone is annoyed or upset. Teach students how to use "for Pete's sake" with a call-and-response strategy.

→ *You forgot your homework!* (Oh, for Pete's sake.)

→ *I missed the bus again!* (Oh, for Pete's sake.)

→ Have students point out when the queen tells Paulina that she has "a big mouth." Guide students to understand that if you have a big mouth, you talk too much. Model using the idiom in a sentence frame. *I did not tell my friend the secret. She has a _____ _____.*

Develop Comprehension

8 Skill: Sequence

Paraphrase what happens after Paulina is locked in her room. (She gives up on mixing ingredients and takes a nap. Then the queen comes to tell her that losers will be beheaded.) Add this detail to the chart.

Character
Paulina

Setting
a small kingdom

Beginning
Paulina enters a competition to marry a prince and is confident she will win.

Middle
Paulina wants to give up and carelessly mixes the ingredients. But the Queen tells her that the losers will be beheaded.

End

A servant escorted Paulina to her room and locked the door. "Hey! How can I cook without a bowl or spoons or pots?"

There was no reply.

Paulina tried to make bread, kneading the flour, water, and yeast together; but it only stuck to the tray in a **flattened** mess. She squished the tomatoes over the dough to brighten it up. It looked awful. She sprinkled cheese gratings over the top. It was still a mess, and Paulina was exhausted.

"For Pete's sake, where's your fairy godmother when you need her? I'm going to take a nap." She reached under the pile of mattresses, pulled out the offending pea, and climbed into bed.

She hadn't been sleeping long when there was a knock at the door.

"Only twenty minutes left," called Queen Zelda. "I don't smell anything cooking."

"I'm not cooking," said Paulina. "I'm napping. Then I'm going home."

"You're not going anywhere," said the queen. "The losers will be beheaded."

Paulina sat bolt upright. "Beheaded! You didn't tell us that!"

"I forgot," said the queen.

18

A C T Access Complex Text

▶ Organization

Point out that Paulina speaks to multiple people on pages 18 and 19. Review each of Paulina's quotes and to whom she is speaking in each.

→ *When Paulina says, "How can I cook without a bowl or spoons or pots?", who is she speaking to?* (the servant) *How do you know?* (The servant had just escorted her to her room and locked the door.)

→ *When Paulina says, "Where's your fairy godmother when you need her?", who is she speaking to?* (herself) *How do you know?* (She is alone and she feels frustrated.)

→ *When Paulina says, "But that's not fair!", who is she speaking to?* (Queen Zelda) *How do you know?* (She is responding to the queen.)

"Can't I have a second chance? How about I try to spin straw into gold? Or maybe I could guess a weird little man's name?"

"No second chances," declared the queen.

"But that's not fair!" Paulina cried.

"Who needs to be fair? I'm the queen."

8 **9**

19

LITERATURE ANTHOLOGY, pp. 18–19

9 Genre: Fairy Tale

How is Paulina like characters you would find in other fairy tales? (She is a princess. She faces a difficult task.) **How is she different from characters in other fairy tales?** (She doesn't seem to really care about winning or marrying the prince. She makes fun of other fairy tales.)

What other fairy tales can you think of that are a part of this one? Share your list with a partner. (The fairy godmother is a reference to "Cinderella." Pulling the pea from beneath the mattress is a reference to "The Princess and the Pea." Spinning straw into gold and guessing the name of a weird little man are references to "Rumpelstiltskin.")

ELL Have students reread the third paragraph on page 18. Use gestures to reinforce the meaning of the action verbs in this paragraph.

→ *Is Paulina trying to make bread in the first sentence?* (yes) *What does she do to the flour, water, and yeast?* (She kneads it.)

→ Use a gesture to show kneading. *Look at the picture on page 18. Does the dough look like it was kneaded?* (yes)

→ Continue using gestures to reinforce the meanings of *squished* and *sprinkled*.

Develop Comprehension

 Skill: Sequence

How does Paulina respond to the threat of being beheaded? (First, she tries to escape through the window. Then she throws the pizza into the fireplace to cook and paces back and forth. She is clearly worried.) What time-order word do you see on page 20? (Finally)

Paulina leaped out of bed and ran to the window, but it was an unbelievably long drop to the ground. The meal was her only hope. She rushed the tray over to the fireplace, stirred the few remaining hot coals, then crushed her garlic and sprinkled it over the mess for good luck. Finally, Paulina tossed on the herbs to cover up the garlic smell.

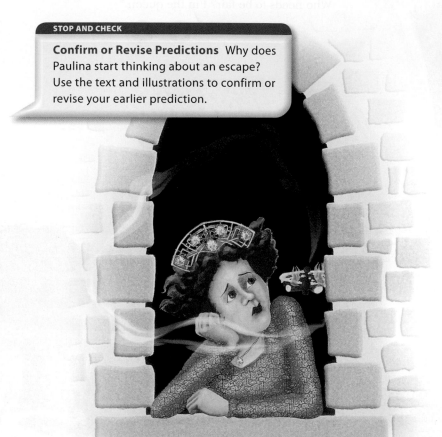

STOP AND CHECK

Confirm or Revise Predictions Why does Paulina start thinking about an escape? Use the text and illustrations to confirm or revise your earlier prediction.

20

A C T Access Complex Text

▶ **Connection of Ideas**

Point out the second sentence on page 20. Tell students that they will have to connect what they read on pages 18 and 19 to understand why Paulina feels this way.

→ *What inference can you make about how Paulina feels on page 20?* (Paulina is worried, afraid, and desperate.)

→ *Which text clues helped you make that inference?* (Queen Zelda told Paulina that the losers would be beheaded. There is no way to escape. Paulina has no choice but to cook a meal with the ingredients she has.)

Paulina paced back and forth, planning her escape. Perhaps she could make a deal with the long-haired princess to climb down her braid. She didn't notice that the goopy dough had browned into a crust, the tomatoes were bubbling, the hard bits of cheese had melted, and the fragrance of garlic and herbs filled the room.

A page opened the door. "Time's up."

Paulina took a deep breath and carried her tray into the great dining room.

21

LITERATURE ANTHOLOGY, pp. 20–21

STOP AND CHECK

Confirm or Revise Predictions Why does Paulina start thinking about an escape?

Teacher Think Aloud The first prediction we made was that Paulina would try to become a princess again. We were right, but now Paulina is planning to escape because she doesn't think she will win. Do you think her pizza will be a winning entry, allowing her to become a princess again? How do you think Paulina would respond if she does win? Explain your answer.

Prompt students to apply the strategy in a Think Aloud by paraphrasing text details to revise the prediction made earlier.

Student Think Aloud I can tell Paulina is really nervous about losing the competition because she tries to escape. Then she paces back and forth. But the more I read about her pizza cooking, the more I think she might win. Her pizza sounds delicious. I think that the author includes details like the browned crust, bubbling tomatoes, and fragrant garlic and herbs to show us that her entry will be a success. At this point, I don't think Paulina would care much if she does win except that she won't be beheaded. I will read to confirm my prediction.

▶ Sentence Structure

Tell students that they will need to unpack information in long sentences to understand them. Have students reread the first paragraph on page 21.

→ *What is the purpose of the long sentence?* (to show that the pizza is cooking) *Who is the she in the beginning of the sentence?* (Paulina) *Why doesn't she notice all of the events listed in the sentence?* (She's trying to plan her escape.)

ELL Encourage students to point out cognates on pages 20–21: princess/*princesa*, herbs/*hierbas*, escape/*escape,* tomatoes/*tomates.*

→ *Do you put herbs on a pizza?* (yes)

→ *Complete this sentence frame. The princess tries to make an _____ from the castle.* (escape)

LITERATURE ANTHOLOGY **T25L**

Develop Comprehension

11 Skill: Sequence

Does Paulina's attitude toward the competition change after the prince likes the dish she created? (No. She shrugs and responds to the queen only when she remembers the threat of being beheaded.)

Character
Paulina

Setting
a small kingdom

Beginning
Paulina enters a competition to marry a prince and is confident she will win.

Middle
Paulina wants to give up and carelessly mixes the ingredients. But the Queen tells her that the losers will be beheaded. Paulina's dish is good.

End

The other princesses had made lovely feasts, especially the one who had the seven strange little men to help her.

Prince Drupert went right to Paulina's tray. "It's not pretty, but it smells scrumptious." He helped himself to an unusually generous piece. "What do you call this dish?"

22

A C T Access Complex Text

▶ **Purpose**

Remind students that the purpose of the story is to entertain the audience with playful language and references to other fairy tales.

→ *How does the author humorously lighten the mood on pages 22 and 23?* (by creating wordplay with the phrase, "For Pete's sake")

→ *Despite the mood, why does the action remain tense?* (Paulina remembers that she will be beheaded if she loses.)

Paulina shrugged. "I don't know."

"It can't be an **official** entry in the contest if it doesn't have a name," said the queen.

"Oh, for Pete's sake," Paulina **muttered**.

"What's that?" snapped the queen. "Pete's what?"

Remembering the beheading threat, Paulina **frantically** tried to think of a name. "It's Pete's . . . ah . . ." 13

23

LITERATURE ANTHOLOGY, pp. 22–23

12 Vocabulary: Context Clues

What context clues surrounding *official* can help you remember the word's meaning? (The words *entry* and *contest* tell that it has something to do with competition. The "it" the queen is referring to in the sentence is Paulina's pizza, so *official* has to do with the cooking competition. I can infer that the queen has the authority to say whether the pizza can be an entry, so an official entry must be one that is properly authorized.)

13 Ask and Answer Questions

Generate a question about the text and share it with a partner. Find the answer and paraphrase the text to state your answer. For example, you might ask, "Why were the other princesses' feasts not good enough?" (The prince thought Paulina's pizza was especially tasty.)

ELL Point out the phrase "he helped himself." Fill a bowl with a classroom object such as markers. Pick up the bowl and take one while modeling. Then have students use the phrase in a sentence frame.

→ *I helped myself to a marker.*

→ *Prince Drupert is hungry, so he _____ to pizza.* (helps himself)

Develop Comprehension

14 Author's Craft: Alliteration

What sound is repeated at the beginning of words in this sentence? (the *p* sound)

15 Skill: Sequence

What happens after Paulina wins the contest? (She decides to open a pizza shop instead of marrying Prince Drupert.)

Character
Paulina

Setting
a small kingdom

Beginning
Paulina enters a competition to marry a prince and is confident she will win.

↓

Middle
Paulina wants to give up and carelessly mixes the ingredients. But the Queen tells her that the losers will be beheaded. Paulina's dish is good.

↓

End
Paulina wins the competition but opens a pizza shop instead of marrying Prince Drupert.

"Pizza?" The queen took a big bite. "Odd name, but it's tasty. The winner is Paulina's pizza."

"You mean I won't be beheaded?"

"I was only kidding about the beheading," said the queen.

"Then I was only kidding about wanting to marry Prince Drupert. Who needs him? I have other plans."

"Will you leave your recipe?" asked the queen.

"No way," said Paulina. "It's just become a family secret." She headed for the door.

"I liked you best," whined the queen, following close behind.

"Oh, for Pete's sake," muttered Paulina as she stomped across the drawbridge.

Princess Paulina's Pizza Palace opened a few weeks later. It featured unusual, carved furniture and fifty kinds of pizza.

14

Every Thursday, on the royal chef's night off, Queen Zelda and Prince Drupert came to Paulina's for popcorn-pineapple pizza. They often stayed to play cards with Paulina's father. **15**

24

A C T Access Complex Text

▶ Connection of Ideas

Sometimes authors include details that add to a text's richness. If a reader is not paying attention, he or she will miss out on important details in the story. Have students reread the last two paragraphs on page 24.

→ *What is something humorous about the name of Paulina's pizza shop?* (It is called Princess Paulina's

Pizza Palace even though she decided not to become a princess again.)

→ *Why would the Pizza Palace's furniture be carved "unusually"? Why is this humorous?* (Paulina's father is a wood-carver and is still learning. People might interpret his carvings to be unusual because he's not very good at it.)

From then on, whenever Paulina drove her pizza delivery cart through town doing the princess wave, everybody waved back and ran after her, asking about the day's specials.

Life was good. Paulina was grateful not to have Queen Zelda for a mother-in-law, but she still worried about one little thing.

She worried about getting Queen Zelda as her stepmother!

STOP AND CHECK

Confirm or Revise Predictions How does Paulina's story end? Confirm or revise your prediction about whether Paulina would win the competition.

25

LITERATURE ANTHOLOGY, pp. 24–25

STOP AND CHECK

Confirm Predictions How does Paulina's story end? (Paulina's story ends with her winning the competition but deciding to open up a pizza shop instead.)

Student Think Aloud Paulina's pizza turns out to taste as good as it was described while cooking. It is surprising that she manages to win despite the fact that the recipe is an accident, but I can confirm my prediction that the pizza would turn out well. I can also confirm that she does not care much that she wins. As a result, she is happy because she gets to open up her own pizza place.

Return to Predictions

Review students' predictions and purposes for reading. Ask them to answer the Essential Question. (Sometimes we don't think of ideas; instead, they seem to come out of nowhere. In this story, Paulina does not think of the idea for pizza; she stumbles upon it when forced to use leftover ingredients. She is smart to recognize that she should make use of the recipe and what everyone thinks is her "idea.")

ELL Help students use the illustrations and text to understand the ending of the story. Reread the last two paragraphs on page 25.

→ *Why does Paulina think life is good?* (She opened her own pizza shop and does not have Queen Zelda for a mother-in-law.)

→ *What does Paulina worry about?* (She worries that she will have Queen Zelda for a stepmother.)

About the Author

Meet the Author and Illustrator

Mary Jane and Herm Auch

Have students read the biography of the author and illustrator. Ask:

→ How might Mary Jane's love of reading as a child have affected how she writes stories as an adult?

→ How might a husband and wife working together make for a more interesting book?

Author's Purpose

To Entertain

Remind students of the many references in the story to other fairy tales. Then discuss Paulina's attitude toward the typical fairy tale events. Ask students why the author would choose to write the story this way. Students may say the author wanted to make Paulina's story more interesting and unexpected by making her more modern than a fairy-tale character.

Author's Craft

Humor

Have students find places where the author uses humor to lighten the mood.

→ The author uses Paulina's responses to create a humorous mood: *How about I try to spin straw into gold? Or maybe I could guess a weird little man's name?* (page 19)

→ The author lightens the mood with humorous descriptions: *After the royal page made his way around the room with the slippers, two big-footed princesses were sent home.* (page 16)

About the Author and Illustrator

Mary Jane Auch and Herm Auch are a wife and husband author-illustrator team. Mary Jane's love for books and art began at an early age. She could always be found sketching characters from her imagination into notebooks. When a polio epidemic kept Mary Jane home from school for the first half of second grade, her mother taught her how to read. By the time she returned to school, her teacher was introducing her to books that excited and challenged her. Mary Jane believes, "The writer in me was probably born the year that I almost missed second grade."

Mary Jane began collaborating with her husband, Herm, after finishing a number of young adult novels. Before then, Herm had spent years working as a graphic artist, editorial cartoonist, and digital artist. He photographs Mary Jane's artistic creations and works on the images in his digital studio.

Author's Purpose

The Princess and the Pizza is a special kind of fairy tale called a fractured fairy tale. Fractured fairy tales are based on fairy tales you know, but they change the characters, setting, points of view, and/or events, usually for humor. Why would the author choose to write Paulina's story this way?

(t) Herm Auch

26

LITERATURE ANTHOLOGY, pp. 26–27

Respond to Reading

Summarize

Use your Character, Setting, and Plot Chart to help you summarize the important events in the *The Princess and the Pizza*.

Character
Setting
Beginning
Middle
End

Text Evidence

1. How do you know that *The Princess and the Pizza* is a fairy tale? **GENRE**

2. Sequence the settings in the story. **SEQUENCE**

3. When Prince Drupert sees Paulina's dish, he says, "It's not pretty, but it smells scrumptious." What is a synonym for *scrumptious*? Use context clues to explain how you know. **SYNONYMS**

4. Write about how Paulina's character changes over the course of the story. **WRITE ABOUT READING**

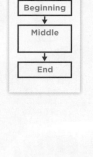

Make Connections

How did Paulina get out of a difficult situation and win the competition? **ESSENTIAL QUESTION**

Fairy tales and fables often include characters who think of clever ideas to solve a problem. What can these tales teach us about where good ideas come from? **TEXT TO WORLD**

27

Make Connections *Analytical Writing*

Essential Question Have partners write about Paulina's main problem in the story and how she used a good idea and a lot of luck to solve it.

Text to World Students should list how good ideas can come from a variety of sources—observation, quick-thinking, brainstorming, having a discussion, sharing information, feeling pressured, and at times out of the blue!

Respond to Reading

Summarize

Review with students the information from their graphic organizers. Model how to use the sequence of events to summarize *The Princess and the Pizza*.

Analytical Writing **Write About Reading: Summarize**
Remind students that a summary of a story is a restatement of all the major events. You can summarize an entire story or just a section of the story.

Ask students to write a summary of the selection, using the events in the plot that they identified. Remind them that the events in their summary must be in the correct order, or sequence. Have students share their summaries with a partner.

Text Evidence

1. **Genre** <u>Answer</u> The story takes place long ago in a kingdom and a character has to complete a difficult task. <u>Evidence</u> Paulina is a former princess who must complete several difficult tasks to win a competition.

2. **Sequence** <u>Answer</u> The sequence of the settings is Paulina's original kingdom, the neighboring kingdom, Blom Castle, and the pizza shop. <u>Evidence</u> Paulina moved to the next kingdom over, went to Blom Castle for the contest, then opened a pizza shop.

3. **Synonyms** <u>Answer</u> "delicious" <u>Evidence</u> Context clues, such as Prince Drupert going directly to Paulina's tray and helping himself to a large piece

 4. **Write About Reading: Sequence** Paulina learns what she truly wants out of life. Paulina changes from wanting to marry Prince Drupert to wanting to open her own pizzeria.

Develop Comprehension

"Tomás and His Sons"

Text Complexity Range

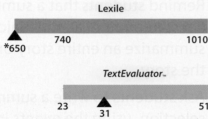

Lexile

*650   740   1010

TextEvaluator™

23   31   51

Literature Anthology
*Although the selection score falls below the Lexile range, the organization of the fable may be challenging to students.

Options for Close Reading

→ Whole Class

→ Small Group

→ Independent

CCSS Genre · Fable

Compare Texts
Read to find out how Tomás and Maria come up with an idea to solve their problem.

TOMÁS AND HIS SONS

28

A C T Access Complex Text

What makes this text complex?

▶ **Organization**

▶ **Genre**

▶ **Organization**

Explain to students that authors tell stories in different ways. It is up to the reader to identify how a text is organized in order to understand the story. Flashbacks and foreshadowing can help readers determine how a text is organized. Reread the last three paragraphs on page 29 with students.

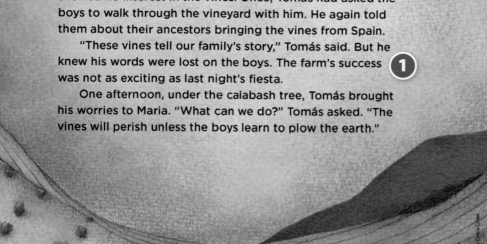

Tomás was a hardworking farmer. His vines produced the best grapes of any vineyard around. "It is the soil, which has been tilled for years," he told people if they asked him his secret. Other times, he said, "Mexico's sun gives the grapes no choice but to grow large and juicy."

Over the years, Tomás's stories became more inventive. But Tomás knew why his grapes were the best. Generations of hard work had kept the land plentiful.

Hard work was something Tomás knew well. But his sons, Eduardo, Miguel, and Luis, were the three laziest boys in all of Mexico.

While their parents tilled the earth under the hot afternoon sun, the boys slept. As the sun bent toward evening, the brothers rose. They stumbled into the kitchen. They filled their plates with eggs and tortillas. By nightfall they were wide awake. Soon, they were off to the village to sing and dance until morning.

Tomás worried about the land. What would happen once he and his wife, Maria, were too old to work? Their sons showed no interest in the vines. Once, Tomás had asked the boys to walk through the vineyard with him. He again told them about their ancestors bringing the vines from Spain.

"These vines tell our family's story," Tomás said. But he knew his words were lost on the boys. The farm's success was not as exciting as last night's fiesta. **1**

One afternoon, under the calabash tree, Tomás brought his worries to Maria. "What can we do?" Tomás asked. "The vines will perish unless the boys learn to plow the earth."

29

LITERATURE ANTHOLOGY, pp. 28–29

Compare Texts ✎ Analytical Writing

Students will read another traditional story, a fable, about people who must think creatively to solve a problem. Explain that a fable, like a fairy tale, may have mythical creatures. It also has a moral, or a lesson to be learned. Ask students to do a close reading of the text, rereading to deeply understand the content. Encourage them to use the making predictions strategy or other strategies they know to help them. They will also take notes about the characters, setting, and plot. Then students will use the text evidence they gathered to compare this text with *The Princess and the Pizza*.

1 **Ask and Answer Questions**

How are Tomás's values different from those of his sons? Why is this an important problem for Tomás?

✎ Analytical Writing **Write About Reading** Create a chart that shows how Tomás and his sons are alike and different. Then write a sentence that summarizes his problems with his sons. (Tomás is hardworking and respectful of the land and vineyards, but his sons prefer to sleep late and avoid work.)

→ *Why does the author use a flashback on the first page of the story?* (The author uses a flashback to tell the reader why Tomás is worried.)

→ *How does the flashback help you to determine how the author organized this story?* (It tells the reader about the character's problem. The rest of the story will focus on solving the problem.)

ELL Have students point to and identify the grapes in the picture on page 28. *The setting of this fable is in a vineyard. Point to the vineyard.* Clarify the different terms associated with vineyards using the illustrations.

→ *Grapes grow on _____.* (vines) *Many vines together make up a _____.* (vineyard)

Develop Comprehension

2 Ask and Answer Questions

What is Maria's idea for persuading her sons to work? How does she come up with the idea?

With a partner, paraphrase the part of the story where Maria comes up with a plan to make her sons work. (Maria and Tomás try to think of a solution for weeks, until one day Maria sees a gourd falling from a tree. The gourd makes her think of a time when Luis was motivated to clean his room because he needed to find his gourd drum.)

3 Ask and Answer Questions

What treasure have Luis and his brothers found at the end of the story?

Analytical Writing **Write About Reading** Write a sentence or two that summarizes the lesson Tomás's sons learned in the story. (The sons learned that hard work can bring more rewards than anything.)

Maria knew the boys valued a warm night under the stars. Why would they want to work in the heat of the day?

"There must be a way to get the boys to plow," Maria said. "Let's **brainstorm** ideas to find one that will work."

Each day, Tomás and Maria sat under a calabash tree and talked over their problem. One day, when it seemed no **original** ideas would ever come to them, a gourd fell from the tree. Maria picked up the gourd. Turning it in her hands, she remembered something that had worked in the past.

"Of course, Tomás!" said Maria. "The boys need a purpose, a real reason for doing something. Last year, Luis could not find his gourd drum. His room was a mess. His clothes were lying all around. It was not possible to find his bed, much less a small gourd drum! The only way to find his drum was to clean his room."

"And did he?" asked Tomás.

Maria smiled. "He did. Once he had cleaned, Luis **2** found his great treasure buried under a pile of shirts."

Tomás thought about this. "Maria," he said after a while, "what if the boys believe a treasure is buried in the vineyard? Would they dig to find it?"

"I think that's just the motivation they need," Maria said.

The next day Tomás told his sons he had been keeping a secret. "When our ancestors brought the vines to this land, they also brought a great treasure. I believe it is buried in the vineyard. For years I have tilled the earth to find it. We will be rich beyond belief once it is found." Right away his sons declared they would help Tomás find the treasure.

30

A C T Access Complex Text

▶ **Genre**

Remind students that fables are short stories that teach a moral, or lesson. Point out that there is often a turn of events that brings the story to a close and tells the lesson.

→ *What is the turning point in this story?* (when Tomás tells his sons that there is a treasure buried in the vineyard)

→ *How do you know this is the turning point?* (The sons have not been motivated to work in the vineyard until this point.)

→ *What lesson did Tomás teach his sons?* (The family vineyard is a treasure.)

Many happy seasons passed with the family digging together in the vineyard. The sons were amazed each year to see the big, juicy grapes. Even more, they were thrilled by the wealth the crop had brought them.

One day, long after the farmer's sons had taken over the vineyard, Luis asked his brothers, "Have we found the great treasure yet?"

The three brothers began to laugh. They had forgotten that they were digging to find treasure. Yet all their hard work made them realize that their vineyard was a treasure.

Make Connections

How did Tomás and Maria come up with an idea to solve their problem? **ESSENTIAL QUESTION**

Compare the ways in which characters come up with ideas. **TEXT TO TEXT**

31

LITERATURE ANTHOLOGY, pp. 30–31

Make Connections • *Analytical Writing*

Essential Question Have students list specific details from the event that sparked Maria's idea about how to get the boys involved in the vineyard. If students have trouble answering, suggest they review and paraphrase Maria's story about Luis's messy room and what prompted her to tell it.

Text to Text Have groups of students compare their responses to the Ask and Answer Questions prompts with the characters and events in *The Princess and the Pizza.* Each group can report back to the whole class. Ask one group to compare the problems in both stories. (Both Paulina and Tomás were not satisfied with their prospects for the future.) Have another group compare the solutions in both stories. (Paulina's solution was to compete to marry a prince and leave her home and father, while Tomás's solution was to trick his sons into working hard on his land.) Ask a third group to compare the final outcome of each story and how the characters felt. (Paulina became a success without being a princess. Tomás got to see his sons working hard and his land preserved for the future.)

ELL Students might have trouble with the way the word *treasure* is used in this story. Tell students that treasures come in many forms.

→ Have students point to and identify the treasure that the brothers find. *Is it gold?* (no) *What type of treasure do the brothers find?* (the family vineyard)

→ *What do the brothers think about the vineyard?* (Their hard work made them appreciate the vineyard and made them realize that the vineyard was the treasure.)

→ Encourage students to write complete sentences describing a treasure they found.

Phonics/Fluency

MINILESSON
20 Mins

Short Vowels

Go Digital

Short Vowels

Present the Lesson

View "The Dragon Problem"

OBJECTIVES

CCSS Use combined knowledge of all letter-sound correspondences, syllabication patterns, and morphology (e.g., roots and affixes) to read accurately unfamiliar multisyllabic words in context and out of context. **RF.4.3a**

CCSS Read on-level prose and poetry orally with accuracy, appropriate rate, and expression on successive readings. **RF.4.4b**

Rate: 84–104 WCPM

ACADEMIC LANGUAGE

• intonation
• Cognate: entonación

ELL

Refer to the sound transfers chart in the **Language Transfers Handbook** to identify sounds that do not transfer in Spanish, Cantonese, Vietnamese, Hmong, and Korean.

1 Explain

Display the *Apple, Egg, Insect, Octopus,* and *Umbrella* **Sound-Spelling Cards**. Point to each card and say the short-vowel sound. Provide a sample word for each spelling. Explain that the /e/ sound has two different spellings: *e* as in *egg* and *ea* as in *head*. Explain that the /i/ sound also has two different spellings: *i* as in *ink* and *y* as in *gym*.

2 Model

Write the word *strap* on the board. Underline the letter *a* and model how to pronounce the short-vowel sound /a/. Then model pronouncing the whole word. Run your finger under the word as you sound it out, emphasizing the short-vowel sound.

3 Guided Practice

Write the following list of words with short-vowel sounds on the board. Help students identify the short-vowel sound in each word. Then have students pronounce each word.

spent	wish	strung
crack	blond	myth
drill	bread	splash

Read Multisyllabic Words

Transition to Longer Words Draw a T-chart on the board. In the first column, write *net, test,* and *fish*. In the second column, write *magnet, contest,* and *selfish*. Have students chorally read the words in the first column. Point to the words in the second column and explain that they contain the shorter words from the first column.

Underline the shorter words *net, test,* and *fish* in *magnet, contest,* and *selfish*. Model how to blend the two syllables to read the words. Point to each word in random order and have students read the words chorally.

Inflectional Endings

1 Explain

Adding -ed, -s, and -ing to verbs creates new verb forms and tenses.

→ For many base words, adding -ed, -s, or -ing does not change the spelling of the base word: *spill/spilled/spills/spilling*.

→ Adding -ed to a base word puts the action in the past tense: *pack/packed*.

→ Adding -s or -ing to a base word puts the action in the present tense: *stop/stops, jump/jumping*.

2 Model

Write and say *wish*. Have students repeat it. Model creating new words by adding the endings -ed, -s, and -ing.

3 Guided Practice

Write the inflected forms of *spread* and *crush*. Have students underline the endings, say the words, and discuss their tenses.

Intonation

Explain/Model Explain that part of reading with intonation is changing the tone of your voice. Stressing important words will help students to express the meaning of what they are reading. Reading a word slowly can show it is important. Reading a word loudly can show excitement.

Model reading the first six paragraphs on page 24 of "The Dragon Problem." Change the tone of your voice to express how Liang feels. Then change it again to make an important announcement. Exaggerate intonation when asking a question.

Practice/Apply Divide students into groups. Have each group read one paragraph from the passage. Remind students to use correct intonation based on what happens in the story and how the characters feel. Offer feedback as needed.

Daily Fluency Practice

Students can practice fluency using **Your Turn Practice Book.**

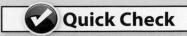

Monitor and *Differentiate*

✔ Quick Check

Can students decode multisyllabic words with short-vowel spellings? Can students read words with inflectional endings? Can students read fluently?

Small Group Instruction

If No →	**Approaching Level**	Reteach pp. T42, T46
	ELL	Develop pp. T58, T62
If Yes →	**On Level**	Review p. T48
	Beyond Level	Extend p. T52

ON-LEVEL PRACTICE BOOK p. 8

A. Read each sentence. Circle the word that has a short-vowel sound. Write the word on the line.

1. The strange (bell) always chimes so late! bell

2. My poor (health) was a good reason to stay home. health

3. The tire was (flat) so we needed to wait. flat

4. I could hear the (crunch) of the toy falling down the stairs. crunch

5. She gave the team (hints) so they could find the clue. hints

B. Write the correct -ed, -s, and -ing forms for each verb.

Verb	+ ed	+ s	+ ing
1. float	floated	floats	floating
2. work	worked	works	working
3. start	started	starts	starting
4. follow	followed	follows	following
5. answer	answered	answers	answering

APPROACHING p. 8	BEYOND p. 8	ELL p. 8

Go Digital

www.connected.mcgraw-hill.com
RESOURCES
Research and Inquiry

Wrap Up the Week
Integrate Ideas

Tim Macpherson/Stone +/Getty Images

RESEARCH AND INQUIRY

Clever Ideas

OBJECTIVES

CCSS Recall relevant information from experiences or gather relevant information from print and digital sources; take notes and categorize information, and provide a list of sources. **W.4.8**

CCSS Differentiate between contexts that call for formal English (e.g., presenting ideas) and situations where informal discourse is appropriate (e.g., small-group discussion); use formal English when appropriate to task and situation. **SL.4.6**

- Follow roles in a discussion.
- Take notes from sources.
- Practice interviewing skills.

ACADEMIC LANGUAGE

interview, collaborate, formal language

Interview a Classmate

COLLABORATE

Explain that students will work in pairs and conduct interviews to find out how their partners come up with clever ideas. They will then collaborate to create a list of ideas they discussed and share that list with another student group. Discuss the following steps:

1 Prepare for the Interview Have students prepare written interview questions that require their partners to recall relevant information from their own experiences and to give examples. As a starting point for their questions, encourage students to review this week's reading selections and recall how different characters came up with ideas.

2 Conduct the Interview Remind students that it is appropriate to use formal language while interviewing their partners. Have them ask their partners to elaborate on ideas when necessary.

3 Guided Practice Have student interviewers take notes while their partners are speaking. Remind them to keep their notes organized and legible so they can refer back to them easily.

4 Create the List Have pairs use their interview notes to make a list of ways that people can come up with clever ideas. Tell students to include only the most important or relevant ideas in their lists.

Present the List

Have students present their lists to another pair or group and answer any questions other students may have. Encourage them to build on each other's ideas and to express their own ideas clearly. Have students use the online Listening Checklist to evaluate their roles in listening to and discussing the projects.

TEXT CONNECTIONS  *Analytical Writing*

OBJECTIVES

CCSS Compare and contrast the treatment of similar themes and topics (e.g., opposition of good and evil) and patterns of events (e.g., the quest) in stories, myths, and traditional literature from different cultures. **RL.4.9**

CCSS Review the key ideas expressed and explain their own ideas and understanding in light of the discussion. **SL.4.1d**

Text to Text

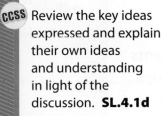

Cite Evidence Explain to students that they will work in groups to compare information they have learned about where good ideas come from in all the texts they have read. Model how to compare this information by using examples from the week's **Leveled Readers** and from *The Dragon Problem*, **Reading/Writing Workshop** pages 22–25. Review class notes and completed graphic organizers. You may also wish to model going back into the text for more information. You can use an Accordion Foldable® to record comparisons.

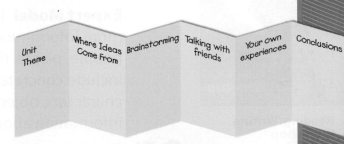

Students should cite at least three examples from each text.

Dinah Zike's
FOLDABLES®
Study Organizer

Present Information Ask groups of students to present their findings to the class. Encourage discussion, asking students to comment on personal experiences with coming up with good ideas.

WRITE ABOUT READING  *Analytical Writing*

OBJECTIVES

CCSS Apply *grade 4 Reading standards* to literature (e.g., "Describe in depth a character, setting, or event in a story or drama, drawing on specific details in the text [e.g., a character's thoughts, words, or actions]"). **W.4.9a**

CCSS Identify the reasons and evidence a speaker provides to support particular points. **SL.4.3**

Write an Analysis

Cite Evidence Using evidence from a text they have read, students will analyze how the author uses the events in the story to develop the characters and the plot.

Discuss how to analyze a text by asking *how* and *why* questions.

→ How will understanding the events in the story help you to understand the characters and plot?

→ Why is the sequence of events important to the story?

Read and discuss the student model on **Your Turn Practice Book** page 9. Then have students select a text and review the details they recorded about the sequence of the story events. Have them write an analysis that explains how the sequence of events helps them to understand the characters and the plot. Remind students that strong explanatory writing clearly states the topic and is written in complete sentences.

Present Your Ideas Ask partners to share their paragraphs and discuss how the evidence they cited from the text supports their ideas.

Readers to Writers

MINILESSON 10 Mins

Writing Traits: Ideas

Descriptive Details

Expert Model Explain that good writers use descriptive details to give more information and help readers create a picture in their minds of people, places, things, or events. In narrative writing, descriptive details include concrete words and phrases and sensory details that describe characters, objects, settings, and actions in a story. They may give information about size, number, shape, or color.

 Read aloud the expert model from "The Dragon Problem." Ask students to listen for the descriptive details that help the reader picture the toys Liang made: *flapping wings, sharp claws, red eyes*. Have students talk with partners to identify these details.

Student Model Remind students that adding descriptive details helps readers picture what is happening in a story. Read aloud the student draft "The Lost Prince." As students follow along, have them focus on descriptive details the writer added to his draft.

 Invite partners to talk about the draft and the descriptive details that Martin added. Ask them to suggest places where Martin could add more descriptive details.

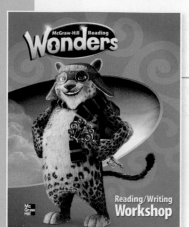

Reading/Writing Workshop

OBJECTIVES

CCSS Write routinely over extended time frames (time for research, reflection, and revision) and shorter time frames (a single sitting or a day or two) for a range of discipline-specific tasks, purposes, and audiences. **W.4.10**

CCSS Use concrete words and phrases and sensory details to convey experiences and events precisely. **W.4.3d**

- Analyze models to understand how descriptive details add information.
- Write about a personal experience.
- Add descriptive details to revise writing.

ACADEMIC LANGUAGE

descriptive details, topic

Expert Model

Student Model

 Genre Writing

Narrative Text

For full writing process lessons and rubrics, see:

→ Friendly Letter, pages T344–T349

→ Personal Narrative, pages T350–T355

Go Digital

CCSS **Writing Traits** Ideas

Readers to...

Writers

Writers include specific, concrete, and sensory details when writing stories. These details provide a visual picture for the reader. Reread the excerpt below from "The Dragon Problem."

Martin wrote a story about a prince. Read Martin's revisions to a section of his story.

Editing Marks

⌐⌐ Switch order.

∧ Add.

⌄ Add a comma.

⊙ Add a period.

◞ Take out.

SP Check spelling.

≡ Make a capital letter.

Grammar Handbook

Sentences

See page 450.

Descriptive Details

Identify the **descriptive details** in the story. How do the details help readers picture what is happening in the story?

Expert Model

During the day, Liang helped his father build furniture. At night, he made unique, original toys for the children in the village. He made birds with flapping wings. He carved dragons with rippling, moving scales, sharp claws, and red eyes. Every child in the village had one of Liang's dragons.

Student Model

THE LOST PRINCE

Once there was a prince who *in a faraway Kingdom* always got lost. He turned left when he meant to turn right. He walked ten miles instead of one. He got lost *every day of his life* a lot.

The King hired a wise man to help his son. First, the wise man *wrote* an R on the prince's right hand and an L on his left. Next, he gave him a compass *that showed all four directions*. Finally, he invented a machine to tell the prince when he had gone too far.

Your Turn

COLLABORATE

✔ Identify the details.
✔ Did Martin use complete sentences?
✔ Tell how revisions improved his writing.

Go Digital!
Write online in Writer's Workspace

30

31

READING/WRITING WORKSHOP, pp. 30–31

ELL ENGLISH LANGUAGE LEARNERS SCAFFOLD

As English Language Learners write during the week, provide support to help them respond to the prompts. For example:

Beginning	**Intermediate**	**Advanced/High**
Write Help students complete the sentence frames. *The story takes place in a____ kingdom. The prince walked ____ miles instead of one. The wise man wrote an R on the Prince's ____ hand. Another descriptive detail is ____.*	**Describe** Ask students to complete the sentence frames. Encourage students to provide details. *The story takes place ____. The prince walked ____. The wise man wrote ____. Some descriptive details are ____.*	**Discuss** Check for understanding. Ask: *Where does the story take place? How far does the prince walk? What does the wise man write on the prince's hands? What are some descriptive details in the story?*

Writing Every Day: Ideas

DAY 1

Writing Entry: Descriptive Details

Prewrite Provide students with the prompt below.

Tell about a time when a good idea came from an unexpected place. Include descriptive details that tell about this experience.

Have partners think of a time when they or someone they know or read about had a good idea. Ask them to jot down descriptive details about the experience that they might include in their drafts.

Draft Have each student select an experience to write about. Remind students to include descriptive details in their drafts.

DAY 2

Focus on Descriptive Details

Use **Your Turn Practice Book** page 10 to model adding details.

Once there was a princess who lived in a castle. She was tired of climbing stairs. She asked her father for a platform she could stand on that would carry her from floor to floor. Today we call it an elevator.

Model adding descriptive details by revising the first sentence.

Once there was a clever princess who lived in a huge castle.

Discuss how adding descriptive details creates a clearer picture in the reader's mind. Guide students to add more descriptive details to the rest of the model.

Writing Entry: Descriptive Details

Revise Have students revise their writing from Day 1 by adding two or three descriptive details.

Use the **Conferencing Routines**. Circulate among students and stop briefly to talk with individuals. Provide time for peer reviews.

Edit Have students use Grammar Handbook page 450 in the **Reading/Writing Workshop** to edit for errors in sentences.

Conferencing Routines

Teacher Conferences

STEP 1

Talk about the strengths of the writing.

The introduction makes me want to read more. You introduced the characters and the problem they face. I want to read on to find out how they solve the problem.

STEP 2

Focus on how the writer uses the target trait for the week.

These descriptive details help me picture the characters in the story. It would help me if you added some descriptive details to tell more about the setting.

STEP 3

Make concrete suggestions for revisions. Have students work on a specific assignment, such as those to the right, and then meet with you to review progress.

DAY 3

Writing Entry: Descriptive Details

Prewrite Ask students to search their Writer's Notebook for topics to write a draft. Or, provide a prompt, such as the following:

Tell about a time when a good idea helped solve a problem. Give descriptive details that tell about the experience.

Draft Ask students to create a sequence chart with the events written in the order they happened. Then have them think about the descriptive details that they might include in their writing. Students can then use their sequence charts to begin their drafts.

DAY 4

Writing Entry: Descriptive Details

Revise Have students revise the draft writing from Day 3 by adding two or three descriptive details to describe the events more clearly. As students are revising their drafts, hold teacher conferences with individual students. You may also wish to have students work with partners to peer conference.

Edit Invite students to review the rules for sentences on Grammar Handbook page 450 in the **Reading/Writing Workshop** and then edit their drafts for errors.

DAY 5

Share and Reflect

Discuss with the class what they learned about adding descriptive details to help readers create a picture in their minds. Invite volunteers to read and compare draft text with text that has been revised. Have students discuss the writing by focusing on how the descriptive details help them picture what is happening in the story. Allow time for individuals to reflect on their own writing progress and record observations in their Writer's Notebooks.

McGraw-Hill Companies, Inc. Ken Karp, photographer

Suggested Revisions

Provide specific direction to help focus young writers.

Focus on a Sentence
Read the draft and target one sentence for revision. *Rewrite this sentence by adding descriptive details that tell about the _____.*

Focus on a Section
Underline a section that needs to be revised. Provide specific suggestions. *This section is very interesting. I want to know more about the _____. Provide descriptive details to help me picture that more clearly in my mind.*

Focus on a Revision Strategy
Underline a section of the writing and ask students to use a specific revision strategy, such as substituting. *Some of these words could be more descriptive. Try changing a few to give more information.*

Peer Conferences

Focus peer response groups on adding descriptive details to help readers create a picture in their minds. Provide this checklist to frame discussion.

- ☑ Does the writing include descriptive details?
- ☑ Are any parts of the writing unclear?
- ☑ What descriptive details can be added to give more information?

Grammar: Sentences

Reading/Writing Workshop

OBJECTIVES

CCSS Produce complete sentences, recognizing and correcting inappropriate fragments and run-ons. **L.4.1f**

CCSS Choose punctuation for effect. **L.4.3b**

- Distinguish sentences and sentence fragments.
- Identify sentence types.
- Capitalize and punctuate sentences correctly.

Go Digital

Sentences

Grammar Activities

DAY 1

DAILY LANGUAGE ACTIVITY

Sam brot his lunch to school. He played with his friend's.
(1: brought; 2: friends)

Introduce Sentences

Present the following:

→ A **sentence** is a group of words that shows a complete thought:
  Lynn went to softball practice.

→ A **sentence fragment** is a group of words that does not show a complete thought:
  went to softball practice

→ Every sentence begins with a **capital letter** and ends with a **punctuation mark**:
  Does Lynn like softball**?**

Have partners discuss sentences and sentence fragments using page 450 of the Grammar Handbook in **Reading/Writing Workshop**.

DAY 2

DAILY LANGUAGE ACTIVITY

you feed the cat? alice is finish with her chores.
(1: Did; 2: Alice; 3: finished)

Review Sentences

Review what a sentence is. Have students explain how sentences and sentence fragments differ.

Introduce Types of Sentences

Explain that different types of sentences serve different purposes:

→ A **statement** tells something:
  I like to play soccer.

→ A **question** asks something:
  Do you like to play soccer?

→ A **command** tells someone to do something:
  Give me the soccer ball.

→ An **exclamation** expresses surprise, excitement, or strong feeling:
  Juan scored the winning goal!

 TALK ABOUT IT

COLLABORATE

IDENTIFY SENTENCES

Ask partners to take turns reading different passages from a book aloud. The first partner reads some complete sentences and then just parts of other sentences. The second partner should identify if what is read is a sentence or sentence fragment.

SAY THE ENDING

Have students in pairs each select one paragraph from a newspaper, magazine, or book. Tell them to take turns reading a random sentence from their selection. The other student must say which punctuation mark goes at the end of the sentence that was read.

Spelling: Short Vowels

DAY 3

Where is my comic book! that was a great story!
(1: book?; 2: That)

Mechanics and Usage: Sentence Punctuation

→ Every sentence begins with a capital letter.

→ A statement ends with a period. (.)

→ A question ends with a question mark. (?)

→ A command ends with a period or exclamation mark. (. or !)

→ An exclamation ends with an exclamation mark. (!)

As students write, refer them to Grammar Handbook pages 450 and 477.

DAY 4

bring the video games to my howse? How many games can you fit into you're backpack?
(1: Bring; 2: house.; 3: your)

Proofread

Have students correct errors in these sentences.

1. Wow, he runs fast. (1: fast!)

2. i thought Jack took my lunch? (1: I; 2: lunch.)

3. the food on the table. (1: Put)

4. the movie was about too friends helping each other (1: The; 2: two; 3: other.)

Have students check their work using Grammar Handbook pages 450 and 477 on sentences, sentence fragments, and end punctuation.

DAY 5

Meet me in class tumorrow before school? that was a wonderful first day of school!
(1: tomorrow; 2: school.; 3: That)

Assess

Use the Daily Language Activity and **Grammar Practice Reproducibles** page 5 for assessment.

Reteach

Use Grammar Practice Reproducibles pages 1–4 and selected pages from the Grammar Handbook for additional reteaching. Remind students to use sentences correctly as they speak and write.

Check students' writing for use of the skill and listen for it in their speaking. Assign Grammar Revision Assignments in their Writer's Notebooks as needed.

See Grammar Practice Reproducibles pages 1–5.

ON THE SPOT

Ask students in small groups to pick a theme, such as playground. Have them take turns choosing another student in the group to say a theme-related sentence. The student who chooses decides which end punctuation mark the student being chosen has to use.

COMPLETE THE THOUGHTS

Ask partners to write down sentence fragments about everyday things people do. Then have them trade lists and write complete sentences using these fragments. Have them read each list of complete sentences aloud.

PICTURE SENTENCES

Have students in small groups cut out images from a magazine and place them in a bag. Then have each student reach into the bag, pull out an image, and write a sentence to describe the image. Have students read their sentences aloud and ask the group to identify the end punctuation mark.

Spelling: Short Vowels

OBJECTIVES

CCSS Spell grade-appropriate words correctly, consulting references as needed. **L.4.2d**

Spelling Words

flat	grim	sum
cash	mill	plum
band	hint	bluff
bell	plot	crunch
left	dock	build
shelf	blot	gym
wealth	odd	

Review snack, step, pond
Challenge heavy, shovel

Differentiated Spelling

Approaching Level

flat	smell	blot
tax	when	odd
band	list	plum
cash	mill	mud
past	hint	lunch
bell	plot	gym
left	rot	

Beyond Level

sandwich	grimace	smudge
clamped	miller	plum
shelves	skimming	bluff
sketches	slipped	culprit
heavy	plots	crunches
wealthy	dock	typical
alibi	blot	

DAY 1

Assess Prior Knowledge

Display the spelling words. Read them aloud, drawing out the short-vowel sounds in each word.

Point out that words with one vowel usually have a short-vowel sound. (Remind students that y can also act as a vowel.) Next, show students how sometimes two vowels together create a short vowel sound, like the short e in *wealth* and the short i in *build*.

Demonstrate sorting the spelling words by pattern under key words *flat, bell, grim, plot* and *sum*. (Write the words on index cards or the IWB.) Sort a few words. Point out the different short-vowel sounds in the different words.

Then use the Dictation Sentences from Day 5 to give the Pretest. Say the underlined word, read the sentence, and repeat the word. Have students write the words. Then have students check and correct their spelling.

WORD SORTS

COLLABORATE

OPEN SORT

Have students cut apart the **Spelling Word Cards BLM** in the Teacher Resource Book and initial the back of each card. Have them read the words aloud with a partner. Then have partners do an open sort. Have them record the sort in their word study notebook.

DAY 2

Spiral Review

Review the short *a, e* and *o* vowel sounds in *snack, step* and *pond*. Use the Dictation Sentences below for the review words. Read the sentence, say the word, and have students write the words.

1. We ate a <u>snack</u> of cheese.
2. We had to <u>step</u> carefully.
3. Frogs lived in the <u>pond</u>.

Have students trade papers and check the spellings.

Challenge Words Review this week's short-vowel spelling patterns. Use these Dictation Sentences for challenge words. Say the word, read the sentence, and say the word again. Have students write the word.

1. The table was <u>heavy</u>.
2. He dug a hole with a <u>shovel</u>.

Have students check and correct their spelling before writing the words in their word study notebook.

PATTERN SORT

Complete the **pattern sort** from Day 1 using the key words, pointing out the short-vowel spellings. Have students use Spelling Word Cards to do their own pattern sort. Ask partners to compare and check their sorts.

DAY 3

Word Meanings

Have students copy the three sentences below into their word study notebooks. Say the sentences aloud; ask students to fill in the blanks with a spelling word.

1. The trophy sat on a special ____. (*shelf*)
2. My sister and I are going to ____ a clubhouse. (*build*)
3. The well-known actor had fame and ____. (*wealth*)

Challenge students to come up with at least three other sentences for spelling, review, or challenge words. Have them write the sentences, leaving a blank for the word. Then have them trade with a partner and fill in the missing word. Ask for volunteers to share sentences with the class.

See Phonics/Spelling Reproducibles pp. 1–6.

SPEED SORT

Have partners do a **speed sort** to see who is faster. Then have them do a word hunt in the week's reading for words with the short-vowel pattern. Ask them to sort the new words and add the final sort to the word study notebook.

DAY 4

Proofread and Write

Write these sentences on the board. Have students circle and correct each misspelled word. They can use print or electronic dictionaries or other resources to help them.

1. He looked grimb after he lost his welth. (*grim, wealth*)
2. Will you help me bild a new dok? (*build, dock*)
3. We played od music in our rock bande. (*odd, band*)
4. Put the plumm on the top shef. (*plum, shelf*)

Error Correction Some students will leave off the first letter of a final blend, such as the letter *l* in *shelf*. Help them segment the word by orally stretching the individual sounds. Then have students attach a spelling to each sound they hear.

BLIND SORT

Have partners do a **blind sort**: one reads a Spelling Word Card; the other tells under which key word it belongs. Have them take turns until both have sorted all their words. Then have students write a reflection on the process of sorting the different short-vowel sounds.

DAY 5

Assess

Use the Dictation Sentences for the Posttest. Have students list misspelled words in their word study notebooks. Look for students' use of these words in their writings.

Dictation Sentences

1. We know Earth is not <u>flat</u>.
2. Sid deposited <u>cash</u> in the bank.
3. She plays the trumpet in the <u>band</u>.
4. Class begins when the <u>bell</u> rings.
5. I know I <u>left</u> my coat on the chair.
6. Get the book on the top <u>shelf</u>.
7. The lottery brought her <u>wealth</u>.
8. The losing players had <u>grim</u> faces.
9. The <u>mill</u> grinds wheat into flour.
10. If he can't guess the answer, I'll give him a <u>hint</u>.
11. The story had an amazing <u>plot</u>.
12. Tie the sailboat to the <u>dock</u>.
13. <u>Blot</u> the stain with a towel.
14. Is three an <u>odd</u> or even number?
15. The <u>sum</u> of two plus two is four.
16. The ripe <u>plum</u> fell off the tree.
17. Can you really run faster than him, or is that just a <u>bluff</u>?
18. Some birds can <u>crunch</u> hard seeds.
19. How do you <u>build</u> a birdhouse?
20. We played soccer in <u>gym</u> class.

Have students self-correct the tests.

Build Vocabulary

DAY 1

DAY 2

OBJECTIVES

CCSS Use context (e.g., definitions, examples, or restatements in text) as a clue to the meaning of a word or phrase. **L.4.4a**

CCSS Demonstrate understanding of words by relating them to their opposites (antonyms) and to words with similar but not identical meanings (synonyms). **L.4.5c**

Expand vocabulary by adding inflectional endings and affixes.

Vocabulary Words

brainstorm	muttered
flattened	official
frantically	original
gracious	stale

Go Digital

Vocabulary

Vocabulary Activities

Connect to Words

Practice this week's vocabulary.

1. What ideas can you **brainstorm** to raise money?
2. What would a **flattened** cardboard box look like?
3. Show how acting **frantically** is different than acting calmly.
4. Show how a **gracious** person would welcome someone new.
5. What would it sound like if a person **muttered**?
6. Describe why a judge's decision would be **official**.
7. Is something **original** very common? Why or why <u>not</u>?
8. What foods can go **stale**?

Expand Vocabulary

Help students generate different forms of this week's words by adding, changing, or removing inflectional endings.

→ Draw a four-column chart on the board. Write *muttered* in the last column. Then write *mutter, mutters, muttering* in the first three columns. Read aloud the words with students.

→ Have students share sentences using each form of *mutter*.

→ Students can fill in the chart for *brainstorm* and *flattened* and then share sentences using the different forms of the word.

→ Have students copy the chart in their word study notebook.

BUILD MORE VOCABULARY

COLLABORATE

ACADEMIC VOCABULARY

Discuss important academic words.

→ Display *humor, fantasy, synonym*.

→ Define each word and discuss the meanings with students.

→ Display *humor* and *humorous*. Have partners look up and define related words.

→ Write the related words on the board. Have partners ask and answer questions using the words. Repeat with *fantasy* and *synonym*.

SYNONYMS

→ Discuss synonyms, or words with the same or similar meanings. Give examples as necessary, such as *small, little, tiny*.

→ Have partners use a thesaurus to find synonyms of *original*, such as *new*.

→ Have students use a dictionary to check meanings.

→ Have them add synonyms with the same or similar meanings to their word study notebook.

DAY 3

Reinforce the Words

Review this week's vocabulary words. Have students orally complete each sentence stem.

1. Put the <u>flattened</u> _____ in the recycling bin.

2. This _____ is <u>stale</u> and as hard as a rock!

3. My father <u>muttered</u> to himself as he tried to fix the _____.

4. My brother and I <u>frantically</u> cleaned the _____ before our parents got home.

5. This is the <u>official</u> form to fill out if you want to get a _____.

6. I tried to be <u>gracious</u> after beating my _____ in checkers.

DAY 4

Connect to Writing

→ Have students write sentences in their word study notebooks using this week's vocabulary.

→ Tell them to write sentences that provide word information they learned from this week's readings.

→ Provide the Day 3 sentence stems 1–6 for students needing extra support.

Write About Vocabulary
Have students write something they learned from this week's words in their word study notebook. For example, they might write about how a character in a story was *gracious*, or how the character came up with an *original* idea for solving a problem.

DAY 5

Word Squares

Ask students to create Word Squares for each vocabulary word.

→ In the first square, students write the word. (example: *flattened*)

→ In the second square, students write their own definition of the word and any related words, such as synonyms. (example: *squashed, crushed*)

→ In the third square, students draw a simple illustration that will help them remember the word. (example: drawing of a flattened can or cardboard box)

→ In the fourth square, students write nonexamples, including antonyms for the word. (example: *whole, filled up, round*)

→ Have partners compare and discuss their Word Squares.

SYNONYMS

Remind students to look for clues in a sentence, such as synonyms, to help figure out the meaning of unfamiliar words.

→ Display **Your Turn Practice Book** pages 3–4. Read the first paragraph. Model figuring out the meaning of *explored*.

→ Have students complete page 7 and then find clues for *morsel* and *perform* on pages 3–4, using a print or online dictionary to confirm meanings.

SHADES OF MEANING

Help students generate words related to *gracious*. Draw a word web. Label the web "Gracious."

→ Have partners generate words to add to the word web. Ask students to use a thesaurus.

→ Add words not included, such as *courteous* or *generous*.

→ Ask students to copy the words in their word study notebook.

MORPHOLOGY

Use *brainstorm* as a springboard for students to learn more words. Draw a three-column chart.

→ Write *brain* in the first column, *storm* in the second, and *brainstorm* in the third. Discuss how the words combined to create a new compound word.

→ Have students search for other compound words and add them to the chart. Discuss the meanings of suggested words.

→ Approaching Level

Lexile 530
TextEvaluator™ 28

OBJECTIVES

(CCSS) Follow agreed-upon rules for discussions and carry out assigned roles. **SL.4.1b**

(CCSS) Paraphrase portions of a text read aloud or information presented in diverse media and formats, including visually, quantitatively, and orally. **SL.4.2**

(CCSS) Make connections between the text of a story or drama and a visual or oral presentation of the text, identifying where each version reflects specific descriptions and directions in the text. **RL.4.7**

ACADEMIC LANGUAGE

- *confirm, revise predictions, fairy tale, sequence*
- Cognates: *confirmar, revisar predicciones, secuencia*

Leveled Reader:
Clever Puss

Leveled Readers

Before Reading

Preview and Predict

Have students read the Essential Question. Give students a copy of *Clever Puss,* and have them read the title and respond to the cover illustrations. Ask students to discuss what they can see in the illustrations that shows them the cat is clever.

Review Genre: Fairy Tale

Have students recall that fairy tales have main characters that must complete a difficult task or journey and usually contain imaginary characters. Have students identify features of a fairy tale in *Clever Puss*.

During Reading

Close Reading

Note Taking Ask students to use their graphic organizer while they read.

Use Graphic Organizer

Pages 2–3 *Reread pages 2–3. In your graphic organizer, paraphrase the gifts the father gives in order.* (The father first gives each of his two older sons a bag of money. Then he gives the youngest son his cat.)

Pages 4–5 *Turn to a partner and explain why Puss is a fairy tale character that could not exist in real life. Use the illustrations on pages 4–5 to form your answer.* (He stands up and wears boots. He also talks. Cats cannot do these things in real life.)

Pages 6–10 *Read pages 6–9. Turn to a partner and make a prediction about what the cat whispers in Tom's ear. Then read page 10 and confirm or revise your prediction.* (I predict the cat will tell Tom a way to count faster. When I read page 10, I see the cat told Tom to skip numbers.)

Page 12 *What synonym can help you find the meaning of the word* dissolved *on page 12? Use it to tell a definition to a partner.* ("disappeared"; *dissolved* means "disappeared into a liquid")

Pages 13–14 *Do you think Puss will make a good king? Why or why not? Read pages 13–14 to answer the question.* (I think Puss will make a good king because he is very clever, but also kind and helps Tom.)

After Reading

Respond to Reading

Have students complete Respond to Reading on page 16 after they have finished reading.

Write About Reading *Analytical Writing* Have students work with a partner to write a short paragraph describing the steps that led to Tom entering the contest to become the next king. Ask them to check that they have included all the steps and that the steps are listed in order.

Fluency: Intonation

Model Reread page 6. Model reading the passage with proper intonation. Next, read the passage aloud and have students read along with you.

Apply Have students practice reading the passage with a partner.

PAIRED READ

"Rabbit and the Well"

Make Connections: Write About It *Analytical Writing*

Before reading, ask students to note that the genre of this text is a folktale, which is similar to a fairy tale. In a folktale, there is often a lesson. Then discuss the Essential Question. After reading, ask students to make and list connections between the ways Puss solved problems and the ways Rabbit does in "Rabbit and the Well."

Leveled Reader

Analytical Writing

COMPARE TEXTS

→ Have students use text evidence to compare a fairy tale to a folktale.

Literature Circles

Ask students to conduct a literature circle using the Thinkmark questions to guide the discussion. You may wish to have a whole-class discussion on what students learned about characters overcoming problems with clever ideas from both selections in the leveled reader.

Level Up

Level-up lessons available online.

IF students read the **Approaching Level** fluently and answered the questions

THEN pair them with students who have proficiently read the **On Level** and have students

• echo-read the **On Level** main selection.

• use self-stick notes to mark at least one new detail they would like to discuss in each section.

A C T **A**ccess **C**omplex **T**ext

The **On Level** challenges students by including more **domain-specific words** and **complex sentence structures**.

Approaching Level
Phonics/Decoding

DECODE WORDS WITH SHORT *e*

 TIER 2

OBJECTIVES

(CCSS) Use combined knowledge of all letter-sound correspondences, syllabication patterns, and morphology (e.g., roots and affixes) to read accurately unfamiliar multisyllabic words in context and out of context. **RF.4.3a**

Decode words with short *e*.

 I Do
Explain that when a vowel appears between two consonants, it usually makes a short-vowel sound. Write *pen* on the board and read it aloud. Underline the letter *e*. Point out that in *pen*, the letter *e* appears between two consonants and stands for /e/, a short-vowel sound. Repeat with *den, ten, set,* and *met*. Review the letter and sound for each short vowel.

 We Do
Write *tell, sell, fell, left,* and *bend* on the board. Model how to decode *tell*. Have students identify the short- or long-vowel sound. Help students choral-read the rest of the words aloud and identify the vowel sounds.

 You Do
Add these words to the board: *bread, tread, lead,* and *head*. Have students read each word aloud and identify the short *e* sound. Point out the spelling of the short *e* sound in these words. Then point to the words in random order for students to choral-read. Repeat several times.

REVIEW SHORT VOWELS

 TIER 2

OBJECTIVES

(CCSS) Use combined knowledge of all letter-sound correspondences, syllabication patterns, and morphology (e.g., roots and affixes) to read accurately unfamiliar multisyllabic words in context and out of context. **RF.4.3a**

Decode words with short vowels.

 I Do
Remind students that short words containing one vowel usually have a short-vowel sound. Write *pin* and *pan*. Point out that both of these words contain a short-vowel sound. Underline the *i* in *pin* while saying /iii/, to show why it is a short vowel. Underline the *a* in *pan* while saying /aaa/.

We Do
Write the syllables *sun* and *set* on the board. Guide students as they decode the syllables. Point out that each syllable has a short-vowel sound. Then have students say the syllables together to form the word *sunset*. Write these words on the board, separated into syllables to help students read the words one syllable at a time: *win/ter, cen/ter, ten/nis, splen/did, pen/cil, sis/ter*. Have students identify the vowel sounds and decode the words.

 You Do
Add the following examples to the board: *after, member,* and *hopscotch*. Ask students to decode each word. Then point to all of the words on the board in random order for students to choral-read. Repeat several times.

PRACTICE SHORT VOWELS

OBJECTIVES

Use combined knowledge of all letter-sound correspondences, syllabication patterns, and morphology to read accurately unfamiliar multisyllabic words in context and out of context. **RF.4.3a**

 I Do Remind students of the sounds that short vowels make. Show the *camel, lemon, hippo,* and *jump* **Sound-Spelling Cards.** Then read the words aloud. Point to the short-vowel spelling in each word as you pronounce it.

 We Do Write the words *dash, lead* (metal), *symbol, posh,* and *hush* on the board. Model how to decode *dash,* then guide students as they decode the remaining words. Help them identify the short-vowel sound in each word and say it.

 You Do Afterward, point to the words in random order for students to choral-read.

INFLECTIONAL ENDINGS

OBJECTIVES

Use combined knowledge of all letter-sound correspondences, syllabication patterns, and morphology (e.g., roots and affixes) to read accurately unfamiliar multisyllabic words in context and out of context. **RF.4.3a**

Decode words with inflectional endings *-ing, -s,* and *-ed.*

 I Do Review that the endings *-ed, -s,* and *-ing* are added to verbs to create new verb forms and tenses. For many verbs, adding *-ed* or *-ing* does not change the spelling: *crack, cracked, cracks, cracking.* Adding *-ed* to a base word puts the action in the past tense: *drill, drilled.* Adding *-s* or *-ing* to a base word puts the action in the present tense: *center, centers, centering.*

 We Do Write *twisted* on the board. Model how to decode the word. Give other examples of words with inflectional endings. Guide students as they decode the words. Divide multisyllabic words into syllables using the syllable-scoop technique by using your finger to draw an arc under each syllable as you read it aloud. This technique helps students read one syllable at a time.

 You Do Write the words *snow, step,* and *rate* on the board. Have students add an inflectional ending to each word. Point to the words in random order for students to choral-read.

ENGLISH LANGUAGE LEARNERS

For the **ELLs** who need **phonics, decoding,** and **fluency** practice, use scaffolding methods as necessary to ensure students understand the meaning of the words. Refer to the **Language Transfers Handbook** for phonics elements that may not transfer in students' native languages.

Approaching Level
Vocabulary

REVIEW HIGH-FREQUENCY WORDS

OBJECTIVES

(CCSS) Read with sufficient accuracy and fluency to support comprehension. Read on-level text with purpose and understanding. **RF.4.4a**

Review high-frequency words.

 I Do Use **Word Cards 1–10.** Display one word at a time, following the routine: Display the word. Read the word. Then spell the word.

 We Do Ask students to state the word and spell the word with you. Model using the word in a sentence and have students repeat after you.

 You Do Display the word. Ask students to say the word and then spell it. When completed, quickly flip through the word card set as students choral-read the words. Provide opportunities for students to use the words in speaking and writing. For example, provide sentence starters such as *I will always _____.* Ask students to write each word in their Writer's Notebook.

REVIEW VOCABULARY WORDS

OBJECTIVES

(CCSS) Acquire and use accurately grade-appropriate general academic and domain-specific words and phrases, including those that signal precise actions, emotions, or states of being (e.g., *quizzed, whined, stammered*) and that are basic to a particular topic (e.g., *wildlife, conservation,* and *endangered* when discussing animal preservation). **L.4.6**

 I Do Display each **Visual Vocabulary Card** and state the word. Explain how the photograph illustrates the word. State the example sentence and repeat the word.

 We Do Point to the word on the card and read the word with students. Ask them to repeat the word. Engage students in structured partner-talk about the image as prompted on the back of the vocabulary card.

 You Do Display each visual in random order, hiding the word. Have students match the definitions and context sentences of the words to the visuals displayed.

ANSWER CHOICE QUESTIONS

OBJECTIVES

(CCSS) Acquire and use accurately grade-appropriate general academic and domain-specific words and phrases, including those that signal precise actions, emotions, or states of being (e.g., *quizzed, whined, stammered*) and that are basic to a particular topic (e.g., *wildlife, conservation,* and *endangered* when discussing animal preservation). **L.4.6**

Display the *muttered* **Visual Vocabulary Card** and say aloud the following choice question: *In which location might you have muttered: the library or the baseball park?* Point out that one would *mutter* in the library because it is a way of speaking softly.

Display the vocabulary card for the word *stale*. Say aloud the following question: *If you had a piece of stale bread, would you rather eat it or throw it away?* With students, identify the correct choice and justify why.

Using the questions below, display the remaining cards one at a time and say the question. Ask students to identify the correct choice.

→ Where would you find a *flattened* piece of paper: in the trash or in a book?

→ If someone were *frantically* looking for a hat, would he or she be calm or anxious?

→ Where are you more likely to find an *original* piece of art: in an art museum or on a friend's wall?

→ If someone you knew were *gracious,* would you be more or less likely to be his or her friend?

CONTEXT CLUES: SYNONYMS

OBJECTIVES

(CCSS) Demonstrate understanding of words by relating them to their opposites (antonyms) and to words with similar but not identical meanings (synonyms). **L.4.5c**

Use context clues to determine the meanings of unfamiliar words.

Display the Comprehension and Fluency passage on **Approaching Reproducibles** pages 3–4. Read aloud the third paragraph. Point to the word *cautiously*. Explain to students that they can use surrounding words, including possible synonyms, to figure out the meaning of the word.

Think Aloud I do not know the word *cautiously*, but I see some clues that might help me figure out its meaning. I see that *cautiously* describes how the boy walked. The boy also walked "slowly" and "with care." I think *cautiously* must mean slowly and with care.

Ask students to point to the word *perform* at the bottom of the page. Discuss how to use synonyms to figure out the word's meaning.

Have students use clues from the passage to find the meanings of *howling* in the last paragraph on page 3 and *stumbled* in the fourth paragraph on page 4.

Approaching Level

Comprehension

FLUENCY

 OBJECTIVES

CCSS Read on-level prose and poetry orally with accuracy, appropriate rate, and expression on successive readings. **RF.4.4b**

Read fluently with good intonation.

 I Do Explain that reading out loud is not just about getting the words right. Readers should change the sound of their voice to show the meaning of what they read. Read the first paragraph of the Comprehension and Fluency passage on **Approaching Reproducibles** pages 3–4. Tell students to listen for when you read more slowly or raise your voice.

 We Do Read the rest of the page aloud. Have students repeat what the characters say after you, using the same intonation. Explain that you changed the tone of your voice to express how Grandmother, the boy, and Coyote feel.

 You Do Have partners take turns reading sentences from the Approaching Reproducibles passage. Remind them to focus on their intonation. Listen in and provide corrective feedback by modeling proper fluency as needed.

IDENTIFY IMPORTANT EVENTS

 OBJECTIVES

CCSS Describe in depth a character, setting, or event in a story or drama, drawing on specific details in the text (e.g., a character's thoughts, words, or actions). **RL.4.3**

Identify important events.

 I Do Reread the first three paragraphs of the Comprehension and Fluency passage in **Approaching Reproducibles.** Write the title on the board. Then write: "Event: The boy decides to follow Blue Jay." Explain that to identify a sequence of events, students must determine the important events in a story. Explain that the sequence begins when the boy leaves the farm, not when he is eating his lunch.

 We Do Reread the remainder of the first page of the passage. Ask: *What character do we meet on this page?* Point out that identifying characters and their actions can help identify important events. Ask: *What is the major event that happens after the boy leaves the farm?* Explain that this event is the next important event. Help students identify the coyote as a trickster, and that the boy does not fall for his tricks at first.

 You Do Have students read the rest of the passage, writing down the most important events as they read. Review the lists. Help students explain why the events they chose are important. Then put the events in sequence.

REVIEW SEQUENCE

OBJECTIVES

 CCSS Describe in depth a character, setting, or event in a story or drama, drawing on specific details in the text (e.g., a character's thoughts, words, or actions). **RL.4.3**

Identify a story's sequence of events.

I Do Remind students that sequence is the order in which the events of a story take place. Putting a story's events in sequence will help you to summarize the plot. Explain that identifying a story's sequence involves describing the most important events that happen in the beginning, middle, and end.

We Do Read the first page of the Comprehension and Fluency passage in the **Approaching Reproducibles.** Model how to decide which events are the most important. Then, work with students to identify where in the sequence the events would be placed: beginning, middle, or end.

You Do Have students complete a sequence of the story's main events and summarize the passage.

SELF-SELECTED READING

OBJECTIVES

 CCSS Describe in depth a character, setting, or event in a story or drama, drawing on specific details in the text (e.g., a character's thoughts, words, or actions). **RL.4.3**

Make, confirm, or revise predictions to increase understanding.

Read Independently

Have students choose a fiction book for sustained silent reading. Remind students that:

→ the sequence is the order in which the events of a story take place. Stories have a beginning, middle, and end.

→ by making, confirming, and revising predictions about plot and characters' actions, they will gain a deeper understanding of the story. Putting events in a sequence will also help them understand the story.

Read Purposefully

Have students record details about character, setting, and the sequence of plot events on a Story Map as they read independently. After they finish, they can conduct a Book Talk, each telling about the book they read.

→ Students should share their maps and answer this question: *What happens in this story?*

→ They should also tell the group if the predictions they made about the story were correct and how they might revise them after reading.

→ On Level

Lexile 750
TextEvaluator 32

OBJECTIVES

 Follow agreed-upon rules for discussions and carry out assigned roles. **SL.4.1b**

 Paraphrase portions of a text read aloud or information presented in diverse media and formats, including visually, quantitatively, and orally. **SL.4.2**

 Explain major differences between poems, drama, and prose, and refer to the structural elements of poems (e.g., verse, rhythm, meter) and drama (e.g., casts of characters, settings, descriptions, dialogue, stage directions) when writing or speaking about a text. **RL.4.5**

ACADEMIC LANGUAGE

- *confirm, revise predictions, fairy tale, sequence*
- Cognates: *confirmar, revisar predicciones*

Leveled Reader:
Jack and the Extreme Stalk

Before Reading

Preview and Predict

Have students read the Essential Question. Then have students read the title and the first two pages of *Jack and the Extreme Stalk*. Ask students to discuss if they think there is something special about the beans Jack has bought.

Review Genre: Fairy Tale

Review with students that a fairy tale features a main character that must complete a difficult task or journey. Fairy tales often have happy endings. Have students identify features of a fairy tale in *Jack and the Extreme Stalk* and tell how this genre differs from other fiction genres.

During Reading

Close Reading

Note Taking Ask students to use their graphic organizer while they read.

Pages 2–3 *Turn to a partner and make a prediction about what will happen to the beans. Read pages 2–3 to form your prediction.* (I think the beans will grow and something special will happen to them.)

Pages 4–5 *Reread pages 4–5. Turn to a partner and confirm or revise your prediction about the beans.* (I read that one bean did grow into an extremely tall stalk, like I predicted. Based on what I know about this fairy tale, I predict that Jack will try to climb the stalk.)

Pages 6–10 *In your graphic organizer, list the sequence of events that happens after Jack climbs the giant stalk.* (Jack finds a magic castle. He meets a giant and a hen that lays golden eggs. Jack learns that the giant is lonely. He gets a tour of the castle. Jack brainstorms ways to help the giant grow a garden in his castle.)

Page 11 *What synonym can help you find the meaning of the word* contraption *on page 11? Use the synonym to tell a definition to a partner.* ("machine"; a contraption is a machine or special tool made by people)

Go Digital

Leveled Readers

Use Graphic Organizer

Pages 12–13 *Paraphrase how Jack's machine works and how it helps the giant. Reread pages 12–13.* (The hen's golden egg triggers a machine that uses a giant fan to blow the clouds away, so that the castle can get sunshine. The machine helps the giant because now he can plant a garden.)

After Reading

Respond to Reading Have students complete Respond to Reading on page 16 after they have finished reading.

Analytical Writing **Write About Reading** Have students work with a partner to write a short paragraph describing the steps Jack took to solve the giant's problem. Ask them to check that they have included all the steps and that they are listed in order.

Fluency: Intonation

Model Model reading page 2 with proper intonation. Next, read the passage aloud and have students read along with you.

Apply Have partners do repeated rereadings of the passage.

PAIRED READ

"Stone Soup"

Make Connections:
Write About It *Analytical Writing*

Before reading, ask students to note that the genre of this story is a folktale, which is similar to a fairy tale. A folktale is a story from a certain tradition or culture that contains a lesson. Then discuss the Essential Question. After reading, ask students to make and list connections between how the characters in both stories overcome difficult obstacles.

Leveled Reader

Analytical Writing

COMPARE TEXTS

→ Have students use text evidence to compare a fairy tale to a folktale.

Literature Circles

Ask students to conduct a literature circle using the Thinkmark questions to guide the discussion. You may wish to have a whole-class discussion on how characters use cleverness to solve problems from both leveled reader selections.

Level Up

Level-up lessons available online.

IF students read the `On Level` fluently and answered the questions

THEN pair them with students who have proficiently read the `Beyond Level` and have students

- partner-read the `Beyond Level` main selection.
- identify a part of the story they would like to learn more about.

A C T Access Complex Text

The `On Level` challenges students by including more **domain-specific words** and **complex sentence structures**.

On Level

Vocabulary

REVIEW VOCABULARY WORDS

OBJECTIVES

 Acquire and use accurately grade-appropriate general academic and domain-specific words and phrases, including those that signal precise actions, emotions, or states of being (e.g., *quizzed, whined, stammered*) and that are basic to a particular topic (e.g., *wildlife, conservation,* and *endangered* when discussing animal preservation). **L.4.6**

 Use the **Visual Vocabulary Cards** to review key selection words *brainstorm, flattened, frantically, gracious, muttered, official,* and *stale*. Point to each word, read it aloud, and have students chorally repeat it.

 Display the word card for *gracious*. Say aloud the word set *gracious, kind, selfish, giving*. Identify the word that does not belong and discuss why.

 Using the word sets below, ask students to identify the word that does not belong and explain why.

brainstorm, rest, think, analyze

muttered, whispered, shouted, grumbled

flattened, smoothed, spread, crumpled

official, forged, proper, correct

frantically, calmly, hastily, wildly

stale, old, fresh, moldy

CONTEXT CLUES: SYNONYMS

OBJECTIVES

 Demonstrate understanding of words by relating them to their opposites (antonyms) and to words with similar but not identical meanings (synonyms). **L.4.5c**

 Remind students they can often figure out the meaning of an unknown word by looking at surrounding words and sentences for clues. Use the Comprehension and Fluency passage on **Your Turn Practice Book** pages 3–4 to model using synonyms to determine the meaning of *cautiously*.

Think Aloud I want to know what the word *cautiously* means. *Cautiously* describes how the boy walks. I know that he has to be careful because of the many hills and heat. The sentence states that he walks "slowly" and "with care." I think *cautiously* probably means slowly and with care.

 Have students read the third paragraph on page 4, where they encounter *depart*. Have students figure out the definition by looking for a synonym. Guide students by telling them to look in the same sentence for a clue.

 Have students work in pairs to determine the meaning of the words *accustomed* and *burdened* on page 4 of the selection.

Comprehension

REVIEW SEQUENCE

OBJECTIVES

 Determine a theme of a story, drama, or poem from details in the text; summarize the text. **RL.4.2**

 Describe in depth a character, setting, or event in a story or drama, drawing on specific details in the text (e.g., a character's thoughts, words, or actions). **RL.4.3**

 I Do Remind students that sequence is the order in which the events of a story take place. Explain that stories have a beginning, middle, and end. Along with describing the characters and setting, putting events in order will help students understand the story. They can use the sequence to summarize the plot.

We Do Have a volunteer read the first three paragraphs of the Comprehension and Fluency passage on **Your Turn Practice Book** pages 3–4. Have students name the first event of the story. Then model how to describe the main character and setting, and how to identify the next event. Then work with students to identify the next event.

 You Do Have partners identify the sequence in the rest of the story. Then have them summarize the plot using the sequence.

SELF-SELECTED READING

OBJECTIVES

 Describe in depth a character, setting, or event in a story or drama, drawing on specific details in the text (e.g., a character's thoughts, words, or actions). **RL.4.3**

Make, confirm, or revise predictions to increase understanding.

Read Independently

Have students choose a fiction book for sustained silent reading.

→ Before they read, have students preview the book, reading the title and viewing the front and back cover.

→ Remind students to make predictions about the characters and events before they read, and to revise and confirm predictions while reading.

Read Purposefully

Encourage students to read different books in order to examine different characters and plot.

→ As students read, have them fill in the main character, setting, and sequence on a Story Map.

→ They can use this map to help them write a summary of the book.

→ Ask students to share their reactions to the book with classmates.

→ Beyond Level

Lexile 860
TextEvaluator™ 41

OBJECTIVES

 Follow agreed-upon rules for discussions and carry out assigned roles. **SL.4.1b**

 Paraphrase portions of a text read aloud or information presented in diverse media and formats, including visually, quantitatively, and orally. **SL.4.2**

 Compare and contrast the treatment of similar themes and topics (e.g., opposition of good and evil) and patterns of events (e.g., the quest) in stories, myths, and traditional literature from different cultures. **RL.4.9**

ACADEMIC LANGUAGE

• *confirm, revise predictions, fairy tale, sequence*

• Cognates: *confirmar, revisar predicciones, secuencia*

Leveled Reader:
Charming Ella

Before Reading

Preview and Predict

Have students read the Essential Question. Then have students read the title and the first two pages of *Charming Ella*. Ask students to predict how Ella might use her special talents.

Review Genre: Fairy Tale

Review with students that a fairy tale features a main character who must complete a difficult task or journey. Fairy tales often have a happy ending. Have students identify features of a fairy tale in *Charming Ella*.

During Reading

Close Reading

Note Taking Ask students to use their graphic organizer while they read.

Pages 2–3 *What clues tell you this story is a fairy tale? Read pages 2–3 to answer the question.* (Ella will have to overcome a difficult obstacle—her stepsisters who make her work all the time.)

Pages 4–5 *Read pages 4–5. Turn to a partner and make a prediction about whether Ella will be able to participate in the contest.* (I predict that Ella will make an outfit for the contest because she is so talented at making things. I bet she will find some old clothes to make a new outfit out of.)

Pages 6–11 *Turn to a partner and confirm or revise your prediction about whether Ella will enter the fashion contest. Read pages 6–11 for details.* (I was right that Ella makes an outfit out of old clothes. I think she will enter the contest. I didn't predict that Ella would use a bike-sharing program to get there. I will read on to confirm that she gets to the contest on time.)

Page 12 *What synonym can help you find the meaning of the word* gaping *on page 12? Use it to tell a definition to a partner.* ("wide-open"; gaping means being wide open)

Go Digital

Leveled Readers

Use Graphic Organizer

Pages 12–15 *Read pages 12–15, looking for the sequence of events in the last chapter. Paraphrase the sequence of events using your graphic organizer.* (Ella makes it to the fashion contest just in time. The audience cheers for her and she is named the winner. Troy Charming loves Ella's design so much that he asks Ella to work with him on an official fashion label.)

After Reading

Respond to Reading

Have students complete Respond to Reading on page 16.

 Analytical Writing **Write About Reading** Have students work with a partner to write a short paragraph describing the steps Ella took to get to the contest. Ask them to check that they have included all the steps and that they are listed in order.

Fluency: Intonation

Model Model reading page 2 with proper intonation. Next, read the passage aloud and have students read along with you.

Apply Have partners do repeated rereadings of the passage.

PAIRED READ

Leveled Reader

"Ivana and the Ogre"

Make Connections: Write About It

Before reading, ask students to note that the genre of this story is a folktale, which is similar to a fairy tale. A folktale is a story from a certain tradition or culture and contains a lesson. Then discuss the Essential Question. After reading, ask students to make and write about connections between how the characters in both stories overcome difficult obstacles.

Analytical Writing

COMPARE TEXTS

→ Have students use text evidence to compare a fairy tale to a folktale.

Literature Circles

Ask students to conduct a literature circle using the Thinkmark questions to guide the discussion. You may wish to have a whole-class discussion on how characters use their cleverness to solve problems from both selections in the leveled reader.

Gifted and Talented

Synthesize *Charming Ella* is similar to a classic fairy tale, Cinderella, but it uses more modern characters and settings. Have students choose a classic fairy tale and write a modern version about one page long. Ask volunteers to share their fairy tales with the class.

Beyond Level

Vocabulary

REVIEW DOMAIN-SPECIFIC WORDS

OBJECTIVES

 Acquire and use accurately grade-appropriate general academic and domain-specific words and phrases, including those that signal precise actions, emotions, or states of being and that are basic to a particular topic. **L.4.6**

 Model Use the **Visual Vocabulary Cards** to review the meanings of the words *original* and *brainstorm*. Think of two well-known characters and write a sentence about them using these two adjectives.

Write the words *creative* and *imagination* on the board and discuss the meanings with students. Then help students write sentences about the same two characters using these words.

 Apply Have students work in pairs to review the meanings of the words *develop* and *inventive*. Then have partners write sentences using the words.

CONTEXT CLUES: SYNONYMS

OBJECTIVES

 Use context (e.g., definitions, examples, or restatements in text) as a clue to the meaning of a word or phrase. **L.4.4a**

 Demonstrate understanding of words by relating them to their opposites (antonyms) and to words with similar but not identical meanings (synonyms). **L.4.5c**

 Model Read aloud the fourth paragraph of the Comprehension and Fluency passage on **Beyond Reproducibles** pages 3–4.

Think Aloud When I read this paragraph, I want to understand the word *morsel*. I know I can look for a word close to *morsel* that might give me a clue to its meaning. The coyote is looking for food, but can't find a "single morsel, or crumb." The text offers a synonym, *crumb*. So a morsel must be like a crumb, or a very small piece of food.

With students, read the seventh paragraph. Help them figure out the meaning of *perform*.

 Apply Have pairs of students read the rest of the passage. Ask them to use synonyms as context clues to determine the meanings of *depart*, *accustomed*, and *burdened* on page 4.

 Synthesize Using their definition of *perform*, have partners write a short fairy tale about a character who has special abilities to perform. Encourage them to use artwork to add meaning to the story.

Comprehension

REVIEW SEQUENCE

OBJECTIVES

Describe in depth a character, setting, or event in a story or drama, drawing on specific details in the text (e.g., a character's thoughts, words, or actions). **RL.4.3**

Identify the sequence of events in a story.

Model Remind students that sequence is the order in which the events of a story take place. Explain that stories have a beginning, middle, and end. Analyzing the sequence of plot events and how the main character changes during the story will increase their understanding.

Have students read the first page of the Comprehension and Fluency passage in **Beyond Reproducibles** pages 3–4. Ask open-ended questions to facilitate discussion, such as *Why does Coyote want to help the boy?* Students should support their responses with details in the text.

Apply Have students identify the sequence of plot events in the story as they independently fill in a Story Map. Then have partners use their work to summarize the plot.

SELF-SELECTED READING

OBJECTIVES

Describe in depth a character, setting, or event in a story or drama, drawing on specific details in the text (e.g., a character's thoughts, words, or actions). **RL.4.3**

Make, confirm, or revise predictions to increase understanding.

Read Independently

Have students choose a fiction book for sustained silent reading.

→ As students read, have them fill in a Story Map.

→ Remind them to make predictions about plot events and characters, and to confirm or revise their predictions as they continue reading.

Read Purposefully

Encourage students to keep a reading journal. Ask them to read different books in order to learn about a variety of subjects.

→ Students can write summaries of the books in their journals.

→ Ask students to share their reactions to the books with classmates.

Independent Study Challenge students to discuss how their books relate to the weekly concept of clever ideas. Have students compare the character traits of the main characters in the books they read. How do the characters use ingenuity to solve their problems or conflicts? Do the characters make use of cleverness or are they taken advantage by it?

→ English Language Learners

Reading/Writing Workshop

OBJECTIVES

 Refer to details and examples in a text when explaining what the text says explicitly and when drawing inferences from the text. **RL.4.1**

LANGUAGE OBJECTIVE

 Demonstrate understanding of words by relating them to their opposites (antonyms) and to words with similar but not identical meanings (synonyms). **L.4.5c**

ACADEMIC LANGUAGE

• synonyms, sequence, predict

• Cognates: sinónimos, secuencia, predecir

Shared Read
The Dragon Problem

Before Reading

Build Background

Read the Essential Question: Where do good ideas come from?

→ Explain the meaning of the Essential Question. Point out the cognate for *ideas* is *ideas.*

→ **Model an answer:** *Sometimes good ideas come from thinking about ways to fix a problem. Sometimes good ideas come from talking to others. Good ideas can also come from studying or watching something closely.*

→ Ask students a question that ties the Essential Question to their own background knowledge: *Turn to a partner and discuss where you get your ideas. Give one or two examples of an idea that led you to create something new.* Call on several pairs.

During Reading

Interactive Question-Response

→ Ask questions that help students understand the meaning of the text after each paragraph.

→ Reinforce the meanings of key vocabulary.

→ Ask students questions that require them to use key vocabulary.

→ Reinforce strategies and skills of the week by modeling.

Go Digital

View "The Dragon Problem"

Page 22

Explain and Model Making Predictions *Before I read, I look at the title and pictures and make predictions about the story and characters. What is the title?* ("The Dragon Problem") *I see a dragon in the picture. I can predict that the story will be about a dragon. The dragon might be a problem. Now I can read to see if my prediction is correct.*

Page 23

Paragraph 1
When does the story take place? (long ago) *How do you know?* (It begins with "once upon a time, long before.") *Who is the main character?* (Liang) *What does he do?* (He helps his father build furniture and makes toys for the children in the village.)

Paragraph 2
Why does Liang know a lot about dragons? (There is a dragon nearby.) *What does the dragon eat?* (He eats water buffalo, pigs, and sometimes people.) *Is the dragon a problem?* (Yes) Point out that this information confirms the earlier prediction that the dragon might be a problem.

Paragraph 3
Explain and Model Sequence Model putting events in order to help students understand the characters and the plot. *I see that something important happens in this paragraph. First, the Emperor and his family arrive at his summer palace. Then Princess Peng smiles at Liang, and Liang falls in love with the princess.*

Paragraphs 4–7
What happens next? (Liang tells his father that he wants to marry the princess.) *Does his father think Liang will marry the princess?* (No)

Page 24

Paragraphs 2 and 3
 Have students chorally read the Emperor's announcement. *What do you predict Liang will do after hearing the announcement?* (Possible answer: Liang will try to get rid of the dragon.)

Paragraph 4
Have students take turns reading the sentences. *Was your prediction correct?* (Possible answer: Yes, Liang wants to get rid of the dragon.)

Point out the word *brainstorm* in the paragraph and provide a definition.

Paragraph 7
What is Ling Ling's idea? (Liang should carve a giant dragon. The giant dragon will scare the real dragon away.)
Explain and Model Synonyms Point out the word *alarm*. Ask advanced students to identify a word with a similar meaning in the same sentence. (scare) Ask a volunteer to use *alarm* in a sentence.

Page 25

Paragraphs 1–4
Demonstrate *glare*. Glare *means "to stare angrily or fiercely."* *What does the real dragon do when Liang hides in the bushes and pretends to be a dragon?* (Possible answer: At first the dragon tells him to go away, but when the giant dragon continues to glare, the real dragon gets scared and decides to take a long trip.)

 How does the story end? (Liang and the princess marry. They open a toy shop.) *Are you surprised by the ending?* (Possible answer: I am surprised that they opened a toy store.)

After Reading

Make Connections
→ Review the Essential Question: Where do good ideas come from?

→ Make text connections.

→ Have students complete **ELL Reproducibles** pages 3–5.

→ English Language Learners

Lexile 430
TextEvaluator™ 11

Leveled Reader:
Jack and the Extreme Stalk

Go Digital

Leveled Readers

Before Reading

Preview

→ Read the Essential Question: Where do good ideas come from?

→ Refer to Creative Thinking: How is this boy being creative?

→ Preview *Jack and the Extreme Stalk* and "Stone Soup": *Our purpose for reading is to find out how characters come up with good ideas.*

Vocabulary

Use the **Visual Vocabulary Cards** to preteach the ELL vocabulary: *inventive, machine, wondered.* Use the routine found on the cards. Point out the cognate: *máquina.*

During Reading

Interactive Question-Response

Note Taking Have students use the graphic organizer in the **ELL Reproducibles**, page 2. Use the questions below after reading each page with students.

Use Graphic Organizer

Pages 2–3 Reread the first sentence of the second paragraph on page 3. Remind students that *to brainstorm* means "to think of many ideas or solutions." *Why does Jack brainstorm?* (He wants to think of ideas for growing beans.)

Pages 4–5 Have students look at the pictures on page 5. Ask students to point to the cloud, beanstalk, and the field as you read the labels. *What helps Jack's beanstalk grow?* (fertilizer, field)

Pages 6–10 *Describe the picture on page 7.* (The giant is wringing out his wet clothes.) *What is the giant's problem?* (Everything is wet.) *Why is everything wet?* (The giant lives in a castle in the clouds.)

Pages 11–13 Remind students that *machine* has a cognate: *máquina. Describe the machine that Jack builds for the giant.* (The chicken lays an egg. The egg moves the spring, which moves gears. The gears move a giant fan that blows the clouds away.)

OBJECTIVES

 Refer to details and examples in a text when explaining what the text says explicitly and when drawing inferences from the text. **RL.4.1**

 Make connections between the text of a story or drama and a visual or oral presentation of the text, identifying where each version reflects specific descriptions and directions in the text. **RL.4.7**

ACADEMIC LANGUAGE

• *make, confirm, and revise predictions, fairy tale, sequence*

• Cognates: *confirmar, revisar predicciones, secuencia*

Pages 14–15 *How will the giant's life be different now than it was before? Turn to a partner and make a prediction.* (Possible answers: The giant will be able to grow a garden. His clothes will be dry. He has a new friend in Jack.)

After Reading

Respond to Reading Help students complete the graphic organizer in the **ELL Reproducibles**, page 2. Revisit the Essential Question. Ask students to work with partners to summarize and answer the Text Evidence Questions. Support students as necessary and review all responses as a group.

Analytical Writing **Write About Reading** Have students work with a partner to write a short paragraph describing how Jack solves the giant's problem. Remind them to include supporting details and write events in order.

Fluency: Intonation

Model Model reading page 2 with proper intonation. Next, read the passage aloud and have students read along with you.

Apply Have students practice reading with a partner.

PAIRED READ

Leveled Reader

"Stone Soup"

Make Connections: Write About It
Analytical Writing

Before reading, ask students to note that the genre of this story is a folktale. A folktale is a story based on the traditions and customs of a group of people and is passed down from one generation to another. Then discuss the Essential Question. After reading, ask students to list connections between how the characters in both stories overcome difficult obstacles.

Analytical Writing

COMPARE TEXTS

→ Have students use text evidence to compare a fairy tale to a folktale.

Literature Circles

Ask students to conduct a literature circle using the Thinkmark questions to guide the discussion. You may wish to have a whole-class discussion about the ways the characters in both selections use their cleverness to solve problems.

Level Up

Level-up lessons available online.

IF students read the **ELL Level** fluently and answered the questions

THEN pair them with students who have proficiently read the **On Level** and have students

• echo-read the **On Level** main selection with their partners.

• list words with which they have difficulty.

• discuss these words with their partners.

A C T Access Complex Text

The **On Level** challenges students by including more **complex sentence structures** and **descriptive language**.

English Language Learners

Vocabulary

PRETEACH VOCABULARY

OBJECTIVES

 CCSS Acquire and use accurately grade-appropriate general academic and domain-specific words and phrases, including those that signal precise actions, emotions, or states of being and that are basic to a particular topic. **L.4.6**

LANGUAGE OBJECTIVE
Use vocabulary words.

 I Do Preteach vocabulary from "The Dragon Problem," following the Vocabulary Routine found on the **Visual Vocabulary Cards** for the words *brainstorm, flattened, frantically, gracious, muttered, official, original,* and *stale.*

 We Do After completing the Vocabulary Routine for each word, point to the word on the Visual Vocabulary Card and read the word with students. Ask students to repeat the word.

 You Do Have students work with a partner to use two or more words in sentences. Then have each pair read the sentences aloud.

Beginning	Intermediate	Advanced/High
Help students write the sentences correctly and read them aloud.	Challenge students to write a sentence for all of the words.	Challenge students to write one sentence and one question for each word.

REVIEW VOCABULARY

OBJECTIVES

 CCSS Acquire and use accurately grade-appropriate general academic and domain-specific words and phrases, including those that signal precise actions, emotions, or states of being and that are basic to a particular topic. **L.4.6**

LANGUAGE OBJECTIVE
Use vocabulary words.

 I Do Review the week's vocabulary and high-frequency words. The words can be reviewed over a few days. Read each word aloud, and point to the word on the flash card. Have students repeat after you.

 We Do Make a flash card for one of the words. Write the word on the front and the definition on the back. Show students the word and ask them for the definition.

 You Do In pairs, have students make flash cards for two or more words. Assign students into small groups and have them quiz each other.

Beginning	Intermediate	Advanced/High
Help students write definitions and read them aloud.	Have students write definitions for each word.	Ask students to include synonyms along with definitions.

CONTEXT CLUES: SYNONYMS

OBJECTIVES
Demonstrate understanding of words by relating them to their opposites (antonyms) and to words with similar but not identical meanings (synonyms). **L.4.5c**

LANGUAGE OBJECTIVE
Use context clues.

I Do Read aloud the first and second paragraphs of the Comprehension and Fluency passage on **ELL Reproducibles** pages 3–4, while students follow along. Point to the word *cautiously*. Explain that students can use the surrounding sentences to figure out the meaning of an unfamiliar word.

Think Aloud I am not sure what *cautiously* means, but I can look for clues near the word. I see that the words "slowly" and "with care" describe the way the boy walked. *Cautiously* must mean "with care."

We Do Have students point to the word *howling* on page 3. Help students find a synonym for *howling*. Write the definition of the word on the board.

You Do Have pairs find synonyms for *depart* and *stumbled* on page 4. Have students write a definition and use each word in a sentence.

Beginning	Intermediate	Advanced/High
Help students locate the word and its synonym on the page.	Ask students to locate and read aloud the synonyms on the page.	Have students explain how they found the synonyms on the page.

ADDITIONAL VOCABULARY

OBJECTIVES
Choose words and phrases to convey ideas precisely. **L.4.3a**

LANGUAGE OBJECTIVE
Use academic and high-frequency words.

I Do List academic and high-frequency words from "The Dragon Problem": *problem, around, soon;* and *Jack and the Extreme Stalk: once, different, live, materials.* Define each word for students: *Soon means "within a short time from now." When we say as soon as possible, we mean quickly or right away.*

We Do Model using the word *soon* in a sentence: *I will read a new story soon. Soon it began to rain hard.* Then provide sentence frames and complete them with students: *If we finish our work soon, we can _____.*

You Do Have students work with a partner to write their own sentence frames, using the remaining words. Then have each pair share them with the class.

Beginning	Intermediate	Advanced/High
Help students copy sentence frames and complete them.	Provide sentence starters for students.	Have students use the words in a question.

English Language Learners
Writing/Spelling

WRITING TRAIT: IDEAS

OBJECTIVES

 Use concrete words and phrases and sensory details to convey experiences and events precisely. **W.4.3d**

LANGUAGE OBJECTIVE
Add details to writing.

 I Do Explain that good writers use descriptive details to create a vivid picture of the characters, settings, and events in stories. Read the Expert Model passage aloud as students follow along. Identify the descriptive details.

 We Do Read aloud page 23 of "The Dragon Problem" beginning with the second paragraph. Identify descriptive details, such as "swoop down" and "stale, hard rice ball." Help students visualize the details. Then use a sequence chart to put the events in order.

 You Do Have pairs use a sequence chart to write about a problem they solved. Ask students to use descriptive details. Edit each pair's writing.

Beginning	Intermediate	Advanced/High
Have students copy the edited sentences.	Have students revise, using complete sentences.	Have students revise, using details to clarify.

SPELL WORDS WITH SHORT VOWELS

OBJECTIVES

 Spell grade-appropriate words correctly, consulting references as needed. **L.4.2d**

LANGUAGE OBJECTIVE
Spell words with short vowels.

 I Do Read aloud the Spelling Words on page T36. Elongate the sound of the short vowel, and spell out each sound. Have students repeat the words. Explain that vowels in words with only one vowel are usually short vowels.

 We Do Read the Dictation Sentences on page T37 aloud for students. With each sentence, read the underlined word slowly, stressing the short-vowel sound. Have students repeat after you and write the word.

 You Do Display the words. Have students exchange their list with a partner to check the spelling and write the words correctly.

Beginning	Intermediate	Advanced/High
Have students copy the corrected words and say the words aloud.	After students have corrected their words, have pairs quiz each other.	After they have corrected their words, have pairs use each word in a sentence.

Grammar

SENTENCES

OBJECTIVES

CCSS Produce complete sentences, recognizing and correcting inappropriate fragments and run-ons. **L.4.1f**

CCSS Choose punctuation for effect. **L.4.3b**

Use and punctuate sentences correctly.

LANGUAGE OBJECTIVE

Write sentences.

Language Transfers Handbook

Speakers of Cantonese may have difficulties with preposition placement and may sometimes omit prepositions altogether. For students who have trouble, emphasize how prepositions show where things are by having students form sentences describing location.

I Do Remind students that a sentence is a group of words that shows a complete thought. Write the following on the board: *Julian likes to read stories about baseball.* Underline the *J* and circle the period. Explain that a sentence begins with a capital letter and ends with a punctuation mark, such as a period. Then write: *likes to play baseball* with no punctuation. Read the fragment aloud and explain that it does not give a complete thought because it does not say who likes to play baseball.

Review sentence types and punctuation marks. Provide sample sentences and have students circle the punctuation marks.

We Do Write the sentences below. Have volunteers identify the sentences as complete or fragment. Then have them explain how they identified each sentence. Correct the sentence fragments with students. Then read the corrected sentences aloud and have students repeat.

likes to eat pea soup for lunch.

I can't believe we didn't win the game!

who will sit next to?

You Do Have partners write a sentence fragment, a question, and a statement. Then have them exchange with another pair and correct the fragment.

Beginning	Intermediate	Advanced/High
Help students complete their sentences. Read each sentence aloud and have students point to the capital letters and punctuation marks.	Ask students to circle the punctuation and identify each complete sentence as a statement, question, or exclamation.	Have students explain the difference between a complete sentence and a sentence fragment.

For extra support, have students complete the activities in the **Grammar Practice Reproducibles** during the week, using the routine below:

→ Explain the grammar skill.

→ Model the first activity in the Grammar Practice Reproducibles.

→ Have the whole group complete the next couple of activities. Then have students complete the rest with a partner.

→ Review the activities with correct answers.

PROGRESS MONITORING

Weekly Assessment

CCSS TESTED SKILLS

✔ COMPREHENSION:	✔ VOCABULARY:	✔ WRITING:
Sequence **RL.4.3**	Context Clues: Synonyms **L.4.5c**	Writing About Text **RL.4.3, W.4.9a**

Assessment Includes

→ Pencil-and-paper administration

→ On-line administration

→ Approaching-Level Weekly Assessment also available

Fluency Goal 84 to 104 words correct per minute (WCPM)

Accuracy Rate Goal 95% or higher

Administer oral reading fluency assessments using the following schedule:

→ **Weeks 1, 3, 5** Provide Approaching-Level students at least three oral reading fluency assessments during the unit.

→ **Weeks 2 and 4** Provide On-Level students at least two oral reading fluency assessments during the unit.

→ **Week 6** If necessary, provide Beyond-Level students an oral reading fluency assessment at this time.

Also Available: Selection Tests online PDFs

Go Digital! www.connected.mcgraw-hill.com

Using Assessment Results

TESTED SKILLS	If ...	Then ...
COMPREHENSION	Students answer 0–6 multiple-choice items correctly ...	... assign Lessons 40–42 on Sequence from the *Tier 2 Comprehension Intervention online PDFs.*
VOCABULARY	Students answer 0–6 multiple-choice items correctly ...	... assign Lesson 137 on Context Clues from the *Tier 2 Vocabulary Intervention online PDFs.*
WRITING	Students score less than "3" on the constructed response ...	... assign Lessons 40–42 and/or Write About Reading Lesson 194 from the *Tier 2 Comprehension Intervention online PDFs.*
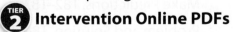	Students have a WCPM score of 76–83 ...	... assign a lesson from Section 1 or 7–10 of the *Tier 2 Fluency Intervention online PDFs.*
	Students have a WCPM score of 0–75 ...	... assign a lesson from Sections 2–6 of the *Tier 2 Fluency Intervention online PDFs.*

Response to Intervention

Use the appropriate sections of the *Placement and Diagnostic Assessment* as well as students' assessment results to designate students requiring:

TIER 2 Intervention Online PDFs

TIER 3 WonderWorks Intervention Program

Text Complexity Range for Grades 4–5

Lexile	
740	1010
TextEvaluator™	
23	51

Reading/Writing Workshop

TEACH AND MODEL

CCSS Shared Read › Genre • Realistic Fiction

THE Talent Show

Essential Question
How do your actions affect others?
Read about how Tina's actions affect Maura.

36

"Tina, there's a school talent show in three weeks," I shouted to my best friend. My older brother had been teaching me juggling, and I knew he'd help me with my act for the show.

Tina ran over to the bulletin board and read the poster. "Maura, what's our act going to be?" Tina asked me.

"Our act?" I said, taking a tighter grip on my books.

Tina grinned, pointed to the poster and said "It says acts can be individuals, partners, or small groups."

My grip on my books became uncomfortably tight. "You want to do an act together?"

"It'll be fun," Tina said.

I hesitated for a second before continuing. "I've got an idea and. . . ."

Tina interrupted me. "Yeah, me too; let's talk at lunch."

During math, I tried to think of how I would tell Tina that I wanted to do my own act. After all, we are best friends; we should be able to see eye to eye about this. The problem is Tina always takes charge, I don't speak up, and then I end up feeling resentful about the whole situation.

I desperately wanted to win, but it was more than that. I wanted to win on my own—with an act that was all mine.

37

✓ Vocabulary

accountable

advise

desperately

hesitated

humiliated

inspiration

self-esteem

uncomfortably

🔍 Close Reading of Complex Text

Shared Read "The Talent Show," 36–39

Genre Realistic Fiction

Lexile 620

ETS *TextEvaluator™* 38

Minilessons   ✓ Tested Skills **CCSS**

✓ **Comprehension Strategy** .... Make Predictions, T82–T83

✓ **Comprehension Skill** .... Problem and Solution, T84–T85

✓ **Genre** .... Realistic Fiction, T86–T87

✓ **Vocabulary Strategy** .... Idioms, T88–T89

✓ **Writing Traits** .... Ideas, T94–T95

Grammar .... Subjects and Predicates, T98–T99

☞ **Go** Digital

www.connected.mcgraw-hill.com

APPLY WITH CLOSE READING

Complex Text

Literature Anthology

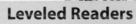

Experts, Incorporated, 32–43
Genre Realistic Fiction
Lexile 730
(ETS) *TextEvaluator*™ 44

PAIRED READ

"Speaking Out to Stop Bullying," 44–47
Genre Expository Text
Lexile 800
(ETS) *TextEvaluator*™ 27

Differentiated Text

Leveled Readers *Include Paired Reads*

APPROACHING
Lexile 530
(ETS) *TextEvaluator*™ 27

ON LEVEL
Lexile 710
(ETS) *TextEvaluator*™ 35

BEYOND
Lexile 810
(ETS) *TextEvaluator*™ 39

ELL
Lexile 540
(ETS) *TextEvaluator*™ 12

Extended Complex Text

The Skirt
Genre Realistic Fiction
Lexile 540
(ETS) *TextEvaluator*™ 27

Accidental Hero
Genre Fiction
Lexile 780
(ETS) *TextEvaluator*™ 50

Classroom Library

Classroom Library lessons available online.

TEACH AND MANAGE

How You Teach

INTRODUCE

Weekly Concept
Think of Others

Reading/Writing Workshop
32–33

TEACH

Close Reading
"The Talent Show"

Minilessons
Make Predictions, Problem and
Solution, Realistic Fiction, Idioms,
Writing Traits

Reading/Writing Workshop
36–39

APPLY

Close Reading
Experts, Incorporated
"Speaking Out to Stop
Bullying"

Literature Anthology
32–47

 Go Digital

Interactive Whiteboard

 Interactive Whiteboard

Mobile

How Students Practice

WEEKLY CONTRACT

PDF Online

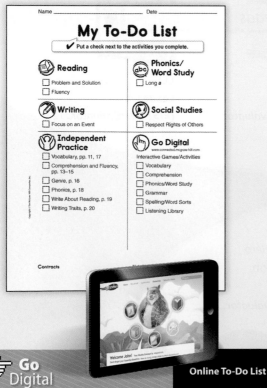

My To-Do List
✔ Put a check next to the activities you complete.

Reading
☐ Problem and Solution
☐ Fluency

Phonics/Word Study
☐ Long *a*

Writing
☐ Focus on an Event

Social Studies
☐ Respect Rights of Others

Independent Practice
☐ Vocabulary, pp. 11, 17
☐ Comprehension and Fluency, pp. 13–15
☐ Genre, p. 16
☐ Phonics, p. 18
☐ Write About Reading, p. 19
☐ Writing Traits, p. 20

Go Digital
www.connected.mcgraw-hill.com
Interactive Games/Activities
☐ Vocabulary
☐ Comprehension
☐ Phonics/Word Study
☐ Grammar
☐ Spelling/Word Sorts
☐ Listening Library

Contracts

LEVELED PRACTICE AND ONLINE ACTIVITIES

Your Turn Practice Book
11–20

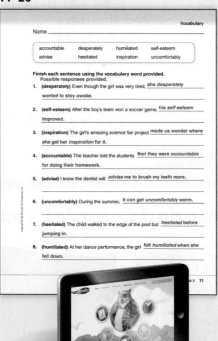

Leveled Readers

 **Go Digital**

Online To-Do List

Leveled Activities

Writer's Workspace

Go Digital! www.connected.mcgraw-hill.com

DIFFERENTIATE

SMALL GROUP INSTRUCTION
Leveled Readers

Mobile

INTEGRATE

Research and Inquiry
Charts, T92

Text Connections
Compare How Actions Affect
Others, T93

Analytical Writing **Write About Reading**
Write an Analysis, T93

Online Research
and Writing

ASSESS

Wonders
Grade 4

Weekly
Assessment

Assessing the Common Core
State Standards

**Weekly Assessment
13–24**

Online
Assessment

LEVELED WORKSTATION CARDS

 More
Activities
on back

2

Respect the Rights of Others

SOCIAL ST

- With a partner, discuss common
situations in which a person might
not be treated fairly. Make a list of at
least four situations. Make sure to
describe each carefully.

2

Ideas: Focus on an Event

Read this paragraph of Kim's narrative about
an important event. Identify details about the
day, the location, and the people. Revise the
paragraph to give the event better focus.

WRITING

When ... andma Williams

2

Idioms, Proverbs, Adages

abc

PHONICS/WORD STUDY

- Write these idioms: *a bad apple, caught
red-handed,* and *pain in the neck.* Talk
about the difference between the common
meaning of each idiom and the
literal meaning of the words it uses.

A Bad Apple

- Write the meaning of each idiom.

- Write these adages and proverbs:
*No news is good news; Where there's
smoke, there's fire;* and
Better to be safe than sorry.

You need
20 minutes
> paper
> pencils

- Choose one adage or proverb
and use it in a short paragraph
that shows its meaning.

Go Digital! www.connected.mcgraw-hill.com • Interactive Games and Activities • Grade 4   2

2

Problem and Solution

READING

- Think about a story you have read
in which a character—either a person
or an animal—solves a problem.

- Reread the story. Identify the problem
and write it down. Then list steps the
character took to find a solution.

- Write a short sequel to the
story. What other problem
might the character face?
In your conclusion, explain
how the character
solved the problem.

You need
20 minutes
> fictional story
> paper
> pencils or pens

Go Digital! www.connected.mcgraw-hill.com • Interactive Games and Activities • Grade 4   2

DEVELOPING READERS AND WRITERS

Write to Sources and Research

Paraphrase, T84–T85

Note Taking, T89B, T89N

Summarize, T89L

Make Connections: Essential Question, T89L, T89P, T93

Key Details, T89N, T89O

Problem and Solution, T89L

Research and Inquiry, T92

Analyze to Share an Opinion, T93

Comparing Texts, T105, T113, T117, T123

Predictive Writing, T89A

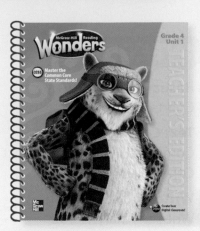

Teacher's Edition

Literature Anthology

Summarize, 43
Problem and Solution, 43

Interactive Whiteboard

Leveled Readers
Comparing Texts
Problem and Solution

Your Turn Practice Book

Problem and Solution, 13–15
Genre, 16
Analyze to Share, 19

Narrative Text
Friendly Letter, T344–T349

Conferencing Routines
Teacher Conferences, T346
Peer Conferences, T347

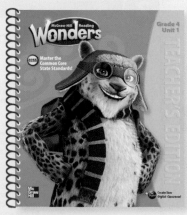

Interactive Whiteboard

Teacher's Edition

Leveled Workstation Card
Letter, Card 24

Writer's Workspace
Narrative Text: Letter
Writing Process
Multimedia Presentations

Writing Traits • Write Every Day

Writing Trait: Ideas
Focus on an Event, T94–T95

Conferencing Routines
Teacher Conferences, T96
Peer Conferences, T97

Teacher's Edition

Ideas: Focus on an Event, 44–45

Reading/Writing Workshop

Go Digital

Interactive Whiteboard

Ideas: Focus, Card 2

Leveled Workstation Card

Ideas: Focus on an Event, 20

Your Turn Practice Book

Grammar and Spelling

Grammar
Subjects and Predicates, T98–T99

Spelling
Long *a*, T100–T101

Go Digital

Interactive Whiteboard

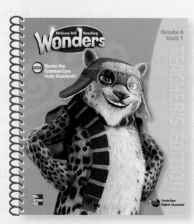

Teacher's Edition

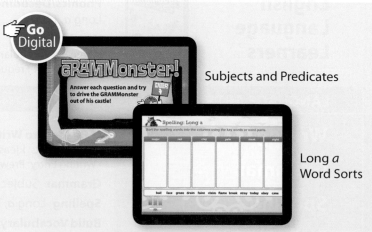

Go Digital

Subjects and Predicates

Long *a* Word Sorts

Online Spelling and Grammar Games

SUGGESTED LESSON PLAN

	DAY 1	DAY 2

Whole Group

Teach, Model and Apply

Reading/Writing Workshop

READING

DAY 1

Build Background Think of Others, T74–T75

Listening Comprehension Interactive Read Aloud: "Say Something," T76–T77

Comprehension
• Preview Genre: Realistic Fiction
• Preview Strategy: Make Predictions

✔**Vocabulary** Words in Context, T78–T79

Practice Your Turn, 11

Close Reading of Complex Text "The Talent Show," 36–39

DAY 2

✔**Comprehension**
• Strategy: Make Predictions, T82–T83
• Skill: Problem and Solution, T84–T85
• Write About Reading ● Analytical Writing
• Genre: Realistic Fiction, T86–T87

✔**Vocabulary** Strategy: Figurative Language, T88–T89

Practice Your Turn, 12–17

DIFFERENTIATED INSTRUCTION   Choose across the week to meet your students' needs.

Small Group

Approaching Level

Leveled Reader The Dream Team, T104–T105

Phonics/Decoding Decode Words with Long a, T106 TIER 2

Vocabulary
• Review High-Frequency Words, T108 TIER 2
• Identify Related Words, T109

Leveled Reader The Dream Team, T104–T105

Vocabulary Review Vocabulary Words, T108 TIER 2

Comprehension
• Plot: Identify Problems, T110 TIER 2
• Review Problem and Solution, T111

On Level

Leveled Reader Rosa's Garden, T112–T113

Vocabulary Review Vocabulary Words, T114

Leveled Reader Rosa's Garden, T112–T113

Comprehension Review Problem and Solution, T115

Beyond Level

Leveled Reader Saving Grasshopper, T116–T117

Vocabulary Review Domain-Specific Words, T118

Leveled Reader Saving Grasshopper, T116–T117

Comprehension Review Problem and Solution, T119

English Language Learners

Shared Read "The Talent Show," T120–T121

Phonics/Decoding Decode Words with Long a, T106

Vocabulary
• Preteach Vocabulary, T124
• Review High-Frequency Words, T108

Leveled Reader Rosa's Garden, T122–T123

Vocabulary Review Vocabulary, T124

Writing Writing Trait: Ideas, T126

Grammar Subjects and Predicates, T127

Whole Group

LANGUAGE ARTS   Writing Process: Friendly Letter, T344–T349   Use with Weeks 1–3

Writing
Grammar
Spelling
Build Vocabulary

DAY 1

✔**Readers to Writers**
• Writing Traits: Ideas/Focus on an Event, T94–T95
• Writing Entry: Prewrite and Draft, T96

Grammar Subjects and Predicates, T98

Spelling Long a, T100

Build Vocabulary
• Connect to Words, T102
• Academic Vocabulary, T102

DAY 2

Readers to Writers
• Writing Entry: Revise, T96

Grammar Subjects and Predicates, T98

Spelling Long a, T100

Build Vocabulary
• Expand Vocabulary, T102
• Review Synonyms, T102

| **DAY 3** | **DAY 4** | **DAY 5 Review and Assess** |

READING

Phonics/Decoding • Long *a*, T90 • Inflectional Endings, T91 **Practice** *Your Turn*, 18 **Close Reading** *Experts, Incorporated*, 32–43 ● ⧉*Analytical Writing* Literature Anthology	**Fluency** Expression and Rate, T91 **Integrate Ideas** ● ⧉*Analytical Writing* • Research and Inquiry, T92 **Practice** *Your Turn*, 13–15 **Close Reading** "Speaking Out to Stop Bullying," T44–T47 ● ⧉*Analytical Writing*	**Integrate Ideas** ● ⧉*Analytical Writing* • Research and Inquiry, T92 • Text Connections, T93 • Write About Reading, T93 **Practice** *Your Turn*, 19 

DIFFERENTIATED INSTRUCTION

Leveled Reader *The Dream Team*, T104–T105 **Phonics/Decoding** Review Open Syllables, T106 ② **Fluency** Expression and Rate, T110 ② **Vocabulary** Idioms, T109	**Leveled Reader** Paired Read: "Making a Difference," T105 ● ⧉*Analytical Writing* **Phonics/Decoding** Practice Words with Long *a*, T107	**Leveled Reader** Literature Circles, T105 **Comprehension** Self-Selected Reading, T111 **Phonics/Decoding** Inflectional Endings, T107
Leveled Reader *Rosa's Garden*, T112–T113 **Vocabulary** Idioms, T114	**Leveled Reader** Paired Read: "Fresh from the City," T113 ● ⧉*Analytical Writing*	**Leveled Reader** Literature Circles, T113 **Comprehension** Self-Selected Reading, T115
Leveled Reader *Saving Grasshopper*, T116–T117 **Vocabulary** • Idioms, T118 • Independent Study, T118 ⭐*Gifted and Talented*	**Leveled Reader** Paired Read: "Backyard Bird Habitats," T117 ● ⧉*Analytical Writing*	**Leveled Reader** Literature Circles, T117 **Comprehension** • Self-Selected Reading, T119 • Analyze: Think of Others, T119 ⭐*Gifted and Talented*
Leveled Reader *Rosa's Garden*, T122–T123 **Phonics/Decoding** Review Open Syllables, T106 **Vocabulary** Idioms, T125 **Spelling** Words with Long *a*, T126	**Leveled Reader** Paired Read: "Fresh from the City," T123 ● ⧉*Analytical Writing* **Vocabulary** Additional Vocabulary, T125 **Phonics/Decoding** Practice Words with Long *a*, T107	**Leveled Reader** Literature Circles, T123 **Phonics/Decoding** Inflectional Endings, T107

LANGUAGE ARTS

Readers to Writers • Writing Entry: Prewrite and Draft, T97 **Grammar** Mechanics and Usage, T99 **Spelling** Long *a*, T101 **Build Vocabulary** • Reinforce the Words, T103 • Idioms, T103	**Readers to Writers** • Writing Entry: Revise, T97 **Grammar** Subjects and Predicates, T99 **Spelling** Long *a*, T101 **Build Vocabulary** • Connect to Writing, T103 • Shades of Meaning, T103	**Readers to Writers** • Writing Entry: Share and Reflect, T97 **Grammar** Subjects and Predicates, T99 **Spelling** Long *a*, T101 **Build Vocabulary** • Word Squares, T103 • Morphology, T103

DIFFERENTIATE TO ACCELERATE

A C T Scaffold to Access Complex Text

Qualitative · Quantitative
Reader and Task
TEXT COMPLEXITY

IF the text complexity of a particular selection is too difficult for students

THEN see the references noted in the chart below for scaffolded instruction to help students Access Complex Text.

	Reading/Writing Workshop	Literature Anthology	Leveled Readers		Classroom Library
Quantitative	 "The Talent Show" **Lexile** 620 *TextEvaluator* 38	 *Experts, Incorporated* **Lexile** 730 *TextEvaluator* 44 "Speaking Out to Stop Bullying" **Lexile** 800 *TextEvaluator* 27	 **Approaching Level** **Lexile** 530 *TextEvaluator* 27 **Beyond Level** **Lexile** 810 *TextEvaluator* 39	**On Level** **Lexile** 710 *TextEvaluator* 35 **ELL** **Lexile** 540 *TextEvaluator* 12	 *The Skirt* **Lexile** 540 *TextEvaluator* 27 *The Accidental Hero* **Lexile** 780 *TextEvaluator* 50
Qualitative	**What Makes the Text Complex?** • **Genre** Dialogue T81 • **Connection of Ideas** Characters and Problems T85 **A C T** *See Scaffolded Instruction in Teacher's Edition T81 and T85.*	**What Makes the Text Complex?** • **Genre** Realistic Fiction T89A • **Purpose** Point of View T89C; Expository Text T89M; Author's Perspective T89O • **Sentence Structure** T89E • **Organization** Events T89F • **Specific Vocabulary** Figurative Language T89G • **Connection of Ideas** Earlier Details T89I **A C T** *See Scaffolded Instruction in Teacher's Edition T89A–T89P.*	**What Makes the Text Complex?** • **Specific Vocabulary** • **Sentence Structure** • **Connection of Ideas** • **Genre** **A C T** *See Level Up lessons online for Leveled Readers.*		**What Makes the Text Complex?** • **Genre** • **Specific Vocabulary** • **Prior Knowledge** • **Sentence Structure** • **Organization** • **Purpose** • **Connection of Ideas** **A C T** *See Scaffolded Instruction in Teacher's Edition T360–T361.*
Reader and Task	The Introduce the Concept lesson on pages T74–T75 will help determine the reader's knowledge and engagement in the weekly concept. See pages T80–T89 and T92–T93 for questions and tasks for this text.	The Introduce the Concept lesson on pages T74–T75 will help determine the reader's knowledge and engagement in the weekly concept. See pages T89A–T89P and T92–T93 for questions and tasks for this text.	The Introduce the Concept lesson on pages T74–T75 will help determine the reader's knowledge and engagement in the weekly concept. See pages T104–T105, T112–T113, T116–T117, T122–T123, and T92–T93 for questions and tasks for this text.		The Introduce the Concept lesson on pages T74–T75 will help determine the reader's knowledge and engagement in the weekly concept. See pages T360–T361 for questions and tasks for this text.

Go Digital! www.connected.mcgraw-hill.com

Monitor and *Differentiate*

IF you need to differentiate instruction

THEN use the Quick Checks to assess students' needs and select the appropriate small group instruction focus.

 Quick Check

Comprehension Strategy Make, Confirm, or Revise Predictions T83

Comprehension Skill Character, Setting, Plot: Problem and Solution T85

Genre Realistic Fiction T87

Vocabulary Strategy Figurative Language T89

Phonics/Fluency Long *a* T91

If No →

| Approaching Level | Reteach T104–T111 |
| ELL | Develop T120–T127 |

If Yes →

| On Level | Review T112–T115 |
| Beyond Level | Extend T116–T119 |

Level Up with Leveled Readers

IF students can read their leveled text fluently and answer comprehension questions

THEN work with the next level up to accelerate students' reading with more complex text.

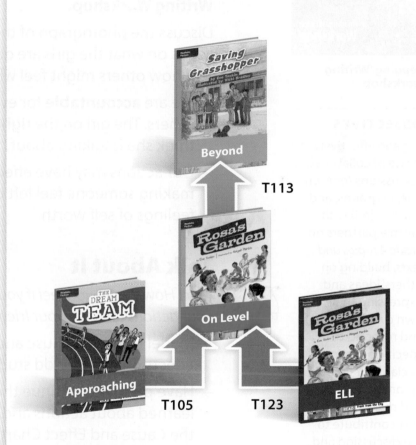

Beyond — T113

On Level

T105   T123

Approaching   ELL

ENGLISH LANGUAGE LEARNERS
SCAFFOLD

IF ELL students need additional support **THEN** scaffold instruction using the small group suggestions.

Reading/Writing Workshop "The Talent Show" T120–T121	Leveled Reader *Rosa's Garden* T122–T123 "Fresh from the City" T123	Additional Vocabulary T125 another neighborhood group safe idea work	Using Idioms T125	Writing Ideas T126	Spelling Words with Long *a* T126	Grammar Subjects and Predicates T127

Note: Include ELL Students in all small groups based on their needs.

→ # Introduce the Concept

Reading/Writing Workshop

OBJECTIVES

CCSS Engage effectively in a range of collaborative discussions (one-on-one, in groups, and teacher-led) with diverse partners on *grade 4 topics and texts,* building on others' ideas and expressing their own clearly. Pose and respond to specific questions to clarify or follow up on information, and make comments that contribute to the discussion and link to the remarks of others. **SL.4.1c**

CCSS Paraphrase portions of a text read aloud or information presented in diverse media and formats, including visually, quantitatively, and orally. **SL.4.2**

Build background knowledge on actions and their effects.

MINILESSON 10 Mins

Build Background

ESSENTIAL QUESTION
How do your actions affect others?

Have students read the Essential Question on page 32 of the **Reading/Writing Workshop.**

Discuss the photograph of the girl whispering to another student. Focus on what the girls are doing, what they might be talking about, and how others might feel when they see them.

→ We are **accountable** for everything we do because it may affect others. The girl on the right is whispering to her friend. What do you think she is talking about?

→ Our actions may have effects we don't intend. The girls could be making someone feel left out and lowering his or her **self-esteem,** or feelings of self worth.

Talk About It

 Ask: *How would you feel if you were sitting next to these girls? When have your actions affected your friends?* Have students discuss in pairs.

→ Model using the Cause and Effect Chart to generate actions and their effects on others. Add students' contributions in their own words.

→ Have partners continue the discussion by sharing what they have learned about actions and their effects on others. They can complete the Cause and Effect Chart, generating additional words and phrases.

Collaborative Conversations

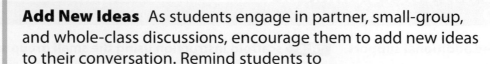

Add New Ideas As students engage in partner, small-group, and whole-class discussions, encourage them to add new ideas to their conversation. Remind students to

→ stay on topic and express their ideas clearly.

→ connect their own ideas to things their peers have said.

→ look for ways to connect their personal experiences or prior knowledge to the conversation.

Go Digital

Discuss the Concept

Watch Video

View Photos

Use Graphic Organizer

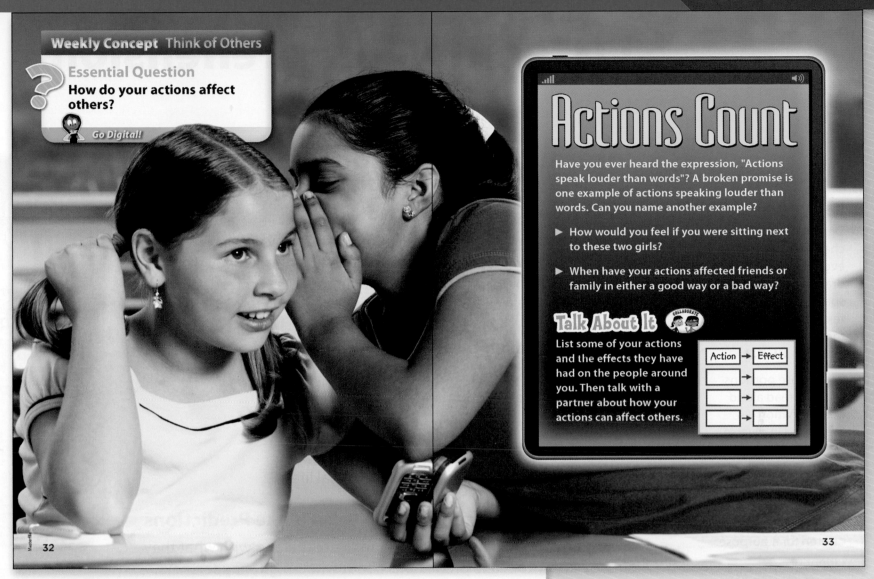

READING/WRITING WORKSHOP, pp. 32–33

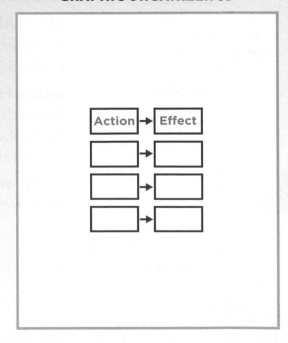

ENGLISH LANGUAGE LEARNERS SCAFFOLD

ELL

Beginning	Intermediate	Advanced/High
Use Visuals Write and say the word *affect*. Point to the girls. Say: *The girls' actions affect others. Do you think their actions would make someone feel good or bad?* Elaborate on students' answers. Point out the cognates for *affect (afectar)* and *actions (acciones)*.	**Describe** Have students describe the photograph. *What are the girls doing? How do you think their actions affect others?* Prompt students to give a more comprehensive response by asking additional questions or guiding them to get an answer.	**Discuss** Have students elaborate on their actions and the effects they can have on others. *When have your actions affected others? How can we think of others before we act in a negative, or bad, way?* Elicit details to support students' responses.

Listening Comprehension

 MINILESSON 10 Mins

Interactive Read Aloud

Go Digital

OBJECTIVES

CCSS Describe in depth a character, setting, or event in a story or drama, drawing on specific details in the text (e.g., a character's thoughts, words, or actions). **RL.4.3**

CCSS Paraphrase portions of a text read aloud or information presented in diverse media and formats, including visually, quantitatively, and orally. **SL.4.2**

- Listen for a purpose.
- Identify characteristics of realistic fiction.

ACADEMIC LANGUAGE

- *realistic fiction, make, confirm, and revise predictions*
- Cognates: *ficción realista, confirmar, revisar predicciones*

Connect to Concept: Think of Others

Tell students that our actions affect others in many ways. Let students know that you will be reading aloud a passage about a boy who decides to speak up and help a fellow student. As you read, students should listen for examples of how the characters' actions affect others.

Preview Genre: Realistic Fiction

Explain that the text you will read aloud is realistic fiction. Discuss features of realistic fiction:

→ includes characters whose behavior is realistic

→ is set in a real-life place

→ includes events that could happen in real life

Preview Comprehension Strategy: Make Predictions

Explain that good readers use clues in the text along with what they already know to make predictions about what might happen next. As they continue to read, they may confirm or revise their predictions based on new information.

Use the Think Alouds on page T77 to model the strategy.

Respond to Reading

Think Aloud Clouds Display Think Aloud Master 3: *I predicted _____ because . . .* to reinforce how you used the make, confirm, and revise predictions strategy to understand content.

Genre Features With students, discuss the elements of the Read Aloud that let them know it is realistic fiction. Ask them to think about other texts that you have read or they have read independently that were realistic fiction stories.

Summarize Have students paraphrase the story "Say Something" in their own words.

View Illustrations

Model Think Alouds

Fill in Genre Chart

Say Something

Mr. Benz was checking attendance when the principal came to the door with a new student. I looked up from my seat near the back and saw a kid step into the classroom. "Class, this is Eli Tate," Mrs. Scalia said, and then pointed toward the empty desk next to me.

I nodded and gave the kid a smile. Last year I had been a new student, and I still remembered that feeling of walking into a new classroom for the first time, with everybody watching me, trying to size me up and make some judgment. Was I cool? A brain? An athlete? A loser? **1**

Within a month I had adjusted pretty well. One important reason for this was Kent, a kid who became my best friend until he moved away over the summer. Kent had introduced himself right away and made sure I had somebody to sit with at lunch that long first day.

At ten our class was herded into the gym, but since the P.E. teacher was out, Mr. Benz said to run laps. On my third lap I noticed the new kid, Eli, standing against the wall. In front of him was Tad Scott. As I got nearer, I heard Tad say, "So you lie? I mean your name is e–LIE, right?" **2**

I ran past them. Maybe Tad would knock it off. Or maybe Eli would tell him to stop being a jerk. Nobody likes getting on the wrong side of Tad. He always finds a way to make you pay if you do. On my next lap I saw that Tad was still at it. Eli wasn't backing down, but he wasn't saying anything either. *Okay*, I said to myself, *if Tad's still bothering him when I come back around, I'll definitely say something.*

As I came back around, Tad was still giving Eli a hard time. I stopped and said, "It's Eli, right? I'm Darius. You want to shoot some hoops? I'm tired of running." Eli shrugged and said sure so we headed off to grab a ball. "You want to come too, Tad?" I asked, turning back. But Tad had already lost interest and was heading over to bother some girls. **3**

Yellow Dog Productions/Digital Vision/Getty Images

> **1** **Think Aloud** Will Eli and the narrator be friends? I **predict** that they will be friends because the narrator was new once. After I read, I can **confirm my prediction**.

> **2** **Think Aloud** Will the narrator do anything when he hears Tad teasing Eli? I **predict** that the narrator will do something to stop Tad because Kent helped him when he was a new student.

> **3** **Think Aloud** My predictions were correct. Darius, the narrator, is helping the new kid by getting him away from Tad. I **predict** that they will probably become friends because Darius's friend Kent moved away.

→ Vocabulary

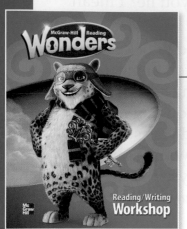

**Reading/Writing
Workshop**

OBJECTIVES

CCSS Acquire and use accurately grade-appropriate general academic and domain-specific words and phrases, including those that signal precise actions, emotions, or states of being (e.g., *quizzed, whined, stammered*) and that are basic to a particular topic (e.g., *wildlife, conservation,* and *endangered* when discussing animal preservation). **L.4.6**

MINILESSON 10 Mins

Words in Context

Model the Routine

Introduce each vocabulary word using the Vocabulary Routine found on the Visual Vocabulary Cards.

Visual Vocabulary Cards

Vocabu...
Define:
Example:
Ask:

Vocabulary Routine

Define: To be **accountable** means to be responsible.

Example: Sam is held accountable for washing his dog.

Ask: How are the words *accountable* and *responsible* similar?

Definitions

→ **advise**	To **advise** means to give one's opinion or to inform.
→ **desperately**	To act **desperately** means to try anything to change a hopeless situation.
→ **hesitated**	If you **hesitated** you waited or stopped, especially because of feeling unsure.
→ **humiliated**	To be **humiliated** means to be made to feel ashamed or foolish. Cognate: *humillado*
→ **inspiration**	An **inspiration** is a person or thing that stirs the mind, feelings, or imagination. Cognate: *inspiración*
→ **self-esteem**	To have **self-esteem** is to have respect for oneself.
→ **uncomfortably**	**Uncomfortably** means "uneasily."

Talk About It

Have students work with a partner and look at each picture and discuss the definition of each word. Then ask students to choose three words and write questions for their partner to answer using each word.

Go Digital

accountable

Use Visual Glossary

CCSS Words to Know

Vocabulary

Use the picture and the sentences to talk with a partner about each word.

accountable

Sam is held **accountable** for washing his dog.

How are the words accountable and responsible similar?

advise

A coach can **advise** you on how to improve your swimming.

What is a synonym for advise?

desperately

The woman was **desperately** trying to remember where she had left her keys.

Describe a time when you desperately tried to remember something.

hesitated

The dog **hesitated** before jumping up to grab the food off the counter.

When have you hesitated before doing something?

humiliated

Sarah felt **humiliated** when she forgot her lines.

How is humiliated similar to embarrassed?

inspiration

The girl found **inspiration** for her drawing in nature.

When you have to write a story where does your inspiration come from?

self-esteem

Winning the soccer championship helped improve Billy's confidence and **self-esteem**.

What else builds self-esteem?

uncomfortably

Sonya's throat felt **uncomfortably** sore.

What are some things that can feel uncomfortably tight?

Your Turn COLLABORATE

Pick three words. Write three questions for your partner to answer.

Go Digital! Use the online visual glossary

34

35

READING/WRITING WORKSHOP, pp. 34–35

ENGLISH LANGUAGE LEARNERS SCAFFOLD

Beginning

Use Visuals Elicit that another word for *humiliated* is *embarrassed*. Act out or pantomime its meaning and have students repeat. Help students complete the sentence frame: *The girl feels ____. Humiliated* in Spanish is *humillado*.

Intermediate

Describe Have students describe the picture for the word *humiliated*. *How does the girl feel?* Ask students to turn to a partner and describe why the girl might feel humiliated. If a student's response is correct, repeat it slowly and clearly for the class to hear.

Advanced/High

Discuss Have partners describe a time when they felt humiliated. Ask questions to help them elaborate. *What happened to make you feel humiliated? What happened to make you feel better?*

ON-LEVEL PRACTICE BOOK p. 11

| accountable | desperately | humiliated | self-esteem |
| advise | hesitated | inspiration | uncomfortably |

Finish each sentence using the vocabulary word provided.
Possible responses provided.

1. (desperately) Even though the girl was very tired, she *desperately* wanted to stay awake.
2. (self-esteem) After the boy's team won a soccer game, his *self-esteem* improved.
3. (inspiration) The girl's amazing science fair project *made us wonder where* she got her *inspiration* for it.
4. (accountable) The teacher told the students *that they were accountable* for doing their homework.
5. (advise) I know the dentist will *advise me to brush my teeth more.*
6. (uncomfortably) During the summer, *it can get uncomfortably* warm.
7. (hesitated) The child walked to the edge of the pool but *hesitated* before jumping in.
8. (humiliated) At her dance performance, the girl *felt humiliated* when she fell down.

APPROACHING p. 11 | BEYOND p. 11 | ELL p. 11

READING/WRITING WORKSHOP, pp. 36–37

Reading/Writing Workshop

Shared Read

Lexile 620L   *TextEvaluator™* 38

Connect to Concept: Think of Others

Explain to students that "The Talent Show" will tell them more about how people's actions can affect others. Read "The Talent Show" with students. Note the vocabulary words previously taught are highlighted in the text.

Close Reading

Reread Paragraphs 1 and 2: Tell students that you are going to make predictions about the text based on the first two paragraphs. Reread the paragraphs together. Ask: *What does Maura want to do in the talent show?* (She wants to perform a juggling act.) *What does Tina want to do in the show?* (She wants to perform an act with Maura.) *What do you think will happen?* Model how to cite evidence to answer the question.

I think they will have a disagreement about what their talent show act should be. Since Tina is her best friend, Maura might not want to disappoint her by telling her she wants to do an act alone.

Reread Paragraph 8: Reread paragraph 8 with students. Model how to confirm a prediction. Remind students that if a prediction is not supported by the text, they can revise their prediction as they continue reading.

Tina interrupts Maura when Maura tries to tell her about her idea for the act. This information confirms my prediction that Maura may not tell Tina that she wants to perform an act alone.

At lunch, Tina started talking as soon as we sat down. "I have it all planned out. My inspiration came from that new TV show, 'You've Got Talent.' We can sing along to a song and do a dance routine, and my mother can make us costumes."

"Yeah, that's good," I said. "But I had another idea." I told her about my juggling act.

Tina considered it. "Nah, I don't think I can learn to juggle in three weeks and I'd probably drop the balls," she said. "We don't want to be humiliated, right?"

At recess, I ran around the track a couple of times just to let off steam.

When my grandmother picked me up after school, she drove a few minutes and finally said, "Cat got your tongue?"

I explained about the talent show as she listened carefully. "So, Tina is not being respectful of your ideas, but it sounds as if you aren't either."

"What?" I shouted. "I told Tina her idea was good."

"No," said my grandmother, "I said that you weren't respectful of your *own* ideas, or you would have spoken up. I understand that you're friends, but you're still accountable for your own actions."

I thought about this. "So what should I do?" I asked.

"I advise you to tell the truth," she said. "It wouldn't hurt to let Tina know what you want. Besides," my grandmother added, "it will be good for your self-esteem!"

When we got home, I took 12 deep breaths, called Tina, and told her that I was going to do my juggling act. She was curt on the phone, and I spent all night worrying she would be mad at me.

The next day, she described her act and her costume. But the biggest surprise came at recess, when we played a game that I chose, not Tina.

I guess standing up for myself did pay off.

Make Connections

Talk about how Maura was affected by Tina's actions.
ESSENTIAL QUESTION

Tell about a time when someone wouldn't listen to your ideas. What did you do? **TEXT TO SELF**

38   39

READING/WRITING WORKSHOP, pp. 38–39

Make Connections

ESSENTIAL QUESTION

Have student pairs review their purpose for reading and discuss what they have learned about how a person's actions affect others. Encourage them to use information from the text as evidence. Have students discuss a time when someone didn't listen to their ideas and how they responded.

Continue Close Reading

Use the following lessons for focused rereadings.

→ Make, Confirm, or Revise Predictions, T82–T83

→ Problem and Solution, T84–T85

→ Realistic Fiction, T86–T87

→ Figurative Language, T88–T89

A C T **A**ccess **C**omplex **T**ext

▶ **Genre**

Explain that by using dialogue, students can compare characters' words and their actions in order to learn more about how they think.

→ Read the third paragraph on page 37. *Why is Maura's grip tightening on her books?* (She's nervous because Tina wants to do an act with her.)

→ *Do you think Maura asks "Our act?" because she is curious, or because she is surprised and alarmed?* (She asks because she is surprised and alarmed.)

Comprehension Strategy

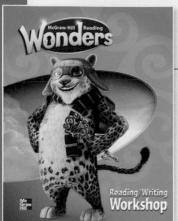

Reading/Writing Workshop

OBJECTIVES

 Refer to details and examples in a text when explaining what the text says explicitly and when drawing inferences from the text. **RL.4.1**

Use text clues and illustrations to predict future events within a selection and identify events that confirm or challenge predictions.

ACADEMIC LANGUAGE

• *make, confirm, and revise predictions; realistic fiction*

• Cognates: *confirmar, revisar predicciones, ficción realista*

MINILESSON **10** Mins

Make, Confirm, or Revise Predictions

1 Explain

Explain that when they read realistic fiction, students may use story details to predict what will happen next. Remind students that making predictions will help them better understand the characters and plot of a story.

→ Good readers use clues from the story to make predictions.

→ Students may stop, confirm, and revise their predictions if necessary.

→ Often, students may find that making predictions will help them understand and remember why events happen in a certain way.

Point out that making predictions will help students set a purpose for reading.

2 Model Close Reading: Text Evidence

Model how to find text evidence to confirm your predictions by rereading the first three paragraphs on page 37 with students. Have students explain how this evidence supports your prediction.

3 Guided Practice of Close Reading

 Have students work in pairs to predict how Maura will solve a future problem. Ask them to reread the text, focusing on how Maura has handled problems in the past and how she handles her most recent problem. Remind students to record their predictions and any supporting evidence. Once they are finished, have partners compare their evidence and their predictions.

Go Digital

View "The Talent Show"

CCSS **Comprehension Strategy**

Make Predictions

When you read, use story details to make predictions about what will happen. As you read "The Talent Show," make predictions.

Find Text Evidence

You predicted that Tina is the kind of friend who is bossy. Reread page 37 of "The Talent Show" to find the text evidence that confirms your prediction.

page 37

I read that Tina always takes charge. This confirms my prediction that Tina is bossy.

 COLLABORATE

Your Turn

Using clues you find in the text, how do you predict Maura will solve a future problem? As you read, use the strategy Make Predictions.

40

READING/WRITING WORKSHOP, p. 40

 **Monitor and Differentiate**

 ✓ **Quick Check**

Do students use evidence within the text to predict future plot events?

⬇

Small Group Instruction

If No → | Approaching Level | Reteach p. T104
| ELL | Develop p. T120

If Yes → | On Level | Review p. T112
| Beyond Level | Extend p. T116

ELL ENGLISH LANGUAGE LEARNERS SCAFFOLD

Beginning	Intermediate	Advanced/High
Clarify the Meaning Help students reread the first paragraph on page 37. Define *talent show, juggling,* and *act.* Point to the illustration on page 36 and explain that the girl is juggling in a talent show. Ask: *What does Maura want to do in the talent show?* Define other difficult words and help students replace the words with words they know.	**Describe** Have students reread page 37. Ask: *What does Maura want to do in the talent show? What does Tina say to upset Maura?* Point out why the passage is confusing. *Maura wants to juggle in the talent show, but her friend Tina has other ideas.* Explain that this passage points to a conflict, or problem, between Maura and Tina.	**Discuss** Have students reread page 37. Elicit from students why the passage is confusing. Ask: *Why does Maura get upset? What do her feelings tell you about Tina?* Have students discuss their answers with a partner.

ON-LEVEL PRACTICE BOOK pp. 13–14

Read the passage. Use the make predictions strategy to check your understanding.

The Cyber Bully

15 Every time I got on the school bus, I felt sick and got butterflies in
30 my stomach. I had recently moved to a new school, and no one on the
44 bus talked to me. I was certain I would never make any new friends.
59 Right off the bat, the very first week of school, I was in deep trouble.
72 It all started when my teacher, Mr. Evers, took us to the computer
85 lab to do an assignment. I was logging in when I noticed my
96 classmate, Corey, watching my fingers on the keyboard. He looked at
105 me and smirked. I could tell something was wrong.
112 "I know your password, Aaron," Corey said.
116 "Um…ok," I said.
126 Right away he logged into his computer using my password!
140 I thought about telling Mr. Evers, but I didn't want the other kids to
155 think I was a tattle-tale. After all, I was the new kid, and I didn't
170 want to get off on the wrong foot or make a bad impression. I decided
176 to just focus on my work.
188 A few minutes later I heard Mr. Evers say, "Aaron? Could you
193 come here for a second?"
207 Just as I was getting up, I got a message. "You better keep your
221 mouth shut," it said. I couldn't tell who it came from since it was
225 from my own account.
238 "What is the meaning of this e-mail you sent me?" said Mr. Evers.
246 I read it but couldn't believe my eyes!
261 "But I haven't been on e-mail at all!" I said. Then I realized that it
     was Corey using my e-mail!

APPROACHING pp. 13–14	BEYOND pp. 13–14	ELL pp. 13–14

Comprehension Skill

MINILESSON
10 Mins

Character, Setting, Plot: Problem and Solution

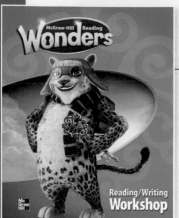

Reading/Writing Workshop

OBJECTIVES

CCSS Describe in depth a character, setting, or event in a story or drama, drawing on specific details in the text (e.g., a character's thoughts, words, or actions). **RL.4.3**

Identify problem and solution within a story.

ACADEMIC LANGUAGE

• *character, setting, plot, problem, solution, event*

• Cognates: *problema, solución*

SKILLS TRACE

CHARACTER, SETTING, PLOT

Introduce Unit 1 Week 1

Review Unit 1 Weeks 2, 6; Unit 2 Week 6; Unit 3 Week 6; Unit 4 Week 6; Unit 5 Weeks 1, 2; Unit 6 Week 6

Assess Units 1, 5

1 Explain

Explain to students that plot is the series of events that take place in a story. Students need to identify several story elements in order to find the story's plot.

→ Students need to identify the story's problem. The problem is what the main characters want to do, change, or find out.

→ Students need to identify the steps that the characters take to solve their problem. Characters reveal their traits through the steps they take to solve their problem.

→ The way in which the problem is finally solved is called the solution.

2 Model Close Reading: Text Evidence

First, model finding Maura's problem on page 37. Then model using the information from the graphic organizer to identify the events in the story and how they lead to the solution.

 Write About Reading: Paraphrase Model for students how to use their graphic organizers to paraphrase Maura's problem in "The Talent Show." Be sure students include the characters and setting in their writing.

3 Guided Practice of Close Reading

 Have students reread "The Talent Show." Have them find other important story events and use them to identify the solution. Students can work in pairs. Discuss each event as students complete the graphic organizer.

 Write About Reading: Paraphrase Ask pairs to work together to write a paragraph that paraphrases the events in the text that lead to the solution. Make sure students include a concluding sentence in their paragraphs.

Go Digital

Present the Lesson

Comprehension Skill CCSS

Problem and Solution

The main **character** in a story usually has a problem that needs to be solved. The steps the character takes to solve the problem make up the **story's events**, the plot of the story.

Find Text Evidence

As I reread pages 37 and 38 of "The Talent Show," I can see that Maura has a problem. I will list the events in the story. Then I can figure out how Maura finds a solution.

Character
Maura

Setting
Maura's school

Problem
Maura does not want to do an act with Tina.

Event
Tina tells Maura that they will do a dance act together.

Event

Solution

Your Turn COLLABORATE

Reread "The Talent Show." Find other important story events. Use these events to identify the solution.

Go Digital!
Use the interactive graphic organizer

41

READING/WRITING WORKSHOP, p. 41

A C T Access Complex Text

▶ Connection of Ideas

Students may have difficulty understanding how characters affect the story's problem.

→ *What is the story's problem?* (Maura wants to do an act by herself, but Tina wants to do an act together.)

→ *What does Maura say about Tina's personality?* (Tina always takes charge; they always do what Tina wants.)

→ *Tina contributes to the problem by always wanting to do things her way. Maura adds to it by not speaking up for herself.*

Monitor and *Differentiate*

✓ Quick Check

As students complete the graphic organizer, are they able to correctly identify events that lead to the solution?

⬇

Small Group Instruction

If No → **Approaching Level** Reteach p. T111
ELL Develop p. T120

If Yes → **On Level** Review p. T115
Beyond Level Extend p. T119

ON-LEVEL PRACTICE BOOK pp. 13–15

A. Reread the passage and answer the questions. Possible responses provided.

1. What problem does Aaron face?
Aaron has to decide whether or not to tell the teacher that he is being cyber bullied.

2. Why is Aaron worried about telling Mr. Evers the truth?
Aaron is the new kid. He does not want the other kids to think he is a tattle-tale.

3. What is the solution to Aaron's problem?
He tells the teacher the truth about being bullied.

B. Work with a partner. Read the passage aloud. Pay attention to expression and rate. Stop after one minute. Fill out the chart.

	Words Read	–	Number of Errors	=	Words Correct Score
First Read		–		=	
Second Read		–		=	

APPROACHING pp. 13–15	BEYOND pp. 13–15	ELL pp. 13–15

→ # Genre: Literature

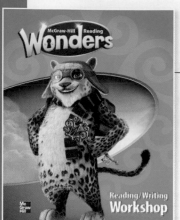

Reading/Writing Workshop

Realistic Fiction

1 Explain

Share with students the following key characteristics of **realistic fiction**.

→ Realistic fiction tells a made-up story.

→ Realistic fiction features characters, settings, and events that could exist in real life.

→ Realistic fiction usually includes dialogue.

2 Model Close Reading: Text Evidence

Model finding the characteristics that identify a work of realistic fiction on page 37 of "The Talent Show." Realistic fiction is set in a place that could exist in real life. Point out that "The Talent Show" is mostly set in a school. Realistic fiction also uses dialogue, or the exact words characters say when they talk to each other.

3 Guided Practice of Close Reading

COLLABORATE

Have students work with partners to find and list two examples from "The Talent Show" that identify it as realistic fiction. Remind students to pay attention to dialogue, character, and setting. Then have them share their work with a partner or with the class. Discuss how realistic fiction is different from other fiction genres they may have read, such as fantasy.

OBJECTIVES

 Explain major differences between poems, drama, and prose, and refer to the structural elements of poems (e.g., verse, rhythm, meter) and drama (e.g., casts of characters, settings, descriptions, dialogue, stage directions) when writing or speaking about a text. **RL.4.5**

CCSS By the end of the year, read and comprehend literature, including stories, dramas, and poetry, in the grades 4–5 text complexity band proficiently, with scaffolding as needed at the high end of the range. **RL.4.10**

Recognize the characteristics of realistic fiction.

ACADEMIC LANGUAGE

• *realistic fiction, dialogue*

• Cognate: *diálogo*

CCSS Genre Literature

Realistic Fiction

The selection "The Talent Show" is realistic fiction.

Realistic Fiction:
- Is a made-up story.
- Has characters, settings, and events that could exist in real life.
- Includes dialogue.

 Find Text Evidence

I can tell that "The Talent Show" is realistic fiction. The story mostly takes place at school. On page 37, Maura and Tina act and speak like real people who might go to my school.

Dialogue Dialogue is the exact words the characters say.

Your Turn

With a partner, list two examples from "The Talent Show" that let you know it is realistic fiction.

42

READING/WRITING WORKSHOP, p. 42

Monitor and *Differentiate*

 Quick Check

Are students able to list two examples from "The Talent Show" that show it is realistic fiction?

Small Group Instruction

If No → | Approaching Level | Reteach p. T104
ELL | Develop p. T120

If Yes → | On Level | Review p. T112
Beyond Level | Extend p. T116

ELL ENGLISH LANGUAGE LEARNERS SCAFFOLD

Beginning	Intermediate	Advanced/High
Understand Point to the illustration on page 37. Say: *Maura and Tina are talking.* Then point to the quotation marks in the first line. Explain that the quotation marks show when someone is speaking. Read the first sentence. Say: *This is called dialogue. Maura is speaking.* Have students point out more examples of dialogue on the page.	**Identify** Have students reread page 37 and identify examples that make the story realistic fiction. Then have partners work together to discuss the examples. *This story is realistic fiction because _____.* Elicit details to support students' responses.	**Discuss** Reread page 37. Ask: *Are the characters and setting in "The Talent Show" realistic?* Have students work with a partner to discuss the key characteristics that make the story realistic fiction. Elaborate on students' responses.

ON-LEVEL PRACTICE BOOK p. 16

Paul's Mix-Up

"You're going to be at the show next week, right, Paul?" Rosa asked as the students packed up their instruments.

"Of course I am!" Paul said. "We've been practicing for months!"

Luis looked at Paul with curiosity. "You said you might not be able to make it. What about the trip you're taking with your family?"

Paul froze. All week long he had been thinking about their show. He had forgotten about his family trip!

Answer the questions about the text.

1. How can you tell this story is realistic fiction?

   It has characters and events that could exist in real life.

2. What literary elements does the text include?

   Dialogue, character, setting, plot

3. How does the dialogue make the story realistic?

   It lets you know what the characters are saying; it shows that they talk

   the way people talk in real life.

4. What details about Paul make him a believable character?

   Possible response: Paul forgets about a trip, which is believable; Paul

   faces a problem one might face in real life.

| APPROACHING p. 16 | BEYOND p. 16 | ELL p. 16 |

→ Vocabulary Strategy

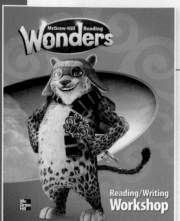

Reading/Writing Workshop

Reading/Writing Workshop

OBJECTIVES

CCSS Demonstrate understanding of figurative language, word relationships, and nuances in word meanings. Recognize and explain the meaning of common idioms, adages, and proverbs. **L.4.5b**

CCSS Determine the meaning of words and phrases as they are used in a text, including those that allude to significant characters found in mythology (e.g., Herculean). **RL.4.4**

MINILESSON 10 Mins — Figurative Language

1 Explain

Tell students that they will occasionally encounter phrases called **idioms**, whose meanings cannot be understood by reading and interpreting the words as they are commonly used.

→ Tell students that an idiom probably will not make sense in context if it is read as though it were an ordinary phrase.

→ When students find idioms, they should look for clues in the sentence or paragraph to help find their figurative meaning.

2 Model Close Reading: Text Evidence

Model using context clues to find the meaning of the idiom *see eye to eye* on page 37. Explain that the phrase means "to agree."

3 Guided Practice of Close Reading

Have students work in pairs to find the meanings of the idioms *let off steam*, *cat got your tongue*, and *standing up for myself* in "The Talent Show." Remind students to use context clues in order to find the meanings. Then have partners list some other idioms and their meanings.

Go Digital

Present the Lesson

SKILLS TRACE

FIGURATIVE LANGUAGE: IDIOMS

Introduce Unit 1 Week 2

Review Unit 1 Weeks 2, 3; Unit 4 Week 2; Unit 5 Week 3

Assess Units 1, 4

Vocabulary Strategy CCSS

Idioms

Idioms are phrases that have a meaning different from the meaning of each word in them. Sometimes context clues can help you figure out the meaning of an idiom.

🔍 Find Text Evidence

When I read the idiom see eye to eye *on page 37 in "The Talent Show," the words* After all, we are best friends *help me figure out its meaning. To* see eye to eye *means to agree.*

 After all, we are best friends; we should be able to see eye to eye about this.

Your Turn COLLABORATE

Use context clues to help you understand the meanings of the following idioms in "The Talent Show":

let off steam, *page 38*
cat got your tongue, *page 38*
standing up for myself, *page 39*
List some other idioms and their meanings.

43

Chris Vallo

READING/WRITING WORKSHOP, p. 43

Monitor and *Differentiate*

✔ Quick Check

Do students use context clues to determine the meanings of the idioms *let off steam, cat got your tongue,* and *standing up for myself*?

Small Group Instruction

If No → | **Approaching Level** | Reteach p. T109
| **ELL** | Develop p. T125
If Yes → | **On Level** | Review p. T114
| **Beyond Level** | Extend p. T118

 ## ENGLISH LANGUAGE LEARNERS SCAFFOLD

Beginning	**Intermediate**	**Advanced/High**
Understand Reread the fifth paragraph on page 38. Point out the idiom *cat got your tongue.* Ask: *What do you think would happen if a cat got your tongue? Would you still be able to talk?* Have students act out the idiom. Then ask if there is a similar idiom in their native language. Repeat with other idioms.	**Determine** Read the sentence, "At recess, . . ." on page 38. Point out the idiom *let off steam.* Explain that it means to release one's emotions, such as anger or frustration. Ask: *Why does Maura need to let off steam?* (She is angry at Tina.) Have partners determine the meanings of *cat got your tongue* and *stand up for myself.*	**Actively Engage** Have students work with a partner to locate the idioms in the story. Help them look for clues to determine the meanings of the idioms. Then have them act out the idioms using gestures and body language.

ON-LEVEL PRACTICE BOOK p. 17

A. Read the idioms in the box. Find and underline an idiom in each sentence below. Then circle the context clues that help you understand the idiom.

butterflies in my stomach	between a rock and a hard place
right off the bat	get off on the wrong foot

1. Every time I got on the school bus, I felt sick and got butterflies in my stomach. I had recently moved to a new school, and no one on the bus talked to me. I was certain I would never make any new friends.

2. Right off the bat, the very first week of school, I was in deep trouble.

3. I felt like I was stuck between a rock and a hard place. I wanted desperately to tell the truth, but that would mean getting Corey into trouble.

4. I didn't want to get off on the wrong foot or make a bad impression.

B. Read the sentences below. Underline each idiom. For each idiom, write a definition in your own words. Possible responses provided.

1. The test was a piece of cake because the questions were so easy.
a simple task, no problem

2. He kept bothering me until I told him to cut it out.
stop altogether

APPROACHING p. 17	**BEYOND** p. 17	**ELL** p. 17

Develop Comprehension

Literature Anthology

Experts, Incorporated

Text Complexity Range

Lexile

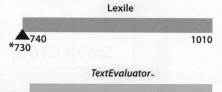

▲740
*730   1010

*Although the selection score falls below the Lexile range, the genre and connection of ideas may be challenging to students.

TextEvaluator™

23   44   51

Options for Close Reading

→ Whole Class
→ Small Group
→ Independent

Predictive Writing

Have students read the title, preview the illustrations, and write their predictions about what the story will be about.

CCSS Genre · Realistic Fiction

EXPERTS, Incorporated

by Sarah Weeks · illustrated by Chuck Gonzales

That's me.

Lucas (my best friend)

Essential Question

How do your actions affect others?

Read to find out if Rodney's actions will affect his class and his future.

Go Digital!

32

Experts, Incorporated © 2004 by Sarah Weeks.

ⒶⒸⓉ Access Complex Text

What makes this text complex?

▶ **Genre**
▶ **Purpose**
▶ **Sentence Structure**
▶ **Specific Vocabulary**
▶ **Connection of Ideas**

▶ **Genre**

Remind students that a characteristic of realistic fiction is the use of dialogue. Explain that dialogue is what the characters in a story say to one another. It helps readers understand the characters, and can also be used to reveal events that have already happened.

Things I can't stand

There are three things in this world I can't stand—cucumber salad, wool sweaters, and creative writing. Cucumbers make me burp and wool makes me itch, but if you gave me a choice, I would rather burp and itch at the same time than have to write something creative.

"You finished your essay, right, Rodd-o?" my friend Lucas asked me as we walked toward school together early one morning.

I **hesitated**. Lucas is my best friend and we always shoot straight with each other.

"Yeah, I finished it," I said.

"Phew, that's a relief," he said. "If you hadn't, I would never forgive you, you know."

"Yeah, I know," I said.

The problem began on the first day of the school year when our humanities teacher, Mrs. Greenberg, promised that if nobody got an F in her class all semester she would give us a pizza party.

"Just remember," she'd laughed, "there are no F's in *pizza*."

Here it was, the last week of the semester and I was about to earn not just an F, but the F that would ruin everything. Because, you see, I hadn't done the assignment. Not one word of it.

STOP AND CHECK

Make Predictions Use what you have read so far to make a prediction about whether or not Rodney will complete the assignment.

33

LITERATURE ANTHOLOGY, pp. 32–33

ESSENTIAL QUESTION

Ask students to read aloud the Essential Question. Have students discuss how the story might help them answer the question.

Note Taking: Use the Graphic Organizer

As students read the selection, ask them to take notes by filling in the graphic organizer on **Your Turn Practice Book page 12** to record the character, setting, plot, problem, and solution.

STOP AND CHECK

Make Predictions Use what you have read so far to make a prediction about whether or not Rodney will complete the assignment. (He hates creative writing, so he might not do it.)

Teacher Think Aloud As I begin reading, I can make a prediction about Rodney. The first sentence says that he doesn't enjoy creative writing. The illustration of the pencil and paper next to the label "the worst" confirms that he dislikes it. I predict that he will write his essay only if he finds a topic that interests him.

→ Have students identify the dialogue on page 33. *Who is speaking?* (the narrator, Lucas, Mrs. Greenberg)

→ *What does the dialogue tell us about the narrator?* (We learn that the narrator is lying to his best friend. He did not write a paper.)

ELL Point out the idiom "shoot straight." Explain that it means "to talk or deal with honestly and truthfully."

→ Reread page 33. *Does Rodney tell the truth when Lucas asks him if he has finished his essay?* Explain. (No; Rodney did not write the essay.)

→ *Is he shooting straight with Lucas?* (no)

LITERATURE ANTHOLOGY **T89B**

Develop Comprehension

1 Skill: Problem and Solution

Who is telling this story? (Rodney) What other characters have we met? (Lucas, Mrs. Greenberg, Jeremy, Russell) Where does the story take place? (at their school) What is the main character's problem? (The students have an assignment that Rodney has not completed. If he does not do the assignment, his class will not get a pizza party.)

2 Author's Craft: Figurative Language

Authors can use figurative language to express what characters are thinking or feeling. Figurative language has a meaning different from the literal meaning of the words. Reread the text and find examples of figurative language. What does Jeremy mean when he says he "can taste the pepperoni already"? (Jeremy means that, since he and Russell finished their assignment, he knows they will get the pizza party. He does not mean that he literally can taste pepperoni.)

1 As we rounded the corner and headed up the block toward school, Jeremy and Russell, two friends from our class, caught up with us.

"You guys did the assignment, right?" Russell asked us.

"Yep," Lucas answered for us both. "How about you?"

2 "Of course," said Jeremy. "What do we look like, idiots? I can taste that pepperoni already. Last year's class got the party and somebody told me she let them have all the soda they wanted too."

When I get nervous, I sometimes get hives on my neck, and I could feel one beginning to prickle up under my collar.

34

Huge hive growing on my neck!

A C T Access Complex Text

▶ Purpose

Remind students that understanding the author's purpose helps the reader to better understand the characters and how their actions shape the story.

→ *From what point of view is the story told?* (first person) *How do you know?* (The main character is the narrator. He refers to himself as *I* or *me*.)

→ *Why do you think the author chose to tell this story from Rodney's point of view?* (The author wanted to write a realistic story by showing how Rodney deals with a problem. In order to show how Rodney feels about things, the author has him describe the events as he sees them.)

"What profession did you pick?" Lucas asked.

"Doctor," Jeremy said. "'Cause they get to save people and stuff."

"I picked truck driver," said Russell. "They get to travel and eat at diners. I love diners, but my mom says they're too greasy, so we never get to go. What about you, Lucas?"

"Star pitcher for the New York Yankees," he said. "Man, can you imagine getting paid to play baseball?"

The assignment had been to write an essay about what you want to be when you grow up. Sounds easy enough, unless you're like me and have no idea what you want to be, and no matter how hard you try, you can't think of even one thing that feels the least bit right.

"I bet all the girls are going to say they want to be teachers 'cause they know Mrs. Greenberg will eat that up with a spoon," Russell said with disgust.

"Yeah, probably," Lucas agreed. "So, what did you pick, Rodd-o?" he asked, turning to me.

We were just starting up the steps of the school, when a familiar cry went up from the playground.

"Hey look, everybody! There goes Mucus! Hey, Mucus!"

Lucas blushed and hung his head as we walked up the steps and into the building. It happens to him all the time, poor guy. He has one of the worst names. Not only does *Lucas* rhyme with *mucus*, but even if you shorten it to *Luke*, you're still in trouble because then it rhymes with *puke*. He's been tortured his whole life on account of that name.

4 **3**

Lucas...

guess what his name rhymes with?

35

LITERATURE ANTHOLOGY, pp. 34–35

3 Text Features: Illustrations

Look at the illustrations on pages 34 and 35. Turn to a partner and discuss how Rodney uses his drawings and labels to help the reader get to know him. What are Rodney and his friends doing? (They are discussing the assignment that is due.) How does Rodney show us what happens to him when he gets nervous? (He points out his neck and draws a hive.) How does he show what happens when Lucas gets called names? (He shows a picture of Lucas's unhappy face and adds a label about what his name rhymes with.) How do these illustrations help the reader understand the events in the story? (They help the reader to visualize what is going on and to point out important details of the story.)

4 Genre: Realistic Fiction

Realistic fiction tells a made-up story with characters, settings, and events that could happen in real life. Is the dialogue on page 35 realistic? (Yes; Jeremy, Russell, and Lucas speak like kids in our class.)

 Help students understand the expression "hung his head." Explain that it means to be ashamed or embarrassed. Demonstrate by showing a gesture. Then have students repeat the gesture.

→ *Why does Rodney say, "Lucas blushed and hung his head"?* (Someone called him a name.)

→ *How does the name-calling make Lucas feel?* (embarrassed, sad, or ashamed) *Does he like these names?* (no)

Develop Comprehension

5 **Skill: Problem and Solution**

Why does Rodney feel there is "still hope left" to solve his problem? (Mrs. Greenberg announces that she will collect papers after lunch.) Add this information to your chart.

Character
Rodney

Setting
school

Problem
The class has to write an essay in order to get a pizza party. Rodney has not completed the assignment.

Event
Mrs. Greenberg announces that she will collect papers after lunch.

6 **Author's Craft: Word Choice**

Authors carefully choose the words they use. Reread paragraph 4 on page 36. Why does the author use the word *scribble* instead of *write*? (*Scribble* is a more descriptive word. *Scribble* tells us that Rodney is in a hurry while he is writing.)

Having a bad name is something Lucas and I have in common and probably part of the reason we became friends all the way back on the first day of kindergarten. My name is Rodney Curtain. My parents and my teachers call me Rod, my friends call me Rodd-o, and my sister, who's only two, calls me Rah-rah. Rodney Curtain may not be the greatest name in the world, but front-ward like that it's not so bad. The thing is, at school when they call out your name for attendance they say it backward. Lucas Bromberg becomes Bromberg, Lucas. Samantha Smith becomes Smith, Samantha.

Unfortunately, I become Curtain, Rod. That's bad.

As we made our way down the hall to homeroom, I felt sorry for Lucas on account of the teasing, but secretly I was relieved that he'd forgotten about the question he'd asked me. How was he going to take it when he found out I hadn't done the assignment?

5 After she took attendance, Mrs. Greenberg—we have her for homeroom as well as humanities—announced that she would be collecting our papers after lunch. There was still hope left. All I had to do was come up with an idea between now and **6** then, scribble it down in time to hand it in with the others, and maybe I wouldn't have to ruin the party after all. The problem was, I still didn't have any ideas.

That's me.

36

A C T Access Complex Text

▶ **Sentence Structure**

Point out the dashes that are used in the first sentence of the last paragraph on page 36. The dash comes before and after a phrase that gives further explanation or further emphasizes a point. Think about why the writer uses dashes on this page.

→ *Does the author give information or emphasize a point with these dashes?* (gives information)

→ *What do we learn about Mrs. Greenberg by reading the text between the dashes?* (The students have her for homeroom and humanities. They will see her again later in the day when they go to her class to hand in their essays.)

Pencil maker?

sweat

Clock fixer?

Desk builder?

"What do I want to be?" I asked myself. "Come on, Curtain, think."

I thought about it during math, history, and science lab, but with lunchtime only minutes away, my mind was still a complete blank. The only thing I could think of that I wanted to be was someone else. Someone who had written the stupid essay already.

As I looked around the room **desperately** hoping to find some **inspiration** somewhere, I asked myself, "Do I want to be a scientist? Do I want to fix clocks? Write books? Build desks? Make pencils?" No, no, no. And then suddenly without warning, everything shifted into slow motion as my eyes came to rest on the face of the girl sitting in the second seat in the third row from the left. That's when it hit me. I knew what I wanted to be. What the world needed me to be.

7

8

When the bell for lunch rang, I didn't join the others in the cafeteria.

Instead I took out my notebook and began to write. When the fifth-period bell rang, I was already in my seat in Mrs. Greenberg's room with a stack of four handwritten sheets of paper in front of me and a huge grin on my face.

37

LITERATURE ANTHOLOGY, pp. 36–37

7 Ask and Answer Questions

Generate a question of your own and share it with a partner. Continue reading to find your answer. Paraphrase the text to support your answer. For example, your question may be "Why does seeing the girl in his class help Rodney?" (Seeing the girl helps Rodney because he suddenly realizes what he wants to be. As I continue reading, I will look for more details.)

8 Vocabulary: Idioms

What clues can help you figure out the meaning of the idiom *hit me* on page 37? (the phrases: "then suddenly," "without warning," "I knew.") What does Rodney mean when he says "That's when it hit me"? (It became clear to Rodney what he wanted to be.) How do we know that this phrase is an idiom? (Its literal meaning is different from its nonliteral meaning. Rodney is not physically hit by something. Rather, he thinks of an idea.)

▶ Organization

Tell students that the text on page 37 is organized in a way that helps us to follow the story's events.

→ *Where is Rodney when he thinks of a good idea for his paper?* (science lab) *When does he write his essay?* (during lunch) *How can you tell his essay is complete?* (He is early to class with four handwritten sheets and a "huge grin.")

 Students may have difficulty with the concept of *picking a profession.*

→ Point out that the Spanish word for *profession* is *profesión.* Say: *My profession is a teacher.*

→ Have students list professions and circle one they would choose. *I pick a _____ as my profession.*

Develop Comprehension

9 **Skill: Problem and Solution**

How does Rod solve his problem? (He comes up with an idea for his paper. He decides that he wants to become a name expert.) What happens when he tells Lucas about his idea? (Lucas does not think it is a good profession. He does not think people will pay Rod to name their kids.) Add these events to your chart. Use your chart to paraphrase the text you have read so far.

Character
Rodney

Setting
school

Problem
If Rodney does not complete the assignment, there will be no pizza party.

Event 1
Mrs. Greenberg announces that she'll be collecting papers after lunch.

↓

Event 2
Rodney comes up with an idea for his paper and tells Lucas.

"Why are you sitting there smiling like a dork?" Lucas asked as he slid into the seat next to me. "And where were you at lunch anyway? And another thing, you never answered my question from before, what did you choose as your profession?"

"Name expert," I told him happily. "That's definitely what I want to be, a name expert."

"A name expert? Whoever heard of that?" he said.

"Nobody. It hasn't been invented yet. But I'm going to be the first one," I told him.

"Oh, yeah? And what exactly are you going to do?" he asked me.

9 "I'm going to **advise** people about what not to name their kids."

"No offense, but that is so dumb. Why would anybody pay you to tell them what not to name their kid?" he asked.

"Because I'm an expert," I said.

"Says who?" he said.

"What's your name?"

"What do you mean, what's my name? You know my name, fish-for-brains." Lucas snorted.

"Come on, just answer the question. What's your name?"

"Lucas," he said.

"And what do all the kids call you?"

He hesitated **uncomfortably** for a second before answering.

"Mucus," he said quietly.

"Exactly," I said. "See? If I had been around when your parents were deciding what to name you, I could have warned them that every name needs to be checked for bad rhymes. A kid named Leo is gonna end up getting called B.O., anybody named Gabby is gonna get called Flabby, it doesn't take a rocket scientist to figure that out. Your name is particularly bad, because it's a double whammy."

I'm an expert!

38

A C T Access Complex Text

▶ **Specific Vocabulary**

Students may have difficulty distinguishing literal and nonliteral meanings. Remind students that sometimes what characters say is not exactly what they mean. *In realistic fiction, authors use the language that we encounter in everyday life.* Examine how the author uses everyday language on pages 38 and 39.

→ *Is the language used in the story formal or informal?* (informal)

→ *What does Rodney mean when he says that Melody Adams "sings like a moose"?* (She is not a good singer.)

"Tell me about it," said Lucas, shaking his head sadly.

"The way I see it, a name expert should be hired every time a baby gets born, to protect it from being saddled with a name that could ruin its life," I went on.

"How much do you think you'll get paid?" he asked.

"A lot. Parents pay a bundle for braces to straighten their kids' teeth. Don't you think they'd shell out even more to save their kids from being **humiliated** at school?"

"Here's a question for you—do you think there's any way a name expert could figure out whether a name is going to fit when the kid gets older?" Lucas asked me.

"What do you mean?" I said.

"Well, for instance, you know how Melody Adams is tone-deaf?"

"Yeah, she sings like a moose," I said.

"If her parents had known she was going to be unmusical, maybe they wouldn't have given her a musical name like Melody."

"Maybe they would have named her Moose," I said. We both laughed.

STOP AND CHECK

Confirm Predictions Why does Rodney want to be a name expert? Confirm or revise your prediction about Rodney.

LITERATURE ANTHOLOGY, pp. 38–39

STOP AND CHECK

Confirm Predictions Why does Rodney want to be a name expert? Confirm or revise your prediction about Rodney.(Rodney feels it would be helpful for kids, and it is a topic in which he is interested.)

Teacher Think Aloud Let's review the prediction that we made that Rodney would only complete the essay if he could find a topic he was interested in writing about. We can see how the events in the story have led him to make the choice for his profession. We can add to our prediction that he will hand in the paper to Mrs. Greenberg. If she likes Rodney's idea for a profession, the class will get their pizza party.

Prompt students to apply the strategy in a Think Aloud by revising their prediction about Rodney's essay.

Student Think Aloud I can see that Rodney's initial reaction to writing the essay has changed now that he has come up with an idea that he believes in. I will not have to change the prediction I made. I still predict that Rodney will complete the assignment.

 Students may have difficulty following the dialogue in the story.

→ Remind students that quotation marks show dialogue. Read the first line on page 38 and explain that Lucas is speaking the words. Have students point out other examples of dialogue.

→ Have pairs read the dialogue between Rodney and Lucas. Help students understand difficult words or phrases.

Develop Comprehension

10 Skill: Problem and Solution

Working with a partner, use your charts to paraphrase the plot of the text. How are the problems of the characters solved? (Rodney has come up with an idea for his essay. He decides that he wants to become a name expert. He finishes his paper in time to turn it in.) Add these solutions to your chart.

Character
Rodney

Setting
school

Problem
If Rodney does not complete the assignment, there will be no pizza party.

Event 1
Mrs. Greenberg announces that she'll be collecting papers after lunch.

Event 2
Rodney comes up with an idea for his paper.

Solution
He hands in his paper and comes up with the idea of *Experts, Incorporated* with Lucas.

"I suppose a name expert could be trained to look carefully at the parents for signs of what's to come," I said. "Like for instance, if there's a history of baldness in a family, it's probably not a very good idea to use the name Harry."

"Yeah, or like if the parents have big noses they shouldn't name their kid Honker," said Lucas.

"Who names their kid Honker?" I said. "That's not even a real name."

"Oh, and Curtain Rod is?"

I punched him in the arm, but not too hard because like I said, we're best friends.

"Hyphenated names would have to be looked at very carefully too, don't you think?" Lucas said. "Like Jessica's, for instance."

"Exactly," I said. "She's the one I was looking at in science lab when this whole idea came to me."

Jessica's dad's name is Charlie Mintz and her mom's name is Sylvia Pepper.

How hard could it have been to name her Jessica Mintz-Pepper instead of Jessica Pepper-Mintz? If they'd had a name expert around, trust me, it never would have happened.

"You know, I take back what I said about this idea being dumb," Lucas said. "I think maybe you're onto something big here."

"Yeah? You think?" I said.

10 "Yeah. And you know, once business takes off, you might even need a partner," Lucas said excitedly. "We could call it Experts, Incorporated."

"We?" I laughed. "I thought you were going to pitch for the Yankees."

Lucas smiled and shrugged.

Harry

Honker

Jessica Pepper-Mintz

40

A C T Access Complex Text

▶ Connection of Ideas

Remind students that they need to connect details they have already read in order to understand what happens. Work with students to recall earlier details.

→ *How does teasing influence Rodney's idea for his essay?* (Rodney sees how the students make jokes about Lucas's name. He does not want to see other students get teased because of the names their parents give them.)

→ *Why is it so important that Rodney complete the assignment?* (If he does not complete it, the class will not get a pizza party.)

"I doubt I'll get picked up; I can't even throw a slider. But if you want a partner who really understands why the world needs name experts, I'm your man, Rodd-o."

Mrs. Greenberg came down the aisle collecting the papers. As I handed her mine, I heaved a huge sigh of relief. Not only had I avoided ruining the pizza party, I'd managed to plan my entire future too, and it was looking pretty bright, if I do say so myself.

Success!

pizza!

EXPERTS INC

pizza!

STOP AND CHECK

Make Predictions Why does Lucas change his opinion about Rodney's profession? Make a prediction about Lucas's future using details from the story.

41

LITERATURE ANTHOLOGY, pp. 40–41

STOP AND CHECK

Make Predictions Why does Lucas change his opinion about Rodney's profession? Make a prediction about Lucas's future using details from the story. (Rodney changes Lucas's mind because he convinces him that his idea could be a good business. Possible prediction: I predict that Lucas will not become a star pitcher because he says he can't even throw a slider.)

Student Think Aloud My prediction was that Rod would complete the assignment and he has. He is able to do so because he found he is very interested in the topic of name-calling. As a result, Rodney is also able to convince Lucas that his idea is a good one. Since he has so much interest in the topic, I believe that Rodney will think of more things to do with his new business.

Return to Predictions

Review students' predictions and purposes for reading. Ask them to answer the Essential Question. (Rodney comes up with an idea that he feels could have made the lives of some people he knows easier. Lucas agrees with his idea and they plan on starting a business, *Experts, Incorporated*.)

ELL Help students understand what is meant by the term "name expert." Explain that an expert is a person who knows more about something than most people.

→ *Rodney wants to be an expert on names. He is a name _____. (expert)*

→ Have students list other ways that people can be experts.

About the Author

Meet the Author

Sarah Weeks

Have students read the biography of the author. Ask:

→ How did Sarah Weeks learn about the behaviors of kids?

→ How did the pictures in the story help you to visualize what Sarah has written?

Author's Purpose

To Entertain

Remind students that authors who write to entertain include interesting characters and exciting events. Students may say that the author includes dialogue to make the story more realistic and to provide insights into the characters' actions and traits.

Author's Craft

Point of View

Explain that authors use points of view for different purposes. Point of view is the perspective of the narrator, or the person telling the story. Discuss the difference between first-person and third-person narrators.

→ A first-person narrator allows the reader to gain unique insights into the person telling the story. Example: *There are three things in this world I can't stand—cucumber salad, wool sweaters, and creative writing.* (page 33)

→ Have students compare the first-person narrator in *Experts, Incorporated* with the third-person narrator in *The Princess and the Pizza* in Week 1.

About the Author

SARAH WEEKS, Incorporated

For **Sarah Weeks,** the best thing about writing is that she gets to spend all day doing what she enjoys most. Sarah prefers writing books about things she knows or has experienced. She has written about animals and the environment as well as about kids and their experiences.

When Sarah is not writing picture books or novels, she loves to bake, watch movies and little league games, and spend time with family and friends. She also visits classrooms around the country to talk about her stories.

That's me, the author! ↓

I love baking!

Matthew Peyton/Getty Images

42

Author's Purpose
The author uses a lot of dialogue in *Experts, Incorporated*. How does the dialogue make the story more realistic?

LITERATURE ANTHOLOGY, pp. 42–43

Respond to Reading

Summarize

Use details from *Experts, Incorporated* to summarize what happened in the story. Information from your Problem and Solution Chart may help you.

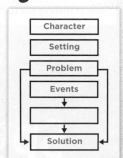

| Character |
| Setting |
| Problem |
| Events |
| |
| Solution |

Text Evidence

1. How do you know that *Experts, Incorporated* is realistic fiction? **GENRE**

2. What is Rodney Curtain's main problem in the story? What will happen if he cannot solve this problem? **PROBLEM AND SOLUTION**

3. On page 33, Rodney says that he and Lucas "always shoot straight with each other." What is the meaning of the idiom "shoot straight"? Use context clues to help you figure out the meaning. **IDIOMS**

4. Write about how Rodney resolved his problem. **WRITE ABOUT READING**

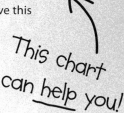

This chart can help you!

Make Connections

How did Rodney's actions affect others in this story? **ESSENTIAL QUESTION**

Rodney saw a real-world problem in his school and turned it into a future career. Make a list of jobs in which people make a difference or solve problems. Talk with a partner about why people might do these special jobs. **TEXT TO WORLD**

43

Make Connections *Analytical Writing*

Essential Question Have partners tell how Rodney's completing his essay affected his classmates. Then have them list the ways in which Rodney's idea will affect his class and his future.

Text to World After students list the jobs in which people make a difference or solve problems, discuss other problems that students might be able to turn into future careers.

Respond to Reading

Summarize

Review with students the information in their problem and solution graphic organizers. Model how to use the information to summarize the events in the story.

Analytical Writing **Write About Reading: Summarize** Remind students that you can write a summary of a section of text or of an entire text. Ask students to write a summary of what happened in the story. They can use their completed graphic organizers to help them write their summaries. Have students share their summaries with a partner.

Text Evidence

1. **Genre** <u>Answer</u> Readers can relate to the story's settings and problems. <u>Evidence</u> The story takes place on the way to school and in a classroom. The problems include completing an assignment and teasing.

2. **Problem and Solution** <u>Answer</u> Rodney's main problem is that he has not written an essay. The class will not get a pizza party unless he writes it. <u>Evidence</u> He can't think of a profession to write about. His class only gets a pizza party if no one gets an F.

3. **Idioms** <u>Answer</u> "Shoot straight" means to be honest with each other. <u>Evidence</u> Rodney hesitates to answer Lucas's question. Since Rodney didn't do the assignment, he lies to Lucas, which is something he would not normally do.

4. **Write About Reading: Problem and Solution** Rodney solves his problem by discovering a profession. He was able to write his assignment and can change the lives of students when he starts his name expert business.

Develop Comprehension

Literature Anthology

"Speaking Out to Stop Bullying"

Text Complexity Range

Lexile

740 ▲ 1010
800

TextEvaluator™

23 ▲ 51
27

Options for Close Reading

→ Whole Group

→ Small Group

→ Independent

CCSS Genre • Expository Text

Compare Texts
Read to find out about how people are standing up to bullying.

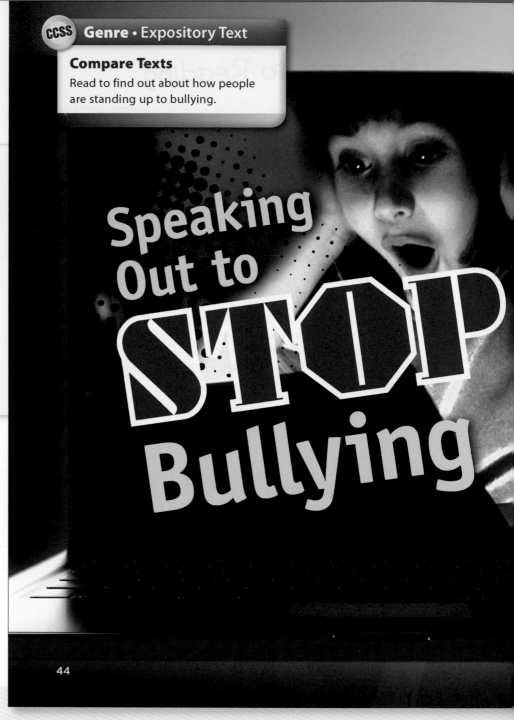

Speaking
Out to
STOP
Bullying

44

A C T Access Complex Text

What makes this text complex?

▶ **Purpose**

▶ **Purpose**

Remind students that the purpose of expository text is to provide the reader with information about a topic. Help students understand the purpose of the selection.

→ *From what point of view is the selection told?* (third-person)

Victims of bullying often feel powerless, or unable to do anything about their problem.

Raising the Issue

One of the toughest issues facing students today is bullying. Bullying occurs when a person uses aggressive behavior to hurt others on purpose. Acts of bullying often happen over and over. The victim usually feels powerless. A bully's power may stem from being older, bigger, or stronger. Bullies may also seem to have more friends or resources than the person they target.

Bullying comes in many forms. Calling someone names or teasing them can be a form of bullying. Other forms include spreading stories that aren't true about a person. Some bullies hurt people by ignoring them or leaving them out. They may also hurt their victims by shoving, hitting, or kicking. Bullying can take place anywhere, even in cyberspace. Victims may be targeted online, in e-mails, or over cell phones.

1

45

LITERATURE ANTHOLOGY, pp. 44–45

Compare Texts

Students will read an expository text about bullying. Ask students to do a close reading of the text. Students should reread to deeply understand the content. As students reread "Speaking Out to Stop Bullying," encourage them to use the make predictions strategy and take notes on their predictions. As they reread the selection, ask students to compare the information they learn in the selection with what they learned from *Experts, Incorporated*.

1 **Ask and Answer Questions**

What are different forms that bullying can take?

Analytical Writing **Write About Reading** Make a list of the different forms bullying can take. Share your list with a partner. (Bullying can include name-calling, teasing, spreading untrue stories about someone, ignoring someone, leaving someone out, shoving, hitting, and kicking.)

→ *What words or phrases does the writer use to let the reader know the importance of the topic?* (toughest issues, aggressive behavior, hurt, victim)

→ *Read the first pargraph on page 46. How does the writer introduce solutions to the problem?* (asks the reader how students can stop bullying, then gives some examples)

ELL Help students use the image on the top of page 45 to understand the meaning of *bullying*. Have them point to and identify the bullies and their actions. Ask: *How does the girl feel?* (hurt, sad)

→ Help students list words that describe bullies and bullying.

Develop Comprehension

Students should report any signs of bullying to an adult they trust.

② Ask and Answer Questions

What does the law passed in New Hampshire require? What message have police officers in Midland, Texas brought to schools?

Analytical Writing **Write About Reading** Write a short paragraph explaining the laws passed in New Hampshire and Texas. Paraphrase the information on page 46 to support your answer. (New Hampshire requires teachers to be trained on what bullying looks like. It also requires people who see bullying to report it. Police officers in Midland want students to know that bullying is a crime and that students who see bullying should report it.)

③ Ask and Answer Questions

What has Julia Kordon done to help stop bullying? Discuss with a partner. (Julia started a group called The Bullying Ends Now. She talks to students about how bullying affects people's self-esteem.)

How can students stop bullying from becoming a problem? The most important thing students can do is to tell a trusted adult when they are bullied. The same strategy applies if they see someone else being bullied. Power can also be taken away from bullies by ignoring them, agreeing with them, or using humor. Participating in anti-bullying programs may help resolve bullying issues.

Communities Take a Stand

New Hampshire passed a law to stop bullies. The law states that all school staff must be trained to know what bullying looks like. People learn to spot the signs of bullying. The law tells people who see bullying ② to report it. The state hopes that the law will create bully-free schools.

In Midland, Texas, the police take their message to the schools. Police officers make sure to tell students that bullying can be a crime. They want bullies to know that they are **accountable** for what they do. This means that bullies will be punished if they are caught. The officers tell students who have been bullied or who have seen bullying to report it right away. They make it clear that people have choices. They tell students that anyone can choose to stop being a bully.

(t) Ocean Corbis/Ocean/Corbis

46

A C T Access Complex Text

▶ **Purpose**

Tell students that authors have different viewpoints that may influence the way they present information in a text.

→ *How does the author feel about bullying?* (The author feels that people should speak up to stop bullying.)

→ *How do you know author feels this way?* (The author includes suggestions on how to stand up to bullying in the article and concludes by stating that everyone has a right to feel safe.)

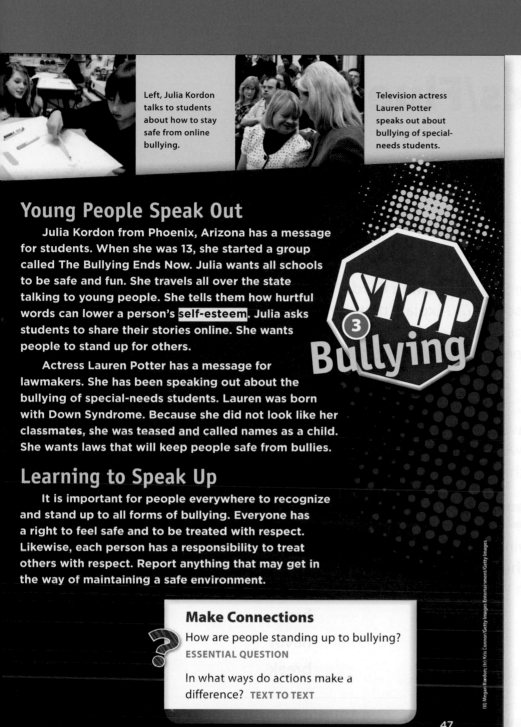

Left, Julia Kordon talks to students about how to stay safe from online bullying.

Television actress Lauren Potter speaks out about bullying of special-needs students.

Young People Speak Out

Julia Kordon from Phoenix, Arizona has a message for students. When she was 13, she started a group called The Bullying Ends Now. Julia wants all schools to be safe and fun. She travels all over the state talking to young people. She tells them how hurtful words can lower a person's self-esteem. Julia asks students to share their stories online. She wants people to stand up for others.

Actress Lauren Potter has a message for lawmakers. She has been speaking out about the bullying of special-needs students. Lauren was born with Down Syndrome. Because she did not look like her classmates, she was teased and called names as a child. She wants laws that will keep people safe from bullies.

Learning to Speak Up

It is important for people everywhere to recognize and stand up to all forms of bullying. Everyone has a right to feel safe and to be treated with respect. Likewise, each person has a responsibility to treat others with respect. Report anything that may get in the way of maintaining a safe environment.

Make Connections

How are people standing up to bullying? **ESSENTIAL QUESTION**

In what ways do actions make a difference? **TEXT TO TEXT**

47

(tl) Megan Kordon; (tr) Kris Connor/Getty Images Entertainment/Getty Images

LITERATURE ANTHOLOGY, pp. 46–47

Make Connections Analytical Writing

Essential Question Make sure students give specific details from the text to write about how people are standing up to bullying. Students can look back at the headings in the text to identify how their actions can make a difference.

Text to Text Have groups of students compare this selection with what they read in *Experts, Incorporated*. Each group will report back to the whole class. Ask one group to compare the way Lucas is teased in *Experts, Incorporated* with the way "Speaking Out to Stop Bullying" describes how actress Lauren Potter was teased. (Lucas is teased because of his name. Lauren was called names because she looks different than her classmates.) Have another group compare the information given in each text. (The information in *Experts, Incorporated* was entertaining, but it did not include much information on bullying. "Speaking Out to Stop Bullying" gave me more information on bullying and how to stop it.) Encourage a class discussion on the most beneficial ways to stop bullying.

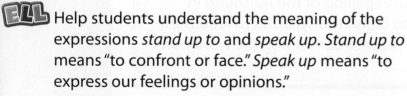

ELL Help students understand the meaning of the expressions *stand up to* and *speak up*. *Stand up to* means "to confront or face." *Speak up* means "to express our feelings or opinions."

→ Model how to stand up to and speak up. Say: *I stand up to bullies by saying no to bullying!* Have students repeat, using the proper expression and intonation.

→ Then have students complete the sentence frames: *I stand up to _____. I speak up for _____.*

→ Phonics/Fluency

20 Mins MINILESSON

Long *a*

OBJECTIVES

CCSS Use combined knowledge of all letter-sound correspondences, syllabication patterns, and morphology (e.g., roots and affixes) to read accurately unfamiliar multisyllabic words in context and out of context. **RF.4.3a**

CCSS Read on-level prose and poetry orally with accuracy, appropriate rate, and expression on successive readings. **RF.4.4b**

Rate: 84–104 WCPM

ACADEMIC LANGUAGE
• *expression*
• Cognate: *expresión*

Refer to the sound transfers chart in the **Language Transfers Handbook** to identify sounds that do not transfer in Spanish, Cantonese, Vietnamese, Hmong, and Korean.

1 Explain

Display the *Train* **Sound-Spelling Card**. Point to the card and say the long-vowel sound /ā/. Explain that the /ā/ sound has different spellings: *a, ay, ai, a_e, ea, ei, eigh,* and *ey*. Provide a sample word for each spelling: *apron, stay, train, cake, great, reins, sleigh,* and *they*.

2 Model

Write the word *weight* on the board. Underline the letters *eigh* and say the long-vowel sound /ā/. Run your finger under the word as you sound out the whole word.

3 Guided Practice

Write the following list of words on the board. Help students identify the spelling of the /ā/ sound in each word. Then have students pronounce each word.

clay	freight	hey
trade	rail	flavor
brain	grape	break

Read Multisyllabic Words

Transition to Longer Words Draw a three-column chart on the board. In the first column, write *dis, es, com,* and *en*. In the second column, write *play, cape, plain,* and *able*. Have students chorally read the word parts in the columns. Then have students combine the word parts to create longer words: *display, escape, complain,* and *enable*. Write these words in the third column.

Ask volunteers to underline the spelling of the /ā/ sound in each new word. Model how to blend the syllables to read these longer words. Have partners practice combining the word parts and pronouncing the words.

Inflectional Endings

1 Explain

Adding -ed or -ing to verbs creates new verb forms and tenses.

→ For many base words, adding -ed or -ing does not change the spelling of the base word: *blink, blinked, blinking*.

→ For a base word that ends with a consonant and e, drop the final e before adding -ed or -ing: *hike, hiked, hiking*.

2 Model

Write and say *name*. Have students repeat it. Note that *name* ends with a consonant and e. Model adding the endings -ed and -ing. Ask students to read the new words. Point out that you dropped the final e before adding the endings.

3 Guided Practice

Write the words *vote, care,* and *surprise* on the board. Have students add the endings -ed and -ing to each word and take turns saying each new word.

Expression and Rate

Explain/Model Explain that reading with expression includes changing the volume, tone, and pitch of your voice to show emotion. Tell students it is important to read at a moderate rate so others can easily understand the text.

Model reading the first eight paragraphs of "The Talent Show" on page 37. Read at a steady rate with expression to show how the characters feel about the talent show. Point out that you did not read the text too quickly or slowly. Discuss how reading with expression made the text more interesting.

Practice/Apply Divide students into two groups. Have one group read what Tina says and the other read what Maura says, while you act as the narrator. Before beginning, remind students to monitor their reading rate and to use expression to show how their characters feel.

Daily Fluency Practice

Students can practice fluency using **Your Turn Practice Book.**

Monitor and *Differentiate*

✓ **Quick Check**

Can students decode multisyllabic words with long *a* spellings? Can students read words with inflectional endings? Can students read fluently?

Small Group Instruction

If No → | Approaching Level | Reteach pp. T106, T110
| ELL | Develop pp. T122, T126
If Yes → | On Level | Review p. T112
| Beyond Level | Extend p. T116

ON-LEVEL PRACTICE BOOK p. 18

A. Circle the word with a long a vowel sound to complete each sentence. Then write it on the line to complete the sentence.

1. She had a big smile on her _____ face
   (face)   hand   fan

2. The show will begin at _____ eight _____ tonight.
   nine   five   (eight)

3. The drum _____ major _____ marched with the band.
   (major)   manner   jam

4. My feet _____ ache _____ after walking so much!
   halt   (ache)   sleep

5. The cars stopped at the _____ railway _____ crossing.
   cattle   (railway)   street

B. Circle the correct form of the verb in the right column. Then match the verb in the left column to its correct form.

Verb	Verb + -ed or -ing
1. dive	createing / (creating)
2. shake	(carved) / carveed
3. believe	(diving) / diveing
4. create	shacking / (shaking)
5. carve	believeed / (believed)

| APPROACHING p. 18 | BEYOND p. 18 | ELL p. 18 |

☞ **Go** Digital

www.connected.mcgraw-hill.com
RESOURCES
Research and Inquiry

→ **Wrap Up the Week**
Integrate Ideas

RESEARCH AND INQUIRY

Think of Others

OBJECTIVES

CCSS Conduct short research projects that build knowledge through investigation of different aspects of a topic. **W.4.7**

CCSS Pose and respond to specific questions to clarify or follow up on information, and make comments that contribute to the discussion and link to the remarks of others. **SL.4.1c**

CCSS Paraphrase portions of a text read aloud or information presented in diverse media and formats, including visually, quantitatively, and orally. **SL.4.2**

• Gather resources for research.

• Organize information.

Research the Effects of Human Actions

Explain that students will work in groups of three, four, or five and research a human action that has both positive and negative effects on people or the environment. They will then fill in Graphic Organizer 85 to display the information they found. Discuss the following steps:

① **Choose a Topic** Have groups brainstorm ways that humans affect their environment, such as building suburbs or spraying for insects. They may recall relevant topics from their reading or from their own experiences. Ask them to choose one topic from their list to research.

② **Find Resources** Review how to locate and use reliable print and online resources. Students should verify all facts in multiple sources.

③ **Guided Practice** Have students record their ideas in a two-column chart. One column should list the positive effect the action has on people or the environment. The other column should show the negative effect the action has on people or the environment.

④ **Complete the Charts** As students fill in their graphic organizers, remind them to paraphrase the information they have found and to use facts instead of opinions to support their judgments.

Present the Charts

Have students present their graphic organizers to other student groups. Ask them to display the charts, read them aloud, and pose and respond to specific questions to clarify information. Have students use the online Listening Checklist to evaluate their roles in listening to and discussing the projects.

TEXT CONNECTIONS  *Analytical Writing*

OBJECTIVES

 Compare and contrast the treatment of similar themes and topics (e.g., opposition of good and evil) and patterns of events (e.g., the quest) in stories, myths, and traditional literature from different cultures. **RL.4.9**

Text to Text

 **Cite Evidence** Explain to students that they will work in groups to compare information they have learned about how actions affect others from all the texts they have read. Model how to compare this information by using examples from the week's **Leveled Readers** and *The Talent Show*, **Reading/Writing Workshop** pages 36–39. Review class notes and completed graphic organizers. You may also wish to model going back into the text for more information. You can use a Two-Tab Foldable® to record comparisons.

positive effects   negative effects

Dinah Zike's
FOLDABLES
Study Organizer

Students should cite at least three examples from each text.

Present Information Ask groups of students to present their findings to the class. Encourage discussion, asking students to comment on information on the charts that is similar and ideas that are different.

WRITE ABOUT READING *Analytical Writing*

OBJECTIVES

Draw evidence from literary or informational texts to support analysis, reflection, and research. Apply *grade 4 Reading standards* to literature (e.g., "Describe in depth a character, setting, or event in a story or drama, drawing on specific details in the text [e.g., a character's thoughts, words, or actions]"). **W.4.9a**

Write an Analysis

Cite Evidence Using text evidence, students will analyze how well the author used details to develop realistic characters and events in the story.

Discuss how to analyze a text by asking *how* and *why* questions.

→ How did the author make the characters in the story seem realistic?

→ Why are the events in the story realistic?

Read and discuss the student model on **Your Turn Practice Book** page 19. Then have students choose a text they have read and review their notes on the story events. Have them write a paragraph analyzing how well the author used realistic characters and events in the story. Remind students that good opinion writing includes reasons supported by details and uses subjects and predicates correctly.

Present Your Ideas Ask partners to share their paragraphs and discuss how the evidence they cited from the texts supports their opinion.

→ Readers to Writers

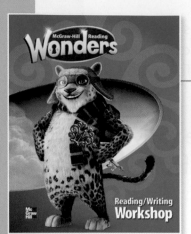

Reading/Writing Workshop

OBJECTIVES

CCSS Orient the reader by establishing a situation and introducing a narrator and/or characters; organize an event sequence that unfolds naturally. **W.4.3a**

CCSS Use dialogue and description to develop experiences and events or show the responses of characters to situations. **W.4.3b**

- Understand how to focus on an event.
- Write about a time when you stood up for yourself.
- Add details to revise.

ACADEMIC LANGUAGE
- *focus, event, sequence*
- Cognate: *secuencia*

 MINILESSON 10 Mins

Writing Traits: Ideas

Focus on an Event

Expert Model Explain that when writing a narrative, good writers focus on a central event and describe the small moments that create that event. All the details they include relate to the event. They also make sure the event sequence unfolds naturally, and they may include dialogue to show the characters' responses to the situation.

 Read aloud the expert model from "The Talent Show." Ask students to listen to identify the event that is taking place: *two friends are talking about entering a talent show*. Have students meet with partners to talk about the small moments that make up the event.

Student Model Remind students that when writing a story, it is important to focus on a central event and describe the small moments that create the event. Read aloud the student draft "Dogs or Kids?" As students follow along, have them identify the event that is taking place and think about the small moments that create it.

 Invite partners to talk about the draft and the revisions that Kyra made. Ask them to suggest places where Kyra could add more details to describe the small moments that create the event.

Go Digital

Expert Model

Student Model

 **Genre Writing**

Narrative Text

For full writing process lessons and rubrics, see:

→ Friendly Letter, pages T344–T349

→ Personal Narrative, pages T350–T355

Writing Traits Ideas

Readers to ...

Writers know that many small moments make up an event. When a writer focuses on an event, he or she describes the small moments that create the event. Reread the excerpt from "The Talent Show" below.

Focus on an Event
Identify the **event**. What small moments help to describe the event?

Expert Model

"Our act?" I said, taking a tighter grip on my books.

Tina grinned and pointed to the poster. "It says acts can be individuals, partners, or small groups."

My grip on my books became uncomfortably tight. "You want to do an act together?"

"It'll be fun," Tina said.

I hesitated for a second before continuing. "I've got an idea and . . . ."

Tina interrupted me. "Yeah, me, too! Let's talk at lunch."

Chris Vallo

44

Writers

Kyra wrote a story about two friends. Read Kyra's revisions to a section of her story.

Student Model

Dogs or Kids?

and Selena
Nan needed to earn some extra money. ~~Selena needed to earn money, too.~~

"How about baby-sitting?" Nan asked when they were trying to come up with ideas. Selena's eyes lit up, and she smiled. "How about ^a
business
dog-walking?"

Nan frowned. "But I am allergic to dogs. That idea won't work for me."

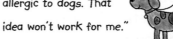

45 Chris Vallo

Editing Marks

⌒ Switch order.
∧ Add.
⌄ Add a comma.
✗ Take out.
SP Check spelling.
≡ Make a capital letter.

Grammar Handbook

Subjects and Predicates See page 451.

Your Turn COLLABORATE

✔ Identify the event.
✔ Find a compound subject.
✔ Tell how revisions improved Kyra's writing.

Go Digital!
Write online in Writer's Workspace

READING/WRITING WORKSHOP, pp. 44–45

ENGLISH LANGUAGE LEARNERS SCAFFOLD

As English Language Learners write during the week, provide support to help them respond to the prompts. For example:

Beginning	**Intermediate**	**Advanced/High**
Write Help students complete the sentence frames. *Nan and Selena need to earn ____. ____ suggests baby-sitting. ____ suggests dog-walking. The event is ____.*	**Describe** Ask students to complete the sentence frames. Encourage students to provide details. *Nan and Selena need to ____. Nan suggests ____. Selena suggests ____. The event is ____.*	**Discuss** Check for understanding. Ask: *What do Nan and Selena need to do? What is the event? Can you name a few small moments that make up the event?*

Writing Every Day: Ideas

 DAY
1

DAY
2

Writing Entry: Focus on an Event

Prewrite Provide students with the prompt below.

Tell about an experience when you stood up for yourself.

Have partners list occasions when they stood up for themselves. Ask them to jot down details about each event that they might include in their drafts.

Draft Have each student choose an experience to write about. Remind students to include details that describe the small moments that make up the event.

Focus on an Event

Use **Your Turn Practice Book** page 20 to model adding details about an event.

Dan wanted to run for class president. He asked his friend to help him. He needed good ideas. "How about proposing a school-wide dance day?" his friend said, excitedly.

Model adding details by revising the first sentence.

Dan wanted to run for class president of his elementary school.

Discuss how adding details helps the reader better understand and picture the event. Guide students to add more details to the model.

Writing Entry: Focus on an Event

Revise Have students revise their writing from Day 1 by adding two or three details related to the event.

Use the **Conferencing Routines**. Circulate among students and stop briefly to talk with individuals. Provide time for peer reviews.

Edit Have students use Grammar Handbook page 451 in the **Reading/Writing Workshop** to edit for errors in subjects and predicates.

Conferencing Routines

Teacher Conferences

STEP 1

Talk about the strengths of the writing.

This is a strong paragraph. You used transition words to make the sequence of events clear, and you included descriptive details.

STEP 2

Focus on how the writer uses the target trait for the week.

These details help create the event, but some of the details you included don't relate to the event. Deleting those details will make your story better.

STEP 3

Make concrete suggestions for revisions. Have students work on a specific assignment, such as those to the right, and then meet with you to review progress.

DAY 3

Writing Entry: Focus on an Event

Prewrite Ask students to search their Writer's Notebook for topics to write a draft. Or, provide a prompt, such as the following:

Tell about a time when you teamed up with another person to do something. Give details about the event.

Draft Once students have chosen their topics, ask them to create a story map. Then have them think about the small moments that make up the event and the details that they might include in their writing. Students can then use their story maps to begin their drafts.

DAY 4

Writing Entry: Focus on an Event

Revise Have students revise the draft writing from Day 3 by adding two or three details to tell more about the event. As students are revising their drafts, hold teacher conferences with individual students. You may also wish to have students work with partners to peer conference.

Edit Invite students to review the rules for subjects and predicates on Grammar Handbook page 451 in the **Reading/Writing Workshop** and then edit their drafts for errors.

DAY 5

Share and Reflect

Discuss with the class what they learned about focusing on an event and the small moments that create it. Invite volunteers to read and compare draft text with text that has been revised. Have students discuss the writing by focusing on the importance of the details that have been added. Allow time for individuals to reflect on their own writing progress and record observations in their Writer's Notebooks.

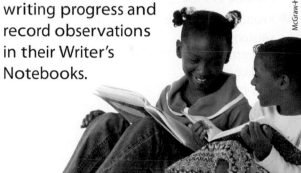

McGraw-Hill Companies, Inc. Ken Karp, photographer

Suggested Revisions

Provide specific direction to help focus young writers.

Focus on a Sentence
Read the draft and target one sentence for revision. *Rewrite this sentence by adding details that tell about _____.*

Focus on a Section
Underline a section that needs to be revised. Provide specific suggestions. *This section is interesting. I want to know more about _____. Add details that help describe the event.*

Focus on a Revision Strategy
Underline a section of the writing and ask students to use a specific revision strategy, such as rearranging. *The events in this section seem to be out of order. Rearrange some of the sentences so that the sequence of events is clearer.*

Peer Conferences

Focus peer response groups on adding details that describe an event. Provide this checklist to frame discussion.

- ☑ Does the writing focus on an event?
- ☑ Do all the details relate to that event?
- ☑ Is the sequence of events clear?

Grammar: Subjects and Predicates

Reading/Writing Workshop

OBJECTIVES

CCSS Produce complete sentences, recognizing and correcting inappropriate fragments and run-ons. **L.4.1f**

CCSS Produce simple, compound, and complex sentences. **L.3.1i**

• Identify subjects and predicates.

• Punctuate compound subjects and predicates.

• Proofread sentences for errors.

Go Digital

Subjects and Predicates

Grammar Activities

DAY 1

DAILY LANGUAGE ACTIVITY

what a great song that was. Hope they play it again.
(1: What; 2: was!; 3: I hope)

Introduce Subjects and Predicates

Present the following:

→ The **subject** names the person or thing the sentence is about. A **simple subject** is the main noun or pronoun in the **complete subject.**

    My friend <u>Lucy</u> lives there.

→ The **predicate** tells what the subject is or does. The **simple predicate** is the main verb or verb phrase in the **complete predicate.**

    My friend Lucy **<u>lives</u> there.**

Have partners discuss subjects and predicates using pages 451–452 of the Grammar Handbook in **Reading/Writing Workshop.**

DAY 2

DAILY LANGUAGE ACTIVITY

Have to finish my homework tonight. Julie has to fed her dog before she can go out to play
(1: I have; 2: feed; 3: play.)

Review Subjects and Predicates

Review subjects and predicates. Have students explain how they function in a sentence.

Introduce Compound Subjects and Predicates

→ A **compound subject** is two or more subjects with the same predicate. The subjects are usually joined by **and** or **or.**

    Bananas and oranges are my favorite fruits.

→ A **compound predicate** is two or more predicates with the same subject. The simple predicates in a compound predicate are usually joined by **and**, **but**, or **or.**

    The baby **screamed and cried.**

 TALK ABOUT IT

COLLABORATE

PASS THE SENTENCES

Have students in small groups each write two sentences on an index card. Each person passes the card to the next person. That person must read the sentences aloud and identify the simple subject and predicate in each sentence.

CREATE COMPOUND SUBJECTS AND PREDICATES

Ask partners to each write three sentences. Have them trade papers and rewrite each other's sentences so they include a compound subject and predicate. Have them read aloud the new sentences.

Spelling: Long a

DAY **3**

Chose an animal to write about? Their are many animals that live only in cold climates.
(1: Choose; 2: about.; 3: There)

Mechanics and Usage: Punctuate Compound Subjects and Predicates

→ If a **compound subject** has two subjects, the subjects are not separated by a comma. If it has three or more subjects, they are separated by commas.

→ If a **compound predicate** has two predicates, the predicates are not separated by a comma. If it has three or more predicates, they are separated by commas.

As students write, refer them to Grammar Handbook pages 451–452 and 479.

DAY **4**

My father mother and sister went on a trip. They swam, and sunbathed.
(1: father, mother, and sister; 2: swam and sunbathed)

Proofread

Have students correct errors in these sentences.

1. My back, and legs hurt after doing those exercises? (1: back and; 2: exercises.)

2. The cook served us eggs toast and orange juice for brekfast! (1: eggs, toast,: 2: breakfast.)

3. The recipe said to mix milk sugar and flour in a bowl. (1: milk, sugar, and)

4. In the woods, there are raccoons, and bears (1: raccoons and; 2: bears.)

Have students check their work using Grammar Handbook page 479 on commas.

DAY 5

Joan, and George live in Boston. When is the best time to visit them.
(1: Joan and; 2: them?)

Assess

Use the Daily Language Activity and **Grammar Practice Reproducibles** page 10 for assessment.

Reteach

Use Grammar Practice Reproducibles pages 6–9 and selected pages from the Grammar Handbook for additional reteaching. Remind students to use subjects and predicates correctly as they speak and write.

Check students' writing for use of the skill and listen for it in their speaking. Assign Grammar Revision Assignments in their Writer's Notebooks as needed.

See Grammar Practice Reproducibles pages 6–10.

SAY A COMPLETE SENTENCE

Have students in small groups list subjects and predicates on separate index cards. Have them take turns choosing two cards (two subjects, two predicates, or one of each) and using the words in a complete sentence.

IDENTIFY SENTENCE PARTS

Ask partners to select a paragraph from a book. Have them take turns reading a sentence from the paragraph aloud. Have the student reading ask the other student to identify the simple subject and predicate in the sentence.

IT'S YOUR TURN

Have students work in small groups. Have one student say a simple subject, a second student say a simple predicate, and a third student say a complete sentence using the subject and predicate spoken by the first two students.

Spelling: Long *a*

CCSS OBJECTIVES
Spell grade-appropriate words correctly, consulting references as needed.
L.4.2d

Spelling Words

major	faint	ache
clay	claim	steak
stray	pale	break
today	face	eight
bail	graze	they
rail	cane	obey
drain	slate	

Review grim, plum, cash
Challenge neighbor, railway

Differentiated Spelling

Approaching Level

major	faint	crate
clay	aim	late
today	rain	mane
tray	save	break
paid	cane	weigh
rail	pale	they
drain	face	

Beyond Level

major	frail	ache
display	fainting	nickname
stray	claimed	break
railway	remain	steak
relay	pale	eighteen
bail	parade	obeyed
wailing	mistake	

DAY 1

Assess Prior Knowledge

Display the spelling words. Read them aloud, drawing out the long *a* sound in each.

Point out the spelling patterns in *stray* and *bail*. Segment the words sound by sound, and then attach a spelling to each sound. Point out that the long *a* spelling *ay* is found at the end of a word or syllable, and the long *a* spelling *ai* is not.

Demonstrate sorting the spelling words by pattern under key words *major, rail, clay, pale, steak, eight* and *they*. (Write the words on index cards or the IWB.) Sort a few words. Point out how some letter combinations can create the long *a* sound without using the letter *a*.

Then use the Dictation Sentences from Day 5 to give the Pretest. Say the underlined word, read the sentence, and repeat the word. Have students write the words. Then have students check and correct their spelling.

DAY 2

Spiral Review

Review the short-vowel sounds in *flat, grim, bell, plot* and *sum*. Use the Dictation Sentences below for the review words. Read the sentence, say the word, and have students write the words.

1. The <u>grim</u> news made her cry.
2. He baked a <u>plum</u> cake.
3. I'll pay for that with <u>cash</u>.

Have partners check the spellings.

Challenge Words Review this week's long *a* spelling patterns. Use these Dictation Sentences for challenge words. Say the word, read the sentence, and say the word again. Have students write the word.

1. My <u>neighbor</u> is moving away.
2. We walked under a <u>railway</u>.

Have students check and correct their spelling before writing the words in their word study notebook.

 WORD SORTS

COLLABORATE

OPEN SORT

Have students cut apart the **Spelling Word Cards BLM** in the Teacher Resource Book and initial the back of each card. Have them read the words aloud with a partner. Then have partners do an open sort. Have them record the sort in their word study notebook.

PATTERN SORT

Complete the **pattern sort** from Day 1 using the key words and pointing out the long *a* spellings. Have students use Spelling Word Cards to do their own pattern sort. Ask partners to compare and check their sorts.

DAY 3

Word Meanings

Have students copy the three sentences below into their word study notebook. Say the sentences aloud; ask students to fill in the blanks with a spelling word.

1. Yesterday is the day before ____. (*today*)
2. I asked my mom if I could keep the ____ dog I found. (*stray*)
3. If a color is faint, you could also say it is ____. (*pale*)

Challenge students to come up with at least three other sentences for spelling, review, or challenge words. Have them write the sentences, leaving a blank for the word. Then have them trade with a partner and fill in the missing words. Ask volunteers to write sentences on the board for the class to complete.

See Phonics/Spelling Reproducibles pp. 7–12.

SPEED SORT

Have partners do a **speed sort** to see who is faster and record their sorts in their word study notebook. Then have them do a word hunt in the week's reading for other words with the long *a* vowel sound. Ask them to discuss how they would sort the new words they find.

DAY 4

Proofread and Write

Write these sentences on the board. Have students circle and correct each misspelled word. They can use print or electronic dictionaries or other resources to help them.

1. He cooked a stake todai. (*steak, today*)
2. The clae was too thick to go down the drane. (*clay, drain*)
3. The eyght sheep like to graize near the pond. (*eight, graze*)
4. Thay made a meijor mistake in the book report. (*they, major*)

Error Correction Remind students that the *ai* spelling for the long *a* sound never appears at the end of a word or syllable. However, the *ay* spelling often appears at the end. Create underscore hints on the board or IWB (e.g., *ai_* and *_ay*) to reinforce this principle.

BLIND SORT

Have partners do a **blind sort**: one reads a Spelling Word Card; the other tells under which key word it belongs. Have them take turns until both have sorted all their words. Ask them to discuss their sorts, then play Word Match using both sets of their Spelling Word Cards.

DAY 5

Assess

Use the Dictation Sentences for the Posttest. Have students list misspelled words in their word study notebooks. Look for students' use of these words in their writings.

Dictation Sentences

1. Her dad was a <u>major</u> in the army.
2. Myra made a <u>clay</u> pot in art class.
3. Our family took in a <u>stray</u> kitten.
4. The special for <u>today</u> is meatloaf.
5. Use a bucket to <u>bail</u> out the water.
6. The fence <u>rail</u> needed to be fixed.
7. The <u>drain</u> was clogged with peas.
8. I heard a <u>faint</u> scratching sound.
9. They <u>claim</u> to make the best pie.
10. The baby bird was a <u>pale</u> pink color.
11. She has the cutest little <u>face</u>!
12. The sheep <u>graze</u> in the pasture.
13. The woman leaned on her <u>cane</u>.
14. I wrote in chalk on a <u>slate</u>.
15. The <u>ache</u> in her ankle worsened.
16. I prefer a <u>steak</u> over a burger.
17. I wonder what else she will <u>break</u>!
18. Today my sister turns <u>eight</u>.
19. <u>They</u> all sat down to watch their favorite show.
20. You must <u>obey</u> the doctor's orders.

Have students self-correct the tests.

→ Build Vocabulary

DAY

DAY
1

DAY
2

OBJECTIVES

CCSS Recognize and explain the meaning of common idioms, adages, and proverbs. **L.4.5b**

CCSS Demonstrate understanding of words by relating them to their opposites (antonyms) and to words with similar but not identical meanings (synonyms). **L.4.5c**

Expand vocabulary by adding inflectional endings and affixes.

Vocabulary Words

accountable	humiliated
advise	inspiration
desperately	self-esteem
hesitated	uncomfortably

Go Digital

Vocabulary

Vocabulary Activities

Connect to Words

Practice this week's vocabulary.

1. How are you **accountable** for the choices you make?

2. What would you ask a friend to **advise** you about?

3. Describe how someone acting **desperately** would behave.

4. If a person **hesitated**, did he or she act right away or pause?

5. Show how someone who feels **humiliated** might look.

6. When you need an idea, what things give you **inspiration**?

7. How can practicing hard build confidence and **self-esteem**?

8. Why might someone squirm **uncomfortably**?

Expand Vocabulary

Help students generate different forms of this week's words by adding, changing, or removing inflectional endings.

→ Draw a four-column chart on the board. Write *advise* in the first column. Then write *advises, advised, advising* in the other three columns. Read aloud the words with students.

→ Have students share sentences using each form of *advise*.

→ Students can fill in the chart for *hesitate* and then share sentences using the different forms of the word.

→ Have students copy the chart in their word study notebook.

BUILD MORE VOCABULARY

COLLABORATE

ACADEMIC VOCABULARY

Discuss important academic words.

→ Display *inspiration, apology.*

→ Define each word and discuss the meanings with students.

→ Display *inspiration* and *inspirational.* Have partners look up and define related words.

→ Write the related words on the board. Have partners ask and answer questions using the words. Repeat with *apology.*

SYNONYMS

→ Remind students that synonyms are words with similar meanings. Ask, *What are some synonyms for* warm? *For* cold?

→ Have partners use a thesaurus to find synonyms of *advise*, such as *suggest* or *recommend.*

→ Have partners use *advise* and the synonyms they have found to write sentences to people they know. For example, students could offer to advise friends on what books they recommend.

DAY 3

Reinforce the Words

Review last week's and this week's vocabulary words. Have students orally complete each sentence stem.

1. Jimmy <u>hesitated</u> when the teacher called on him because he couldn't think of the ____.

2. After the long race, Teresa <u>desperately</u> looked for ____.

3. I asked my friend to <u>advise</u> me about a ____.

4. I can't finish this ____ until I find some <u>inspiration</u>!

5. He felt a little <u>humiliated</u> when he ____ in front of his friends.

6. My brother sat <u>uncomfortably</u> on the ____.

DAY 4

Connect to Writing

→ Have students write sentences in their word study notebooks using this week's vocabulary.

→ Tell them to write sentences that provide word information they learned from this week's readings.

→ Provide the Day 3 sentence stems 1–6 for students needing extra support.

Write About Vocabulary Have students write something they learned from this week's words in their word study notebook. For example, they might write about a friend, acquaintance, or family member who found *inspiration* or had high or low *self-esteem*.

DAY 5

Word Squares

Ask students to create Word Squares for each vocabulary word.

→ In the first square, students write the word. (example: *humiliated*)

→ In the second square, students write their own definition of the word and any related words, such as synonyms. (example: *embarrassed, ashamed*)

→ In the third square, students draw a simple illustration that will help them remember the word. (example: feeling embarrassed after losing a game)

→ In the fourth square, students write nonexamples, including antonyms for the word. (example: *proud, happy, full of pride*)

→ Have partners compare and discuss their Word Squares.

IDIOMS

Define idioms and remind students to use context clues or resources to help find the meanings of idioms.

→ Display **Your Turn Practice Book** pages 13–14. Read the first paragraph. Model finding the meaning of the first idiom, *butterflies in my stomach*.

→ Have students complete page 17, then find clues for *right off the bat* and *get off on the wrong foot* on pages 13–14, using a dictionary to confirm meanings.

SHADES OF MEANING

Help students generate words related to *hesitated*. Draw a T-chart. Head one column "Slowed down" and the other column "Sped up."

→ Have partners generate words to add to the T-chart. Ask students to use a thesaurus.

→ Add words not included, such as (Slowed down) *paused, delayed* and (Sped up) *quickened*.

→ Ask students to copy the words in their word study notebook.

MORPHOLOGY

Use *desperately* as a springboard for students to learn more words. Draw a T-chart. Label the columns "Root word" and "Suffixes."

→ In the left column, put *desperate*. In the right column, write the suffixes -*ation* and -*ly*.

→ Have students define the root word *desperate* and then add the suffixes. Review the meanings of the new words.

→ Ask partners to do a search for other words with these suffixes.

→ Approaching Level

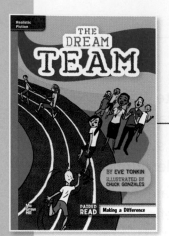

Lexile 530
TextEvaluator™ 27

OBJECTIVES

 Describe in depth a character, setting, or event in a story or drama, drawing on specific details in the text (e.g., a character's thoughts, words, or actions). **RL.4.3**

 Paraphrase portions of a text read aloud or information presented in diverse media and formats, including visually, quantitatively, and orally. **SL.4.2**

ACADEMIC LANGUAGE

- *prediction, character, setting, plot, problem and solution, realistic fiction*
- Cognates: *predicción, problema, solución, ficción realista*

Leveled Reader:
The Dream Team

Go Digital

Leveled Readers

Before Reading

Preview and Predict

Have students read the Essential Question. Give students a copy of *The Dream Team* and have them read the title and respond to the cover illustrations. Ask students to discuss what they think the selection will be about. Ask students why it is important for members of a sports team to get along.

Review Genre: Realistic Fiction

Have students recall that realistic fiction is a made-up story that contains characters, settings, and plots that could exist in real life. Have students identify features of realistic fiction in *The Dream Team*.

During Reading

Close Reading

Note Taking Ask students to use their graphic organizer while they read.

Pages 2–3 *Turn to a partner and explain what it means when the author says Cody's "heart sank" on page 3.* (It means that Cody is very disappointed.)

Pages 4–6 *Read pages 4–6. Paraphrase what Cody's problem is.* (Cody thinks that River is going to mess around and ruin the team's chances of winning.)

Pages 7–8 *Read pages 7–8. With a partner, compare and contrast Tony's and Cody's attitudes about winning.* (Both try to win. Tony believes that having fun can be more important than winning. Cody believes that winning is the most important thing.)

Pages 9–11 *Paraphrase what happens during the relay race.* (Cody's team loses the race because Cody trips and River isn't present for the race.)

Use Graphic Organizer

Pages 12–15 *Read page 12. Make a prediction to a partner about what you think will happen in the final race.* (Sample answer: I predict that Cody's team will win the final race.) *Then read pages 14–15 and confirm or revise your prediction.* (Sample answer: My prediction was incorrect. Cody's team came in second in the final race.)

After Reading

Respond to Reading

Have students complete Respond to Reading on page 16 after they have finished reading.

Write About Reading Have students work with a partner to write a short paragraph describing how Cody and River resolved their problem. Remind them to use details from the story to support their statements. Check that students cite proper text evidence when describing the problem and solution in their paragraphs.

Fluency: Expression and Rate

Model Reread page 12. Model reading the passage with proper expression and rate. Next, read the passage aloud and have students read along with you.

Apply Have students practice reading the passage with a partner.

PAIRED READ

"Making a Difference"

Make Connections:
Write About It

Before reading, ask students to note that the genre of this text is expository, which means that it explains something about a topic. Then discuss the Essential Question. After reading, ask students to make connections between how the different texts show how actions affect others.

Leveled Reader

FOCUS ON LITERARY ELEMENTS

Students can extend their knowledge of idioms by completing the activity on page 20.

Literature Circles

Ask students to conduct a literature circle using the Thinkmark questions to guide the discussion. You may wish to have a whole-class discussion on what students learned about getting along from the characters in *The Dream Team*.

Level Up

Level-up lessons available online.

IF students read the **Approaching Level** fluently and answered the questions

THEN pair them with students who have proficiently read the **On Level** and have students

• echo-read the **On Level** main selection.

• use self-stick notes to mark at least one new detail they would like to discuss in each section.

A C T Access Complex Text

The **On Level** challenges students by including more **domain-specific words** and **complex sentence structures.**

Approaching Level

Phonics/Decoding

DECODE WORDS WITH LONG *a*

 TIER 2

OBJECTIVES

 Use combined knowledge of all letter-sound correspondences, syllabication patterns, and morphology (e.g., roots and affixes) to read accurately unfamiliar multisyllabic words in context and out of context. **RF.4.3a**

Decode words with long vowels.

 I Do
Write *main* on the board. Slowly run your finger under the word as you elongate the vowel sound: /māāān/. Read the word normally. Then underline the letters *ai*. Explain to students that these two letters together are one way to write the long *a* sound, or /ā/. Repeat with *mail, play,* and *day.* Point out the *ay* spelling of long *a.* Review both spellings of long *a.*

 We Do
Write *say, plain, plan, gray, sand,* and *snail* on the board. Model how to decode *say.* Work with students to choral-read the remaining words. Have students raise their hands when they read a word with the long *a* sound.

 You Do
Add these words to the board: *lay, pan, hail, bay,* and *gain.* Have students read each word aloud and identify words with the long *a* sound. Then point to the words in random order. Have students read aloud only the words with /ā/. Repeat several times.

REVIEW OPEN SYLLABLES

TIER 2

OBJECTIVES

 Use combined knowledge of all letter-sound correspondences, syllabication patterns, and morphology (e.g., roots and affixes) to read accurately unfamiliar multisyllabic words in context and out of context. **RF.4.3a**

Decode words with open syllables.

 I Do
Remind students that every syllable in a word has only one vowel sound. Write *a* and *me.* Point out that when syllables are made of only one vowel or begin with a consonant and end with a vowel, the syllable usually has the long-vowel sound. These are called open syllables because the vowel is not "closed in" by consonants. Underline the *m* in *me* and circle the *e,* saying /ēēē/, to show students why *me* is an open syllable.

 We Do
Write the syllables *la* and *bor* on the board. Guide students as they decode the syllables. Point out the open syllable. Have students say the syllables together to form *labor.* Write these words on the board, separated into syllables: *ba/con, be/gan, mo/tor, pa/per.* Have students identify the vowel sounds and the open syllables, then decode the words.

 You Do
Add *tiger, pilot,* and *baby* to the board. Have students decode each word. Point to the words in random order for students to choral-read.

PRACTICE WORDS WITH LONG *a*

OBJECTIVES

CCSS Use combined knowledge of all letter-sound correspondences, syllabication patterns, and morphology to read accurately unfamiliar multisyllabic words in context and out of context. **RF.4.3a**

 I Do Remind students that the long *a* sound, or /ā/, can be spelled in a variety of ways. Write *rain, stay, favor, made, great, they,* and *eight* on the board. Underline the letter or letters in each word that make the sound /ā/. Point to the letters while reading aloud each word and elongating the sound /ā/. Review with students each spelling of the long *a* sound.

 We Do Write the words *stain, weight, acorn, awake, today, break,* and *shaken* on the board. Model how to decode the first word. Help students as they decode the remaining words. Help them distinguish the different spellings for the long-vowel sound. Explain that each spelling stands for the same sound.

 You Do Afterward, point to the words in random order for students to choral-read.

INFLECTIONAL ENDINGS

OBJECTIVES

CCSS Use combined knowledge of all letter-sound correspondences, syllabication patterns, and morphology to read accurately unfamiliar multisyllabic words in context and out of context. **RF.4.3a**

Decode words with inflectional endings *-ing* and *-ed*.

 I Do Review that the endings *-ed* and *-ing* are added to verbs to create new verb forms and tenses. For many verbs, adding *-ed* or *-ing* does not change the spelling: *rain, rained, raining.* For verbs that end with a consonant and *e*, drop the final *e* before adding *-ed* or *-ing: bike, biked, biking.* For most verbs that end with a short vowel and a consonant, double the final consonant before adding *-ed* or *-ing: stop, stopped, stopping.*

 We Do Write *ripped* on the board. Model how to decode the word. Write other words with inflectional endings on the board. Help students decode these words. Use the syllable-scoop technique to help students read one syllable at a time.

 You Do Write the words *plan, fail,* and *make* on the board. Have students add an inflectional ending to each word. Point to the words in random order for students to choral-read. Repeat several times.

ELL ENGLISH LANGUAGE LEARNERS

For the **ELLs** who need **phonics**, **decoding**, and **fluency** practice, use scaffolding methods as necessary to ensure students understand the meaning of the words. Refer to the **Language Transfers Handbook** for phonics elements that may not transfer in students' native languages.

Approaching Level
Vocabulary

TIER **2**

REVIEW HIGH-FREQUENCY WORDS

OBJECTIVES

 Read with sufficient accuracy and fluency to support comprehension. Read on-level text with purpose and understanding. **RF.4.4a**

Review high-frequency words.

 I Do Use **Word Cards 11–20.** Display one word at a time, following the routine: Display the word. Read the word. Then spell the word.

 We Do Ask students to state the word and spell the word with you. Model using the word in a sentence and have students repeat after you.

 You Do Display the word. Ask students to say the word then spell it. When completed, quickly flip through the word card set as students choral-read the words. Provide opportunities for students to use the words in speaking and writing. For example, provide sentence starters such as *I would like another ____.* Ask students to write each word in their Writer's Notebook.

TIER **2**

REVIEW VOCABULARY WORDS

OBJECTIVES

Acquire and use accurately grade-appropriate general academic and domain-specific words and phrases, including those that signal precise actions, emotions, or states of being and that are basic to a particular topic. **L.4.6**

 I Do Display each **Visual Vocabulary Card** and state the word. Explain how the photograph illustrates the word. State the example sentence and repeat the word.

 We Do Point to the word on the card and read the word with students. Ask them to repeat the word. Engage students in structured partner-talk about the image as prompted on the back of the vocabulary card.

 You Do Display each visual in random order, hiding the word. Have students match the definitions and context sentences of the words to the visuals displayed.

IDENTIFY RELATED WORDS

OBJECTIVES

CCSS Demonstrate understanding of words by relating them to their opposites (antonyms) and to words with similar but not identical meanings (synonyms). **L.4.5c**

 I Do

Display the *advise* **Visual Vocabulary Card** and say aloud the word set *advise, inform, lie, coach*.

Point out that the word *lie* does not belong.

 We Do

Display the vocabulary card for the word *inspiration*. Say aloud the word set *inspiration, boredom, idea, motivation*. With students, identify the word that does not belong and discuss why.

 You Do

Using the word sets below, display the remaining cards one at a time. Read aloud the word set. Have students identify the word that does not belong.

accountable, lazy, obligated, responsible

humiliated, embarrassed, ashamed, rested

desperately, hopefully, wildly, worriedly

hesitated, rushed, delayed, avoided

self-esteem, confidence, pride, uncertainty

uncomfortably, roughly, sleepily, painfully

IDIOMS

OBJECTIVES

CCSS Demonstrate understanding of figurative language, word relationships, and nuances in word meanings. Recognize and explain the meaning of common idioms, adages, and proverbs. **L.4.5b**

 I Do

Display the Comprehension and Fluency passage on **Approaching Reproducibles** pages 13–14. Read aloud the first paragraph. Point to the phrase *butterflies in my stomach*. Tell students that this phrase is an idiom. Explain that an idiom is a group of words that mean something different than the meaning of each individual word. Tell students that they can use words and phrases in sentences near the idiom to understand its meaning.

Think Aloud I don't know what *butterflies in my stomach* means. I know the narrator doesn't have real butterflies in his stomach. I read that he feels sick when he gets on the bus. I see he is starting at a new school. *Butterflies in my stomach* must mean to be nervous and have an upset stomach.

 We Do

Have students point to the phrase *between a rock and a hard place* on page 14. Discuss how to use context clues to figure out the idiom's meaning.

 You Do

Have students reread page 13 and find the meaning of *right off the bat*.

→ Approaching Level
Comprehension

FLUENCY

OBJECTIVES

 Read with sufficient accuracy and fluency to support comprehension. Read on-level prose and poetry orally with accuracy, appropriate rate, and expression on successive readings. **RF.4.4b**

Read fluently with appropriate expression and rate.

 I Do Explain that effective readers use expression, or emphasize words to show meaning and emotion. They also slow down or speed up the rate at which they read. Read the first paragraph of the Comprehension and Fluency passage on **Approaching Reproducibles** pages 13–14. Tell students to listen for when you read more slowly or emphasize certain words.

 We Do Read the rest of the page aloud and have students repeat each sentence after you, using the same expression and rate.

You Do Have partners take turns reading sentences from the Approaching Reproducibles passage. Remind them to focus on their expression and rate. Listen in and provide any necessary corrective feedback by modeling proper fluency.

PLOT: IDENTIFY PROBLEMS

OBJECTIVES

 Describe in depth a character, setting, or event in a story or drama, drawing on specific details in the text (e.g., a character's thoughts, words, or actions). **RL.4.3**

Identify plot events.

 I Do Write *Problem* on the board. Under *Problem,* write *Aaron is new at school* and *Aaron misses his friends.* Explain to students that the main character in a story usually has a problem that needs to be solved. Each step that the character takes to solve the problem is a part of the story's plot, or the events that make up a story.

 We Do Read the first page of the Comprehension and Fluency passage in **Approaching Reproducibles.** Ask: *So far, what has happened to Aaron?* Explain that how a character solves a problem makes up the story's plot. These events lead to the problem's solution. Help students identify how each event relates to the previous one.

 You Do Have students read the rest of the passage. After each paragraph, they should list the most important events. Once they have completed their lists, review the story's plot together and then identify the solution.

REVIEW PROBLEM AND SOLUTION

OBJECTIVES

 Describe in depth a character, setting, or event in a story or drama, drawing on specific details in the text (e.g., a character's thoughts, words, or actions). **RL.4.3**

 I Do Remind students that a story's main character usually has a problem to solve. Each step that the character takes to solve the problem is an event in the story, and these events make up the story's plot. Remind students that a story's setting can play a part in the resolution of the character's problem. It can make a problem easier to solve or even harder.

 We Do Read the first paragraph of the Comprehension and Fluency passage in the **Approaching Reproducibles** together. Identify the characters and the setting. Then model how to identify the character's main problem. Continue reading and work with students to identify each event that leads up to the story's solution.

 You Do Have students use the character's problem and the events leading up to the story's conclusion to summarize the story.

SELF-SELECTED READING

OBJECTIVES

Describe in depth a character, setting, or event in a story or drama, drawing on specific details in the text (e.g., a character's thoughts, words, or actions). **RL.4.3**

Make, confirm, or revise predictions about a text.

Read Independently

Have students choose a realistic fiction book for sustained silent reading. Remind students that:

→ the main character in a story usually has a problem that needs to be solved. The steps the character takes to solve the problem make up the story's events, which make up the story's plot.

→ they should use story details and their own experiences to make predictions about what will happen as they read.

Read Purposefully

Have students record examples of problem and solution on a Character, Plot, Setting: Problem and Solution Chart as they read independently. After they finish, they can conduct a Book Talk, each telling about the book they read.

→ Students should share their charts and answer this question: *What is the main character's problem?*

→ They should share any predictions they made while reading the book and share if their predictions were accurate.

On Level

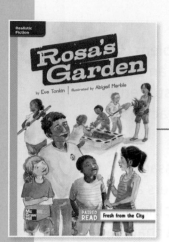

Lexile 710
TextEvaluator™ 35

 OBJECTIVES

Describe in depth a character, setting, or event in a story or drama, drawing on specific details in the text (e.g., a character's thoughts, words, or actions). **RL.4.3**

Paraphrase portions of a text read aloud or information presented in diverse media and formats, including visually, quantitatively, and orally. **SL.4.2**

ACADEMIC LANGUAGE

• *prediction, character, setting, plot, problem and solution, realistic fiction*

• Cognates: *predicción, problema, solución, ficción realista*

Leveled Reader:
Rosa's Garden

Before Reading

Preview and Predict

Read the Essential Question with students. Give students a copy of *Rosa's Garden* and have them read the title and respond to the cover illustrations. Have students predict what the story will be about. Ask students to discuss how a garden could help people in a community get along.

Review Genre: Realistic Fiction

Have students recall that realistic fiction is a made-up story that contains characters, settings, and plots that could exist in real life. Have students identify features of realistic fiction in *Rosa's Garden*.

During Reading

Close Reading

Note Taking Ask students to use their graphic organizer while they read.

Pages 2–3 *Read pages 2–3. What does Rosa's mom mean when she says, "Don't get me started!" on page 3? Turn to a partner and explain.* (She means that she's frustrated with the state of the empty lot. She is so frustrated she could go on and on about it.)

Pages 4–5 *Read page 4. How does the phrase "giant pot of trash soup" help you picture the abandoned lot? Describe what you see to a partner.* (I can picture a lot of garbage jumbled together.)

Pages 6–7 *Read pages 6–7. Paraphrase the steps the community takes to turn the lot into a garden.* (The neighbors pick up the remaining trash and then build garden beds. Then a dump truck arrives to deliver the dirt for the garden.)

Pages 9–11 *Read pages 9–10. Turn to a partner and make a prediction about what has happened to all of the plants.* (Sample answer: I predict that an animal ate and trampled the plants.) *Then read page 11 and confirm or revise your predictions.* (Sample answer: My prediction was correct. A raccoon ate and trampled the plants.)

Go Digital

Leveled Readers

Use Graphic Organizer

Pages 12–15 *How is the community better off at the end of the story? Read pages 12–15.* (The dirty, vacant lot has been turned into a beautiful garden. The neighborhood now has a place where people can celebrate and relax. They also have fresh vegetables to share.)

After Reading

Respond to Reading Have students complete Respond to Reading on page 16 after they have finished reading.

Write About Reading Have students work with a partner to reread pages 9 and 10 and write a short paragraph describing the problem. Then have students write about how Rosa and her neighbors solve the problem. Check that students cite appropriate details when describing the problem and solution.

Fluency: Expression and Rate

Model Model reading page 9 with proper expression and rate. Next, read the passage aloud and have students read along with you.

Apply Have partners do repeated rereadings of the passage.

PAIRED READ

Leveled Reader

"Fresh from the City"

Make Connections: Write About It

Before reading, ask students to note that the genre of this story is expository text. Expository text explains something about a topic. Have students discuss the Essential Question. After reading, ask students to use the information from "Fresh from the City" to write about and discuss how Rosa's garden can help her neighborhood.

FOCUS ON LITERARY ELEMENTS

Students can extend their knowledge of idioms by completing the activity on page 20.

Literature Circles

Ask students to conduct a literature circle using the Thinkmark questions to guide the discussion. You may wish to have a whole-class discussion on ways to help the community.

Level Up

Level-up lessons available online.

IF students read the On Level fluently and answered the questions

THEN pair them with students who have proficiently read the Beyond Level and have students

• partner-read the Beyond Level main selection.

• list ways Amy gets along with others.

• compare and contrast how Rosa and Amy help others.

A C T Access Complex Text

The Beyond Level challenges students by including more **domain-specific words** and **complex sentence structures**.

On Level

Vocabulary

REVIEW VOCABULARY WORDS

OBJECTIVES
 Acquire and use accurately grade-appropriate general academic and domain-specific words and phrases, including those that signal precise actions, emotions, or states of being and that are basic to a particular topic. **L.4.6**

I Do Use the **Visual Vocabulary Cards** to review key selection words *advise, desperately, hesitated, humiliated, self-esteem,* and *uncomfortably*. Point to each word, read it aloud, and have students chorally repeat it.

We Do Ask these questions and help students respond and explain their answers.
→ Would being *humiliated* help or hurt your *self-esteem*?
→ If I *hesitated* to tell you your test score, would you be worried?

You Do Have students work in pairs to respond to these questions and explain their answers.
→ Who would you ask to *advise* you on what to read?
→ Why would a bird be *desperately* looking for sticks and twigs?
→ Name a place that might be *uncomfortably* loud.

IDIOMS

OBJECTIVES
 Demonstrate understanding of figurative language, word relationships, and nuances in word meanings. Recognize and explain the meaning of common idioms, adages, and proverbs. **L.4.5b**

I Do Remind students that idioms are phrases that have a meaning different from the meaning of each individual word in the phrase. They can use text clues to figure out the meaning of an idiom. Use the Comprehension and Fluency passage on **Your Turn Practice Book** pages 13–14 to model.

Think Aloud I do not understand what *butterflies in my stomach* means. The character doesn't have real butterflies in his stomach. I see that he is nervous about starting a new school. When he says he has *butterflies in his stomach*, he means that he feels nervous and his stomach is upset.

We Do Have students read the fifth paragraph, and figure out the meaning of *get off on the wrong foot*. Have students point out the context clues they used to figure out the meaning of the phrase.

You Do Have students work in pairs to determine the meaning of *between a rock and a hard place* on page 14.

Comprehension

REVIEW PROBLEM AND SOLUTION

OBJECTIVES

 Describe in depth a character, setting, or event in a story or drama, drawing on specific details in the text (e.g., a character's thoughts, words, or actions). **RL.4.3**

 I Do
Remind students that a story's main character usually has a problem to solve. Explain to students that each step that the character takes to solve the problem is an event in the story, or part of the story's plot. Remind students that a story's setting can play a part in the resolution of the character's problem.

 We Do
Read the first paragraph of the Comprehension and Fluency passage in **Your Turn Practice Book** together. Have students discuss the characters, the setting, and the main character's problems so far. Guide them in identifying how the characters' problems are related to the plot. Then work with students to identify the key events of the story and how they are connected.

 You Do
Have students continue to list the story's events and identify the solution when they finish reading. Have students explain how the characters, setting, and plot are related to Aaron's problem and eventual solution.

SELF-SELECTED READING

OBJECTIVES

Describe in depth a character, setting, or event in a story or drama, drawing on specific details in the text (e.g., a character's thoughts, words, or actions). **RL.4.3**

Make predictions about a text.

Read Independently

Have students choose a realistic fiction book for sustained silent reading.

→ Before they read, have students preview the book, reading the title and viewing the front and back cover.

→ As students read, remind them to make predictions about the text.

Read Purposefully

Encourage students to read different books in order to identify the problems and solutions that drive each book's plot.

→ As students read, have them fill in story details on a Character, Plot, Setting: Problem and Solution Chart.

→ They can use this chart to help them write a summary of the book.

→ Ask students to share their reactions to the book with classmates.

→ Beyond Level

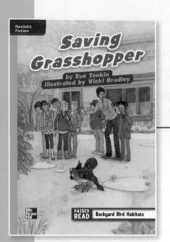

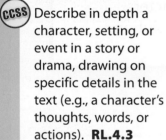

Lexile 810
TextEvaluator™ 39

OBJECTIVES

 Describe in depth a character, setting, or event in a story or drama, drawing on specific details in the text (e.g., a character's thoughts, words, or actions). **RL.4.3**

Paraphrase portions of a text read aloud or information presented in diverse media and formats, including visually, quantitatively, and orally. **SL.4.2**

ACADEMIC LANGUAGE

• *prediction, character, setting, plot, problem and solution, realistic fiction*

• Cognates: *predicción, problema, solución, ficción realista*

Leveled Reader:
Saving Grasshopper

Before Reading

Preview and Predict

Read the Essential Question with students. Have students read the title and the first two pages of *Saving Grasshopper*. Ask them to make predictions about what the title means and what the story will be about.

Review Genre: Realistic Fiction

Have students recall that realistic fiction is a made-up story that contains characters, settings, and plots that could exist in real life. Have students identify features of realistic fiction in *Saving Grasshopper*.

During Reading

Close Reading

Note Taking Ask students to use their graphic organizer while they read.

Pages 2–3 *Read pages 2–3. Paraphrase the problem Amy has in the beginning of the story.* (The other students think Amy is strange for talking to birds.)

Pages 4–5 *Read pages 4–5. Make a prediction about how Mr. Martinez might help Amy. Tell your prediction to a partner.* (Sample answer: I think Mr. Martinez will have the class study birds. This will help the other students understand why Amy likes birds.)

Page 6 *What does the phrase "raining cats and dogs" tell you about the weather? Describe the weather to a partner.* (It means that it was raining very heavily.)

Pages 7–11 *Confirm or revise your prediction about how Mr. Martinez helps Amy.* (Sample answer: My prediction was incorrect. Mr. Martinez asks Amy what to do when the class finds the hurt hawk. He lets Amy stay with the bird while they wait for the bird rescue center to arrive.)

Go Digital

Leveled Readers

Use Graphic Organizer

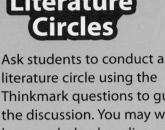

Pages 12–14 *Read pages 12–14. What clues does the author give you that show Amy is a natural at helping birds? Turn to a partner and explain.* (Amy correctly identifies the species of bird. She also helps set the bird's wing and seems to know how to do it immediately.)

Page 15 *How can you tell that the other students are treating Amy differently than they did at the beginning of the story?* (The other students in Amy's class ask her questions about Grasshopper. Now they want to help out and feed and protect the birds.)

After Reading

Respond to Reading

Have students complete Respond to Reading on page 16 after they have finished reading.

Analytical Writing **Write About Reading** Have students work with a partner to write a short paragraph explaining why Amy's classmates change the way they think about her. Make sure students cite text evidence when explaining the resolution of the problem.

Fluency: Expression and Rate

Model Model reading page 3 with proper expression and rate. Next read the passage aloud and have students read along with you.

Apply Have partners do repeated rereadings of the passage.

PAIRED READ

"Backyard Bird Habitats"

Make Connections:
Write About It **Analytical Writing**

Before reading, ask students to note that the genre of this text is expository text, which means it explains about a topic. Then discuss the Essential Question. After reading, ask students to use the information from *Saving Grasshopper* and "Backyard Bird Habitats" to write about and discuss why it's important to preserve the habitats of birds in the wild.

Leveled Reader

FOCUS ON LITERARY ELEMENTS

Students can extend their knowledge of idioms by completing the activity on page 20.

Literature Circles

Ask students to conduct a literature circle using the Thinkmark questions to guide the discussion. You may wish to have a whole-class discussion on information learned about why it's important to take care of birds and ways that students can help.

Gifted and Talented

Synthesize In *Saving Grasshopper,* Amy finds a way to rescue a hawk. Challenge students to research some birds in your local area and make a list of the foods, types of habitats, and other conditions they need to survive. Then have each student choose one of the birds and write a short paragraph telling how they could help it survive.

→ Beyond Level

Vocabulary

REVIEW DOMAIN-SPECIFIC WORDS

OBJECTIVES

 Acquire and use accurately grade-appropriate general academic and domain-specific words and phrases, including those that signal precise actions, emotions, or states of being and that are basic to a particular topic. **L.4.6**

 Model Use the **Visual Vocabulary Cards** to review the meaning of the words *self-esteem* and *accountable*. Write sentences on the board using the words.

Write the words *confidence* and *respect* on the board and discuss the meanings with students. Then help students write sentences using these words.

 Apply Have students work in pairs to review the meanings of the words *capable* and *responsible*. Then have partners write sentences using the words.

IDIOMS

OBJECTIVES

CCSS Demonstrate understanding of figurative language, word relationships, and nuances in word meanings. Recognize and explain the meaning of common idioms, adages, and proverbs. **L.4.5b**

 Model Read aloud the first paragraph of the Comprehension and Fluency passage on **Beyond Reproducibles** pages 13–14.

Think Aloud I do not understand what *right off the bat* means, but I can use context clues to help me understand the idiom. After the phrase is used the narrator says "the very first week of school." This clue helps me understand that when the narrator says *right off the bat,* he means immediately or very early on.

With students, read the second paragraph. Help them figure out the meaning of *get off on the wrong foot.*

 Apply Have pairs of students read the rest of the passage. Have them determine the meaning of *between a rock and a hard place* on page 14.

 Independent Study Have students look up other examples of idioms, either in a book or online. Then have students write a short story using at least one of the idioms they learned.

Comprehension

REVIEW PROBLEM AND SOLUTION

OBJECTIVES

Describe in depth a character, setting, or event in a story or drama, drawing on specific details in the text (e.g., a character's thoughts, words, or actions). **RL.4.3**

Model Remind students that a story's main character usually has a problem to solve. Explain to students that each step that the character takes to solve the problem is an event in the story, or part of the story's plot. Remind students that a story's setting can play a part in the resolution of the character's problem.

Have students read the first paragraph of the Comprehension and Fluency passage of **Beyond Reproducibles** pages 13–14. Ask open-ended questions to facilitate discussion, such as *How does the setting of the story affect Aaron's situation?* Students should support their responses with details from the text.

Apply Have students identify the character, setting, problem, events, and solution in the rest of the passage as they independently fill in a Character, Plot, Setting: Problem and Solution Chart. Then have partners use their work to discuss how all of these story elements are related.

SELF-SELECTED READING

OBJECTIVES

Describe in depth a character, setting, or event in a story or drama, drawing on specific details in the text (e.g., a character's thoughts, words, or actions). **RL.4.3**

Reread difficult sections in a text to increase understanding.

Read Independently

Have students choose a realistic fiction book for sustained silent reading.

→ As students read, have them fill in a Character, Plot, and Setting: Problem and Solution Chart.

→ Remind them to reread difficult sections of the text.

Read Purposefully

Encourage students to keep a reading journal. Ask them to read different books in order to learn about a variety of subjects.

→ Students can write summaries of the books in their journals.

→ Ask students to share their reactions to the books with classmates.

Analyze Challenge students to discuss how their books relate to the weekly theme of how one person's actions affect others. How do characters in their books relate to others? How do their relationships with others affect the plot? Have students write a book report analyzing how the main character interacts with others.

English Language Learners

Reading/Writing Workshop

Shared Read
The Talent Show

Go Digital

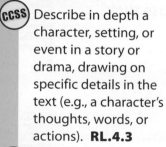

View "The Talent Show"

 OBJECTIVES

Describe in depth a character, setting, or event in a story or drama, drawing on specific details in the text (e.g., a character's thoughts, words, or actions). **RL.4.3**

Determine the meaning of words and phrases as they are used in a text, including those that allude to significant characters found in mythology (e.g., Herculean). **RL.4.4**

LANGUAGE OBJECTIVE

Identify a problem and its solution.

ACADEMIC LANGUAGE

• *problem, solution, prediction*

• Cognates: *problema, solución, predicción*

Before Reading

Build Background

Read the Essential Question: How do your actions affect others?

→ Explain the meaning of the Essential Question, and point out the cognates *action (acción)* and *affect (afectar)*. Demonstrate that our actions affect how others feel or act.

→ **Model an answer:** *Our actions can affect others in many ways. If we do something good for someone, that person will feel good. But if we do something bad, our actions can hurt others and make others feel bad. For example, if I cheat and do not play fair, it might upset my teammates. If I say something kind, I can make others feel good about themselves.*

→ Ask students a question that ties the Essential Question to their own background knowledge: *Turn to a partner and think of a time when your actions affected someone in a good or bad way. Discuss or act out the situation with your partner. How did your own actions make you feel?* Call on several pairs to share with the class.

During Reading

Interactive Question-Response

→ Ask questions that help students understand the meaning of the text after each paragraph.

→ Reinforce the meanings of key vocabulary.

→ Ask students questions that require them to use key vocabulary.

→ Reinforce strategies and skills of the week by modeling.

Page 37

Paragraph 1
What event is happening at the school in three weeks? (a talent show)

Paragraphs 2–5
Explain and Model Making Predictions *I see that Maura and Tina want to be in their school's talent show. Tina asks Maura if she wants to do an act together. Is Maura comfortable with Tina's idea?* (no) *I can predict that Maura does not want to be in the show with Tina.*

Paragraph 7
Maura hesitates, or waits, before telling Tina about her idea for the talent show. Demonstrate hesitating. *Why do you think she hesitates?* (Maura wants to do an act by herself.)

Paragraphs 9 and 10
Explain and Model Problem and Solution
In many stories, the main character tries to solve a problem. We learn that Maura wants to do her own act in the talent show, but Tina wants to do an act together. Is this a problem? (yes) *Who can find another problem on this page?* (Possible answers: Tina always takes charge and makes the decisions. Maura does not tell her about how she feels.)

Have students revisit their predictions. *Are the predictions you made about the story correct so far? What do you think will happen next?* (Possible answer: My prediction was correct. Maura wants to do an act by herself, but she doesn't know how to tell Tina. I predict that Maura will tell Tina how she feels.)

Page 38

Paragraphs 1–3
Have students chorally read the first three paragraphs on page 38. Review the definitions of *inspiration* and *humiliated*. Point out the cognates *inspiración* and *humillado(a)*.

What does Tina want to do in the talent show? (Tina wants to sing and dance.) *Why is this a problem?*

(Maura wants to juggle.)
Does Tina listen to Maura's idea? (no) *How does Maura feel?* (Maura is upset.)

Paragraphs 4–8
Explain and Model Idioms Ask an advanced student to answer the following question: *What does Maura's grandmother mean when she says, "Cat got your tongue?"* (She wants to know why Maura is not speaking.) Ask another student to find another idiom. ("let off steam")

Has Maura tried to solve the problem? How would you solve this problem? (Possible answer: Maura has not tried to solve her problem. If I were Maura, I would talk to my friend about doing my own act.)

Page 39

Paragraphs 1–5

Point out and say the word *curt*. *Tina was curt when Maura told her she was going to do her juggling act. When someone is curt, he or she gives short or rude responses.* Model being curt. *How did Tina's reaction make Maura feel?* (She was worried that Tina would be mad at her.) Have students role-play the interaction between Maura and Tina.

The idiom stand up for myself *means "to defend myself against someone or something." How does Maura stand up for herself? Does she solve her problem?* (Maura solves her problem. She decides to tell Tina what she wants to do in the talent show.)

After Reading

Make Connections

→ Review the Essential Question: How do your actions affect others?

→ Make text connections.

→ Have students complete **ELL Reproducibles** pages 13–15.

→ English Language Learners

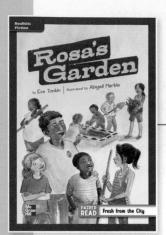

Lexile 540
TextEvaluator™ 12

 OBJECTIVES

Describe in depth a character, setting, or event in a story or drama, drawing on specific details in the text (e.g., a character's thoughts, words, or actions). **RL.4.3**

 Paraphrase portions of a text read aloud or information presented in diverse media and formats, including visually, quantitatively, and orally. **SL.4.2**

ACADEMIC LANGUAGE

• *prediction, character, setting, plot, problem and solution, realistic fiction*

• Cognates: *predicción, problema, solución, ficción realista*

Leveled Reader:
Rosa's Garden

Before Reading

Preview

→ Read the Essential Question: How do your actions affect others?

→ Refer to Actions Count: *How can you help your community?*

→ Preview *Rosa's Garden* and "Fresh from the City": *Our purpose for reading is to learn about how people's actions can help others.*

Vocabulary

Use the **Visual Vocabulary Cards** to pre-teach the ELL vocabulary: *community, gardening, neighborhood.* Use the routine found on the cards. Point out the cognates: *comunidad* and *jardinería.*

During Reading

Interactive Question-Response

Note Taking Have students use the graphic organizer in **ELL Reproducibles,** page 12 while they read the selection.

Pages 2–3 Lot *means "an area of land." What makes the lot unsafe?* (holes in the ground, trash) *Is the lot a problem?* (yes) Discuss the problem and possible solutions with students.

Pages 4–5 Read page 4 aloud and point to the pictures. *What do you predict Rosa will do with the lot?* (Possible answer: She will plant flowers.) Have students discuss their predictions with a partner. Then read page 5 and help them find details to confirm or revise their predictions.

Pages 6–8 *A community garden is a garden that people in a community share.* Remind students that *community* has a Spanish cognate (*comunidad*). *Who helps plant the garden?* (Rosa's family and their neighbors) *Who can use the garden?* (the community) Compare the illustration of the lot on page 7 with the way it is described on page 2.

Pages 9–10 *What happens to the garden?* (Some of the vegetables are ruined and others are missing.) *What clues on the page tell you what might have caused this problem?* (animal tracks)

**Go
Digital**

Leveled Readers

**Use Graphic
Organizer**

Pages 11–12 Point to and say the word *desperately* on page 11. Have students repeat after you. Read the line of dialogue with a normal voice and then with a desperate voice. Ask students to echo-read.

Pages 13–15 Point to and discuss the illustration on page 13. *How did the community solve the raccoon problem?* (They put up a fence and built a gate.)

After Reading

Respond to Reading Help students complete the graphic organizer. Revisit the Essential Question. Ask students to work with partners to summarize and answer the Text Evidence Questions. Support students as necessary and review all responses as a group.

Analytical Writing **Write About Reading** Have partners write a short paragraph that describes one of the problems in the story and how Rosa and her neighbors solve the problem. Encourage students to reread the text and use notes from their graphic organizer to support their responses.

Fluency: Expression and Rate

Model Model reading page 2 with proper expression and rate. Next, read the passage aloud and have students read along with you.

Apply Have students practice reading with a partner.

PAIRED READ

"Fresh from the City"

Make Connections:
Write About It *Analytical Writing*

Leveled Reader

Before reading ask students to note that the genre of this text is expository text, which means that it explains a topic. Then discuss the Essential Question. After reading, ask students to use the information in "Fresh from the City" to list and discuss additional ways Rosa's garden could help her community.

FOCUS ON LITERARY ELEMENTS

Students can extend their knowledge of idioms by completing the activity on page 20.

Literature Circles

Ask students to conduct a literature circle using the Thinkmark questions to guide the discussion. You may wish to have a whole-class discussion on information learned about how Rosa and her neighbors helped others by building the garden.

Level Up

Level-up lessons available online.

IF students read the **ELL Level** fluently and answered the questions

THEN pair them with students who have proficiently read **On Level** and have ELL students

• echo-read the **On Level** main selection with their partners.

• list difficult words and discuss these words with their partners.

A C T Access Complex Text

The **On Level** challenges students by including **complex sentence structures**.

English Language Learners
Vocabulary

PRETEACH VOCABULARY

OBJECTIVES

 Acquire and use accurately grade-appropriate general academic and domain-specific words and phrases, including those that signal precise actions, emotions, or states of being. **L.4.6**

Preteach vocabulary words.

LANGUAGE OBJECTIVE
Use vocabulary words.

 I Do Preteach vocabulary from "The Talent Show," following the Vocabulary Routine found on the **Visual Vocabulary Cards** for the words *accountable, advise, desperately, hesitated, humiliated, inspiration, self-esteem,* and *uncomfortably.*

 We Do After completing the Vocabulary Routine for each word, point to the word on the card and read it with students. Ask students to repeat the word.

 You Do Have students work with a partner to use two or more words in sentences or questions. Then have each pair read the sentences aloud.

Beginning	Intermediate	Advanced/High
Help students write the sentences correctly and read them aloud.	Ask students to write one sentence and one question.	Challenge students to write a question for each word and then trade with another pair and answer the questions.

REVIEW VOCABULARY

OBJECTIVES

Acquire and use accurately grade-appropriate general academic and domain-specific words and phrases, including those that signal precise actions, emotions, or states of being and that are basic to a particular topic. **L.4.6**

LANGUAGE OBJECTIVE
Use vocabulary words.

 I Do Review the previous week's vocabulary words. The words can be reviewed over a few days. Read each word aloud, pointing to the word on the **Visual Vocabulary Card.** Have students repeat after you. Then follow the Vocabulary Routine on the back of each card.

 We Do Use gestures or physical expressions to pantomime clues for each word. Have students guess the word that you act out and use it in a sentence.

 You Do In pairs, have students act out clues for two words. Then have them pantomime the clues for the class. Have the class guess the word.

Beginning	Intermediate	Advanced/High
Model gestures for words and help students read the words aloud.	Ask students to provide clues for an additional word.	Ask students to provide clues for two additional words.

FIGURATIVE LANGUAGE: IDIOMS

OBJECTIVES

 CCSS Demonstrate understanding of figurative language, word relationships, and nuances in word meanings. Recognize and explain the meaning of common idioms, adages, and proverbs. **L.4.5b**

LANGUAGE OBJECTIVE

Recognize idioms.

I Do Reread the first paragraph of the Comprehension and Fluency passage in the **ELL Reproducibles** pages 13–14. Point out the idiom *butterflies in my stomach*. Explain that an idiom is a group of words with a meaning different than the meaning of each word by itself. Tell students that context clues in the surrounding sentences and paragraphs can help them figure out the meaning of an idiom.

Think Aloud I am not sure what *butterflies in my stomach* means, but context clues can help me understand the meaning. I know the narrator feels sick when he gets on the bus. He is nervous because he has moved to a new school. *Butterflies in my stomach* must mean "to feel nervous."

We Do Have students point to the idiom *right off the bat* on page 13. Work with students to find context clues to figure out the idiom's meaning.

You Do In pairs, have students write a definition for *between a rock and a hard place* on page 14 using context clues.

Beginning	Intermediate	Advanced/High
Help students locate the idiom and the clues on the page.	Ask students to locate and read aloud the clues on the page.	Have students explain how they found the clues on the page.

ADDITIONAL VOCABULARY

OBJECTIVES

CCSS Use knowledge of language and its conventions when writing, speaking, reading, or listening. Choose words and phrases to convey ideas precisely. **L.4.3a**

LANGUAGE OBJECTIVE

Use academic and high-frequency words.

I Do List academic and high-frequency words from "The Talent Show" and *Rosa's Garden: another, idea, group, neighborhood, work,* and *safe*. Define each word: *An idea is a thought, plan, or suggestion about what to do.*

We Do Model using the words in a sentence: *My idea was to leave early. Miranda has an idea for a movie.* Then provide sentence frames and complete them with students: *I have an idea about _____.*

You Do Have pairs describe Rosa's garden, using at least two of the words. Have pairs share their sentences with the class.

Beginning	Intermediate	Advanced/High
Help students write the sentences correctly and read them aloud.	Have students define the words they used.	Ask students to write two sentences about "The Talent Show."

English Language Learners
Writing/Spelling

WRITING TRAIT: IDEAS

 OBJECTIVES
Use dialogue and description to develop experiences and events or show the responses of characters to situations. **W.4.3b**

Clarify ideas.

LANGUAGE OBJECTIVE
Add description to writing.

 I Do
Explain that good writers understand that many small moments can make up an event. Writers use descriptive words to describe each small moment that creates an event. Read the Expert Model passage aloud as students follow along and identify the event.

 We Do
Read aloud page 38 from "The Talent Show" as students follow along. Use a story map to describe what happens when Tina and Maura sit for lunch. Model sentences to describe the event and its individual parts.

 You Do
Have pairs write about an important event or lesson they learned, using their story maps as a reference. Ask them to include details that describe each moment. Edit each pair's writing. Then ask students to revise.

Beginning	Intermediate	Advanced/High
Have students copy the edited sentences.	Have students revise, using relevant details and editing for errors.	Have students revise, expanding on details and editing for errors.

SPELL WORDS WITH LONG *a*

 OBJECTIVES
Spell grade-appropriate words correctly, consulting references as needed. **L.4.2d**

LANGUAGE OBJECTIVE
Spell words with long vowels.

 I Do
Read aloud the Spelling Words on page T100. Elongate the vowel sound. Point out each spelling of long *a*. Have students repeat the words.

 We Do
Read the Dictation Sentences on page T101 aloud for students. With each sentence, read the underlined word slowly. Have students repeat after you and write the word. Repeat the activity with the remaining sentences.

 You Do
Display the words. Have students exchange their list with a partner to check the spelling and write any incorrect words correctly.

Beginning	Intermediate	Advanced/High
Have students copy the words with correct spelling and say the words aloud.	After students have corrected their words, have pairs quiz each other.	After they have corrected their words, have pairs use each word in a sentence.

Grammar

SUBJECTS AND PREDICATES

OBJECTIVES

CCSS Produce complete sentences, recognizing and correcting inappropriate fragments and run-ons. **L.4.1f**

Identify subjects and predicates.

LANGUAGE OBJECTIVES

Write sentences.

Language Transfers Handbook

Speakers of Cantonese and Korean might have difficulty with word order, especially with adverb placement. Write each word on three separate index cards: *Tara, read,* and *silently.* Work with students to build a sentence from the cards and reinforce the adverb placement.

I Do Remind students that every sentence is made up of two parts: a subject and a predicate. Explain that a subject names the person or the thing that the sentence is about and a predicate tells what that person or thing is or does. Write on the board: *Gordon walked.* Underline the subject. Tell students that *Gordon* is the subject of the sentence. Then circle the predicate. Explain that *walked* is the predicate because it describes what Gordon did.

We Do Draw a two-column chart on the board with the heads *Subjects* and *Predicates.* Under *Subjects,* write *The frog, Tara, The dog.* Under *Predicates,* write *barked, hopped,* and *read.* Work with students to match each subject with its predicate, and then read the sentences aloud.

You Do Brainstorm a list of subjects with students. Have students work in pairs, using subjects from the list and adding predicates to form complete sentences.

Beginning	Intermediate	Advanced/High
Have students copy their sentences and help them identify the subject and the predicate. Read the sentences aloud and have students repeat.	Ask students to underline the subjects and circle the predicates in their sentences.	Ask students to underline the subjects and circle the predicates in their sentences. Then have students state the definitions of a subject and a predicate.

For extra support, have students complete the activities in the **Grammar Practice Reproducibles** during the week, using the routine below:

→ Explain the grammar skill.

→ Model the first activity in the Grammar Practice Reproducibles.

→ Have the whole group complete the next couple of activities. Then have students complete the rest with a partner.

→ Review the activities with correct answers.

PROGRESS MONITORING

Weekly Assessment

CCSS TESTED SKILLS

| ✓ **COMPREHENSION:** Problem and Solution **RL.4.3** | ✓ **VOCABULARY:** Idioms **L.4.5b** | ✓ **WRITING:** Writing About Text **RL.4.3, W.4.9a** |

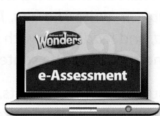

Assessment Includes

→ Pencil-and-paper administration

→ On-line administration

→ Approaching-Level Weekly Assessment also available

 FLUENCY ←

Fluency Goal 84 to 104 words correct per minute (WCPM)

Accuracy Rate Goal 95% or higher

Administer oral reading fluency assessments using the following schedule:

→ **Weeks 1, 3, 5** Provide Approaching-Level students at least three oral reading fluency assessments during the unit.

→ **Weeks 2 and 4** Provide On-Level students at least two oral reading fluency assessments during the unit.

→ **Week 6** If necessary, provide Beyond-Level students an oral reading fluency assessment at this time.

Also Available: Selection Tests online PDFs

Go Digital! www.connected.mcgraw-hill.com

Using Assessment Results

TESTED SKILLS	If ...	Then ...
COMPREHENSION	Students answer 0–6 multiple-choice items correctly ...	... assign Lessons 46–48 on Problem and Solution from the *Tier 2 Comprehension Intervention online PDFs.*
VOCABULARY	Students answer 0–6 multiple-choice items correctly ...	... assign Lesson 166 on Idioms, Proverbs, and Adages from the *Tier 2 Vocabulary Intervention online PDFs.*
WRITING	Students score less than "3" on the constructed response ...	... assign Lessons 46–48 and/or Write About Reading Lesson 194 from the *Tier 2 Comprehension Intervention online PDFs.*
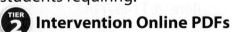	Students have a WCPM score of 76–83 ...	... assign a lesson from Section 1 or 7–10 of the *Tier 2 Fluency Intervention online PDFs.*
	Students have a WCPM score of 0–75 ...	... assign a lesson from Sections 2–6 of the *Tier 2 Fluency Intervention online PDFs.*

Response to Intervention

Use the appropriate sections of the *Placement and Diagnostic Assessment* as well as students' assessment results to designate students requiring:

TIER 2 **Intervention Online PDFs**

TIER 3 **WonderWorks Intervention Program**

WEEKLY OVERVIEW

Text Complexity Range for Grades 4–5

Lexile

740 — 1010

TextEvaluator™

23 — 51

Reading/Writing Workshop

TEACH AND MODEL

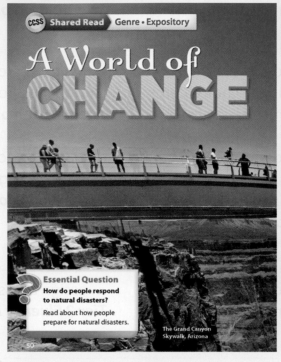

CCSS **Shared Read** Genre · Expository

A World of CHANGE

Essential Question
How do people respond to natural disasters?

Read about how people prepare for natural disasters.

The Grand Canyon Skywalk, Arizona

50

Earth may seem as if it is a large rock that never changes. Actually, our planet is in a constant state of change. Natural changes take place every day. These activities **alter** the surface of Earth. Some of these changes take place slowly over many years. Others happen in just minutes. Whether they are slow or fast, both kinds of changes have a great effect on our planet.

Slow and Steady

Some of Earth's biggest changes can't be seen. That is because they are happening very slowly. Weathering, erosion, and deposition are three natural processes that change the surface of the world. They do it one grain of sand at a time.

Weathering occurs when rain, snow, sun, and wind break down rocks into smaller pieces. These tiny pieces of rock turn into soil, but they are not carried away from the landform.

Erosion occurs when weathered pieces of rock are carried away by a natural force such as a river. This causes landforms on Earth to get smaller. They may even completely **collapse** over time. The Grand Canyon is an example of the effect of erosion. It was carved over thousands of years by the Colorado River.

After the process of erosion, dirt and rocks are then dropped in a new location. This process is called deposition. Over time, a large collection of deposits may occur in one place. Deposition by water can build up a beach. Deposition by wind can create a **substantial** landform, such as a sand dune.

51

✔ Vocabulary

alter

collapse

crisis

destruction

hazard

severe

substantial

unpredictable

Close Reading of Complex Text

Shared Read "A World of Change," 50–53

Genre Expository Text

Lexile 790

 TextEvaluator™ 44

Minilessons

✔ Tested Skills CCSS

✔ **Comprehension Strategy** .... Reread, T146–T147

✔ **Comprehension Skill** .... Compare and Contrast, T148–T149

✔ **Genre** .... Expository Text, T150–T151

✔ **Vocabulary Strategy** .... Context Clues: Multiple-Meaning Words, T152–T153

✔ **Writing Traits** .... Ideas, T158–T159

Grammar .... Compound Sentences, T162–T163

 **Go Digital**

www.connected.mcgraw-hill.com

TAKE ACTION
Essential Question
How do people respond to
natural disasters?

WEEK 3

APPLY WITH CLOSE READING

Complex Text

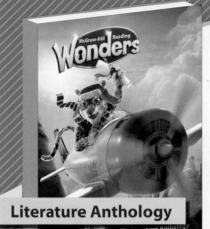

Literature Anthology

Earthquakes, 48–59
Genre Expository Text
Lexile 870
ETS *TextEvaluator* 36

PAIRED READ

"Tornado," 60–61
Genre Expository Text
Lexile 950
ETS *TextEvaluator* 27

Differentiated Text

Leveled Readers *Include Paired Reads*

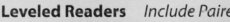

APPROACHING
Lexile 670
ETS *TextEvaluator* 23

ON LEVEL
Lexile 840
ETS *TextEvaluator* 32

BEYOND
Lexile 920
ETS *TextEvaluator* 32

ELL
Lexile 740
ETS *TextEvaluator* 20

Extended Complex Text

*America's Champion
Swimmer: Gertrude
Ederle*
Genre Biography
Lexile 580
ETS *TextEvaluator* 38

*Happy Birthday,
Martin Luther King*
Genre Biography
Lexile 800
ETS *TextEvaluator* 9

Classroom
Library
lessons available
online.

Classroom Library

TEACH AND MANAGE

How You Teach

INTRODUCE

Weekly Concept
Take Action

Reading/Writing Workshop
46–47

 Go Digital

Interactive Whiteboard

TEACH

Close Reading
"A World of Change"

Minilessons
Reread, Compare and Contrast,
Expository, Multiple-Meaning Words,
Writing Traits

Reading/Writing Workshop
50–53

Interactive Whiteboard

APPLY

Close Reading
Earthquakes
"Tornado"

Literature Anthology
48–61

Mobile

How Students Practice

WEEKLY CONTRACT

PDF Online

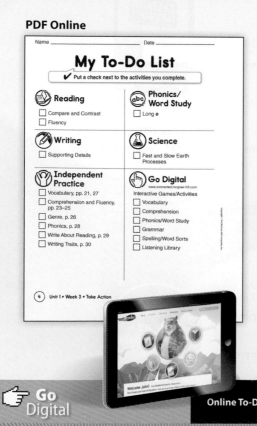

Name _____ Date _____

My To-Do List
✓ Put a check next to the activities you complete.

Reading
☐ Compare and Contrast
☐ Fluency

Phonics/Word Study
☐ Long e

Writing
☐ Supporting Details

Science
☐ Fast and Slow Earth Processes

Independent Practice
☐ Vocabulary, pp. 21, 27
☐ Comprehension and Fluency, pp. 23–25
☐ Genre, p. 26
☐ Phonics, p. 28
☐ Write About Reading, p. 29
☐ Writing Traits, p. 30

Go Digital
www.connected.mcgraw-hill.com
Interactive Games/Activities
☐ Vocabulary
☐ Comprehension
☐ Phonics/Word Study
☐ Grammar
☐ Spelling/Word Sorts
☐ Listening Library

4 Unit 1 • Week 3 • Take Action

 Go Digital
Online To-Do List

LEVELED PRACTICE AND ONLINE ACTIVITIES

Your Turn Practice Book
21–30

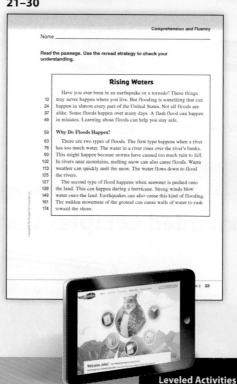

Comprehension and Fluency

Name _____

Read the passage. Use the reread strategy to check your understanding.

Rising Waters

Have you ever been in an earthquake or a tornado? These things may never happen where you live. But flooding is something that can happen in almost every part of the United States. Not all floods are alike. Some floods happen over many days. A flash flood can happen in minutes. Learning about floods can help you stay safe.

Why Do Floods Happen?

There are two types of floods. The first type happens when a river has too much water. The water in a river rises over the river's banks. This might happen because storms have caused too much rain to fall. In rivers near mountains, melting snow can also cause floods. Warm weather can quickly melt the snow. The water flows down to flood the rivers.

The second type of flood happens when seawater is pushed onto the land. This can happen during a hurricane. Strong winds blow water onto the land. Earthquakes can also cause this kind of flooding. The sudden movement of the ground can cause walls of water to rush toward the shore.

Leveled Activities

Leveled Readers

Writer's Workspace

DIFFERENTIATE

SMALL GROUP INSTRUCTION
Leveled Readers

Mobile

INTEGRATE

Research and Inquiry
Poster, T156

Text Connections
Compare Responses to Natural Disasters, T157

Analytical Writing **Write About Reading**
Write an Analysis, T157

Online Research and Writing

ASSESS

Weekly Assessment
25–36

Online Assessment

LEVELED WORKSTATION CARDS

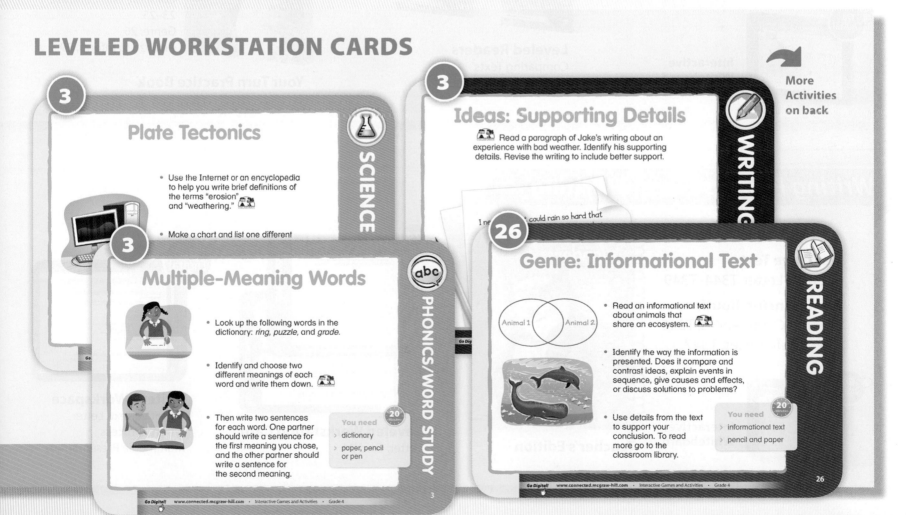

3

Plate Tectonics

SCIENCE

- Use the Internet or an encyclopedia to help you write brief definitions of the terms "erosion" and "weathering."

- Make a chart and list one different

3

Multiple-Meaning Words

PHONICS/WORD STUDY

- Look up the following words in the dictionary: *ring*, *puzzle*, and *grade*.

- Identify and choose two different meanings of each word and write them down.

- Then write two sentences for each word. One partner should write a sentence for the first meaning you chose, and the other partner should write a sentence for the second meaning.

You need
- dictionary
- paper, pencil or pen

20

3

Ideas: Supporting Details

WRITING

Read a paragraph of Jake's writing about an experience with bad weather. Identify his supporting details. Revise the writing to include better support.

I need . . . could rain so hard that

More Activities on back

26

Genre: Informational Text

READING

Animal 1   Animal 2

- Read an informational text about animals that share an ecosystem.

- Identify the way the information is presented. Does it compare and contrast ideas, explain events in sequence, give causes and effects, or discuss solutions to problems?

- Use details from the text to support your conclusion. To read more go to the classroom library.

You need
- informational text
- pencil and paper

20

26

Go Digital! www.connected.mcgraw-hill.com • Interactive Games and Activities • Grade 4

DEVELOPING READERS AND WRITERS

Write About Reading • Analytical Writing

Write to Sources and Research

Summary, T148–T149

Note Taking, T153B, T153M

Summarize, T153L

Compare and Contrast, T153L

Make Connections: Essential Question, T153L, T153N, T157

Research and Inquiry, T156

Analyze to Inform/Explain, T157

Comparing Texts, T159, T177, T181, T187

Predictive Writing, T153B

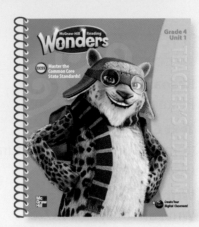

Teacher's Edition

Literature Anthology

Summarize, 59
Compare and Contrast, 59

Interactive Whiteboard

Leveled Readers
Comparing Texts
Compare and Contrast

Your Turn Practice Book

Compare and Contrast, 23–25
Genre, 26
Analyze to Inform, 29

Writing Process • Genre Writing

Narrative Text
Friendly Letter, T344–T349

Conferencing Routines
Teacher Conferences, T346
Peer Conferences, T347

Interactive Whiteboard

Teacher's Edition

Leveled Workstation Card
Letter, Card 24

Writer's Workspace
Narrative Text: Letter
Writing Process
Multimedia Presentations

Writing Traits • Write Every Day

Writing Trait: Ideas
Supporting Details, T158–T159

Conferencing Routines
Teacher Conferences, T160
Peer Conferences, T161

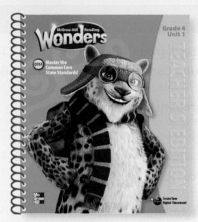

Teacher's Edition

Ideas: Supporting
Details, 58–59

Reading/Writing Workshop

**Interactive
Whiteboard**

Ideas:
Supporting
Details, 3

Leveled Workstation Card

Ideas: Supporting
Details, 30

Your Turn Practice Book

Grammar and Spelling

Grammar
Compound Sentences,
T162–T163

Spelling
Long *e*, T164–T165

**Interactive
Whiteboard**

Teacher's Edition

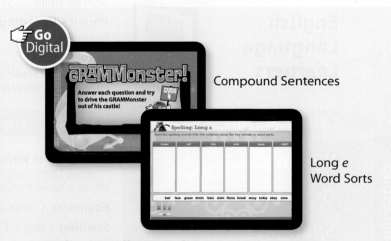

Compound Sentences

Long *e*
Word Sorts

Online Spelling and Grammar Games

SUGGESTED LESSON PLAN

		DAY 1	DAY 2

READING

Whole Group

Teach, Model and Apply

Reading/Writing Workshop

DAY 1

Build Background Take Action, T138–T139

Listening Comprehension Interactive Read Aloud: "Avalanche!", T140–T141

Comprehension
• Preview Genre: Expository Text
• Preview Strategy: Reread

✔ **Vocabulary** Words in Context, T142–T143

Practice *Your Turn*, 21

Close Reading of Complex Text "A World of Change," 50–53

DAY 2

✔ **Comprehension**
• Strategy: Reread, T146–T147
• Skill: Compare and Contrast, T148–T149
• Write About Reading *Analytical Writing*
• Genre: Expository Text, T150–T151

✔ **Vocabulary** Strategy: Multiple-Meaning Words, T152–T153

Practice *Your Turn*, 22–27

DIFFERENTIATED INSTRUCTION   Choose across the week to meet your students' needs.

Small Group

Approaching Level

DAY 1

Leveled Reader *Changing Landscapes*, T168–T169

Phonics/Decoding Decode Words with Double *e*, T170 **TIER 2**

Vocabulary
• Review High-Frequency Words, T172 **TIER 2**
• Answer Yes/No Questions, T173

DAY 2

Leveled Reader *Changing Landscapes*, T168–T169

Vocabulary Review Vocabulary Words, T172 **TIER 2**

Comprehension
• Identify Details to Compare and Contrast, T174 **TIER 2**
• Review Compare and Contrast, T175

On Level

DAY 1

Leveled Reader *Changing Landscapes*, T176–T177

Vocabulary Review Vocabulary Words, T178

DAY 2

Leveled Reader *Changing Landscapes*, T176–T177

Comprehension Review Compare and Contrast, T179

Beyond Level

DAY 1

Leveled Reader *Changing Landscapes*, T180–T181

Vocabulary Review Domain-Specific Words, T182

DAY 2

Leveled Reader *Changing Landscapes*, T180–T181

Comprehension Review Compare and Contrast, T183

English Language Learners

DAY 1

Shared Read "A World of Change," T184–T185

Phonics/Decoding Decode Words with Double *e*, T170

Vocabulary
• Preteach Vocabulary, T188
• Review High-Frequency Words, T172

DAY 2

Leveled Reader *Changing Landscapes*, T186–T187

Vocabulary Review Vocabulary, T188

Writing Writing Trait: Ideas, T190

Grammar Simple and Compound Sentences, T191

LANGUAGE ARTS   Writing Process: Friendly Letter, T344–T349   Use with Weeks 1–3

Whole Group

Writing

Grammar

Spelling

Build Vocabulary

DAY 1

✔ **Readers to Writers**
• Writing Traits: Ideas/Supporting Details, T158–T159
• Writing Entry: Prewrite and Draft, T160

Grammar Compound Sentences, T162

Spelling Long *e*, T164

Build Vocabulary
• Connect to Words, T166
• Academic Vocabulary, T166

DAY 2

Readers to Writers
• Writing Entry: Revise, T160

Grammar Compound Sentences, T162

Spelling Long *e*, T164

Build Vocabulary
• Expand Vocabulary, T166
• Review Idioms, T166

DAY 3	DAY 4	DAY 5 Review and Assess

READING

Phonics/Decoding
• Long e, T154
• Plurals, T155

Practice Your Turn, 28

Close Reading Earthquakes, 48–59 • *Analytical Writing*

Literature Anthology

Fluency Accuracy, T155
Integrate Ideas • *Analytical Writing*
• Research and Inquiry, T156

Practice Your Turn, 23–25

Close Reading "Tornado," 60–61 • *Analytical Writing*

Integrate Ideas • *Analytical Writing*
• Research and Inquiry, T156
• Text Connections, T157
• Write About Reading, T157

Practice Your Turn, 29

DIFFERENTIATED INSTRUCTION

Leveled Reader Changing Landscapes, T168–T169
Phonics/Decoding Review Words with Long e, T170 **TIER 2**
Fluency Accuracy, T174 **TIER 2**
Vocabulary Context Clues: Multiple-Meaning Words, T173

Leveled Reader Paired Read: "Students Save Wetlands," T169 • *Analytical Writing*
Phonics/Decoding Practice Words with Long e, T171

Leveled Reader Literature Circles, T169
Comprehension Self-Selected Reading, T175
Phonics/Decoding Plural Nouns, T171

Leveled Reader Changing Landscapes, T176–T177
Vocabulary Context Clues: Multiple-Meaning Words, T178

Leveled Reader Paired Read: "Students Save Wetlands," T177 • *Analytical Writing*

Leveled Reader Literature Circles, T177
Comprehension Self-Selected Reading, T179

Leveled Reader Changing Landscapes, T180–T181
Vocabulary
• Context Clues: Multiple-Meaning Words, T182
• Synthesize, T182

Gifted and Talented

Leveled Reader Paired Read: "Students Save Wetlands," T181 • *Analytical Writing*

Leveled Reader Literature Circles, T181
Comprehension
• Self-Selected Reading, T183
• Evaluate: Take Action, T183

Leveled Reader Changing Landscapes, T186–T187
Phonics/Decoding Review Words with Long e, T170
Vocabulary Context Clues: Multiple-Meaning Words, T189
Spelling Words with Long e, T190

Leveled Reader Paired Read: "Students Save Wetlands," T187 • *Analytical Writing*
Vocabulary Additional Vocabulary, T189
Phonics/Decoding Practice Words with Long e, T171

Leveled Reader Literature Circles, T187
Phonics/Decoding Plural Nouns, T171

LANGUAGE ARTS

Readers to Writers
• Writing Entry: Prewrite and Draft, T161

Grammar Mechanics and Usage, T163

Spelling Long e, T165

Build Vocabulary
• Reinforce the Words, T167
• Multiple-Meaning Words, T167

Readers to Writers
• Writing Entry: Revise, T161

Grammar Compound Sentences, T163

Spelling Long e, T165

Build Vocabulary
• Connect to Writing, T167
• Shades of Meaning, T167

Readers to Writers
• Writing Entry: Share and Reflect, T161

Grammar Compound Sentences, T163

Spelling Long e, T165

Build Vocabulary
• Word Squares, T167
• Morphology, T167

DIFFERENTIATE TO ACCELERATE

A C T Scaffold to Access Complex Text

IF ➤ the text complexity of a particular selection is too difficult for students

THEN ➤ see the references noted in the chart below for scaffolded instruction to help students Access Complex Text.

Qualitative · Quantitative
Reader and Task
TEXT COMPLEXITY

Reading/Writing Workshop	Literature Anthology	Leveled Readers	Classroom Library
		 Approaching · On Level · Beyond · ELL	

Quantitative

Reading/Writing Workshop

"A World of Change"
Lexile 790
TextEvaluator™ 44

Literature Anthology

Earthquakes
Lexile 870
TextEvaluator™ 36

"Tornado"
Lexile 950
TextEvaluator™ 27

Leveled Readers

Approaching Level
Lexile 670
TextEvaluator™ 23

Beyond Level
Lexile 920
TextEvaluator™ 32

On Level
Lexile 840
TextEvaluator™ 32

ELL
Lexile 740
TextEvaluator™ 20

Classroom Library

America's Champion Swimmer: Gertrude Ederle
Lexile 580
TextEvaluator™ 38

Happy Birthday, Martin Luther King
Lexile 800
TextEvaluator™ 9

Qualitative

What Makes the Text Complex?
- **Specific Vocabulary** Greek and Roman Myths T145
- **Purpose** Diagrams T151

A C T *See Scaffolded Instruction in Teacher's Edition T145 and T151.*

What Makes the Text Complex?
- **Organization** Text Structure T153A
- **Purpose** Firsthand Account T153D
- **Genre** Maps; Sidebar T153I
- **Connection of Ideas** Information T153E; Tornadoes T153N
- **Specific Vocabulary** Unfamiliar Words T153G, T153M

A C T *See Scaffolded Instruction in Teacher's Edition T153A–T153N.*

What Makes the Text Complex?
- **Specific Vocabulary**
- **Prior Knowledge**
- **Sentence Structure**
- **Connection of Ideas**
- **Genre**

A C T *See Level Up lessons online for Leveled Readers.*

What Makes the Text Complex?
- **Genre**
- **Specific Vocabulary**
- **Prior Knowledge**
- **Sentence Structure**
- **Organization**
- **Purpose**
- **Connection of Ideas**

A C T *See Scaffolded Instruction in Teacher's Edition T360–T361.*

Reader and Task

The Introduce the Concept lesson on pages T138–T139 will help determine the reader's knowledge and engagement in the weekly concept. See pages T144–T153 and T156–T157 for questions and tasks for this text.

The Introduce the Concept lesson on pages T138–T139 will help determine the reader's knowledge and engagement in the weekly concept. See pages T153A–T153N and T156–T157 for questions and tasks for this text.

The Introduce the Concept lesson on pages T138–T139 will help determine the reader's knowledge and engagement in the weekly concept. See pages T168–T169, T176–T177, T180–T181, T186–T187, and T156–T157 for questions and tasks for this text.

The Introduce the Concept lesson on pages T138–T139 will help determine the reader's knowledge and engagement in the weekly concept. See pages T360–T361 for questions and tasks for this text.

Monitor and *Differentiate*

IF you need to differentiate instruction

THEN use the Quick Checks to assess students' needs and select the appropriate small group instruction focus.

 Quick Check

Comprehension Strategy Reread T147

Comprehension Skill Text Structure: Compare and Contrast T149

Genre Expository Text T151

Vocabulary Strategy Context Clues T153

Phonics/Fluency Long *e* T155

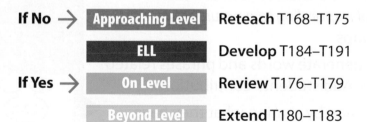

If No →	Approaching Level	Reteach T168–T175
	ELL	Develop T184–T191
If Yes →	On Level	Review T176–T179
	Beyond Level	Extend T180–T183

Level Up with Leveled Readers

IF students can read their leveled text fluently and answer comprehension questions

THEN work with the next level up to accelerate students' reading with more complex text.

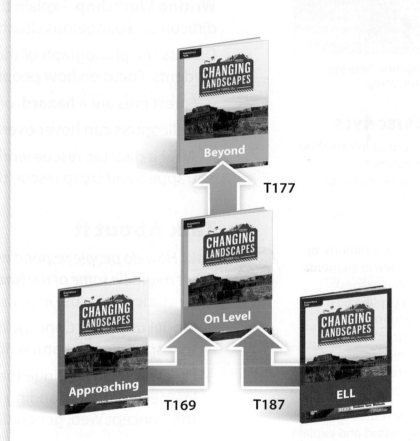

T177

On Level

T169   T187

ENGLISH LANGUAGE LEARNERS
SCAFFOLD

IF ELL students need additional support **THEN** scaffold instruction using the small group suggestions.

Reading/Writing Workshop "A World of Change" T184–T185	Leveled Reader *Changing Landscapes* T186–T187 "Students Save Wetlands" T187	Additional Vocabulary T189 landscape change constant natural remove shape surface	Using Context Clues: Multiple-Meaning Words T189	Writing Ideas T190	Spelling Words with Long *e* T190	Grammar Simple and Compound Sentences T191

Note: Include ELL Students in all small groups based on their needs.

Introduce the Concept

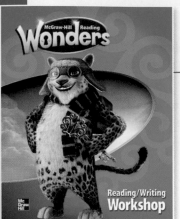

Reading/Writing Workshop

OBJECTIVES

CCSS Interpret information presented visually, orally, or quantitatively (e.g., in charts, graphs, diagrams, time lines, animations, or interactive elements on Web pages) and explain how the information contributes to an understanding of the text in which it appears. **RI.4.7**

CCSS Review the key ideas expressed and explain their own ideas and understanding in light of the discussion. **SL.4.1d**

Build background knowledge on responding to natural disasters.

 MINILESSON 10 Mins

Build Background

ESSENTIAL QUESTION
How do people respond to natural disasters?

Have students read the Essential Question on page 46 of the **Reading/Writing Workshop**. Explain that a natural disaster can cause a **crisis**, a difficult and dangerous situation.

Discuss the photograph of the helicopter responding to a fire with students. Focus on how people respond to natural disasters.

→ Forest fires are a **hazard**, or danger, during the dry, windy season.

→ Helicopters can hover over a fire and drop water on it.

→ After a disaster, rescue workers search for people who may be trapped and try to rescue them.

Talk About It

 COLLABORATE

Ask: *How do people respond when there is a **crisis** or natural disaster? What might be some of the **hazards** of responding to a natural disaster?* Have students discuss in pairs or groups.

→ Model using the Concept Web to generate words and phrases related to responding to natural disasters. Add students' contributions.

→ Have partners continue the discussion by sharing what they have learned about responding to natural disasters. They can complete the Concept Web, generating additional related words and phrases.

 Go Digital

Discuss the Concept

Watch Video

Natural Disasters

Use Graphic Organizer

Collaborative Conversations

Listen Carefully As students engage in partner, small-group, and whole-class discussions, encourage them to follow discussion rules by listening carefully to speakers. Remind students to

→ always look at the person who is speaking.

→ respect others by not interrupting them.

→ repeat peers' ideas to check understanding.

Weekly Concept Take Action

Essential Question
How do people respond to natural disasters?

Go Digital!

To the Rescue

Natural disasters are events such as hurricanes, earthquakes, floods, and forest fires. When these kinds of events occur, it can cause a huge crisis in a community. Luckily, there are people who are trained to respond to natural disasters.

► How might people respond to a forest fire?

► How do you think people are rescued during a flood?

► What are some ways that people might respond during other kinds of natural disasters?

Talk About It

Write words you have learned about responding to natural disasters. Then talk to a partner about what you might do to help after a natural disaster.

Natural Disasters

46 | 47

READING/WRITING WORKSHOP, pp. 46–47

GRAPHIC ORGANIZER 62

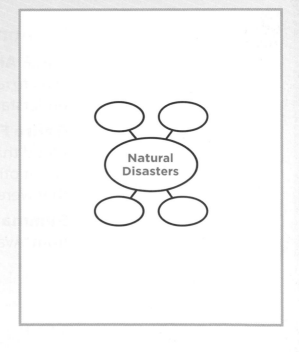

Natural Disasters

ELL ENGLISH LANGUAGE LEARNERS SCAFFOLD

Beginning	**Intermediate**	**Advanced/High**
Use Visuals Point to the fire. Say: *This is a forest fire. It is a natural disaster. Fires can be dangerous.* Help students fill in the sentence frame: *A fire is a ____. It is dangerous.* Repeat slowly and clearly for the class to hear.	**Describe** Have students describe the photograph. Ask: *Why are forest fires a hazard? How is the person in the helicopter responding to the crisis?* Elicit details to support students' responses.	**Discuss** Ask students to think of ways that people respond to natural disasters. *How might rescue workers respond to a natural disaster?* Ask questions to help them elaborate.

Listening Comprehension

MINILESSON
10 Mins

Interactive Read Aloud

View Photos

OBJECTIVES

CCSS Paraphrase portions of a text read aloud or information presented in diverse media and formats, including visually, quantitatively, and orally. **SL.4.2**

• Listen for a purpose.
• Identify characteristics of expository text.

ACADEMIC LANGUAGE

• *expository text, reread*
• Cognate: *texto expositivo*

Connect to Concept: Take Action

Tell students that an avalanche is a natural event that can be dangerous. Let students know that you will be reading aloud a passage about how avalanches form and ways that people take action to prevent and control them. As students listen, have them think about how the passage answers the Essential Question.

Preview Genre: Expository Text

Explain that the passage you will read aloud is an expository text. Discuss features of expository text:

→ provides facts and details about a topic

→ may have headings and subheadings to help readers locate information

→ may include text features such as photographs, maps, or graphs

Preview Comprehension Strategy: Reread

Point out that when reading expository text, good readers can read the text again, or reread, to help them better understand anything that was unclear. They can also reread to help them remember important facts and details.

Use the Think Alouds on page T141 to model the strategy.

Respond to Reading

Think Aloud Clouds Display Think Aloud Master 4: *When I read _____, I had to reread . . .* to reinforce how you used the reread strategy to understand content.

When I read _____, I had to reread...

Model Think Alouds

Genre Features With students, discuss the elements of the Read Aloud that let them know it is an expository text. Ask them to think about other texts that you have read or they have read independently that were expository text.

Genre	Features

Fill in Genre Chart

Summarize Have students restate the most important information from "Avalanche!" in their own words.

Avalanche!

An avalanche is a slab of snow that slides quickly down a mountain. As the snow mass moves, it picks up more snow. It grows larger and more deadly as it plunges down the slope. Each year more than 150 people die when they become trapped under the sliding snow. **1**

Common Triggers

An avalanche must be triggered by another force. New snow, brisk wind, or a loud noise can cause a heavy snow mass to break away. More often, people on skis, snowboards, or snowmobiles act as a trigger. **2**

Prevention and Rescue

Trees are the best natural defense against an avalanche. But in many places trees have been cut for wood or to form ski slopes. In some areas experts create small, controlled snow slides. Before the slopes are open to skiers, they use cannons or other blasts to break up a large snow mass. **3**

Taking a safety course is the best way to avoid or live through an avalanche. Skiers and others on the slopes are told to go with a friend. It is also key to have the right tools. A beacon sends out a beep that tells searchers where to dig. A probe helps find someone who has been buried. It can also tell the depth of snow. A shovel can be used to dig out. With these avalanche safety tips in mind, people can continue enjoying winter sports—and nature at its finest.

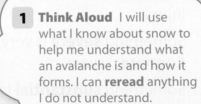

1 **Think Aloud** I will use what I know about snow to help me understand what an avalanche is and how it forms. I can **reread** anything I do not understand.

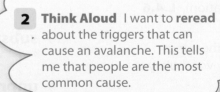

2 **Think Aloud** I want to **reread** about the triggers that can cause an avalanche. This tells me that people are the most common cause.

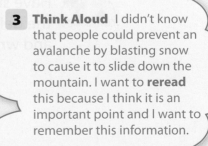

3 **Think Aloud** I didn't know that people could prevent an avalanche by blasting snow to cause it to slide down the mountain. I want to **reread** this because I think it is an important point and I want to remember this information.

→ Vocabulary

Reading/Writing Workshop

Wonders

McGraw-Hill Reading

Reading/Writing Workshop

MINILESSON 10 Mins

Words in Context

Model the Routine

Introduce each vocabulary word using the Vocabulary Routine found on the Visual Vocabulary Cards.

Visual Vocabulary Cards

Vocabu...
Define:
Example:
Ask:

Vocabulary Routine

Define: To **alter** means to make different or change.

Example: The ocean waves slowly alter the shoreline by carving away the rocks.

Ask: How can people alter their appearance?

CCSS OBJECTIVES

Acquire and use accurately grade-appropriate general academic and domain-specific words and phrases, including those that signal precise actions, emotions, or states of being (e.g., *quizzed, whined, stammered*) and that are basic to a particular topic (e.g., *wildlife, conservation,* and *endangered* when discussing animal preservation). **L.4.6**

- Learn meanings of new vocabulary words.
- Use new words in sentences.

Definitions

→ **collapse**   To **collapse** means to fall down or cave in.

→ **crisis**   A **crisis** is a difficult or dangerous situation.

→ **destruction**   **Destruction** is great damage or ruin.
    Cognate: *destrucción*

→ **hazard**   A **hazard** is something that can cause harm or injury.

→ **severe**   Something **severe** is very harsh or serious.
    Cognate: *severo*

→ **substantial**   Something **substantial** is of a great amount or size.
    Cognate: *sustancial*

→ **unpredictable**   **Unpredictable** means not able to tell beforehand.

Talk About It

COLLABORATE

Have students work with a partner and look at each picture and discuss the definition of each word. Then ask students to choose three words and write questions for their partner to answer.

alter

Use Visual Glossary

Go Digital

CCSS Words to Know

Vocabulary

Use the picture and the sentences to talk with a partner about each word.

alter

The ocean waves slowly **alter** the shoreline by carving away the rocks.

How can people alter their appearance?

collapse

Flood waters caused the bridge to **collapse**.

What might cause a tent to collapse?

crisis

Rescue workers help people during an emergency or a **crisis,** such as a flood.

How would you react to a crisis?

destruction

The tornado destroyed buildings and caused a lot of other **destruction**.

What is a synonym for destruction?

hazard

The water was a **hazard** to people driving on the street.

What else might be a hazard to people who are driving?

severe

Severe weather can include very strong winds and heavy rain.

Describe severe winter weather.

substantial

We got a **substantial** amount of snow last night.

What is an antonym for substantial?

unpredictable

The **unpredictable** weather turned suddenly from sun to rain.

What is an antonym for unpredictable?

Your Turn

COLLABORATE

Pick three words. Write three questions for your partner to answer.

Go Digital! *Use the online visual glossary*

48

49

READING/WRITING WORKSHOP, pp. 48–49

ELL ENGLISH LANGUAGE LEARNERS SCAFFOLD

Beginning

Use Visuals *Let's look at the picture for the word* alter. Point to the waves and rocks. Say: *The waves alter the rocks.* Elicit that another word for *alter* is *change.* Demonstrate the word *alter* by drawing on a copy of a picture. Say: *I have altered the picture.* Have students repeat.

Intermediate

Describe Have students describe the picture for the word *alter.* Help them with the pronunciation. Say: *Think about ways you can alter, or change, your appearance.* Turn to a partner and give two examples.

Advanced/High

Discuss Have students write a definition for the word *alter* and share their definitions with the class. Correct students' responses as needed. Then have partners make a list of ways they can alter the classroom.

ON-LEVEL PRACTICE BOOK p. 21

| alter | collapse | destruction | severe |
| substantial | unpredictable | hazard | crisis |

Finish each sentence using the vocabulary word provided.
Possible responses provided.

1. **(alter)** When she saw that it was going to rain, she had to *alter* what she was wearing.

2. **(collapse)** The fort we made of sticks was so fragile, we knew it would *collapse* when the wind hit it.

3. **(destruction)** When the tidal wave hit the trees on the beach, there was total *destruction*.

4. **(severe)** The show was interrupted with the announcement that a *severe* storm was coming.

5. **(substantial)** Having to rebuild after the storm would take a *substantial* amount of work.

6. **(unpredictable)** We tried to catch the firefly, but its movements were *unpredictable*.

7. **(hazard)** When our neighborhood flooded, the roads became a *hazard*.

8. **(crisis)** When all the lights went out in town, we found ourselves in a *crisis*.

| APPROACHING | BEYOND | ELL |
| p. 21 | p. 21 | p. 21 |

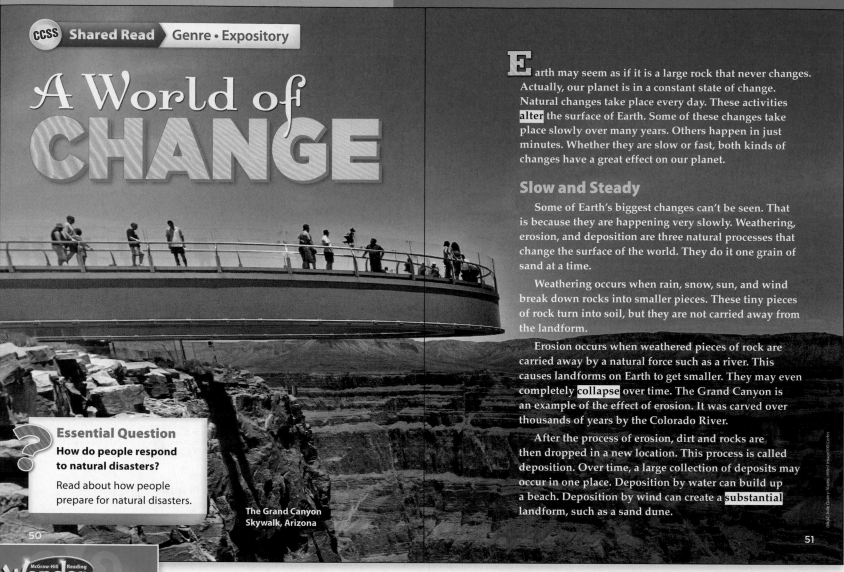

CCSS Shared Read | Genre · Expository

A World of CHANGE

Essential Question

How do people respond to natural disasters?

Read about how people prepare for natural disasters.

The Grand Canyon Skywalk, Arizona

50

Earth may seem as if it is a large rock that never changes. Actually, our planet is in a constant state of change. Natural changes take place every day. These activities **alter** the surface of Earth. Some of these changes take place slowly over many years. Others happen in just minutes. Whether they are slow or fast, both kinds of changes have a great effect on our planet.

Slow and Steady

Some of Earth's biggest changes can't be seen. That is because they are happening very slowly. Weathering, erosion, and deposition are three natural processes that change the surface of the world. They do it one grain of sand at a time.

Weathering occurs when rain, snow, sun, and wind break down rocks into smaller pieces. These tiny pieces of rock turn into soil, but they are not carried away from the landform.

Erosion occurs when weathered pieces of rock are carried away by a natural force such as a river. This causes landforms on Earth to get smaller. They may even completely **collapse** over time. The Grand Canyon is an example of the effect of erosion. It was carved over thousands of years by the Colorado River.

After the process of erosion, dirt and rocks are then dropped in a new location. This process is called deposition. Over time, a large collection of deposits may occur in one place. Deposition by water can build up a beach. Deposition by wind can create a **substantial** landform, such as a sand dune.

51

McGraw-Hill Reading Wonders

Reading/Writing Workshop

READING/WRITING WORKSHOP, pp. 50–51

Shared Read

Lexile 790L   *TextEvaluator*™ 44

Connect to Concept: Take Action

Explain to students that "A World of Change" will tell them more about natural disasters and how people respond to them. Read "A World of Change" with students. Note the vocabulary words previously taught are highlighted in the text.

Close Reading

Reread Paragraph 1: Tell students that you are going to take a closer look at the first paragraph. Reread the first paragraph together. Ask: *How are the natural changes that affect Earth different? What do they have in common?* Model how to cite evidence to answer the question.

The speed of the changes can be different. The author states that some changes take place slowly over many years and some can happen very fast. But the author says that both fast and slow changes have a great effect on the planet.

Reread Paragraph 2: Model how to use text features in the second paragraph. Remind students that headings often give clues about the topic of the next section.

The second paragraph has a heading called "Slow and Steady." The second paragraph also lists three different changes that happen slowly. This section will probably be about slow changes.

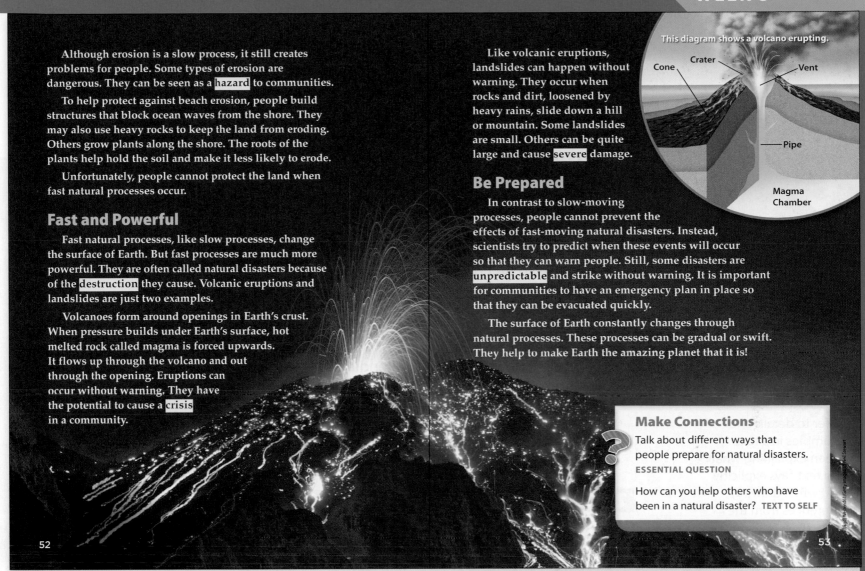

Although erosion is a slow process, it still creates problems for people. Some types of erosion are dangerous. They can be seen as a hazard to communities.

To help protect against beach erosion, people build structures that block ocean waves from the shore. They may also use heavy rocks to keep the land from eroding. Others grow plants along the shore. The roots of the plants help hold the soil and make it less likely to erode.

Unfortunately, people cannot protect the land when fast natural processes occur.

Fast and Powerful

Fast natural processes, like slow processes, change the surface of Earth. But fast processes are much more powerful. They are often called natural disasters because of the destruction they cause. Volcanic eruptions and landslides are just two examples.

Volcanoes form around openings in Earth's crust. When pressure builds under Earth's surface, hot melted rock called magma is forced upwards. It flows up through the volcano and out through the opening. Eruptions can occur without warning. They have the potential to cause a crisis in a community.

Like volcanic eruptions, landslides can happen without warning. They occur when rocks and dirt, loosened by heavy rains, slide down a hill or mountain. Some landslides are small. Others can be quite large and cause severe damage.

Be Prepared

In contrast to slow-moving processes, people cannot prevent the effects of fast-moving natural disasters. Instead, scientists try to predict when these events will occur so that they can warn people. Still, some disasters are unpredictable and strike without warning. It is important for communities to have an emergency plan in place so that they can be evacuated quickly.

The surface of Earth constantly changes through natural processes. These processes can be gradual or swift. They help to make Earth the amazing planet that it is!

This diagram shows a volcano erupting.

Cone · Crater · Vent · Pipe · Magma Chamber

Make Connections

Talk about different ways that people prepare for natural disasters. **ESSENTIAL QUESTION**

How can you help others who have been in a natural disaster? **TEXT TO SELF**

52 · 53

READING/WRITING WORKSHOP, pp. 52–53

Make Connections

ESSENTIAL QUESTION

Encourage students to go back into the text for evidence as they talk about the different ways that people respond to natural disasters. Ask students to explain how people prepare for natural disasters as well.

Continue Close Reading

Use the following lessons for focused rereadings.

→ Reread, T146–T147

→ Compare and Contrast, T148–T149

→ Expository Text, T150–151

→ Context Clues, T152–T153

ACT Access Complex Text

▶ Specific Vocabulary

Explain that words can come from names in Greek or Roman myth. Point to the words *volcanic* and *volcanoes* on page 52. Tell students that these words come from the name of the Roman god of fire, Vulcan.

→ *How is Vulcan related to what you know about volcanoes?* (Both are related to fire.)

→ *Find out more about Vulcan. Use the information to write a definition of* volcano. (A volcano is an opening in Earth's crust where fiery magma and ash come out.)

Comprehension Strategy

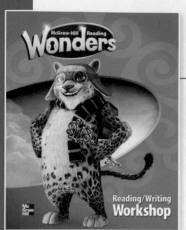

Reading/Writing Workshop

 OBJECTIVES

CCSS Refer to details and examples in a text when explaining what the text says explicitly and when drawing inferences from the text. **RI.4.1**

Reread difficult sections to increase understanding.

ACADEMIC LANGUAGE

• *reread, informational text*

• Cognate: *texto informativo*

MINILESSON 10 Mins

Reread

1 Explain

Explain that when they read informational text, students may come across facts and explanations that are new to them. Remind students that they can reread challenging sections of the text to increase their understanding.

→ Good readers reread something that they do not understand.

→ When they encounter challenging text, students can reread that section. They may need to reread more than once to make sure they understand.

→ Students may find that that rereading improves their comprehension of informational texts.

2 Model Close Reading: Text Evidence

Model how rereading can help you understand why a volcano erupts. Reread the section called "Fast and Powerful" on page 52 of "A World of Change."

3 Guided Practice of Close Reading

Have students work in pairs to explain what happens to rock during weathering. Direct them to reread the "Slow and Steady" section of "A World of Change." Partners can reread the section and find out what happens to rock during weathering. Have partners discuss other sections of "A World of Change" that they might want to reread.

Go Digital

View "A World of Change"

Comprehension Strategy

Reread

When you read an informational text, you may come across facts and ideas that are new to you. As you read "A World of Change," you can reread the difficult sections to make sure you understand them and to help you remember key details.

Find Text Evidence

You may not be sure why a volcano erupts. Reread the section "Fast and Powerful" on page 52 of "A World of Change."

page 52

Fast and Powerful

Fast natural processes, like slow processes, change the surface of Earth. But fast processes are much more powerful. They are often called natural disasters because of the **destruction** they cause. Volcanic eruptions and landslides are just two examples.

Volcanoes form around openings in Earth's crust. When pressure builds under Earth's surface, hot melted rock called magma is forced upwards. It flows up through the volcano and out through the opening. Eruptions can occur without warning. They have the potential to cause a **crisis** in a community.

I read that when pressure builds under Earth's surface, magma is forced upwards. From this I can draw the inference that pressure below the surface causes a volcano to erupt.

 Your Turn

What happens to rock during weathering? Reread the section "Slow and Steady" on page 51 to find out. As you read, remember to use the strategy Reread.

54

READING/WRITING WORKSHOP, p. 54

 Monitor and *Differentiate*

✓ Quick Check

Do students reread informational text that they do not understand? Do they read it more than once if necessary?

⬇

Small Group Instruction

If No → | Approaching Level | Reteach p. T168
| ELL | Develop p. T184

If Yes → | On Level | Review p. T176
| Beyond Level | Extend p. T180

ENGLISH LANGUAGE LEARNERS SCAFFOLD

Beginning	**Intermediate**	**Advanced/High**
Clarify the Meaning Help students reread "Fast and Powerful" on page 52. Point out difficult words, such as *processes, surface,* and *pressure*. Define the words and give examples for students. Then help students replace the words with words they know and use them in a sentence.	**Describe** Have students reread "Fast and Powerful" on page 52. Ask: *What causes volcanoes to erupt?* (pressure under Earth's surface) Point out why this text is difficult. The passage describes the fast natural process of volcanic eruptions, using specific vocabulary.	**Explain** Have students reread "Fast and Powerful" on page 52. Elicit from students why the text is challenging. Ask: *What causes volcanoes to erupt? Why is this important? Turn to a partner and explain.*

ON-LEVEL PRACTICE BOOK pp. 23–24

Read the passage. Use the reread strategy to check your understanding.

Rising Waters

Have you ever been in an earthquake or a tornado? These things
12 may never happen where you live. But flooding is something that can
24 happen in almost every part of the United States. Not all floods are
37 alike. Some floods happen over many days. A flash flood can happen
49 in minutes. Learning about floods can help you stay safe.

59 **Why Do Floods Happen?**

63 There are two types of floods. The first type happens when a river
76 has too much water. The water in a river rises over the river's banks.
90 This might happen because storms have caused too much rain to fall.
102 In rivers near mountains, melting snow can also cause floods. Warm
113 weather can quickly melt the snow. The water flows down to flood
125 the rivers.
127 The second type of flood happens when seawater is pushed onto
138 the land. This can happen during a hurricane. Strong winds blow
149 water onto the land. Earthquakes can also cause this kind of flooding.
161 The sudden movement of the ground can cause walls of water to rush
174 toward the shore.

| APPROACHING pp. 23–24 | BEYOND pp. 23–24 | ELL pp. 23–24 |

→ Comprehension Skill

MINILESSON
10 Mins

Text Structure: Compare and Contrast

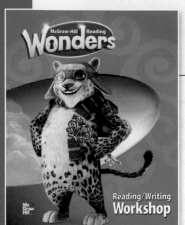

Reading/Writing Workshop

OBJECTIVES

CCSS Describe the overall structure (e.g., chronology, comparison, cause/ effect, problem/ solution) of events, ideas, concepts, or information in a text or part of a text. **RI.4.5**

Identify comparisons and contrasts.

ACADEMIC LANGUAGE
- compare, contrast
- Cognates: *comparar, contrastar*

1 Explain

Explain that text structure is a way that authors organize a text. Comparison and contrast is one kind of text structure. It shows how things are alike and different.

→ When you compare, you tell how things are alike.

→ When you contrast, you tell how things are different.

→ An author may use signal words such as *same, but, both,* and *like* to signal comparisons.

2 Model Close Reading: Text Evidence

Identify similarities between slow and fast natural processes on pages 51–52 of "A World of Change." Then identify the differences. Model using this information to fill out the graphic organizer to compare and contrast slow and fast natural processes.

 Write About Reading: Summary Model for students how to use the notes from the graphic organizer to summarize how slow and fast natural processes are similar and different.

3 Guided Practice of Close Reading

 Have students reread the section "Fast and Powerful" on page 52. Then have them list details in a Venn diagram to compare and contrast volcanoes and landslides. Students can work in pairs. Have students use the completed graphic organizer to orally compare volcanoes and landslides.

 Write About Reading: Summary Ask pairs to work together to write a summary of "Fast and Powerful." Select pairs of students to share their summaries with the class.

Go Digital

Present the Lesson

SKILLS TRACE

TEXT STRUCTURE

Introduce Unit 1 Week 3

Review Unit 1 Weeks 4, 6; Unit 2 Week 6; Unit 3 Week 6; Unit 4 Weeks 1, 4; Unit 5 Weeks 3, 4, 5, 6; Unit 6 Week 6

Assess Units 1, 4, 5

Comprehension Skill **CCSS**

Compare and Contrast

Authors use text structure to organize the information in a text. Comparison is one kind of text structure. Authors who use this text structure show how things are alike and different.

Find Text Evidence

Looking back at pages 51–52 of "A World of Change, " I can reread to learn how slow natural processes and fast natural processes are alike and different. Words such as some, but, both, *and* like *let me know that a comparison is being made.*

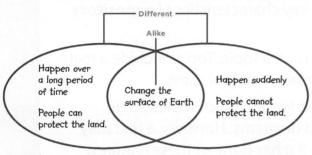

Different
Alike

Happen over a long period of time

People can protect the land.

Change the surface of Earth

Happen suddenly

People cannot protect the land.

Your Turn
COLLABORATE

Reread the section "Fast and Powerful." Compare and contrast volcanoes and landslides. List the information in the graphic organizer.

Go Digital! Use the interactive graphic organizer

55

READING/WRITING WORKSHOP, p. 55

 **Monitor and Differentiate**

 Quick Check

As students complete the Venn diagram about volcanoes and landslides, are they able to identify similarities and differences?

Small Group Instruction

If No → | **Approaching Level** | Reteach p. T175
| **ELL** | Develop p. T184
If Yes → | **On Level** | Review p. T179
| **Beyond Level** | Extend p. T183

ELL ENGLISH LANGUAGE LEARNERS SCAFFOLD

Beginning	Intermediate	Advanced/High
Respond Orally Help students reread pages 51–52. Ask questions to help students compare and contrast slow and fast natural processes. Ask: *Is weathering a slow natural process? Is a volcanic eruption a fast natural process?* Have students use the frame: *A slow natural process happens very slowly. A _____ happens fast.* (fast natural process)	**Demonstrate Understanding** Have students reread pages 51–52. Ask: *What is one way slow and fast natural processes are alike? What is one way they are different? Explain to a partner.* Then have partners summarize the similarities and differences. *Slow and fast natural processes are alike because _____. Slow and fast natural processes are different because _____.*	**Compare and Contrast** Have students compare and contrast slow and fast natural processes. Then have them explain how they identified the similarities and differences to a partner. Ask them to use words from "A World of Change," including vocabulary words.

ON-LEVEL PRACTICE BOOK pp. 23–25

A. Reread the passage and answer the questions.
Possible responses provided.

1. What are the two things being compared in the second and third paragraphs?

The two things being compared are a river flood and a flood from the ocean.

2. What do these two things have in common?

They both involve too much water. They can both happen because of strong storms.

3. How are these two things different?

One happens when water overflows the sides of rivers. The other happens when water from the ocean gets pushed onto the shore.

B. Work with a partner. Read the passage aloud. Pay attention to accuracy. Stop after one minute. Fill out the chart.

	Words Read	–	Number of Errors	=	Words Correct Score
First Read		–		=	
Second Read		–		=	

APPROACHING pp. 23–25	BEYOND pp. 23–25	ELL pp. 23–25

Genre: Informational Text

Reading/Writing Workshop

OBJECTIVES

By the end of year, read and comprehend informational texts, including history/ social studies, science, and technical texts, in the grades 4–5 text complexity band proficiently, with scaffolding as needed at the high end of the range. **RI.4.10**

Recognize the characteristics and text features of expository text.

ACADEMIC LANGUAGE
- *expository, headings, diagrams, labels*
- Cognates: *expositivo, diagrama*

Expository Text

MINILESSON 10 Mins

1 Explain

Share with students the following key characteristics of **expository text**.

→ Expository text explains facts about a topic. Topics include a real person, an actual event, a real place, or a real thing.

→ Expository text may include text features such as headings, photographs and captions, and diagrams. However, a text may still be an expository text even if it has none of these features.

2 Model Close Reading: Text Evidence

Model identifying and using the text features on page 53 of "A World of Change."

Diagrams Point out the diagram of the volcanic eruption. Explain that diagrams show the parts of something or how a process works. Labels help explain the diagram.

Headings Point out the heading "Be Prepared." Explain that headings tell what a section is mostly about. Ask: *What do you think this section will be about?*

3 Guided Practice of Close Reading

Have students work with partners to find and list three text features in "A World of Change." Partners should discuss the information they learned from each feature. Then have them share their work with the class.

Go Digital

Present the Lesson

Genre Informational Text

Expository

The selection "A World of Change" is an expository text.

Expository text:
- Explains facts about a topic.
- Includes text features.

 Find Text Evidence

"A World of Change" is an expository text. It gives many facts about Earth's processes. Each section has a heading that tells me what the section is about. The diagram gives me more information.

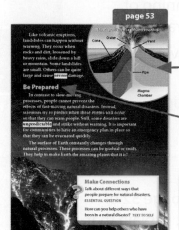

page 53

Text Features

Diagrams Diagrams show the parts of something or how a process works. They have labels that tell about their different parts.

Headings Headings tell what a section of text is mostly about.

Your Turn

COLLABORATE

List three text features in "A World of Change." Tell your partner what information you learned from each of the features.

56

READING/WRITING WORKSHOP, p. 56

 Access Complex Text

▶ **Purpose**

Remind students that the purpose of "A World of Change" is to explain natural disasters and how people respond to them. Point out that text features can help authors share information and meet their purpose.

→ *What does the diagram show?* (The diagram shows a volcano erupting.)

→ *How does the diagram relate to the author's purpose?* (It shows the reader how a natural disaster occurs.)

Monitor and *Differentiate*

✓ **Quick Check**

Are students able to identify three text features in "A World of Change"? Can they identify what they learned from each feature?

Small Group Instruction

If No → | Approaching Level | Reteach p. T168
| ELL | Develop p. T184
If Yes → | On Level | Review p. T176
| Beyond Level | Extend p. T180

ON-LEVEL PRACTICE BOOK p. 26

Forest Fires

Forest fires start and spread in different ways. The type of fire and the plants affect how it spreads. There are three types of forest fires. The first is a ground fire. It moves along the ground, sometimes below the leaf cover. Dead plant matter along the ground can burn for weeks and months. In a surface fire, low plants, twigs, and rotten logs catch fire. The flames can sometimes become tall and spread. The third type is a crown fire. It burns and spreads across the tops of trees and can be carried by the wind.

Answer the questions about the text.

1. How do you know this is an expository text?
   It gives facts about forest fires.

2. What text features does the text include?
   heading; diagram

3. What is the heading of this text? How could it be made more specific?
   "Forest Fires"; it could be changed to "Types of Forest Fires"

4. What does the diagram show? How does it add to the text?
   It shows the three types of forest fires. Possible answer: It supports the text by comparing where the plants burn.

| APPROACHING | BEYOND | ELL |
| p. 26 | p. 26 | p. 26 |

→ # Vocabulary Strategy

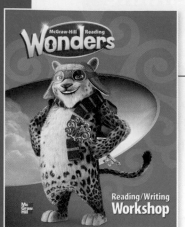

Reading/Writing Workshop

MINILESSON
10 Mins

Context Clues

1 Explain

Remind students that they can often figure out the meaning of an unknown word by using context clues within the paragraph.

→ Some words are **multiple-meaning words.** They have more than one meaning.

→ Students can use the words and phrases near a multiple-meaning word to figure out its meaning.

2 Model Close Reading: Text Evidence

Model using context clues in the second paragraph on page 52 of "A World of Change" to determine the meaning of *block*. Explain that the word *protect* and the phrase "ocean waves from the shore" are clues to the meaning.

3 Guided Practice of Close Reading

COLLABORATE

Have students work in pairs to find the meanings of *place*, *shore*, and *strike* in "A World of Change." Note that these words have multiple meanings. Encourage partners to go back into the text and use context clues within the paragraphs to help them determine which meaning is being used for each word.

OBJECTIVES

CCSS Determine the meaning of general academic and domain-specific words or phrases in a text relevant to a *grade 4 topic or subject area.* **RI.4.4**

CCSS Use context (e.g., definitions, examples, or restatements in text) as a clue to the meaning of a word or phrase. **L.4.4a**

ACADEMIC LANGUAGE

context clues, multiple-meaning words

SKILLS TRACE

CONTEXT CLUES: MULTIPLE-MEANING WORDS

Introduce Unit 1 Week 3

Review Unit 1 Week 4; Unit 2 Week 1

Assess Unit 1

Go Digital

Present the Lesson

Vocabulary Strategy CCSS

Multiple-Meaning Words

As you read "A World of Change," you will come across some **multiple-meaning words**. These are words that have more than one meaning. To figure out the meaning of a multiple-meaning word, check the words and phrases near it for clues.

 Find Text Evidence

When I read page 52 of "A World of Change," I see the word block. *There are a few different meanings for* block, *so this is a multiple-meaning word. The word* protect *and the phrase "ocean waves from the shore" help me figure out which meaning is being used in the sentence.*

To help protect against beach erosion, people build structures that block ocean waves from the shore.

Your Turn

 COLLABORATE

Use context clues to figure out the meanings of the following words in "A World of Change."
- **place,** *page 51*
- **shore,** *page 52*
- **strike,** *page 53*

57

(bc) Denis Jr. Tangney/Vetta/Getty Images

READING/WRITING WORKSHOP, p. 57

 Monitor and *Differentiate*

 Quick Check

Can students identify and use context clues to determine the meanings of *place*, *shore*, and *strike*?

Small Group Instruction

If No → | Approaching Level | Reteach p. T173
| ELL | Develop p. T189
If Yes → | On Level | Review p. T178
| Beyond Level | Extend p. T182

ENGLISH LANGUAGE LEARNERS
ELL SCAFFOLD

Beginning	Intermediate	Advanced/High
Derive Meaning Help students find the words *place*, *shore*, and *strike*. Read aloud the sentence or sentences in which each word is found. Use pictures, demonstration, or restatement to help students understand the meaning of each word. Give the definition for each word and have students echo.	**Distinguish** Ask students to find clues for the words *place*, *shore*, and *strike* in the text. Then have them choose between two definitions for each word. For example, ask: *Does* shore *mean "a piece of land next to water" or "to support something"?* (land next to water) Have partners talk about how they used context clues to find each word's meaning.	**Clarify the Meaning** Point out the words *place*, *shore*, and *strike*. Brainstorm with students two possible meanings for each word. Have them find the words in the text and decide which meaning is being used. Have students work with a partner to write a short sentence for each word, using it the same way as it is used in "A World of Change."

ON-LEVEL PRACTICE BOOK p. 27

Read each passage. Underline the context clues that help you figure out the meaning of each multiple-meaning word in bold. Then write the word's meaning on the line.

1. Have you ever been in an earthquake or a tornado? These things may never happen where you live. But flooding is something that can happen in almost every **part** of the United States.

   a piece of something

2. Not all floods are alike. Some floods happen over many days. A **flash** flood can happen in minutes. Learning about floods can help you stay safe.

   happen very quickly

3. Floods also cause damage to buildings and bridges. They can even **wash** away entire roads! This can make it hard for rescue workers to help people who are trapped by the water.

   carry away with water

4. The water in a river rises over the river's **banks**. This might happen because storms have caused too much rain to fall.

   sides of the river

APPROACHING p. 27	BEYOND p. 27	ELL p. 27

Develop Comprehension

Literature Anthology

Earthquakes

Text Complexity Range

Lexile

740   ▲   1010
      870

TextEvaluator™

23   ▲   51
   36

Options for Close Reading

→ Whole Class

→ Small Group

→ Independent

This selection is suggested for use as an Extended Complex Text. See pages T356–T361.

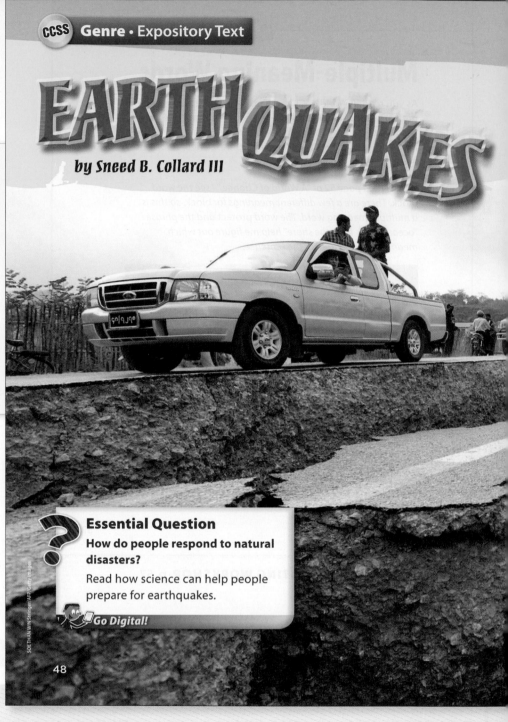

CCSS **Genre** · Expository Text

EARTHQUAKES
by Sneed B. Collard III

? Essential Question

How do people respond to natural disasters?

Read how science can help people prepare for earthquakes.

Go Digital!

48

A C T Access Complex Text

What makes this text complex?

▶ **Purpose**

▶ **Genre**

▶ **Connection of Ideas**

▶ **Specific Vocabulary**

▶ **Organization**

▶ Organization

Explain that authors of expository text organize information in a meaningful way. Reread page 49 with students and use the questions to guide them in identifying how the text is organized.

→ *How does the author introduce the information about Earth's crust and the upper mantle?*

A Shifting Planet

We like to believe that the ground under our feet is solid and secure. People who have felt the ground shake know differently. They have lived through an earthquake.

Earth's crust resembles a jigsaw puzzle more than a solid sphere. Like a puzzle, the crust is divided into different pieces that fit together. These pieces are called plates. Earth's plates float on top of a layer just below the crust called the upper mantle. The upper mantle is solid rock, but it behaves like a thick gel. Heat from deep inside the earth moves through the rock and causes it to slowly swirl and flow.

 Myanmar residents inspect large cracks on a road after an earthquake struck the area.

49

LITERATURE ANTHOLOGY, pp. 48–49

Predictive Writing

Have students read the title, preview the photos and diagram, and write their predictions about what the selection will be about. Encourage them to share what they already know about earthquakes.

ESSENTIAL QUESTION

Ask a student to read aloud the Essential Question. Have students discuss what information they expect to learn.

Note Taking: Use the Graphic Organizer

Analytical Writing

As students read the selection, ask them to take notes by filling in the graphic organizer on **Your Turn Practice Book page 22** to compare and contrast details in each section.

① Text Features: Photographs

Look at the caption and photograph on pages 48–49. What happened to this road in the Asian country of Myanmar? How could an earthquake cause this?

(The author says that the crust is like a jigsaw puzzle and the upper mantle behaves like a thick gel.)

→ *What does this tell you about how the author organized the information?* (The author uses a compare and contrast text structure to help readers understand the information.)

ELL Help students understand the meaning of science terms in the text, such as *crust, plates,* and *upper mantle.* Have students create a word wall or picture glossary with challenging terms.

→ *What do we call Earth's crust?* (plates)

→ *What is the upper mantle?* (solid rock that acts like thick gel)

Develop Comprehension

2 Skill: Compare and Contrast

How are Earth's plates and boiling milk similar? (Heat causes milk to boil and to move the layer of cream that floats on top of it. Heat also causes the upper mantle to push and pull, or move, the plates that float on top of it.) What difference does Dr. Cifuentes point out? (The Earth's crust is much harder than a layer of cream.) Use this information to fill in the Venn diagram.

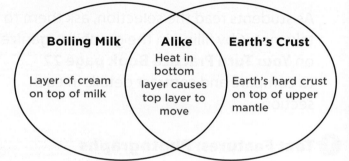

Boiling Milk
Layer of cream on top of milk

Alike
Heat in bottom layer causes top layer to move

Earth's Crust
Earth's hard crust on top of upper mantle

Dr. Inés Cifuentes is a seismologist—someone who studies earthquakes. She likes to compare the movement of Earth's plates to boiling milk. "When you boil milk," she says, "you get that little surface layer of cream on top that moves and dances around. That's what's going on in the earth, except that Earth's crust is much harder than the layer of cream."

As the mantle "boils," it pushes and pulls the plates above it. "It's at the edges of these plates," Dr. Cifuentes explains, "where we have most earthquakes."

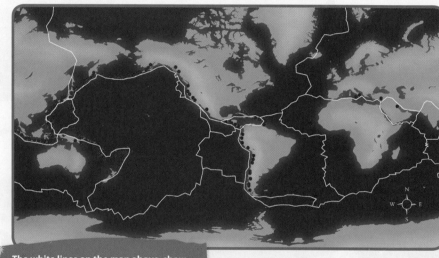

The white lines on the map above show plates on Earth's surface. The red dots show where earthquakes have occurred.

Neil Stewart

50

A C T Access Complex Text

▶ Genre

Remind students that maps can help readers to better understand expository text.

→ *What is shown on the map?* (the plates on Earth's surface; locations of earthquakes)

→ Reread the last sentence: *"It's at the edges of these plates," Dr. Cifuentes explains, "where we have most earthquakes."*

→ Ask students to use Dr. Cifuentes's explanation and the map features to identify where on the map most earthquakes around the world usually take place. (Students should identify the edges of Earth's plates on the map. Edges identified should have a large number of symbols indicating earthquakes have occurred nearby.)

People stare at a gigantic crack on a street in Valdivia caused by the 1960 Chilean earthquake.

Earth's Largest Quake: A Firsthand Account

Dr. Inés Cifuentes became a seismologist for a very good reason—she and her family lived through the largest recorded earthquake in history. This was the 1960 earthquake that struck Chile. As Dr. Cifuentes explains: "In April, 1960, my family moved to Santiago, Chile. Just a few weeks later, on May 21st, we were woken up by strong shaking. Then, thirty-three hours later a gigantic earthquake hit the southern part of Chile, and with it, an enormous tsunami. About a year later, we took a trip to the northern end of the earthquake zone. And that's where I saw that the land had actually been raised up a meter or so. I saw these huge changes, and that impressed me— that the earth could actually do that! Later, as a graduate student I wanted to know how big that earthquake was, how long it lasted, and whether it was preceded by a "slow" earthquake. I worked on this problem for four years. I was able to calculate that Earth's largest recorded earthquake had a magnitude of 9.5. I also confirmed that a slow precursor [forerunner] had occurred 15 minutes before the main earthquake. I am very proud of this work."

③

④

51

STF Staff/AFP/Getty Images

LITERATURE ANTHOLOGY, pp. 50–51

③ **Genre: Informational Text**

An informational text can have both firsthand and secondhand accounts of an event to give readers different perspectives. What information about earthquakes is provided in Dr. Cifuentes's firsthand account on page 51? (She describes feeling the shaking and seeing the giant crack in the earth.) How is this description different than the secondhand information you have learned elsewhere in this selection? (It allows me to experience the earthquake myself. The other parts of the selection use examples to explain how it happens.)

④ **Strategy: Reread**

Teacher Think Aloud   I can reread this section to make sure I understand the main details about the earthquake. Then I can paraphrase what I have learned. The earthquake happened on May 22, 1960, and was accompanied by a tsunami. It was Earth's largest recorded earthquake. Dr. Cifuentes calculated that the earthquake had a magnitude of 9.5 and that there was a slow precursor earthquake 15 minutes before the main earthquake.

▶ **Purpose**

Students may be confused by the insertion of a firsthand account feature in the middle of this expository text. Discuss why an author might do this and what it adds to the selection.

→ *Why did the author give Dr. Cifuentes's account?* (to explain why Dr. Cifuentes became a seismologist)

→ *How would the selection have been different without the firsthand account?* (The selection would have only given the scientific explanation of earthquakes and would not have allowed the reader to understand the personal experience that led Dr. Cifuentes to study them.)

Develop Comprehension

5 **Vocabulary: Multiple-Meaning Words**

Turn to a partner and discuss the different meanings of the word *fault*. What is the meaning of *fault* in the text? (a break in Earth's crust) What is another meaning of the word *fault*? (mistake or blame)

6 **Author's Craft: Word Choice**

Sometimes an author uses more than one meaning of a multiple-meaning word. Reread page 52. How does the author use multiple meanings of the word *fault* to make a pun, or joke, in the section's heading? (Faults are at fault, or to blame, for earthquakes.)

7 **Text Features: Diagrams**

Turn to a partner and discuss the diagram. What does the diagram show? (a fault) What do the arrows in the diagram show? (movement along the fault)

Whose Fault Is It?

5 Earth's plates crash together, spread apart, and slide against each other. Wherever they do this, they cause breaks in Earth's crust. Seismologists call these breaks faults. Usually, the blocks of rock on each side of a fault just sit there stuck together. But when enough pressure builds, the two sides of the fault can suddenly shift, or slip. This sudden movement releases waves of energy. These waves travel through the earth. We feel them as earthquakes.

6 Most faults do not slip and cause earthquakes. Around the globe, however, active faults cause hundreds of earthquakes every day. Most are too small for us to notice. Once in a while, Earth unleashes a whopper.

The diagram below shows a normal fault, which is a crack or fracture in the Earth's surface. Movement along the fault can sometimes cause earthquakes.

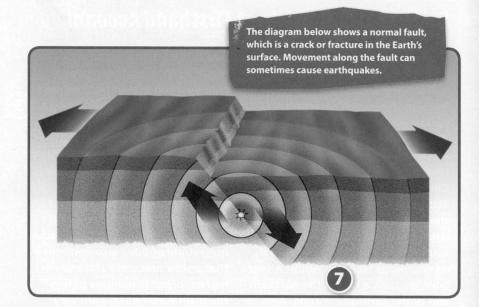

7

Neil Stewart

52

A C T Access Complex Text

▶ Connection of Ideas

Tell students that when they read a complex text, they should try to connect new information to information they have already learned.

→ *Compare the magnitude of the 2011 Japan earthquake mentioned on page 53 with the magnitude of the earthquake that hit Chile in 1960.* (The Japan earthquake had a magnitude of 9.0

and was the fourth largest recorded earthquake. The earthquake in Chile had a magnitude of 9.5 and was the largest earthquake ever recorded.)

→ *Was the earthquake in Chile 5 or 50 times larger than the earthquake in Japan?* (5 times larger) *How do you know?* (Each whole number on the magnitude scale is 10 times greater than the

Measuring Earthquakes

Seismologists record earthquakes using machines called seismographs. These measure shaking, or ground motion. After an earthquake, scientists read their seismographs. They use their readings to calculate the earthquake's size, or magnitude. Magnitude scales are set up so that each whole number is ten times larger than the number before it. A magnitude 7.0 earthquake, for instance, is ten times larger than a magnitude 6.0 quake.

Truly giant earthquakes happen about once a year. These are quakes with a magnitude of 8.0 or greater. They occur only on very large faults and can cause **severe destruction**.

Dr. Cifuentes explains, "The only way you can get an earthquake like the 2011 Japan earthquake is where one of Earth's plates is sliding under another one. This is the only kind of place where you have a fault long enough and wide enough to release that kind of energy."

Seismologists gave the 2011 Japan earthquake a 9.0 magnitude. It was the fourth largest earthquake ever recorded. They believe that the earthquake occurred on a fault more than 150 miles (250 kilometers) long. It shook Japan for three to five minutes. It was so powerful that it **altered** the geography of the country. Surprisingly, it wasn't the shaking of the ground that did the most damage. A massive wave proved much more destructive.

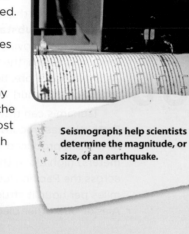

Seismographs help scientists determine the magnitude, or size, of an earthquake.

Guy Croft/SciTech/Alamy

STOP AND CHECK

Reread How do scientists measure earthquakes? Reread to check your understanding.

53

LITERATURE ANTHOLOGY, pp. 52–53

STOP AND CHECK

Reread How do scientists measure earthquakes?

Teacher Think Aloud I can reread the first paragraph to better understand how seismologists measure an earthquake's size. The text says that seismologists, who measure earthquakes, use seismographs. Seismographs measure shaking and ground motion, and the readings are used to calculate an earthquake's size. How do scientists compare the sizes of different earthquakes by using their magnitude?

Prompt students to apply the strategy in a Think Aloud by rereading to confirm their understanding of magnitude scales and how earthquakes are measured.

Student Think Aloud I know *magnitude* is another word for *size*. A scale is a set of numbers used to measure and compare sizes. A magnitude scale must be the numbers used to measure earthquakes. The text says that each whole number on a magnitude scale is ten times larger than the whole number before it. So a magnitude 7.0 earthquake is ten times larger than a magnitude 6.0 earthquake.

one before it, so half of a whole number on the magnitude scale, or .5, must be 5 times greater.)

 Define difficult science terms in this section, such as *fault*, *seismologist*, *seismograph*, and *magnitude*.

→ Point out the cognates energy/*energía*, magnitude/*magnitud*, and calculate/*calcular*.

→ Read the captions on pages 52–53. Help students describe the images, using science terms.

Develop Comprehension

The disaster zone in Kesennuma, Japan, 2011, 100 days after the massive earthquake and tsunami

8 Skill: Compare and Contrast

Compare and contrast a tsunami and an earthquake. (They are both natural disasters caused by faults shifting or slipping. But an earthquake happens in Earth's crust, and a tsunami travels through oceans.) Use this information to fill in the Venn diagram.

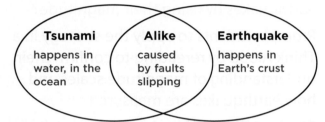

Tsunami
happens in water, in the ocean

Alike
caused by faults slipping

Earthquake
happens in Earth's crust

9 Literary Device: Figurative Language

In the first paragraph, how does the author use figurative language to describe a tsunami? (The author compares a tsunami to a towering monster to describe how tall and powerful a tsunami can become.)

Tsunami Terror

8 9

When an earthquake occurs under the ocean, it often moves a **substantial** amount of water above it. This creates a fast-moving wave called a tsunami (soo-NAH-mee). Out at sea, the wave may be only a few feet high. As it reaches shore, however, the wave can tower into a monster. It can hurl water for miles inland.

Tsunamis can travel thousands of miles. In 1960, Earth's largest recorded earthquake struck the country of Chile. It produced tsunami waves up to 82 feet (25 meters) high along the coast. The tsunami also raced across the Pacific Ocean at a speed of more than 150 miles per hour. It struck the shorelines of Hawaii, Japan, Alaska, and other places. Hundreds of people drowned.

KAZUHIRO NOGI Staff/AFP/Getty Images

54

A C T Access Complex Text

▶ Specific Vocabulary

Review strategies for finding the meaning of unfamiliar words, such as using context clues, word parts, or a dictionary.

→ Reread the sentence: *It can hurl water for miles inland.* Discuss the meaning of *hurl.* (throw) *Find the pronunciation, part of speech, and definitions of the word in a print or digital dictionary.*

→ *When the tsunami reaches shore, where does the water then travel?* (across miles of land)

→ *What does* inland *mean?* (the land that is not close to the ocean, or not on the shore)

The 2011 Japan earthquake produced tsunami waves more than 30 feet (10 meters) high. The 2004 Indian Ocean earthquake in southern Asia produced 50-foot (15-meter) tsunamis. These tsunamis engulfed entire cities and shorelines. The waves swept away buildings, cars, and people.

Japan, southern Asia, and Chile had experienced many powerful earthquakes and tsunamis before. Why were so many people unprepared?

Predicting Earthquakes

Seismologists are very good at measuring earthquakes. However, they still can't predict when earthquakes will happen.

"There was a time," Dr. Cifuentes explains, "when I think scientists felt that predicting earthquakes was just around the corner—that we were going to be able to predict earthquakes very soon. But it's clear now that it's not around the corner. In fact, some have given up entirely on predicting earthquakes."

One reason that earthquakes are **unpredictable** is that scientists cannot collect enough information to understand where and when an earthquake might happen next. Although scientists have placed special instruments in many earthquake zones, earthquakes still surprise us. Scientists, for example, had believed the next big earthquake in Japan would happen farther to the south, closer to Tokyo. Instead, it struck farther north.

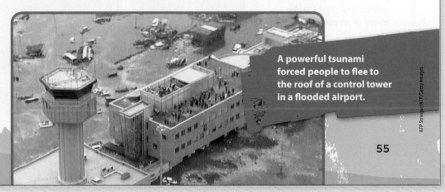

A powerful tsunami forced people to flee to the roof of a control tower in a flooded airport.

AFP Stringer/AFP/Getty Images

55

LITERATURE ANTHOLOGY, pp. 54–55

ELL Help students use the expression *just around the corner* in a sentence. For example: *Winter break is just around the corner.* Then have students echo-read the second paragraph of "Predicting Earthquakes." Help students understand that scientists no longer believe that predicting earthquakes is "just around the corner."

⑩ Skill: Make Inferences

Turn to a partner. Discuss why you think so many people were swept away by the tsunamis in 2011 and 2004. (Many people were probably living and working close to the ocean and did not have enough time to escape.)

⑪ Strategy: Reread

Are scientists able to predict the exact time and place of an earthquake?

Student Think Aloud I can reread the section on predicting earthquakes and paraphrase the information. The text says that seismologists are good at measuring earthquakes. Unfortunately, it also says they still can't reliably predict earthquakes.

SCIENCE

CONNECT TO CONTENT
CHANGING EARTH'S SURFACE

Erosion is a slow process that changes the surface of Earth. Earthquakes and tsunamis can not only cause destruction to buildings and harm people, but they can also change the surface of Earth very quickly. On page 51, Dr. Cifuentes described how the earthquake in Chile in 1960 raised the land in the earthquake zone about a meter. In this section, students read about how tsunamis can strike shorelines thousands of miles away from where the earthquake happens. Tsunamis can carry away sand and soil from inland areas as well as change the landscape of the shorelines where they hit.

STEM

Develop Comprehension

⑫ Skill: Compare and Contrast

Compare and contrast how people can plan ahead for earthquakes and tsunamis. Paraphrase what Dr. Cifuentes tells people to do to prepare for a tsunami. How can we be prepared for earthquakes? Use this information to fill in a Venn diagram.

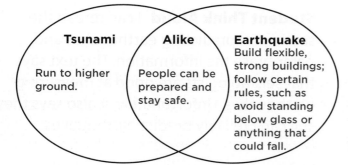

Tsunami
Run to higher ground.

Alike
People can be prepared and stay safe.

Earthquake
Build flexible, strong buildings; follow certain rules, such as avoid standing below glass or anything that could fall.

⑬ Ask and Answer Questions

Generate a question of your own about the text and share it with a partner. To find the answer, try rereading the text. For example, you might ask "Why is the way a city is built important if an earthquake happens?"

Planning for Earthquakes

⑫ Even though we can't predict earthquakes, we can prepare for them. Many seismologists help make information **available** to people so they can plan for and respond to earthquakes. This is especially important near coastal areas.

"Once the shaking goes on for more than thirty seconds," Dr. Cifuentes says, "it's pretty simple. You have to run away from the ocean and run up hill. You have maybe fifteen or twenty minutes to reach higher ground."

How cities are built also affects how many people survive an earthquake. Cities in many countries have special building laws. Buildings must be strong and flexible. That way, they won't **collapse** during an earthquake. In some countries, however, buildings are often poorly built. The 2010 Haiti earthquake, for example, killed between 46,000 and 316,000 people. Unlike the earthquake in Japan, many of these people were killed by collapsing buildings and falling debris.

However, earthquakes don't just destroy. They also create. "They help make the mountains, coasts, and other landscapes we see around us," Dr. Cifuentes explains. ⑬ This is worth remembering as we learn how to predict and survive earthquakes in the future.

Utility ducts like this one are being constructed to protect underground wires, cables, and pipes in the event of an earthquake.

(t) Heath Korvola/Aurora/Getty Images; (b) Koichi Kamoshida Staff/Getty Images NewsGetty Images

56

A C T Access Complex Text

▶ Genre

Remind students that an expository text informs readers about a topic and organizes information in a way that is easy to follow. Point out the sidebar "What to Do During an Earthquake."

→ *What do the first six bullets tell us?* (how to stay safe if you are indoors during an earthquake)

→ *What do the last three bullets tell us?* (how to stay safe if you are outdoors during an earthquake)

→ *Where would you find information about what to do if you are in bed during an earthquake?* (below the subheading "If you are indoors")

What to Do During an Earthquake

If you are indoors

- Drop to the ground and crawl under a sturdy piece of furniture until the shaking stops.

- Stay away from glass, windows, outside doors and walls, and anything that could fall, such as a hanging light or fan.

- Stay in bed if you are there when the earthquake strikes. Protect your head with a pillow. Only move from the bed if there is a heavy light or fan above you.

- Use a doorway for shelter only if you know it is strongly supported.

- Stay inside until the shaking stops and it is safe to go outside.

- Do not use elevators.

If you are outdoors (14)

- Move away from buildings, streetlights, and utility wires.

- Avoid any space where there is falling debris, such as glass.

- Once in the open, stay there until the shaking stops.

STOP AND CHECK

Reread How can you protect yourself if you are indoors during an earthquake? Reread to check your understanding.

Students raise awareness about earthquakes by participating in a nation-wide earthquake drill.

57

LITERATURE ANTHOLOGY, pp. 56–57

STOP AND CHECK

Reread How can you protect yourself if you are indoors during an earthquake? (Stay inside, stay away from glass and anything that could fall, and don't use elevators.)

(14) Author's Craft: Text Structure

Authors writing informational texts often put instructions or important information in lists. This helps the information stand out and makes it easier to read. Reread page 57. Then turn to a partner and discuss why the section is a list. (It is important to know what to do in an earthquake. Making the information part of a list makes it easier to read and understand.)

Return to Predictions

Review students' predictions and purposes for reading. Ask them to answer the Essential Question. (Earthquakes and tsunamis are natural disasters that can cause great destruction. Studying these natural disasters helps us understand how they happen and what we can do to prepare for them.)

ELL Point out the photograph and caption on page 57.

→ Read the caption with students. Point out the cognate participating/*participando*. Explain that *drill* is another word for *practice* or *exercise*.

→ *What does the caption tell about the students in the photograph?* (Students participate in earthquake drills.)

→ Ask students to describe the photograph. *How do students protect themselves during the earthquake drill?* (They drop to the ground and stay below desks.)

About the Author

Meet the Author

Sneed B. Collard III

Have students read the biography of the author. Ask:

→ Sneed B. Collard's parents were biologists. How might that have led him to be interested in writing about science for kids?

→ What might have inspired Sneed B. Collard to write about earthquakes?

Author's Purpose

To Inform

Remind students that authors who write to inform interview experts who have studied a certain topic for a long time. Students may say how Dr. Cifuentes makes earthquakes more relatable by describing her own experiences. She is able to describe the science of earthquakes in a way that is easy to understand.

Author's Craft

Text Features

Explain how authors use photographs and captions to add depth to their descriptions of events.

→ In addition to providing facts and details about an event in the text, authors also can provide photographs to show what an event, or the effects of an event, looked like. Example: photograph of a city street after the 1960 Chilean earthquake. (p. 51)

→ Have students find other examples of photographs that illustrate an event described in the text, such as the photograph of Kesennuma, Japan, after being hit by a tsunami in 2011. (p. 54)

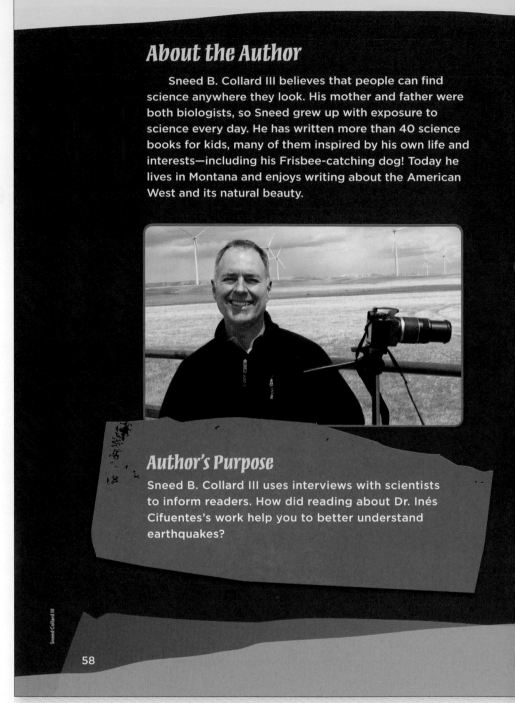

About the Author

Sneed B. Collard III believes that people can find science anywhere they look. His mother and father were both biologists, so Sneed grew up with exposure to science every day. He has written more than 40 science books for kids, many of them inspired by his own life and interests—including his Frisbee-catching dog! Today he lives in Montana and enjoys writing about the American West and its natural beauty.

Sneed Collard III

Author's Purpose

Sneed B. Collard III uses interviews with scientists to inform readers. How did reading about Dr. Inés Cifuentes's work help you to better understand earthquakes?

58

LITERATURE ANTHOLOGY, pp. 58–59

Respond to Reading

Summarize

Summarize what you learned about earthquakes. Information from your Venn Diagram may help you.

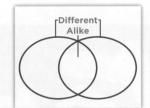

Text Evidence

1. How can you tell that *Earthquakes* is an expository text? **GENRE**

2. How is the movement of Earth's plates similar to boiling milk? How is it different? Use details from the selection to support your answer. **COMPARE AND CONTRAST**

3. What is the meaning of *plates* on page 49? Use context clues to help you figure out the correct definition. **MULTIPLE-MEANING WORDS**

4. Write about the impact of the 2010 and 2011 earthquakes in Haiti and Japan. Compare and contrast the earthquakes' destruction and outcome. **WRITE ABOUT READING**

Make Connections

How can science help people prepare for earthquakes? **ESSENTIAL QUESTION**

Why should people take warnings about tsunamis seriously? **TEXT TO WORLD**

59

Make Connections

Essential Question Science can help us to build stronger, more flexible structures that can withstand earthquakes. Science may also someday help us to predict earthquakes and improve warning systems.

Text to World Students should write about the dangers of tsunamis and how people who are near a coastline should move to higher ground to stay safe.

Respond to Reading

Summarize

Review with students the information from their graphic organizers. Model how to use the information to summarize *Earthquakes*.

Write About Reading: Summarize Remind students that a summary is a restatement of the main ideas of the text. You can write a summary of a section of a text or write a summary about a whole text.

Ask students to write a summary of the selection, using the main ideas of each section of the text. Remind them to start with a sentence that names the selection title and the genre. Have students share their summaries with a partner.

Text Evidence

1. **Genre** Answer The selection gives facts about earthquakes. Evidence The selection includes photographs, captions, a map, a diagram, and headings.

2. **Compare and Contrast** Answer Heat causes both Earth's plates and the cream in boiling milk to move, but the hardness of each makes them different. Evidence Dr. Cifuentes's explanations on page 50

3. **Multiple-Meaning Words** Answer Plates are sections of Earth's hard outer layer, or crust. Evidence The text says that Earth's crust is divided into different pieces that fit together, called plates.

4. **Write About Reading: Compare and Contrast** Both earthquakes were destructive, but in different ways. In Haiti, collapsing buildings and falling debris caused many deaths. In Japan, the earthquake caused a tsunami that drowned many people.

Develop Comprehension

Literature Anthology

"Tornado"

Text Complexity Range

Lexile

740 ▲ 1010
950

TextEvaluator™

23 ▲ 51
27

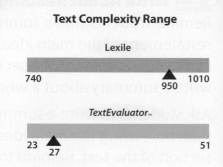

Compare Texts ✎ *Analytical Writing*

Students will read another informational text on natural disasters. Ask students to do a close reading of the text to understand the content. Encourage them to use the reread strategy. Students will also take notes. They will use the text evidence they gathered to compare this text with *Earthquakes*.

CCSS Genre · Expository Text

Compare Texts
Read to find out what to do in the event of a tornado.

TORNADO

When warm and cold air masses collide, the result can be a fast-moving, dangerous force of nature—a tornado. A tornado is a violent windstorm over land. Wind makes a rotating, funnel-shaped cloud that extends toward the ground. As it moves, it picks up debris and objects in its path.

Tornadoes are a natural process, especially in flat areas such as the middle of the United States. But tornadoes can also be **unpredictable**. They may cause **destruction** on one side of a street yet leave the other side untouched.

One way you can tell a tornado is coming is if you spot a funnel cloud. Other warning signs include sounds. An approaching tornado may sound like the rumble of a fast-moving train. It may also sound like a waterfall or like wind whipping into the open windows of a speeding car.

Even after a tornado has passed, there are many **hazards**. Avoid stepping on glass, sharp objects, or, especially, fallen power lines. Stay out of heavily damaged buildings that may **collapse**. It is important to treat a tornado as a serious **crisis**, as warnings may come quickly with little time to act.

(bkgd) Alan R Moller/Stone/Getty Images

60

A C T **A**ccess **C**omplex **T**ext

What makes this text complex?
▶ **Specific Vocabulary**
▶ **Connection of Ideas**

▶ Specific Vocabulary

Have students read the first sentence aloud and point out "air masses."

→ *What can collide and result in a tornado?* (warm and cold air masses)

→ *What do you think "air mass" means in this text?* (air that is the same temperature and moves as one mass)

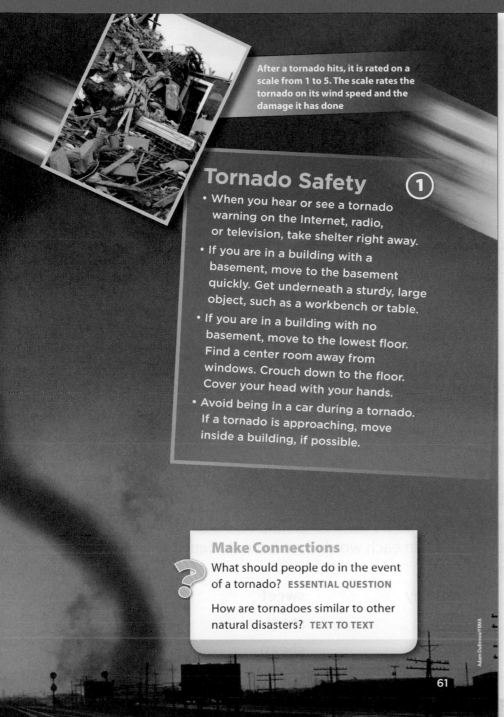

After a tornado hits, it is rated on a scale from 1 to 5. The scale rates the tornado on its wind speed and the damage it has done

Tornado Safety ①

- When you hear or see a tornado warning on the Internet, radio, or television, take shelter right away.
- If you are in a building with a basement, move to the basement quickly. Get underneath a sturdy, large object, such as a workbench or table.
- If you are in a building with no basement, move to the lowest floor. Find a center room away from windows. Crouch down to the floor. Cover your head with your hands.
- Avoid being in a car during a tornado. If a tornado is approaching, move inside a building, if possible.

Make Connections

What should people do in the event of a tornado? **ESSENTIAL QUESTION**

How are tornadoes similar to other natural disasters? **TEXT TO TEXT**

Adam DuBrowa/FEMA

61

LITERATURE ANTHOLOGY, pp. 60–61

① Ask and Answer Questions

What makes a tornado dangerous? What can people do to stay safe when a tornado forms?

 Write About Reading (A tornado moves fast and picks up objects and debris. It is unpredictable. To stay safe you should go inside a building and find cover.)

Make Connections

Essential Question Have students reread the sidebar "Tornado Safety" and paraphrase what to do in the event of a tornado.

Text to Text Have groups of students compare their written responses to the Ask and Answer Questions prompt with what they learned in *Earthquakes*. Each group can report back to the class. Ask one group to compare indoor safety suggestions for tornados and earthquakes. (In both, the authors suggest crawling under sturdy furniture and staying away from windows.) Ask another group to contrast why tornados and earthquakes are dangerous. (An earthquake shakes the ground and can cause tsunamis. A tornado is fast-moving air that can pick up objects and debris.)

▶ Connection of Ideas

Have students reread the last paragraph and the list under the heading "Tornado Safety."

→ *How do both sections help you know what to do if there is a tornado? How is the information different?* (Both include ways to stay safe. The list tells what to do when a tornado is coming. The paragraph tells how to stay safe after the tornado has passed.)

 Students may have difficulty with the vocabulary the author uses to describe tornadoes. Use the photograph on pages 60 and 61 to explain the meaning and movement of *funnel-shaped cloud*. Have a volunteer demonstrate a rotating motion that moves toward the ground.

→ Phonics/Fluency

MINILESSON
20 Mins

Long *e*

OBJECTIVES

CCSS Use combined knowledge of all letter-sound correspondences, syllabication patterns, and morphology (e.g., roots and affixes) to read accurately unfamiliar multisyllabic words in context and out of context. **RF.4.3a**

CCSS Use context to confirm or self-correct word recognition and understanding, rereading as necessary. **RF.4.4c**

Rate: 84–104 WCPM

1 Explain

Display the *Tree* **Sound-Spelling Card**. Point to the card and say the long-vowel sound /ē/. Explain that the /ē/ sound has different spellings: *e, ea, ee, e_e, ie, ei, ey,* and *y*. Provide a sample word for each spelling: *we, seat, teeth, these, grief, receive, key,* and *scary*.

2 Model

Write the word *happy* on the board. Underline the letter *y* and say the long-vowel sound /ē/. Then model pronouncing each syllable and blending the word. Remind students that *y* is the only spelling of /ē/ that does not include the letter *e*.

3 Guided Practice

Write the following list of words on the board. Help students identify the spelling of the /ē/ sound in each word. Then have students pronounce each word.

brief	monkey	sweet
ceiling	zebra	story
maybe	athlete	cheap

> **Read Multisyllabic Words**
>
> **Transition to Longer Words** Write the following words in one column on the board: *mean, greed, week, treat*. Point out the /ē/ sound and spelling in each word. Then have students partner-read the words.
>
> Next, list the following word parts in another column on the board: *ment, y, end, ing*. Have partners work together to combine word parts and create longer /ē/ words, such as: *meaning, greedy, weekend, treatment, treaty,* and *treating*. Have partners read their lists to the group.

ELL

Refer to the sound transfers chart to identify sounds that do not transfer in Spanish, Cantonese, Vietnamese, Hmong, and Korean.

Grades K–6

Language Transfers Handbook

Language Transfers Handbook

Go Digital

Long *e*

Present the Lesson

View "A World of Change"

Plurals

1 Explain

Adding -s or -es to a noun makes it plural. A plural noun names more than one.

→ For most nouns, add -s to form the plural: *cards, books*.

→ For nouns ending in *sh, ch, s, ss, z,* and *x,* add -es to form the plural: *dishes, boxes*.

→ For nouns ending in a consonant and *y,* change the *y* to *i* and add -es to form the plural: *babies, ladies*.

2 Model

Write and say *beach*. Have students repeat the word. Model forming the plural by adding -es.

3 Guided Practice

Write the words *bus, team,* and *family* on the board. Have students write the plural form of each word and read their words to a partner.

Accuracy

Explain/Model Explain that reading with accuracy means pronouncing words correctly and reading every word in the text. Reading with accuracy improves comprehension of a text.

Model reading the first three paragraphs under the heading "Slow and Steady" on page 51 of "A World of Change." Carefully pronounce domain-specific words. Point out that you did not skip over any words in the text.

Practice/Apply Divide students into groups to practice choral-reading the passage. Have each student read one sentence, focusing on accurately pronouncing each word and not leaving out any words. Tell students to use the context of the passage to help them recognize and pronounce difficult words.

Daily Fluency Practice

Students can practice fluency using **Your Turn Practice Book**.

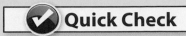

Monitor and *Differentiate*

✓ Quick Check

Can students decode multisyllabic words with long *e* spellings? Can students read plural words? Can students read fluently?

Small Group Instruction

If No →	**Approaching Level**	Reteach pp. T170, T174
	ELL	Develop pp. T186, T190
If Yes →	**On Level**	Review p. T176
	Beyond Level	Extend p. T180

ON-LEVEL PRACTICE BOOK p. 28

A. Read the words in each row. Circle the word with the long e vowel sound. Then write the letters that make the long e sound on the line.

1.	(league)	large	growl	ea
2.	deck	sled	(sleek)	ee
3.	(scheme)	shelf	sky	e_e
4.	marked	(maybe)	melted	e
5.	claim	dense	(honey)	ey
6.	farming	(family)	laying	y

B. Write the correct plural form of each noun. Use the plural ending -s, -es, or -ies.

Noun	Plural Form
1. kiss	kisses
2. zebra	zebras
3. buddy	buddies
4. match	matches
5. stone	stones
6. box	boxes

APPROACHING p. 28	BEYOND p. 28	ELL p. 28

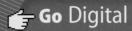

Go Digital

www.connected.mcgraw-hill.com
RESOURCES
Research and Inquiry

 Wrap Up the Week

Integrate Ideas

RESEARCH AND INQUIRY

Take Action

OBJECTIVES

CCSS Recall relevant information from experiences or gather relevant information from print and digital sources; take notes and categorize information, and provide a list of sources. **W.4.8**

CCSS Add audio recordings and visual displays to presentations when appropriate to enhance the development of main ideas or themes. **SL.4.5**

• Gather resources for research.

• Present information visually.

ACADEMIC LANGUAGE

resources, collaborate, visuals

Make a Poster

Explain that students will work in small groups and research how to prepare for a specific type of natural disaster. They will then collaborate to make a poster that demonstrates to others how to stay safe during that type of disaster. Discuss the following steps:

1 **Choose a Topic** Have student groups brainstorm different natural disasters that people can prepare for. Ask them to take a group vote to decide which one they will research for their project.

2 **Find Resources** Tell students to use the selections they read this week along with other reliable print and online resources to gather information for their project. Students should verify all facts in multiple sources.

3 **Guided Practice** Have students take notes as they research, focusing on relevant facts and helpful tips for how to stay safe before, during, and after a natural disaster. Remind them to list each source in their notes and include page numbers or web addresses where the information can be verified.

4 **Create the Poster** Encourage collaborative efforts when students make the posters based on their research. They should use precise language and domain-specific vocabulary on their posters when appropriate. They may want to add visuals to illustrate their tips, such as illustrations or cut-out photos from magazines or newspapers.

Present the Poster

Have students share their posters with another group. Tell them to orally present the information shown on their posters. Have students use the online Listening Checklist to evaluate their roles in the discussion.

TEXT CONNECTIONS

OBJECTIVES

CCSS Integrate information from two texts on the same topic in order to write or speak about the subject knowledgeably. **RI.4.9**

CCSS Review the key ideas expressed and explain their own ideas and understanding in light of the discussion. **SL.4.1d**

Text to Text

COLLABORATE

Cite Evidence Explain to students that they will work in groups to compare information they have learned about responding to natural disasters from all the texts they have read. Model how to compare this information by using examples from the week's **Leveled Readers** and *A World of Change*, **Reading/ Writing Workshop** pages 50–53. Review class notes and completed graphic organizers. You may also wish to model going back into the text for more information. You can use a Four-Door Foldable® to record comparisons.

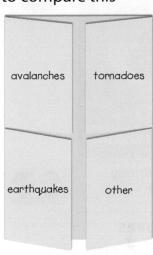

Students should cite at least three examples from each text.

Present Information Ask groups of students to present their findings to the class. Encourage discussion, asking students to comment on information on the charts that is similar and ideas that are different.

Dinah Zike's
FOLDABLES
Study Organizer

WRITE ABOUT READING

OBJECTIVES

CCSS Draw evidence from literary or informational texts to support analysis, reflection, and research. Apply *grade 4 Reading standards* to informational texts (e.g., "Explain how an author uses reasons and evidence to support particular points in a text"). **W.4.9b**

CCSS Identify the reasons and evidence a speaker provides to support particular points. **SL.4.3**

Write an Analysis

Cite Evidence Using evidence from a text they have read, students will analyze how the author used an illustration to provide more details about a topic.

Discuss how to analyze a text by asking *how* and *why* questions.

→ How does the illustration add more details about the topic?

→ Why is the illustration an important part of the text?

Read and discuss the student model on **Your Turn Practice Book** page 29. Then have students select a nonfiction text that has an illustration. Have them write an analysis that explains how the illustration provides more details about the topic. Remind students that strong explanatory writing includes transitions that link ideas and uses both simple and compound sentences.

COLLABORATE

Present Your Ideas Ask partners to share their paragraphs and discuss how the evidence they cited from the text supports their ideas. Partners may suggest additional text evidence if necessary.

→ Readers to Writers

Reading/Writing Workshop

OBJECTIVES

CCSS Write routinely over extended time frames (time for research, reflection, and revision) and shorter time frames (a single sitting or a day or two) for a range of discipline-specific tasks, purposes, and audiences. **W.4.10**

CCSS Develop the topic with facts, definitions, concrete details, quotations, or other information and examples related to the topic. **W.4.2b**

• Analyze models to understand how supporting details explain main ideas.

• Write about how to help people after a natural disaster.

• Add details to revise writing.

ACADEMIC LANGUAGE
main idea, topic

Writing Traits: Ideas

Supporting Details

Expert Model Explain that good writers use details to support and explain a main idea. Supporting details include facts, examples, definitions, quotations, and other details that give important information about the topic. They help readers better understand the topic.

 Read aloud the expert model from "A World of Change." Ask students to listen for the details that support and explain the topic, such as *Natural changes take place every day.* Have students talk with partners to identify the supporting details.

Student Model Remind students that adding supporting details, such as facts and examples, helps readers better understand the topic, or main idea. Read aloud the student draft "Yellowstone National Park." As students follow along, have them focus on supporting details the writer added to his draft.

 Invite partners to talk about the draft and the supporting details that Jake added. Ask them to suggest places where Jake could add more supporting details.

 Genre Writing

Narrative Text

For full writing process lessons and rubrics, see:

→ Friendly Letter, pages T344–T349

→ Personal Narrative, pages T350–T355

Expert Model

Student Model

Go Digital

CCSS Writing Traits › Ideas

Readers to...

Writers make sure they focus on a topic by providing a main idea when they write expository text. They use important details to support the main idea. Reread the first paragraph of "A World of Change" below.

Focus on a Topic

Identify supporting details for the main idea that Earth is in a constant state of change.

Expert Model

A World of Change

Earth may seem as if it is a large rock that never changes. Actually, our planet is in a constant state of change. Natural changes take place every day. These activities alter the surface of Earth. Some of these changes take place slowly over many years. Others happen in just minutes. Whether they are slow or fast, both kinds of changes have a great effect on our planet.

58

Writers

Jake wrote an expository text. Read Jake's revision of a section of it.

Student Model

Yellowstone National Park

Yellowstone National Park is

Millions of people visit this park every year.

popular. People come from all over

the world.

Yellowstone is a beautiful park

to visit. People photograph the

waterfalls and the animals, and they

This famous geyser erupts every 1–2 hours.

make sure to visit Old Faithful, too. ∧

There are lots of different

animals at Yellowstone,

including elk, bison,

and grizzly bears.

59

Editing Marks

⊓ Switch order.
∧ Add.
⌃ Add a comma.
⌿ Take out.
(SP) Check spelling.
≡ Make a capital letter.

Grammar Handbook

Compound Sentences See page 451.

Your Turn COLLABORATE

☑ Identify the details that Jake included.
☑ Identify a compound sentence.
☑ Tell how Jake's revisions improved his writing.

Go Digital!
Write online in Writer's Workspace

READING/WRITING WORKSHOP, pp. 58–59

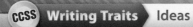

ENGLISH LANGUAGE LEARNERS SCAFFOLD

As English Language Learners write during the week, provide support to help them respond to the prompts. For example:

Beginning	Intermediate	Advanced/High
Write Help students complete the sentence frames. *People come from all over the ____. People photograph the ____ and the ____. There are lots of different animals at Yellowstone, including ____ and ____. Another supporting detail is ____.*	**Describe** Ask students to complete the sentence frames. Encourage students to provide details. *People come from ____. People photograph the ____. There are lots of different ____ at Yellowstone, including ____. Another supporting detail is ____.*	**Discuss** Check for understanding. Ask: *From where do people come to visit Yellowstone? What do people photograph at the park? What kinds of animals live in Yellowstone? What is another supporting detail?*

Writing Every Day: Ideas

DAY 1

Writing Entry: Supporting Details

Prewrite Provide students with the prompt below.

Explain how you could help people who have experienced a natural disaster. Include details that give facts and examples.

Have partners think of what they could do to help people who have experienced natural disasters. Ask them to jot down details about ways they could help people that they might include in their drafts.

Draft Have each student select a topic to write about. Remind them to include supporting details in their drafts.

DAY 2

Focus on Supporting Details

Use **Your Turn Practice Book** page 30 to model adding supporting details.

The park near my house is a great place to spend time. Many people enjoy hiking or walking in the park and looking at nature. The park has baseball fields.

Model adding a supporting detail after the last sentence.

Families enjoy using the playground and the covered picnic area.

Discuss how adding supporting details helps explain the topic. Guide students to add supporting details to the rest of the model.

Writing Entry: Supporting Details

Revise Have students revise their writing from Day 1 by adding two or three supporting details.

Use the **Conferencing Routines**. Circulate among students and stop briefly to talk with individuals. Provide time for peer reviews.

Edit Have students use Grammar Handbook page 451 in the **Reading/Writing Workshop** to edit for errors in compound sentences.

Conferencing Routines

Teacher Conferences

STEP 1

Talk about the strengths of the writing.

The opening paragraph is well organized. You expressed your main idea clearly and included several supporting details.

STEP 2

Focus on how the writer uses the target trait for the week.

These examples explain the topic. It would help if you also included some facts to support the main idea.

STEP 3

Make concrete suggestions for revisions. Have students work on a specific assignment, such as those to the right, and then meet with you to review progress.

DAY 3

Writing Entry: Supporting Details

Prewrite Ask students to search their Writer's Notebook for topics to write a draft. Or, provide a prompt, such as the following:

Explain how people who volunteer at animal shelters help pets in need. Include supporting details that give examples.

Draft Once students have chosen their topics, ask them to create a word web with the topic in the center. Then have them think about the information about the topic that they might include in their writing. Students can then use their word webs to begin their drafts.

DAY 4

Writing Entry: Supporting Details

Revise Have students revise the draft writing from Day 3 by adding two or three supporting details to explain and support their main idea. As students are revising their drafts, hold teacher conferences with individual students. You may also wish to have students work with partners to peer conference.

Edit Invite students to review the rules for compound sentences and their punctuation on Grammar Handbook pages 451 and 479 in the **Reading Writing/Workshop** and then edit their drafts for errors.

DAY 5

Share and Reflect

Discuss with the class what they learned about adding supporting details to explain the topic. Invite volunteers to read and compare draft text with text that has been revised. Have students discuss the writing by focusing on the importance of the supporting details that have been added. Allow time for individuals to reflect on their own writing progress and record observations in their Writer's Notebooks.

McGraw-Hill Companies, Inc. Ken Karp, photographer

Suggested Revisions

Provide specific direction to help focus young writers.

Focus on a Sentence
Read the draft and target one sentence for revision. *Rewrite this sentence by adding supporting details to explain _____.*

Focus on a Section
Underline a section that needs to be revised. Provide specific suggestions. *This section is interesting. I want to know more about _____. Add supporting details that give more information.*

Focus on a Revision Strategy
Underline a section of the writing and ask students to use a specific revision strategy, such as adding. *There are very few facts and examples in this section. Try adding some supporting details to better explain the topic.*

Peer Conferences

Focus peer response groups on adding supporting details to help explain the topic. Provide this checklist to frame discussion.

- ☑ Does the writing include supporting details that explain the main idea?
- ☑ Are all the details related to the topic?
- ☑ What supporting details can be added to explain and support the main idea?

Grammar: Compound Sentences

Reading/Writing Workshop

___

OBJECTIVES

CCSS Use a comma before a coordinating conjunction in a compound sentence. **L.4.2c**

CCSS Use coordinating and subordinating conjunctions. **L.3.1h**

CCSS Produce simple, compound, and complex sentences. **L.3.1i**

___

• Identify simple and compound sentences.

• Use conjunctions in sentences.

Go Digital

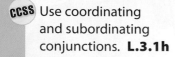

Compound Sentences

Grammar Activities

DAY 1

DAILY LANGUAGE ACTIVITY

We plan to camp out, hike and go rock climbing. Sheila, and Pam are on vacation.

(1: hike, and; 2: Sheila and Pam)

Introduce Simple and Compound Sentences

Present the following:

→ A **clause** is a group of words that has a subject and a verb.

→ An **independent clause** can stand alone as a sentence.

→ A **simple sentence** has one independent clause:
   The sun came out today.

→ A **compound sentence** has two or more independent clauses:
   The sun came out today, and the flowers blossomed.

Have partners discuss simple and compound sentences using page 451 of the Grammar Handbook in **Reading/Writing Workshop**.

DAY 2

DAILY LANGUAGE ACTIVITY

The people where fishing on the pier! one person caught a fish that was three feet long?

(1: were; 2: pier.; 3: One; 4: long!)

Review Simple and Compound Sentences

Review simple and compound sentences. Have students explain how they are different.

Introduce Conjunctions

The independent clauses in compound sentences are usually joined by a coordinating conjunction.

→ Some **coordinating conjunctions** used to connect clauses are **and**, **but**, **or**, **for**, **nor**, and **yet**:
   I called you, **but** you did not answer.

   We took our seats, **and** the concert started.

TALK ABOUT IT

COLLABORATE

ADD TO SIMPLE SENTENCES

Have students in small groups each write a simple sentence and pass it one person to the right. That person adds an independent clause to create a compound sentence. Have students read aloud their compound sentences.

CREATE THEMED SENTENCES

Ask students in small groups to pick a theme, such as music. Have each student create a theme-related compound sentence using a coordinating conjunction. Have students take turns reading their sentences aloud.

DAY

3

DAY
5

DAILY LANGUAGE ACTIVITY

My friend opened her presents and I took pictures. She received a game, a doll and a sweater!
(1: presents, 2: doll, and; 3: sweater.)

DAILY LANGUAGE ACTIVITY

marty rides the bus to school, I walk. Sit next to each other in math class.
(1: Marty; 2: school, but; 3: We sit)

DAILY LANGUAGE ACTIVITY

Max collects stamps and Tori collects coins. I like soccer, my friend likes baseball.
(1: stamps, and; 2: soccer; my)

Mechanics and Usage: Punctuating Compound Sentences

→ Use a **comma** and a coordinating conjunction to join two independent clauses to form a compound sentence.

→ You can also use a **semicolon** to join two independent clauses.

As students write, refer them to Grammar Handbook pages 451 and 479.

Proofread

Have students correct errors in these sentences.

1. David is a great guitar player, he learned to play when he was five? (1: player; he; 2: five.)

2. i was going to cleen the garage but my dad took us camping. (1: I; 2: clean; 3: garage, but)

3. I have a digital camera, it connects to my computer. (1: camera; it)

4. I studied for the math test and I got an A. (1: test, and)

Have students check their work using Grammar Handbook page 478 on compound sentences and semicolons.

Assess

Use the Daily Language Activity and **Grammar Practice Reproducibles** page 15 for assessment.

Reteach

Use Grammar Practice Reproducibles pages 11–14 and selected pages from the Grammar Handbook for additional reteaching. Remind students it is important to form compound sentences correctly as they write.

Check students' writing for use of the skill. Assign Grammar Revision Assignments in their Writer's Notebooks as needed.

See Grammar Practice Reproducibles pages 11–15.

EXPLAIN PUNCTUATION

Ask partners to each write two compound sentences—one using a coordinating conjunction and one using a semicolon. Have them trade sentences, read each other's sentences aloud, and explain the punctuation in each sentence.

USE CONJUNCTIONS

List coordinating conjunctions on the board. Have students in small groups write compound sentences using each conjunction once. Ask a volunteer from each group to read the group's sentences aloud. Have the class identify the conjunctions.

DESCRIBE PICTURES

Ask partners to cut out five pictures from a magazine. Have them take turns writing two simple sentences to describe a picture. The other student combines the sentences to form a compound sentence and reads aloud the new sentence.

Spelling: Long e

OBJECTIVES

CCSS Spell grade-appropriate words correctly, consulting references as needed. **L.4.2d**

Spelling Words

evening	indeed	belief
zebra	reef	chief
breathe	deed	honey
league	speech	donkey
squeaky	wheeze	family
healer	concrete	weary
sleek	scheme	

Review bail, pale, eight
Challenge appeal, freedom

Differentiated Spelling

Approaching Level

maybe	seem	chief
zebra	reef	either
beam	deed	key
heal	speech	money
please	feet	busy
leak	gene	only
weep	scene	

Beyond Level

evening	tea	belief
feline	eerie	chief
breathe	thirteen	donkey
league	succeed	honeybee
creature	wheeze	mystery
increased	concrete	weary
appealing	scheme	

DAY 1

Assess Prior Knowledge

Display the spelling words. Read them aloud, drawing out the long *e* sound in each.

Point out the spelling patterns in *squeaky*. Segment the word sound by sound, then attach a spelling to each sound. Point out that the word contains two long *e* sounds with different spellings: the *ea* in the middle and the *y* at the end.

Demonstrate sorting the spelling words by pattern under key words *zebra, deed, scheme, chief, healer, honey* and *family*. (Write the words on index cards or the IWB.) Sort a few words. Point out that most long *e* sounds use the letter *e*, but some, like the *y* in *family*, do not.

Then use the Dictation Sentences from Day 5 to give the Pretest. Say the underlined word, read the sentence, and repeat the word. Have students write the words. Then have students check and correct their spelling.

DAY 2

Spiral Review

Review the long *a* sound in *major, rail, clay, pale, steak, eight* and *they*. Use the Dictation Sentences below for the review words. Read the sentence, say the word, and have students write the words.

1. The prisoner could not post <u>bail</u>.
2. Your face is getting very <u>pale</u>.
3. Tosha's sister is <u>eight</u> years old.

Have partners check the spellings.

Challenge Words Review this week's long *e* spelling patterns. Use these Dictation Sentences for challenge words. Say the word, read the sentence, and say the word again. Have students write the word.

1. Does this color <u>appeal</u> to you?
2. People struggled for <u>freedom</u>.

Have students check and correct their spelling before writing the words in their word study notebook.

WORD SORTS

COLLABORATE

OPEN SORT

Have students cut apart the **Spelling Word Cards BLM** in the Teacher Resource Book and initial the back of each card. Have them read the words aloud with a partner. Then have partners do an open sort. Have them record the sort in their word study notebook.

PATTERN SORT

Complete the **pattern sort** from Day 1 using the key words, pointing out the different long *e* spellings. Have students use Spelling Word Cards to do their own pattern sort. Ask partners to compare and check their sorts.

DAY **3**

Word Meanings

Remind students that analogies show relationships between two pairs of words. Read each analogy below. Have students copy the analogies into their word study notebooks. Tell them to complete each analogy with a spelling word.

1. *Water* is to *drink* as *air* is to _____. *(breathe)*

2. *Players* are to *team* as *teams* are to _____. *(league)*

3. *Sing* is to *song* as *speak* is to _____. *(speech)*

Challenge students to come up with other analogies for spelling, review, or challenge words. Encourage them to use synonyms and antonyms in the analogies. Have students write the analogies, leaving a blank space for the word. Ask volunteers to share analogies for the class to complete as a group.

See Phonics/Spelling Reproducibles pp. 13–18.

DAY **4**

Proofread and Write

Write these sentences on the board. Have students circle and correct each misspelled word. They can use print or electronic dictionaries or other resources to help them.

1. The heeler said she could help the familie dog. *(healer, family)*

2. The police cheif discovered their scheam. *(chief, scheme)*

3. The hunny was very, very sticky indeid. *(honey, indeed)*

4. The zeebra ran too hard and began to whieze. *(zebra, wheeze)*

Error Correction Remind students that the *ie* spelling for long *e* is not as common at the end of an English word as *y*.

DAY **5**

Assess

Use the Dictation Sentences for the Posttest. Have students list misspelled words in their word study notebooks. Look for students' use of these words in their writings.

Dictation Sentences

1. It was a cold, moonless <u>evening</u>.
2. The <u>zebra</u> had a lot of stripes.
3. People can't <u>breathe</u> under water.
4. I joined the baseball <u>league</u>.
5. That door was loud and <u>squeaky</u>.
6. The <u>healer</u> bandaged the cut.
7. That's a <u>sleek</u> new car.
8. Wet floors are very slippery <u>indeed</u>!
9. We can't fish near the <u>reef</u>.
10. Are you sorry for that <u>deed</u>?
11. Did you listen to the <u>speech</u>?
12. The runner started to <u>wheeze</u>.
13. The sidewalk is made of <u>concrete</u>.
14. Your <u>scheme</u> needs more planning.
15. Kevin thinks it is beyond <u>belief</u>.
16. Who is the <u>chief</u> here?
17. Do you want <u>honey</u> in your tea?
18. This <u>donkey</u> will carry our tent.
19. Let's go home to your <u>family</u>.
20. I am too <u>weary</u> to play.

Have students self-correct the tests.

SPEED SORT

Have partners do a **speed sort** to see who is faster. Then have them do a word hunt in the week's reading for words with the long *e* vowel sound. Have them sort the new words and record both sorts in the word study notebook.

BLIND SORT

Have partners do a **blind sort**: one reads a Spelling Word Card; the other tells under which key word it belongs. Have them take turns until both have sorted all their words. Ask them to review their sorts and then discuss how they sorted the words and if any changes are needed.

Build Vocabulary

DAY
1

DAY
2

OBJECTIVES

CCSS Use context (e.g., definitions, examples, or restatements in text) as a clue to the meaning of a word or phrase. **L.4.4a**

CCSS Recognize and explain the meaning of common idioms, adages, and proverbs. **L.4.5b**

Expand vocabulary by adding inflectional endings and affixes.

Vocabulary Words

alter	hazard
collapse	severe
crisis	substantial
destruction	unpredictable

Go Digital

Vocabulary

Vocabulary Activities

Connect to Words

Practice this week's vocabulary.

1. How would you **alter** the school's dress code? Why?

2. What things can **collapse** during an earthquake?

3. How do you think you would react to a **crisis**? Why?

4. What kinds of natural events can cause a lot of **destruction**?

5. What is one possible **hazard** for people who ski?

6. Describe a **severe** storm you have seen or heard about.

7. How can storms cause **substantial** damage?

8. Why do you think earthquakes are so **unpredictable**?

Expand Vocabulary

Help students generate different forms of this week's words by adding, changing, or removing inflectional endings.

→ Draw a three-column T-chart on the board. Write *predict* in the left column. Then write *predictable* and *unpredictable* in the other columns. Read aloud the words with students.

→ Have students share sentences with each form of *predict*.

→ Students can fill in the chart for *alter* (*alterable, unalterable*), then share sentences using different forms of the word.

→ Have students copy the chart in their word study notebook.

 BUILD MORE VOCABULARY

COLLABORATE

ACADEMIC VOCABULARY

Discuss important academic words.

→ Display *erosion, predict*.

→ Define each word and discuss the meanings with students.

→ Display *predict* and *prediction*. Have partners look up and define related words.

→ Write the related words on the board. Have partners ask and answer questions using the words. Repeat with *erosion*.

IDIOMS

→ Remind students that idioms are figurative language.

→ Give the example *to fall in love*. Explain that no one actually falls—it is just a way to describe the feeling of being in love.

→ Have partners find other examples of idioms in the readings or other resources.

→ Have partners show you the idioms they have found. Read examples aloud for the class.

DAY 3

Reinforce the Words

Review last week's and this week's vocabulary words. Have students orally complete each sentence stem.

1. The hurricane caused <u>substantial</u> damage to the ____.

2. The <u>severe</u> storm blew over the big tree in the ____.

3. ____ are <u>unpredictable</u> and can happen at any time.

4. We saw the ____ <u>collapse</u> from the weight of too much snow.

5. A ____ can cause a lot of <u>destruction</u> in a short time.

6. We had to <u>alter</u> our route when the ____ flooded.

DAY 4

Connect to Writing

→ Have students write sentences in their word study notebooks using this week's vocabulary.

→ Tell them to write sentences that provide word information they learned from this week's readings.

→ Provide the Day 3 sentence stems 1–6 for students needing extra support.

Write About Vocabulary Have students write something they learned from this week's words in their word study notebook. For example, they might write about a *severe* storm they saw on the news or experienced in person. They might describe any *destruction*, or if it caused anything to *collapse*.

DAY 5

Word Squares

Ask students to create Word Squares for each vocabulary word.

→ In the first square, students write the word. (example: *collapse*)

→ In the second square, students write their own definition of the word and any related words, such as synonyms. (example: *fall down, break*)

→ In the third square, students draw a simple illustration that will help them remember the word. (example: drawing of a house or building falling down)

→ In the fourth square, students write nonexamples, including antonyms for the word. (example: *stay up, stay intact*)

→ Have partners compare and discuss their Word Squares.

MULTIPLE-MEANING WORDS

When a word has more than one possible meaning, remind students to use context clues to determine which meaning is being used.

→ Display **Your Turn Practice Book** pages 23–24. Read the first paragraph. Model figuring out the meaning of *part*.

→ Have students complete page 27, then find clues for *safe* and *banks* on pages 23–24, using a print or online dictionary to confirm meanings.

SHADES OF MEANING

Help students generate words related to *alter*. Draw a word web. Label the web "Alter."

→ Have partners generate words related to *alter* to add to the web. Ask students to use a dictionary or thesaurus.

→ Add words not included, such as *revise* or *convert*.

→ Ask students to copy the words in their word study notebook.

MORPHOLOGY

Use *crisis* as a springboard for students to learn more words. Draw a T-chart. Label one column "Singular" and the other "Plural."

→ In the columns, write *crisis* and *crises*. Note the spelling change.

→ Explain that *crisis* comes from the Greek word *krisis*. Have students look up other words with Greek origins. (*axis, axes*)

→ Discuss any singular/plural spelling patterns they notice for words with Greek origins.

→ Approaching Level

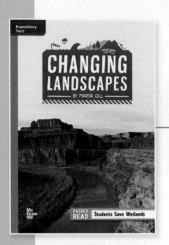

Lexile 670
TextEvaluator™ 23

Leveled Reader:
Changing Landscapes

Go Digital

Leveled Readers

Before Reading

Preview and Predict

Have students read the Essential Question. Give students a copy of *Changing Landscapes* and have them read the title and respond to the cover photograph. Ask students to discuss what they think the selection will be about. Ask students why it is important to respond to natural disasters.

Review Genre: Expository Text

Have students recall that expository text provides information about a topic. Expository text includes headings and diagrams that help the reader understand that topic. Have students identify features of expository text in *Changing Landscapes.*

During Reading

Close Reading

Note Taking Ask students to use their graphic organizer while they read.

Pages 2–3 *Why does the author want you to imagine going back in time?* (to picture the land in the past) *What do you see?* (how big changes to the land can happen slowly)

Pages 4–7 *What does the diagram on page 4 show?* (how erosion makes a river wider over many years) *How are sand dunes and wetlands similar?* (Both protect against erosion.) *How are they different?* (Dunes are on beaches. Wetlands are marshes or swamps.)

Pages 8–11 *Read pages 8–9. Paraphrase how landslides affect people.* (They can destroy the property in their path.) *Compare and contrast how landslides and hurricanes affect land.* (Both cause damage to the land and threaten people. Landslides occur in hilly areas with few trees or plants and can wipe out all buildings in their path. Hurricanes occur in coastal areas and can cause flooding.)

Use Graphic Organizer

OBJECTIVES

Refer to details and examples in a text when explaining what the text says explicitly and when drawing inferences from the text. **RI.4.1**

Paraphrase portions of a text read aloud or information presented in diverse media and formats, including visually, quantitatively, and orally. **SL.4.2**

ACADEMIC LANGUAGE

• compare, contrast, context clues

• Cognates: *comparar, contraste, contexto*

Pages 12–13 *How do people work against natural protections from landslides?* (They remove plants and trees and clear out wetlands.) *What does* hazards *mean on page 12?* (potential dangers)

Page 14 *Read page 14. Contrast land changes from weathering with land changes from natural disasters.* (Land changes from weathering happen slowly. Land changes from natural disasters happen quickly.)

After Reading

Respond to Reading

Have students complete Respond to Reading on page 15 after they have finished reading.

Analytical Writing **Write About Reading** Have students work with a partner to write a short paragraph comparing and contrasting landslides and hurricanes. Make sure students cite supporting evidence from the text. Call on partners to read their responses.

Fluency: Accuracy

Model Model reading page 6 with accuracy, being sure to pronounce every word clearly and correctly. Next, read the passage aloud and have students read along with you.

Apply Have partners do repeated rereadings of the passage.

PAIRED READ

"Students Save Wetlands"

Make Connections: Write About It *Analytical Writing*

Before reading, ask students to note that the genre of this story is expository text, which means it explains about a topic. Have students discuss the Essential Question. After reading, ask students to use the information from both texts to explain why it is important to keep the wetlands intact.

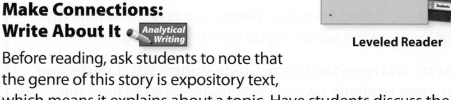
Leveled Reader

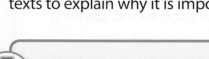
FOCUS ON SCIENCE

Students can extend their knowledge of how to prepare for natural disasters by completing the activity on page 20. **STEM**

Literature Circles

Ask students to conduct a literature circle using the Thinkmark questions to guide the discussion. You may wish to have a whole-class discussion on how students can help prevent natural disasters.

Level Up

Level-up lessons available online.

IF students read the **Approaching Level** fluently and answered the questions

THEN pair them with students who have proficiently read the **On Level** and have students

• echo-read the **On Level** main selection.

• use self-stick notes to mark at least one detail they would like to discuss in each section.

A C T ccess omplex ext

The **On Level** challenges students by including more **domain-specific words** and **complex sentence structures**.

Approaching Level

Phonics/Decoding

DECODE WORDS WITH DOUBLE *e*

TIER 2

 OBJECTIVES

Use combined knowledge of all letter-sound correspondences, syllabication patterns, and morphology (e.g., roots and affixes) to read accurately unfamiliar multisyllabic words in context and out of context. **RF.4.3a**

Decode words with long *e*.

 I Do Explain that the long *e* vowel sound is spelled with the letters *ee* in many words. Write the word *see* on the board, underline *ee*, and explain that the spelling *ee* stands for the sound /ē/. Blend the sounds as you read the word aloud.

 We Do Write *teen, meet, deep,* and *three* on the board. Model how to decode *teen*. Have students identify the vowel sound as long *e* and the sound-spelling *ee* in the word. Have them read the remaining words aloud.

 You Do Add these words to the board: *reef, seem, feet, weep,* and *deed*. Have students read each word aloud and identify the long *e* vowel sound. Then point to the words in random order for students to read chorally. Repeat several times.

REVIEW WORDS WITH LONG *e*

TIER 2

 OBJECTIVES

Use combined knowledge of all letter-sound correspondences, syllabication patterns, and morphology (e.g., roots and affixes) to read accurately unfamiliar multisyllabic words in context and out of context. **RF.4.3a**

Decode words with long *e*.

 I Do Display the *tree* **Sound-Spelling Card**. Explain that the long *e* sound has several different spellings, and point to each sound-spelling on the card: *ee, ea, e_e, ei, ie, e, ey,* and *y*. Write sample words with each spelling on the board: *free, sea, gene, ceiling, chief, me, money,* and *only*. Underline the sound-spelling for long *e* in the words as you read them aloud.

 We Do Write the syllables *sto* and *ry* on the board. Guide students as they decode the syllables. Then have students say the syllables together to form the word *story*. Write these words on the board, breaking each into syllables to help students read one syllable at a time: *sea/son, in/deed/, be/lief, re/ceive, con/crete/, fe/line,* and *don/key*. Have students identify the sound-spelling for long *e* in each word and then decode the words.

 You Do Add the following examples on the board: *maybe, honey,* and *zebra*. Ask students to decode each word. Then point to all the words in random order for students to choral-read. Repeat several times.

PRACTICE WORDS WITH LONG *e*

OBJECTIVES

(CCSS) Use combined knowledge of all letter-sound correspondences, syllabication patterns, and morphology to read accurately unfamiliar multisyllabic words in context and out of context. **RF.4.3a**

I Do Remind students that every syllable in a word has only one vowel sound, and that the long *e* sound has different spellings. Write *please* on the board, and read the word aloud. Point out that *please* has one syllable and its vowel sound is long *e* spelled *ea*.

We Do Write the words *evening, treatment, he, thirteen, many, grief,* and *honey.* Model how to decode the first word, and guide students as they decode the remaining words. Help them divide each multisyllabic word into syllables using the syllable-scoop technique.

You Do Afterward, point to the words in random order for students to choral-read.

PLURAL NOUNS

OBJECTIVES

(CCSS) Use combined knowledge of all letter-sound correspondences, syllabication patterns, and morphology to read accurately unfamiliar multisyllabic words in context and out of context. **RF.4.3a**

Decode words with plural endings -*s* and -*es*.

I Do Review that the endings -*s* and -*es* are added to singular nouns to create plural nouns. Explain that adding -*s* to most singular nouns makes them plural: *pencils, desks,* and *stairs.* For singular nouns that end in the letters *sh, ch, s, ss, z,* or *x,* add -*es* to form the plural: *dresses, brushes, bunches,* and *foxes.* For singular nouns that end in a consonant and *y,* change the *y* to *i* and add -*es* to form the plural: *cities* and *babies.*

We Do Write *speeches* on the board. Model how to decode the word. Give other examples of plural nouns and guide students as they decode these words. Divide multisyllabic words into syllables using the syllable-scoop technique to help students read one syllable at a time.

You Do Write the words *cherry, box, zebra,* and *watch* on the board. Have students add a plural ending to each word. Then point to the words in random order for students to choral-read.

ELL ENGLISH LANGUAGE LEARNERS

For the **ELLs** who need **phonics, decoding,** and **fluency** practice, use scaffolding methods as necessary to ensure students understand the meaning of the words. Refer to the **Language Transfers Handbook** for phonics elements that may not transfer in students' native languages.

→ Approaching Level

Vocabulary

REVIEW HIGH-FREQUENCY WORDS

TIER 2

OBJECTIVES

CCSS Read with sufficient accuracy and fluency to support comprehension. Read on-level text with purpose and understanding. **RF.4.4a**

Review high-frequency words.

 I Do Use **Word Cards 21–30.** Display one word at a time, following the routine: Display the word. Read the word. Then spell the word.

 We Do Ask students to state the word and spell the word with you. Model using the word in a sentence and have students repeat after you.

 You Do Display the word. Ask students to say the word and then spell it. When completed, quickly flip through the word card set as students choral-read the words. Provide opportunities for students to use the words in speaking and writing. For example, provide sentence starters such as *I do my homework before _____.* Ask students to write each word in their Writer's Notebook.

REVIEW VOCABULARY WORDS

TIER 2

OBJECTIVES

 CCSS Acquire and use accurately grade-appropriate general academic and domain-specific words and phrases, including those that signal precise actions, emotions, or states of being (e.g., *quizzed, whined, stammered*) and that are basic to a particular topic (e.g., *wildlife, conservation,* and *endangered* when discussing animal preservation). **L.4.6**

 I Do Display each **Visual Vocabulary Card** and state the word. Explain how the photograph illustrates the word. State the example sentence and repeat the word.

 We Do Point to the word on the card and read the word with students. Ask them to repeat the word. Engage students in structured partner-talk about the image as prompted on the back of the vocabulary card.

 You Do Display each visual in random order, hiding the word. Have students match the definitions and context sentences of the words to the visuals displayed.

ANSWER YES/NO QUESTIONS

OBJECTIVES

CCSS Acquire and use accurately grade-appropriate general academic and domain-specific words and phrases, including those that signal precise actions, emotions, or states of being (e.g., *quizzed, whined, stammered*) and that are basic to a particular topic (e.g., *wildlife, conservation,* and *endangered* when discussing animal preservation). **L.4.6**

 I Do Display the *hazard* **Visual Vocabulary Card.** Ask students the following question: *Is broken glass a hazard?*

Point out that broken glass is a hazard because it is dangerous.

We Do Display the vocabulary card for the word *destruction*. Ask: *Can a forest fire cause a lot of destruction?* With students, discuss how forest fires can burn down trees and other plants and cause destruction to life in a forest.

You Do Help students explain their answers to these questions.

→ Will a sturdy, or strong, chair *collapse* when a person sits in it?

→ Will baseball teams cancel a game in a *severe* rainstorm?

→ Does a *substantial* amount of rain fall during a hurricane?

→ Is our class's schedule *unpredictable*?

→ Would new plants and desks *alter* how our classroom looks?

→ Can family members help in a *crisis*?

CONTEXT CLUES: MULTIPLE-MEANING WORDS

OBJECTIVES

CCSS Use context (e.g., definitions, examples, or restatements in text) as a clue to the meaning of a word or phrase. **L.4.4a**

Use context clues to determine the correct meaning of a multiple-meaning word in the text.

 I Do Display the Comprehension and Fluency passage on **Approaching Reproducibles** pages 23–24. Read aloud the first page of the passage. Point to the word *type*. Explain that students can use the words in the same paragraph to find the correct meaning of a multiple-meaning word.

Think Aloud I know that *type* can mean to write on a keyboard. It also can mean a group of things that are alike. The first sentence in the paragraph says that there are "two types of floods." From this clue, I know that *type* means a group of things that are alike.

 We Do Ask students to point to the word *waves* on the same page. With students, discuss how to use the clues in the text to figure out the correct meaning of the multiple-meaning word. Write the definition of the word.

 You Do Have students read page 24 and use context clues to find the meanings of *wash* in the first paragraph and *sponges* in the second paragraph.

Approaching Level

Comprehension

 FLUENCY

TIER 2

OBJECTIVES

 CCSS Use context to confirm or self-correct word recognition and understanding, rereading as necessary. **RF.4.4c**

Read aloud with accuracy.

I Do
Explain that reading aloud with accuracy means pronouncing words correctly and reading every word in the text. Read the first paragraph of the Comprehension and Fluency passage on **Approaching Reproducibles** pages 23–24. Tell students to listen to how you pronounce each word in the text with accuracy.

 We Do
Read the rest of the passage aloud, and have students read each sentence after you. Use pitch and phrasing to enhance the meaning of what you are reading. Provide adequate time for students to read sentences aloud with accuracy after you.

 You Do
Have partners take turns reading sentences from the Approaching Reproducibles passage. Remind them to focus on pronouncing each word with accuracy. Listen and provide corrective feedback as needed.

 IDENTIFY DETAILS TO COMPARE AND CONTRAST

TIER 2

OBJECTIVES

CCSS Describe the overall structure (e.g., chronology, comparison, cause/effect, problem/solution) of events, ideas, concepts, or information in a text or part of a text. **RI.4.5**

Identify details to compare and contrast in a text.

 I Do
Write "a river has too much water" and "the sea pushes water on to land." Explain that these are two types of floods that students can compare and contrast in the text: floods caused by rivers and floods caused by the sea.

 We Do
Read the first page of the Comprehension and Fluency passage in **Approaching Reproducibles**. Point out that the heading "Why Do Floods Happen?" is the topic of the text so far. Then ask: *What facts tell how rivers flood? What facts tell how the sea floods the land?* Discuss how you can compare and contrast these facts.

 You Do
Have students read the rest of the passage. After each paragraph, they should write down the details that seem most important. Review their lists and help students determine how they can compare and contrast information, such as how people around the world work to avoid flooding.

REVIEW COMPARE AND CONTRAST

OBJECTIVES

 Describe the overall structure (e.g., chronology, comparison, cause/effect, problem/solution) of events, ideas, concepts, or information in a text or part of a text. **RI.4.5**

I Do Remind students that comparing information involves telling how details are alike and contrasting information involves telling how details are different. Authors may use signal words such as *some, but, both,* and *like* to signal comparisons they make in a text.

We Do Read the first paragraph of the Comprehension and Fluency passage in **Approaching Reproducibles** together. Pause to point out the detail "not all floods are alike" and the signal word "some." Model how to compare and contrast details about floods in the first paragraph. Then work with students to compare and contrast details in each paragraph in the passage.

You Do Have students use the details they have compared and contrasted to come up with a summary of the key details in the passage.

SELF-SELECTED READING

OBJECTIVES

 Describe the overall structure (e.g., chronology, comparison, cause/effect, problem/solution) of events, ideas, concepts, or information in a text or part of a text. **RI.4.5**

Reread difficult sections in a text to increase understanding.

Read Independently

Have students choose a nonfiction book for sustained silent reading. Remind students that:

→ compare and contrast is one kind of text structure; it tells how things are alike and different.

→ if they have trouble identifying similarities and differences in the information presented in the text, they should reread a paragraph or section to help them understand it better.

Read Purposefully

Have students record details that are alike and different on a Venn diagram as they read independently. After they finish, they can conduct a Book Talk, telling about the book they read.

→ Students should share their Venn diagrams and answer this question: *What was the most interesting comparison you learned from reading this book?*

→ They should also tell the group if there were any sections they reread to increase their understanding.

On Level

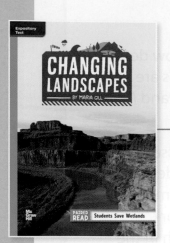

Lexile 840
TextEvaluator™ 32

OBJECTIVES

 Refer to details and examples in a text when explaining what the text says explicitly and when drawing inferences from the text. **RI.4.1**

Paraphrase portions of a text read aloud or information presented in diverse media and formats, including visually, quantitatively, and orally. **SL.4.2**

Leveled Reader:
Changing Landscapes

Before Reading

Preview and Predict

Read the Essential Question with students. Give students a copy of *Changing Landscapes* and have them read the title and table of contents, and respond to the cover photograph. Have students predict what the book will be about. Ask students to discuss how they think people respond to sudden changes.

Review Genre: Expository Text

Have students recall that expository text provides information about a topic. Expository text includes headings and diagrams that help the reader understand that topic. Have students identify features of expository text in *Changing Landscapes*.

During Reading

Close Reading

Note Taking Ask students to use their graphic organizer while they read.

Pages 2–3 *Why does the author ask you to imagine you are in a time machine?* (To allow the reader to identify with the text more closely.) *What does the author describe?* (how Earth's surface changes over time)

Pages 4–6 *Look at the diagram on page 4. How are the young and elderly rivers the same or different?* (In both phases, the river runs in the middle. In the older phase, the river goes back and forth more. The valley has a wider plain.) *What does the sidebar on page 6 tell about the topic?* (how a plant lives in the wetlands)

Pages 8–11 *Read pages 8–9. How do landslides affect people?* (They can cause damage.) *Compare and contrast how landslides and hurricanes affect land.* (Both cause damage and threaten people. Landslides occur in hilly areas with few trees or plants. Hurricanes occur in coastal areas and can cause flooding and change the shape of beaches.)

Go Digital

Leveled Readers

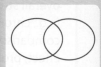

Use Graphic Organizer

Pages 12–13 *How do people work against natural protections from landslides?* (They remove plants and trees and clear out wetlands.) *What does* features *mean on page 12?* (characteristics)

Page 14 *Read page 14. Paraphrase to contrast land changes from weathering with land changes from natural disasters.* (Land changes from weathering happen slowly. Land changes from natural disasters happen quickly.)

After Reading

Respond to Reading Have students complete Respond to Reading on page 15 after they have finished reading.

Write About Reading *Analytical Writing* Have students work with a partner to write a short paragraph comparing and contrasting landslides and hurricanes. Make sure students cite supporting evidence from the text. Call on partners to read their responses.

Fluency: Accuracy

Model Model reading page 6 with accuracy, being sure to pronounce every word clearly and correctly. Next, read the passage aloud and have students read along with you.

Apply Have partners do repeated rereadings of the passage.

PAIRED READ

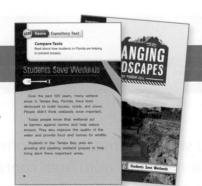

"Students Save Wetlands"

Make Connections:
Write About It *Analytical Writing*

Leveled Reader

Before reading, ask students to note that the genre of this story is expository text, which means it explains about a topic. Have students discuss the Essential Question. After reading, ask students to use the information from both texts to explain why it is important to keep the wetlands intact.

FOCUS ON SCIENCE

Students can extend their knowledge of how to prepare for natural disasters by completing the activity on page 20. **STEM**

Literature Circles

Ask students to conduct a literature circle using the Thinkmark questions to guide the discussion. You may wish to have a whole-class discussion on how students can help prevent natural disasters.

Level Up

Level-up lessons available online.

IF students read the On Level fluently and answered the questions

THEN pair them with students who have proficiently read the Beyond Level and have students

- partner-read the Beyond Level main selection.
- identify a part of *Changing Landscapes* they would like to learn more about.

A C T Access Complex Text

The Beyond Level challenges students by including more **domain-specific words** and **complex sentence structures**.

On Level

Vocabulary

REVIEW VOCABULARY WORDS

OBJECTIVES

 Acquire and use accurately grade-appropriate general academic and domain-specific words and phrases, including those that signal precise actions, emotions, or states of being (e.g., *quizzed, whined, stammered*) and that are basic to a particular topic (e.g., *wildlife, conservation,* and *endangered* when discussing animal preservation). **L.4.6**

 I Do Use the **Visual Vocabulary Cards** to review key selection words *alter, collapse, destruction, severe, substantial,* and *unpredictable*. Point to each word, read it aloud, and have students chorally repeat it.

 We Do Ask these questions and help students respond and explain their answers.
→ What makes a story *unpredictable*?
→ What types of *severe* weather have you seen or read about?
→ Why do sports teams spend a *substantial* amount of time practicing?

You Do Have students respond to these questions and explain their answers.
→ Why would people want to make an old building *collapse*?
→ How does fire safety prevent *destruction* to nature and property?
→ Why would an author decide to *alter* a story before it is finished?

CONTEXT CLUES: MULTIPLE-MEANING WORDS

OBJECTIVES

 Use context (e.g., definitions, examples, or restatements in text) as a clue to the meaning of a word or phrase. **L.4.4a**

 I Do Remind students that they can often figure out the correct meaning of a multiple-meaning word from context clues. Use the Comprehension and Fluency passage on **Your Turn Practice Book** pages 23–24 to model.

Think Aloud The multiple-meaning word *type* appears in the text. I know that *type* can mean to write on a keyboard or a group of things that are alike. The first sentence in the paragraph says that there are "two types of floods." From this clue, I think *type* means a group of things that are alike.

 We Do Have students continue reading. When they encounter *banks*, help them identify the context clues to its correct meaning in the text such as "too much water" and "water in a river rises."

 You Do Have students work in pairs to determine the context clues for the multiple-meaning words *wash* and *sponges* on page 24.

Comprehension

REVIEW COMPARE AND CONTRAST

OBJECTIVES

CCSS Describe the overall structure (e.g., chronology, comparison, cause/effect, problem/solution) of events, ideas, concepts, or information in a text or part of a text. **RI.4.5**

Summarize key details in a passage.

I Do Remind students that comparing information tells how details are alike and contrasting information tells how details are different. Authors may use signal words such as *some, but, both,* and *like* to signal comparisons they make in a text.

We Do Read the first page of the Comprehension and Fluency passage in **Your Turn Practice Book** together. Model how to compare and contrast details related to why floods occur: *What are two events that may cause a river to flood? What two events may cause a sea to flood land? How are these details similar and how are they different?* Then work with students to compare and contrast details in each paragraph in the passage.

You Do Have students use the details they have compared and contrasted to write a summary of the key details in the passage.

SELF-SELECTED READING

OBJECTIVES

CCSS Describe the overall structure (e.g., chronology, comparison, cause/effect, problem/solution) of events, ideas, concepts, or information in a text or part of a text. **RI.4.5**

Reread difficult sections in a text to increase understanding.

Read Independently

Have students choose an informational book for sustained silent reading.

→ Before they read, have students preview the book, reading the title and viewing the front and back cover.

→ As students read, remind them to reread difficult sections.

Read Purposefully

Encourage students to read different books in order to learn about a variety of subjects.

→ As students read, have them fill in the key details in a Venn diagram.

→ They can use a Venn diagram to help them analyze the information they have read and to write a summary of the book.

→ Ask students to share their reactions to the book with classmates.

→ Beyond Level

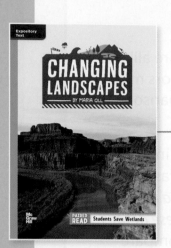

Lexile 920
TextEvaluator™ 32

OBJECTIVES

CCSS Refer to details and examples in a text when explaining what the text says explicitly and when drawing inferences from the text. **RI.4.1**

CCSS Use context (e.g., definitions, examples, or restatements in text) as a clue to the meaning of a word or phrase. **L.4.4a**

Leveled Reader:
Changing Landscapes

Before Reading

Preview and Predict

Have students read the Essential Question. Have students read the title and the first two pages of *Changing Landscapes*. Ask them to make predictions about what the title means and what the selection will be about.

Review Genre: Expository Text

Have students recall that expository text provides information about a topic. Expository text includes headings and diagrams that help the reader understand that topic. Have students identify features of expository text in *Changing Landscapes*.

During Reading

Close Reading

Note Taking Ask students to use their graphic organizer while they read.

Pages 2–3 *Why does the author set up the selection with the time machine passage?* (To help the reader visualize the drastic changes to the land over time.) *Reread page 3. What are three natural disasters that can alter the landscape?* (hurricanes, floods, and landslides)

Pages 4–7 *What does* sediment *mean on page 4?* (a mixture of rocks, sand, and silt) *Read page 6. Why are there insect-eating plants in the wetlands?* (The soil is low in nutrients.)

Pages 8–11 *How are landslides and hurricanes similar?* (They can both cause erosion.) *How are they different?* (Landslides move lots of rock and soil down hillsides at once. Hurricanes are strong storms that bring heavy rain and high winds. They can cause major flooding.)

Go Digital

Leveled Readers

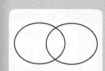

Use Graphic Organizer

Pages 12–14 *How do people play a role in environmental damage?* (They build on wetlands and dunes.) *How are others working to restore the wetlands and dunes?* (They plant grasses in wetlands or build sand dunes.)

After Reading

Respond to Reading

Have students complete Respond to Reading on page 15 after they have finished reading.

Analytical Writing **Write About Reading** Have students work with a partner to write about the similarities and differences between landslides and hurricanes. Make sure students cite three or four supporting details from the text.

Fluency: Accuracy

Model Model reading page 6 with accuracy, being sure to pronounce every word clearly and correctly. Next, read the passage aloud and have students read along with you.

Apply Have partners do repeated rereadings of the passage.

PAIRED READ

"Students Save Wetlands"

Make Connections:
Write About It • **Analytical Writing**

Before reading, ask students to note that the genre of this story is expository text, which means it explains about a topic. Have students discuss the Essential Question. After reading, ask students to use the information from both texts to explain why it is important to keep the wetlands intact.

Leveled Reader

Literature Circles

Ask students to conduct a literature circle using the Thinkmark questions to guide the discussion. You may wish to have a whole-class discussion on information learned about why it's important to help maintain the wetlands.

Gifted and Talented

Synthesize In *Changing Landscapes*, students learn about natural disasters and erosion. Challenge students to research ways to reduce the impact of such natural disasters on communities and the surrounding landscapes. Have each student write a short paragraph telling how he or she could help reduce the damage of natural disasters.

FOCUS ON SCIENCE

Students can extend their knowledge of how to prepare for natural disasters by completing the activity on page 20. **STEM**

Beyond Level

Vocabulary

REVIEW DOMAIN-SPECIFIC WORDS

OBJECTIVES

 Acquire and use accurately grade-appropriate general academic and domain-specific words and phrases, including those that signal precise actions, emotions, or states of being and that are basic to a particular topic. **L.4.6**

 Model Use the **Visual Vocabulary Cards** to review the meanings of the words *crisis* and *hazard*. Write sentences related to natural disasters on the board using these words.

Write the words *destruction* and *severe* on the board and discuss the meanings with students. Then help students write sentences using these words.

Apply Have students work in pairs to review the meanings of the words *disaster* and *substantial*. Then have partners write sentences about natural disasters using the words.

CONTEXT CLUES: MULTIPLE-MEANING WORDS

OBJECTIVES

 Use context (e.g., definitions, examples, or restatements in text) as a clue to the meaning of a word or phrase. **L.4.4a**

 Model Read aloud the first two paragraphs of the Comprehension and Fluency passage on **Beyond Reproducibles** pages 23–24.

Think Aloud The multiple-meaning word *fall* appears in the text. I know that *fall* is a season in the year, but *fall* also means to move down toward the ground. The text is discussing rainwater falling during storms, so I know the meaning of *fall* in the text is the action of rain moving down toward the ground.

With students, read the next paragraph. Help them identify the context clues for the multiple-meaning words *flash* and *banks*.

 Apply Have student pairs read the rest of the passage. Ask them to identify the context clues for the multiple-meaning words *wash* and *sponges*.

 Gifted and Talented **Synthesize** Have students compare and contrast how people respond to different natural disasters, such as flooding, earthquakes, and tornadoes. Encourage students to discuss how people around the world work to anticipate and be prepared for such events.

Comprehension

REVIEW COMPARE AND CONTRAST

OBJECTIVES

 Determine the main idea of a text and explain how it is supported by key details; summarize the text. **RI.4.2**

 Describe the overall structure (e.g., chronology, comparison, cause/effect, problem/solution) of events, ideas, concepts, or information in a text or part of a text. **RI.4.5**

Model

Remind students that comparison is one type of text structure that authors use to organize information. Explain how comparing information involves telling how details are alike and contrasting information involves telling how details are different. Review signal words that may help them recognize when an author uses the compare-and-contrast text structure, such as *some, but, both,* and *like*.

Have students read the first paragraph of the Comprehension and Fluency passage in **Beyond Reproducibles** pages 23–24. Ask open-ended questions to facilitate discussion, such as *What is the author comparing?* Students should support their responses with details in the text.

Apply

Have students compare and contrast details in each paragraph in the rest of the passage as they independently fill in a Venn diagram. Then have partners use their work to summarize the whole passage.

SELF-SELECTED READING

OBJECTIVES

 Describe the overall structure (e.g., chronology, comparison, cause/effect, problem/solution) of events, ideas, concepts, or information in a text or part of a text. **RI.4.5**

Reread difficult sections in a text to increase understanding.

Read Independently

Have students choose an informational book for sustained silent reading.

→ As students read, have them fill in a Venn diagram.

→ Remind them to reread difficult sections of the text.

Read Purposefully

Encourage students to keep a reading journal. Ask them to read different books in order to learn about a variety of subjects.

→ Students can write summaries of the books in their journals.

→ Ask students to share their reactions to the books with classmates.

 Evaluate Challenge students to discuss how their books relate to the weekly concept: Take Action. Have students discuss how they can take action to help make their school or community a safer place.

English Language Learners

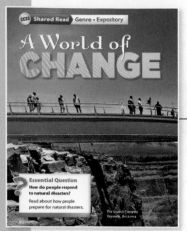

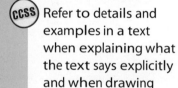

Reading/Writing Workshop

Shared Read
A World of Change

Before Reading

Build Background

Read the Essential Question: How do people respond to natural disasters?

→ Explain the meaning of the Essential Question. Respond *can mean to answer (for example, you answer, or respond to, a question). Respond can also mean to take action. Nature is everything around you that is not made by people, including the earth, the sea, and the weather. A natural disaster is when nature causes great destruction and harm.*

→ **Model an answer:** *People respond to natural disasters by helping others stay safe and by rebuilding what has been damaged or destroyed in a natural disaster. People may also respond by making sure they are prepared the next time a natural disaster happens.*

→ Ask students a question that ties the Essential Question to their own background knowledge: *Turn to a partner and think of a type of natural disaster you have learned about, such as an earthquake. Discuss what happens in an earthquake and how people can stay safe in an earthquake.* Call on several pairs.

During Reading

Interactive Question-Response

→ Ask questions that help students understand the meaning of the text after each paragraph.

→ Reinforce the meanings of key vocabulary.

→ Ask students questions that require them to use key vocabulary.

→ Reinforce strategies and skills of the week by modeling.

OBJECTIVES

CCSS Refer to details and examples in a text when explaining what the text says explicitly and when drawing inferences from the text. **RI.4.1**

CCSS Explain events, procedures, ideas, or concepts in a historical, scientific, or technical text, including what happened and why, based on specific information in the text. **RI.4.3**

CCSS Use context (e.g., definitions, examples, or restatements in text) as a clue to the meaning of a word or phrase. **L.4.4a**

LANGUAGE OBJECTIVE

Compare and contrast key details in the text.

Page 51

Paragraph 1
Chorally read the title and the first two lines on page 51. *When something is constant, it is always happening. Is our planet constantly changing?* (yes)

Point out the synonym *change* for *alter*. *Alter means to change.* Discuss everyday changes (for example, changes in weather or in the community). Tell students that they are going to learn about changes that happen on Earth.

Slow and Steady

Paragraph 1
This paragraph names three slow natural processes that change Earth's surface. Demonstrate the meaning of *surface* by pointing to the top of a desk. *This is the desk's surface. It is on the outside.* Have students say the word *surface. What are three examples of slow natural processes?* (weathering, erosion, and deposition)

Paragraph 2
Echo-read the first line. *When does weathering occur?* (when rain, snow, sun, and wind break down rocks into smaller pieces) Define *landform* as different shapes of land on Earth, such as a hill or mountain. Show pictures of landforms.

Paragraph 3
Explain and Model Multiple-Meaning Words
I know that weather *can refer to the temperature outside, but it can also mean "to be affected by the elements." The clues "pieces of rock" tell me that* weathered *means "broken down."*

Explain how erosion is the cause of the Grand Canyon. Encourage students to use the visuals on the page to demonstrate how the Colorado River carved the Grand Canyon over time.

Paragraph 4
To clarify the term *deposition,* demonstrate the act of taking away small quantities of objects, such as paper clips, and depositing them in another pile.

Have partners describe wind and water deposition. (Possible answer: Deposition by water can build up a beach. Deposition by wind can create a landform, such as a sand dune.)

Page 52

Fast and Powerful

Heading and Paragraph 1
Chorally read the heading. *What do you think this section describes?* (fast and powerful changes to Earth's surface)

Model Compare and Contrast *How are slow and fast natural processes different? How are they similar?* (Similar: both change the surface of the Earth; Different: slow processes happen over time; fast processes are fast and more powerful) Ask students to find clue words that show a comparison is being made. (like, But)

Page 53

Diagram
Have students identify the magma chamber and crater in the diagram as you read the labels. *What happens when a volcano erupts?* (Magma flows through the crater, or opening, of the volcano.)

Be Prepared

Paragraph 1
What is another difference between slow and fast natural processes? (People cannot prevent the effects in fast natural processes.)

After Reading

Make Connections
→ Review the Essential Question: How do people respond to natural disasters?

→ Make text connections.

→ Have students complete **ELL Reproducibles** pages 23–25.

→ English Language Learners

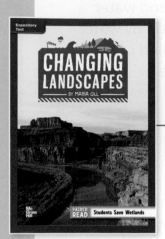

Lexile 740
TextEvaluator™ 20

OBJECTIVES

 Refer to details and examples in a text when explaining what the text says explicitly and when drawing inferences from the text. **RI.4.1**

CCSS Explain events, procedures, ideas, or concepts in a historical, scientific, or technical text, including what happened and why, based on specific information in the text. **RI.4.3**

Leveled Reader:
Changing Landscapes

Before Reading

Preview

→ Read the Essential Question: How do people respond to natural disasters?

→ Refer to To the Rescue: *What are some ways natural disasters can alter, or change, the surface of Earth?*

→ Preview *Changing Landscapes* and "Students Save Wetlands": *Our purpose for reading is learn about different changes to Earth's surface.*

Vocabulary

Use the **Visual Vocabulary Cards** to preteach the ELL vocabulary: *damage, force.* Use the routine found on the cards. Point out the cognate: *fuerza.*

During Reading

Interactive Question-Response

Note Taking Have students use their graphic organizer in **ELL Reproducibles,** page 22. Use the questions below after reading each section. As you read, define vocabulary, using visuals and examples.

Pages 2–3 Have students point to the labels on page 2. *The picture shows a landscape, or area of land. Natural disasters can change the landscape. What are two natural disasters?* (landslides, hurricanes)

Pages 4–5 Have students complete the sentence frame: ____ *happens when rocks and sand are carried away.* (Erosion) Explain that water can break, or crumble, rocks into smaller pieces. *What causes large rocks to break down into smaller pieces?* (weathering)

Pages 6–7 *Wetlands and dunes are land features. They slow down erosion.* Provide the frame and repeat with students: ____ (wetlands) *and* ____ (dunes) *slow down erosion. What does the diagram show on page 7?* (how wetlands work) Have students echo-read the diagram.

Pages 8–11 *How are hurricanes and landslides similar?* (Both are natural disasters that change the land quickly.) *How are they different?*

Go Digital

Leveled Readers

Use Graphic Organizer

(Landslides cause hillsides to collapse. Hurricanes bring heavy rain and cause a lot of destruction on land.)

Pages 12–14 *Can erosion be a problem?* (yes) *What can people do to prevent erosion?* (They can plant trees and other plants with long roots. They can replant wetlands and restore dunes to slow down erosion.)

After Reading

Respond to Reading Help students complete the graphic organizer. Revisit the Essential Question. Have pairs summarize and answer the Text Evidence Questions.

Analytical Writing **Write About Reading** Have partners write a short paragraph that describes the similarities between landslides and hurricanes. Encourage students to reread the text and use notes from their graphic organizer to support their responses.

Fluency: Accuracy

Model Model reading page 6 with accuracy, being sure to pronounce every word clearly and correctly. Next, read the passage aloud and have students read along with you.

Apply Have students practice reading a passage with a partner.

PAIRED READ

Leveled Reader

"Students Save Wetlands"

Make Connections:
Write About It *Analytical Writing*

Before reading, ask students to note that the genre of this story is expository text, which means it explains a topic. Then discuss the Essential Question. After reading, ask students to use the information from both texts to explain why it is important to keep the wetlands intact.

FOCUS ON SCIENCE

Students can extend their knowledge of preparing for natural disasters by completing the activity on page 20.
STEM

Literature Circles

Ask students to conduct a literature circle using the Thinkmark questions to guide the discussion. You may wish to have a whole-class discussion on ways that people can prevent erosion, drawing from both selections in the leveled reader.

Level Up

Level-up lessons available online.

IF students read the **ELL Level** fluently and answered the questions

THEN pair them with students who have proficiently read **On Level** and have ELL students

• echo-read the **On Level** main selection with their partners.

• list difficult words and phrases and discuss them with their partners.

A C T ccess omplex ext

The **On Level** challenges students by including more **domain-specific words** and **complex sentence structures**.

English Language Learners
Vocabulary

PRETEACH VOCABULARY

OBJECTIVES

 Acquire and use accurately grade-appropriate general academic and domain-specific words and phrases, including those that signal precise actions, emotions, or states of being and that are basic to a particular topic. **L.4.6**

LANGUAGE OBJECTIVE

Use vocabulary words.

I Do Preteach vocabulary from "A World of Change," following the Vocabulary Routine found on the **Visual Vocabulary Cards** for the words *alter, collapse, crisis, destruction, hazard, severe, substantial,* and *unpredictable.*

We Do After completing the routine for each word, point to the word on the Visual Vocabulary Card and read it. Ask students to repeat the word.

You Do Have small groups use *crisis* in a sentence. Then have each group read the sentence aloud. Repeat until at least four of the words have been used.

Beginning	Intermediate	Advanced/High
Help students write the sentences correctly and read them aloud.	Ask students to write one sentence for each word.	Challenge students to write synonyms for two of the words.

REVIEW VOCABULARY

OBJECTIVES

 Acquire and use accurately grade-appropriate general academic and domain-specific words and phrases, including those that signal precise actions, emotions, or states of being and that are basic to a particular topic. **L.4.6**

LANGUAGE OBJECTIVE

Use vocabulary words.

I Do Review the previous week's vocabulary words. The words can be reviewed over a few days. Read each word aloud, pointing to the word on the **Visual Vocabulary Card**. Have students repeat after you. Then follow the Vocabulary Routine on the back of each card.

We Do Make flash cards for each word, using synonyms, examples, nonexamples, or other clues. Have students read the clues and guess the word. Define and use each word in a sentence.

You Do Have small groups play the game with the words face up. Have students give clues for the word, then compare their clues with those on the card.

Beginning	Intermediate	Advanced/High
Help students list clue words and read them aloud.	Have students write sentences using the vocabulary from the cards.	Ask students to make their own set of flash cards with different clues.

CONTEXT CLUES: MULTIPLE-MEANING WORDS

OBJECTIVES

CCSS Use context (e.g., definitions, examples, or restatements in text) as a clue to the meaning of a word or phrase. **L.4.4a**

LANGUAGE OBJECTIVE

Use context clues to find the correct meaning of multiple-meaning words.

 I Do Read aloud the first paragraph of the Comprehension and Fluency passage on **ELL Reproducibles** pages 23–24, while students follow along. Summarize the paragraph. Point to the word *flash* and tell students that it is a multiple-meaning word. Explain that context clues, or words in the same sentence or paragraph, can help you figure out the meaning of *flash*.

Think Aloud I know that *flash* can mean to shine. *Flash* can also describe when something happens fast. I see the phrase "happens fast," so this tells me that a flash flood does not mean to shine.

 We Do Have students point to the word *safe* on page 23. Find the context clues for the word with students. Write the definition of the word on the board.

 You Do In pairs, have students identify the context clues for the words *waves* on page 23 and *wash* on page 24.

Beginning	Intermediate	Advanced/High
Help students locate the word and context clues on the page.	Ask students to locate and read aloud the context clues on the page.	Have students explain how "away" is a clue to the meaning of *wash*.

ADDITIONAL VOCABULARY

OBJECTIVES

CCSS Choose words and phrases to convey ideas precisely. **L.4.3a**

LANGUAGE OBJECTIVE

Use academic and high-frequency words.

 I Do List academic and high-frequency words from "A World of Change" and *Changing Landscapes: change, constant, natural, landscape, remove, shape,* and *surface.* Define each word for students: Natural *means not made or changed by people. When something is natural, it is part of nature.*

 We Do Model using the words in a sentence: *We can prepare for natural disasters.* Point to the picture of the volcano on pages 52–53 of "A World of Change." Provide sentence frames and complete them with students: *A volcano is a natural disaster. It can cause _____ .*

 You Do Have pairs write about three changes they read about in "A World of Change" or *Changing Landscapes,* using at least two words on the list.

Beginning	Intermediate	Advanced/High
Help students write sentences correctly and read them aloud.	Ask students to read their sentences aloud to the class.	Challenge students to write two questions, using the vocabulary words.

English Language Learners
Writing/Spelling

WRITING TRAIT: IDEAS

 OBJECTIVES
Develop the topic with facts, definitions, concrete details, quotations, or other information and examples related to the topic. **W.4.2b**

Add supporting details to revise writing.

LANGUAGE OBJECTIVE
Add supporting details to writing.

 I Do Explain that good writers use details to support the topic and to tell how things look, sound, smell, taste, and feel. Read the Expert Model aloud as students identify the main idea and details.

We Do Read a passage from "A World of Change." Identify the main idea. Then use a word web to generate details. Model using the main idea and details.

You Do Have pairs write a short paragraph about a natural disaster they have read about or witnessed. Ask them to use a word web with the main idea in the center and list at least three details. Edit each pair's writing.

Beginning	Intermediate	Advanced/High
Have students copy the edited sentences.	Have students revise supporting details for clarity and errors.	As they revise, challenge students to add another detail to their paragraphs.

SPELL WORDS WITH LONG *e*

 OBJECTIVES
Spell grade-appropriate words correctly, consulting references as needed. **L.4.2d**

LANGUAGE OBJECTIVE
Spell words with long *e*.

 I Do Read aloud the Spelling Words on page T164. Segment them into syllables, and attach a spelling to each sound. Point out that the vowel sound for (at least) one syllable in each word is long *e*. Have students repeat the words.

 We Do Read the Dictation Sentences on page T165 aloud for students. With each sentence, read the underlined word slowly and segment it into syllables with emphasis on the long *e* sound. Have students repeat after you and write the word. Repeat the activity with the remaining sentences.

 You Do Display the words. Have students exchange their list with a partner to check the spelling and write the words correctly.

Beginning	Intermediate	Advanced/High
Have students copy the words with correct spelling and say the words aloud.	After students have corrected their words, have pairs quiz each other.	After they have corrected their words, have pairs use each word in a sentence.

Grammar

SIMPLE AND COMPOUND SENTENCES

OBJECTIVES

 Use a comma before a coordinating conjunction in a compound sentence. **L.4.2c**

 Use coordinating and subordinating conjunctions. **L.3.1h**

 Produce simple, compound, and complex sentences. **L.3.1i**

Write simple and compound sentences.

LANGUAGE OBJECTIVE

Write sentences.

Language Transfers Handbook

Speakers of Cantonese, Haitian Creole, Hmong, Korean, and Vietnamese may make errors in subject-verb agreement as it is not used in the native language.

I Do Remind students that a simple sentence has one complete thought. Write on the board: *Juan plays the violin.* Identify the subject and verb in the simple sentence. Tell students that a compound sentence has two or more complete thoughts. Write on the board: *Juan plays the violin, and his sister plays the guitar.* Read aloud each clause and identify the subjects and verbs. Underline the comma and *and* in the sentence. Point out that compound sentences are often combined with a comma and a coordinating conjunction, such as *and, but, or, for, nor*, or *yet*.

We Do Write the pairs of simple sentences below on the board. Ask volunteers to combine the simple sentences with a conjunction to make compound sentences. Write students' responses on the board, pointing out the use of a comma. Read the compound sentences aloud and have students repeat.

> *Today is sunny. It is also warm outside.*
>
> *Miguel and I play soccer. We are on the same team.*
>
> *We wanted to play outside. It started to rain.*

You Do Have students work in pairs to write two compound sentences about their likes and dislikes. Challenge them to write a compound sentence in which they make a comparison using the conjunction *but*. For example: *I like apples, but she prefers oranges.* Provide sentence frames if necessary.

Beginning	**Intermediate**	**Advanced/High**
Have students copy their sentences and help them underline the conjunctions. Read the sentences aloud for students to repeat.	Ask students to explain why their sentences are examples of compound sentences.	Have students define simple and compound sentences. Then have them identify each complete thought in their compound sentences.

For extra support, have students complete the activities in the **Grammar Practice Reproducibles** during the week, using the routine below:

→ Explain the grammar skill.

→ Model the first activity in the Grammar Practice Reproducibles.

→ Have the whole group complete the next couple of activities. Then have students complete the rest with a partner.

→ Review the activities with correct answers.

PROGRESS MONITORING
Weekly Assessment

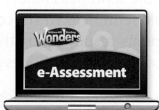

CCSS TESTED SKILLS

✔ **COMPREHENSION:** Compare and Contrast **RI.4.5**	✔ **VOCABULARY:** Context Clues: Multiple-Meaning Words **L.4.4a**	✔ **WRITING:** Writing About Text **RI.4.5, W.4.9b**

Grade 4

Wonders
Weekly Assessment

Assessing the Common Core State Standards

Wonders
e-Assessment

Assessment Includes

→ Pencil-and-paper administration

→ On-line administration

→ Approaching-Level Weekly Assessment also available

FLUENCY ←

Grades 1-6

Wonders
Fluency Assessment

Assessing the Common Core State Standards

Fluency Goal 84 to 104 words correct per minute (WCPM)

Accuracy Rate Goal 95% or higher

Administer oral reading fluency assessments using the following schedule:

→ **Weeks 1, 3, 5** Provide Approaching-Level students at least three oral reading fluency assessments during the unit.

→ **Weeks 2 and 4** Provide On-Level students at least two oral reading fluency assessments during the unit.

→ **Week 6** If necessary, provide Beyond-Level students an oral reading fluency assessment at this time.

Also Available: Selection Tests online PDFs

Go Digital! www.connected.mcgraw-hill.com

Using Assessment Results

TESTED SKILLS	If ...	Then ...
COMPREHENSION	Students answer 0–6 multiple-choice items correctly ...	... assign Lessons 79–81 on Compare and Contrast from the *Tier 2 Comprehension Intervention online PDFs.*
VOCABULARY	Students answer 0–6 multiple-choice items correctly ...	... assign Lesson 138 on Using Homograph Clues from the *Tier 2 Vocabulary Intervention online PDFs.*
WRITING	Students score less than "3" on the constructed response ...	... assign Lessons 79–81 and/or Write About Reading Lesson 200 from the *Tier 2 Comprehension Intervention online PDFs.*
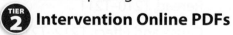	Students have a WCPM score of 76–83 ...	... assign a lesson from Section 1 or 7–10 of the *Tier 2 Fluency Intervention online PDFs.*
	Students have a WCPM score of 0–75 ...	... assign a lesson from Sections 2–6 of the *Tier 2 Fluency Intervention online PDFs.*

Response to Intervention

Use the appropriate sections of the *Placement and Diagnostic Assessment* as well as students' assessment results to designate students requiring:

TIER 2 **Intervention Online PDFs**

TIER 3 **WonderWorks Intervention Program**

WEEKLY OVERVIEW

McGraw-Hill Reading

Wonders

Reading/Writing Workshop

TEACH AND MODEL

Shared Read Genre • Narrative Nonfiction

The Big Race

This race car simulator is cool.

Let's try it!

Essential Question
How can science help you understand how things work?

Read how Alex and Liam want to use science to help them win a race.

64

GRAVITY AND FRICTION

Clara smiled, "Right! Another force acting on your car is **gravity**. Gravity is a pulling force between two objects." Clara took a tennis ball out of her pocket. "When I drop this ball, gravity pulls it towards the floor. It's the same force that pulls your car down the hill."

"So, a big push gives us an **advantage** over other cars, and gravity will keep us going. How do we stop?" Liam asked.

"You'll need **friction**. Friction is a force between two surfaces that slows objects down or stops them from moving. For example, I lean back on my skates, and the friction between the rubber stoppers and the floor slows me down," said Clara.

"Thanks, Clara! The virtual race car was cool! I knew we had the skills and **capabilities** to win the race, but now we have science on our side, too," Liam grinned.

You need friction.

Make Connections
Talk about ways that science can help you understand how objects move. ESSENTIAL QUESTION

How can science help you understand your favorite activities? TEXT TO SELF

67

✓ Vocabulary

accelerate

advantage

capabilities

friction

gravity

identity

inquiry

thrilling

 ## Close Reading of Complex Text

Shared Read "The Big Race," 64–67

Genre Narrative Nonfiction

Lexile 690

ETS *TextEvaluator™* 18

Minilessons ✓ Tested Skills CCSS

✓ **Comprehension Strategy** .... Reread, T210–T211

✓ **Comprehension Skill** .... Cause and Effect, T212–T213

✓ **Genre** .... Narrative Nonfiction, T214–T215

✓ **Vocabulary Strategy** .... Context Clues: Definitions and Restatements, T216–T217

✓ **Writing Traits** .... Organization, T222–T223

Grammar .... Clauses and Complex Sentences, T226–T227

 ☞ **Go Digital**

www.connected.mcgraw-hill.com

IDEAS IN MOTION
Essential Question
How can science help you
understand how things work?

WEEK 4 →

APPLY WITH CLOSE READING

Complex Text

Literature Anthology

PAIRED READ

*A Crash Course in Forces and Motion with
Max Axiom, Super Scientist,* 62–79
Genre Narrative Nonfiction
Lexile 630
(ETS) *TextEvaluator*™ 27

"The Box-Zip Project," 80–83
Genre Science Fiction
Lexile 620
(ETS) *TextEvaluator*™ 31

Differentiated Text

Leveled Readers   *Include Paired Reads*

APPROACHING
Lexile 550
(ETS) *TextEvaluator*™ 13

ON LEVEL
Lexile 810
(ETS) *TextEvaluator*™ 33

BEYOND
Lexile 910
(ETS) *TextEvaluator*™ 39

ELL
Lexile 610
(ETS) *TextEvaluator*™ 20

Extended Complex Text

*America's Champion
Swimmer: Gertrude
Ederle*
Genre Biography
Lexile 580
(ETS) *TextEvaluator*™ 38

Classroom Library

*Happy Birthday,
Martin Luther King*
Genre Biography
Lexile 800
(ETS) *TextEvaluator*™ 9

Classroom
Library
lessons available
online.

TEACH AND MANAGE

How You Teach

INTRODUCE

Weekly Concept
Ideas in Motion

**Reading/Writing Workshop
60–61**

TEACH

Close Reading
"The Big Race"

Minilessons
Reread, Cause and Effect, Narrative
Nonfiction, Context Clues,
Writing Traits

**Reading/Writing
Workshop
64–67**

APPLY

Close Reading
*A Crash Course in Forces and
Motion with Max Axiom, Super
Scientist* "The Box-Zip Project"

**Literature
Anthology
62–83**

 Go Digital

Interactive Whiteboard

Interactive Whiteboard

Mobile

How Students Practice

WEEKLY CONTRACT

PDF Online

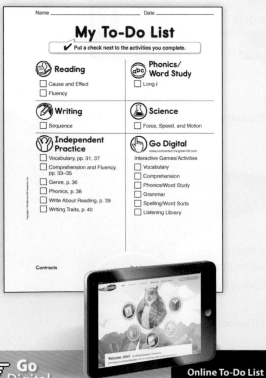

LEVELED PRACTICE AND ONLINE ACTIVITIES

**Your Turn Practice Book
31–40**

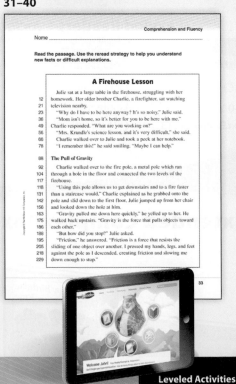

Leveled Readers

Go Digital

Online To-Do List

Leveled Activities

Writer's Workspace

DIFFERENTIATE

SMALL GROUP INSTRUCTION
Leveled Readers

Mobile

INTEGRATE

Research and Inquiry
Visual Display, T220

Text Connections
Compare How Things Work, T221

 Write About Reading
Write an Analysis, T221

**Online Research
and Writing**

ASSESS

**Weekly Assessment
37–48**

**Online
Assessment**

LEVELED WORKSTATION CARDS

More
Activities
on back

4

Speed and Motion

- Working with a partner, place a piece of chalk on the floor and gently tap it. Use the ruler to measure how far it rolled. Record the results.

- Next, place the chalk on fabric or carpet. Tap it with the

SCIENCE

6

Organization: Sequence

Read Mandi's paragraph about how to make a shadow box. Identify the sequence. Revise the paragraph to make the directions clear.

Your _box will look perfect on your

WRITING

4

Context Clues

barbecue

- Look up the words *rumble, stoops, barbecue,* and *strut* in a dictionary. Write a sentence for one. Include context clues to the word's meaning. (Example for *mango*: "He enjoyed eating the juicy sweet mango.")

- Write a paragraph using two of the other words. For the first word, include a context clue in a sentence other than the one in which the word is used. For the second word, include a definition or restatement as a clue to its meaning.

  You need
  20 minutes
  > dictionary
  > paper, pencils

- Exchange paragraphs. Identify your partner's context clues.

PHONICS/WORD STUDY

Go Digital! www.connected.mcgraw-hill.com • Interactive Games and Activities • Grade 4

7

Cause and Effect

- Choose an informational text that you have enjoyed reading in class. As you reread, identify pairs of events that have cause-and-effect relationships.

- For each pair of events, write the cause on one side of a note card and its related effect on the other side.

- Take turns reading one side of a card and asking your partner to identify the cause or effect that goes with it.

  You need
  15 minutes
  > informational text
  > note cards
  > pencils or pens

READING

Go Digital! www.connected.mcgraw-hill.com • Interactive Games and Activities • Grade 4

DEVELOPING READERS AND WRITERS

Write to Sources and Research

Paraphrase, T212–T213

Note Taking, T217B, T217T

Summarize, T217R

Cause and Effect, T217R

Make Connections: Essential Question, T217R, T217V, T221

Key Details, T217U

Research and Inquiry, T220

Analyze to Inform/Explain, T221

Comparing Texts, T233, T241, T245, T251

Predictive Writing, T217B

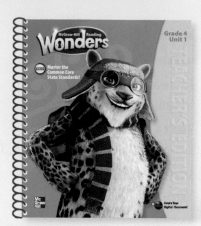

Teacher's Edition

Summarize, 79
Cause and Effect, 79

Literature Anthology

Leveled Readers
Comparing Texts
Cause and Effect

Cause and Effect, 33–35
Genre, 36
Analyze to Inform, 39

Your Turn Practice Book

Interactive Whiteboard

Narrative Text
Personal Narrative, T350–T355

Conferencing Routines
Teacher Conferences, T352
Peer Conferences, T353

Interactive Whiteboard

Teacher's Edition

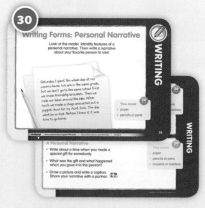

Leveled Workstation Card
Personal Narrative, Card 30

Writer's Workspace
Personal Narrative
Writing Process
Multimedia Presentations

Writing Traits • Write Every Day

Writing Trait: Organization
Sequence, T222–T223

Conferencing Routines
Teacher Conferences, T224
Peer Conferences, T225

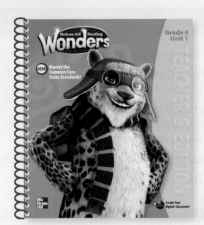

Teacher's Edition

Organization:
Sequence, 72–73

Reading/Writing Workshop

Interactive Whiteboard

Organization:
Sequence,
Card 6

Leveled Workstation Card

Organization:
Sequence, 40

Your Turn Practice Book

Grammar and Spelling

Grammar
Clauses and Complex
Sentences, T226–T227

Spelling
Long *i*, T228–T229

Interactive Whiteboard

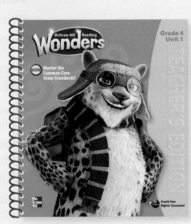

Teacher's Edition

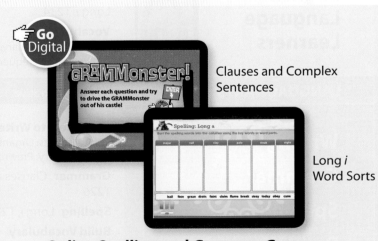

Clauses and Complex
Sentences

Long *i*
Word Sorts

Online Spelling and Grammar Games

SUGGESTED LESSON PLAN

✔ **TESTED SKILLS**

	DAY 1	DAY 2

READING

Whole Group

Teach, Model and Apply

Reading/Writing Workshop

DAY 1

Build Background Ideas in Motion, T202–T203

Listening Comprehension Interactive Read Aloud: "Look Out Below!", T204–T205

Comprehension
• Preview Genre: Narrative Nonfiction
• Preview Strategy: Reread

✔ **Vocabulary** Words in Context, T206–T207

Practice *Your Turn*, 31

Close Reading of Complex Text "The Big Race," 64–67

DAY 2

✔ **Comprehension**
• Strategy: Reread, T210–T211
• Skill: Cause and Effect, T212–T213
• Write About Reading ● *Analytical Writing*
• Genre: Narrative Nonfiction, T214–T215

✔ **Vocabulary** Strategy: Context Clues, T216–217

Practice *Your Turn*, 32–37

DIFFERENTIATED INSTRUCTION Choose across the week to meet your students' needs.

Small Group

Approaching Level

DAY 1

Leveled Reader *George's Giant Wheel*, T232–T233

Phonics/Decoding Decode Words with Long *i*, T234 (TIER 2)

Vocabulary
• Review High-Frequency Words, T236 (TIER 2)
• Identify Related Words, T237

DAY 2

Leveled Reader *George's Giant Wheel*, T232–T233

Vocabulary Review Vocabulary Words, T236 (TIER 2)

Comprehension
• Identify Important Effects, T238 (TIER 2)
• Review Cause and Effect, T239

On Level

DAY 1

Leveled Reader *George's Giant Wheel*, T240–T241

Vocabulary Review Vocabulary Words, T242

DAY 2

Leveled Reader *George's Giant Wheel*, T240–T241

Comprehension Review Cause and Effect, T243

Beyond Level

DAY 1

Leveled Reader *George's Giant Wheel*, T244–T245

Vocabulary Review Domain-Specific Words, T246

DAY 2

Leveled Reader *George's Giant Wheel*, T244–T245

Comprehension Review Cause and Effect, T247

English Language Learners

DAY 1

Shared Read "The Big Race," T248–T249

Phonics/Decoding Decode Words with Long *i*, T234

Vocabulary
• Preteach Vocabulary, T252
• Review High-Frequency Words, T236

DAY 2

Leveled Reader *George's Giant Wheel*, T250–T251

Vocabulary Review Vocabulary, T252

Writing Writing Trait: Organization, T254

Grammar Clauses and Complex Sentences, T255

LANGUAGE ARTS Writing Process: Personal Narrative, T350–T355 Use with Weeks 4–6

Whole Group

Writing

Grammar

Spelling

Build Vocabulary

DAY 1

✔ **Readers to Writers**
• Writing Traits: Organization/Sequence, T222–T223
• Writing Entry: Prewrite and Draft, T224

Grammar Clauses and Complex Sentences, T226

Spelling Long *i*, T228

Build Vocabulary
• Connect to Words, T230
• Academic Vocabulary, T230

DAY 2

Readers to Writers
• Writing Entry: Revise, T224

Grammar Clauses and Complex Sentences, T226

Spelling Long *i*, T228

Build Vocabulary
• Expand Vocabulary, T230
• Review Multiple-Meaning Words, T230

DAY 3	DAY 4	DAY 5 Review and Assess

READING

Phonics/Decoding
• Long *i*, T218
• Inflectional Endings, T219

Practice *Your Turn,* 38

Close Reading *A Crash Course in Forces and Motion with Max Axiom,* 62–79 • *Analytical Writing*

Literature Anthology

Fluency Phrasing and Rate, T219

Integrate Ideas *Analytical Writing*
• Research and Inquiry, T220

Practice *Your Turn,* 33–35

Close Reading "The Box-Zip Project," 80–83 • *Analytical Writing*

Integrate Ideas • *Analytical Writing*
• Research and Inquiry, T220
• Text Connections, T221
• Write About Reading, T221

Practice *Your Turn,* 39

DIFFERENTIATED INSTRUCTION

Leveled Reader *George's Giant Wheel,* T232–T233
Phonics/Decoding Review Long *i*, T234 **TIER 2**
Fluency Phrasing and Rate, T238 **TIER 2**
Vocabulary Context Clues, T237

Leveled Reader Paired Read: "3001: A Space Mystery," T233 • *Analytical Writing*
Phonics/Decoding Practice Long *i*, T235

Leveled Reader Literature Circles, T233
Comprehension Self-Selected Reading, T239
Phonics/Decoding Inflectional Endings, T235

Leveled Reader *George's Giant Wheel,* T240–T241
Vocabulary Context Clues, T242

Leveled Reader Paired Read: "3001: A Space Mystery," T241 • *Analytical Writing*

Leveled Reader Literature Circles, T241
Comprehension Self-Selected Reading, T243

Leveled Reader *George's Giant Wheel,* T244–T245
Vocabulary
• Context Clues, T246
• Synthesize, T246 *Gifted and Talented*

Leveled Reader Paired Read: "3001: A Space Mystery," T245 • *Analytical Writing*

Leveled Reader Literature Circles, T245
Comprehension
• Self-Selected Reading, T247
• Independent Study: Ideas in Motion, T247

Leveled Reader *George's Giant Wheel,* T250–T251
Phonics/Decoding Review Long *i*, T234
Vocabulary Context Clues, T253
Spelling Words with Long *i*, T254

Leveled Reader Paired Read: "3001: A Space Mystery," T251 • *Analytical Writing*
Vocabulary Additional Vocabulary, T253
Phonics/Decoding Practice Long *i*, T235

Leveled Reader Literature Circles, T251
Phonics/Decoding Inflectional Endings, T235

LANGUAGE ARTS

Readers to Writers
• Writing Entry: Prewrite and Draft, T225

Grammar Mechanics and Usage, T227

Spelling Long *i*, T229

Build Vocabulary
• Reinforce the Words, T231
• Context Clues, T231

Readers to Writers
• Writing Entry: Revise, T225

Grammar Clauses and Complex Sentences, T227

Spelling Long *i*, T229

Build Vocabulary
• Connect to Writing, T231
• Shades of Meaning, T231

Readers to Writers
• Writing Entry: Share and Reflect, T225

Grammar Clauses and Complex Sentences, T227

Spelling Long *i*, T229

Build Vocabulary
• Word Squares, T231
• Morphology, T231

DIFFERENTIATE TO ACCELERATE

A C T Scaffold to Access Complex Text

IF → the text complexity of a particular selection is too difficult for students

THEN → see the references noted in the chart below for scaffolded instruction to help students Access Complex Text.

Qualitative — Quantitative
Reader and Task
TEXT COMPLEXITY

	Reading/Writing Workshop	Literature Anthology	Leveled Readers	Classroom Library

Quantitative	**"The Big Race"** Lexile 690 *TextEvaluator*™ 18	***A Crash Course in Forces and Motion with Max Axiom*** Lexile 630 *TextEvaluator*™ 26 **"The Box-Zip Project"** Lexile 620 *TextEvaluator*™ 31	**Approaching Level** Lexile 550 *TextEvaluator*™ 13 **Beyond Level** Lexile 910 *TextEvaluator*™ 39 **On Level** Lexile 810 *TextEvaluator*™ 33 **ELL** Lexile 610 *TextEvaluator*™ 20	***America's Champion Swimmer: Gertrude Ederle*** Lexile 580 *TextEvaluator*™ 36 ***Happy Birthday, Martin Luther King*** Lexile 800 *TextEvaluator*™ 9
Qualitative	**What Makes the Text Complex?** • **Genre** Headings T209 • **Organization** Demonstrations T217 **A C T** *See Scaffolded Instruction in Teacher's Edition T209 and T217.*	**What Makes the Text Complex?** • **Organization** Sequence T217A, T217G; Compare T217O; Dialogue T217U • **Purpose** Illustrations T217C • **Connection of Ideas** Information T217E, T217H, T217M • **Genre** Text Features T217I • **Specific Vocabulary** Illustrations T217N; Unfamiliar Words T217S **A C T** *See Scaffolded Instruction in Teacher's Edition T217A–T217V.*	**What Makes the Text Complex?** • **Specific Vocabulary** • **Prior Knowledge** • **Sentence Structure** • **Connection of Ideas** • **Genre** **A C T** *See Level Up lessons online for Leveled Readers.*	**What Makes the Text Complex?** • **Genre** • **Specific Vocabulary** • **Prior Knowledge** • **Sentence Structure** • **Organization** • **Purpose** • **Connection of Ideas** **A C T** *See Scaffolded Instruction in Teacher's Edition T360–T361.*
Reader and Task	The Introduce the Concept lesson on pages T202–T203 will help determine the reader's knowledge and engagement in the weekly concept. See pages T208–T217 and T220–T221 for questions and tasks for this text.	The Introduce the Concept lesson on pages T202–T203 will help determine the reader's knowledge and engagement in the weekly concept. See pages T217A–T217V and T220–T221 for questions and tasks for this text.	The Introduce the Concept lesson on pages T202–T203 will help determine the reader's knowledge and engagement in the weekly concept. See pages T232–T233, T240–T241, T244–T245, T250–T251, and T220–T221 for questions and tasks for this text.	The Introduce the Concept lesson on pages T202–T203 will help determine the reader's knowledge and engagement in the weekly concept. See pages T360–T361 for questions and tasks for this text.

Go Digital! www.connected.mcgraw-hill.com

Monitor and *Differentiate*

IF ▶ you need to differentiate instruction

THEN ▶ use the Quick Checks to assess students' needs and select the appropriate small group instruction focus.

✓ Quick Check

Comprehension Strategy Reread T211

Comprehension Skill Text Structure: Cause and Effect T213

Genre Narrative Nonfiction T215

Vocabulary Strategy Context Clues T217

Phonics/Fluency Long *i* T219

If No →	**Approaching Level**	**Reteach** T232–T239
	ELL	**Develop** T248–T255
If Yes →	**On Level**	**Review** T240–T243
	Beyond Level	**Extend** T244–T247

Level Up with Leveled Readers

IF ▶ students can read their leveled text fluently and answer comprehension questions

THEN ▶ work with the next level up to accelerate students' reading with more complex text.

T241

T233   T251

ENGLISH LANGUAGE LEARNERS
SCAFFOLD

IF ELL students need additional support **THEN** ▶ scaffold instruction using the small group suggestions.

Reading/Writing Workshop "The Big Race" T248–T249	Leveled Reader *George's Giant Wheel* T250–T251 "3001: A Space Mystery" T251	Additional Vocabulary T253 force invention machine science speed technology	Using Context Clues T253	Writing Organization T254	Spelling Words with Long *i* T254	Grammar Clauses and Complex Sentences T255

Note: Include ELL Students in all small groups based on their needs.

→ Introduce the Concept

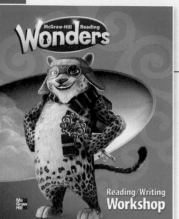

Reading/Writing Workshop

OBJECTIVES

CCSS Pose and respond to specific questions to clarify or follow up on information, and make comments that contribute to the discussion and link to the remarks of others. **SL.4.1c**

Build background knowledge on forces and motion.

ACADEMIC LANGUAGE
• accelerate, inquiry
• Cognate: acelerar

 MINILESSON **10** Mins

Build Background

ESSENTIAL QUESTION
How can science help you understand how things work?

Have students read the Essential Question on page 60 of the **Reading/Writing Workshop**. Explain that science is about **inquiry**, or asking questions and trying to find out the answers.

Discuss the photograph of the roller coaster. Focus on how science can help explain the forces that make it work.

→ Gravity is what makes roller coasters so thrilling. As a roller coaster starts down a hill, gravity causes it to **accelerate**.

→ The force created by the acceleration presses you against the seat of the coaster. This keeps you in place during a loop-the-loop.

Talk About It

COLLABORATE

Ask: *How do gravity and **acceleration** combine to make roller coasters more fun? How did your **inquiry** into the science of roller coasters help you better understand them?* Have students discuss in pairs or groups.

→ Model using the Concept Web to generate words and phrases related to the science of motion. Add students' contributions.

→ Have partners continue the discussion by sharing what they have learned about the science of motion. They can complete the Concept Web, generating additional words and phrases.

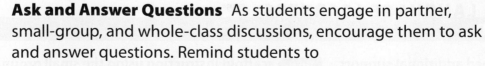

Collaborative Conversations

Ask and Answer Questions As students engage in partner, small-group, and whole-class discussions, encourage them to ask and answer questions. Remind students to

→ ask questions to clarify information they do not understand

→ wait a few seconds after asking a question to give others a chance to think before responding.

→ answer questions thoughtfully with complete ideas, not one-word answers.

Go Digital

Discuss the Concept

Watch Video

View Photos

Motion
Use Graphic Organizer

Essential Question
How can science help you understand how things work?

Go Digital!

HOW DOES IT WORK?

Science can help us understand a lot of things—from how to throw a curve ball to what happens when you ride a roller coaster. Look at this picture. What keeps these people from falling out? Let's use science to find out!

▶ How do you stay in place during the loop-the-loops? The force created by the acceleration presses you against the seat of the coaster.

▶ What kind of rides have you ridden on at an amusement park? Why did you like them?

Talk About It

Write words that you have learned about motion. Talk to your partner about a ride that you would design.

Motion

60 · 61

READING/WRITING WORKSHOP, pp. 60–61

ENGLISH LANGUAGE LEARNERS SCAFFOLD

Beginning	Intermediate	Advanced/High
Use Visuals Point to the roller coaster. Say: *This is a roller coaster. A roller coaster goes very fast. See how it goes around a loop.* Demonstrate the motion of a roller coaster. Ask students to describe the movements of the roller coaster. Allow ample time to respond.	**Describe** Have students describe what they know about roller coasters. Ask: *Have you ever gone on a roller coaster ride? Describe how it felt.* Encourage students to use concept words in their descriptions.	**Discuss** Ask students to come up with questions that can help them understand how roller coasters move. For example: *What makes a roller coaster go fast? How do roller coasters stop? How can roller coasters turn upside down?* Then discuss the answers.

GRAPHIC ORGANIZER 62

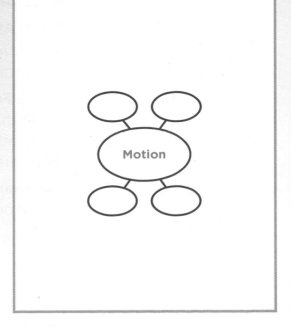

Motion

Listening Comprehension

MINILESSON
10 Mins

Interactive Read Aloud

Go Digital

View Photos

OBJECTIVES

 Determine the main idea of a text and explain how it is supported by key details; summarize the text. **RI.4.2**

CCSS Explain events, procedures, ideas, or concepts in a historical, scientific, or technical text, including what happened and why, based on specific information in the text. **RI.4.3**

• Listen for a purpose.
• Identify characteristics of narrative nonfiction.

ACADEMIC LANGUAGE

narrative nonfiction; reread

Connect to Concept: Ideas in Motion

Tell students that science helps people understand how things work. Let students know that you will be reading aloud a passage that tells how an apple helped a man better understand gravity. Explain that their purpose in listening is to gain information and to think about how the passage answers the Essential Question.

Preview Genre: Narrative Nonfiction

Explain that the passage you will read aloud is narrative nonfiction. Discuss features of narrative nonfiction:

→ its main purpose is to inform
→ may include an introduction that provides background
→ may use an interesting story to tell facts about an event

Preview Comprehension Strategy: Reread

Explain that when reading informational text, readers can read the text again, or reread, if they feel they may have missed an important point. They can also reread to better understand any facts or details that were unclear.

Use the Think Alouds on page T205 to model the strategy.

Respond to Reading

Think Aloud Clouds Display Think Aloud Master 4: *When I read _____, I had to reread . . .* to reinforce how you used the reread strategy to understand content.

Genre Features With students, discuss the elements of the Read Aloud that let them know it is narrative nonfiction. Ask them to think about other texts that you have read or they have read independently that were narrative nonfiction.

Summarize Have students restate the most important information from "Look Out Below!" in their own words.

When I read _____,
I had to reread...

Model Think Alouds

Genre	Features

Fill in Genre Chart

Look Out Below!

"Kyle, lunch!" Mom called up through the leaves to where I sat in the tree house reading. When my mom, a science writer, was working on a new article, it was best if I stayed out of her way.

"I'm here!" I yelled as I leaned out and let down the basket. Mom placed a wrapped sandwich and an apple inside, and I started to haul the basket up. But right before it got to the top, it got caught on a limb and began to tip. I reached to grab it and got the sandwich but not the apple. "Look out below!" I called as the apple landed at her feet. "Sorry, Mom! Are you okay?"

"I'm fine," she said, laughing. "It's funny. I was just writing about Isaac Newton!"

"The guy who invented gravity, right?" I said. She gave me a look. **1**

"He didn't invent gravity. The story goes that he fell asleep in his garden one day and an apple fell on his head, which caused him to start thinking about the force of gravity and how it works.

I imagine he may have asked himself, 'Why did the apple fall down instead of up, or even sideways?'" **2**

"Hey, yeah, that's a good question," I said.

"Certainly Newton thought so," Mom said. "He wondered if this force called gravity applied to every object—for example, the moon, the sun, and the planets. Can't you see him sitting there holding the apple and asking, 'What keeps the moon from falling to Earth as this apple did?' By asking questions and, as he once said, thinking continually about how to solve a problem, he figured out the Law of Universal Gravitation. It was a huge development, and it eventually led to a new understanding of how and why planets orbit the sun. He went on to study other forces of nature and figured out how to measure their effects. What a guy!" **3**

Mom threw the apple up to me, and I caught it. "Thanks for the inspiration," she said. "I'm ready to get back to work!"

1 **Think Aloud** I want to go back and **reread** the paragraph about the apple falling out of the basket. Maybe this will help me understand the connection Kyle's mom makes to Isaac Newton.

2 **Think Aloud** I want to **reread** the previous paragraph to make sure I understand who Isaac Newton was and how he solved problems.

3 **Think Aloud** I guess before Newton made these discoveries, people didn't understand what gravity was or how it worked. I want to **reread** this section because I think it gives important information.

Stockbroker/SuperStock

→ Vocabulary

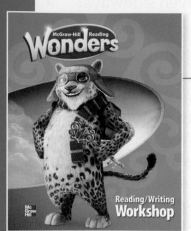

Reading/Writing Workshop

McGraw-Hill Reading
Wonders
Reading/Writing
Workshop

OBJECTIVES

CCSS Acquire and use accurately grade-appropriate general academic and domain-specific words and phrases, including those that signal precise actions, emotions, or states of being (e.g., *quizzed, whined, stammered*) and that are basic to a particular topic (e.g., *wildlife, conservation,* and *endangered* when discussing animal preservation). **L.4.6**

ACADEMIC LANGUAGE

- *accelerate, inquiry*
- Cognate: *acelerar*

MINILESSON 10 Mins

Words in Context

Model the Routine

Introduce each vocabulary word using the Vocabulary Routine found on the Visual Vocabulary Cards.

Visual Vocabulary Cards

Vocab...
Define:
Example:
Ask:

Vocabulary Routine

Define: To have **capabilities** means to have the needed skills, powers, or abilities.

Example: The capabilities of a potter include strength and creativity.

Ask: What capabilities would an athlete need?

Definitions

→ **accelerate**   To **accelerate** means to move or cause to move faster.

→ **advantage**   An **advantage** is something that is helpful or useful.

→ **friction**   **Friction** is a force between surfaces that slows objects or stops them from moving.
   Cognate: *fricción*

→ **gravity**   **Gravity** is a force that pulls objects toward each other.

→ **identity**   An **identity** is who a person is or what a thing is.
   Cognate: *identidad*

→ **inquiry**   An **inquiry** is a search for information.

→ **thrilling**   To be **thrilling** means to be exciting.

Talk About It

COLLABORATE

Have students work with a partner and look at each picture and discuss the definition of each word. Then ask students to choose three words and write questions for their partner to answer.

Go Digital

capabilities
Use Visual Glossary

CCSS Words to Know

Vocabulary

Use the picture and the sentences to talk with a partner about each word.

accelerate
I saw the race car **accelerate**, or speed up, across the finish line.

What is an antonym for accelerate?

advantage
The father's size gave him a big **advantage** over his son.

What is a synonym for advantage?

capabilities
The **capabilities** of a potter include strength and creativity.

What capabilities would an athlete need?

friction
The **friction** between the tires and the pavement slows down the airplane.

How is using the brakes on a bike an example of friction?

gravity
Gravity helps pull the batter down into the baking pan.

Describe what would happen if there were no gravity on Earth.

identity
The woman showed her passport to prove her **identity**.

Why might somebody want to keep his or her identity a secret?

inquiry
Reporters ask questions at the beginning of any **inquiry** or investigation.

How are the words inquiry and investigation similar?

thrilling
Going on a roller coaster can be exciting and **thrilling**.

What is an antonym for thrilling?

Your Turn

Pick three words. Write three questions for your partner to answer.

Go Digital! *Use the online visual glossary*

62   63

READING/WRITING WORKSHOP, pp. 62–63

ELL ENGLISH LANGUAGE LEARNERS SCAFFOLD

Beginning

Use Visuals *Let's look at the picture for the word* friction. *Friction is a force that stops or slows down two objects.* Have a volunteer demonstrate friction by rubbing his or her shoes against the floor. Say: *Friction causes the shoes to slow down.* Have students repeat.

Intermediate

Describe Have students describe the picture. Help them with the pronunciation of *friction.* Ask: *Who can give me another example of friction?* Ask them to turn to a partner and tell each other what they learned about friction. Clarify students' responses.

Advanced/High

Discuss Ask students to define the word *friction.* Then have partners experiment with friction using classroom materials. Have volunteers demonstrate their experiments in front of the class and explain how friction works. Restate students' responses.

ON-LEVEL PRACTICE BOOK p. 31

| thrilling | capabilities | friction | gravity |
| accelerate | inquiry | identity | advantage |

Finish each sentence using the vocabulary word provided.
Possible responses provided.

1. (friction) I use the brakes on my roller skates to create *friction* to slow me down.

2. (identity) The policeman asked me to show my ID card to prove my *identity*.

3. (thrilling) At the amusement park, the roller coaster was the most *thrilling* ride.

4. (advantage) The fact that the basketball player is very tall is an *advantage* for him and his team.

5. (gravity) The apple fell from the tree because it was pulled down by *gravity*.

6. (accelerate) When traveling downhill, my skateboard tends to *accelerate*.

7. (inquiry) I used the Internet to find the answer to my *inquiry*.

8. (capabilities) My friend is good at math and English and he showed his *capabilities* when he got an 'A' on both exams.

| APPROACHING p. 31 | BEYOND p. 31 | ELL p. 31 |

CCSS **Shared Read** | Genre • Narrative Nonfiction

THE BIG Race

This race car simulator is cool.

Let's try it!

I'm Clara. Welcome!

Essential Question

How can science help you understand how things work?

Read how Alex and Liam want to use science to help them win a race.

64

Alex and Liam planned to build a car for the soap box derby. As a result of their **inquiry** into how to build a fast car, they had come to the science museum today for answers. Last week, Alex's mother had called one of the museum's scientists. When they walked into the museum, a woman in a lab coat and inline skates zoomed up and greeted them.

"Hi, I'm Clara. Are you the boys who want to know what will make a car go fast?"

"Yes, I'm Alex, and that's Liam," Alex responded.

"Why are you wearing inline skates, Clara?" Liam asked.

"I'm a champion skater!" Clara claimed, doing a spin. Then she whispered, "That's not my true **identity**. I'm a scientist. Skates make it easier to get around. Follow me!"

IT'S ABOUT SPEED

"Welcome to our On the Move exhibit," Clara announced as they entered a large room. "So, tell me about the race."

"There will be 20 cars in the race. We'll be going down the steepest hill in town!" Alex said.

"Sounds **thrilling**! It must be exciting to go fast!" Clara answered as she pressed buttons on a machine. "This is a virtual race car, and this screen shows you the virtual race course and your speed. Speed is the distance an object moves in a certain amount of time."

65

READING/WRITING WORKSHOP, pp. 64–65

Reading/Writing Workshop

Shared Read

Lexile 690   *TextEvaluator* 18

Connect to Concept: Ideas in Motion

Explain to students that "The Big Race" will tell them more about how science can help them understand how objects move. Read "The Big Race" with students. Note the vocabulary words previously taught are highlighted in the text.

Close Reading

Reread Paragraph 1: Tell students that you are going to take a closer look at the introduction to "The Big Race." Reread the first paragraph together. Ask: *Why are Alex and Liam at the science museum?* Model how to cite evidence to answer the question.

An inquiry is a search for information, so Alex and Liam are at the museum to get information about how to build a fast car.

Reread Section 2: Model how to paraphrase the information in the section "It's About Speed." Remind students that paraphrasing or restating the text in your own words helps to ensure that you understand what you are reading about.

Clara takes Alex and Liam to the On the Move exhibit. She asks them about the race, and they tell her they will be going down the steepest hill in town. Then she shows them a virtual race car and explains what speed is.

FORCES AT WORK

Alex and Liam climbed into the machine. Each seat had a steering wheel and a screen in front of it.

Clara said, "Since you want to build a fast car, you need to know about forces and how they affect motion."

"What's a force?" asked Liam.

Clara continued, "A force is a push or a pull. Forces cause things to move or cause a change in motion. When I apply a big enough force on an object, like this stool, it moves. If two objects are exactly the same, the object that receives a bigger force will **accelerate**, or increase its speed," Clara said, pushing two stools at the same time.

"Which stool received a bigger force?" Clara asked.

"The one on the right. It went farther," said Liam.

"So, giving our car a big push at the top of the hill will cause it to accelerate and go faster," Alex summarized.

A force is a push or pull.

There's a sharp curve coming up!

I'm going to accelerate now!

66

GRAVITY AND FRICTION

Clara smiled, "Right! Another force acting on your car is **gravity**. Gravity is a pulling force between two objects." Clara took a tennis ball out of her pocket. "When I drop this ball, gravity pulls it towards the floor. It's the same force that pulls your car down the hill."

"So, a big push gives us an **advantage** over other cars, and gravity will keep us going. How do we stop?" Liam asked.

"You'll need **friction**. Friction is a force between two surfaces that slows objects down or stops them from moving. For example, I lean back on my skates, and the friction between the rubber stoppers and the floor slows me down," said Clara.

"Thanks, Clara! The virtual race car was cool! I knew we had the skills and **capabilities** to win the race, but now we have science on our side, too," Liam grinned.

You need friction.

Make Connections

? Talk about ways that science can help you understand how objects move. **ESSENTIAL QUESTION**

How can science help you understand your favorite activities? **TEXT TO SELF**

67

Craig Phillips

READING/WRITING WORKSHOP, pp. 66–67

Make Connections

ESSENTIAL QUESTION

Have students review their purpose for reading and tell a partner what they have learned about how science can help them understand how things move.

Continue Close Reading

Use the following lessons for focused rereadings.

→ Reread, T210–T211

→ Cause and Effect, T212–T213

→ Narrative Nonfiction, T214–T215

→ Context Clues: Definitions and Restatements, T216–T217

A C T Access Complex Text

▶ **Genre**

Remind students "The Big Race" is narrative nonfiction. Ask students to find the heading on page 65.

→ *How does this heading relate to the section of text beneath it?* (In this section, Clara explains what speed is.)

→ *What is the purpose of headings?* (They organize the text and give the reader an idea of what the text is about.)

→ Comprehension Strategy

Reading/Writing Workshop

OBJECTIVES

CCSS Refer to details and examples in a text when explaining what the text says explicitly and when drawing inferences from the text. **RI.4.1**

Reread difficult sections to increase understanding.

ACADEMIC LANGUAGE
reread, narrative nonfiction

MINILESSON 10 Mins — Reread

1 Explain

Explain that when students read narrative nonfiction, they may come across facts and explanations that are new to them. Remind students that they can reread challenging sections of the text to increase their understanding.

→ Good readers reread something they do not understand.

→ When students encounter unclear or difficult text, they can reread that section. They may need to reread more than once to make sure they understand.

→ Students may find that rereading improves their understanding of narrative nonfiction.

Point out that rereading will also help them remember the most important ideas and details.

2 Model Close Reading: Text Evidence

Model how rereading can help you understand the meaning of a challenging word, such as *accelerate*. Reread the section "Forces at Work" on page 66 of "The Big Race."

3 Guided Practice of Close Reading

COLLABORATE

Have students work in pairs to explain what gravity does. Direct them to reread the "Gravity and Friction" section of "The Big Race." Partners can reread the section and find out how gravity affects a soapbox derby car. Have partners discuss other sections of "The Big Race" that they might want to reread.

Go Digital

View "The Big Race"

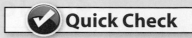
 CCSS Comprehension Strategy

Reread

When you read an informational text, you often come across information that is new to you. As you read "The Big Race," reread key sections of text to make sure you understand them and remember the information they contain.

Find Text Evidence

As you read "The Big Race," the concept of acceleration may be new to you. Reread the "Forces at Work" section on page 66 to help you remember what *accelerate* means.

I read that accelerate *means to increase the speed of something. Rereading will help me to understand and remember this concept.*

Your Turn

COLLABORATE

What does gravity do? Reread the "Gravity and Friction" section of "The Big Race" to find out. As you read, remember to use the strategy Reread.

68

READING/WRITING WORKSHOP, p. 68

Monitor and *Differentiate*

✓ Quick Check

Do students reread narrative nonfiction text when they do not understand? Do they reread more than once if necessary?

⬇

Small Group Instruction

If No →

Approaching Level	Reteach p. T232
ELL	Develop p. T248

If Yes →

On Level	Review p. T240
Beyond Level	Extend p. T244

ELL ENGLISH LANGUAGE LEARNERS SCAFFOLD

Beginning	Intermediate	Advanced/High
Clarify the Meaning Point to the word *accelerate*. Read the sentence where it appears. Say: *Accelerate means to go faster.* Demonstrate by moving slowly and then quickly. Ask: *Do I move faster when I accelerate?* Model other words such as *force* and *motion*.	**Summarize** Help students reread the section "Forces at Work" on page 66. Ask: *Who can tell me what it means to accelerate?* Explain that rereading text can help clarify the meaning of difficult words such as *accelerate*. Have partners summarize "Forces at Work."	**Explain** Have students reread "Forces at Work." Elicit from students why the text is challenging. Ask: *How does force affect motion? What is the meaning of* accelerate? Then have partners explain how a force works. Elicit details to support students' responses.

ON-LEVEL PRACTICE BOOK pp. 33–34

Read the passage. Use the reread strategy to help you understand new facts or difficult explanations.

A Firehouse Lesson

12	Julie sat at a large table in the firehouse, struggling with her
21	homework. Her older brother Charlie, a firefighter, sat watching
23	television nearby.
36	"Why do I have to be here anyway? It's so noisy," Julie said.
49	"Mom isn't home, so it's better for you to be here with me,"
56	Charlie responded. "What are you working on?"
66	"Mrs. Krandle's science lesson, and it's very difficult," she said.
78	Charlie walked over to Julie and took a peek at her notebook.
	"I remember this!" he said smiling. "Maybe I can help."

88	**The Pull of Gravity**
92	Charlie walked over to the fire pole, a metal pole which ran
104	through a hole in the floor and connected the two levels of the
117	firehouse.
118	"Using this pole allows us to get downstairs and to a fire faster
131	than a staircase would," Charlie explained as he grabbed onto the
142	pole and slid down to the first floor. Julie jumped up from her chair
156	and looked down the hole at him.
163	"Gravity pulled me down here quickly," he yelled up to her. He
175	walked back upstairs. "Gravity is the force that pulls objects toward
186	each other."
188	"But how did you stop?" Julie asked.
195	"Friction," he answered. "Friction is a force that resists the
205	sliding of one object over another. I pressed my hands, legs, and feet
218	against the pole as I descended, creating friction and slowing me
229	down enough to stop."

APPROACHING pp. 33–34	BEYOND pp. 33–34	ELL pp. 33–34

Comprehension Skill

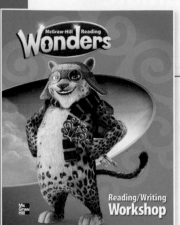

Reading/Writing Workshop

 OBJECTIVES

CCSS Describe the overall structure (e.g., chronology, comparison, cause/ effect, problem/ solution) of events, ideas, concepts, or information in a text or part of a text. **RI.4.5**

Identify cause and effect text structures.

ACADEMIC LANGUAGE

- *text structures, cause, effect*
- Cognates: *causa, efecto*

SKILLS TRACE

TEXT STRUCTURE

Introduce Unit 1 Week 3

Review Unit 1 Weeks 4, 6; Unit 2 Week 6; Unit 3 Week 6; Unit 4 Weeks 1, 4; Unit 5 Weeks 3, 4, 5, 6; Unit 6 Week 6

Assess Units 1, 4, 5

MINILESSON 10 Mins

Text Structure: Cause and Effect

1 Explain

Explain to students that cause and effect is one kind of text structure authors use to organize information that tells how or why something happens.

→ A cause is why something happens. An effect is what happens.

→ Students can look for signal words such as *because*, *due to*, *so*, and *as a result* to find causes and effects in a text.

→ Then they can use the cause-and-effect relationships they find to understand how or why things happen in the text.

Point out that "The Big Race" explains challenging science concepts using simple, everyday examples. To understand these concepts, students will need to pay careful attention to specific information in the text about causes and effects, or what happens and why.

2 Model Close Reading: Text Evidence

Identify causes and effects in the section "Forces at Work" on page 66. Then model using the information written on the graphic organizer to state cause-and-effect relationships using signal words.

 Write About Reading: Paraphrase Model for students how to use the notes from the graphic organizer to paraphrase the cause-and-effect relationships using signal words.

3 Guided Practice of Close Reading

 Have students work in pairs to complete a graphic organizer for each section of "The Big Race," rereading the text and looking for words that signal causes and effects. Students can work in pairs. Discuss each section as students complete the graphic organizer.

 Write About Reading: Paraphrase Ask pairs to work together to paraphrase the cause-and-effect relationships in the section "Gravity and Friction." Select pairs of students to share their writing with the class.

 **Go Digital**

Present the Lesson

Comprehension Skill CCSS

Cause and Effect

Text structure is the way that authors organize information in a selection. Cause and effect is one kind of text structure. The author explains how and why something happens. A cause is why something happens. An effect is what happens.

Find Text Evidence

I can reread "Forces at Work" in "The Big Race" on page 66 to find actions that cause something to happen. Then I can figure out the effects of those actions.

Cause	→	Effect
Clara applies force to one stool.	→	The stool moves.
Clara pushes both stools.	→	Both stools move.
Clara applies more force to one of the stools.	→	One stool moves farther.

Your Turn COLLABORATE

Reread each section of "The Big Race." Find events or actions that cause something to happen and their effects. List each cause and effect in the graphic organizer.

Go Digital!
Use the interactive graphic organizer

69

READING/WRITING WORKSHOP, p. 69

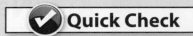

Monitor and *Differentiate*

 Quick Check

As students complete the graphic organizer, can they differentiate between cause and effect?

⬇

Small Group Instruction

If No →	Approaching Level	Reteach p. T239
	ELL	Develop p. T248
If Yes →	On Level	Review p. T243
	Beyond Level	Extend p. T247

ELL ENGLISH LANGUAGE LEARNERS SCAFFOLD

Beginning

Understand Reread the fourth paragraph on page 66. Demonstrate how a force causes an object to move by pushing a chair or a small object. Say: *When I pushed the chair, I caused it to move.* Help students describe the cause-and-effect relationship. *The force is the _____. The movement of the object is the _____.*

Intermediate

Describe Reread "Forces at Work." Ask: *What happens when a force is applied to an object?* (It causes something to move or causes a change in motion.) *Turn to a partner and describe the causes and effects on page 66.* Have students fill in the frame. *The force is the _____. The movement of the object is the _____.*

Advanced/High

Write Have students work in pairs to write sentences describing the cause-and-effect relationships on page 66. Ask students to use vocabulary words to explain the relationships.

ON-LEVEL PRACTICE BOOK pp. 33–35

A. Reread the passage and answer the questions.
Possible responses provided.

1. What is the cause in the following sentence from the passage?
Charlie pushed the ball with his hand, and it rolled across the floor.

Charlie pushed the ball with his hand.

2. What is the effect in the following sentence from the passage?
Charlie pushed the ball with his hand, and it rolled across the floor.

It rolled across the floor.

3. What is one example of an effect in the section "The Pull of Gravity"? What is the cause of this effect?

An example of an effect is Charlie sliding down the pole. Gravity is the cause of this effect.

B. Work with a partner. Read the passage aloud. Pay attention to phrasing and rate. Stop after one minute. Fill out the chart.

	Words Read	–	Number of Errors	=	Words Correct Score
First Read		–		=	
Second Read		–		=	

APPROACHING pp. 33–35	BEYOND pp. 33–35	ELL pp. 33–35

Genre: Informational Text

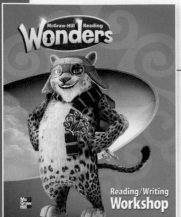

 MINILESSON **10** Mins

Narrative Nonfiction

Go Digital

1 Explain

Share with students the following key characteristics of **narrative nonfiction**.

→ Narrative nonfiction tells a story that includes facts and examples about a topic. The characters in the story share or learn facts.

→ Narrative nonfiction may include text features such as headings, photographs and captions, and speech balloons. However, even if a text has none of these features, it may still be narrative nonfiction.

2 Model Close Reading: Text Evidence

Model identifying and using the text features on page 66 of "The Big Race."

Headings Point out the heading "Forces at Work." Explain that headings tell the main topic of a section. Ask: *Why does this heading fit this section?*

Speech Balloons Point out the speech balloons at the bottom of the page. Explain that speech balloons can be a way for characters in narrative nonfiction to point out key details. Ask: *How do the speech balloons help you understand the topic of this section?*

3 Guided Practice of Close Reading

COLLABORATE

Have students work with partners to find and list two text features in "The Big Race." Partners should discuss the information they learned from each feature. Then have them share their work with the class.

Present the Lesson

Reading/Writing Workshop

OBJECTIVES

CCSS Interpret information presented visually, orally, or quantitatively (e.g., in charts, graphs, diagrams, time lines, animations, or interactive elements on Web pages) and explain how the information contributes to an understanding of the text in which it appears. **RI.4.7**

Recognize the characteristics and text features of narrative nonfiction.

ACADEMIC LANGUAGE
narrative nonfiction, text features, speech balloons, headings

CCSS Genre Informational Text

Narrative Nonfiction

The selection "The Big Race" is narrative nonfiction.

Narrative nonfiction:
- Tells a story.
- Includes facts and examples about a topic.
- Often includes text features.

Find Text Evidence

Even though "The Big Race" reads like a story, I can tell that it is an informational text because it includes facts and text features.

Text Features

Headings Headings tell what a section of text is mostly about.

Speech Balloons Speech Balloons tell what the characters are saying or thinking.

Your Turn COLLABORATE

Find two examples of text features in "The Big Race." Tell your partner what information you learned from the features.

70

READING/WRITING WORKSHOP, p. 70

Beginning

Respond Orally Point to the heading on page 66. *Look at the heading. It says "Forces at Work." The heading tells us that we will learn about forces. Headings tell us what we will read.* Ask students to fill in the sentence frames: *The heading is _____. We will read about _____.*

Intermediate

Demonstrate Understanding Have students point to the heading. Ask: *What does the heading tell us?* (that we will read about forces) *Turn to a partner and explain why the heading fits this section.*

Advanced/High

Discuss Ask students to work in pairs to describe how the illustrations and text on page 66 relate to the heading "Forces at Work." Have them share the main points from their discussion with the class.

Monitor and *Differentiate*

✓ Quick Check

Are students able to identify two text features in "The Big Race"? Can they identify what they learned from each feature?

⬇

Small Group Instruction

If No →	**Approaching Level**	Reteach p. T232
	ELL	Develop p. T248
If Yes →	**On Level**	Review p. T240
	Beyond Level	Extend p. T244

ON-LEVEL PRACTICE BOOK p. 36

Science in a Soda Bottle

"You look bored. I know something fun you can make," Mom said.

"What?" I asked.

"I'll show you. You need an empty soft drink bottle and a catsup packet," Mom said as she got the supplies. "Put the packet in the bottle and fill the bottle all the way to the top with water. Then close the bottle."

When she picked up the bottle and squeezed it, the packet sank!

The water pressure squeezes the air in the packet, making it sink.

Answer the questions about the text.

1. How do you know this is narrative nonfiction?

   It tells a story about a real-life topic that includes facts and examples.

2. What text features does the text include?

   heading, illustration, and speech bubble

3. What is the heading? How could it be better?

   "Science in a Soda Bottle"; Possible response: It could be better if it told more about the topic.

4. What information do the illustration and speech bubble give you?

   The illustration shows you what the girl and her mom are making. The speech bubble tells you what is happening in the bottle.

| **APPROACHING** p. 36 | **BEYOND** p. 36 | **ELL** p. 36 |

→ Vocabulary Strategy

 MINILESSON 10 Mins

Context Clues

Go Digital

Reading/Writing Workshop

OBJECTIVES

CCSS Use context (e.g., definitions, examples, or restatements in text) as a clue to the meaning of a word or phrase. **L.4.4a**

CCSS Consult reference materials (e.g., dictionaries, glossaries, thesauruses), both print and digital, to find the pronunciation and determine or clarify the precise meaning of key words and phrases. **L.4.4c**

ACADEMIC LANGUAGE
- *definitions, restatements*
- Cognate: *definiciones*

1 Explain

Explain to students that they can look for context clues to help define an unfamiliar word.

→ To find context clues, students can look at words surrounding the unfamiliar word. These words might be **definitions, examples,** or **restatements** of the word's meaning.

→ Context clues can appear in the same sentence as an unfamiliar word or somewhere in the same paragraph.

2 Model Close Reading: Text Evidence

Model using context clues in the fourth paragraph on page 66 of "The Big Race" to find the meaning of *force*. Point out the phrase "a push or a pull" as a definition for the word.

3 Guided Practice of Close Reading

 COLLABORATE

Have students work in pairs to figure out the meanings of *speed, friction,* and *surfaces* in "The Big Race." Encourage partners to go back into the text and use context clues surrounding the words to help them determine each word's definition.

Present the Lesson

SKILLS TRACE

CONTEXT CLUES: DEFINITIONS AND RESTATEMENTS

Introduce Unit 1 Week 4

Review Unit 1 Weeks 4, 5; Unit 3 Week 2; Unit 6 Week 2

Assess Units 1, 3

Use Reference Sources

Print and Digital Dictionaries Have students check an online or print dictionary and compare the meanings they find there for *speed, friction,* and *surfaces* with the meanings they came up with from context. If the dictionary gives more than one meaning, ask students to choose the meaning closest to that used in the selection.

Review a dictionary entry for the word *surface*. Discuss each part of the entry: the meanings and example sentences; the syllabication and phonetic respelling; and the part of speech label. Then have students identify each of these parts in a dictionary entry for *friction*.

Vocabulary Strategy CCSS

Context Clues

When you are not sure what a word means, you can look at the other words around it to figure out the meaning. These other words, called context clues, may be **definitions**, **examples**, or **restatements** of the word's meaning.

 Find Text Evidence

When I read the fourth paragraph on page 66 of "The Big Race," I am not sure what the word force *means. The phrase "a push or a pull" defines what the word* force *means.*

Clara continued, "A force is a push or a pull. Forces cause things to move or cause a change in motion."

Your Turn COLLABORATE

Use context clues to figure out the meanings of the following words in "The Big Race":

speed, *page 65*
friction, *page 67*
surfaces, *page 67*

71

Craig Phillips

READING/WRITING WORKSHOP, p. 71

A C T Access Complex Text

▶ Specific Vocabulary

Domain-specific words can prove challenging for students. Guide them in using context clues in the surrounding sentences to define unfamiliar words. Point out that authors who introduce new science terms often provide definitions or examples to help readers understand a word's meaning.

→ *What context clues tell you what the word* gravity *means?* (The second sentence on page 67 defines what gravity is: "Gravity is a pulling force between two objects." Also, the example of the ball being pulled down helps the reader understand gravity.)

Monitor and *Differentiate*

 Quick Check

Can students identify and use context clues to determine the meanings of *speed*, *friction*, and *surfaces*?

Small Group Instruction

If No → | Approaching Level | **Reteach p. T237**

| ELL | **Develop p. T253**

If Yes → | On Level | **Review p. T242**

| Beyond Level | **Extend p. T246**

ON-LEVEL PRACTICE BOOK p. 37

Read each sentence below. Underline the context clues in the sentence that help you define each word in bold. Then, in your own words, write the definition of the word. Possible responses provided.

1. Charlie walked over to the **fire pole,** a metal pole which ran through a hole in the floor and connected the two levels of the firehouse.
   a metal pole between floors

2. **Inertia** means that an object at rest tends to stay at rest.
   a law of motion

3. "A **force** is something that moves, stops, or changes the motion of an object," he said.
   something that affects an object

4. **Speed** is the distance an object moves in a certain amount of time.
   how fast something goes

5. **Gravity** is the force that pulls objects toward each other.
   Earth's pull on us

| APPROACHING p. 37 | BEYOND p. 37 | ELL p. 37 |

Develop Comprehension

Literature Anthology

A Crash Course in Forces and Motion with Max Axiom

Text Complexity Range

Lexile

*630   740   1010

TextEvaluator™

23   27   51

Literature Anthology
*Although the selection score falls below the Lexile range, this selection includes domain-specific vocabulary. Also, the narrative nonfiction genre may be challenging to students.

Options for Close Reading

→ Whole Class

→ Small Group

→ Independent

CCSS Genre · Narrative Nonfiction

? Essential Question

How can science help you find out how things work?

Read how forces and motion affect our lives.

Go Digital!

62

A C T Access Complex Text

What makes this text complex?

▶ **Sentence Structure**

▶ **Connection of Ideas**

▶ **Organization**

▶ **Genre**

▶ **Specific Vocabulary**

▶ **Genre**

Explain to students that this selection is an informational text presented as a graphic novel. This means that factual information about forces and motion will be presented in the form of a story, with illustrations much like a comic book. Point out the boxed text about Max Axiom on page 63.

A CRASH COURSE IN FORCES AND MOTION with MAX AXIOM SUPER SCIENTIST

About Max

Real Name: Maxwell J. Axiom
Hometown: Seattle, Washington
Height: 6' 1"   **Weight:** 192 lbs
Eyes: Brown   **Hair:** None

Super capabilities: Super intelligence; able to shrink to the size of an atom; sunglasses give x ray vision; lab coat allows for travel through time and space.

Origin: Since birth, Max Axiom seemed destined for greatness. His mother, a marine biologist, taught her son about the mysteries of the sea. His father, a nuclear physicist and volunteer park ranger, schooled Max on the wonders of earth and sky.

One day on a wilderness hike, a megacharged lightning bolt struck Max with blinding fury. When he awoke, Max discovered a newfound energy and set out to learn as much about science as possible. He traveled the globe earning degrees in every aspect of the field. Upon his return, he was ready to share his knowledge and new **identity** with the world. He had become Max Axiom, Super Scientist.

BY **Emily Sohn**
ILLUSTRATED BY **Steve Erwin and Charles Barnett III**

63

LITERATURE ANTHOLOGY, pp. 62–63

Predictive Writing

Have students read the title and preview the sidebars, headings, and illustrations. Tell students to write their predictions about what they will learn in the selection. Encourage them to share what they already know about force and motion.

ESSENTIAL QUESTION

Ask a student to read aloud the Essential Question. Have students discuss what information they expect to learn.

Note Taking: Use the Graphic Organizer

As students read the selection, ask them to fill in the graphic organizer on **Your Turn Practice Book page 32** to record the causes and effects in each section.

❶ Text Features: Illustrations

Look at the illustration on page 62. What are Max and the child doing? (They are riding a roller coaster.) What might the roller coaster have to do with force and motion? (Roller coasters move fast in many different directions.)

→ *Is Max Axiom a real person or a fictional character? How do you know?* (Max Axiom is a fictional character. The box provides information about him that could not be true, such as being able to shrink, having x-ray vision, and being able to travel through time.)

→ *What is the purpose of the box about Max Axiom? Is it part of the story?* (The box is not part of the story. The box serves to introduce the reader to Max Axiom, Super Scientist. Since Max earned degrees in every science field, he will teach the reader about forces and motion in this story.)

Develop Comprehension

❷ Text Features: Headings

What is the heading on page 64? (Forces That Move Us) What do you think this section will be about? (It will explain how forces cause people and objects to move.)

A C T Access Complex Text

▶ Sentence Structure

Explain to students that this story is told mostly through dialogue, but it also includes headings and informational sidebars. Readers must pay close attention to the boxed illustrations and text to follow the story. Tell students that just as they read running text from left to right and top to bottom, the same strategy applies to this selection.

→ *How do you know when a character is speaking?* (white speech bubbles point toward the character)

→ *What is the purpose of the rest of the text on page 64?* (heading introduces topic; boxed sentence serves as a narration about Max; "SKRAWW" is a sound word for the bird)

3 Author's Craft: Word Choice

Authors of informational text choose words carefully to make concepts clear to their readers. Reread this sentence on page 65: *A force is any push or pull on an object.* How does the author's word choice help the reader understand what a force is? (The author uses simple words that clearly define what a force is.) In what sentence does the author use simple words to clearly explain what gravity does? (in the sentence *It pulls objects toward each other, and it keeps us on the earth.*)

ELL Demonstrate the concept of gravity by picking up a book and letting it fall to the ground. Point out that gravity is the force that makes things fall to the ground.

→ Have students point to the word *gravity* on page 65 and say it aloud. *The book fell to the ground because of _____.*

→ Have students point to the image of the bungee jumper. *Why is he falling?* (Gravity is pulling him to the ground.)

Develop Comprehension

4 Skill: Cause and Effect

According to the law of inertia, what happens when an object is at rest? (It stays at rest until a force gets it moving.) What happens when an object is in motion? (It stays in motion until another force causes it to change direction, slow down, or come to a stop.) Add the causes and effects to your chart.

Cause	→	Effect
An object is still.	→	It stays at rest until acted on by a force.
An object is in motion.	→	The object stays in motion until another force causes it to change direction, slow down, or come to a stop.

A C T Access Complex Text

▶ **Connection of Ideas**

Tell students that when they read complex text, they should try to connect new information to information they have already learned. Remind students that bungee jumping depends on gravity.

→ *How does gravity allow Max to bungee jump at the amusement park?* (Gravity causes Max to fall toward the earth.)

→ *Reread the definition of* inertia *on page 67 and recall when Max bungee jumps on page 65.*

→ *Why does Max keep falling until the bungee cord acts on him?* (Max will stay in motion until a force acts on him to slow him down or stop him.)

LITERATURE ANTHOLOGY, pp. 66–67

5 Text Features: Sidebars

What information do you learn about Isaac Newton in the sidebar that is not included in the text? (He was the first person to realize that certain laws of nature explain how things move on Earth and in space. He was also the first to explain gravity.)

STOP AND CHECK

Reread Why does a moving object need a force in order to change direction, slow down, or stop?

Teacher Think Aloud I want to make sure I understand what I have read about force and motion. Rereading a text can help me more clearly understand what I have read. I will reread the part about inertia. It says that an object at rest tends to stay at rest until a force is applied to get it moving. Inertia also keeps a moving object in motion until a force is applied to get it to change direction, slow down, or stop. Now I understand that part of the text better.

ELL Students may have difficulty with the word *inertia*.

→ Demonstrate *inertia* by rolling a ball from one end of the classroom to the other end.

→ Tell students to look at the way the ball rolls across the classroom floor and does not stop until it reaches the other end of the room. Help students complete the sentence frame: *The ball keeps rolling across the floor because of _____.*

→ Point out the cognate for *inertia* is *inercia*.

Develop Comprehension

6 Skill: Cause and Effect

Remember that a cause is why something happens and an effect is what happens. What causes the forward motion of the chair during the roller coaster ride? (the roller coaster moving forward) What is the effect of inertia on the riders? (It makes the riders feel like they are being pushed to the back of their seats.) Add the cause and effect to your chart.

Cause →	Effect
The roller coaster moves forward. →	Inertia makes the riders feel like they are being pushed to the back of their seats.

A C T Access Complex Text

▶ **Connection of Ideas**

Remind students that they learned about *force, gravity,* and *inertia* on pages 65 and 67. Guide them in connecting what they learned to understand the new terms introduced on page 69.

→ *How do inertia, gravity, speed, and acceleration affect the roller coaster and riders?* (On page 65, we learn that a still object needs a force to get it

moving and that a moving object needs a force to stop it. When the roller coaster ride starts the riders are not moving, so they feel as though they are being pushed to the back of their seats. As the roller coaster gets to the top of the hill, gravity acts as a force and pulls the cars down. The roller coaster speeds up as it goes down the

LITERATURE ANTHOLOGY, pp. 68–69

7 Vocabulary: Context Clues

What context clues can help you determine the definition of *acceleration*? (Max explains what *acceleration* is. He says, "Acceleration is how much speed we pick up as we go down the hill." The definition of *acceleration* must be "an increase in speed.")

hill, causing it to accelerate faster at the bottom. All of these factors keep the roller coaster in motion until the ride stops. As the roller coaster slows and stops, the lap bar acts as a force to keep riders in the cars.)

→ *What is necessary for the ride stop?* (A force must be used to stop the roller coaster.)

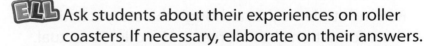 Ask students about their experiences on roller coasters. If necessary, elaborate on their answers.

→ *When does a roller coaster begin to go faster?* (when it goes downhill)

→ *Why does the coaster go faster and faster?* (It is accelerating.)

Develop Comprehension

8 **Skill: Cause and Effect**

What causes the riders to remain in their seats when the roller coaster stops? (The lap bars apply a force on the moving riders.) Look at the illustration at the top of page 70. What effect does friction have on the stone? (Friction stops the forward motion of the stone.) Add the causes and effects to your chart.

Cause	→	Effect
Lap bar applies a force to the riders.	→	Riders remain in their seats.
The force of friction is applied to the stone.	→	The stone stops.

STOP AND CHECK

Reread How does friction stop a roller coaster? (The brakes squeeze against the fins and cause friction. Friction makes the roller coaster slow down and stop.)

A C T Access Complex Text

▶ **Genre**

Remind students that although this story is fictional, the information about forces and motion is factual. Tell students that text features can help them understand informational text. Guide students in moving between the fiction and nonfiction elements in the selection. Point out the side bar at the bottom of page 70.

→ *How is the explanation of friction in the story related to the sidebar about friction?* (Max Axiom talks about friction on Earth and how it works with gravity to slow things down and make them stop. The sidebar informs readers that there is no friction in space.)

LITERATURE ANTHOLOGY, pp. 70–71

9 **Strategy: Reread**

Teacher Think Aloud I just read a lot of information about friction and how it affects an object in motion. How can rereading the text help you understand how friction works?

Prompt students to apply the strategy in a Think Aloud by rereading the text to better understand friction. Have them turn to a partner to paraphase what they reread.

Student Think Aloud I can reread the text to make sure that I did not miss any important information about friction. Friction works with gravity to slow things down and make them stop. Now I understand why the roller coaster slows down as it approaches the station.

10 **Skill: Make Inferences**

What would happen if there was no friction when the brake fins slid between the brake rails? (The roller coaster would stay in motion.) Based on the information you just read, why is it important for a roller coaster to have brakes? (The brakes use friction to slow the roller coaster down and stop it at the end of the ride.)

ELL Students may have difficulty understanding *friction*. Have students slide a small object, such as a paper clip, across a desk. Ask: *Why did the paper clip stop?* (friction) Point out that the paper clip and the desk rubbed against each other, causing friction.

→ Help students complete the sentence frame: *When two surfaces rub against each other, they cause ____.*

→ Point out the cognate for *friction* is *fricción*.

Develop Comprehension

11 Skill: Cause and Effect

What happens when the juggler on the right juggles the bowling balls? (He has to use more force to throw and catch the bowling balls because they are heavy.) Read the sidebar on page 73. If you traveled to Saturn, why would your weight change even though your mass stays the same? (because gravity determines weight, and each planet in our solar system has a different gravitational pull) Add the causes and effects to your chart.

Cause	→	Effect
The juggler is juggling heavy bowling balls.	→	The juggler has to use more force to throw and catch the balls.
Saturn has a different gravitational pull than Earth.	→	Your mass stays the same, but your weight changes on Saturn.

CONNECT TO CONTENT
PLANETS AND GRAVITATIONAL PULL

The gravitational pull on an object determines its weight. Each planet in the solar system has a different gravitational pull. Point out the captions under the photograph of the planets. Explain that these numbers can help students figure out how much they would weigh on each planet. Have each student calculate what his or her weight would be on each planet.

STEM

LITERATURE ANTHOLOGY, pp. 72–73

12 Author's Craft: Text Structure

Words such as *because, since,* and *as a result* signal causes and effects. What word does the author use on page 72 to signal a cause-and-effect relationship? Turn to a partner and identify the word, as well as the cause and effect. (The author uses the word *because.* The cause is the juggler using more force to throw and catch heavier balls. The effect is that the juggler is tired.)

13 Genre: Informational Text

Informational text often includes features that give additional information about a topic. Look at the feature about gravitational pull on page 73. What information does this feature provide? (how the different gravitational pull on each planet in our solar system affects weight) If you weighed 100 pounds on Earth, what would you weigh on Venus? (88 pounds)

ELL Students may have difficulty with the concept of *mass.* Tell students that matter is the material that something is made of, and mass is the amount of matter in something.

→ *Say it with me:* mass.

→ Pick up a light object and a heavy object, such as a book and a pencil. *Which object has more mass?*

How do you know? (The book has more mass. I know this because the book is heavier than the pencil. The book has more matter in it than the pencil, so it has more mass.)

→ Have students complete the sentence frame: *The pencil is lighter than the book because it has less _____.*

Develop Comprehension

14 **Strategy: Reread**

Reread the text to explain why Max needed to use the same amount of force to demonstrate Newton's second law. Turn to your partner and paraphrase the explanation given in the text.

Student Think Aloud At the top of page 75, Max points out that both his arms "are equally strong" and that the "amount of force will be the same." He seems to be making a point about this fact. I know that Max's experiment has to do with the effect of a force on two people that have different masses. So in order to show that Jenny will move faster, he has to be sure that he is being fair by applying the same amount of force to each of them.

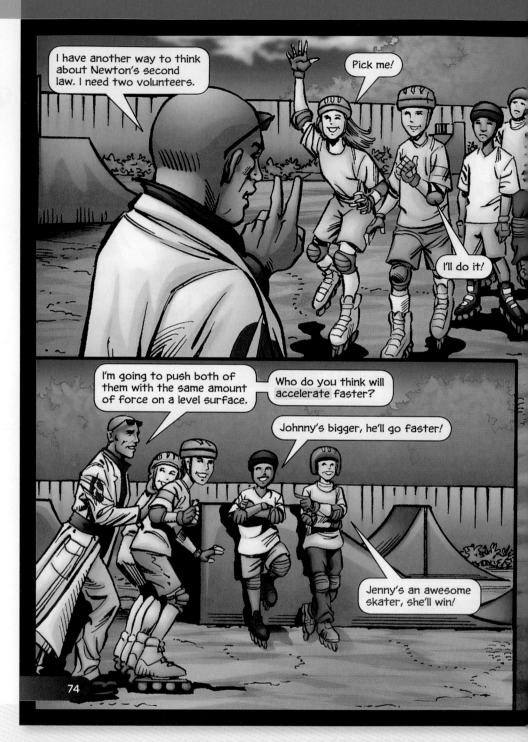

A C T Access Complex Text

▶ Connection of Ideas

Remind students that according to Newton's second law, the amount of acceleration that a force can produce depends on an object's mass.

→ *How does Max demonstrate Newton's second law?* (Max pushes Jenny and Johnny with the same amount of force to show who will accelerate faster.)

→ *What do the children learn at the end of the demonstration?* (They learn that Jenny has less mass than Johnny, so she gets a faster start even though they were pushed with the same force. They also learn that Johnny would need a stronger force to get moving as fast as Jenny.)

LITERATURE ANTHOLOGY, pp. 74–75

15 Skill: Cause and Effect

What happens when equal force is applied to two people with different masses? (The force causes the person with less mass to accelerate faster.) Add this cause and effect to your chart.

Cause	→	Effect
Equal force is applied to two people with different masses.	→	The person with less mass accelerates faster.

▶ Specific Vocabulary

Point out the word *level* on page 74.

→ *Is the definition of* level *stated in the text?* (No.)

→ *Use the illustrations on page 75 as context clues to figure out the meaning of* level. (It means "flat.")

ELL Help students understand Newton's second law.

→ *Remember that mass is the amount of matter in an object or a person. Who has more mass, Johnny or Jenny?* (Johnny)

→ *When Max pushes Johnny and Jenny, who gets a faster start?* (Jenny) *Why?* (She has less mass.)

Develop Comprehension

Make Predictions Who will travel farther when released down the ramp? (Johnny will win the race because he has more mass. He will need more force to slow down or stop.)

16 Skill: Cause and Effect

What cause-and-effect relationships can you find on pages 76 and 77, beginning with when Max pushes Johnny and Jenny down the ramp? Add the causes and effects to your chart.

Cause	→	Effect
Max pushes Johnny and Jenny down the ramp.	→	Gravity pulls them down the ramp.
Johnny has more mass than Jenny.	→	More force is needed to slow down Johnny, so he travels farther.
Friction occurs between their wheels and the ground.	→	Johnny and Jenny slow down.

A C T Access Complex Text

▶ Organization

Tell students that the author includes two races between Johnny and Jenny so the reader can compare the races and understand the concepts of force, mass, acceleration, and friction.

→ *What difference between Johnny and Jenny affects their second race?* (Johnny has more mass, so it takes more force to stop him. This means he travels farther than Jenny does before friction stops them.)

→ *What is the main difference between the two races?* (In the first race, Max applies an equal force to Jenny and Johnny to see how fast they accelerate. In the second race, Jenny and Johnny skate down a ramp to see who travels farther.)

LITERATURE ANTHOLOGY, pp. 76–77

Return to Predictions

Review students' predictions and purposes for reading. Ask them to answer the Essential Question. (Science can help us find out how force affects the way people and objects move.)

ELL Point out the idiom *in the bag* on page 76. Explain that *in the bag* means success is certain. Tell students that it's another way to say you are sure you will win or achieve something.

→ Help students use the idiom by completing the sentence frames: *We've practiced for the game and know we'll win. We've got it _____. I've studied for the test and know I'll get an A. It's _____.*

About the Author

Meet the Author and Illustrator

Emily Sohn and Steve Erwin

Have students read the biographies of the author and illustrator. Ask:

→ How do you think Emily Sohn's background helped her write *A Crash Course in Forces and Motion with Max Axiom?*

→ How do Steve Erwin's comic book illustrations help you understand the science concepts Emily Sohn explains in the text?

Author's Purpose

To Inform

Remind students that authors who write to inform present facts about a topic and often use text features to give additional information. Discuss with students how the illustrations in this graphic novel help the reader visualize and understand science concepts that may be difficult to grasp based on the text alone.

Author's Craft

Dialogue

Discuss what the author's use of dialogue adds to the text.

→ Having the characters talk to each other about science makes it easier and more fun for the reader to learn about science concepts. For example, Jenny and Max have this exchange: "Max, what happened? I got a good start, but Johnny just passed right by me." (Max replies) "Johnny's larger mass takes more force to slow down or stop than your smaller mass." (page 77)

About the Author and Illustrator

EMILY SOHN lives in Minneapolis, Minnesota. She writes mostly about science and health for kids and adults. Emily studied science in school. She even spent a few seasons following sea lions and seals to learn about them. When not writing and learning more about science, she loves rock climbing and running triathlons.

There's a lot of science behind that!

STEVE ERWIN is a comic book artist. Early in his career, Steve contributed art to many superhero comic series, including *Batman Returns* and *Superman: The Man of Steel*. For his accomplishments in comics, he was inducted into the Oklahoma Cartoonists Hall of Fame.

Author's Purpose

A Crash Course in Forces and Motion with Max Axiom, Super Scientist is an informational text written in the form of a graphic novel. This means that the information is presented graphically, or in words and pictures that tell a story, much like a comic book. Why would the author choose to teach science concepts in a graphic novel format?

78

LITERATURE ANTHOLOGY, pp. 78–79

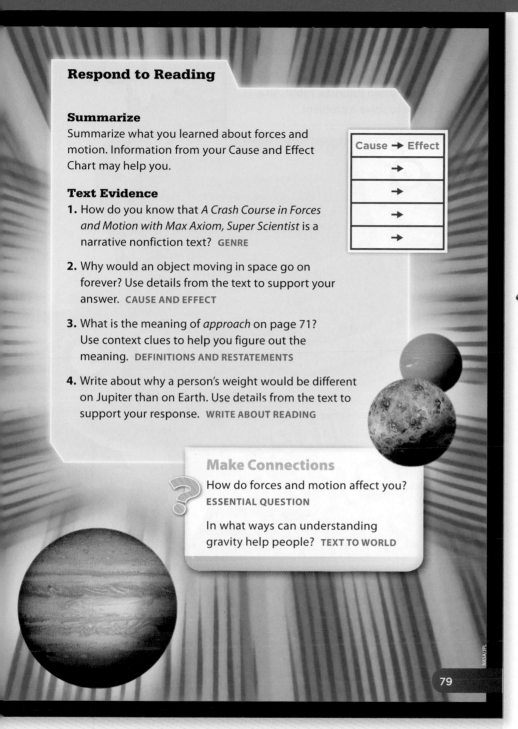

Respond to Reading

Summarize

Summarize what you learned about forces and motion. Information from your Cause and Effect Chart may help you.

Cause → Effect
→
→
→
→

Text Evidence

1. How do you know that *A Crash Course in Forces and Motion with Max Axiom, Super Scientist* is a narrative nonfiction text? **GENRE**

2. Why would an object moving in space go on forever? Use details from the text to support your answer. **CAUSE AND EFFECT**

3. What is the meaning of *approach* on page 71? Use context clues to help you figure out the meaning. **DEFINITIONS AND RESTATEMENTS**

4. Write about why a person's weight would be different on Jupiter than on Earth. Use details from the text to support your response. **WRITE ABOUT READING**

Make Connections

How do forces and motion affect you? **ESSENTIAL QUESTION**

In what ways can understanding gravity help people? **TEXT TO WORLD**

79

NASA/JPL

Make Connections *Analytical Writing*

Essential Question Have student pairs describe to each other how the laws of forces and motion affect their lives. (Forces and motion help to explain how things work. For example, understanding gravity tells us why things fall.)

Text to World After students discuss their knowledge of forces and motion, write about how understanding gravity can help people.

Respond to Reading

Summarize

Review with students the information from their cause and effect graphic organizers. Model how to use the information to summarize *A Crash Course in Forces and Motion with Max Axiom.*

Analytical Writing Write About Reading: Summarize
Remind students that a summary is a restatement of the main ideas of a text. You can write a summary of a section of text or of an entire text.

Ask students to write a summary of the selection, using the information on their graphic organizers. Remind them to start with a sentence that names the selection title and the genre. Have students share their summaries with a partner.

Text Evidence

1. **Genre** <u>Answer</u> It has fictional characters presenting factual information and uses text features. <u>Evidence</u> The character Max Axiom explains motion and forces and the text includes headings and sidebars.

2. **Cause and Effect** <u>Answer</u> In space there is no friction to slow the object down. <u>Evidence</u> Friction comes from two surfaces rubbing together. There is nothing for the object to rub against in space.

3. **Context Clues** <u>Answer</u> *Approach* means "move toward." <u>Evidence</u> The example on page 71 talks about slowing the cars down. The cars slow down at the end of the ride, when they are moving toward the station.

4. **Analytical Writing Write About Reading: Cause and Effect** Weight is determined by gravity's pull on a person. Jupiter's gravitational pull is different than Earth's, so a person would have a different weight on each planet.

Develop Comprehension

"The Box-Zip Project"

Text Complexity Range

Lexile

▲ 740   1010
*620

TextEvaluator™

23   ▲ 31   51

Literature Anthology
*Although the selection score falls below the Lexile range, elements of science fiction may be unfamiliar to students.

Options for Close Reading

→ Whole Class

→ Small Group

→ Independent

CCSS Genre · Science Fiction

Compare Texts

Read how two futuristic robots use science to solve a problem.

DR. TANK

The Box-Zip Project

SHINE

80   up

A C T   **A**ccess **C**omplex **T**ext

What makes this text complex?

▶ **Specific Vocabulary**

▶ **Genre**

▶ **Specific Vocabulary**

Review strategies for finding the meaning of an unfamiliar word, such as using context clues or a dictionary. Point out the word *warp* in the last paragraph on page 81.

→ Identify context clues to figure out what *warp* means. (*accelerate, moved faster*)

The thirteenth sun of Xyport rose in the orange-tinted sky as Dr. Tank and his assistant, Shine, arrived for work.

"Good morning," Shine said, slipping into his lab coat. "Today's the day! I feel it in my battery!"

Dr. Tank smiled and said, "Now, Shine, we don't feel. We are robots, remember?"

Shine's robot laughter clattered like marbles inside a can. "You got me, Dr. Tank! But, honestly, I think we'll figure out the problem with this silly machine today."

The silly machine, known as Box-Zip, stood in the middle of the science laboratory looking like a ticket booth.

"Let's hope so, Shine. This project will be history if we're not successful pronto!"

For months, the robots had been attempting to travel in the Box-Zip to Earth. A voyage to planet Xto was no problem, and it was twice the distance. They could land on Grolon in a heartbeat. When they traveled to Vinzine, they returned ten minutes before they even left!

But Earth? Every time they attempted landing on that bizarre planet they could only get so close.

"Time for the morning checklist," Dr. Tank said.

"Ready-o," Shine answered.

"Inertia?" inquired Dr. Tank.

"Check," said Shine. "This baby is definitely at rest."

"Superb. Now let's apply force to move it," Dr. Tank said. Together, they pushed Box-Zip, which slid easily.

"Now use force to stop it," Dr. Tank said. Shine held out his enormous robot hand and immediately stopped the sliding Box-Zip.

"Let's do a trial run to Klugger and back," said Dr. Tank. Both robots stepped into Box-Zip and buckled up.

"Accelerate to warp times five blinkers," Dr. Tank advised. As Box-Zip moved faster, the seat belts kept the robots in place.

Lance Lekander

81

LITERATURE ANTHOLOGY, pp. 80–81

Compare Texts

Analytical Writing

Students will read another selection that includes science information. Ask students to do a close reading of the text, rereading to deeply understand the content. As they reread, encourage them to use the reread strategy or other strategies they know to help them. They will also take notes. Then students will use the text evidence they gathered to compare this text with *A Crash Course in Forces and Motion with Max Axiom.*

❶ Ask and Answer Questions

When Dr. Tank asks, "Inertia?" how does Shine's answer show that he understands what inertia is? (Inertia is the tendency of an object to stay at rest unless acted upon by a force. When Shine says, "This baby is definitely at rest," that shows he understands what inertia is.)

→ Reread this sentence: *"Accelerate to warp times five blinkers," Dr. Tank advised.*

→ Help students state the definition of *warp* as used in this sentence. Have them look up the word in a print or digital dictionary and identify the definition, pronunciation, and part of speech. (*Warp* means a very fast speed.)

ELL Point out the idiom *in a heartbeat*.

→ Explain to students that if something happens in a heartbeat, it happens right away.

→ Have students point out clues in the text that can help them define *in a heartbeat*. (no problem; returned ten minutes before they even left)

Develop Comprehension

2 Ask and Answer Questions

What does *accelerate* mean on page 82?

 **Write About Reading** List context clues that help you determine the meaning of *accelerate*. (warp times seven blinkers, then twelve blinkers; blur of colorful motion)

3 Ask and Answer Questions

Why is gravity the solution Dr. Tank and Shine need?

Write About Reading With a partner, paraphrase what happens after Dr. Tank and Shine talk to Mortimer. (The robots move back and forth until Box-Zip moves down fast due to gravity and finally lands on Earth.)

Almost instantly Box-Zip glided onto a dusty purple planet. Shine wanted a purple frozen beverage from the 7-0-12 store, but Dr. Tank explained that there was simply no time. In five blinkers, they were back in the laboratory.

"Klugger is no problem, yet we can't manage an Earth landing!" the frustrated Dr. Tank said. "It's ridiculous!"

"Come on," Shine encouraged. "Giving up is not an option."

Dr. Tank couldn't help but smile at his unfailingly cheerful assistant. Now he regretted not letting Shine get a purple frozen beverage on Klugger.

"You're absolutely right," said Dr. Tank. "Let's try Earth again."

2 Buckled safely in Box-Zip, Shine began to **accelerate** to warp times seven blinkers, then twelve blinkers. The world was a distorted blur of colorful motion. The robots' chrome teeth chattered as they whizzed through the galaxies, finally landing with a thud. They peered out the window.

"Drats!" Dr. Tank shouted in frustration. "It's happened again! We'll never make it all the way down."

Shine looked down. There was Earth below, yet Box-Zip remained at least fifteen feet above, stuck in the many arms of some enormous green and brown structure.

"Why can't we get to Earth?" Dr. Tank cried.

"Yoo-hoo, there!" came a voice from below.

The robots looked at each other. Something was attempting communication!

"Yoo-hoo!" the voice called again.

"Maybe 'yoo-hoo' means hello," said Shine. "Let's try to communicate!"

Shine leaned out the window, calling, "Yoo-hoo!"

"Might I possibly make an **inquiry**?" the Earth creature said.

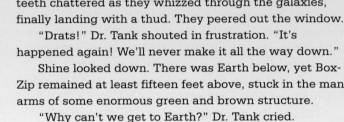

82

A C T ccess Complex Text

▶ Genre

Tell students that "The Box-Zip Project" is science fiction. Science fiction stories tell of imagined events based on science or technology. Guide students in identifying elements of the science fiction genre in the selection.

→ *How do you know that "The Box-Zip Project" is science fiction?* (The story is about two robots on a distant planet who are attempting to use a machine to travel to Earth. The robots use science to prepare the machine for travel. At the end of the story, the robots use gravity to solve their problem.)

"An inquiry?" asked Shine.

"A question, might I ask a question?"

"Certainly," answered Dr. Tank. "And then we'll ask you a question."

"Very well," said the creature. "Did you mean to land in a tree?"

"Tree!" said Shine. "What a hilarious name for this funny-looking thing!"

"Your tree prevents us from landing on your planet," said Dr. Tank. "Is there something we can do about it?"

The creature nodded his head. "I believe that gravity might offer a solution. Try rocking back and forth a bit. Once you start falling, I'm sure you'll come all the way down."

The robots looked at each other doubtfully. Still, they shifted from side to side until Box-Zip began to move. Then it moved down. In fact, it moved down rather quickly.

3 "Yes!" Dr. Tank shouted. "We've landed on Earth at last!"

To prove their successful landing, the robots had photographs made with the Earth creature, whose name turned out to be Mortimer. With some special sticky tape, Box-Zip was soon patched up and ready to go home. Before leaving Earth, Dr. Tank bought Shine a delicious green frozen beverage for the trip home.

Earth friend Mortimer

Make Connections

How did science help the robots solve their problem? **ESSENTIAL QUESTION**

What are a few ways that science can help us answer questions and solve problems? **TEXT TO TEXT**

83

LITERATURE ANTHOLOGY, pp. 82–83

Make Connections Analytical Writing

Essential Question Make sure students list evidence from the text to show how the robots use gravity to solve their problem. Suggest students look back at the text on page 83 to try to identify how gravity helps Shine and Dr. Tank.

Text to Text Have groups of students compare their responses to the Ask and Answer Questions prompts with what they learned in *A Crash Course in Forces and Motion with Max Axiom*. Each group can report back to the whole class. Ask one group to compare how inertia is explained in each text. (Max gives a full explanation of inertia; Shine briefly explains what inertia is in his reply to Dr. Tank.) Have another group compare how force is explained. (In both texts, force is explained as a push or a pull that changes an object's motion.) Ask a third group to compare how gravity is explained in each text. (In both texts, gravity is explained as a force that pulls objects downward.) Discuss with students why it is helpful to understand these science concepts.

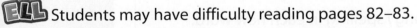

ELL Students may have difficulty reading pages 82–83.

→ Before reading, help students identify difficult words or phrases. Define the words or phrases and use them in a sentence. If possible, act them out for students.

→ For example, act out or demonstrate the phrases "whizzed through," "landing with a thud," and "peered out the window." Say the words using proper intonation and have students repeat after you.

Phonics/Fluency

 MINILESSON 20 Mins

Long *i*

OBJECTIVES

CCSS Use combined knowledge of all letter-sound correspondences, syllabication patterns, and morphology (e.g., roots and affixes) to read accurately unfamiliar multisyllabic words in context and out of context. **RF.4.3a**

CCSS Read on-level prose and poetry orally with accuracy, appropriate rate, and expression on successive readings. **RF.4.4b**

Rate: 84–104 WCPM

ACADEMIC LANGUAGE
phrasing

1 Explain

Display the *Five* **Sound-Spelling Card**. Point to the card and say the long-vowel sound /ī/. Explain that the /ī/ sound has different spellings and provide a sample word for each: *i (mind), ie (pie), igh (night), i_e (pride),* and *y (fly)*. Point out that the letters *gh* are silent in the /ī/ spelling *igh*.

2 Model

Write the word *might* on the board. Underline the letters *igh* and say the long-vowel sound /ī/. Run your finger under the word as you sound out the whole word.

3 Guided Practice

Write the following list of words on the board. Help students identify the spelling of the /ī/ sound in each word. Then have students pronounce each word.

alive	item	shine
sight	spy	kind
tie	high	cry

Read Multisyllabic Words

Transition to Longer Words Draw a three-column chart on the board. In the first column, write *frighten, final, like,* and *widen*. In the second column, write *ing* and *ly*. Have students chorally read the words in the first column. Then have students add an ending from the second column to each word in the first column to form a new word. Write these words in the third column.

Ask students to circle the long *i* spelling in each new word. Model how to read each word in the third column. Have students echo-read the words after you.

Refer to the sound transfers chart in the **Language Transfers Handbook** to identify sounds that do not transfer in Spanish, Cantonese, Vietnamese, Hmong, and Korean.

Go Digital

Long *i*

Present the Lesson

View "The Big Race"

Inflectional Endings

1 Explain

Adding *-es* or *-ed* to verbs creates new verb forms and tenses.

→ For base words that end in a consonant and *y*, change the *y* to *i* before adding *-es* or *-ed*: *spy/spies/spied, carry/carries/carried*.

2 Model

Write and say *study*. Have students repeat it. Point out that the word *study* is a verb that ends in a consonant and *y*. Model creating new forms of the verb by replacing the *y* with *i* and adding *-es* or *-ed*. Ask students to read the new words.

3 Guided Practice

Write inflected forms of *try (tries, tried)* and *apply (applies, applied)* on the board. Have students circle the word endings, say each word, and identify the base form of the verb.

Phrasing and Rate

Explain/Model Explain that phrasing involves an awareness of punctuation so that readers know when to pause and stop in the text. Commas indicate pauses. Periods and other end punctuation require readers to come to a stop. Connect phrasing to rate. Explain that pauses and stops must be of consistent lengths to maintain an appropriate reading rate.

Model reading the first five paragraphs of "The Big Race" on page 65. Read at a steady rate with correct phrasing.

Practice/Apply Have students take turns partner-reading the passage. Partners should follow along in the text and give specific feedback about phrasing and rate. Offer help and suggestions as you walk around the class.

Daily Fluency Practice

Students can practice fluency using **Your Turn Practice Book.**

Monitor and *Differentiate*

 Quick Check

Can students decode multisyllabic words with long *i* spellings? Can students read words with inflectional endings? Can students read fluently?

⬇

Small Group Instruction

If No → **Approaching Level** Reteach pp. T234, T238

ELL Develop pp. T250, T254

If Yes → **On Level** Review p. T240

Beyond Level Extend p. T244

ON-LEVEL PRACTICE BOOK p. 38

A. Read each sentence. Underline the word with the long *i* vowel sound. Then sort the words by their long *i* spellings in the chart below.

1. Which of these is a prime number?

2. Make a slight turn at the next street.

3. She was minding the baby for you.

Long *i* spelled *i*	Long *i* spelled *i_e*	Long *i* spelled *igh*
4. minding	5. prime	6. slight

B. Write the correct -es and -ed forms for each verb ending in y.

Verb	+ es	+ ed
1. cry	cries	cried
2. fry	fries	fried
3. apply	applies	applied
4. deny	denies	denied
5. worry	worries	worried

APPROACHING p. 38	BEYOND p. 38	ELL p. 38

→ **Wrap Up the Week**

Integrate Ideas

www.connected.mcgraw-hill.com
RESOURCES
Research and Inquiry

RESEARCH AND INQUIRY

Ideas in Motion

OBJECTIVES

CCSS Conduct short research projects that build knowledge through investigation of different aspects of a topic. **W.4.7**

CCSS Add audio recordings and visual displays to presentations when appropriate to enhance the development of main ideas or themes. **SL.4.5**

CCSS Differentiate between contexts that call for formal English (e.g., presenting ideas) and situations where informal discourse is appropriate (e.g., small-group discussion); use formal English when appropriate to task and situation. **SL.4.6**

ACADEMIC LANGUAGE
visual display

Research a Topic

COLLABORATE

Explain that students will collaborate as they work in groups to research one of the following topics: motion, force, friction, acceleration, or gravity. They will then create a visual display that shows their understanding of the topic. Discuss the following steps:

❶ Form Groups Divide students into five groups and assign each group one of the topics. Each group should consist of diverse learners collaborating on the assignment.

❷ Find Resources Have students use the selections they read this week along with other reliable print and online resources to gather information for their project. Have students take notes and verify all facts in multiple sources.

❸ Guided Practice Have groups discuss the best way to present their information in a visual display. They may want to create a poster, booklet, or comic strip. Ask them to first plan out a draft that incorporates information from their notes along with visuals.

❹ Create the Visual Display After students in each group have created a draft, have them discuss how they can improve it. Be sure all members work together to create the final visual display.

Present the Visual Display

Have students share their visual displays with the class. Ask them whether formal or informal language is appropriate for the presentation and discuss ways students can use formal language. Afterward have groups share feedback. Have students use online Presentation Checklist 1 to evaluate their presentations.

STEM

TEXT CONNECTIONS  *Analytical Writing*

OBJECTIVES

CCSS Integrate information from two texts on the same topic in order to write or speak about the subject knowledgeably. **RI.4.9**

Text to Text

COLLABORATE

Cite Evidence Explain to students that they will work in groups to compare information they have learned about how science helps us understand how things work from all the texts they have read. Model how to compare this information by using examples from the week's **Leveled Readers** and *The Big Race*, **Reading/Writing Workshop** pages 64–67.

Review class notes and completed graphic organizers. You may also wish to model going back into the text for more information. You can use an Accordion Foldable® to record comparisons.

Students should cite at least three examples from each text.

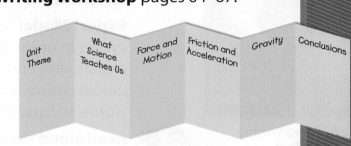

Dinah Zike's
FOLDABLES
Study Organizer

Present Information Ask groups of students to present their findings to the class. Encourage discussion, asking students to comment on information on the charts that helps them understand the science concepts they have learned about this week.

WRITE ABOUT READING *Analytical Writing*

OBJECTIVES

CCSS Draw evidence from literary or informational texts to support analysis, reflection, and research. Apply *grade 4 Reading standards* to informational texts (e.g., "Explain how an author uses reasons and evidence to support particular points in a text"). **W.4.9b**

Write an Analysis

Cite Evidence Using evidence from a text they have read, students will analyze how the author uses headings to tell what a section of text is mostly about.

Discuss how to analyze a text by asking *how* or *why* questions.

→ Why are headings an important part of the text?

Read and discuss the student model on **Your Turn Practice Book** page 39. Then have students select a text that uses headings. Have them write an analysis that explains how the use of headings provides information about different sections of the text. Remind students that good explanatory writing includes a strong concluding statement and uses clauses correctly.

COLLABORATE

Present Your Ideas Ask partners to share their paragraphs and discuss how the evidence they cited from the text supports their ideas. Partners may suggest additional text evidence if necessary.

→ Readers to Writers

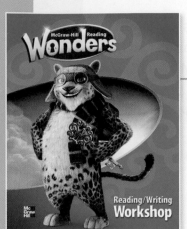
 MINILESSON
10 Mins

Writing Traits: Organization

Sequence

Expert Model Explain that in narrative writing, writers usually tell the events in order, or **sequence**. Good narratives have a clear beginning, middle, and end. Writers organize the sequence of events so they unfold naturally and make sense to the reader. Writers use time-order words, such as *first, next,* and *last,* to tell when things happen.

 COLLABORATE

Read aloud the expert model from "The Big Race." Ask students to listen for the time-order words that help the reader understand the order of events. Have students talk with partners to identify the sequence of events.

Student Model Remind students that sequencing events and using time-order words helps readers understand what is happening in a story. Read aloud the student draft "Boating." As students follow along, have them focus on the time-order words the writer used in his draft.

 COLLABORATE

Invite partners to talk about the sequence of events in the draft and the time-order words that Jonah used. Ask them to suggest places where Jonah could add more time-order words.

Go Digital

Expert Model

Student Model

OBJECTIVES

CCSS Orient the reader by establishing a situation and introducing a narrator and/or characters; organize an event sequence that unfolds naturally. **W.4.3a**

CCSS Use a variety of transitional words and phrases to manage the sequence of events. **W.4.3c**

- Analyze models to understand how events are sequenced.

- Write about a time when science helped you have fun.

- Add time-order words to revise writing.

ACADEMIC LANGUAGE

- *sequence, transitions*
- Cognate: *secuencia*

 Genre Writing

Narrative Text

For full writing process lessons and rubrics, see:

→ Friendly Letter, pages T344–T349

→ Personal Narrative, pages T350–T355

Readers to...

Writers choose the best way to organize their information. One way to organize information is to present events in the order in which they happen. Reread the section from "The Big Race" below.

Sequence

Identify the **sequence** of information in this excerpt. What time-order words does the author use?

Expert Model

Alex and Liam planned to build a car for the soap box derby. As a result of their inquiry into how to build a fast car, they had come to the science museum today for answers. Last week, Alex's mother had called one of the museum's scientists. When they walked into the museum, a woman in a lab coat and inline skates zoomed up and greeted them.

Craig Phillips

72

Writers

Jonah wrote a narrative nonfiction piece. Read Jonah's revision of a section of it.

Student Model

BOATING

My grandfather asked me to go boating today. I love to go boating. ^but

I was scared we would sink. First, he told me about buoyancy force ⊙ ^

Buoyancy force pushes an object For example, if I drop a ball in the water it won't sink. upward when it is in water. Buoyancy forces it up to the water's surface.

Now, I wanted to go boating!

Next, he explained that the lake was not very deep. ←

73

Editing Marks

⌐⌐	Switch order.
∧	Add.
∧	Add a comma.
⊙	Add a period.
ℐ	Take out.
SP	Check spelling.
≡	Make a capital letter.

Grammar Handbook

Complex Sentences
See page 453.

Your Turn

COLLABORATE

- ☑ How does Jonah present new information?
- ☑ Identify a complex sentence he uses.
- ☑ How did the revisions improve his writing?

Go Digital!
Write online in Writer's Workspace

READING/WRITING WORKSHOP, pp. 72–73

ENGLISH LANGUAGE LEARNERS SCAFFOLD

As English Language Learners write during the week, provide support to help them respond to the prompts. For example:

Beginning	**Intermediate**	**Advanced/High**
Write Help students complete the sentence frames. *Jonah's grandfather asked him to go boating ____. The ____ thing Jonah's grandfather did was tell him about buoyancy force. One time-order word Jonah used is ____.*	**Describe** Ask students to complete the sentence frames. Encourage students to provide details. *Jonah's grandfather asked him to ____. The first thing Jonah's grandfather did was ____. Some time-order words Jonah used are ____.*	**Discuss** Check for understanding. Ask: *When did Jonah go boating with his grandfather? What is the first thing Jonah's grandfather did? Can you identify some of the time-order words that Jonah used?*

Writing Every Day: Organization

Writing Entry: Sequence

Prewrite Provide students with the prompt below.

Write about a time when science helped you have fun. Put events in the order they happened.

Have partners list times when they had fun because of science. Ask them to write down how the sequence of events of each experience unfolded.

Draft Have each student choose an experience to write about. Remind students to sequence events and to include time-order words in their drafts.

Focus on Sequence

Use **Your Turn Practice Book** page 40 to model adding time-order words to sequence events.

We went to a dairy farm. We saw a farmer milk a cow. He showed us how he turns milk into butter. We learned how cheese is made from milk.

Model adding time-order words by revising the first sentence.

We went to a dairy farm last weekend.

Discuss how adding time-order words makes the sequence of events clearer. Guide students to add more time-order words to the rest of the model.

Writing Entry: Sequence

Revise Have students revise their writing from Day 1 by adding two or three time-order words.

Use the **Conferencing Routines**. Circulate among students and stop briefly to talk with individuals. Provide time for peer reviews.

Edit Have students use Grammar Handbook page 453 in the **Reading/Writing Workshop** to edit for errors in complex sentences.

Conferencing Routines

Teacher Conferences

STEP 1

Talk about the strengths of the writing.

You have a strong voice in your writing. I like how you share your feelings about the fun experience you had.

STEP 2

Focus on how the writer uses the target trait for the week.

This time-order word helps me understand the order of events. It would help if you added more time-order words so that the sequence of events is clearer and flows more naturally.

STEP 3

Make concrete suggestions for revisions. Have students work on a specific assignment, such as those to the right, and then meet with you to review progress.

DAY 3

Writing Entry: Sequence

Prewrite Ask students to search their Writer's Notebook for topics to write a draft. Or, provide a prompt, such as the following:

Write about a time when you built something for school or just for fun. Put events in the order they happened.

Draft Once students have chosen their topics, ask them to create a sequence chart. Then have them think about the details about the topic that they might include in their writing and the time-order words they could use. Students can then use their sequence charts to begin their drafts.

DAY 4

Writing Entry: Sequence

Revise Have students revise the draft writing from Day 3 by adding time-order words to make the sequence of events clearer. As students are revising their drafts, hold teacher conferences with individual students. You may also wish to have students work with partners to peer conference.

Edit Invite students to review the rules for complex sentences on Grammar Handbook page 453 in the **Reading/Writing Workshop** and then edit their drafts for errors. Students should also use relative pronouns and relative adverbs correctly.

DAY 5

Share and Reflect

Discuss with the class what they learned about using time-order words and sequencing events so they unfold naturally. Invite volunteers to read and compare draft text with text that has been revised. Have students discuss the writing by focusing on the importance of the time-order words that have been added. Allow time for individuals to reflect on their own writing progress and record observations in their Writer's Notebooks.

McGraw-Hill Companies, Inc./Ken Karp, photographer

Suggested Revisions

Provide specific direction to help focus young writers.

Focus on a Sentence
Read the draft and target one sentence for revision. *Rewrite this sentence by adding time-order words that tell when _____.*

Focus on a Section
Underline a section that needs to be revised. Provide specific suggestions. *This section confuses me. I can't tell when _____ happened. Add time-order words to help sequence the events.*

Focus on a Revision Strategy
Underline a section of the writing and ask students to use a specific revision strategy, such as rearranging. *I think the sequence of events would make more sense if you moved this sentence so it comes before this sentence.*

Peer Conferences

Focus peer response groups on adding time-order words to make the sequence of events clear. Provide this checklist to frame discussion.

- ☑ Does the writing include time-order words?
- ☑ Does the event sequence unfold naturally?
- ☑ What time-order words can be added to clarify the sequence of events?

Grammar: Clauses and Complex Sentences

Reading/Writing Workshop

- Distinguish relative pronouns and relative adverbs.
- Punctuate complex sentences correctly.

Go Digital

Clauses and Complex Sentences

Grammar Activities

DAY 1

DAILY LANGUAGE ACTIVITY

The rain stopped, the sun came out. Lina, Sue and I rowed our bikes. (1: stopped, and; 2: Sue, and; 3: rode)

Introduce Clauses

Present the following:

→ A **clause** is a group of words that has a subject and a verb. An **independent clause** can stand alone as a sentence, but a **dependent clause** cannot:

   He arrived. (independent)
   before I did (dependent)

→ A dependent clause usually begins with a **subordinating conjunction,** such as **before, when,** or **because**.

   He arrived **before** I did.

Have partners discuss clauses using page 453 of the Grammar Handbook in **Reading/Writing Workshop**.

DAY 2

DAILY LANGUAGE ACTIVITY

The birds flyed south and the weather grew colder. The days turned gray? (1: flew; 2: south, and; 3: gray.)

Review Clauses

Review clauses. Have students explain how the two kinds differ.

Introduce Complex Sentences

→ A **complex sentence** includes an independent clause and one or more dependent clauses.

→ The subordinating conjunctions **who**, **whose**, **whom**, **which**, and **that** are called **relative pronouns**.

   I like people **who** are friendly.

→ The subordinating conjunctions **where**, **when**, and **why** are called **relative adverbs**.

   Say "thank you" **when** someone helps you.

TALK ABOUT IT

COLLABORATE

COMPLETE THE SENTENCES

Have partners each write five dependent clauses using subordinating conjunctions. Taking turns, have one partner read a clause from the list while the other partner completes the sentence by adding an independent clause.

USE RELATIVE PRONOUNS

Have students in small groups choose a theme, such as science, and write the relative pronouns on index cards. They should take turns drawing a card and saying aloud a theme-related complex sentence using the relative pronoun.

DAY **3**

Mechanics and Usage: Punctuate Complex Sentences

→ When an independent clause begins a complex sentence, it is usually not followed by a comma:

Eva wore a sweater because it was cold outside.

→ When a dependent clause begins a complex sentence, it is usually followed by a comma:

Before I go to bed, I brush my teeth.

As students write, refer them to Grammar Handbook pages 453 and 479.

DAY **4**

Proofread

Have students correct errors in the following sentences.

1. Ricky wants a blue bike, because that is his favorite color! (1: bike because; 2: color.)

2. When the kittens where six months old we let them play in the grass. (1: were; 2: old,)

3. Greg studies in his room, before he plays video games? (1: room before; 2: games.)

4. Before he gave his speech Charlie rehearsed severel times. (1: speech,; 2: several)

Have students check their work using Grammar Handbook page 479 on complex sentences and commas.

DAY **5**

Assess

Use the Daily Language Activity and **Grammar Practice Reproducibles** page 20 for assessment.

Reteach

Use Grammar Practice Reproducibles pages 16–19 and selected pages from the Grammar Handbook for additional reteaching. Remind students to use complex sentences correctly as they speak and write.

Check students' writing for use of the skill and listen for it in their speaking. Assign Grammar Revision Assignments in their Writer's Notebooks as needed.

See Grammar Practice Reproducibles pages 16–20.

USE A COMMA OR NOT?

Ask partners to take turns saying complex sentences that begin or end with a dependent clause using the conjunctions **before, when,** or **because**. The other partner should tell whether or not a comma should be used in the sentence.

BE THE TEACHER

Have students in small groups each write two complex sentences, one with a comma and one without. Each student then chooses another student to act as the teacher and explain the punctuation in his or her two sentences.

ACT OUT A SCENE

Have students in small groups write a short scene from a play that includes at least five complex sentences. Then have them act out the scene for the rest of the class. Have students discuss the complex sentences the characters used.

Spelling: Long *i*

DAY 1

DAY 2

OBJECTIVES
Spell grade-appropriate words correctly, consulting references as needed. **L.4.2d**

Spelling Words

climb	slight	twice
minding	drive	wipe
pies	file	pry
die	kite	sly
height	prime	shy
sigh	pride	spy
fright	slice	

Review chief, zebra, sleek
Challenge highway, wildlife

Differentiated Spelling

Approaching Level

minding	kite	time
climb	file	twice
mind	wipe	cry
pies	inside	sly
die	pride	shy
flight	line	spy
sigh	alike	

Beyond Level

shiny	frightened	prime
climb	lightning	pride
minding	sigh	twice
reminded	slightly	slyly
wiping	tightly	pry
die	filed	spy
height	likely	

Assess Prior Knowledge

Display the spelling words. Read them aloud, drawing out the long *i* sound in each.

Point out the spelling patterns in *climb* and *slight*. Segment the words sound by sound, attaching a spelling to each sound. Point out how the long *i* sound can be made by a single letter *i* or by a combination of letters, as in *slight*.

Demonstrate sorting the spelling words by pattern under key words *climb, wipe, die, slight, height* and *spy*. (Write the words on index cards or the IWB.) Sort a few words. Point out how the letters *i* and *e* are often used together to make the long *i* sound, like in *wipe, die* and *height*.

Then use the Dictation Sentences from Day 5 to give the Pretest. Say the underlined word, read the sentence, and repeat the word. Have students write the words. Then have students check and correct their spelling.

Spiral Review

Review the long *e* sound in *chief, zebra, deed, healer, honey, family* and *scheme*. Use the Dictation Sentences below for the review words. Read the sentence, say the word, and have students write the words.

1. The police <u>chief</u> is in charge.
2. The <u>zebra</u> was new to the zoo.
3. Sharks swim very fast because of their <u>sleek</u> body shapes.

Have partners check the spellings.

Challenge Words Review this week's long *i* spelling patterns. Use these Dictation Sentences for challenge words. Say the word, read the sentence, and say the word again. Have students write the word.

1. We hit traffic on the <u>highway</u>.
2. We need to protect <u>wildlife</u>.

Have students check and correct their spelling before writing the words in their word study notebook.

 WORD SORTS

COLLABORATE

OPEN SORT

Have students cut apart the **Spelling Word Cards BLM** in the Teacher Resource Book and initial the back of each card. Have them read the words aloud with a partner. Then have partners do an open sort. Have them record the sort in their word study notebook.

PATTERN SORT

Complete the **pattern sort** from Day 1 using the key words, pointing out the different long *i* spellings. Have students use Spelling Word Cards to do their own pattern sort. Ask partners to compare and check their sorts.

DAY 3

Word Meanings

Ask students to copy the following words into their word study notebooks. Explain that each word has an antonym, or word that has the opposite meaning. Say the words aloud; ask students to write an antonym for each word using the spelling list.

1. honest (sly)
2. walk (drive)
3. fall (climb)
4. depth (height)

Challenge students to come up with at least three other antonym pairs using spelling, review, or challenge words. Students can use a thesaurus or other resource to help them. Have them write the antonyms, leaving a blank for the word from the spelling list. Have partners trade papers and fill in the missing words.

See Phonics/Spelling Reproducibles pp. 19–24.

SPEED SORT

Have partners do a **speed sort** to see who is faster. Have them compare any differences in their sorts. Then have them write the sort results and a reflection of why they sorted the words as they did in their word study notebook.

DAY 4

Proofread and Write

Write these sentences on the board. Have students circle and correct each misspelled word. They can use print or electronic dictionaries or other resources to help them.

1. She had to prie open the fighyl cabinet. (*pry, file*)
2. It took a long time to clymb the mountain because of its hite. (*climb, height*)
3. The wonderful smell of the pys made the boy siygh. (*pies, sigh*)
4. The new girl likes to fligh her kyt in the park. (*fly, kite*)

Error Correction Remind students that the *y* spelling for the long *i* sound never appears at the beginning of a word or syllable. Rather, it appears at the end.

BLIND SORT

Have partners do a **blind sort**: one reads a Spelling Word Card; the other tells under which key word it belongs. Have them take turns until both have sorted all their words. Ask them to review their sorts and discuss how they sorted the words and if any changes are needed.

DAY 5

Assess

Use the Dictation Sentences for the Posttest. Have students list misspelled words in their word study notebooks. Look for students' use of these words in their writings.

Dictation Sentences

1. She started to <u>climb</u> the rock wall.
2. I was <u>minding</u> my own business.
3. She baked two blueberry <u>pies</u>.
4. Water the rose, or it will <u>die</u>.
5. Amy measured the door's <u>height</u>.
6. She gave a <u>sigh</u> as she waited.
7. The movie gave us a <u>fright</u>.
8. The baby had a <u>slight</u> fever.
9. Do you know how to <u>drive</u> a car?
10. Please use a <u>file</u> cabinet.
11. It is a perfect day to fly a <u>kite</u>.
12. October is the <u>prime</u> month to see fall colors.
13. He carried the flag with <u>pride</u>.
14. Carlos cut a <u>slice</u> of pie.
15. We only went to the pool <u>twice</u>.
16. Use a rag to <u>wipe</u> up that spill.
17. Use a screwdriver to <u>pry</u> it open.
18. The three <u>sly</u> pigs tricked the wolf.
19. The <u>shy</u> toddler hid in his room.
20. The detective will <u>spy</u> on the thief.

Have students self-correct the tests.

→ Build Vocabulary

DAY 1

DAY 2

OBJECTIVES

CCSS Use context (e.g., definitions, examples, or restatements in text) as a clue to the meaning of a word or phrase. **L.4.4a**

Expand vocabulary by adding inflectional endings and affixes.

Vocabulary Words

accelerate	gravity
advantage	identity
capabilities	inquiry
friction	thrilling

Connect to Words

Practice this week's vocabulary.

1. When cars **accelerate**, do they slow down or speed up?
2. What would be an **advantage** for a runner?
3. Describe some **capabilities** of a home computer.
4. What things create **friction** on a car's tires?
5. How does **gravity** affect you?
6. What can you use to prove your **identity** to someone?
7. How can an **inquiry** help you learn more about something?
8. Describe a book or movie that you found **thrilling**.

Expand Vocabulary

Help students generate different forms of this week's words by adding, changing, or removing inflectional endings.

→ Draw a T-chart on the board. Write *identity* in the left column. Then write *identities* in the right column. Read aloud the words with students.

→ Have students share sentences using each form of *identity*.

→ Students can fill in the chart for *inquiry* and *capabilities*, then share sentences using the different forms of the words.

→ Have students copy the chart in their word study notebook.

Go Digital

Vocabulary

Vocabulary Activities

BUILD MORE VOCABULARY

COLLABORATE

ACADEMIC VOCABULARY

Discuss important academic words.

→ Display *hypothesis, force*.

→ Define each word and discuss the meanings with students.

→ Display *hypothesis, hypothesize,* and *hypothetical*. Have partners look up and define related words.

→ Write the related words on the board. Have partners ask and answer questions using the words. Repeat with *force*. Elicit examples from students.

MULTIPLE-MEANING WORDS

→ Ask, *What are some different meanings of the word* force?

→ Have partners use a dictionary to find different meanings for *force*. (something that moves a body; to make someone do something against their wishes)

→ Have partners use the different meanings of *force* in sentences. Have them write the sentences in their word study notebook.

DAY

Reinforce the Words

Review last week's and this week's vocabulary words. Have students orally complete each sentence stem.

1. The photo on her ____ proved her <u>identity</u>.

2. Being a fast runner is an <u>advantage</u> when you're playing ____.

3. Car brakes use <u>friction</u> to ____ the car.

4. The ____ was so <u>thrilling</u>, I wanted to read it twice!

5. Astronauts ____ around in space because there is very little <u>gravity</u>.

6. This new ____ has many <u>capabilities</u> that the older version does not.

DAY

Connect to Writing

→ Have students write sentences in their word study notebooks using this week's vocabulary.

→ Tell them to write sentences that provide word information they learned from this week's readings.

→ **ELL** Provide the Day 3 sentence stems 1–6 for students needing extra support.

Write About Vocabulary Have students write something they learned from this week's words in their word study notebook. For example, they might write about how using technology gives you an *advantage* or how seeing science fiction movies can be *thrilling*.

DAY

Word Squares

Ask students to create Word Squares for each vocabulary word.

→ In the first square, students write the word. (example: *friction*)

→ In the second square, students write their own definition of the word and any related words, such as synonyms. (example: *rub against, resist*)

→ In the third square, students draw a simple illustration that will help them remember the word. (example: drawing of two hands rubbing together)

→ In the fourth square, students write nonexamples, including antonyms for the word. (example: *smooth, easy, slippery*)

→ Have partners compare and discuss their Word Squares.

CONTEXT CLUES

Remind students to look for restatements or definitions to help them understand unfamiliar words or concepts as they read.

→ Display **Your Turn Practice Book** pages 33–34. Read the seventh paragraph. Model finding the meaning of *fire pole*.

→ Have students complete page 37 and find clues for *gravity, inertia* and *speed* on pages 33–34, using a print or online dictionary to confirm meanings.

SHADES OF MEANING

Help students generate words related to *accelerate*. Draw a T-chart. Label one side "Speed up" and the other side "Slow down."

→ Have partners generate words to add to the T-chart. Ask students to use a dictionary or thesaurus.

→ Add words not included, such as *escalate, build up* (Speed up) and *decelerate* (Slow down).

→ Ask students to copy the words in their word study notebook.

MORPHOLOGY

Use *advantage* as a springboard for students to learn more words. Draw a three-column chart labeled "Root," "Prefix," and "Suffix."

→ Fill in the columns with *advantage, dis-* and *-ous.*

→ Discuss how each prefix or suffix changes the word's meaning.

→ Have students suggest root words with similar prefixes and suffixes, such as *appear.* (*disappear, disappearance*)

→ Approaching Level

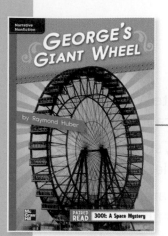

Lexile 550
TextEvaluator™ 13

OBJECTIVES

CCSS Interpret information presented visually, orally, or quantitatively (e.g., in charts, graphs, diagrams, time lines, animations, or interactive elements on Web pages) and explain how the information contributes to an understanding of the text in which it appears. **RI.4.7**

CCSS Paraphrase portions of a text read aloud or information presented in diverse media and formats, including visually, quantitatively, and orally. **SL.4.2**

ACADEMIC LANGUAGE
• *cause, effect*
• Cognates: *causa, efecto*

Leveled Reader:
George's Giant Wheel

Go Digital

Leveled Readers

Before Reading

Preview and Predict

Have students read the Essential Question. Give students a copy of *George's Giant Wheel* and have them read the title and respond to the cover illustrations. Ask students to discuss how a Ferris wheel moves.

Review Genre: Narrative Nonfiction

Have students recall that narrative nonfiction gives facts about a topic, but does so in the form of a narrative, or story. Have students identify features of narrative nonfiction in *George's Giant Wheel*.

During Reading

Close Reading

Note Taking Ask students to use their graphic organizer while they read.

Use Graphic Organizer

Pages 2–3 *Read pages 2–3 and look at the picture on page 3. How was George Ferris's idea for a structure different than the Eiffel Tower? Turn to a partner and explain.* (The Eiffel Tower is tall and narrows to a point. George Ferris wanted to make a big wheel that people could ride on.)

Pages 4–7 *Read pages 4-7. Turn to a partner and paraphrase how a Ferris wheel is similar to a bike wheel.* (The design is similar. It has an axle, spokes, and rims.)

Pages 8–10 *Read page 10 and look for causes and effects with a partner. What causes the wheel to turn?* (two steam engines) *What causes the wheel to stop?* (friction from the brake)

Page 11 *Read "Flying Off Into the Air" on page 11. Tell a partner how centripetal force prevents things from flying off into the air.* (Centripetal force pulls an object toward the center of a circle.)

Pages 12–14 *Look at the box on page 12. How does it help you learn about the Ferris wheel? Turn to a partner and explain.* (It gives the measurements for the Ferris wheel. It helps me understand how big it is.)

After Reading

Respond to Reading Have students complete Respond to Reading on page 15 after they have finished reading.

Write About Reading Have students work with a partner to write a short paragraph describing how people felt about the wheel after it had been invented.

Fluency: Phrasing and Rate

Model Reread page 6. Model reading the passage with appropriate phrasing and rate. Next, read the passage aloud and have students read along with you.

Apply Have students practice reading the passage with a partner.

PAIRED READ

Leveled Reader

"3001: A Space Mystery"

Make Connections: Write About It

Before reading, ask students to note that the genre of this story is science fiction.
Science fiction is a form of fiction that contains some sort of scientific element. Have students discuss the Essential Question. After reading, ask students to make connections between the scientific concepts in *George's Giant Wheel* and "3001: A Space Mystery."

FOCUS ON SCIENCE

Students can extend their knowledge of centripetal force by completing the activity on page 20. **STEM**

Literature Circles

Ask students to conduct a literature circle using the Thinkmark questions to guide the discussion. You may wish to have a whole-class discussion on where you have seen the technology used in the Ferris wheel around the world.

Level Up

Level-up lessons available online.

IF students read the **Approaching Level** fluently and answered the questions

THEN pair them with students who have proficiently read the **On Level** and have students

- echo-read the **On Level** main selection.
- use self-stick notes to mark at least one new detail they would like to discuss in each section.

A C T Access Complex Text

The **On Level** challenges students by including more **domain-specific words** and **complex sentence structures**.

Approaching Level

Phonics/Decoding

DECODE WORDS WITH LONG *i*

 OBJECTIVES

Use combined knowledge of all letter-sound correspondences, syllabication patterns, and morphology (e.g., roots and affixes) to read accurately unfamiliar multisyllabic words in context and out of context. **RF.4.3a**

Decode words with long *i*.

 I Do Display the **Sound-Spelling Card** for the word *fly*. Explain that long *i* has different spellings. Write *fly* on the board and read it aloud. Underline the letter *y*. Point out that in *fly* the long *i* sound is spelled with a *y*. Repeat with *my* and *by*.

 We Do Write *sly* on the board. Model how to decode the word. Have students identify the vowel sound and underline the long *i* sound. Guide students as they decode the words *cry* and *shy*.

 You Do Write these words on the board: *sky, dry, pry,* and *spy*. Have students read each word aloud and identify the long *i* spelling. Then point to the words in random order for students to choral-read. Repeat several times.

REVIEW LONG *i*

 OBJECTIVES

Use combined knowledge of all letter-sound correspondences, syllabication patterns, and morphology (e.g., roots and affixes) to read accurately unfamiliar multisyllabic words in context and out of context. **RF.4.3a**

Decode words with long *i*.

 I Do Tell students that long *i* can also be spelled with *igh* as in *light*, *i_e* as in *dime*, *ie* as in *tie,* and *i* as in *child*. Point out that the letters *gh* are silent in the word *light* and the letter *e* is silent in the word *tie*. Write *light, dime, tie,* and *child* on the board. Underline the long *i* spelling in each word.

 We Do Display the **Word-Building Cards** for *night, high, kind, life, sky, pride, ness, ful, like,* and *light*. Have students use the cards to build as many multisyllabic long *i* words as possible. Have them identify the long *i* spellings and decode each word.

 You Do Write the following examples on the board: *alive, crying,* and *nighttime*. Ask students to decode each word. Then point to all of the words on the board in random order for students to choral-read. Repeat several times.

PRACTICE LONG *i*

OBJECTIVES

CCSS Use combined knowledge of all letter-sound correspondences, syllabication patterns, and morphology to read accurately unfamiliar multisyllabic words in context and out of context. **RF.4.3a**

Decode words with long *i*.

I Do Remind students that the long *i* sound has the spellings *igh, y, i_e, ie,* and *i*. Write the word *widen* on the board and read the word aloud. Point out that the first syllable *wi* has the long *i* sound spelled *i*.

We Do Write the words *scientist, frightened, driveway,* and *minding* on the board. Model how to decode the first word and then guide students as they decode the remaining words. Help them divide each word into syllables using the syllable-scoop technique to read one syllable at a time.

You Do Afterward, point to the words in random order for students to choral-read.

INFLECTIONAL ENDINGS

OBJECTIVES

CCSS Use combined knowledge of all letter-sound correspondences, syllabication patterns, and morphology to read accurately unfamiliar multisyllabic words in context and out of context. **RF.4.3a**

Decode words with inflectional endings -s, -es, -d, and -ed.

I Do Review that adding endings *-s, -es, -d,* and *-ed* to verbs creates new verb forms and tenses. For base words that end in a consonant + *y*, the *y* is changed to *i* before adding *-es* and *-ed*; for example: *apply/applies/applied* and *worry/worries/worried*. For base words that end in a vowel + *y*, the *y* does not change to *i* before adding *-s*; for example: *monkeys*.

We Do Write *carry* on the board. Model how to decode the word. Give some examples of words with inflectional endings, such as *dry/dries/dried*. Guide students as they decode these words. Divide multisyllabic words into syllables using the syllable-scoop technique.

You Do Write the words *marry, empty, vary, reply,* and *study* on the board. Have students add an inflectional ending to each word. Point to the words in random order for students to choral-read.

ELL **ENGLISH LANGUAGE LEARNERS**

For the **ELLs** who need **phonics**, **decoding**, and **fluency** practice, use scaffolding methods as necessary to ensure students understand the meaning of the words. Refer to the **Language Transfers Handbook** for phonics elements that may not transfer in students' native languages.

Approaching Level

Vocabulary

REVIEW HIGH-FREQUENCY WORDS

 TIER 2

OBJECTIVES

 Read with sufficient accuracy and fluency to support comprehension. Read on-level text with purpose and understanding. **RF.4.4a**

Review high-frequency words.

 I Do Use **Word Cards 31–40**. Display one word at a time, following the routine:

Display the word. Read the word. Then spell the word.

 We Do Ask students to say the word and spell it with you. Model using the word in a sentence and have students repeat after you.

 You Do Display the word. Ask students to say the word, then spell it. When completed, quickly flip through the word card set as students choral-read the words. Provide opportunities for students to use the words in speaking and writing. For example, provide sentence starters, such as *I asked Dad to buy ____*. Ask students to write each word in their Writer's Notebook.

REVIEW VOCABULARY WORDS

TIER 2

OBJECTIVES

 Acquire and use accurately grade-appropriate general academic and domain-specific words and phrases, including those that signal precise actions, emotions, or states of being and that are basic to a particular topic. **L.4.6**

 I Do Display each **Visual Vocabulary Card** and state the word. Explain how the photograph illustrates the word. State the example sentence and repeat the word.

 We Do Point to the word on the card and read the word with students. Ask them to repeat the word. Engage students in structured partner-talk about the image as prompted on the back of the vocabulary card.

 You Do Display each card in random order, hiding the word. Have students match the definitions and context sentences of the words to the cards displayed.

IDENTIFY RELATED WORDS

OBJECTIVES

CCSS Demonstrate understanding of words by relating them to their opposites (antonyms) and to words with similar but not identical meanings (synonyms). **L.4.5c**

 I Do

Display the *thrilling* **Visual Vocabulary Card**. Tell which word has almost the same meaning as the first word in the word set: *thrilling, exciting, happy*, and *boring*.

Point out that the word *exciting* means almost the same as *thrilling*.

 We Do

Display the vocabulary card for the word *friction*. Say aloud the word set *friction, elastic, rubbing, looseness*. With students, identify the word that means almost the same as *friction* and discuss why.

 You Do

Using the word sets below, display the remaining cards one at a time, as you say aloud the word set. Ask students to identify the word or words that mean almost the same as the first word in each word set.

advantage, benefit, gain, disadvantage   *gravity, force, light, significance*

identity, status, someone, self   *inquiry, investigation, ask, reply*

capabilities, skills, faults, inabilities   *accelerate, increase, slow, speed*

CONTEXT CLUES

OBJECTIVES

 CCSS Use context (e.g., definitions, examples, or restatements in text) as a clue to the meaning of a word or phrase. **L.4.4a**

Use context clues to determine the meaning of unfamiliar words.

 I Do

Display the Comprehension and Fluency passage on **Approaching Reproducibles** pages 33–34. Read aloud the section "The Pull of Gravity." Point to the word *gravity*. Explain to students that they can use the words in the sentence and from the other sentences in the paragraph to figure out the meaning of *gravity*.

Think Aloud   I want to understand the word *gravity*. Two clues help me: "pulled me down" and "pulls objects toward each other." I can guess from these clues that *gravity* is a force that pulls objects toward each other.

Write the definition of the word from the clues.

 We Do

Ask students to point to the word *inertia* on page 34. With students, discuss how to use the clues in the text to figure out the meaning of the word. Write the definition of the word.

 You Do

Have students find the meanings of *force* and *motion* in the fifth paragraph on page 34 using clues from the passage.

Approaching Level

Comprehension

FLUENCY

TIER 2

 OBJECTIVES

CCSS Read on-level prose and poetry orally with accuracy, appropriate rate, and expression on successive readings. **RF.4.4b**

Read fluently with good phrasing and rate.

I Do Explain that phrasing involves awareness of punctuation and when to pause and stop in a text. Readers should know that commas indicate pauses, and periods and other end punctuation require them to stop. Pauses and stops should be of consistent lengths to maintain an appropriate rate. Read aloud the first paragraph of the Comprehension and Fluency passage on **Approaching Reproducibles** pages 33–34. Tell students to listen to how you use phrasing and rate.

We Do Read the rest of the page aloud and have students repeat each sentence after you, using the same phrasing and rate. Explain that you emphasized pauses and stops at an appropriate rate.

You Do Have partners take turns reading sentences from the passage. Remind them to focus on their phrasing and rate. Listen in and provide corrective feedback by modeling proper fluency as needed.

IDENTIFY IMPORTANT EFFECTS

TIER 2

 OBJECTIVES

CCSS Describe the overall structure (e.g., chronology, comparison, cause/effect, problem/solution) of events, ideas, concepts, or information in a text or part of a text. **RI.4.5**

Identify effects in text structures.

I Do Write the topic "The Pull of Gravity" on the board. Then write: "pulled me down here," "pulls objects toward each other," and "walked back upstairs." Explain that the first two phrases are about the effects of gravity. Help students understand that "walked back upstairs" is not an effect of gravity and remind them that gravity pulls objects down.

We Do Read aloud the first page of the Comprehension and Fluency passage. Ask: *So far, what is this passage about?* Point out that this is the topic of the passage. Then ask, *What effects of gravity did you read about in the passage?* Explain that these effects describe what happens when gravity is applied to an object.

You Do Have students read the rest of the passage. After each paragraph, they should write down the effects of force that seem most important. Review their lists and help them explain why the effects they chose are important. Then have them determine the cause of each effect.

REVIEW CAUSE AND EFFECT

OBJECTIVES

 Describe the overall structure (e.g., chronology, comparison, cause/effect, problem/solution) of events, ideas, concepts, or information in a text or part of a text. **RI.4.5**

Identify causes and effects in a text.

 I Do Remind students that a cause is why something happens and an effect is what happens. Signal words, such as *because, due to, so,* and *as a result* can be used to find causes and effects in a text. Explain that cause-and-effect relationships can be used to understand why something happens.

 We Do Read the second section in the Comprehension and Fluency passage in **Approaching Reproducibles** together. Pause to point to the causes and effects in this section. Model how to decide what information in the text is a cause and what is an effect. Then work with students to explain each cause and each effect.

 You Do Have students identify the causes and effects in the next section of the passage.

SELF-SELECTED READING

OBJECTIVES

CCSS Describe the overall structure (e.g., chronology, comparison, cause/effect, problem/solution) of events, ideas, concepts, or information in a text or part of a text. **RI.4.5**

Reread difficult sections in a text to increase understanding.

Read Independently

Have students choose an informational text for sustained silent reading. Remind students that:

→ a cause is why something happens and an effect is what happens as a result.

→ if they have trouble identifying cause and effect, they should reread a paragraph or section and look for more information to help them understand the cause and effect better.

Read Purposefully

Have students record the cause and effect on a Cause and Effect Chart as they read independently. After they finish, they can have a discussion, each telling about the book they read.

→ Students should share their charts and answer this question: *What was the most interesting fact you learned from this text?*

→ They should also tell the rest of the class if there were any sections they reread to increase their understanding.

On Level

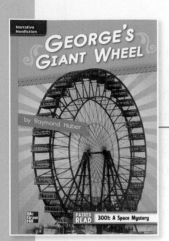

Lexile 810
TextEvaluator 33

OBJECTIVES

 Interpret information presented visually, orally, or quantitatively (e.g., in charts, graphs, diagrams, time lines, animations, or interactive elements on Web pages) and explain how the information contributes to an understanding of the text in which it appears. **RI.4.7**

Paraphrase portions of a text read aloud or information presented in diverse media and formats, including visually, quantitatively, and orally. **SL.4.2**

ACADEMIC LANGUAGE

- *cause, effect*
- Cognates: *causa, efecto*

Leveled Reader:
George's Giant Wheel

Leveled Readers

Before Reading

Preview and Predict

Read the Essential Question with students. Give students a copy of *George's Giant Wheel* and have them read the title and respond to the cover illustrations. Ask students to discuss how a Ferris wheel moves.

Review Genre: Narrative Nonfiction

Have students recall that narrative nonfiction gives facts about a topic in the form of a story. It often has captions and headings to help them better understand the information. Have students identify features of narrative nonfiction in *George's Giant Wheel*.

During Reading

Close Reading

Note Taking Ask students to use their graphic organizer while they read.

Pages 2–3 *Reread pages 2–3. What was the Eiffel Tower originally used for?* (the entrance to the world's fair in Paris) *Where did you find this information?* (the caption on page 3)

Pages 4–7 *Turn to a partner and tell how Ferris's wheel was designed to be similar to a bicycle wheel and how it was different.* (The two were similar because both had metal frames that revolved around axles and long metal spokes that connected them. The Ferris wheel was different because it had passenger cars between the rims.)

Pages 8–10 *Turn to a partner and tell the cause-and-effect relationships related to how the Ferris wheel was built. What features did the wheel need to have as a result of it being so heavy?* (It needed a solid base and braces because it was so heavy.)

Page 11 *Read the Centripetal Force box on page 11. Tell your partner a definition of centripetal force.* (a force that pulls an object toward the center of a circle when the object is on a circular path)

Use Graphic Organizer

Pages 12–13 *Paraphrase the reaction to Ferris's wheel. Reread pages 12–13.* (The wheel was a huge hit at the fair, and nearly one and a half million people rode it.)

After Reading

Respond to Reading Have students complete Respond to Reading on page 15 after they have finished reading.

Analytical Writing **Write About Reading** Have students work with a partner to write a short paragraph describing the impact that George's invention had on the world.

Fluency: Phrasing and Rate

Model Model reading page 8 with careful phrasing and proper rate. Next read the passage aloud and have students read along with you.

Apply Have partners do repeated rereadings of the passage.

PAIRED READ

"3001: A Space Mystery"

Make Connections:
Write About It *Analytical Writing*

Before reading, ask students to note that the genre of this story is science fiction.
Science fiction is a form of fiction that contains some sort of scientific element. Have students discuss the Essential Question. After reading, ask students to make connections between the scientific concepts in *George's Giant Wheel* and "3001: A Space Mystery."

Leveled Reader

 FOCUS ON SCIENCE

Students can extend their knowledge of centripetal force by completing the activity on page 20. **STEM**

Literature Circles

Ask students to conduct a literature circle using the Thinkmark questions to guide the discussion. You may wish to have a whole-class discussion on where you have seen the technology used in the Ferris wheel around the world.

Level Up

Level-up lessons available online.

IF students read the **On Level** fluently and answered the questions

THEN pair them with students who have proficiently read the **Beyond Level** and have students

- partner-read the **Beyond Level** main selection.
- list vocabulary words they find difficult and look them up with a partner.

A C T ccess **C**omplex **T**ext

The **Beyond Level** challenges students by including more **domain-specific words** and **complex sentence structures**.

On Level

Vocabulary

REVIEW VOCABULARY WORDS

OBJECTIVES

 Acquire and use accurately grade-appropriate general academic and domain-specific words and phrases, including those that signal precise actions, emotions, or states of being (e.g., *quizzed, whined, stammered*) and that are basic to a particular topic (e.g., *wildlife, conservation,* and *endangered* when discussing animal preservation). **L.4.6**

 Use the **Visual Vocabulary Cards** to review the selection words: *advantage, capabilities, friction, gravity, identity,* and *thrilling*. Point to each word, read it aloud, and have students chorally repeat it.

 Ask these questions and help students respond and explain their answers.

→ Does a *thrilling* roller-coaster ride cause someone to feel bored?

→ How would *friction* stop a ball when someone kicks it across the street?

→ Why did his tall height give him an *advantage* on the basketball team?

 Have students respond to these questions and explain their answers.

→ Why did the athlete lose his *capabilities* after his injury?

→ Does *gravity* push objects away from Earth?

→ How can wearing a mask hide your *identity*?

CONTEXT CLUES

OBJECTIVES

 Use context (e.g., definitions, examples, or restatements in text) as a clue to the meaning of a word or phrase. **L.4.4a**

 Remind students that they can often figure out the meaning of an unknown word from context clues in the text. Use the Comprehension and Fluency passage on **Your Turn Practice Book** pages 33–34 to model.

Think Aloud When I read the third paragraph under "The Pull of Gravity," I want to understand the word *gravity*. Two clues help me: "pulled me down" and "pulls objects toward each other." From these clues, I think that *gravity* is a force that pulls objects toward each other.

 Have students finish reading the passage. Point out the word *force* on page 34. Have students figure out the definition of *force* by looking for clues in the paragraph. Point out context clues, such as "something that moves, stops, or changes the motion of an object."

 Have students work in pairs to determine the meanings of *inertia* and *speed* on page 34 of the passage.

Comprehension

REVIEW CAUSE AND EFFECT

OBJECTIVES

 Describe the overall structure (e.g., chronology, comparison, cause/effect, problem/solution) of events, ideas, concepts, or information in a text or part of a text. **RI.4.5**

Identify causes and effects in a text.

 I Do Remind students that cause and effect is one kind of text structure that authors use to tell how or why something happens. A cause is why something happens and an effect is what happens. Signal words, such as *because, due to, so,* and *as a result* can be used to find causes and effects in a text. Explain that cause-and-effect relationships can be used to understand why something happens.

We Do Have a volunteer read the second section of the Comprehension and Fluency passage on **Your Turn Practice Book** pages 33–34. Have students orally list the causes and effects, and help them explain why they are important. Then model how to decide what information in the text is a cause and what is an effect. Next, work with students to explain each cause and effect.

You Do Have partners identify the causes and effects in the next section of the passage.

SELF-SELECTED READING

OBJECTIVES

 Describe the overall structure (e.g., chronology, comparison, cause/effect, problem/solution) of events, ideas, concepts, or information in a text or part of a text. **RI.4.5**

Reread difficult sections in a text to increase understanding.

Read Independently

Have students choose an informational text for sustained silent reading.

→ Before they reread, have students preview the text, reading the title, and viewing the front and back cover.

→ As students read, remind them to reread difficult sections.

Read Purposefully

Encourage students to read different texts in order to learn about a variety of subjects.

→ As students reread, have them fill in the causes and effects on a Cause and Effect Chart.

→ Students can use this chart to help them write a summary of the text.

→ Ask students to share their reactions to the text with classmates.

→ Beyond Level

Lexile 910
TextEvaluator™ 39

OBJECTIVES

(CCSS) Refer to details and examples in a text when explaining what the text says explicitly and when drawing inferences from the text. **RI.4.1**

(CCSS) Determine the meaning of general academic and domain-specific words or phrases in a text relevant to a *grade 4 topic or subject area.* **RI.4.4**

(CCSS) Paraphrase portions of a text read aloud or information presented in diverse media and formats, including visually, quantitatively, and orally. **SL.4.2**

Leveled Reader:
George's Giant Wheel

Before Reading

Preview and Predict

Read the Essential Question with students. Give students a copy of *George's Giant Wheel* and have them read the title and respond to the cover illustrations. Ask students to discuss how a Ferris wheel moves.

Review Genre: Narrative Nonfiction

Have students recall that narrative nonfiction gives facts about a topic in the form of a story. It often has captions and headings to help them better understand the information. Have students identify features of narrative nonfiction in *George's Giant Wheel*.

During Reading

Close Reading

Note Taking Ask students to use their graphic organizer while they read.

Pages 2–3 *Reread pages 2–3. How did the structure of the Eiffel Tower inspire other buildings? Turn to a partner and explain.* (It showed that steel and iron could be used to build tall structures.)

Pages 4–5 *Read pages 4–5. How do context clues help you understand the meaning of* gravity? *Turn to a partner and define the word.* (The definition "the force that attracts things toward Earth" is given in the text.)

Page 6 *Read page 6. What do you think people mean when they call George Ferris "the man with wheels in his head"? Is it a good thing or a bad thing?* (I think they mean that he's always thinking about wheels. I think they mean it in a negative way, to make fun of him.) *Make a prediction to a partner about what these people will think of George Ferris by the end of the text.* (His success will change their minds.)

Pages 8–10 *Turn to a partner and paraphrase the cause and effect relationships that are necessary for the Ferris wheel to work.* (It needed a solid base because it was extremely heavy. Because it was so heavy, it also needed braces. In order to move, it needed the force of two powerful

Go Digital

Leveled Readers

Use Graphic Organizer

steam engines. The steam engines were connected to a chain, which turned the wheel. A brake would cause the wheel to stop.)

Pages 12–14 *Read pages 12–14. What details tell you that the Ferris wheel was a success? Turn to a partner and paraphrase.* (I can tell it was a success because so many people wanted to ride it—almost one and a half million. Also, the ride proved to be safe despite people's fears.)

After Reading

Respond to Reading Have students complete Respond to Reading on page 15 after they have finished reading.

Analytical Writing **Write About Reading** Have students work with a partner to write a short paragraph describing the impact that George's invention had on the world.

Fluency: Phrasing and Rate

Model Model reading page 8 with careful phrasing and proper rate. Next, read the passage aloud and have students read along with you.

Apply Have partners do repeated rereadings of the passage.

PAIRED READ

"3001: A Space Mystery"

Make Connections:
Write About It **Analytical Writing**

Before reading, ask students to note that the genre of this story is science fiction. Science fiction is a form of fiction that contains some sort of scientific element. Have students discuss the Essential Question. After reading, ask students to make connections between the scientific concepts in *George's Giant Wheel* and "3001: A Space Mystery."

Leveled Reader

Literature Circles

Ask students to conduct a literature circle using the Thinkmark questions to guide the discussion. You may wish to have a whole-class discussion on where you have seen the technology used in the Ferris wheel around the world.

Gifted and Talented

Synthesize George Ferris's invention had an impact on people around the world. Have students think of another invention that has changed the way people around the world see and do things. Have them research how the invention works and draw a diagram to show the class.

FOCUS ON SCIENCE

Students can extend their knowledge of centripetal force by completing the activity on page 20. **STEM**

Beyond Level

Vocabulary

REVIEW DOMAIN-SPECIFIC WORDS

 OBJECTIVES

Acquire and use accurately grade-appropriate general academic and domain-specific words and phrases, including those that signal precise actions, emotions, or states of being and that are basic to a particular topic. **L.4.6**

 Model Use the **Visual Vocabulary Cards** to review the meaning of the words *accelerate* and *inquiry*. Write science-related sentences on the board using the words.

Write the words *force* and *motion* on the board and discuss the meanings with students. Then help them write sentences using these words.

 Apply Have students work in pairs to review the meanings of the words *friction* and *gravity*. Then have partners write sentences using these words.

CONTEXT CLUES

OBJECTIVES

Use context (e.g., definitions, examples, or restatements in text) as a clue to the meaning of a word or phrase. **L.4.4a**

 Model Read aloud the first two paragraphs of the Comprehension and Fluency passage on **Beyond Reproducibles** pages 33–34. Remind students that context clues can help them understand unfamiliar words.

Think Aloud I want to understand what *inertia* means. When I read the second paragraph on the second page of the passage, I learn that *inertia* is "when an object at rest tends to stay at rest." Next, I learn that inertia happens when "an object in motion stays in motion, unless acted upon by an outside force." These clues give me the definition of *inertia*.

 Apply Have pairs of students read the rest of the passage. Ask them to use context clues to determine the meaning of *force* and *speed* on page 34.

 Gifted and Talented **Synthesize** Have students imagine that they are interviewing a firefighter about how he or she encounters gravity and friction while fighting fires. Students should create both questions and answers for an interview. Then have students act out their interviews with a partner.

Comprehension

REVIEW CAUSE AND EFFECT

OBJECTIVES

 Describe the overall structure (e.g., chronology, comparison, cause/effect, problem/solution) of events, ideas, concepts, or information in a text or part of a text. **RI.4.5**

Identify the causes and effects in a text.

 Model

Remind students that cause and effect is a kind of text structure that authors use to organize information. Cause and effect tells how or why something happens. A cause is why something happens and an effect is what happens. Signal words, such as *because, due to, so,* and *as a result* can be used to find causes and effects in a text. Explain that cause-and-effect relationships can be used to understand why something happens.

Have students read the first section of the Comprehension and Fluency passage of **Beyond Reproducibles** pages 33–34. Ask open-ended questions to facilitate discussion, such as *What is the author telling us in this section? What does the author want us to know?* Students should support their responses with details in the text.

 Apply

Have partners identify the causes and effects in the next section of the passage.

SELF-SELECTED READING

OBJECTIVES

 Describe the overall structure (e.g., chronology, comparison, cause/effect, problem/solution) of events, ideas, concepts, or information in a text or part of a text. **RI.4.5**

Reread difficult sections in a text to increase understanding.

Read Independently

Have students choose an informational text for sustained silent reading.

→ As students read, have them fill in a Cause and Effect Chart.

→ Remind them to reread difficult sections of the text.

Read Purposefully

Encourage students to keep a reading journal. Ask them to read different texts in order to learn about a variety of subjects.

→ Students can write summaries of the text in their journals.

→ Ask students to share their reactions to the text with classmates.

 Independent Study Challenge students to discuss how their texts relate to the weekly theme of ideas in motion. Ask students to describe how the laws of physics relate to their readings. Have them use specific examples from the text to support their answers.

→ # English Language Learners

Reading/Writing Workshop

OBJECTIVES

CCSS Explain events, procedures, ideas, or concepts in a historical, scientific, or technical text, including what happened and why, based on specific information in the text. **RI.4.3**

CCSS Determine the meaning of general academic and domain-specific words or phrases in a text relevant to a *grade 4 topic or subject area.* **RI.4.4**

LANGUAGE OBJECTIVE

Identify cause and effect text structures.

Shared Read
The Big Race

Go Digital

Before Reading

Build Background

Read the Essential Question: How can science help you understand how things work?

→ Explain the meaning of the Essential Question. Discuss the concept of science, asking students what they know about people and ideas in science. Tell students that science is about **inquiry**, or asking questions and trying to find out the answers.

→ **Model an answer:** *Science can help us understand many things. It can help explain something as simple as how crayons are made, or it can explain something mysterious and challenging like space.*

→ Ask students a question that ties the Essential Question to their own background knowledge. *Turn to a partner and discuss a time when you tried to understand how something works. For example, have you ever taken something apart to see how it works?* Call on several pairs.

View "The Big Race"

During Reading

Interactive Question-Response

→ Ask questions that help students understand the meaning of the text after each paragraph.

→ Reinforce the meanings of key vocabulary.

→ Ask students questions that require them to use key vocabulary.

→ Reinforce strategies and skills of the week by modeling.

Page 65

It's About Speed

Paragraphs 1–3

Explain and Model Rereading Reread this section to help students understand why Alex and Liam are visiting a museum. *Alex and Liam meet Clara, a museum scientist who can help them understand what makes cars go fast. They get to experience a virtual car race. Has anyone ever played a race car game? Tell me about that experience.*

Explain and Model Context Clues *I see that* speed *is defined as the distance an object moves in a certain time.* Have two volunteers demonstrate speed. One student will check the time it takes another student to walk from one side of the room to another side. Measure the distance. Say: *It took __ seconds to travel __ feet.*

Turn to a partner and discuss the meaning of speed. *Make sure your partner understands why time and distance are important.* (Possible answer: To measure speed, we look at the distance an object moves in a certain amount of time.)

Page 66

Forces at Work

Paragraph 4

Have students chorally read the fourth paragraph on page 66. Reread the definitions of *force* and *accelerate*. Point out the cognates: *fuerza* and *acelerar.*

Explain and Model Cause and Effect Explain that the author uses cause and effect to explain forces and speed. *What happens when Clara applies a force to a stool?* (the stool moves) *That's right. Clara's force is the cause. The movement, or motion, is the effect.* Have a student demonstrate the effect of a force on an object. Ask the student push a chair or another object. Have another student explain what caused the chair to move.

Summarize what happens when Clara pushes two stools at the same time. What causes one of the stools to go farther? (When Clara pushed both stools, she gave one a bigger force, or push, which made it go farther.)

Page 67

Gravity and Friction

Paragraph 1

Clara tells the boys that gravity is another force that will pull their car down the hill. What two forces will accelerate, or increase the speed, of the boys' car? (a strong push and gravity)

Paragraph 3

How will friction help the boys during the race? (The boys' car will need friction to slow down and stop the car.)

Turn to a partner and summarize what will happen when the boys' car is pushed at the top of the hill. What kind of force will help accelerate, or increase the speed, of the car? (a push) *What will keep it going downhill?* (gravity) *What will stop the car?* (friction) Call on several pairs to share their summaries with the rest of the class.

After Reading

Make Connections

→ Review the Essential Question: How can science help you understand how things work?

→ Make text connections.

→ Have students complete **ELL Reproducibles** pages 33–35.

English Language Learners

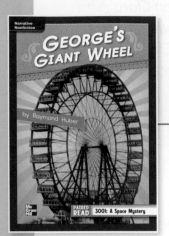

Narrative Nonfiction
GEORGE'S GIANT WHEEL
by Raymond Huber
PAIRED READ 3001: A Space Mystery

Lexile 610
TextEvaluator 20

OBJECTIVES

 CCSS Interpret information presented visually, orally, or quantitatively (e.g., in charts, graphs, digrams, time lines, animations, or interactive elements on Web pages) and explain how the information contributes to an understanding of the text in which it appears. **RI.4.7**

CCSS Paraphrase portions of a text read aloud or information presented in diverse media and formats, including visually, quantitatively, and orally. **SL.4.2**

Leveled Reader:
George's Giant Wheel

Go Digital

| **Before Reading** |

Preview

→ Read the Essential Question: How can science help you understand how things work?

→ Refer to How Does It Work?: *Describe how a roller coaster moves. How is it different than how you normally move?*

→ Preview *George's Giant Wheel* and "3001: A Space Mystery": *Let's read about how science can help us understand how things work.*

Leveled Readers

Vocabulary

Use **Visual Vocabulary Cards** to preteach the ELL vocabulary: *feature, inventions, structure, supported.* Use the routine found on the cards. Point out the cognates: *inventos, estructura.*

| **During Reading** |

Interactive Question-Response

Note Taking Have students use their graphic organizer in **ELL Reproducibles,** page 32. Use the questions below after reading each page with students. Define vocabulary, using visuals and examples.

Pages 2–3 *Inventions are things that are created by people for the first time. Name three inventions.* (Possible answers: phones, TV, cars, lights)

Pages 4–5 Point out where the author writes "one story about the inventions claims. . . ." Explain that this means it is one possible version.

Pages 6–7 *Why did some people think George Ferris's idea was crazy?* (They were afraid that the wheel was too heavy and would fall over.) *How did George Ferris try to get approval for his design?* (He showed his designs to other engineers, and they agreed the wheel would work.)

Pages 8–9 *Turn to a partner and describe the different parts of the wheel. One partner reads the label and the other points to it.*

Pages 10–11 *What causes the passenger cars on a Ferris wheel to move in a circle?* (centripetal force) Point out that *centripetal force* is a cognate: *fuerza centrípeta.*

| Cause → Effect |
| → |
| → |
| → |
| → |

Use Graphic Organizer

Pages 12–14 *Point to the sidebar and caption on page 12. What information does the sidebar give?* (It gives the measurements of Ferris's wheel.) *How tall was Ferris's wheel?* (264 feet tall) *How many people did each passenger car carry?* (60 people)

After Reading

Respond to Reading Help students complete the graphic organizer on **ELL Reproducibles,** page 32. Revisit the Essential Question. Have partners summarize and answer the Text Evidence Questions.

 **Write About Reading** Have partners write a short paragraph describing the impact that George's invention had on the world.

Fluency: Phrasing and Rate

Model Model reading page 8 with careful phrasing and proper rate. Next, reread the passage aloud and have students read along with you.

Apply Have partners do repeated rereadings of the passage.

PAIRED READ

Leveled Reader

"3001: A Space Mystery"

Make Connections: Write About It

Before reading, ask students to note that the genre of this story is science fiction.

Science fiction is a form of fiction that deals with imaginary events and settings. Have students discuss the Essential Question. After reading, ask students to make connections between the scientific concepts in *George's Giant Wheel* and "3001: A Space Mystery."

FOCUS ON SCIENCE

Students can extend their knowledge of centripetal force by completing the activity on page 20. **STEM**

Literature Circles

Ask students to conduct a literature circle using the Thinkmark questions to guide the discussion. You may wish to have a whole-class discussion on where you have seen the technology used in the Ferris wheel around the world.

Level Up

Level-up lessons available online.

IF students read the **ELL Level** fluently and answered the questions

THEN pair them with students who have proficiently read **On Level** and have ELL students

• echo-read the **On Level** main selection with their partners.

• list difficult words and discuss these words with their partners.

A C T Access Complex Text

The **On Level** challenges students by including more **complex sentence structures**.

English Language Learners
Vocabulary

PRETEACH VOCABULARY

OBJECTIVES

 Acquire and use accurately grade-appropriate general academic and domain-specific words and phrases, including those that signal precise actions, emotions, or states of being and that are basic to a particular topic. **L.4.6**

LANGUAGE OBJECTIVE
Use vocabulary words.

I Do Preteach vocabulary from "The Big Race," following the Vocabulary Routine found on the **Visual Vocabulary Cards** for the words *accelerate, advantage, capabilities, friction, gravity, identity, inquiry,* and *thrilling*.

We Do After completing the Vocabulary Routine, point to the word on the Visual Vocabulary Card and read it aloud. Ask students to repeat the word.

You Do Have partners draw a picture for two or more words. Assign students to small groups and have them use the pictures to guess the words.

Beginning	Intermediate	Advanced/High
Help students pronounce the words and generate ideas for their pictures.	Ask students to write clue words along with their pictures.	Challenge students to write sentences for each word.

REVIEW VOCABULARY

OBJECTIVES

 Acquire and use accurately grade-appropriate general academic and domain-specific words and phrases, including those that signal precise actions, emotions, or states of being and that are basic to a particular topic. **L.4.6**

LANGUAGE OBJECTIVE
Use vocabulary words.

I Do Review the previous week's vocabulary words. Read each word aloud, pointing to the word on the **Visual Vocabulary Card.** Have students repeat. Then follow the Vocabulary Routine on the back of each card.

We Do Write the word *hazard* in the center of a word web. Help students identify clues for the word. Write the clues on the web and read the clues aloud.

You Do Provide word webs to small groups. Ask each group to choose a word and write the word in the center. Then have them write one clue. Have groups trade word webs. Instruct them to add a new clue for the word in the center. Repeat until groups have added clues to all words.

Beginning	Intermediate	Advanced/High
Help students write clues. Read the word and clues aloud.	Challenge students to use synonyms as clues.	Challenge students to use examples as clues (e.g., *hazard*/broken glass).

CONTEXT CLUES

OBJECTIVES

Use context (e.g., definitions, examples, or restatements in text) as a clue to the meaning of a word or phrase. **L.4.4a**

LANGUAGE OBJECTIVE

Use context clues.

I Do Read aloud the section "The Pull of Gravity" in the Comprehension and Fluency passage on **ELL Reproducibles** pages 33–34, while students follow along. Summarize the paragraph. Point to the word *gravity*. Explain that context clues, such as definitions, examples, or restatements, can help readers figure out the meaning of an unfamiliar word.

Think Aloud I am not sure what the word *gravity* means. Sometimes writers define difficult words, or they may give examples. I see that the phrase "pulls objects toward each other" defines the word *gravity*.

We Do Have students point to the word *force* on page 34. Help students find context clues for the word. Then write the definition on the board.

You Do In pairs, have students look for context clues for *inertia* and *speed* on page 34. Then have them explain in their own words the meaning of each word.

Beginning	Intermediate	Advanced/High
Help students locate the word and context clues on the page.	Ask students to locate and read aloud the context clues on the page.	Have students identify the type of context clue they found.

ADDITIONAL VOCABULARY

OBJECTIVES

Acquire and use accurately grade-appropriate general academic and domain-specific words and phrases, including those that signal precise actions, emotions, or states of being and that are basic to a particular topic. **L.4.6**

LANGUAGE OBJECTIVE

Use academic language.

I Do List academic and high-frequency words from "The Big Race": *force, machine, speed;* and *George's Giant Wheel: invention, science, technology*. Define each word for students: *A force causes something to move or change its direction.* Demonstrate a force by moving a chair or desk.

We Do Model using the words in a sentence: *If I apply enough force to the chair, I can move it.* Then provide sentence frames and complete them with students: *The force from my push makes the skateboard _____.*

You Do Have pairs make up their own sentence frames and share them with the class. Have the class complete the sentence frames.

Beginning	Intermediate	Advanced/High
Help students copy the sentence frames correctly and complete them.	Provide sentence starters for students, if necessary.	Have students define the words they used.

English Language Learners

Writing/Spelling

WRITING TRAIT: ORGANIZATION

OBJECTIVES

CCSS Use a variety of transitional words and phrases to manage the sequence of events. **W.4.3c**

Add time-order or transitional words to revise writing.

LANGUAGE OBJECTIVE
Organize writing in sequence.

I Do Explain that writers organize the sequence of events so that events unfold naturally and make sense to the reader. Good narratives have a clear beginning, middle, and end. Read the Expert Model passage aloud as students follow along and identify the sequence of events.

We Do Read aloud a passage from "The Big Race" as students follow along. Use a sequence chart to identify the beginning, middle, and end of the events in the passage. Model sentences describing the sequence using the chart.

You Do Have pairs use a sequence chart to write about something they have built at home or school. They should include time-order words to show the sequence of events. Edit each pair's writing. Then ask students to revise.

Beginning	**Intermediate**	**Advanced/High**
Have students copy the sentences. Point out time-order words.	Have students revise, focusing on the sequence of events.	Challenge students to use simple, compound, and complex sentences.

SPELL WORDS WITH LONG *i*

OBJECTIVES

CCSS Spell grade-appropriate words correctly, consulting references as needed. **L.4.2d**

LANGUAGE OBJECTIVE
Spell words with long *i*.

I Do Read aloud the Spelling Words on page T228. Have students repeat the words. Point out that the long *i* sound can be spelled in different ways.

We Do Read the Dictation Sentences on page T229 aloud. Read the underlined word slowly. Have students repeat after you and write the word.

You Do Display the words. Have students exchange their list with a partner to check the spelling and correct misspelled words.

Beginning	**Intermediate**	**Advanced/High**
Have students copy the words with correct spelling and say the words aloud.	After students have corrected their words, have pairs quiz each other.	After they have corrected their words, have pairs use each word in a sentence.

Grammar

CLAUSES AND COMPLEX SENTENCES

OBJECTIVES

CCSS Demonstrate command of the conventions of standard English capitalization, punctuation, and spelling when writing. Use a comma before a coordinating conjunction in a compound sentence. **L.4.2c**

Use clauses and complex sentences.

LANGUAGE OBJECTIVE

Write complex sentences.

Language Transfers Handbook

In Hmong, verbs can be used consecutively without conjunctions or punctuation. Reinforce the use of punctuation and the conjunctions *before, when,* and *because* by helping students use them to form sentences.

I Do Remind students that complex sentences contain an independent clause and one or more dependent clauses. Point out that a clause is a group of words that contains a subject and a verb. Tell students that independent clauses can stand alone as complete sentences. Dependent clauses often begin with the subordinating conjunctions *before, when,* and *because.* Write on the board: *The girl became very shy when she stepped onto the stage.* Circle the independent clause and underline the dependent clause. Tell students that when an independent clause starts a sentence, it is not followed by a comma. Add that when a dependent clause starts a sentence, it is followed by a comma.

We Do Write the sentence frames below on the board. Ask volunteers to complete the sentence frames with the correct subordinating conjunction: *before, when,* or *because.* Identify the independent clause and circle it. Have students underline the dependent clause in each complex sentence. Then read the completed sentence frames aloud and have students repeat.

_____ *our oven was broken, we ordered pizza for dinner.*

Olivia makes her own breakfast _____ *she wakes up in the morning.*

You Do Have students work in small groups to write two complex sentences. Have each group write a complex sentence that begins with an independent clause and one that begins with a dependent clause. Remind students to use correct punctuation.

Beginning	Intermediate	Advanced/High
Have students copy their sentences and help them underline the independent and dependent clauses, and then read them aloud.	Ask students to underline independent clauses once and dependent clauses twice. Then have them circle the subordinating conjunctions.	Have students identify independent and dependent clauses in their sentences. Ask them to explain how they identified the clauses.

For extra support, have students complete the activities in the **Grammar Practice Reproducibles** during the week, using the routine below:

→ Explain the grammar skill.

→ Model the first activity in the Grammar Practice Reproducibles.

→ Have the whole group complete the next couple of activities. Then have students complete the rest with a partner.

→ Review the activities with correct answers.

PROGRESS MONITORING

Weekly Assessment

✔ **COMPREHENSION:**	✔ **VOCABULARY:**	✔ **WRITING:**
Cause and Effect **RI.4.5**	Context Clues: Definitions and Restatements **L.4.4a**	Writing About Text **RI.4.5, W.4.9b**

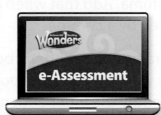

Assessment Includes

→ Pencil-and-paper administration

→ On-line administration

→ Approaching-Level Weekly Assessment also available

Fluency Goal 84 to 104 words correct per minute (WCPM)

Accuracy Rate Goal 95% or higher

Administer oral reading fluency assessments using the following schedule:

→ **Weeks 1, 3, 5** Provide Approaching-Level students at least three oral reading fluency assessments during the unit.

→ **Weeks 2 and 4** Provide On-Level students at least two oral reading fluency assessments during the unit.

→ **Week 6** If necessary, provide Beyond-Level students an oral reading fluency assessment at this time.

Also Available: Selection Tests online PDFs

Go Digital! www.connected.mcgraw-hill.com

Using Assessment Results

TESTED SKILLS	If ...	Then ...
COMPREHENSION	Students answer 0–6 multiple-choice items correctly ...	... assign Lessons 76–78 on Cause and Effect from the *Tier 2 Comprehension Intervention online PDFs.*
VOCABULARY	Students answer 0–6 multiple-choice items correctly ...	... assign Lesson 135 on Using Definition and Example Clues from the *Tier 2 Vocabulary Intervention online PDFs.*
WRITING	Students score less than "3" on the constructed response ...	... assign Lessons 76–78 and/or Write About Reading Lesson 200 from the *Tier 2 Comprehension Intervention online PDFs.*
FLUENCY	Students have a WCPM score of 76–83 ...	... assign a lesson from Section 1 or 7–10 of the *Tier 2 Fluency Intervention online PDFs.*
	Students have a WCPM score of 0–75 ...	... assign a lesson from Sections 2–6 of the *Tier 2 Fluency Intervention online PDFs.*

Response to Intervention

Use the appropriate sections of the *Placement and Diagnostic Assessment* as well as students' assessment results to designate students requiring:

 Intervention Online PDFs

 WonderWorks Intervention Program

WEEKLY OVERVIEW

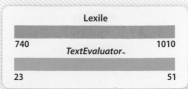

Text Complexity Range for Grades 4–5

Lexile	
740	1010
TextEvaluator™	
23	51

Reading/Writing Workshop

TEACH AND MODEL

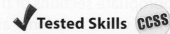

CCSS Shared Read **TIME** *FOR KIDS*

Dollars and $ENSE

Behind the success of these big businesses is a desire to help others.

Good business is not always about the bottom line. A **compassionate** company knows that making money is not the only way to measure success. Many large businesses in the United States and all over the world are finding unusual ways to help people in need.

Hearts and Soles

After starting and running four businesses, Blake Mycoskie wanted a break from his usual **routine**. In 2006, he traveled to Argentina, in South America, and while he was there he learned to sail and dance. He also visited poor villages where very few of the children had shoes. Mycoskie decided he had to do something.

Essential Question
How can starting a business help others?

Read about how two companies are making a difference.

78

"I'm going to start a shoe company, and for every pair I sell, I'm going to give one pair to a kid in need."

For this new **undertaking**, Mycoskie started the business using his own money. He named it TOMS: Shoes for Tomorrow. The slip-on shoes are modeled on shoes that are traditionally worn by Argentine workers.

Mycoskie immediately set up his **innovative** one-for-one program. TOMS gives away one pair of shoes for every pair that is purchased. Later that year, Mycoskie returned to Argentina and gave away 10,000 pairs of shoes. By 2011, TOMS had donated over one million pairs.

79

✓ **Vocabulary**

compassionate

enterprise

exceptional

funds

innovative

process

routine

undertaking

Close Reading of Complex Text

Shared Read "Dollars and Sense," 78–81

Genre Persuasive Article

Lexile 800
ETS *TextEvaluator*™ 31

Minilessons

✓ **Tested Skills** **CCSS**

✓ **Comprehension Strategy**	Reread, T274–T275
✓ **Comprehension Skill**	Main Idea and Key Details, T276–T277
✓ **Genre**	Persuasive Article, T278–T279
✓ **Vocabulary Strategy**	Suffixes, T280–T281
✓ **Writing Traits**	Sentence Fluency, T286–T287
Grammar	Run-On Sentences, T290–T291

👉 **Go Digital**

www.connected.mcgraw-hill.com

APPLY WITH CLOSE READING

Complex Text

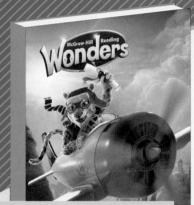

Literature Anthology

PAIRED READ

Kids in Business, 84–87
Genre Persuasive Article
Lexile 790
(ETS) *TextEvaluator™* 33

"Starting a Successful Business," 88–89
Genre Procedural Text
Lexile 770
(ETS) *TextEvaluator™* 39

Differentiated Text

Leveled Readers *Include Paired Reads*

APPROACHING
Lexile 660
(ETS) *TextEvaluator™* 29

ON LEVEL
Lexile 780
(ETS) *TextEvaluator™* 35

BEYOND
Lexile 890
(ETS) *TextEvaluator™* 42

ELL
Lexile 710
(ETS) *TextEvaluator™* 30

Extended Complex Text

*America's Champion
Swimmer: Gertrude Ederle*
Genre Biography
Lexile 580
(ETS) *TextEvaluator™* 38

*Happy Birthday, Martin
Luther King*
Genre Biography
Lexile 800
(ETS) *TextEvaluator™* 9

Classroom Library

Classroom
Library
lessons available
online.

TEACH AND MANAGE

How You Teach

INTRODUCE

Weekly Concept
Putting Ideas to Work

Reading/Writing Workshop
74–75

TEACH

Close Reading
"Dollars and Sense"

Minilessons
Reread, Main Idea and Key Details,
Persuasive Article, Suffixes, Writing
Traits

Reading/Writing
Workshop
78–81

APPLY

Close Reading
Kids in Business
"Starting a Successful
Business"

**Literature
Anthology
84–89**

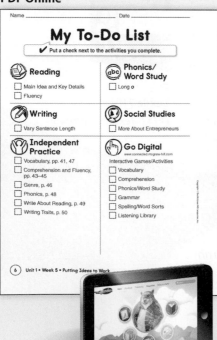 **Go Digital**

Interactive Whiteboard

Interactive Whiteboard

Mobile

How Students Practice

WEEKLY CONTRACT

PDF Online

My To-Do List
✓ Put a check next to the activities you complete.

📖 **Reading**
☐ Main Idea and Key Details
☐ Fluency

🔤 **Phonics/
Word Study**
☐ Long o

✏️ **Writing**
☐ Vary Sentence Length

🌐 **Social Studies**
☐ More About Entrepreneurs

✋ **Independent
Practice**
☐ Vocabulary, pp. 41, 47
☐ Comprehension and Fluency,
pp. 43–45
☐ Genre, p. 46
☐ Phonics, p. 48
☐ Write About Reading, p. 49
☐ Writing Traits, p. 50

👆 **Go Digital**
www.connected.mcgraw-hill.com
Interactive Games/Activities
☐ Vocabulary
☐ Comprehension
☐ Phonics/Word Study
☐ Grammar
☐ Spelling/Word Sorts
☐ Listening Library

6 Unit 1 • Week 5 • Putting Ideas to Work

LEVELED PRACTICE AND ONLINE ACTIVITIES

Your Turn Practice Book
41–50

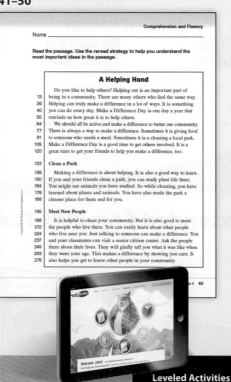

Leveled Readers

Go Digital

Online To-Do List

Leveled Activities

Writer's Workspace

DIFFERENTIATE

SMALL GROUP INSTRUCTION
Leveled Readers

Mobile

INTEGRATE

Research and Inquiry
Poster, T284

Text Connections
Compare How Starting a
Business Can Help Others, T285

 **Write About Reading**
Write an Analysis, T285

**Online Research
and Writing**

ASSESS

**Weekly Assessment
49–60**

**Online
Assessment**

LEVELED WORKSTATION CARDS

More
Activities
on back

5

Entrepreneurs

What do entrepreneurs do?

- Use the Internet to research an important entrepreneur in your state.

- If the person is still living, identify what his or her current business is. If the person is a historical figure, find

SOCIAL STUDIES

12

Sentence Fluency: Sentence Length

Read Ruth's text. Discuss where she used different sentence lengths. Then revise the text, varying the sentence lengths.

I just ... from the water park. We

WRITING

5

Suffixes

| Base Word | Suffix |

- Create a Two-Tab Foldable®. Write *Base Word* on the left top tab and *Suffix* on the right top tab.

- Under the left tab, write the words *bank, break, collect, flex, comic, season,* or words you choose.

- Under the right tab, write 4 or 5 suffixes you learned this week.

- Decide which of the suffixes can be added to each base word to make new words. Check your choices in a dictionary. Define each new word.

You need
> dictionary
> Two-Tab Foldable®
> paper, pencil

PHONICS/WORD STUDY

6

Main Idea and Key Details

| Detail |
| Detail |
| Detail |
| Main Idea |

- Choose a section or paragraph from an informational text you have read.

- As you reread, make a list of the key details in the section or paragraph. Add the key details to a Main Idea and Key Details chart.

- Exchange charts. Compare your details. Think about what they have in common to identify the main idea of the section.

You need
> informational text
> paper
> pencils or pens

READING

DEVELOPING READERS AND WRITERS

Write to Sources and Research

Summarize, T276–T277

Note Taking, T281B, T281E

Research and Inquiry, T284

Analyze to Inform/Explain, T285

Make Connections: Essential Question, T281D, T281F, T285

Comparing Texts, T297, T305, T309, T315

Predictive Writing, T281A

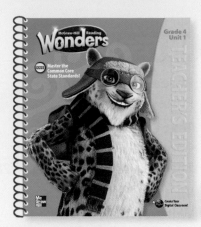

Teacher's Edition

Main Idea and Key Details, 87

Literature Anthology

Interactive Whiteboard

Leveled Readers
Comparing Texts
Main Idea and Key Details

Main Idea and Key Details, 43–45
Genre, 46
Analyze to Inform, 49

Your Turn Practice Book

Writing Process • **Genre Writing**

Narrative Text
Personal Narrative, T350–T355

Conferencing Routines
Teacher Conferences, T352
Peer Conferences, T353

Interactive Whiteboard

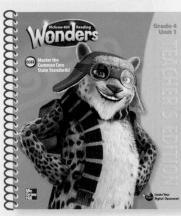

Teacher's Edition

Leveled Workstation Card
Personal Narrative, Card 30

Writer's Workspace
Personal Narrative
Writing Process
Multimedia Presentations

Writing Traits • Write Every Day

Writing Trait: Sentence Fluency
Sentence Length, T286–T287

Conferencing Routines
Teacher Conferences, T288
Peer Conferences, T289

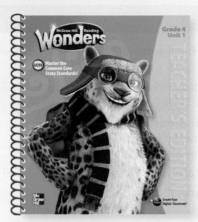

Teacher's Edition

Sentence Fluency:
Sentence Length,
86–87

Reading/Writing Workshop

Interactive Whiteboard

Fluency:
Sentence
Length,
Card 12

Leveled Workstation Card

Sentence Fluency:
Sentence Length, 50

Your Turn Practice Book

Grammar and Spelling

Grammar
Run-On Sentences,
T290–T291

Spelling
Long o, T292–T293

Interactive Whiteboard

Teacher's Edition

Run-On Sentences

Long o
Word Sorts

Online Spelling and Grammar Games

SUGGESTED LESSON PLAN

✔ **TESTED SKILLS**

	DAY 1	**DAY 2**

READING

Teach, Model and Apply

Reading/Writing Workshop

DAY 1

Build Background Putting Ideas to Work, T266–T267

Listening Comprehension Interactive Read Aloud: "Kids Can Help," T268–T269

Comprehension
• Preview Genre: Persuasive Article
• Preview Strategy: Reread

✔ **Vocabulary** Words in Context, T270–T271

Practice *Your Turn,* 41

Close Reading of Complex Text "Dollars and Sense," 78–81

DAY 2

✔ **Comprehension**
• Strategy: Reread, T274–T275
• Skill: Main Idea and Key Details, T276–T277
• Write About Reading ● *Analytical Writing*
• Genre: Persuasive Article, T278–T279

✔ **Vocabulary** Strategy: Suffixes, T280–T281

Practice *Your Turn,* 42–47

DIFFERENTIATED INSTRUCTION   Choose across the week to meet your students' needs.

Small Group

Approaching Level

DAY 1

Leveled Reader *Start Small, Think Big,* T296–T297

Phonics/Decoding Decode Words with Long *o,* T298 **TIER 2**

Vocabulary
• Review High-Frequency Words, T300 **TIER 2**
• Answer Yes/No Questions, T301

DAY 2

Leveled Reader *Start Small, Think Big,* T296–T297

Vocabulary Review Vocabulary Words, T300 **TIER 2**

Comprehension
• Identify Key Details, T302 **TIER 2**
• Review Main Idea and Key Details, T303

On Level

DAY 1

Leveled Reader *Start Small, Think Big,* T304–T305

Vocabulary Review Vocabulary Words, T306

DAY 2

Leveled Reader *Start Small, Think Big,* T304–T305

Comprehension Review Main Idea and Key Details, T307

Beyond Level

DAY 1

Leveled Reader *Start Small, Think Big,* T308–T309

Vocabulary Review Domain-Specific Words, T310

DAY 2

Leveled Reader *Start Small, Think Big,* T308–T309

Comprehension Review Main Idea and Key Details, T311

English Language Learners

DAY 1

Shared Read "Dollars and Sense," T312–T313

Phonics/Decoding Decode Words with Long *o,* T298

Vocabulary
• Preteach Vocabulary, T316
• Review High-Frequency Words, T300

DAY 2

Leveled Reader *Start Small, Think Big,* T314–T315

Vocabulary Review Vocabulary, T316

Writing Writing Trait: Sentence Fluency, T318

Grammar Run-On Sentences, T319

LANGUAGE ARTS   Writing Process: Personal Narrative T350–T355   Use with Weeks 4–6

Writing
Grammar
Spelling
Build Vocabulary

DAY 1

✔ **Readers to Writers**
• Writing Traits: Sentence Fluency/Sentence Length, T286–T287
• Writing Entry: Prewrite and Draft, T288

Grammar Run-On Sentences, T290

Spelling Long *o,* T292

Build Vocabulary
• Connect to Words, T294
• Academic Vocabulary, T294

DAY 2

Readers to Writers
• Writing Entry: Revise, T288

Grammar Run-On Sentences, T290

Spelling Long *o,* T292

Build Vocabulary
• Expand Vocabulary, T294
• Review Context Clues, T294

DAY 3	DAY 4	DAY 5 Review and Assess

READING

Phonics/Decoding
• Long *o*, T282
• Compound Words, T283

Practice *Your Turn,* 48

Close Reading *Kids in Business,* 84–87 • *Analytical Writing*

Literature Anthology

Fluency Phrasing and Rate, T283
Integrate Ideas • *Analytical Writing*
• Research and Inquiry, T284

Practice *Your Turn,* 43–45

Close Reading "Starting a Successful Business," 88–89 • *Analytical Writing*

Integrate Ideas • *Analytical Writing*
• Research and Inquiry, T284
• Text Connections, T285
• Write About Reading, T285

Practice *Your Turn,* 49

DIFFERENTIATED INSTRUCTION

Leveled Reader *Start Small, Think Big,* T296–T297
Phonics/Decoding Review Words with Long *o*, T298 **TIER 2**
Fluency Phrasing and Rate, T302 **TIER 2**
Vocabulary Suffixes, T301

Leveled Reader Paired Read: "Spending and Saving," T297 • *Analytical Writing*
Phonics/Decoding Practice Words with Long *o*, T299

Leveled Reader Literature Circles, T297
Comprehension Self-Selected Reading, T303
Phonics/Decoding Compound Words, T299

Leveled Reader *Start Small, Think Big,* T304–T305
Vocabulary Suffixes, T306

Leveled Reader Paired Read: "Spending and Saving," T305 • *Analytical Writing*

Leveled Reader Literature Circles, T305
Comprehension Self-Selected Reading, T307

Leveled Reader *Start Small, Think Big,* T308–T309
Vocabulary
• Suffixes, T310
• Synthesize, T310

Gifted and Talented

Leveled Reader Paired Read: "Spending and Saving," T309 • *Analytical Writing*

Leveled Reader Literature Circles, T309
Comprehension
• Self-Selected Reading, T311
• Evaluate, T311

Leveled Reader *Start Small, Think Big,* T314–T315
Phonics/Decoding Review Words with Long *o,* T298
Vocabulary Suffixes, T317
Spelling Words with Long *o,* T318

Leveled Reader Paired Read: "Spending and Saving," T315 • *Analytical Writing*
Vocabulary Additional Vocabulary, T317
Phonics/Decoding Practice Words with Long *o,* T299

Leveled Reader Literature Circles, T315
Phonics/Decoding Compound Words, T299

LANGUAGE ARTS

Readers to Writers
• Writing Entry: Prewrite and Draft, T289

Grammar Mechanics and Usage, T291

Spelling Long *o,* T293

Build Vocabulary
• Reinforce the Words, T295
• Suffixes, T295

Readers to Writers
• Writing Entry: Revise, T289

Grammar Run-On Sentences, T291

Spelling Long *o,* T293

Build Vocabulary
• Connect to Writing, T295
• Shades of Meaning, T295

Readers to Writers
• Writing Entry: Share and Reflect, T289

Grammar Run-On Sentences, T291

Spelling Long *o,* T293

Build Vocabulary
• Word Squares, T295
• Morphology, T295

DIFFERENTIATE TO ACCELERATE

  Scaffold to Access Complex Text

IF the text complexity of a particular selection is too difficult for students

THEN see the references noted in the chart below for scaffolded instruction to help students Access Complex Text.

Qualitative / **Quantitative**
Reader and Task
TEXT COMPLEXITY

	Reading/Writing Workshop	**Literature Anthology**	**Leveled Readers**		**Classroom Library**

Quantitative

Reading/Writing Workshop

"Dollars and Sense"
Lexile 800
TextEvaluator 31

Literature Anthology

Kids in Business
Lexile 790
TextEvaluator 33

"Starting a Successful Business"
Lexile 790
TextEvaluator 39

Leveled Readers

Approaching Level
Lexile 660
TextEvaluator 29

Beyond Level
Lexile 890
TextEvaluator 42

On Level
Lexile 780
TextEvaluator 35

ELL
Lexile 710
TextEvaluator 30

Classroom Library

America's Champion Swimmer: Gertrude Ederle
Lexile 580
TextEvaluator 38

Happy Birthday, Martin Luther King
Lexile 880
TextEvaluator 8

Qualitative

What Makes the Text Complex?
- **Connection of Ideas** Chart T273
- **Organization** Supporting Details T277

ACT *See Scaffolded Instruction in Teacher's Edition T273 and T277.*

What Makes the Text Complex?
- **Purpose** Tone T281A
- **Sentence Structure** T281C
- **Specific Vocabulary** Domain-Specific Words T281E

ACT *See Scaffolded Instruction in Teacher's Edition T281A–T281F.*

What Makes the Text Complex?
- **Specific Vocabulary**
- **Prior Knowledge**
- **Sentence Structure**
- **Connection of Ideas**
- **Genre**

ACT *See Level Up lessons online for Leveled Readers.*

What Makes the Text Complex?
- **Genre**
- **Specific Vocabulary**
- **Prior Knowledge**
- **Sentence Structure**
- **Organization**
- **Purpose**
- **Connection of Ideas**

ACT *See Scaffolded Instruction in Teacher's Edition T360–T361.*

Reader and Task

The Introduce the Concept lesson on pages T266–T267 will help determine the reader's knowledge and engagement in the weekly concept. See pages T272–T281 and T284–T285 for questions and tasks for this text.

The Introduce the Concept lesson on pages T266–T267 will help determine the reader's knowledge and engagement in the weekly concept. See pages T281A–T281F and T284–T285 for questions and tasks for this text.

The Introduce the Concept lesson on pages T266–T267 will help determine the reader's knowledge and engagement in the weekly concept. See pages T296–T297, T304–T305, T308–T309, T314–T315, and T284–T285 for questions and tasks for this text.

The Introduce the Concept lesson on pages T266–T267 will help determine the reader's knowledge and engagement in the weekly concept. See pages T360–T361 for questions and tasks for this text.

Go Digital! www.connected.mcgraw-hill.com

Monitor and *Differentiate*

IF you need to differentiate instruction

THEN use the Quick Checks to assess students' needs and select the appropriate small group instruction focus.

 Quick Check

Comprehension Strategy Reread T275

Comprehension Skill Main Idea and Details T277

Genre Persuasive Article T279

Vocabulary Strategy Suffixes T281

Phonics/Fluency Long *o* T283

If No →

Approaching Level	Reteach T296–T303
ELL	Develop T312–T319

If Yes →

On Level	Review T304–T307
Beyond Level	Extend T308–T311

Level Up with Leveled Readers

IF students can read their leveled text fluently and answer comprehension questions

THEN work with the next level up to accelerate students' reading with more complex text.

T305

T297 T315

ENGLISH LANGUAGE LEARNERS
SCAFFOLD

IF ELL students need additional support **THEN** scaffold instruction using the small group suggestions.

Reading/Writing Workshop "Dollars and Sense" T312–T313	Leveled Reader *Start Small, Think Big* T314–T315 "Spending and Saving" T315	Additional Vocabulary T317 courage program similar success support	Using Suffixes T317	Writing Sentence Fluency T318	Spelling Words with Long *o* T318	Grammar Run-On Sentences T319

Note: Include ELL Students in all small groups based on their needs.

Introduce the Concept

Build Background

Go Digital

Reading/Writing Workshop

OBJECTIVES

CCSS Interpret information presented visually, orally, or quantitatively (e.g, in charts, graphs, diagrams, time lines, animations, or interactive elements on Web pages) and explain how the information contributes to an understanding of the text in which it appears. **RI.4.7**

CCSS Follow agreed-upon rules for discussions and carry out assigned roles. **SL.4.1b**

Build background knowledge on inventions.

ACADEMIC LANGUAGE

• innovative
• Cognate: innovador

ESSENTIAL QUESTION
How can starting a business help others?

Have students read the Essential Question on page 74 of the **Reading/ Writing Workshop**. Tell them that a new business can be **innovative**, or something completely new.

Discuss the photograph of the bakery. Focus on how this business could help the community.

→ To start a business, a person must have an idea and a plan to make the idea work.

→ Starting a business can provide goods and services that others need. It can provide things for a community that it didn't have before.

Talk About It

Ask: *What kinds of businesses would you like to start or see in your community? How would they help? In what ways would they be innovative?*

→ Model using the Concept Web to generate words and phrases related to starting a business. Add students' contributions.

→ Have partners continue the discussion by describing how businesses they know of help the community. Students can discuss what businesses they would like to see in their community and why.

Discuss the Concept

Watch Video

Use Graphic Organizer

Collaborative Conversations

Take On Discussion Roles As students engage in partner, small-group, and whole class discussions, encourage them to take on roles. Assigned roles can include

→ a questioner who asks questions in order to keep everyone involved and keep the discussion moving.

→ a recorder who takes notes on the important ideas being discussed and who later reports to the class.

→ a discussion monitor who keeps the group on topic and makes sure everyone gets a turn to talk.

Weekly Concept Putting Ideas to Work

Essential Question
How can starting a business help others?

Go Digital!

TIME FOR KIDS®

RISE
TO THE CHALLENGE

How do you start a business and help people at the same time? A woman in New York did it. She started a bakery that includes a culinary training program for immigrants. Not only has the training program been successful, the bakery's breads are a big hit too.

▶ How do you think a business can give back to the community? What kinds of things could they do?

▶ What kind of business would you start? How would it help people or your community?

Talk About It

Write words that tell how starting a business can help people. Then talk about a business you would like to start.

Starting a Business

74   75

READING/WRITING WORKSHOP, pp. 74–75

GRAPHIC ORGANIZER 62

Starting a Business

ENGLISH LANGUAGE LEARNERS SCAFFOLD

Beginning

Use Visuals Point to the baker. Say: *This woman started a business. What does she sell?* (bread) Have students think about and name other kinds of businesses. Prompt them with questions: *What kind of business sells food? What kind of business sells clothing?* Give students ample time to respond.

Intermediate

Describe Have students discuss the business in the photograph. Ask: *How could this business help a community?* Have students complete the sentence frame: *This business could help a community by ____.* Encourage students to use concept words in their responses.

Advanced/High

Discuss Ask students to discuss with partners how businesses can help communities. Say: *Think about a business in your community. What does it help you get or do? How would your life be different without it?* Encourage them to use the concept word in their responses. Correct their answers for meaning as needed.

→ Listening Comprehension

MINILESSON
10 Mins

Interactive Read Aloud

**Go
Digital**

View
Illustrations

OBJECTIVES

CCSS Refer to details and examples in a text when explaining what the text says explicitly and when drawing inferences from the text. **RI.4.1**

CCSS Paraphrase portions of a text read aloud or information presented in diverse media and formats, including visually, quantitatively, and orally. **SL.4.2**

- Listen for a purpose.
- Identify characteristics of a persuasive article.

ACADEMIC LANGUAGE

- *persuasive article, reread*
- Cognate: *artículo persuasivo*

Connect to Concept: Putting Ideas to Work

Tell students that helping people in need is something that everyone can do. Let students know that you will be reading aloud a passage that tells ways that kids can make a difference. Have them listen for key details in the text as you read.

Preview Genre: Persuasive Article

Explain that the passage you will read aloud is a persuasive article. Discuss features of a persuasive article:

→ is nonfiction

→ tries to get others to agree with the writer's position

→ includes persuasive language and opinion words, such as *should*, *must*, and *best*

Preview Comprehension Strategy: Reread

Explain that when reading persuasive text, readers can read the text again, or reread, if they feel they may have missed an important point that the writer was trying to make. They can also reread to better understand any facts or details that the author uses.

Use the Think Alouds on page T269 to model the strategy.

Respond to Reading

Think Aloud Clouds Display Think Aloud Master 4: *When I read _____, I had to reread…* to reinforce how you used the reread strategy to understand content.

Genre Features With students, discuss the elements of the Read Aloud that let them know it is a persuasive article. Ask them to think about other texts that you have read or they have read independently that were persuasive articles.

Summarize Have students restate the most important information from "Kids Can Help" in their own words.

When I read _____,
I had to reread…

Model Think
Alouds

Genre	Features

Fill in Genre
Chart

Kids Can Help

When disasters such as storms, floods, and earthquakes strike an area, people from all over the world want to help. They know that someday they may need help themselves. They also know that it is the right thing to do and that it is rewarding. I think that when people are in need it is important for all of us to find a way to help out. **1**

One of the best ways we can help others is to find out what our local communities need. Local food banks help feed people who are hungry. Shelters give homeless people a warm and safe place to stay. Sometimes schools need money for art and music programs. Libraries may need money to buy books. Local hospitals often need money for lifesaving equipment.

Kids Can Make a Difference!

We often see adults going to areas around the world to help with disaster relief or raising money to help local communities. But there are many things that kids can do to help, too.

How do you find out what the needs are? Read the newspaper, do online research, and talk to community leaders to see where your help may be most needed. There are many good causes out there. Be smart and do some research before deciding what you want to do to help. **2**

Ways to Raise Money

One good way to help people and communities in need is to have a fundraiser. A garage sale is a great way to get rid of things that your family no longer needs and make some money that can help others.

Lemonade stands and bake sales are two great ways to raise money. It's important to have your stand or bake sale in a visible place with lots of potential customers. Another good idea is to offer dog-walking services and have your customers pay with canned food that can be taken to your local food bank. **3**

These are just a few ideas to get you started. Don't wait! You should plan a brainstorming session with your friends right away. Together you can probably think of many more ways to help!

1 Think Aloud I want to go back and **reread** this first paragraph. I think the writer is trying to persuade me to help out people who are in need. I want to make sure I understand that this is what this piece is about.

2 Think Aloud I should **reread** this paragraph because I think it is making an important point about what steps kids should take when deciding how they would like to help.

3 Think Aloud The author gives several ideas about ways to raise money. **Rereading** this section will help me find some good suggestions that I might be able to use in my own community.

Yellow Dog Productions/Digital Vision/Getty Images

→ Vocabulary

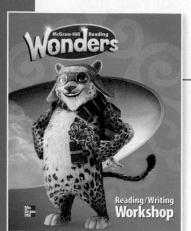

Reading/Writing Workshop

OBJECTIVES

CCSS Acquire and use accurately grade-appropriate general academic and domain-specific words and phrases, including those that signal precise actions, emotions, or states of being (e.g., *quizzed, whined, stammered*) and that are basic to a particular topic (e.g., *wildlife, conservation,* and *endangered* when discussing animal preservation). **L.4.6**

ACADEMIC LANGUAGE

- *innovative, enterprise*
- Cognate: *innovador*

MINILESSON 10 Mins

Words in Context

Model the Routine

Introduce each vocabulary word using the Vocabulary Routine found on the Visual Vocabulary Cards.

Visual Vocabulary Cards

Vocabu...
Define:
Example:
Ask:

Vocabulary Routine

Define: Something that is **innovative** is new or done in a new way.

Example: Sam enjoyed trying out the new innovative racing wheelchair.

Ask: What new technology do you think is innovative?

Definitions

→ **compassionate** To be **compassionate** is to be sympathetic.

→ **enterprise** An **enterprise** is something difficult or important that a person plans or tries to do.

→ **exceptional** To be **exceptional** is to be extraordinary.
Cognate: *excepcional*

→ **funds** **Funds** are money that is ready for use.
Cognate: *fondos*

→ **process** A **process** is a series of actions performed when making or doing something.
Cognate: *proceso*

→ **routine** A **routine** is a fixed way or method of doing something.
Cognate: *rutina*

→ **undertaking** An **undertaking** is something someone decides to do or start.

Talk About It

Have students work with a partner and look at each picture and discuss the definition of each word. Then ask students to choose three words and write questions for their partner to answer.

Go Digital

innovative

Use Visual Glossary

CCSS Words to Know

Vocabulary

Use the picture and the sentences to talk with a partner about each word.

compassionate I could tell she was a **compassionate** and caring person by the way she hugged her sister.

What is an antonym for compassionate?

enterprise Starting a white water rafting business was an exciting new **enterprise** for Tom.

What is the first thing a person starting a new enterprise might do?

exceptional Monica is an **exceptional** and talented flute player.

How does a person become exceptional at doing something?

funds Nicole's class held a bake sale to raise **funds** to buy books for the library.

What project would you like to raise funds for?

innovative Sam enjoyed trying out the new **innovative** racing wheelchair.

What new technology do you think is innovative?

process An important step in the **process** of making a pie is to roll out the crust.

What is one step in the process of baking cookies?

routine Brittany loved the daily **routine** of walking her dog.

Why is it helpful to have a morning routine?

undertaking Cleaning up Tim's messy bedroom was going to be a big **undertaking**.

What would you consider a big undertaking?

Your Turn COLLABORATE

Pick three words. Write three questions for your partner to answer.

Go Digital! Use the online visual glossary

76

77

READING/WRITING WORKSHOP, pp. 76–77

ELL ENGLISH LANGUAGE LEARNERS SCAFFOLD

Beginning

Use Visuals Point to the picture for *innovative*. Say: *This wheelchair is innovative.* Innovative means "using or having new ideas." This wheelchair is new. It can go faster than other wheelchairs. Have students use the sentence frame: *This wheelchair is _____ because it can go faster.* (innovative) Help students with pronunciation. *Innovation* in Spanish is *innovador*.

Intermediate

Describe Point to the picture for *innovative*. Say: *This racing wheelchair is innovative because it is new and different. How might it be different from other wheelchairs?* (faster, lighter, different shape, easy to fold) Correct students' answers for meaning as needed.

Advanced/High

Discuss Discuss the picture for the word *innovative* with students. Then have partners talk about things they think are innovative and how they help people. Ask: *How can innovation help improve people's lives?* Call on pairs to share their answers with the class. Correct students' answers for meaning as needed.

ON-LEVEL PRACTICE BOOK p. 41

| process | routine | undertaking | compassionate |
| funds | enterprise | exceptional | innovative |

Use a word from the box to answer each question. Then use the word in a sentence.
Possible responses provided.

1. What is another word for *a regular series of actions*? routine; My morning *routine* includes eating breakfast, brushing my teeth, and packing my bag.

2. What is a sum of money set aside for something? funds; Our school used the *funds* to pay for new playground equipment.

3. What word might describe something that is out of the ordinary? exceptional; The famous painting showed the artist's *exceptional* skill.

4. What is another word for *something someone decides to do or start*? undertaking; Opening our family restaurant was a huge *undertaking*.

5. What word might describe someone who cares about other people? compassionate; The *compassionate* man always helps his neighbors.

6. What is another word for *a difficult project*? enterprise; Our town's latest *enterprise* is opening a new art museum.

7. What word might describe the steps you take to perform a task? process; The *process* for completing a quilt is very detailed.

8. What word might describe someone who is likely to introduce new ideas? innovative; Everyone knew that the inventor was very *innovative*.

| APPROACHING p. 41 | BEYOND p. 41 | ELL p. 41 |

CCSS **Shared Read** **TIME FOR KIDS**

Dollars and $ENSE

Behind the success of these big businesses is a desire to help others.

Good business is not always about the bottom line. A **compassionate** company knows that making money is not the only way to measure success. Many large businesses in the United States and all over the world are finding unusual ways to help people in need.

Hearts and Soles

After starting and running four businesses, Blake Mycoskie wanted a break from his usual **routine**. In 2006, he traveled to Argentina, in South America, and while he was there he learned to sail and dance. He also visited poor villages where very few of the children had shoes. Mycoskie decided he had to do something.

"I'm going to start a shoe company, and for every pair I sell, I'm going to give one pair to a kid in need."

For this new **undertaking**, Mycoskie started the business using his own money. He named it TOMS: Shoes for Tomorrow. The slip-on shoes are modeled on shoes that are traditionally worn by Argentine workers.

Mycoskie immediately set up his **innovative** one-for-one program. TOMS gives away one pair of shoes for every pair that is purchased. Later that year, Mycoskie returned to Argentina and gave away 10,000 pairs of shoes. By 2011, TOMS had donated over one million pairs.

Essential Question

How can starting a business help others?

Read about how two companies are making a difference.

78

79

Reading/Writing Workshop

READING/WRITING WORKSHOP, pp. 78–79

Shared Read

Lexile 800   *TextEvaluator* 31

Connect to Concept: Putting Ideas to Work

Explain that "Dollars and Sense" will tell about two companies that are making a difference in people's lives. Read "Dollars and Sense" with students. Note that the vocabulary words previously taught are highlighted in the text.

Close Reading

Reread the Title, Subtitle, and Paragraph 1: Tell students that you are going to take a closer look at the introduction. Reread the title, subtitle, and first paragraph together. Ask: *What is the author's opinion about businesses helping people in need?* Model how to find the author's opinion.

The title and subtitle tell me that this selection will focus on businesses that give back to the community. From reading the first paragraph, I think the author believes that good businesses measure their success by the people they help, not just the money they make.

Reread Paragraph 2: Model how to reread to answer questions about the main idea in the second paragraph. Ask, *Why did Blake Mycoskie start a business? How does he use it to help people?*

When Blake visited Argentina, he saw that very few of the kids had shoes. This inspired him to start a shoe company. When someone buys a pair of his shoes, he gives another pair to someone in need.

TOMS' employees unpack shoes to give away.

The company has expanded to sell eyeglasses. In a similar program, one pair of eyeglasses is donated for every pair that is bought.

Mycoskie is pleased and surprised. "I always thought I would spend the first half of my life making money and the second half giving it away," Mycoskie says. "I never thought I could do both at the same time."

Giving Back Rocks!

Have you ever seen a Hard Rock Cafe? The company runs restaurants and hotels. In 1990, the company launched a new **enterprise**: charity. Since then, it has given away millions of dollars to different causes. Its motto is Love All, Serve All.

One way the company raises **funds** for charity is by selling a line of T-shirts. The **process** starts with rock stars designing the art that goes on the shirts. Then the shirts are sold on the Internet. Part of the money that is raised from the sales of the shirts is given to charity.

Employees at Hard Rock Cafe locations are encouraged to raise money for their community. Every store does it differently.

The Hard Rock Cafes are successful and give back to the community.

80

Top Five Biggest Charities

$3,842,018,486	$1,719,268,000	$1,194,350,692	$1,191,965,901	$1,076,390,140
1 United Way Worldwide	2 The Salvation Army	3 AmeriCares	4 Feed the Children	5 Food for the Poor

Source: The Chronicle Of Philanthropy

Individuals as well as businesses are committed to helping people in need. This graph shows the American charities that got the most donations in one recent year and how much money they raised.

The restaurant in Hollywood, Florida, worked with some **exceptional** students from two Florida high schools. Together, they put on an event to raise money for the Make-A-Wish Foundation. The foundation grants wishes to children with serious medical problems.

The Bottom Line

Every day companies are thinking of innovative ways to give back to their community. If you own a business, making a profit is important. However, helping others is just as important as the bottom line. Helping others is good business!

Make Connections

How do the two companies profiled in this article help others? **ESSENTIAL QUESTION**

If you owned a business, how would you use some of your profits to help others? **TEXT TO SELF**

81

READING/WRITING WORKSHOP, pp. 80–81

Make Connections

ESSENTIAL QUESTION

Encourage students to go back into the text for evidence as they talk about how TOMS and Hard Rock Cafe have helped others. Ask students to think of other businesses they know of that give back to the community.

Continue Close Reading

Use the following lessons for focused rereadings.

→ Reread, T274–T275

→ Main Idea and Key Details, T276–T277

→ Persuasive Article, T278–T279

→ Suffixes, T280–T281

A C T Access Complex Text

► Connection of Ideas

Students may have difficulty connecting the chart on page 81 to the rest of the text.

→ *Does this chart show donations to charity from businesses?* (no) *What does it show?* (It shows the top five American charities that people donated to in one year and how much money was given to each charity.)

→ *How does the information in the chart connect to the article's main idea?* (The chart and the article both relate to charity and helping people in need.)

→ # Comprehension Strategy

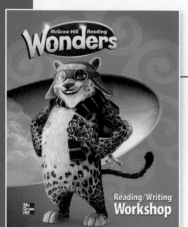

Reading/Writing Workshop

OBJECTIVES
Refer to details and examples in a text when explaining what the text says explicitly and when drawing inferences from the text. **RI.4.1**

Reread informational text to increase comprehension.

ACADEMIC LANGUAGE
- *reread, informational text*
- Cognate: *texto informativo*

 Reread

1 Explain

Remind students that when they read informational text, they can reread to understand details they might have missed or ideas that were confusing at first.

→ Good readers reread parts of text they don't understand.

→ When students have questions or don't understand complex ideas and vocabulary, they can reread to increase their understanding. It may help to reread more than once.

Point out that rereading will help students recall and explain the most important details of a text.

2 Model Close Reading: Text Evidence

Model rereading the section "Hearts and Soles" on page 79 of "Dollars and Sense." Point out the details that explain what a one-for-one program is, and note how this relates to businesses helping people.

3 Guided Practice of Close Reading

 Have partners work together to reread page 80 to find another example of a company giving back to the community. Ask partners to support their answers with details from the text. Have volunteers share their answers with the class.

 # Go Digital

View "Dollars and Sense"

CCSS Comprehension Strategy

Reread

When you read an informational text, you may come across ideas and information that are new to you. As you read "Dollars and Sense," reread sections to make sure you understand the key facts and details in the text.

 Find Text Evidence

As you read, you may want to make sure you understand the ways a business can help others. Reread the section "Hearts and Soles" in "Dollars and Sense."

page 79

I read that TOMS gives one pair of shoes for every pair of shoes someone buys. From this text evidence, I can draw the inference that the more shoes TOMS sells, the more shoes can be given away.

 Your Turn

What is another example of a company giving back to the community? Reread page 80 to answer the question. As you read other selections, remember to use the strategy Reread.

82

READING/WRITING WORKSHOP, p. 82

Monitor and *Differentiate*

✓ **Quick Check**

Are students able to find another example in the text? Do they reread the text more than once if necessary?

⬇

Small Group Instruction

If No →	**Approaching Level**	Reteach p. T296
	ELL	Develop p. T312
If Yes →	**On Level**	Review p. T304
	Beyond Level	Extend p. T308

ELL **ENGLISH LANGUAGE LEARNERS SCAFFOLD**

Beginning	**Intermediate**	**Advanced/High**
Clarify Echo-read the first two sentences in the fourth paragraph of "Hearts and Soles." Say: *The second sentence helps me understand that a one-for-one program means that TOMS gives away one pair of shoes for every pair that they sell.* Help students repeat for understanding. Define difficult words and phrases as needed.	**Describe** Reread the fourth paragraph in "Hearts and Soles." Ask: *What is TOMS' one-for-one program?* (For every pair of shoes people buy, the company gives a pair away.) Have students use the sentence frame to describe another fact they learned by rereading the section: *When I reread, I learned ____.*	**Discuss** Have partners reread page 79. Ask: *What is TOMS' one-for-one program? Why is it innovative?* Have students repeat the definition of *innovative* and discuss with a partner why TOMS is innovative. Call on pairs to share their responses.

ON-LEVEL PRACTICE BOOK pp. 43–44

Read the passage. Use the reread strategy to help you understand the most important ideas in the passage.

A Helping Hand

Do you like to help others? Helping out is an important part of
13 being in a community. There are many others who feel the same way.
26 Helping can truly make a difference in a lot of ways. It is something
40 you can do every day. Make a Difference Day is one day a year that
55 reminds us how great it is to help others.
64 We should all be active and make a difference to better our community.
77 There is always a way to make a difference. Sometimes it is giving food
91 to someone who needs a meal. Sometimes it is a cleaning a local park.
105 Make a Difference Day is a good time to get others involved. It is a
120 great time to get your friends to help you make a difference, too.

133 **Clean a Park**
136 Making a difference is about helping. It is also a good way to learn.
150 If you and your friends clean a park, you can study plant life there.
164 You might see animals you have studied. So while cleaning, you have
176 learned about plants and animals. You have also made the park a
188 cleaner place for them and for you.

195 **Meet New People**
198 It is helpful to clean your community. But it is also good to meet
212 the people who live there. You can easily learn about other people
224 who live near you. Just talking to someone can make a difference. You
237 and your classmates can visit a senior citizen center. Ask the people
249 there about their lives. They will gladly tell you what it was like when
263 they were your age. This makes a difference by showing you care. It
276 also helps you get to know other people in your community.

APPROACHING pp. 43–44	**BEYOND** pp. 43–44	**ELL** pp. 43–44

Comprehension Skill

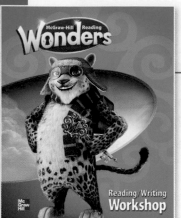

Reading/Writing Workshop

OBJECTIVES

 Determine the main idea of a text and explain how it is supported by key details; summarize the text. **RI.4.2**

ACADEMIC LANGUAGE

main idea, key details

 MINILESSON 10 Mins

Main Idea and Key Details

1 Explain

Tell students that the main idea is the most important idea in a text and that key details give important information to support the main idea.

→ To find the main idea, students can look for important details in a text or part of a text and consider what they have in common.

→ Identifying the main idea and key details will also help students summarize the text.

2 Model Close Reading: Text Evidence

Find the important details in the section "Giving Back Rocks!" on page 80 of "Dollars and Sense" and enter them in the graphic organizer. Then model using the key details to determine the main idea of the section.

 Write About Reading: Summarize Model for students how to use the notes from the graphic organizer to write a summary of the section.

3 Guided Practice of Close Reading

 Have students work in pairs to complete the graphic organizer as they identify key details in the section "Hearts and Soles" on pages 79–80. Then have them use the details to determine the main idea. Discuss the details students enter into their graphic organizers and how they lead students to the main idea.

 Write About Reading: Summarize Ask pairs to work together and use the details in their graphic organizers to write a paragraph summarizing the section "Hearts and Soles." Select pairs of students to share their summaries with the class.

Present the Lesson

SKILLS TRACE

MAIN IDEA AND KEY DETAILS

Introduce Unit 1 Week 5

Review Unit 2 Weeks 3, 4; Unit 4 Week 6; Unit 5 Week 6; Unit 6 Weeks 3, 4

Assess Units 1, 2, 6

Comprehension Skill CCSS

Main Idea and Key Details

The main idea is the most important idea that an author presents in a text or a section of text. Key details give important information to support the main idea.

Find Text Evidence

When I reread the second paragraph in the section "Giving Back Rocks!" on page 80 of "Dollars and Sense," I can identify the key details. Next I can think about what the details have in common. Then I can figure out the main idea of the section.

Main Idea
Hard Rock Cafe sells a line of T-shirts to raise funds for charity.

Key details tell about the main idea.

Detail
Rock stars design the art that goes on the shirts.

Detail
The shirts are sold on the Internet.

Detail
Part of the money that is raised from the sales of the shirts is given to charity.

Your Turn COLLABORATE

Reread the section "Hearts and Soles" on pages 79–80 of "Dollars and Sense." Find the key details in the section and list them in your graphic organizer. Use the details to determine the main idea.

Go Digital!
Use the interactive graphic organizer

83

READING/WRITING WORKSHOP, p. 83

A C T Access Complex Text

▶ Organization

Students may need help understanding that the author of a persuasive article may use examples that are quite different, but that still support the main idea.

→ *How are the two companies in the article different?* (TOMS gives one item to people who need it for every item someone buys. The Hard Rock Cafe has a charity that supports many different causes.)

→ *How are the two companies the same?* (Both companies give back to communities, rather than just earning money.)

Monitor and *Differentiate*

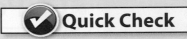

✓ Quick Check

As students complete the graphic organizer, can they identify key details in the section "Hearts and Soles"? Can they identify the main idea?

⬇

Small Group Instruction

If No → | Approaching Level | Reteach p. T303
| ELL | Develop p. T312

If Yes → | On Level | Review p. T307
| Beyond Level | Extend p. T311

ON-LEVEL PRACTICE BOOK pp. 43–45

A. Reread the passage and answer the questions.
Possible responses provided.

1. What are three key details in paragraph 5?

Some people don't have a good meal every day. People can work as a team to collect food. A food bank will be grateful for the donations.

2. How are these details connected?

They all give information about ways to help others.

3. What is the main idea of the whole passage?

We can all find ways to make a difference by helping others in need in our community.

B. Work with a partner. Read the passage aloud. Pay attention to phrasing and rate. Stop after one minute. Fill out the chart.

	Words Read	–	Number of Errors	=	Words Correct Score
First Read		–		=	
Second Read		–		=	

APPROACHING pp. 43–45	BEYOND pp. 43–45	ELL pp. 43–45

→ # Genre: Informational Text

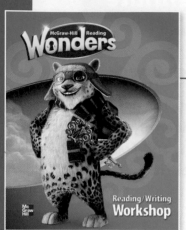

Reading/Writing Workshop

 MINILESSON **10** Mins

Persuasive Article

1 Explain

Share with students the following key characteristics of a **persuasive article**.

→ A persuasive article states the author's opinion on a topic. It is written to convince readers of the validity of this opinion.

→ A persuasive article supports the author's opinion with facts and examples.

→ A persuasive article often includes text features such as headings and bar graphs.

2 Model Close Reading: Text Evidence

Model identifying the features of a persuasive article on page 81 of "Dollars and Sense."

Graph Point out the graph on page 81. Explain that a graph helps the reader picture numerical information. Ask: *How does the graph make it easier to understand the numbers it presents?*

Headings Point out the heading on page 81. Explain that a heading tells what the section is mostly about. Ask: *Based on the heading, what is this section of text mostly about?*

3 Guided Practice of Close Reading

Have students work with partners to find and list two text features in "Dollars and Sense." Partners should discuss what they learned from each feature. Then have them share their work with the class.

OBJECTIVES

CCSS Interpret information presented visually, orally, or quantitatively (e.g., in charts, graphs, diagrams, time lines, animations, or interactive elements on Web pages) and explain how the information contributes to an understanding of the text in which it appears. **RI.4.7**

Identify features of a persuasive article.

ACADEMIC LANGUAGE

• *persuasive article, headings, graph*

• Cognates: *artículo persuasivo, gráfico*

Go Digital

Present the Lesson

CCSS Genre — Informational Text

Persuasive Article

"Dollars and Sense" is a persuasive article.

A persuasive article:
- Is nonfiction.
- States the writer's opinion on a topic.
- Provides facts and examples.
- May include text features such as headings and graphs.

Find Text Evidence

"Dollars and Sense" is a persuasive article. It states the author's opinion and tries to get readers to agree. It includes headings and a graph that shows the amount of money raised by different charities.

page 81 — TIME
Top Five Biggest Charities

Text Features

Graph Graphs help you picture numerical information. A bar graph helps you compare information.

Headings Headings tell you what the section is mostly about.

Your Turn — COLLABORATE

Find and list two text features in "Dollars and Sense." Tell what information you learned from each of the features.

84

READING/WRITING WORKSHOP, p. 84

ELL ENGLISH LANGUAGE LEARNERS SCAFFOLD

Beginning	Intermediate	Advanced/High
Actively Engage Say: *This is a graph. The graph helps us picture numbers.* Chorally read the title and explain that the title gives information about the graph. Ask: *What does this graph show?* (the five biggest charities) Ask students to point to the highest bar on the graph. Go over each charity.	**Recognize** Reread the title of the graph and the caption below. Ask: *Which charity had the most donations?* (United Way Worldwide) *Which charity was second?* (The Salvation Army) Have students fill in the sentence frame: *The graph shows ____.* (the top five biggest charities)	**Discuss** Go over the graph with students. Ask: *What information does the graph show? Why do you think the author included this graph?* Have partners discuss how the graph relates to the rest of the article. Correct their answers as needed.

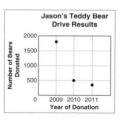

Vocabulary Strategy

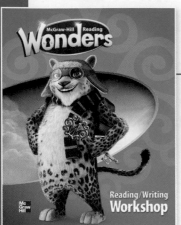
MINILESSON 10 Mins

Suffixes

OBJECTIVES

CCSS Determine the meaning of the new word formed when a known affix is added to a known word. **L.3.4b**

CCSS Determine the meaning of general academic and domain-specific words or phrases in a text relevant to a *grade 4 topic or subject area*. **RI.4.4**

ACADEMIC LANGUAGE

• *suffixes*
• Cognate: *sufijos*

1 Explain

Remind students that understanding suffixes can help them determine the meanings of unfamiliar words.

→ A suffix is a word part added to the end of a word to change its meaning. Students can use the suffix and their knowledge of the root word to help define an unfamiliar word.

→ Three common suffixes are: *-ly* (done in a way of), *-ive* (related or belonging to), and *-ful* (full of or characterized by).

2 Model Close Reading: Text Evidence

Model using the suffix *-ive* to determine the meaning of the word *innovative* on page 79 of "Dollars and Sense."

3 Guided Practice of Close Reading

COLLABORATE

Have students work in pairs to identify and define the suffixes in the words *immediately*, *traditionally*, and *successful* from "Dollars and Sense." Then have partners use suffixes and context clues to determine each word's definition. Ask volunteers to share their work with the class.

Go Digital

Present the Lesson

SKILLS TRACE

SUFFIXES

Introduce Unit 1 Week 5

Review Unit 2 Week 4; Unit 3 Weeks 4, 5

Assess Units 1, 3

Vocabulary Strategy CCSS

Suffixes

A suffix is a word part added to the end of a word to change its meaning. Knowing some common suffixes can help you to figure out the meanings of unfamiliar words. Look at the suffixes below:

-*ly* = done in the way of
-*ive* = related or belonging to
-*ful* = full of or characterized by

 Find Text Evidence

I see the word innovative *on page 79 of "Dollars and Sense." Looking at its word parts, I see the root word* innovate. *The suffix* -ive *changes a word into an adjective. This will help me to figure out what* innovative *means.*

Mycoskie immediately set up his
innovative one-for-one program. TOMS
gives away one pair of shoes for every
pair that is purchased.

Your Turn

Use suffixes and context clues to figure out the meanings of the following words:
immediately, *page 79*
traditionally, *page 79*
successful, *page 80*

85

READING/WRITING WORKSHOP, p. 85

Monitor and *Differentiate*

✓ Quick Check

Can students identify the suffixes in *immediately, traditionally,* and *successful*? Can they define the words using suffixes and context clues?

⬇

Small Group Instruction

If No → | **Approaching Level** | Reteach p. T301
| **ELL** | Develop p. T317

If Yes → | **On Level** | Review p. T306
| **Beyond Level** | Extend p. T310

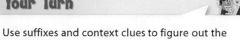

ENGLISH LANGUAGE LEARNERS SCAFFOLD

Beginning

Practice Write the word *traditionally* and circle the suffix -*ly*. Explain that this ending changes the meaning of the root word. Define the root word. Hold an index card with the meaning of the suffix to the end of the word. Have students echo the definition with and without the suffix. Repeat with the words *immediately* and *successful*.

Intermediate

Derive Meaning Point out the words *immediately, traditionally,* and *successful*. Have students write the words in their notebooks and work with partners to circle the suffix in each one. Then have partners work together to define the words using the suffixes and context clues. Monitor their progress and correct their responses for meaning as needed.

Advanced/High

Discuss Ask students to find the words *immediately, traditionally,* and *successful*. Have them identify the suffix in each word. Then ask them to define the words using the suffixes and context clues. Have students share their definitions with a partner and identify cognates (*company, traditionally, immediately, program*).

Develop Comprehension

Literature Anthology

"Kids in Business"

Text Complexity Range

Lexile

740 ▲ 790   1010

TextEvaluator™

23 ▲ 33   51

Predictive Writing

Have students read the title, preview the headings, photographs, and chart, and write their predictions about what this selection will be about. Encourage them to share what they know about being an entrepreneur.

CCSS Genre • Persuasive Article   TIME FOR KIDS®

Kids in Business

Hayleigh Scott/Hayleigh's Cherished Charms

? Essential Question

How can starting a business help others?

Read how kid entrepreneurs are making a difference.

Go Digital!

84

A C T Access Complex Text

What makes this text complex?

▷ **Purpose**

▷ **Sentence Structure**

▷ **Purpose**

Explain to students that authors of persuasive articles use carefully chosen words to support their views. Readers must think about how the author is using the words to determine the overall tone, or attitude, of the selection. Guide students in identifying how the author feels about kids in business.

Starting a business is a huge **undertaking**. That's why these young entrepreneurs who help others are nothing short of amazing.

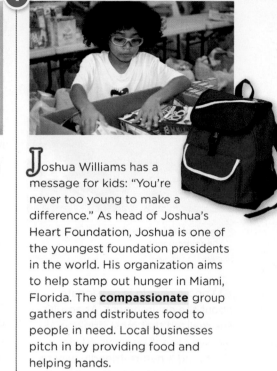

Hayleigh Scott has been wearing hearing aids since she was 18 months old. Hiding the hearing aids behind her hair had become **routine**. At age 5, she decided that she wanted to be proud of them. So Hayleigh began drawing out her ideas to make charms that look like earrings. The charms would hang from her hearing aids and really stand out. Her mother helped Hayleigh bring those drawings to life. Her idea to highlight hearing aids launched a new **enterprise**.

At age 8, Hayleigh began a business with help from her family, including her twin sister. She now sells more than 50 charms in different styles. She even holds patents on her creations.

Joshua Williams has a message for kids: "You're never too young to make a difference." As head of Joshua's Heart Foundation, Joshua is one of the youngest foundation presidents in the world. His organization aims to help stamp out hunger in Miami, Florida. The **compassionate** group gathers and distributes food to people in need. Local businesses pitch in by providing food and helping hands.

Joshua's work includes a backpack program that is aimed especially at helping hungry children. He has plans to start a community garden too. That way, he says, "People can get more fresh food."

STOP AND CHECK

Reread Why did Hayleigh want her charms to stand out? Reread to check your understanding.

(t) Joshua's Heart Foundation; (c) O. Hurst/Alamy; (b) Hayleigh Scott/Hayleigh's Cherished Charms

85

LITERATURE ANTHOLOGY, pp. 84–85

ESSENTIAL QUESTION

Ask a student to read aloud the Essential Question. Have students discuss what information they expect to learn.

Note Taking:
Use the Graphic Organizer *Analytical Writing*

As students read the selection, ask them to take notes by filling in the graphic organizer on **Your Turn Practice Book page 42** to record the main idea and key details of each section.

1 Genre: Persuasive Article

What clues can you find that tell you this is a persuasive article? (The author states an opinion about young entrepreneurs, and provides facts and examples to back it up.)

STOP AND CHECK

Reread Why did Hayleigh want her charms to stand out? (Hayleigh decided that she wanted to be proud of her hearing aids. Charms that look like earrings would be attractive and draw positive attention.)

→ *What is the tone of this selection? Use examples from the text to support your response.* (The tone of the selection is formal, positive, and complimentary. The author's use of the words "amazing" and "compassionate" indicate a favorable regard toward the featured entrepreneurs.)

ELL Preteach economic terms: *business, charities, donate/donations, entrepreneurs, foundation, fund, organizations, patent, program, sell.* Have partners go on a word hunt searching for the terms in the selection. Ask them to define the words or replace them with similar words. Point out cognates: *donación, fundación, fondo, programa, organización.*

Develop Comprehension

❷ Skill: Main Idea and Key Details

On page 86, what do the details in the first two paragraphs have in common? (They all tell about Anna's business.) Determine the main idea of these paragraphs. Determine the details that support the main idea and add them and the main idea to your chart.

Main Idea
Anna's business helps the environment.

Detail
She reuses drinking glasses.

Detail
Her plants purify the air.

Detail
She grows the plants in her backyard and makes her own fertilizer.

❸ Text Features: Charts

What does the chart on page 87 tell you? (the total funds raised by Penny Harvest each year) In which year did Penny Harvest raise the most money? (2009)

Anna's plant business helps the environment.

Ⓐnna Azevedo is passionate about the environment. At age 10, she realized that most drinking glasses cannot be recycled. So, she found a nature-friendly way to reuse old drinking glasses. Anna's budding business, Sprout, sells "plants—in a glass."

Anna hatched her **innovative** idea based on biology. "Plants basically work for you. They purify the air and take out all the bad stuff," Anna says. Her **process**? She collects drinking glasses, grows plants in her backyard, and makes fertilizer. Then she transfers the plants, sand, and soil to the glasses to create a green product for indoors. Anna sells the plants on her Web site. ❷

(t) Anna Azevedo; (b) Jennifer Graylock/AP Photo

86

Ⓒecilia Cassini is an **exceptional** young designer who makes clothes for kids and teens. For her sixth birthday, Cecilia asked for a sewing machine. She wanted to make her own clothes. Cecilia took two sewing lessons. Then, she says, she just started sewing, and she hasn't stopped since.

"I started making clothes for my sister and her friends, and word got around," Cecilia told *TIME For Kids*. Her mom's friend, a store manager, helped Cecilia start her business. Her dream is to have her clothes sold in stores around the world. Cecilia knows there's more to life than just pretty clothes, however. She also donates dresses to raise **funds** for charity. After all, trends come and go, but helping others never goes out of style.

Cecilia often donates dresses she has made to raise funds for charity.

Ⓐ Ⓒ Ⓣ Access Complex Text

▶ Sentence Structure

Point out the dash in the first paragraph on page 86. Explain that a dash often comes before words that give further explanation or emphasize a point.

→ *What do the words after the dash tell?* (They tell how Anna pots her plants.)

→ *Is this dash used to emphasize a point or to give further explanation of something?* (It is used to give more information about Anna's plants.)

Kids Count

If you think you don't have enough money to make a difference, think again. By working with others, you can make a difference! Through a program called Penny Harvest, students gather coins from family and friends. The small change adds up to big donations for charities. The bar graph on the right shows the total amount of money raised by Penny Harvest over five recent years.

Since its start in 1991, students have donated more than $8.1 million to Penny Harvest. The money is then used to create grants for community organizations.

TIME for Kids.

Total funds raised by Penny Harvest per year

○ $802,199.14
○ $799,033.35
○ $711,394.58
○ $694,099.70
○ $543,265.88

2007   2008   2009   2010   2011

Respond to Reading

1. How do you know that *Kids in Business* is a persuasive article? Use details from the selection to support your response. **GENRE**

2. What led Anna Azevedo to start her business? **MAIN IDEA AND KEY DETAILS**

3. What is the definition of *youngest* on page 85? Tell how knowing the suffix helped you figure out the meaning. **SUFFIXES**

4. What are a few ways that young entrepreneurs can help people around the world? **TEXT TO WORLD**

87

LITERATURE ANTHOLOGY, pp. 86–87

ELL Encourage students to notice cognates on page 86: recycled/*reciclado*; biology/*biologia*. Ask if anyone can find another cognate. (exceptional/*excepcional*)

→ Use gestures to reinforce the meaning of the words *drinking* and *glasses*. Ask, *What did Anna put in drinking glasses?* (plants)

Return to Predictions

Review students' predictions and purposes for reading. Ask them to answer the Essential Question. (Starting a business can help others feel better about themselves, improve the environment, and raise money for charity.)

Respond to Reading

1. **Genre** <u>Answer</u> It includes persuasive language when describing each business venture. <u>Evidence</u> The article contains persuasive words and phrases, such as "exceptional young people," "compassionate," and "innovative." These words and phrases encourage readers to think of the young entrepreneurs in a positive way.

2. **Main Idea and Key Details** <u>Answer</u> Anna's passion for the environment led her to start a business that uses drinking glasses that cannot be recycled. <u>Evidence</u> Anna realized that most drinking glasses could not be recycled. She found a use for these glasses in a way that actually helps the environment.

3. **Suffixes** <u>Answer</u> *Youngest* means "one who is the least old." <u>Evidence</u> The suffix *-est* means "most." When it is added to the word *young*, the meaning becomes "most young," which is the same as being the least old.

4. **Text to World** Students should point out that these young entrepreneurs are role models for young people around the world who want to help others by starting businesses. The individuals in the article are hoping to make a difference by showing pride in their differences, helping the environment, collecting food for people who are hungry, and raising money for charities. All of these businesses can have a positive impact on people everywhere.

Develop Comprehension

Literature Anthology

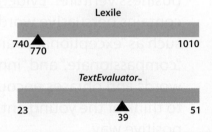

"Starting a Successful Business"

Text Complexity Range

Lexile

Literature Anthology 740 ▲ 770   1010

TextEvaluator™

23   ▲ 39   51

Compare Texts *Analytical Writing*

Students will read a procedural text about entrepreneurs. Ask students to do a close reading of the text. Encourage them to use the reread strategy. Students will also take notes. Then they will use the text evidence they gathered to compare this text with "Kids in Business."

CCSS Genre · Procedural Text   TIME FOR KIDS

Compare Texts
Read about the steps you should take to start a business.

Starting a Successful Business

Becoming an entrepreneur is hard work. But if you're dedicated and have excellent organizational skills, it can be rewarding—sometimes, a small idea can become a very successful business! Neale S. Godfrey, author of *Ultimate Kids' Money Book*, shares these tips for starting a booming business.

(bkgd) LWA/Photographer's Choice/Getty Images

88

A C T Access Complex Text

What makes this text complex?
▶ **Specific Vocabulary**

▶ Specific Vocabulary

Guide students in using context clues to define unfamiliar words.

→ *Identify the context clues that help you figure out the meaning of* market survey. ("questions"; "ask prospective clients about their likes and needs"; "responses to your questionnaire will help you decide if you should move forward with your plan")

Step 1 Have an innovative idea.

Suppose you like dogs, have free time, and feel **compassionate** towards people with busy schedules. Why not start a dog-walking service?

Step 2 Find out if your business has a chance of succeeding.

Come up with questions and do a market survey. Ask prospective clients about their likes and needs. Find out how much they would be willing to pay for your services. The responses to your questionnaire will help you decide if you should move forward with your plan. Also, check out the competition. If there's already another dog-walking service in your neighborhood, your business has a smaller chance at success. **①**

Step 3 Compile a business plan and a budget.

A detailed business plan says what product will be sold, how it will be sold, whom the customers will be, and how much it will cost to start. A budget outlines your finances in detail.

Step 4 Contact potential customers.

Reach out to anyone who could need you. Then, set a work schedule for yourself. Finally, you have to actually start walking dogs!

Step 5 Keep tabs on your business.

Once your business is up and running, look at how it's doing. If you have money left over after your business expenses are paid, you've made a profit. You can consider yourself a successful entrepreneur!

Make Connections

What steps can you take to start a new business? **ESSENTIAL QUESTION**

How can an entrepreneur become successful? **TEXT TO TEXT**

Eric Larsen

89

LITERATURE ANTHOLOGY, pp. 88–89

① Ask and Answer Questions

Why is it important to check out the competition for your business idea?

Analytical Writing **Write About Reading** Write your responses and turn to your partner to compare notes. (If there is another business near you with the same service, your business has a smaller chance at success.)

Make Connections

Essential Question Have students paraphrase and share information about how to start a successful business. Encourage them to review each step in the article to better summarize how to help a new business succeed.

Text to Text Divide the class into four groups. Each group should examine one entrepreneur's business from "Kids in Business." Assign one group to Hayleigh, one to Joshua, one to Anna, and one to Cecilia. Have groups compare their entrepreneur's story with the steps in "Starting a Successful Business." Did the entrepreneur follow all the steps? Did he or she leave any out? Why was each entrepreneur a success? Have each group report back to the entire class.

→ *Identify the context clues that help you figure out the meaning of* clients. ("find out how much they would be willing to pay for your services")

→ *How can a market survey help you gain clients?* (By asking about and providing desired services or products, a business can gain customers and be successful.)

ELL Use the illustrations to help reinforce the concept of each step on page 89. Review what happens during each step of starting a business.

→ *When do you make a budget? Point to the picture.* (Students should point to Step 3.)

→ *When do you check out the competition? Point to the picture.* (Students should point to Step 2.)

→ Phonics/Fluency

MINILESSON
20 Mins

Long *o*

OBJECTIVES

CCSS Use combined knowledge of all letter-sound correspondences, syllabication patterns, and morphology (e.g., roots and affixes) to read accurately unfamiliar multisyllabic words in context and out of context. **RF.4.3a**

CCSS Read on-level text with purpose and understanding. **RF.4.4a**

CCSS Read on-level prose and poetry orally with accuracy, appropriate rate, and expression on successive readings. **RF.4.4b**

Rate: 84–104 WCPM

ACADEMIC LANGUAGE
phrasing

ELL

Refer to the sound transfers chart in the **Language Transfers Handbook** to identify sounds that do not transfer in Spanish, Cantonese, Vietnamese, Hmong, and Korean.

1 Explain

Point to the *boat* **Sound-Spelling Card** and say the long-vowel sound /ō/. Explain that the /ō/ sound has different spellings and provide a sample word for each: *o (cold)*, *ow (low)*, *o_e (note)*, *oa (boat)*, and *oe (toe)*.

2 Model

Write the word *row* on the board. Underline the letters *ow* and model how to pronounce the long-vowel sound /ō/. Run your finger under the word as you model sounding it out.

3 Guided Practice

Write the following list of words on the board. Have students help you circle the long-*o* spelling in each word before reading the list chorally.

most	foe	roam
close	coat	glow
show	old	hope

Read Multisyllabic Words

Transition to Longer Words Draw a T-chart on the board. In the first column, write *road*, *fold*, *froze*, and *slow*. In the second column, write *railroad*, *unfold*, *frozen*, and *slowly*. Have students choral-read the long-*o* words in the first column. Point to the longer words in the second column and underline the words from the first column within these words.

Ask students to use what they know about the long-*o* words to read the longer words in the second column. Model sounding out the first word: *railroad*. Then have students partner-read the remaining words.

Go Digital

Long *o*

Present the Lesson

View "Dollars and Sense"

Compound Words

1 Explain

Compound words are made up of two or more smaller words. Knowing the meaning of the smaller words can help you understand the meaning of the compound word.

→ In some compound words, the smaller words are joined together (ex. *classroom*). In others, the smaller words are combined with hyphens (ex. *son-in-law*). In others, the smaller words are written as separate words (ex. *high school*).

2 Model

Write and say *birdhouse*. Have students repeat it. Note that it is a compound word made up of the smaller words *bird* and *house*. Model pronouncing the smaller words and then combining them.

3 Guided Practice

Write the compound words *nine-year-old*, *firefly*, and *post office* on the board. Have students identify the smaller words before pronouncing each compound word.

Phrasing and Rate

Explain/Model Explain that phrasing involves an awareness of where to pause and stop when reading based on punctuation. Explain that rate involves reading at a consistent speed. A good reading rate is one that is not too fast or too slow.

Model reading the first two paragraphs of "Dollars and Sense" on page 79. Read at a steady rate with correct phrasing. Point out that you paused at commas and stopped at periods while reading.

Practice/Apply Divide the class into two groups. Ask the first group to choral-read the first paragraph very quickly without pausing or stopping. Then have the second group choral-read the second paragraph at a correct rate while using phrasing. Have partners discuss the differences.

Daily Fluency Practice

Students can practice fluency using **Your Turn Practice Book**.

Monitor and _Differentiate_

 Quick Check

Can students decode multisyllabic words with long-*o* spellings? Can students read compound words? Can students read fluently?

↓

Small Group Instruction

If No → | Approaching Level | Reteach pp. T298, T302
| ELL | Develop pp. T314, T318

If Yes → | On Level | Review p. T304
| Beyond Level | Extend p. T308

ON-LEVEL PRACTICE BOOK p. 48

A. Read each sentence. Circle the word that has the long-vowel sound /ō/. Write the letter or letters that make the long-vowel sound /ō/ on the line.

1. Use the crane to (lower) the lumber to the ground. _____ ow
2. The (bolt) of lightning shot across the sky. _____ o
3. The sad movie filled us all with (woe). _____ oe
4. My (shadow) stays behind me when I walk down the stairs. _____ ow
5. Do you smell the chicken (roasting) in the oven? _____ oa
6. My favorite (quote) is from that great author. _____ o_e

B. Read the words in the box. Mark the words that are not compound words with an X. Then list the compound words on the lines below.

| workout | hunter | hands-on | childlike |
| catching | afternoon | half sister | weekend |

1. _____ workout _____ 4. _____ afternoon _____
2. _____ hands-on _____ 5. _____ half sister _____
3. _____ childlike _____ 6. _____ weekend _____

| APPROACHING p. 48 | BEYOND p. 48 | ELL p. 48 |

☞ **Go** Digital

www.connected.mcgraw-hill.com
RESOURCES
Research and Inquiry

→ **Wrap Up the Week**

Integrate Ideas

RESEARCH AND INQUIRY

Putting Ideas to Work

OBJECTIVES

CCSS Conduct short research projects that build knowledge through investigation of different aspects of a topic. **W.4.7**

CCSS Add audio recordings and visual displays to presentations when appropriate to enhance the development of main ideas or themes. **SL.4.5**

• Gather information from print and digital sources.

• Summarize and categorize information.

• Make presentations.

ACADEMIC LANGUAGE

print sources, digital sources, research

Research a Famous Business Owner

Explain that students will collaborate in small groups to research the life of a famous business owner. Students will then summarize their findings in a paragraph and post their paragraphs to the Shared Research Board. Discuss the following steps:

❶ **Form Student Groups** Divide students into small groups, incorporating groups with diverse learning abilities. Ask them to brainstorm a list of famous business owners, keeping in mind what they read about businesses and ideas.

❷ **Research a Topic** Invite students to choose a business owner from their list that they would like to learn more about. Have students gather information about the business owner from print and digital sources, listing their sources as they use them and taking careful notes.

❸ **Guided Practice** Have students sort the information they have gathered, organize it into categories, and then summarize what they have learned. Ask students to pay special attention to the effects the person's business or product had on the community.

❹ **Make a Poster or Slide Show** After students have gathered all of their research materials, have them make a poster or slide show about the business owner.

Present the Poster

Ask students to present their posters or slide shows to the class. Have students use online Presentation Checklist 1 to evaluate their roles in the presentation. Have them use the Listening Checklist to evaluate their roles in listening to and discussing the projects.

TEXT CONNECTIONS  Analytical Writing

OBJECTIVES

CCSS Integrate information from two texts on the same topic in order to write or speak about the subject knowledgeably. **RI.4.9**

Text to Text

Cite Evidence Explain to students that they will work in groups to compare information they have learned about how starting a business helps others from all the texts they have read. Model how to compare this information by using examples from the week's **Leveled Readers** and *Dollars and Sense*, **Reading/Writing Workshop** pages 78–81. Review class notes and completed graphic organizers. You may also wish to model going back into the text for more information. You can use an Accordion Foldable® to record comparisons.

Students should cite at least three examples from each text.

Dinah Zike's
FOLDABLES
Study Organizer

Accordion labels: Unit Theme | Business Helping Others | Help People with Needs | Care for the Environment | Care for Communities | Conclusions

Present Information Ask groups of students to present their findings to the class. Encourage discussion, asking students to comment on information on the charts that is similar and ideas that are different.

WRITE ABOUT READING Analytical Writing

OBJECTIVES

CCSS Determine the main idea of a text and explain how it is supported by key details; summarize the text. **RI.4.2**

CCSS Identify the reasons and evidence a speaker provides to support particular points. **SL.4.3**

Write an Analysis

Cite Evidence Using evidence from a text they have read, students will analyze how the author uses key details to support the main idea.

Discuss how to analyze a text by asking *how* and *why* questions.

→ How do the key details that the author uses connect to the main idea?

→ Why are these details important to understanding the main idea?

Read and discuss the student model on **Your Turn Practice Book** page 49. Then have students select an informational text. Have them write an analysis that explains how the author uses key details to support the main idea. Remind students that good explanatory writing uses precise language to inform about or explain the topic and avoids run-on sentences.

Present Your Ideas Ask partners to share their paragraphs and discuss how the evidence they cited from the text supports their ideas. Partners may suggest additional text evidence if necessary.

Readers to Writers

MINILESSON
10 Mins

Writing Traits: Sentence Fluency

Sentence Length

Expert Model Explain that good writers vary sentence lengths for interest and rhythm. Writers might follow a long sentence with a short sentence to draw attention to an important idea. They may also combine short, related sentences.

COLLABORATE

Read aloud the expert model from "Dollars and Sense." Ask students to listen for long and short sentences and think about how some of the shorter sentences draw attention to an idea. Have students talk with partners to identify these sentences.

Student Model Remind students that varying sentence lengths helps make writing more interesting and rhythmic. It also helps the writer emphasize an important idea. Read aloud the student draft "Soccer Rules!" As students follow along, have them focus on the different sentence lengths the writer used in her draft.

COLLABORATE

Invite partners to talk about the draft and the different sentence lengths that Courtney used. Ask them to suggest more places where Courtney could vary sentence lengths.

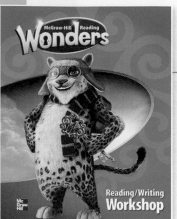

Reading/Writing Workshop

OBJECTIVES

CCSS Write routinely over extended time frames (time for research, reflection, and revision) and shorter time frames (a single sitting or a day or two) for a range of discipline-specific tasks, purposes, and audiences. **W.4.10**

- Analyze models to understand how to vary sentence lengths.
- Write about why people work.
- Vary sentence lengths to revise writing.

ACADEMIC LANGUAGE
rhythm

Go Digital

Expert Model

Student Model

Genre Writing

Narrative Text
For full writing process lessons and rubrics, see:

→ Friendly Letter, pages T344–T349

→ Personal Narrative, pages T350–T355

CCSS **Writing Traits** Sentence Fluency

Readers to ...

Writers often vary the length of their sentences. A writer might follow a long sentence with a short sentence to draw attention to an important idea. Reread the paragraph from "Dollars and Sense" below.

Sentence Lengths

Identify long and short sentences. How do some of the shorter sentences draw attention to an idea?

Expert Model

After starting and running four businesses, Blake Mycoskie wanted a break from his usual routine. In 2006, he traveled to Argentina, in South America, and while he was there he learned to sail and dance. He also visited poor villages where very few of the children had shoes. Mycoskie decided he had to do something. "I'm going to start a shoe company, and for every pair I sell, I'm going to give one pair to a kid in need."

86

Writers

Courtney wrote about her favorite sport. Read Courtney's revisions to a section of her essay.

Student Model

Soccer Rules!

My favorite sport to play is soccer. Soccer is a great sport to play because the action never stops! Last year I joined a soccer team that travels all over the state to play in competitions. My position on the team is striker it's my job to score as many goals as I can. When I score a goal everyone around the field cheers it's such a great feeling!

87

Grammar Handbook

Run-on Sentences
See page 454.

Your Turn COLLABORATE

✔ Describe how Courtney's sentence lengths varied.
✔ Identify the run-on sentences and fragments she corrected.
✔ Tell how other revisions improved her writing.

Go Digital!
Write online in Writer's Workspace

READING/WRITING WORKSHOP, pp. 86–87

ELL ENGLISH LANGUAGE LEARNERS SCAFFOLD

As English Language Learners write during the week, provide support to help them respond to the prompts. For example:

Beginning

Write Help students complete the sentence frames. *My position on the team is _____. It's my job to _____ as many _____ as I can. _____ is a short sentence.*

Intermediate

Describe Ask students to complete the sentence frames. Encourage students to provide precise language. *My position on the team is _____. It's my job to _____. When I score a goal, _____. _____ is a short sentence.*

Advanced/High

Discuss Check for understanding. Ask: *What is Courtney's position on the team? How do people react when she scores a goal? What are some examples of long and short sentences in her essay?*

Writing Every Day: Sentence Fluency

DAY 1

Writing Entry: Sentence Lengths

Prewrite Provide students with the prompt below.

What kind of business would you like to see started in your community? Give reasons for your opinion and vary sentence lengths.

Have partners list different businesses they think should be started in their community. Ask them to jot down reasons and evidence that they might include in their drafts.

Draft Have each student select a business to write about. Remind students to vary sentence lengths in their drafts.

DAY 2

Focus on Sentence Lengths

Use **Your Turn Practice Book** page 50 to model varying sentence lengths.

I think our community needs a frozen yogurt store. We have too many ice cream stores. Frozen yogurt is a healthy alternative to ice cream.

Model varying sentence lengths by combining the second and third sentences.

We have too many ice cream stores, and frozen yogurt is a healthy alternative to ice cream.

Discuss how varying sentence lengths adds interest and rhythm. Guide students to add sentences of varying lengths to the model.

Writing Entry: Sentence Lengths

Revise Have students revise their writing from Day 1 by varying the lengths of some sentences.

Use the **Conferencing Routines**. Circulate among students and stop briefly to talk with individuals. Provide time for peer review.

Edit Have students use Grammar Handbook page 454 to make sure they have not included any run-on sentences.

Conferencing Routines

Teacher Conferences

STEP 1

Talk about the strengths of the writing.

You included many reasons to support your opinion. The transition words you use help me connect ideas.

STEP 2

Focus on how the writer uses the target trait for the week.

Some sentences have different lengths. It would add interest and rhythm to your writing if you varied the lengths of your sentences even more.

STEP 3

Make concrete suggestions for revisions. Have students work on a specific assignment, such as those to the right, and then meet with you to review progress.

DAY

3

Writing Entry: Sentence Lengths

Prewrite Ask students to search their Writer's Notebook for topics to write a draft. Or, provide a prompt, such as the following:

Tell why people should support your favorite business in your community. Be sure to include both long and short sentences.

Draft Once students have chosen their topics, ask them to create a word web with the topic in the center. Then have them think about reasons to support their opinion that they might include in their writing. Students can then use their word webs to begin their drafts.

DAY

4

Writing Entry: Sentence Lengths

Revise Have students revise the draft writing from Day 3 by looking for places to vary sentence lengths. As students are revising their drafts, hold teacher conferences with individual students. You may also wish to have students work with partners to peer conference.

Edit Invite students to review the rules involving run-on sentences on Grammar Handbook page 454 in **Reading/Writing Workshop** and then edit their drafts for errors.

DAY

5

Share and Reflect

Discuss with the class what they learned about varying sentence lengths for interest, rhythm, or to emphasize ideas. Invite volunteers to compare draft text with revised text. Have students discuss the importance of using a variety of sentence lengths. Allow individuals time to reflect on their progress and record observations in their Writer's Notebooks.

McGraw-Hill Companies, Inc./Ken Karp, photographer

Suggested Revisions

Provide specific direction to help focus young writers.

Focus on a Sentence
Read the draft and target one sentence for revision. *Rewrite this sentence by combining it with the next sentence to create a longer sentence.*

Focus on a Section
Underline a section that needs to be revised. Provide specific suggestions. *The sentences in this section are about the same length. Vary the sentence lengths to add interest and rhythm.*

Focus on a Revision Strategy
Underline a section of the writing. Have students use a specific revision strategy, such as adding. *These sentences are long. Try adding a short sentence to emphasize your point.*

Peer Conferences

Focus peer response groups on varying sentence lengths for interest and rhythm. Provide this checklist to frame discussion.

- ☑ Does the writing include long and short sentences?
- ☑ Are short sentences used to call attention to an idea?
- ☑ Are there reasons to support the writer's opinion?
- ☑ Are any parts of the writing unclear?

Grammar: Run-On Sentences

Reading/Writing Workshop

OBJECTIVES

CCSS Produce complete sentences, recognizing and correcting inappropriate fragments and run-ons. **L.4.1f**

- Identify run-on sentences.
- Fix fragments and run-ons.
- Proofread sentences for mechanics and usage errors.

Go Digital

Run-On Sentences

Grammar Activities

DAY 1

DAILY LANGUAGE ACTIVITY

This tree is big but that one is gygantic! It is a giant sequoia?
(1: big, but; 2: gigantic; 3: sequoia.)

Introduce Run-On Sentences

Present the following:

→ A **run-on sentence** has two or more independent clauses that are not combined correctly.

   I haven't seen the cat today he must be hiding.

→ To fix a run-on, write separate sentences or combine the clauses correctly.

   I haven't seen the cat today. He must be hiding.

   I haven't seen the cat today, so he must be hiding.

Have partners discuss run-on sentences using page 454 of the Grammar Handbook in **Reading/ Writing Workshop**.

DAY 2

DAILY LANGUAGE ACTIVITY

When I opened the door; my dog ran outside. Ran to his favorite tree
(1: door, my; 2: He ran; 3: tree.)

Review Run-On Sentences

Review how to recognize run-on sentences. Have students explain how to fix a run-on sentence.

Introduce Types of Run-On Sentences

Present the following types of run-on sentences:

→ Two or more independent clauses joined without a coordinating conjunction or comma

→ Two or more independent clauses joined with a comma but without a coordinating conjunction or connecting word

→ Too many independent clauses joined in one sentence

TALK ABOUT IT

COLLABORATE

FORM A SENTENCE

Have students in a group create a list of ways in which starting a business can help others. Then have students take turns using one of the ideas on the list to create a compound sentence. Students should then explain why their sentence is not a run-on.

USE CONJUNCTIONS AND COMMAS

Ask each student to write five simple sentences about a topic on index cards, then pick two cards and create a compound sentence using a coordinating conjunction and a comma. Have students read their sentence aloud to a partner.

DAY 3

Dan coughed, and sneezed. he had catched a cold.
(1: coughed and; 2: He; 3: caught)

Mechanics and Usage: Correcting Fragments and Run-Ons

→ A sentence has both a subject and a predicate. A fragment is a group of words that is missing a subject, a predicate, or both.

→ A dependent clause by itself is a fragment. Finish the thought or eliminate the conjunction, or connecting word.

→ To correct a run-on sentence, rewrite it as separate sentences or combine the sentences correctly.

As students write, refer them to Grammar Handbook page 454.

DAY 4

DAILY LANGUAGE ACTIVITY

Went to the park. We went swimming, took a walk and fed the Geese.
(1: We went; 2: walk, and; 3: geese)

Proofread

Have students correct errors in these sentences.

1. Joe got up early! Wanted to wash the car. (1: early.; 2: He wanted)

2. Where is Stacy? At the airport. She will be boarding her plain soon. (1: She is at; 2: plane)

3. Try these grapes they are very good. (1: grapes. They)

4. We drove home, and we had dinner, and then we went to bed. (1: dinner. Then we)

Have students check their work using Grammar Handbook pages 450 and 454 on sentence fragments and run-on sentences.

DAY 5

DAILY LANGUAGE ACTIVITY

Ms. Jones is the teacher, that I like the best. She teaches math, and science!
(1: teacher that; 2: math and; 3: science.)

Assess

Use the Daily Language Activity and **Grammar Practice Reproducibles** page 25 for assessment.

Reteach

Use Grammar Practice Reproducibles pages 21–24 and selected pages from the Grammar Handbook for additional reteaching. Remind students that it is important to use complete sentences as they speak and write.

Check students' writing for use of the skill and listen for it in their speaking. Assign Grammar Revision Assignments in their Writer's Notebooks as needed.

See Grammar Practice Reproducibles pages 21–25.

CORRECT RUN-ONS AND FRAGMENTS

Have pairs of students write down two run-on sentences and two fragments. Have students trade sentences, correct them, and then read them aloud. The partner must listen to see if the new sentence is correct.

NAME THE CONJUNCTION

Have partners write five compound sentences about the kind of business they would like to start. Then have students read their sentences aloud. Their partners should name the conjunction that was used to form the compound sentence.

ROLE-PLAY A SCENE

Have students reenact a favorite scene from a story they have read recently that has dialogue. Explain that run-ons and fragments are common in dialogue. As the other students watch, have them listen and identify any run-ons or fragments they hear.

Spelling: Long *o*

DAY 1

OBJECTIVES

CCSS Spell grade-appropriate words correctly, consulting references as needed. **L.4.2d**

Spelling Words

bolt	blown	stole
mold	quote	goal
toll	mole	groan
shadow	stone	load
flow	stove	roasting
mows	chose	woe
lower	sole	

Review kite, fright, climb
Challenge coaster, motor

Differentiated Spelling

Approaching Level

bolt	mows	sole
most	lower	woke
mold	mole	goal
own	stone	groan
flow	stove	foam
tow	chose	woe
know	stole	

Beyond Level

mold	stovetop	floating
toll	chosen	soaked
motionless	poled	groaned
slowly	lonely	loading
lower	whole	coaster
blown	quote	woefully
closer	goalie	

Assess Prior Knowledge

Display the spelling words. Read them aloud, pointing out the long *o* sound in each word.

Point out the spelling patterns in *stone* and *groan*. Circle the letters that create the long *o* sound (*o_e; oa*) in each word. Note that the VCV pattern in *stone* creates the long *o* sound because it ends in a silent *e*.

Demonstrate sorting the spelling words by pattern under key words *toll*, *flow*, *stove*, *goal,* and *woe*. (Write the words on index cards or the IWB.) Sort a few words. Point out that the *oa* spelling for long *o* does not appear at the end of the word.

Then use the Dictation Sentences from Day 5 to give the Pretest. Say the underlined word, read the sentence, and repeat the word. Have students write the words. Then have students check and correct their spelling.

DAY 2

Spiral Review

Review long *i* vowel spellings in *climb, wipe, die, slight, height,* and *spy*. Use the Dictation Sentences below for the review words. Read the sentence, say the word, and have students write the words.

1. Ramón's <u>kite</u> rose higher.
2. The howling outside our tent gave us a <u>fright</u>!
3. He will <u>climb</u> Mt. Everest.

Have partners check the spellings.

Challenge Words Review this week's long *o* spelling pattern. Use these Dictation Sentences for challenge words. Say the word, read the sentence, and say the word again. Have students write the word.

1. The roller <u>coaster</u> is a wild ride!
2. The boat needs a new <u>motor</u>.

Have students check and correct their spelling before writing the words in their word study notebook.

 # WORD SORTS

COLLABORATE

OPEN SORT

Have students cut apart the **Spelling Word Cards BLM** in the Teacher Resource Book and initial the back of each card. Have them read the words aloud with a partner. Then have partners do an open sort. Have them record the sort in their word study notebook.

PATTERN SORT

Complete the **pattern sort** from Day 1 using the key words, pointing out the long *o* vowel spellings. Have students use Spelling Word Cards to do their own pattern sort. Ask partners to compare and check their sorts.

DAY 3

Word Meanings

Have students copy the three sentences below into their word study notebooks. Say the sentences aloud, and ask students to fill in the blanks with a spelling word.

1. I _____ cherry yogurt over vanilla yogurt. (*chose*)
2. Our neighbor _____ his lawn every Monday. (*mows*)
3. The joke was so bad that I could only _____. (*groan*)

Challenge students to come up with at least three other sentences for spelling, review, or challenge words, leaving a blank for the word. Remind them to make the sentences specific enough that only one word from the list will complete the sentence correctly. Then have partners exchange sentences and fill in the blanks. They can trade again to check the answers.

See Phonics/Spelling Reproducibles pp. 25–30.

SPEED SORT

Have partners do a **speed sort** to see who is faster and record the results in their word study notebooks. Then have them do a word hunt for other words with a long *o* sound. Have partners discuss how they would sort the words they find, and why.

DAY 4

Proofread and Write

Write these sentences on the board. Have students circle and correct each misspelled word. They can use print or electronic dictionaries or other resources to help them.

1. A moel ran out of the shaddow. (*mole, shadow*)
2. The water had to flo around the stoan. (*flow, stone*)
3. I smelled the food roesting in the stowv. (*roasting, stove*)
4. The tole to use the bridge is lowr this year. (*toll, lower*)

Error Correction Remind students a word contains the long *o* sound when the *o_e* pattern ends in a silent *e*, as in *mole*. Note that in the other spelling patterns, a silent final *e* does not mean that a word will have a long *o* sound. For example, *woe* and *shoe* both have a silent final *e*; *woe* has a long *o* sound, but *shoe* does not.

BLIND SORT

Have partners do a **blind sort**: one reads a Spelling Word Card; the other tells under which key word it belongs. Have them take turns until both have sorted all their words. Ask them to review their sorts and discuss how they sorted the words and if any changes are needed.

DAY 5

Assess

Use the Dictation Sentences for the Posttest. Have students list misspelled words in their word study notebooks. Look for students' use of these words in their writings.

Dictation Sentences

1. A <u>bolt</u> of lightning lit up the sky.
2. The old bread had <u>mold</u> on it.
3. We pay a <u>toll</u> to cross the bridge.
4. The <u>shadow</u> moved with the light.
5. I love to watch the river <u>flow</u> by.
6. Dana <u>mows</u> the lawn each week.
7. Is that picture <u>lower</u> on the wall?
8. Wind had <u>blown</u> the chair over.
9. Do you know a famous <u>quote</u>?
10. A <u>mole</u> dug holes in our yard.
11. The <u>stone</u> is large and smooth.
12. Ana cooked beans on the <u>stove</u>.
13. Each team captain <u>chose</u> a player.
14. I have gum on the <u>sole</u> of my shoe!
15. A raccoon <u>stole</u> eggs from the farm.
16. Lucie scored the winning <u>goal</u>.
17. I <u>groan</u> every time that happens!
18. The computer program takes time to <u>load</u>.
19. Mom is <u>roasting</u> a turkey.
20. "<u>Woe</u> is me," the actor moaned.

Have students self-correct the tests.

Build Vocabulary

DAY 1

DAY 2

OBJECTIVES

CCSS Use context (e.g., definitions, examples, or restatements in text) as a clue to the meaning of a word or phrase. **L.4.4a**

CCSS Use combined knowledge of all letter-sound correspondences, syllabication patterns, and morphology (e.g., roots and affixes) to read accurately unfamiliar multisyllabic words in context and out of context. **RF.4.3a**

Expand vocabulary by adding inflectional endings and suffixes.

Vocabulary Words

compassionate	innovative
enterprise	process
exceptional	routine
funds	undertaking

Go Digital

Vocabulary

Vocabulary Activities

Connect to Words

Practice this week's vocabulary.

1. Name a person you think is **compassionate**.

2. What kind of **enterprise** would you like to start?

3. Describe someone who is **exceptional**.

4. How could you raise **funds** to help your school?

5. Describe an **innovative** product.

6. What **process** do you use to study for tests?

7. Tell about your daily **routine**.

8. What kind of **undertaking** requires a lot of planning?

Expand Vocabulary

Help students generate different forms of this week's words by adding, changing, or removing inflectional endings.

→ Draw a two-column T-chart on the board. Write *enterprise* (noun) in the left column. Then write *enterprising* (adjective) in the other column. Read aloud the words with students.

→ Have students share sentences using each form of *enterprise*.

→ Students can fill in the chart for *compassionate* and *innovative*, then share sentences using the different forms of the words.

→ Have students copy the chart in their word study notebook.

 BUILD MORE VOCABULARY

COLLABORATE

ACADEMIC VOCABULARY

Discuss important academic words.

→ Display *charitable, donor, recipient*.

→ Define each word and discuss the meanings with students.

→ Display *donor* and *donation*. Have partners look up and define related words.

→ Write the related words on the board. Have partners ask and answer questions using the words. Repeat with *charitable* and *recipient*.

CONTEXT CLUES

→ Write the following sentence: *They had a compassionate teacher who really understood the needs of his students.*

→ Have partners write a definition for *compassionate* using context clues. Ask them to check their definition using a dictionary.

→ Have students write a sentence for another vocabulary word that includes either a definition or a restatement.

DAY 3

Reinforce the Words

Review last week's and this week's vocabulary words. Have students orally complete each sentence stem.

1. It was very <u>compassionate</u> of you to volunteer at the _____.
2. Mr. Tills started an <u>enterprise</u> that became very _____.
3. My brother is an <u>exceptional</u> _____ player.
4. Our class raised <u>funds</u> to buy a new _____.
5. The <u>process</u> of _____ takes a long time.
6. The team members practice their <u>routine</u> every _____.
7. Learning a new _____ is a huge <u>undertaking</u>.

DAY 4

Connect to Writing

→ Have students write sentences in their word study notebooks using this week's vocabulary.

→ Tell them to write sentences that provide word information they learned from this week's readings.

→ Provide the Day 3 sentence stems 1–7 for students needing extra support.

Write About Vocabulary Have students write something they learned from this week's words in their word study notebook. For example, they might write about a person they know who is *compassionate*, or describe how a local business is *innovative* or *exceptional*.

DAY 5

Word Squares

Ask students to create Word Squares for each vocabulary word.

→ In the first square, students write the word. (example: *funds*)

→ In the second square, students write their own definition of the word and any related words, such as synonyms. (example: *money, cash*)

→ In the third square, students draw a simple illustration that will help them remember the word. (example: a dollar sign)

→ In the fourth square, students write nonexamples, including antonyms for the word. (example: *debts*)

→ Have partners compare and discuss their Word Squares.

SUFFIXES

Remind students that recognizing and understanding suffixes can help them figure out the meaning of unfamiliar words.

→ Display **Your Turn Practice Book** pages 43–44. Read the first paragraph. Model figuring out the meaning of *truly*.

→ Have students complete page 47 and find clues for *helpful, easily, gladly, grateful,* and *importantly* on pages 43–44, using a print or online dictionary to confirm meanings.

SHADES OF MEANING

Help students generate words related to *innovative*. Draw a T-chart. Label it "Innovative."

→ Discuss the meaning of the adjective *innovative*. Have students generate related nouns, such as *device, product,* or *person,* for the first column.

→ Ask students to use a thesaurus to find synonyms, such as *new* or *creative*, to add to the second column.

→ Ask students to copy the chart in their word study notebook.

MORPHOLOGY

Use *innovative* as a springboard for students to learn more words. Draw a T-chart. Label the columns "Root words," and "Suffix."

→ Write *innovate* in the first column. Put the suffixes *-ive* and *-ion* in the second column. Discuss how the suffixes change the meaning or part of speech.

→ Write more words that take these suffixes, such as *reflect* and *create*. Note any spelling changes that occur when the suffixes are added.

Approaching Level

Leveled Reader:
Start Small, Think Big

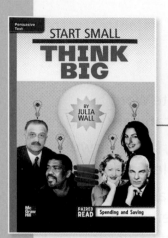

Lexile 660
TextEvaluator™ 29

 OBJECTIVES

Determine the main idea of a text and explain how it is supported by key details; summarize the text. **RI.4.2**

Determine the meaning of the new word formed when a known affix is added to a known word. **L.3.4b**

ACADEMIC LANGUAGE

- *reread, main idea, key details, persuasive article, suffixes, procedural text*
- Cognates:
  artículo persuasivo, sufijos

Go Digital

Leveled Readers

Before Reading

Preview and Predict

Have students read the Essential Question. Then have students read the title and table of contents of *Start Small, Think Big* and make a prediction about the author's position. Have partners share their predictions.

Review Genre: Persuasive Essay

Review with students that a persuasive essay is a type of nonfiction that expresses its author's position on a topic. The author supports his or her position using facts and may use text features like headings or charts. As they preview the book, have students identify features of a persuasive essay in *Start Small, Think Big*.

During Reading

Close Reading

Note Taking Ask students to use their graphic organizer while they read.

Pages 2–5 *What is the main idea of chapter 1?* (Starting a business takes time, energy, and courage.) *Turn to a partner and tell one key detail that supports the main idea.* (Dewitt and Lila Wallace showed courage when they started *Reader's Digest*. It was a new idea because it collected already published articles and shortened them.)

Pages 6–8 *Why was it hard for African Americans to find work in the 1930s? Reread the sidebar on page 6 to find the answer.* (The Great Depression occurred in the 1930s. African Americans often didn't get as good an education, so it was harder for them to find work.)

Pages 9–11 *How did Amadeo Giannini's business help others? Paraphrase to a partner.* (His bank was aimed at the "little fellows" who couldn't get accounts otherwise. Also, after the 1906 earthquake in California, he loaned money to businesses for rebuilding.)

Main Idea
| Detail |
| Detail |
| Detail |

Use Graphic Organizer

Page 12 Remind students that the suffix *-ion* can mean "the result of." *Use this information to define* invention *on page 12*. (*Invention* means "the result of inventing.")

Pages 13–14 *Does the author think that new businesses help a community?* (Yes) *Look at the sidebar on page 13 for evidence.* (The author thinks that businesses bring jobs to an area and help communities grow.)

After Reading

Respond to Reading Have students complete Respond to Reading on page 15 after they have finished reading.

Analytical Writing **Write About Reading** Have students work with a partner to write about how one of the entrepreneurs in the text helped others. Have them use at least two examples from the text.

Fluency: Phrasing and Rate

Model Model reading page 9 with proper phrasing and rate. Next, reread the page aloud and have students read along with you.

Apply Have students practice reading with a partner.

PAIRED READ

Leveled Reader

"Spending and Saving"

Make Connections: Write About It *Analytical Writing*

Before reading, ask students to note that the genre of this text is a procedural text, which explains how to do something. Then discuss the Essential Question. After reading, ask students to use the information from "Spending and Saving" to expand on their discussion about how entrepreneurs succeeded in *Start Small, Think Big*.

FOCUS ON SOCIAL STUDIES

Students can extend their knowledge of how a plan can help raise money by completing the social studies activity on page 20.

Literature Circles

Ask students to conduct a literature circle using the Thinkmark questions to guide the discussion. You may wish to have a whole-class discussion on the type of businesses students might like to start and how they would help others.

Level Up

Level-up lessons available online.

IF students read the **Approaching Level** fluently and answered the questions

THEN pair them with students who have proficiently read **On Level** and have students

- echo-read the **On Level** main selection with their partners.

- use self-stick notes to mark at least one new detail they would like to discuss in each section.

A C T **Access Complex Text**

The **On Level** challenges students by including more **domain-specific words** and **complex sentence structures**.

Approaching Level

Phonics/Decoding

DECODE WORDS WITH LONG *o*

 TIER 2

OBJECTIVES

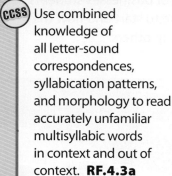 Use combined knowledge of all letter-sound correspondences, syllabication patterns, and morphology to read accurately unfamiliar multisyllabic words in context and out of context. **RF.4.3a**

Decode words with long *o*.

 I Do Explain that the long-*o* vowel sound is spelled with the letters *o_e* in many words. Write the word *stone* on the board, underline *o_e*, and explain that the spelling stands for the sound /ō/. Blend the sounds as you read the word aloud.

 We Do Write *stove, note, sole,* and *hope* on the board. Model how to decode *stove*. Have students identify the vowel sound as long *o* and the sound-spelling *o_e* in the word. Then have them read the remaining words aloud.

 You Do Add these words to the board: *mole, hole,* and *stole*. Have students read each word aloud and identify the long-*o* vowel sound. Then point to the words in random order for students to read chorally. Repeat several times.

REVIEW WORDS WITH LONG *o*

 TIER 2

OBJECTIVES

Use combined knowledge of all letter-sound correspondences, syllabication patterns, and morphology to read accurately unfamiliar multisyllabic words in context and out of context. **RF.4.3a**

Decode words with long *o*.

I Do Display the *boat* **Sound-Spelling Card**. Explain that the long *o* sound has several different spellings, and point to each sound-spelling on the card: *o, ow, o_e, oa,* and *oe*. Write sample words with each spelling on the board: *no, low, rose, boat,* and *toe*. Underline the sound-spelling for long *o* in each word as you read them aloud.

 We Do Display the **Word-Building Cards** *over, flow, load, coat, re, un, ing, told, sold, ed*. Help students use the word parts to build multisyllabic words, such as *overflow, overload, retold, untold, resold*. Guide them as they decode the syllables in each word. Write these words on the board, separated into syllables to help students read the words one syllable at a time: *o/ver/flow, o/ver/load, re/told, un/told, re/sold*. Then have students decode the words.

 You Do Add the following examples to the board: *colder, mowing, hometown, groaning,* and *woeful*. Ask students to decode each word. Then point to all the words in random order for students to choral-read. Repeat several times.

PRACTICE WORDS WITH LONG *o*

OBJECTIVES

 CCSS

Use combined knowledge of all letter-sound correspondences, syllabication patterns, and morphology to read accurately unfamiliar multisyllabic words in context and out of context. **RF.4.3a**

―――――――――――

Decode words with long *o*.

 I Do Remind students that every syllable in a word has only one vowel sound, and that the long *o* sound has different spellings. Write *chose* on the board, and then read the word aloud. Point out that *chose* has one syllable and that its vowel sound is long *o* spelled *o_e*.

 We Do Write the words *hopeful, wholesome, coasting, older, telephone, upload,* and *slowly*. Model how to decode the first word, and then guide students as they decode the remaining words. Help them divide each multisyllabic word into syllables using the syllable-scoop technique. This technique will help students read one syllable at a time.

You Do Afterward, point to the words in random order for students to choral-read.

COMPOUND WORDS

OBJECTIVES

 CCSS

Use combined knowledge of all letter-sound correspondences, syllabication patterns, and morphology to read accurately unfamiliar multisyllabic words in context and out of context. **RF.4.3a**

―――――――――――

Decode compound words.

 I Do Remind students that compound words are made up of two or more smaller words. Explain that some compound words are written with two or more words joined together, such as *snowflake*; some are written with one or more hyphens, such as *nine-year-old*; other compound words are written as two separate words, such as *high school*.

We Do Write *rainbow* on the board. Model how to decode the word. Give other examples of compound words and guide students as they decode these words. Divide multisyllabic words into syllables using the syllable-scoop technique to help students read one syllable at a time.

 You Do Write *raincoat, merry-go-round, bus stop, pillowcase, phone call,* and *ninety-nine* on the board. Have students identify the words in each compound word. Point to the words in random order for students to choral-read.

ELL ENGLISH LANGUAGE LEARNERS

For the **ELLs** who need **phonics**, **decoding**, and **fluency** practice, use scaffolding methods as necessary to ensure students understand the meaning of the words. Refer to the **Language Transfers Handbook** for phonics elements that may not transfer in students' native languages.

Approaching Level

Vocabulary

REVIEW HIGH-FREQUENCY WORDS

 TIER 2

OBJECTIVES

Read with sufficient accuracy and fluency to support comprehension. Read on-level text with purpose and understanding. **RF.4.4a**

Review high-frequency words.

 I Do Use **Word Cards 1–40**. Display one word at a time, following the routine:

Display the word. Read the word. Then spell the word.

 We Do Ask students to state the word and spell the word with you. Model using the word in a sentence and have students repeat after you.

 You Do Display the word. Ask students to say the word and then spell it. When completed, quickly flip through the word card set as students choral-read the words. Provide opportunities for students to use the words in speaking and writing. For example, provide sentence starters such as *I do my homework after _____*. Ask students to write each word in their Writer's Notebook.

REVIEW VOCABULARY WORDS

TIER 2

OBJECTIVES

Acquire and use accurately grade-appropriate general academic and domain-specific words and phrases, including those that signal precise actions, emotions, or states of being (e.g., *quizzed, whined, stammered*) and that are basic to a particular topic (e.g., *wildlife, conservation,* and *endangered* when discussing animal preservation). **L.4.6**

 I Do Display each **Visual Vocabulary Card** and state the word. Explain how the photograph illustrates the word. State the example sentence and repeat the word.

 We Do Point to the word on the card and read the word with students. Ask them to repeat the word. Engage students in structured partner-talk about the image as prompted on the back of the vocabulary card.

 You Do Display each visual in random order, hiding the word. Have students match the definitions and context sentences of the words to the visuals displayed.

ANSWER YES/NO QUESTIONS

OBJECTIVES

CCSS Acquire and use accurately grade-appropriate general academic and domain-specific words and phrases, including those that signal precise actions, emotions, or states of being (e.g., *quizzed, whined, stammered*) and that are basic to a particular topic (e.g., *wildlife, conservation,* and *endangered* when discussing animal preservation). **L.4.6**

 Display the *compassionate* **Visual Vocabulary Card**. Ask students the following question: *Is a* compassionate *person helpful to someone in need?*

Point out that to be *compassionate* means to be sympathetic to someone else's problem or suffering and to want to help that person.

 Display the vocabulary card for the word *exceptional*. Ask: *Is an* exceptional *meal something you eat every day?* With students, discuss how an exceptional meal is an extraordinary meal that you do not eat every day.

 Help students explain their answers to these questions.

→ Do you need *funds* to start a business?

→ Is taking a rest an *undertaking*?

→ Is brushing your teeth part of your morning *routine*?

→ Is following a recipe to make a sandwich a *process*?

→ Do people start *enterprises* carelessly, without planning ahead?

SUFFIXES

OBJECTIVES

CCSS Use combined knowledge of all letter-sound correspondences, syllabication patterns, and morphology (e.g., roots and affixes) to read accurately unfamiliar multisyllabic words in context and out of context. **RF.4.3a**

Use the meanings of suffixes to determine the meaning of unfamiliar words.

 Display the Comprehension and Fluency passage on **Approaching Reproducibles** pages 43–44. Remind students that a suffix is a word part added to the end of a word to change its meaning. Review the meanings of the suffixes *-ly* ("done in the way of"), *-ive* ("related or belonging to"), and *-ful* ("full of or characterized by"). Read aloud the third paragraph. Point to the word *helpful*.

Think Aloud I know that *help* means "to make something easier or better." I know that the suffix *-ful* means "full of or characterized by," and that this suffix turns a noun into an adjective. From these clues, I know that *helpful* is an adjective that describes something that makes something easier or better.

 Ask students to point to the word *active* on the same page. Discuss how students can figure out the meaning of the word by knowing the meanings of the base word *act* and suffix *-ive*. Write the definition of the word.

 Have pairs reread page 43 to determine the meanings of *easily* and *gladly*.

Approaching Level

Comprehension

FLUENCY

 OBJECTIVES

CCSS Read on-level prose and poetry orally with accuracy, appropriate rate, and expression on successive readings. **RF.4.4b**

Read aloud with correct phrasing and at a consistent rate.

 TIER 2

I Do Remind students to pay close attention to punctuation that signals phrasing. They should pause at commas and stop at end punctuation. Point out that correct phrasing will allow them to read text smoothly and clearly. In addition, remind students to read aloud at a consistent speed, or rate. Read the first paragraph of the Comprehension and Fluency passage on **Approaching Reproducibles** pages 43–44. Tell students to listen for your phrasing and consistent reading rate.

We Do Read the rest of the passage aloud. Have students read each sentence after you, paying attention to their phrasing. Provide adequate time for students to read sentences aloud with proper phrasing and rate.

You Do Have partners take turns reading sentences from the Approaching Reproducibles passage. Remind them to focus on phrasing and reading at an appropriate rate. Listen and provide corrective feedback as needed.

IDENTIFY KEY DETAILS

 OBJECTIVES

CCSS Determine the main idea of a text and explain how it is supported by key details; summarize the text. **RI.4.2**

Identify key details.

 TIER 2

I Do Write the topic *Helping Others* on the board. Then write: *help a classmate understand a math problem; help family members around the house; take the bus to school.* Explain that the first two details are both about the topic of helping others. Help students understand that *take the bus to school* is not an important detail because it does not relate to the topic.

We Do Read the first two paragraphs of the Comprehension and Fluency passage. Ask: *So far, what is this selection about?* Point out that this is the topic of the selection. Then ask: *What details do these two paragraphs give about the topic?* Discuss why these details are important.

You Do Have students read the rest of the passage. After each paragraph, they should write down the details that seem most important. Review their lists and help them explain why the details they chose are important.

REVIEW MAIN IDEA AND KEY DETAILS

OBJECTIVES

CCSS Determine the main idea of a text and explain how it is supported by key details; summarize the text. **RI.4.2**

 I Do Remind students that the main idea is the most important point that an author makes about a topic. A paragraph or section has a main idea and a whole selection has a main idea, too. The key details are all the facts and descriptions that tell about the main idea.

 We Do Read the second and third sections of the Comprehension and Fluency passage in **Approaching Reproducibles** together. Pause to point out details in each section. Model how to decide what all the important details have in common, or how they are connected, and how to state the main idea using these details. Then work with students to identify the main idea in each section in the passage.

 You Do Have students use the main ideas of each paragraph to come up with the main idea of the whole passage.

SELF-SELECTED READING

OBJECTIVES

CCSS Determine the main idea of a text and explain how it is supported by key details; summarize the text. **RI.4.2**

Reread difficult sections in a text to increase understanding.

Read Independently

Have students choose an article for sustained silent reading. Remind students that:

→ the main idea is the most important point that the author makes about the topic. Key details provide information about the main idea.

→ if they have trouble identifying the main idea, they should reread a paragraph or section to help them understand it better.

Read Purposefully

Have students record the main idea and key details on a Main Idea and Details Chart as they read independently. After they finish, they can conduct a Book Talk, each telling about the articles they read.

→ Students should share their charts and answer these questions: *What was the most interesting fact you learned from this article? What does the author try to persuade you to do in this article?*

→ They should also tell the group if there were any sections they reread to increase their understanding.

On Level

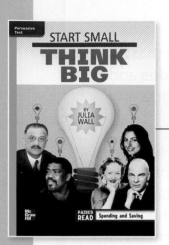

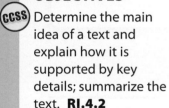

Lexile 780
TextEvaluator 35

OBJECTIVES

 Determine the main idea of a text and explain how it is supported by key details; summarize the text. **RI.4.2**

Determine the meaning of the new word formed when a known affix is added to a known word. **L.3.4b**

ACADEMIC LANGUAGE

• *reread, main idea, key details, persuasive article, suffixes, procedural text*

• Cognates: *artículo persuasivo, sufijos*

Leveled Reader:
Start Small, Think Big

Go Digital

Before Reading

Preview and Predict

Have students read the Essential Question. Have students read the title and table of contents of *Start Small, Think Big* and make a prediction about the author's position. Have partners share their predictions.

Review Genre: Persuasive Essay

Review with students that a persuasive essay is a type of nonfiction that expresses its author's position on a topic. The author supports his or her position using facts and may use text features like headings or charts. As they preview the book, have students identify features of a persuasive essay in *Start Small, Think Big*.

Leveled Readers

During Reading

Close Reading

Note Taking Ask students to use their graphic organizer while they read.

Pages 2–5 *What is the main idea of chapter 1?* (Starting a business takes time, energy, and courage, but when businesses succeed they can help communities.) *How does the example of DeWitt and Lila Wallace support the main idea?* (No one wanted to publish their idea, so they published it themselves. When they became successful, they donated money.)

Pages 6–8 *Why does the author include the sidebar on page 6?* (The sidebar shows that African Americans were having trouble finding jobs in the 1930s. It makes the reader understand the challenges Alvin Ailey had to overcome to create his dance theater.)

Pages 9–11 *Define* successful *on page 10*. (*Successful* means "full of success.") *How does the suffix help you define the word?* (I know the suffix *-ful* means "full of.")

Use Graphic Organizer

Pages 12–13 *What is the main idea of chapter 4?* (Even kids can start businesses that give back.) *How does Kavita's first invention help?* (It keeps dangerous chemicals safe in laboratories.)

Page 14 *What can you conclude about the author's position on businesses on page 14?* (The author says that entrepreneurs are courageous and willing to take big risks. This shows me that the author admires entrepreneurs.)

After Reading

Respond to Reading Have students complete Respond to Reading on page 15 after they have finished reading.

Write About Reading Have students work with a partner to write about how one of the entrepreneurs in the text helped others. Have them use at least two examples from the text.

Fluency: Phrasing and Rate

Model Model reading page 9 with proper phrasing and rate. Next, reread the page aloud and have students read along with you.

Apply Have students practice reading with a partner.

PAIRED READ

Leveled Reader

"Spending and Saving"

Make Connections: Write About It

Before reading, ask students to note that the genre of this text is a procedural text, which explains how to do something. Then discuss the Essential Question. After reading, ask students to use the information from "Spending and Saving" to expand on their discussion about how entrepreneurs succeeded in *Start Small, Think Big*.

FOCUS ON SOCIAL STUDIES

Students can extend their knowledge of how a plan can help raise money by completing the social studies activity on page 20.

Literature Circles

Ask students to conduct a literature circle using the Thinkmark questions to guide the discussion. You may wish to have a whole-class discussion on the type of businesses students might like to start and how they would help others.

Level Up

Level-up lessons available online.

IF students read the On Level fluently and answered the questions

THEN pair them with students who have proficiently read the Beyond Level and have students

- partner-read the Beyond Level main selection.
- list vocabulary words they find difficult and look them up with a partner.

ACT Access Complex Text

The Beyond Level challenges students by including more **domain-specific words** and **complex sentence structures**.

On Level

Vocabulary

REVIEW VOCABULARY WORDS

 OBJECTIVES
Acquire and use accurately grade-appropriate general academic and domain-specific words and phrases, including those that signal precise actions, emotions, or states of being (e.g., *quizzed, whined, stammered*) and that are basic to a particular topic (e.g., *wildlife, conservation,* and *endangered* when discussing animal preservation). **L.4.6**

 I Do
Use the **Visual Vocabulary Cards** to review the words *compassionate, enterprise, exceptional, funds, innovative, process, routine, undertaking.* Point to each word, read it aloud, and have students chorally repeat it.

 We Do
Ask these questions and help students respond and explain their answers.

→ What makes a person *compassionate*?

→ What types of *enterprises* would you perhaps like to start someday?

→ Who has an *exceptional* talent that you have admired?

→ Why does a government need *funds*?

 You Do
Have students respond to these questions and explain their answers.

→ What is a *process* you have followed recently in school or at home?

→ What is one part of your daily *routine*?

→ What is a difficult *undertaking* you have recently completed?

SUFFIXES

 OBJECTIVES
Use combined knowledge of all letter-sound correspondences, syllabication patterns, and morphology (e.g., roots and affixes) to read accurately unfamiliar multisyllabic words in context and out of context. **RF.4.3a**

 I Do
Remind students that they can often figure out the meaning of an unfamiliar word by knowing the meaning of its base word and suffix. Use the fourth paragraph of the Comprehension and Fluency passage on **Your Turn Practice Book** pages 43–44 to model.

Think Aloud I want to know what *helpful* means. I know that *help* means "to make something easier or better." I also know that the suffix *-ful* means "full of or characterized by." This suffix turns a noun into an adjective. I think that *helpful* describes something that makes something easier.

 We Do
Help students use their knowledge of base words and suffixes to define *easily* on page 43.

 You Do
Have student pairs determine the meanings of *gladly* on page 43 and *importantly* on page 44.

Comprehension

REVIEW MAIN IDEA AND KEY DETAILS

OBJECTIVES

CCSS Determine the main idea of a text and explain how it is supported by key details; summarize the text. **RI.4.2**

I Do Remind students that the main idea is the most important point an author makes about a topic. Explain that every paragraph and every section of a selection has a main idea that it is mostly about, and a whole selection has a main idea too. The key details are all the facts, quotations, definitions, and ideas that tell about the main idea.

We Do Have a volunteer read the first section of the Comprehension and Fluency passage on **Your Turn Practice Book** pages 43–44. Ask students to brainstorm key details aloud, and then help them explain why these details are important. Then model how to decide which details are related and how to state the main idea using these details. Then work with students to identify the main idea in the sections "Clean a Park" and "Meet New People."

You Do Have partners identify the main ideas in the remaining sections of the passage. Then have partners write the main idea of the whole passage.

SELF-SELECTED READING

OBJECTIVES

 Determine the main idea of a text and explain how it is supported by key details; summarize the text. **RI.4.2**

Reread difficult sections in a text to increase understanding.

Read Independently

Have students choose an article for sustained silent reading.

→ Before they read, have students preview the article, reading the title and viewing illustrations and other text features.

→ As students read, remind them to reread difficult sections.

Read Purposefully

Encourage students to read different articles in order to learn about a variety of subjects.

→ As students read, have them fill in the key details in a Main Idea and Details graphic organizer.

→ They can use this chart to help them write a summary of the article.

→ Ask students to share their reactions to the article with classmates.

→ Beyond Level

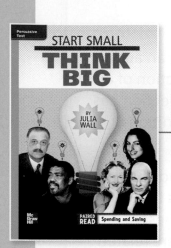

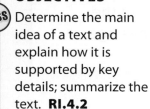

Lexile 890
TextEvaluator™ 42

OBJECTIVES

 Determine the main idea of a text and explain how it is supported by key details; summarize the text. **RI.4.2**

Determine the meaning of the new word formed when a known affix is added to a known word. **L.3.4b**

ACADEMIC LANGUAGE

• *reread, main idea, key details, persuasive article, suffixes, procedural text*

• Cognates: *artículo persuasivo, sufijos*

Leveled Reader:
Start Small, Think Big

Before Reading

Preview and Predict

Have students read the Essential Question. Then have students read the title and table of contents of *Start Small, Think Big* and make a prediction about the author's position. Have partners share their predictions.

Review Genre: Persuasive Essay

Review with students that a persuasive essay is a type of nonfiction that expresses its author's position on a topic. The author supports his or her position using facts and may use text features like headings or charts. As they preview the book, have students identify features of a persuasive essay in *Start Small, Think Big*.

During Reading

Close Reading

Note Taking Ask students to use their graphic organizer while they read.

Pages 2–5 *What is the author's position on people who succeed in a new business?* (When people succeed in a new business, they can make a difference.) *How does the author support this position?* (The author provides the example of the couple that started *Reader's Digest*. They succeeded under tough circumstances and then gave back to the community.)

Pages 6–8 *What is the main idea of chapter 2?* (Alvin Ailey wanted to make dance in the U.S. more exciting and accessible in the 1950s.) *Tell two key details in the chapter.* (Alvin Ailey studied many kinds of dance. He formed a dance theater to celebrate African American heritage.)

Pages 9–11 *Define* eventually *on page 11.* (*Eventually* means "done in an eventual way" or "done after some time.") *How does the suffix help you define the word?* (I know the suffix *-ly* means "done in the way of.")

Go
Digital

Leveled Readers

Main Idea
Detail
Detail
Detail

Use Graphic Organizer

Pages 12–13 *What is the main idea of the sidebar on page 13?* (Successful businesses benefit communities.) *How does Kavita's first invention help?* (It keeps dangerous chemicals safe in laboratories.)

Page 14 *How does the author reinforce her initial position on page 14?* (The author reiterates that starting a business takes courage and carries big risks and then encourages the reader to think big when starting a business.)

After Reading

Respond to Reading Have students complete Respond to Reading on page 15 after they have finished reading.

Analytical Writing **Write About Reading** Have students work with a partner to write about how one of the entrepreneurs in the text helped others. Have them use at least two examples from the text.

Fluency: Phrasing and Rate

Model Model reading page 9 with proper phrasing and rate. Next, reread the page aloud and have students read along with you.

Apply Have students practice reading with a partner.

PAIRED READ

Leveled Reader

"Spending and Saving"

Make Connections: Write About It *Analytical Writing*

Before reading, ask students to note that the genre of this text is a procedural text, which explains how to do something. Then discuss the Essential Question. After reading, ask students to use the information from "Spending and Saving" to expand on their discussion about how entrepreneurs succeeded in *Start Small, Think Big*.

FOCUS ON SOCIAL STUDIES

Students can extend their knowledge of how a plan can help raise money by completing the social studies activity on page 20.

Literature Circles

Ask students to conduct a literature circle using the Thinkmark questions to guide the discussion. You may wish to have a whole-class discussion on the type of businesses students might like to start and how they would help others.

Gifted and Talented

Synthesize Challenge students to create a business plan for a business that would give back to their community. Have them write a summary of what the business would do, what it would provide, and how they would give back once it became successful. Invite volunteers to share their plans.

→ Beyond Level

Vocabulary

REVIEW DOMAIN-SPECIFIC WORDS

OBJECTIVES

 Acquire and use accurately grade-appropriate general academic and domain-specific words and phrases, including those that signal precise actions, emotions, or states of being and that are basic to a particular topic. **L.4.6**

 Model Use the **Visual Vocabulary Cards** to review the meaning of the word *innovative*. Write sentences on the board using the word.

Write the words *funds, process,* and *routine* on the board and discuss the meanings with students. Then help students write sentences using these words.

 Apply Have students work in pairs to review the meanings of the words *enterprise* and *undertaking*. Then have partners write sentences using the words.

SUFFIXES

OBJECTIVES

 Use combined knowledge of all letter-sound correspondences, syllabication patterns, and morphology to read accurately unfamiliar multisyllabic words in context and out of context. **RF.4.3a**

 Model Read aloud the first two paragraphs of the Comprehension and Fluency passage on **Beyond Reproducibles** pages 43–44.

Think Aloud I see the word *active*. I know that its base word is *act* and its suffix is *-ive*. I know the suffix means "related to or belonging to." From these clues, I know that *active* means to be a part of doing something, or to be a part of an activity.

With students, read the fourth paragraph. Help them define *easily* and *gladly* from the base word and suffix of each word.

 Apply Ask students to identify the words *importance* and *importantly* on page 44, and define them using the meanings of their suffixes.

 Synthesize Have students write a journal entry describing a time when they overcame a challenge. Ask them to think and write about what they learned from this experience.

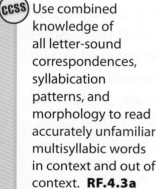

Comprehension

REVIEW MAIN IDEA AND KEY DETAILS

OBJECTIVES

 Determine the main idea of a text and explain how it is supported by key details; summarize the text. **RI.4.2**

 Remind students that the main idea in a passage is the most important idea an author focuses on. Explain that key details support and develop the main idea. Point out how each paragraph and section has a main idea, and that an entire passage or selection also has a main idea.

Have students read the first page of the Comprehension and Fluency passage on **Beyond Reproducibles** pages 43–44. Ask open-ended questions to facilitate discussion, such as *What is the author's position about Make a Difference Day? How can people help their community?* Students should support their responses with details in the text.

 Have students identify the main ideas in each section of the passage as they independently fill in a Main Idea and Details Chart. Then have partners use their work to determine the main idea of the whole passage.

SELF-SELECTED READING

OBJECTIVES

 Determine the main idea of a text and explain how it is supported by key details; summarize the text. **RI.4.2**

Reread difficult sections in a text to increase understanding.

Read Independently

Have students choose an article for sustained silent reading.

→ As students read, have them fill in a Main Idea and Details Chart.

→ Remind them to reread difficult sections of the text.

Read Purposefully

Encourage students to keep a reading journal. Ask them to read different articles in order to learn about a variety of subjects.

→ Students can write summaries of the articles in their journals.

→ Ask students to share their reactions to the articles with classmates.

 Evaluate Challenge students to discuss how their articles relate to the theme of putting ideas to work. Have students discuss how they can take action to help make their school or community a better place.

→ English Language Learners

Dollars and $ENSE

Behind the success of these big businesses is a desire to help others.

Good business is not always about the bottom line. A **compassionate** company knows that making money is not the only way to measure success. Many large businesses in the United States and all over the world are finding unusual ways to help people in need.

Hearts and Soles
After starting and running four businesses, Blake Mycoskie wanted a break from his usual **routine**. In 2006, he traveled to Argentina, in South America, and while he was there he learned to sail and dance. He also visited poor villages where very few of the children had shoes. Mycoskie decided he had to do something.

"I'm going to start a shoe company, and for every pair I sell, I'm going to give one pair to a kid in need."

For this new **undertaking**, Mycoskie started the business using his own money. He named it TOMS: Shoes for Tomorrow. The slip-on shoes are modeled on shoes that are traditionally worn by Argentine workers.

Mycoskie immediately set up his **innovative** one-for-one program. TOMS gives away one pair of shoes for every pair that is purchased. Later that year, Mycoskie returned to Argentina and gave away 10,000 pairs of shoes. By 2011, TOMS had donated over one million pairs.

79

Reading/Writing Workshop

OBJECTIVES

 Interpret information presented visually, orally, or quantitatively and explain how the information contributes to an understanding of the text in which it appears. **RI.4.7**

 Determine the main idea of a text and explain how it is supported by key details; summarize the text. **RI.4.2**

LANGUAGE OBJECTIVE
Identify the main idea and key details of a text.

ACADEMIC LANGUAGE
- *persuasive article, reread, suffix, main idea, details*
- Cognates: *artículo persuasivo, sufijos, detalles*

Shared Read
Dollars and Sense

Go Digital

Before Reading

Build Background

Read the Essential Question: How can starting a business help others?

→ Explain the meaning of the Essential Question. Make a list of local businesses and discuss the ways that these businesses can help people in the community.

→ **Model an answer:** *Starting a business can help in many ways. It can create new jobs in a community. A business can also raise money to help others, or it can donate equipment or some of the products it sells.*

→ Ask students a question that ties the Essential Question to their own background knowledge. *Have you ever volunteered at a local business or with an organization? What did you learn from your experience? Why do you think it is important for people and businesses to help others in need? Turn to a partner and discuss.* Call on several pairs to share their responses with the class.

During Reading

Interactive Question-Response

→ Ask questions that help students understand the meaning of the text after each paragraph.

→ Reinforce the meanings of key vocabulary.

→ Ask students questions that require them to use key vocabulary.

→ Reinforce strategies and skills of the week by modeling.

Dollars and $ENSE

Behind the success of these big businesses is a desire to help others.

View "Dollars and Sense"

Page 79

Paragraph 1

What are many businesses around the world doing to help others? (They are finding unusual ways to help people in need.)

Hearts and Soles

Chorally read the heading. Define the word *soles. Let's read about how one person is giving back to the world one pair of shoes at a time.* Have students point to the shoes in the photographs.

Paragraphs 1–4

Model Main Idea and Key Details *The main idea in this section is that Blake Mycoskie decided to start a shoe company that would give away a pair of shoes for every pair it sold. What detail explains why he decided to do this?* (He visited poor villages where very few of the kids had shoes.) *What other detail supports the main idea?* (One million pairs of shoes have been given away.)

Explain and Model Suffixes *I want to understand what* traditionally *means. I know that the base word* tradition *means "something that has been done over a long period of time." I know that the suffix* -ly *means "done in the way of." So,* traditionally *must mean "done in the way of tradition, or how it has been done for a long time."*

Page 80

Paragraphs 1 and 2

Explain that the word *expanded* means *"has grown." How has Mycoskie's company grown, or expanded?* (They now sell eyeglasses and donate a pair for every pair that is sold.)

Have partners read the caption and discuss how the photograph relates to the information in the text. (The photograph supports the text by showing workers giving away shoes.)

Giving Back Rocks!

Paragraph 1

What is the Hard Rock Cafe? (a company that runs restaurants and hotels)

Paragraph 2

Model Main Idea and Key Details *How does the Hard Rock Cafe raise money for charity?* (The company raises money for charity by selling T-shirts designed by rock stars. The T-shirts are sold on the Internet and part of the money goes to charity.)

Page 81

Paragraph 1

What do the Hard Rock Cafe and students in Hollywood, Florida, do each year? How does this help the community? (They put on an event for the Make-A-Wish Foundation; this foundation grants wishes to children with medical problems.)

Top Five Biggest Charities

Read the caption aloud and paraphrase the information. *What does this bar graph show?* (It shows the five biggest charities and how much money they raised in one year.) *Which charity received the most donations?* (United Way Worldwide) *How does the bar graph support the information in the article?* (Possible answer: The bar graph supports the information by showing how individuals and businesses are giving back and helping others in need.)

After Reading

Make Connections

→ Review the Essential Question: How can starting a business help others?

→ Make text connections.

→ Have students complete **ELL Reproducibles** pages 43–45.

English Language Learners

Lexile 710
TextEvaluator™ 30

 OBJECTIVES

Determine the main idea of a text and explain how it is supported by key details; summarize the text. **RI.4.2**

Determine the meaning of the new word formed when a known affix is added to a known word. **L.3.4b**

ACADEMIC LANGUAGE

• *reread, main idea, key details, persuasive article, suffixes, procedural text*

• Cognates: *artículo persuasivo, sufijos*

Leveled Reader:
Start Small, Think Big

 **Go Digital**

 **Leveled Readers**

Before Reading

Preview

→ Read the Essential Question: How can starting a business help others?

→ Refer to Rise to the Challenge: *How do you think this bakery can help others?*

→ Preview *Start Small, Think Big* and "Spending and Saving": *Let's read about how people have used their time, energy, and courage to succeed and help others.*

Vocabulary

Use the **Visual Vocabulary Cards** to preteach the ELL vocabulary: *borrowed, donated, loaned, operate.* Use the routine found on the cards.

During Reading

Interactive Question-Response

 Use Graphic Organizer

Note Taking Have students use their graphic organizer in **ELL Reproducibles**, page 42. Use the questions below as you read each section with students. As you read, define vocabulary in context and use pictures to help students understand key vocabulary.

Pages 2–5 *What is an entrepreneur?* (a person who starts a business) *Who are the entrepreneurs in this chapter?* (DeWitt and Lila Wallace) *What business did they start?* (a magazine) *Fill in the sentence frame to find the main idea in Chapter 1: Entrepreneurs need to work hard, but when they succeed, they can _____.* (make a big difference)

Pages 6–8 *Reread page 8. How did Alvin Ailey help others? Fill in the sentence frame: Alvin Ailey helped others by _____.* (starting programs that taught children dance and life skills)

Pages 9–11 Point out the word *successful* on page 10. *The suffix* -ful *means "full of." Use this information to define* successful. Successful *means "full of _____."* (success)

Pages 12–13 *What is Chapter 4 about?* (young inventors) *What did Kavita Shukla invent when she was 13 years old?* (the Smart Lid) *How does the Smart Lid help people?* (It keeps dangerous chemicals safe.)

Page 14 *How does the author describe entrepreneurs on page 14? The author says entrepreneurs _____ and _____ .* (take risks; work hard) *This is the author's point of view. Do you agree? Why or why not?* (Possible answer: I agree. It takes courage and determination to be an entrepreneur.)

After Reading

Respond to Reading Help students complete the graphic organizer in **ELL Reproducibles** page 42. Revisit the Essential Question. Have students pairs summarize and answer the Text Evidence Questions. Support students as necessary and review all responses as a group.

Analytical Writing **Write About Reading** Have partners write about how one of the entrepreneurs helped others. Remind them to cite evidence from the text and state a main idea.

Fluency: Phrasing and Rate

Model Model reading page 9 with proper phrasing and rate. Next, reread the page aloud and have students read along with you.

Apply Have students practice reading with a partner.

PAIRED READ

"Spending and Saving"

Make Connections:
Write About It *Analytical Writing*

Leveled Reader

Before reading, ask students to note that the genre of this text is a procedural text, which explains how to do something. Then discuss the Essential Question. After reading, ask students to use the information from "Spending and Saving" to expand on their discussion about how entrepreneurs succeeded in *Start Small, Think Big*.

FOCUS ON SOCIAL STUDIES

Students can extend their knowledge of planning a charity event by completing the social studies activity on page 20.

Literature Circles

Ask students to conduct a literature circle using the Thinkmark questions to guide the discussion. You may wish to have a whole-class discussion on the type of businesses students might like to start and how their businesses would help others.

Level Up

Level-up lessons available online.

IF students read the **ELL Level** fluently and answered the questions

THEN pair them with students who have proficiently read **On Level** and have students

• echo-read the **On Level** main selection with their partners.

• list words with which they have difficulty.

• discuss these words with their partners.

A C T Access Complex Text

The **On Level** challenges students by including more **academic language** and **complex sentence structures**.

English Language Learners
Vocabulary

PRETEACH VOCABULARY

 OBJECTIVES
Acquire and use accurately grade-appropriate general academic and domain-specific words and phrases, including those that signal precise actions, emotions, or states of being and that are basic to a particular topic. **L.4.6**

LANGUAGE OBJECTIVE
Use vocabulary words.

I Do Preteach vocabulary from "Dollars and Sense" following the Vocabulary Routine found on the **Visual Vocabulary Cards** for *compassionate, enterprise, exceptional, funds, process, routine,* and *undertaking.*

We Do After completing the Vocabulary Routine for each word, point to the word on the card and read it aloud. Ask students to repeat the word.

You Do Have partners take turns quizzing each other by spelling the words correctly and giving a definition for each word. Then have students use each word in a sentence.

Beginning	Intermediate	Advanced/High
Work with students to pronounce each word and define it correctly.	Ask students to write their sentences on the board.	Challenge students to write a question for each word.

REVIEW VOCABULARY

 OBJECTIVES
Acquire and use accurately grade-appropriate general academic and domain-specific words and phrases, including those that signal precise actions, emotions, or states of being and that are basic to a particular topic. **L.4.6**

LANGUAGE OBJECTIVE
Use vocabulary words.

I Do Review the previous week's vocabulary words. The words can be reviewed over a few days. Read each word aloud, pointing to the word on the **Visual Vocabulary Card.** Have students repeat after you. Then follow the Vocabulary Routine on the back of each card.

We Do Write each word on an index card. Hold two cards up at a time. Then provide clues for one of the words. Have students point to the word you describe. Ask a volunteer to use the word in a sentence.

You Do Have pairs write clues for three vocabulary words. Assign students to small groups and have them guess the word that goes with the clue.

Beginning	Intermediate	Advanced/High
Help students list clues for each word and read them aloud.	Have students write sentences using the vocabulary.	Ask students to use synonyms or antonyms in their clues.

SUFFIXES

OBJECTIVES

 CCSS Use combined knowledge of all letter-sound correspondences, syllabication patterns, and morphology to read accurately unfamiliar multisyllabic words in context and out of context. **RF.4.3a**

LANGUAGE OBJECTIVE

Use the meanings of suffixes to help determine the meanings of unfamiliar words.

I Do Read aloud the first page of the Comprehension and Fluency passage on **ELL Reproducibles** pages 43–44. Point to the word *helpful* and tell students that it has the suffix *-ful*. Explain that knowing the meaning of a suffix and base word can help you figure out the meaning of an unfamiliar word.

Think Aloud I know that *help* means "to make something easier or better." I know that the suffix *-ful* means "full of or characterized by," and that this suffix turns a noun into an adjective. I think that *helpful* is an adjective that describes something that makes something easier or better.

We Do Have students point to the word *easily* on page 43. Explain its meaning using its base word and suffix. Then write the definition on the board.

You Do In pairs, have students identify the base word and suffixes for *gladly* on page 43 and *importantly* on page 44. Then have them define the word.

Beginning	Intermediate	Advanced/High
Help students locate the word and name the base word and suffix.	Ask students to define the base word and suffix.	Have students define each word and use it in a sentence.

ADDITIONAL VOCABULARY

OBJECTIVES

 CCSS Choose words and phrases to convey ideas precisely. **L.4.3a**

LANGUAGE OBJECTIVE

Use academic and high-frequency words.

I Do List academic and high-frequency words from "Dollars and Sense": *similar, success;* and *Start Small, Think Big: courage, program, support.* Define each word for students: Similar *means alike or having something in common.*

We Do Model using the words for students in a sentence: *I have a similar red shirt. Sue's dog and Jake's dog look similar.* Then provide sentence frames and complete them with students: *We look similar because we both have _____.*

You Do Have pairs write about one of the entrepreneurs they learned about, using at least three words. Have them share their work with the class.

Beginning	Intermediate	Advanced/High
Help students write sentences correctly and read them aloud.	Ask students to include at least two facts they learned about the entrepreneur.	Encourage students to write about how the entrepreneur helped others.

English Language Learners
Writing/Spelling

WRITING TRAIT: SENTENCE FLUENCY

 OBJECTIVES

Produce clear and coherent writing in which the development and organization are appropriate to task, purpose, and audience. **W.4.4**

LANGUAGE OBJECTIVE

Add a variety of sentence lengths to writing.

 I Do
Explain that good writers use a variety of short and long sentences to better express their ideas. Writers may follow a long sentence with a short sentence to draw attention to an important idea. Read the Expert Model aloud as students follow along, paying attention to sentence length.

 We Do
Read the section Giving Back Rocks! from "Dollars and Sense" as students follow along. Have students identify short and long sentences. Point out how the sentences draw attention to important ideas.

 You Do
Have pairs write about ways to help the community. Remind them to vary sentence length to express important ideas. Edit each pair's writing. Then ask students to revise.

Beginning	Intermediate	Advanced/High
Have students copy the edited sentences.	Have students revise for clarity and errors.	Have students edit to add variety to sentence length.

SPELL WORDS WITH LONG o

 OBJECTIVES

Spell grade-appropriate words correctly, consulting references as needed. **L.4.2d**

LANGUAGE OBJECTIVE

Spell words with long o.

 I Do
Read aloud the Spelling Words on page T292. Segment each word into syllables, and attach a spelling to each sound. Point out the long-o spelling in each word. Then have students repeat the words.

 We Do
Read the Dictation Sentences on page T293 aloud for students. With each sentence, read the underlined word slowly, segmenting it into syllables with emphasis on the long-o sound. Have students repeat after you and write the word. Repeat the activity with the remaining sentences.

 You Do
Display the words. Have students exchange their lists with a partner to check the spelling and write the words correctly.

Beginning	Intermediate	Advanced/High
Have students copy the words correctly and say the words aloud.	After students have corrected their words, have pairs quiz each other.	After they have corrected their words, have pairs use each word in a sentence.

Grammar

RUN-ON SENTENCES

OBJECTIVES

 Demonstrate command of the conventions of standard English grammar and usage when writing or speaking. Produce complete sentences, recognizing and correcting inappropriate fragments and run-ons. **L.4.1f**

LANGUAGE OBJECTIVES

Write sentences.

Language Transfers Handbook

Speakers of Cantonese, Haitian Creole, Hmong, Korean, and Vietnamese may make errors in subject-verb agreement as it is not used in the native language.

 I Do Remind students that a compound sentence has two or more independent clauses that are often combined with a comma and a coordinating conjunction, such as *and, or, but,* and *yet.* Write on the board: *Miguel plays soccer, and his sister plays ice hockey.* Read aloud each clause and identify its subject and verb. Remind students that a run-on sentence has two or more independent clauses that are combined incorrectly. Write on the board the following types of run-on sentences and give an example of each: 1) two or more independent clauses joined without a comma or conjunction; 2) two or more independent clauses joined with a comma but not with a conjunction or connecting word; 3) too many independent clauses joined as one sentence.

We Do Write the run-on sentences below on the board. Ask volunteers to correct each run-on sentence and then explain how they corrected it. Read aloud the sentences and have students repeat.

> *Today is cloudy, it is also cold outside.*

> *Tyrone and I play violin we are on the same team.*

> *The puppy is sweet but he needs to be trained.*

 You Do Have students work in pairs to write two run-on sentences. Then have them trade and correct run-on sentences with another student pair.

Beginning	Intermediate	Advanced/High
Have students copy their corrected sentences, and help them underline the conjunctions. Read the sentences aloud, and have students repeat after you.	Ask students to explain why their sentences are examples of compound or simple sentences.	Have students explain which type of run-on sentence they have corrected.

For extra support, have students complete the activities in the **Grammar Practice Reproducibles** during the week, using the routine below:

→ Explain the grammar skill.

→ Model the first activity in the Grammar Practice Reproducibles.

→ Have the whole group complete the next couple of activities. Then have students complete the rest with a partner.

→ Review the activities with correct answers.

PROGRESS MONITORING

Weekly Assessment

CCSS TESTED SKILLS

| ✔ **COMPREHENSION:** Main Idea and Key Details **RI.4.2** | ✔ **VOCABULARY:** Suffixes **L.3.4b** | ✔ **WRITING:** Writing About Text **RI.4.2, W.4.9b** |

Assessment Includes

→ Pencil-and-paper administration

→ On-line administration

→ Approaching-Level Weekly Assessment also available

 FLUENCY ←

Fluency Goal 84 to 104 words correct per minute (WCPM)

Accuracy Rate Goal 95% or higher

Administer oral reading fluency assessments using the following schedule:

→ **Weeks 1, 3, 5** Provide Approaching-Level students at least three oral reading fluency assessments during the unit.

→ **Weeks 2 and 4** Provide On-Level students at least two oral reading fluency assessments during the unit.

→ **Week 6** If necessary, provide Beyond-Level students an oral reading fluency assessment at this time.

Also Available: Selection Tests online PDFs

Go Digital! www.connected.mcgraw-hill.com

Using Assessment Results

TESTED SKILLS	If ...	Then ...
COMPREHENSION	Students answer 0–6 multiple-choice items correctly ...	... assign Lessons 55–57 on Main Idea and Key Details from the *Tier 2 Comprehension Intervention online PDFs.*
VOCABULARY	Students answer 0–6 multiple-choice items correctly ...	... assign Lesson 151 on Suffixes from the *Tier 2 Vocabulary Intervention online PDFs.*
WRITING	Students score less than "3" on the constructed response ...	... assign Lessons 55–57 and/or Write About Reading Lesson 200 from the *Tier 2 Comprehension Intervention online PDFs.*
FLUENCY	Students have a WCPM score of 76–83 ...	... assign a lesson from Section 1 or 7–10 of the *Tier 2 Fluency Intervention online PDFs.*
	Students have a WCPM score of 0–75 ...	... assign a lesson from Sections 2–6 of the *Tier 2 Fluency Intervention online PDFs.*

Response to Intervention

Use the appropriate sections of the *Placement and Diagnostic Assessment* as well as students' assessment results to designate students requiring:

 **TIER 2 Intervention Online PDFs**

 **TIER 3 WonderWorks Intervention Program**

WEEKLY OVERVIEW

The Big Idea: *How can a challenge bring out our best?*

REVIEW AND EXTEND

Reader's Theater

Whodunit? Woo Knows...

Genre Play

Fluency Accuracy, Rate, and Prosody

Reading Digitally

TIME **FOR KIDS** "Bullying: It's Against the Law"

Comprehension Close Reading

Study Skills Skim and Scan

Research Navigate Links to Information

Go Digital!

Level Up Accelerating Progress

From **APPROACHING** To **ON LEVEL**	From **ON LEVEL** To **BEYOND LEVEL**	From **ENGLISH LANGUAGE LEARNERS** To **ON LEVEL**	From **BEYOND LEVEL** To **SELF-SELECTED TRADE BOOK**

Advanced Level **Trade Book**

ASSESS

Presentations

Research and Inquiry
Project Presentations

Project Rubric

Writing
Narrative Text Presentations

Writing Rubric

Unit Assessments

UNIT 1 TEST

FLUENCY

Evaluate Student Progress

Use the McGraw-Hill Reading Wonders eAssessment reports to evaluate student progress and help you make decisions about small group instruction and assignments.

→ Student and Class Assessment Report

→ Student and Class Standards Proficiency Report

→ Student Profile Summary Report

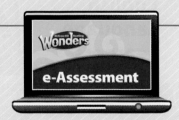

SUGGESTED LESSON PLAN

	DAY 1	DAY 2

READING

Whole Group

Reader's Theater "Whodunit? Woo Knows..."

"Bullying: It's Against the Law"

DAY 1

Reader's Theater, T326

"Whodunit? Woo Knows..."

Assign Roles

Model Fluency: Accuracy, Rate, and Prosody

DAY 2

Reader's Theater, T326

"Whodunit? Woo Knows..."

Model Fluency: Accuracy, Rate, and Prosody

Reading Digitally, T328

TIME "Bullying: It's Against the Law"

Research and Inquiry, T330–T333

Parts of a Library

Research and Inquiry Projects

DIFFERENTIATED INSTRUCTION Level Up to Accelerate

Small Group

Approaching Level

Level Up to On Level

George's Giant Wheel, T336

Spiral Review Comprehension Skills Unit 1 PDFs Online • *Analytical Writing*

Level Up to On Level

George's Giant Wheel, T336

Spiral Review Comprehension Skills Unit 1 PDFs Online • *Analytical Writing*

On Level

Level Up to Beyond Level

George's Giant Wheel, T337

Level Up to Beyond Level

George's Giant Wheel, T337

Beyond Level

Level Up to Self-Selected

Trade Book, T339

Level Up to Self-Selected

Trade Book, T339

English Language Learners

Level Up to On Level

George's Giant Wheel, T338

Level Up to On Level

George's Giant Wheel, T338

LANGUAGE ARTS

Whole Group

Writing

Share Your Writing, T334

Personal Narrative

Prepare to Present Your Writing

Share Your Writing, T334

Personal Narrative

Discuss Peer Feedback

DAY 3	DAY 4	DAY 5
Reading Digitally, T328 TIME. "Bullying: It's Against the Law" Close Reading • *Analytical Writing*	**Reader's Theater,** T326 Performance	**Research and Inquiry,** T332–T333 Presentations ✓ **Unit Assessment,** T340–T341
Research and Inquiry Projects	**Research and Inquiry Projects •** *Analytical Writing*	
Level Up to On Level *George's Giant Wheel,* T336 *Review* **Spiral Review** Comprehension Skills Unit 1 PDFs Online • *Analytical Writing*	**Level Up to On Level** "3001: A Space Mystery," T336	**Level Up to On Level** Literature Circles, T336
Level Up to Beyond Level *George's Giant Wheel,* T337	**Level Up to Beyond Level** "3001: A Space Mystery," T337	**Level Up to Beyond Level** Literature Circles, T337
Level Up to Self-Selected **Trade Book,** T339	**Level Up to Self-Selected** **Trade Book,** T339	**Level Up to Self-Selected** **Trade Book,** T339
Level Up to On Level *George's Giant Wheel,* T338	**Level Up to On Level** "3001: A Space Mystery," T338	**Level Up to On Level** Literature Circles, T338
Share Your Writing, T334 Personal Narrative Rehearse Your Presentation	**Share Your Writing,** T334 Present Your Narrative Evaluate Your Presentation	**Share Your Writing,** T335 Personal Narrative Portfolio Choice

Reader's Theater

WHODUNIT? WOO KNOWS . . .
by Anne M. Miranda

CAST:
Offstage Voice   Ms. Byrd
Ms. Woo   Mr. Lamb
Olivia Woo   Ms. Holstein
Manny the parrot   Mr. Colt
Detective Billie   Mr. Boxer

SETTING:
travel agency

Go Digital!

Teacher's Resource PDF Online, pp 4–24

OBJECTIVES

CCSS Read on-level text with purpose and understanding. **RF.4.4a**

CCSS Read on-level prose and poetry orally with accuracy, appropriate rate, and expression on successive readings. **RF.4.4b**

CCSS Use context to confirm or self-correct word recognition and understanding, rereading as necessary. **RF.4.4c**

Whodunit? Woo Knows...

Introduce the Play

Explain that *Whodunit? Woo Knows…* is a play set in a travel agency during modern times. When a robber strikes several homes while their owners are on vacation, a young sleuth named Olivia becomes suspicious. Distribute scripts and the Elements of Drama handout from the **Teacher's Resource PDF Online, 4–24**.

→ Review the features of a play.

→ Review the list of characters. Build background on the setting, defining the roles of Olivia, Ms. Woo, and the other characters. Note that this play takes place in the present.

→ Point out the prologue.

Shared Reading

Model reading the play as the students follow along in their scripts.

Focus on Vocabulary Stop and discuss any vocabulary words that students may not know. You may wish to teach:

→ burglarized   → clients

→ incognito   → coincidence

→ suspicious   → reassuring

Model Fluency As you read each part, state the name of each character, and read the part emphasizing the appropriate phrasing and expression.

Discuss Each Role

→ Ask students to identify what information the offstage voice is giving about the play.

→ Discuss how the parrot, Manny, can be portrayed.

→ After reading each character's part, ask partners to note the characters' traits. Model how to find text evidence that tells them about the characters.

Assign Roles

Depending on the number of students, you may wish to split the class into two groups. Assign one group parts for the Prologue and ACT I and the other group parts for ACT II. If you need additional roles, you can assign the role of Olivia to more than one student. The gender of the role can change if necessary.

Practice the Play

Each day, allow students time to practice their parts in the play. Pair fluent readers with less fluent readers. Pairs can echo-read or choral-read their parts. As needed, work with less fluent readers to mark pauses in their script using one slash for a short pause and two slashes for longer pauses.

Throughout the week have students work on the Reader's Theater activities on the **Reading Workstation Activity Card 30**.

Once the students have practiced reading their parts several times, allow students time to practice performing the script.

Perform the Reader's Theater

→ Discuss what it is like to play the only animal character. How would you perform Manny's role?

→ Lead a class discussion on ways the sound effects can be created.

ACTIVITIES

BECOMING A SLEUTH

The play *Whodunit? Woo Knows…* presents a mystery. The mystery genre interests readers and the audience through its suspenseful plot.

Review the elements of the genre. Identify the problem to be solved in the play. Then have students reread the play and note the characters and plot structure that are common to mysteries.

Have students work with a partner to answer the following questions:

1. What crime has been committed?
2. What is the setting of the crime?
3. Who are the suspects?
4. Which characters are trying to solve the mystery?
5. What clues does the detective have to investigate?

CRACKING THE CASE OF MYSTERY GENRE VOCABULARY

The play *Whodunit? Woo Knows…* uses mystery-genre vocabulary.

Work with a partner to identify mystery-genre vocabulary in the play. Create definitions for the words. Some words to consider include:

- → detective
- → alibi
- → suspects
- → clue
- → evidence
- → accusation
- → investigation
- → cracked this case

ENGLISH LANGUAGE LEARNERS

- → Review the definitions of difficult words including: *destinations, absolutely, detective, apologize, insulting, impressions, urgent, innocent, alibi*.
- → Discuss the meanings of homophones including: *book (to schedule), forced (affected by force), disks (computer media), connection (relationship)*.
- → Team an ELL student with a fluent reader who is also reading the part of Olivia. Have each reader take turns reading the lines. Determine which reader will read which lines at the performance.

Reading Digitally

OBJECTIVES

 CCSS Interpret information presented visually, orally, or quantitatively (e.g., in charts, graphs, diagrams, time lines, animations, or interactive elements on Web pages) and explain how the information contributes to an understanding of the text in which it appears. **RI.4.7**

 CCSS Conduct short research projects that build knowledge through investigation of different aspects of a topic. **W.4.7**

 CCSS Paraphrase portions of a text read aloud or information presented in diverse media and formats, including visually, quantitatively, and orally. **SL.4.2**

TIME FOR KIDS

Bullying: It's Against the Law

Before Reading

Preview Scroll through the online article "Bullying: It's Against the Law" at www.connected.mcgraw-hill.com and have students identify text features. Clarify how to navigate through the article. Point out the interactive features, such as **links**, **roll-overs**, and **pop-ups**. Explain that you will read the article together first and then access these features.

Close Reading Online

Take Notes Scroll back to the top and read the article aloud. As you read, ask questions to focus students on the problem of bullying and how people are working to solve it. Have students take notes using **Graphic Organizer 26**. After each section, have partners paraphrase the main ideas, giving text evidence. Make sure students understand idioms, such as *stand up for yourself, turn over a new leaf,* or *take the bait.*

Access Interactive Elements Help students access the interactive elements by clicking or rolling over each feature. Discuss what information these elements add to the text.

Tell students they will reread parts of the article to help them answer a specific question: *What can one person do to stop bullying?* Point out they do not need to reread every word. Instead, they can

→ **skim** by reading quickly and focusing on topic sentences, or

→ **scan** by moving their eyes over the text quickly to spot key words

Have students skim the article to find text detailing what one person can do to stop bullying. Have partners share what they find.

Navigate Links to Information Point out that online texts may include **hyperlinks**. Hyperlinks provide a connection from the Web page you are on to another Web page with related information.

Model using a hyperlink to jump to another Web page. Discuss any information on the new Web page related to the question *What can one person do to stop bullying?* Before navigating back, demonstrate bookmarking the page so students can return to it at another time.

WRITE ABOUT READING

Summarize Review students' graphic organizers. Model using the information to summarize "Bullying: It's Against the Law."

Ask students to write a summary of the article, stating the problem and actions people can take to solve it. Partners should discuss their summaries.

Make Connections Have students compare what they learned about the challenges presented by bullying with what they have learned about other challenges in texts they have read in this unit.

CONNECT TO CONTENT

Civic Responsibility

Point out that citizens often face public issues that impact their daily lives. Discuss how the people of a community or state can work together to influence the government and solve local or state issues.

Help students identify information in this article about how citizens and the government are working to prevent bullying.

→ People such as Kathryn Otoshi are teaching kids to stand up for themselves and others.

→ Most states now have anti-bullying laws.

RESEARCH ONLINE

Cyber Safety

Tell students that when they use the Internet, there are safety rules they should follow. Share the following rules for Internet safety with students. Tell them they should

→ Understand which sites they are allowed to visit and which are off limits.

→ Never give out personal information on the Internet, such as their address or phone number, their parents' names, their school's name, pictures, or passwords.

→ Never agree to meet anyone in person that they meet online.

INDEPENDENT STUDY

Investigate

Choose a Topic Students should brainstorm questions related to the article. For example, they might ask: *What can I do about cyberbullying?* Then have students choose a question to research. Help them narrow it.

Conduct Internet Research Review the rules for Internet safety. Then model how to conduct an Internet search. Type in the URL for a search engine. Enter key words and click search. Then click on a link on the results page to go to a site.

Present Have groups present a round-table discussion on the topic of bullying.

RESEARCH AND INQUIRY

The Big Idea: *How can a challenge bring out our best?*

Assign the Projects Break students into five groups. Assign each group one of the five Projects that follow. Before students begin researching, present these minilessons.

Research Skill: Parts of a Library

OBJECTIVES

 CCSS With some guidance and support from adults, use technology, including the Internet, to produce and publish writing as well as to interact and collaborate with others; demonstrate sufficient command of keyboarding skills to type a minimum of one page in a single sitting. **W.4.6**

 CCSS Conduct short research projects that build knowledge through investigation of different aspects of a topic. **W.4.7**

 CCSS Recall relevant information from experiences or gather relevant information from print and digital sources; take notes and categorize information, and provide a list of sources. **W.4.8**

 CCSS Report on a topic or text, tell a story, or recount an experience in an organized manner, using appropriate facts and relevant, descriptive details to support main ideas or themes; speak clearly at an understandable pace. **SL.4.4**

Parts of a Library/Using the Card or Computer Catalog

→ Tell students that they can collect facts from reference texts and online searches for research. Discuss how to use a library and how to use evaluative criteria, such as readability, appropriateness, and special features, to select reference materials.

→ Most reference materials cannot be removed from the library. Remind students that they need to record basic bibliographic information for sources they use while at the library.

→ To use a digital card catalog, students need to identify the author's name or the title of a book or an article, or search by subject. Search results include call numbers and the author's name. Some materials are organized by call number, while others are organized alphabetically by author's last name.

Summarizing and Categorizing Information

Students should take notes that summarize the main idea of a source. Ask students to determine what the most important details in a text are. Have them write a short summary of these details.

→ Remind students to look for important information in different text features, such as sidebars and time lines. Students should also look for bold or italicized text that may contain important information.

→ Remind students that summarizing is not the same as quoting or copying. When summarizing information, they should use their own words to paraphrase the ideas of others.

→ Have students categorize their research according to type of source, topic, background information, or relevance of information. Students can use a graphic organizer to sort and categorize information.

COLLABORATE
Manage and assign Projects online. Students can also work with their group online.

Choose a Project!

Give an Oral Presentation

1

ESSENTIAL QUESTION
Where do good ideas come from?

Goal
Research teams will give an oral presentation on a product or food that came about from work on something else.

STEM

Create a Multimedia Presentation

2

ESSENTIAL QUESTION
How do your actions affect others?

Goal
Research teams will give a multimedia or slideshow presentation on a famous person whose positive actions have affected others.

Create a Newscast

3

ESSENTIAL QUESTION
How do people respond to natural disasters?

Goal
Research teams will create a newscast about how a community responded to a recent natural disaster. The newscast should include a broadcaster, a reporter, and citizens being interviewed.

Do an Experiment

4

ESSENTIAL QUESTION
How can science help you understand how things work?

Goal
Research teams will use an activity or experiment to demonstrate a science topic to the class. Potential science topics include motion, force, friction, or gravity.

STEM

Research a Business

5

ESSENTIAL QUESTION
How can starting a business help others?

Goal
Research teams will create a slideshow about a business owner that they have researched online. Slideshows should focus on how the person's business affects the community.

RESEARCH AND INQUIRY

Distribute the Research Roadmap online PDF. Have students use the roadmap to complete the project.

Conducting the Research

STEP 1 **Set Research Goals**

Discuss with students the Essential Question and the research project. Each group should

→ make sure they are clear on their research focus and end product.

→ decide on each member's role. *Who will do the primary research? Who will categorize the information? Who will summarize the material? Who will be in charge of technology? Who will make the visuals? Who will speak during the presentation? Who will play which part in the newscast?*

STEP 2 **Identify Sources**

Have the group brainstorm where they can find the information for their projects. Sources might include

→ print works, such as informational texts and reference books.

→ digital media, such as online newspapers, maps, and community Web sites.

→ interviews with experts.

Remind students that using a variety of sources will ensure a more complete and accurate presentation.

STEP 3 **Find and Record Information**

Have students review the library-research strategies on page T330. Then have them research their topic. Remind students to categorize their sources.

STEP 4 **Organize**

After team members have completed the research, they can review and analyze all the information they collected. First they should summarize and categorize their notes in order to determine the most useful information. Then they can create a rough graphic organizer as a way to clarify categories of information and sort their notes.

STEP 5 **Synthesize and Present**

Have team members synthesize their research and decide on their final message.

→ Encourage students to use all available technologies, such as audio recordings and visual displays, to enhance their presentations.

→ They should check that the key ideas are included in their presentations and that their findings relate to the Big Idea.

Audience Participation

→ Encourage the audience to make comments and ask clarifying questions.

→ Have students discuss how each presentation relates to the Essential Question.

Review and Evaluate

Distribute the online PDF of the checklists and rubrics. Use the following Teacher Checklist and rubric to evaluate students' research and presentations.

Student Checklist

Research Process

☑ Did you narrow the focus of your research?

☑ Did you create a research plan for your project?

☑ Did you gather information from print and digital sources?

☑ Did you use reliable sources to gather your information?

☑ Did you take notes and sort the information into categories?

Presenting

☑ Did you express your ideas clearly?

☑ Did you support your topic with appropriate facts and details?

☑ Did you make eye contact with your audience?

☑ Did you answer the Essential Question and the Big Idea?

☑ Did you use appropriate visual displays to enhance your presentation?

Teacher Checklist

Assess the Research Process

☑ Selected a focus.

☑ Used multiple sources to gather information.

☑ Cited sources for information.

☑ Used time effectively and collaborated well.

Assess the Presentation

☑ Spoke clearly and at an appropriate pace and volume.

☑ Maintained eye contact.

☑ Established a main message that answered the Essential Question and the Big Idea.

☑ Used appropriate visuals and technology.

Assess the Listener

☑ Listened quietly and politely.

☑ Made appropriate comments and asked clarifying questions.

☑ Responded with an open mind to different ideas.

Project Rubric

4 Excellent	**3** Good	**2** Fair	**1** Unsatisfactory
The project → presents the information clearly. → includes many details. → may include sophisticated observations.	**The project** → presents the information adequately. → provides adequate details. → includes relevant observations.	**The project** → attempts to present information. → may offer few or vague details. → may include few or irrelevant personal observations.	**The project** → may show little grasp of the task. → may present irrelevant information. → may reflect extreme difficulty with research or presentation.

Celebrate Share Your Writing

Publishing Celebrations

Giving Presentations

Now is the time for students to share one of their pieces of narrative writing that they have worked on through the unit.

You may wish to invite parents or students from other classes to the Publishing Celebrations.

Preparing for Presentations

Tell students that they will be presenting their writing and that they will need to prepare in order to provide the best representation of their hard work.

Allow students time to rehearse their presentations. Ask them to reread their presentation piece until they feel familiar with it. Tell students that they should plan to look at the audience and make eye contact rather than simply reading straight from their paper. Remind them that the way they speak and present themselves is as important as the information they are presenting.

Students should also consider any visuals or digital elements that they want to use during their presentation. Discuss a few possible options with students.

→ Do they have photos they want to share? Can they illustrate an important part of the narrative?

→ Are there flyers, souvenirs, or other items that they would want to share with the class?

→ Is there a video related to the topic that they can show?

Students can practice presenting to a partner in the classroom. They can also practice with family members at home or in front of a mirror. Share the following checklist with students to help them focus on important parts of their presentation as they rehearse. Discuss each point on the checklist.

Speaking Checklist

Review the Speaking Checklist with students as they practice.

- ☑ Have all your notes and visuals ready.
- ☑ Take a few deep breaths.
- ☑ Stand up straight.
- ☑ Look at the audience.
- ☑ Speak clearly and slowly.
- ☑ Speak loudly enough that everyone can hear.
- ☑ Speak with excitement.
- ☑ Use appropriate gestures.
- ☑ Hold your visual aids so that everyone can see them.
- ☑ Remember to smile.

Listening to Presentations

Remind students that they will not only take on the role of a presenter, they will also be part of the audience for other students' presentations. As listeners, students have an important role. Review with students the following Listening Checklist.

Listening Checklist

During the presentation

- ☑ Pay attention to how the speaker uses the visuals in the presentation.
- ☑ Take notes on one or two things you liked about the presentation.
- ☑ Write one question or comment you have about the events presented.
- ☑ Listen to the speaker carefully.
- ☑ Do not talk during the presentation.

After the presentation

- ☑ Only comment on the presentation when it is your turn.
- ☑ Tell why you liked the presentation.
- ☑ If someone else makes the same comment first, tell why you agree.
- ☑ Ask your question.

Portfolio Choice

Ask students to select one finished piece of writing and two revised pieces to include in their writing portfolio. As students consider their choices, have them use the questions below.

Published Writing

Does your writing

→ Use the correct structure?

→ Describe ideas and events clearly?

→ Use effective organization?

→ Have few or no spelling and grammatical errors?

→ Have a neat, published appearance?

Writing Entry Revisions

Did you revise your writing to

→ Include a variety of sentence lengths?

→ Add time-order words to show sequence?

→ Provide more descriptive details?

Go Digital

PORTFOLIO
Students can submit their writing to be considered for inclusion in their digital Portfolio. Students' portfolios can be shared with parents.

Level Up Accelerating Progress

Leveled Reader

Level Up
Lessons
also available
online

Approaching Level to On Level

George's Giant Wheel

Before Reading

Preview Discuss what students remember about George Ferris and his passenger wheel. Tell them they will be reading a more challenging version of *George's Giant Wheel*.

Vocabulary Use the routines on the **Visual Vocabulary Cards** to review the vocabulary.

A C T During Reading

▶ **Specific Vocabulary** Review with students the following science-related words that are new to this title: *advances, braces, revolved, suspended*. Provide the meanings of the words for students.

▶ **Connection of Ideas** Students may need help connecting and synthesizing new ideas and information in the On Level reader. Read page 4 with students. Ask pointed questions while reading: *When did Ferris create his plan for the passenger car? How old was Ferris when he started working on it?*

▶ **Sentence Structure** Students may need help understanding the use of the rhetorical questions. See page 6. Choral-read the paragraph on page 6 with students and ask them to state what the paragraph is about. Have students find the sentence before the question. Then ask: *Is the narrator asking the reader a question?* (No) *Who is asking the question?* (It is a question people may have asked about the safety of the passenger car.)

After Reading

Ask students to complete the Respond to Reading on page 15. Have students complete the Paired Read and hold Literature Circles. Students should respond to the questions using the new information from the On Level version of *George's Giant Wheel*.

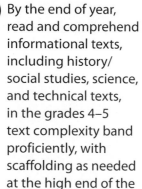

OBJECTIVES

CCSS
By the end of year, read and comprehend informational texts, including history/social studies, science, and technical texts, in the grades 4–5 text complexity band proficiently, with scaffolding as needed at the high end of the range. **RI.4.10**

Leveled Reader

OBJECTIVES

CCSS By the end of year, read and comprehend informational texts, including history/ social studies, science, and technical texts, in the grades 4–5 text complexity band proficiently, with scaffolding as needed at the high end of the range. **RI.4.10**

On Level to Beyond Level

George's Giant Wheel

Level Up Lessons also available online

Before Reading

Preview Discuss what students remember about George Ferris and his passenger wheel. Tell them they will be reading a more challenging version of *George's Giant Wheel*.

Vocabulary Use the routines on the **Visual Vocabulary Cards** to review the vocabulary.

A C T During Reading

▶ **Specific Vocabulary** Review with students the domain-specific vocabulary that is new to this title: *technological, calculated, skeleton*. Model how to use context clues to find the meanings of *technological* and *skeleton*. Provide the definition of *calculated*.

▶ **Sentence Structure** Students may need help understanding more complex sentence structures. See page 7. Choral-read the last sentence in the first paragraph on the page. Point out that there are two ideas in the sentence and ask students to identify them. (Ferris was an expert at making steel structures; he knew his passenger wheel would work) Point out how these ideas are related. Then have students read the compound sentence aloud. Repeat with other compound sentences in the text as needed.

▶ **Connection of Ideas** Students may need help connecting and synthesizing new ideas and information. Read page 5 with students. Have students summarize each paragraph before moving on. Ask: *What is gravity? How would passenger cars remain horizontal as the wheel turned?*

After Reading

Have students complete the Respond to Reading on page 15. Have students complete the Paired Read and hold Literature Circles. Students should respond to the questions using the new information from the Beyond Level version.

Level Up Accelerating Progress

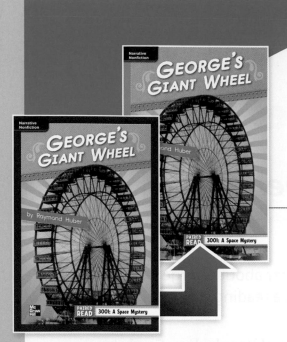

Leveled Reader

 OBJECTIVES

By the end of year, read and comprehend informational texts, including history/social studies, science, and technical texts, in the grades 4–5 text complexity band proficiently, with scaffolding as needed at the high end of the range. **RI.4.10**

English Language Learners to On Level

George's Giant Wheel

Level Up Lessons also available online

Before Reading

Preview Remind students that informational text gives facts about a topic. Discuss what students remember about George Ferris and his passenger wheel. Tell them they will be reading a more challenging version of *George's Giant Wheel*.

Vocabulary Use the routines on the **Visual Vocabulary Cards** to review the vocabulary. Point out the cognates: *acelerar, capacidades, gravedad, identidad, fricción*.

A C T During Reading

▶ **Specific Vocabulary** Show students how to identify context clues that will help them figure out the meaning of domain-specific words such as *advances* in the first paragraph on page 2. Repeat this routine for *achievement, proposed, demolished*.

▶ **Sentence Structure** Point out complex text structures as you read. Reread the fourth paragraph of page 3. Explain that the author uses a dash instead of a comma to emphasize that the Ferris wheel became one of the most popular rides of all time.

▶ **Connection of Ideas** Help students understand how the information in photo captions connects to the content on the page. With students summarize page 4 of the text. Then compare the information with the information in the photo caption. Discuss how the caption gives additional information about the text. Repeat with the photo captions on pages 8, 12, and 13.

After Reading

Respond to Reading Have students complete the Respond to Reading on page 15. Have students complete the Paired Read and hold Literature Circles.

Leveled Reader

OBJECTIVES

 By the end of year, read and comprehend literature/ informational texts, including history/ social studies, science, and technical texts, in the grades 4–5 text complexity band proficiently, with scaffolding as needed at the high end of the range. **RL/RI.4.10**

Advanced Level Trade Book

Beyond Level
to Self-Selected Trade Book

Independent Reading

Level Up Lessons also available online

Before Reading

With students identify a particular focus for their reading based on the text they choose. Students who have chosen the same title will work in groups to closely read the selection and identify its text structure.

Close Reading

Taking Notes Assign a graphic organizer for students to use to take notes as they read. Reinforce a specific comprehension focus from the unit by choosing the graphic organizer that best fits the book.

Examples:

Fiction	Informational Texts
Sequence	Cause and Effect
Graphic Organizer 90	Graphic Organizer 86

Ask and Answer Questions Have students write down any questions they have as they read. As students meet, have them discuss the section that they have read and share the questions they noted. They should work together to find text evidence to support their answers.

After Reading

Write About Reading

Have students respond to the text using their notes and text evidence to support their writing.

Examples:

Fiction	Informational Text
Which words help you understand the sequence of events? Retell the story using the words *first, next,* and *last*.	Which details help you identify the cause-and-effect relationships? How do these relationships form a sequence of events?

SUMMATIVE ASSESSMENT

Unit Assessment

 **TESTED SKILLS**

✓ COMPREHENSION:
- Character, Setting, Plot: Sequence **RL.4.3**
- Character, Setting, Plot: Problem & Solution **RL.4.3**
- Text Structure: Compare & Contrast **RI.4.5**
- Text Structure: Cause and Effect **RI.4.5**
- Main Idea & Key Details **RI.4.2**
- Diagram, Heads, and Subheads **RI.4.7**

✓ VOCABULARY:
- Context Clues: Synonyms **L.4.5c**
- Idioms **L.4.5b**
- Context Clues: Multiple-Meaning Words **L.4.4a**
- Context Clues: Definitions and Restatements **L.4.4a**
- Suffixes **L.3.4b**

✓ ENGLISH LANGUAGE CONVENTIONS:
- Sentences **L.4.1f, L.4.3b**
- Subjects and Predicates **L.4.1f**
- Compound Sentences **L.4.2c**
- Clauses and Complex Sentences **L.4.2c**
- Run-On Sentences **L.4.1f**

✓ WRITING:
- Writing About Text **W.4.9b**
- Narrative **W.4.3a-e**

Assessment Includes

→ Pencil-and-paper administration

→ On-line administration

→ Performance Tasks

→ Writing Prompt

Additional Assessment Options

 FLUENCY

Conduct assessments individually using the differentiated passages in **Fluency Assessment.** Students' expected fluency goal for this Unit is **84–104 WCPM** with an accuracy rate of 95% or higher.

Running Records

Use the instructional reading level determined by the Running Record calculations for regrouping decisions. Students at Level 38 or below should be provided reteaching on specific Comprehension skills.

Using Assessment Results

TESTED SKILLS	If ...	Then ...
COMPREHENSION	Students answer 0–9 multiple-choice items correctly ...	... reteach tested skills using the *Tier 2 Comprehension Intervention online PDFs.*
VOCABULARY	Students answer 0–7 multiple-choice items correctly ...	... reteach tested skills using the *Tier 2 Vocabulary Intervention online PDFs.*
ENGLISH LANGUAGE CONVENTIONS	Students answer 0–7 multiple-choice items correctly ...	... reteach tested skills using the *Tier 2 Writing and Grammar Intervention online PDFs.*
WRITING	Students score less than "2" on short-response items and "3" on extended constructed response items ...	... reteach tested skills using appropriate lessons from the Strategies and Skills and/or Write About Reading sections in the *Tier 2 Comprehension Intervention online PDFs.*
	Students score less than "3" on the writing prompt ...	... reteach tested skills using the *Tier 2 Writing and Grammar Intervention online PDFs.*
FLUENCY	Students have a WCPM score of 0–83 ...	... reteach tested skills using the *Tier 2 Fluency Intervention online PDFs.*

Response to Intervention

Use the appropriate sections of the *Placement and Diagnostic Assessment* as well as students' assessment results to designate students requiring:

 Intervention Online PDFs

 WonderWorks Intervention Program

Reevaluate Student Grouping

View the *McGraw-Hill Reading Wonders eAssessment Class Unit Assessment Report* and *McGraw-Hill Reading Wonders eAssessment Class Standards Proficiency Report* available for this Unit Assessment. Note children who are below the overall proficiency level for the assessment, and use the reports to assign small group instruction for children with similar needs.

Genre Writing

Reading Extended Complex Text

Program Information

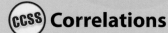

www.connected.mcgraw-hill.com

NARRATIVE TEXT Friendly Letter

EXPERT MODEL

Expert Model • Letter • 1

155 Cooper Street
San Francisco, CA 75025
February 5, 2014

Dear Tracy,

You were absolutely right that I'd love it here. San Francisco is such a charming city! The view of the majestic Golden Gate Bridge from my new apartment is breathtaking. I'm so excited to explore the hilly streets of my new home.

However, shipping everything I own to San Francisco turned out to be a big headache. Thank goodness for my new neighbors, Gina and Marissa. I don't know what I would've done without their help and kindness.

I woke up the morning of my flight feeling as light as a feather. I couldn't wait for my taxi to the airport. Then I received a phone call from the shipping company I'd hired. "This is Fargo Cargo," began the company representative. "I'm so sorry to inform you that the truck carrying your shipment has not arrived in San Francisco." Well, my heart sank hearing this news. Apparently all my possessions were stuck in a snowstorm somewhere in Wyoming!

The sky in San Francisco that day was dark and gray. After a tiring trip, I finally made it to 155 Cooper Street. In the hallway, a woman greeted me with a bright smile. Gina was so warm and welcoming that I found myself telling her about my

Expert Model
PDF Online

OBJECTIVES

CCSS Orient the reader by establishing a situation and introducing a narrator and/or characters; organize an event sequence that unfolds naturally. **W.4.3a**

CCSS Use a variety of transitional words and phrases to manage the sequence of events. **W.4.3c**

ACADEMIC LANGUAGE

sequence, heading, greeting, informal, closing, signature

Read Like a Writer

Point out how friendly letters tell of experiences and events and are exchanged between friends and family. People write friendly letters in order to keep in touch with others and report personal news. Read and discuss the features of a friendly letter.

Features of a Friendly Letter

→ It includes a heading with the sender's address and a date.

→ It includes a greeting.

→ It uses an informal or friendly tone.

→ It shares ideas and events with friends or family.

→ It has a closing and a signature.

Discuss the Expert Model

COLLABORATE

Use the questions below to prompt discussion of friendly letters.

→ When and where was this letter written? (It was written on February 5th in San Francisco, California.)

→ To whom does the writer address her letter? (Tracy)

→ How do you know that this letter was written by Tracy's friend Anne? (The closing, "Your friend," tells that the letter was written by a friend, and Anne's signature identifies her as the writer.)

→ What is the main idea of the first paragraph? (Anne is excited about living in her new home, San Francisco.)

→ What event does Anne go on to describe? (She describes moving to San Francisco and meeting her new neighbors.)

→ Is the tone of the letter friendly or formal? (friendly)

Go Digital

Writer's Workspace

PREWRITE

Discuss and Plan

Purpose Discuss with students the purpose for writing a friendly letter. They can share thoughts and feelings about experiences in their lives and stay in touch with people they know. Friendly letters can also entertain the reader.

Audience Have students think about who will read their friendly letters, such as friends, family members, and classmates. Tell them to consider their audience when communicating their personal experiences. Ask: *Why do you want to tell your readers about your experience?*

Teach the Minilesson

Sequence of Events Explain to students that friendly letters are easier to read when the events of an experience are described in the order they happened. This helps readers understand when and why each event happened. Words and phrases such as *first, after, finally, later,* and *then* can help establish the order of events.

Distribute copies of the Model Sequence Chart found online in the Writer's Workspace. Point out that the events that make up Anne's experience of moving to San Francisco unfold naturally, as they really happened. She organizes the events in order by telling what happened first, next, and last.

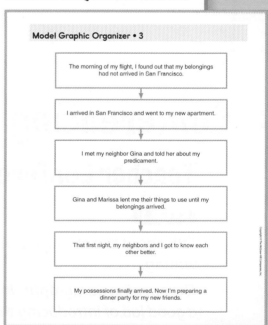

Your Turn

Choose Your Topic Have students work in pairs or small groups to brainstorm experiences in which they faced a challenge. Remind them that the purpose of a friendly letter is to share information about their experiences. Ask questions to prompt thinking. Have students record their topics in their Writer's Notebooks.

→ What made this experience challenging? How did you feel about it?

→ What details about this experience would you like to share?

→ What happened first? What happened next? How did it end?

Plan Provide copies of the blank Sequence Chart found online in Writer's Workspace. Ask students to put the important events in order, or sequence.

ENGLISH LANGUAGE LEARNERS

Beginning

Demonstrate Comprehension Help students draw pictures of the events from their friendly letters.

Intermediate

Describe Have partners make a written list of the events described in the sample friendly letter.

Advanced/High

Expand Have partners write simple sentences responding to the questions about the sample friendly letter.

MODEL SEQUENCE CHART

Model Graphic Organizer • 3

The morning of my flight, I found out that my belongings had not arrived in San Francisco.

I arrived in San Francisco and went to my new apartment.

I met my neighbor Gina and told her about my predicament.

Gina and Marissa lent me their things to use until my belongings arrived.

That first night, my neighbors and I got to know each other better.

My possessions finally arrived. Now I'm preparing a dinner party for my new friends.

NARRATIVE TEXT Friendly Letter

DRAFT

OBJECTIVES

CCSS Orient the reader by establishing a situation and introducing a narrator and/or characters; organize an event sequence that unfolds naturally. **W.4.3a**

CCSS Use concrete words and phrases and sensory details to convey experiences and events precisely. **W.4.3d**

CCSS Provide a conclusion that follows from the narrated experiences or events. **W.4.3e**

ACADEMIC LANGUAGE

draft, introduction, revise, details, sequence

Discuss the Student Model

Review the features of friendly letters. Provide copies of the Student Model found online in Writer's Workspace.

Teach the Minilesson

Introduction Explain that the introductory paragraph in a friendly letter should orient the reader by introducing the topic, which is the experience the writer wants to tell the reader about. It should also establish the friendly tone of the letter and grab the reader's attention by including interesting, descriptive details and expressing strong feelings. The letter should also have a logical conclusion.

Chorally read the first two paragraphs of the Expert Model. Discuss with students how Anne introduces the topic of moving to San Francisco, sets the tone of the letter, and grabs the reader's attention. Point out that Anne shares her feelings about her move and includes an interesting detail about the view from her new home.

Your Turn

Write a Draft Have students review the Sequence Charts they prepared in Prewrite. Remind them to orient the reader by introducing the topic of the letter in the first few paragraphs and offering a conclusion.

Go Digital

Writer's Workspace

Conferencing Routines

Teacher Conferences

STEP 1

Talk about the strengths of the writing.

The opening paragraphs do a good job of introducing the experience you are writing about. You included details that grab the reader's attention.

STEP 2

Focus on how a writer uses a writing trait.

I am able to follow the order of events because you used sequence words to signal what happened first, next, and last.

STEP 3

Make concrete suggestions for revision.

I would be better able to picture this situation in my mind if you used more sensory details to tell what it felt like to be there.

REVISE

Discuss the Revised Model

Distribute copies of the Revised Student Model found online in the Writer's Workspace. Read the model aloud and have students note the revisions that Jimmy made. Use the specific revisions to show how adding details, reviewing word choice, and combining sentences to improve flow all help to make the friendly letter more engaging.

Teach the Minilesson

Details Remind students that including details in a friendly letter helps grab the reader's attention. Details include concrete words and phrases and sensory details. In a friendly letter, writers use details to convey their experiences precisely and to paint a clear picture in the reader's mind.

Have students find an example of a revision in the Revised Student Model that shows the writer added a concrete or sensory detail. Discuss how this revision helps the reader clearly picture the experience the writer is describing.

Your Turn

COLLABORATE

Revise Have students use the peer review routine and questions to review their partners' drafts. Then have students select suggestions from the peer review to incorporate into their revisions. Provide the Revise and Edit Checklist from Writer's Workspace to guide them as they revise. Suggest they consider adding details to explain their experiences more precisely. Circulate among students as they work and conference as needed.

REVISED STUDENT MODEL

Revised Student Model • Friendly Letter • 6

155 President Street
Brooklyn, NY 11201
February 5, 2014

Dear Brad,

Moving from Florida to Brooklyn, New York, was like moving to another world. My family arrived with only what we'd crammed into the trunk of our car. The shipping company was three days late delivering our furniture and boxes of personal stuff. We had to sleep on padding on the floor, and eat on paper plates with plastic forks and knives! This was okay. That was okay. On our first day, my dad got us all to pretend we were camping, my mom let us all have extra dessert too.

Right away, I mist my old house and my friends. My two little sisters complains about being bored, but at least they had each other to play with. On our second day in Brooklyn, Mom announced in a cheerful voice, "It's time to rally the troops!" We played an old bored game, and Dad told us about all the wonderful things we are going to do and see in New York. Somehow, Dad and Mom made us laugh and laugh

I was shocked by how cold it is here? There is snow on the ground and snow that covers the trees. There is snow and ice everywhere.

Mom bundelled us up and took us to a big park called Prospect Park. It was like we were leaving the city and going

---

Peer Conferences

Review with students the routine for peer review of writing: Listen carefully as the writer reads his or her work aloud. Begin by telling what you liked about the writing. Then ask a question that will help the writer think more about the writing. Finally, make a suggestion that will make the writing stronger.

Use these questions for peer review.

☑ Does the writing have an introduction that grabs the reader's attention?

☑ Are sequence words included to help tell events in the order they happened?

☑ Are details included to help you picture events?

☑ Is the letter formatted correctly?

NARRATIVE TEXT Friendly Letter

PROOFREAD/EDIT AND PUBLISH

OBJECTIVES

CCSS With guidance and support from peers and adults, develop and strengthen writing as needed by planning, revising, and editing. **W.4.5**

CCSS With some guidance and support from adults, use technology, including the Internet, to produce and publish writing as well as to interact and collaborate with others; demonstrate sufficient command of keyboarding skills to type a minimum of one page in a single sitting. **W.4.6**

ACADEMIC LANGUAGE

publish, multimedia, rubric

Discuss the Edited Model

Provide copies of the Edited Student Model found online in the Writer's Workspace. Read the model aloud and have students note the editing changes that Jimmy made. Use the specific edits to show how editing for complete sentences, spelling, verb tenses, punctuation, and subject-verb agreement improves the friendly letter.

Your Turn

Edit Have students use the edit questions on the Revise and Edit Checklist to guide them as they review and edit their drafts on their own. Remind them to read for one type of error at a time.

Publish

For the final presentation of their friendly letters, have students choose a format for publishing. Students may want to consider:

Print Publishing	Digital Publishing
Letter (to be mailed)	Writer's Workspace
Personal Book	Class Blog
Collaborative Class Book	Friendly E-mail

Whether students handwrite or use a word-processing program, they should be sure to use standard margins and format their final drafts so that the heading, greeting, closing, and signature are accurate and that the flow of the text is easy for readers to follow. Make sure students demonstrate sufficient keyboarding skills to type their letter in a single sitting.

Explain to students that adding visual and multimedia elements can strengthen their writing and presentation, making them more engaging for their readers. Allow time for students to design and include photos, videos, audio, and other visual or multimedia elements that will enhance their friendly letter.

EDITED STUDENT MODEL

Edited Student Model • Friendly Letter • 7

155 President Street
Brooklyn, NY 11201
February 5, 2014

Dear Brad,

Moving from Florida to Brooklyn, New York, was like moving to another world. My family arrived with only what we'd crammed into the trunk of our car. The shipping company was three days late delivering our furniture and boxes of personal stuff. We had to sleep on padding on the floor, and eat on paper plates with plastic forks and knives. That was okay. On our first day, my dad got us all to pretend we were camping. My mom let us all have extra dessert too.

Right away, I missed my old house and my friends. My two little sisters complained about being bored, but at least they had each other to play with. On our second day in Brooklyn, Mom announced in a cheerful voice, "It's time to rally the troops!" We played an old board game, and Dad told us about all the wonderful things we are going to do and see in New York. Somehow, Dad and Mom made us laugh and laugh.

I was shocked by how cold it is here. There is snow on the ground and snow that covers the trees. There is snow and ice everywhere. One day, Mom bundled us up and took us to a big park called Prospect Park. It was like we were leaving the city and going to a frozen wilderness. Mom said there aren't no bears in the park.

EVALUATE

Discuss Rubrics

Guide students as they use the Student Rubric found online in Writer's Workspace. Help them understand that using a rubric helps them identify and focus on areas that might need further work. Work with the class to review the bulleted points on the rubric.

→ **Focus and Coherence** Does the friendly letter tell about an important experience in the writer's life in an interesting way?

→ **Organization** Are the events told in an order that makes sense? Is there a heading, greeting, closing, and signature?

→ **Ideas and Support** Are ideas developed carefully so readers understand the importance of the experience?

→ **Word Choice** Are concrete or sensory details used? Do sequence words show the order of events?

→ **Voice/Sentence Fluency** Is the tone of the letter friendly and informal? Does the writing include a variety of sentence types?

→ **Conventions** Are errors in grammar, spelling, punctuation, and capitalization corrected?

STUDENT RUBRIC

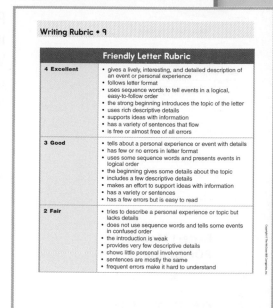

Writing Rubric • 9

	Friendly Letter Rubric
4 Excellent	• gives a lively, interesting, and detailed description of an event or personal experience • follows letter format • uses sequence words to tell events in a logical, easy-to-follow order • the strong beginning introduces the topic of the letter • uses rich descriptive details • supports ideas with information • has a variety of sentences that flow • is free or almost free of all errors
3 Good	• tells about a personal experience or event with details • has few or no errors in letter format • uses some sequence words and presents events in logical order • the beginning gives some details about the topic • includes a few descriptive details • makes an effort to support ideas with information • has a variety or sentences • has a few errors but is easy to read
2 Fair	• tries to describe a personal experience or topic but lacks details • does not use sequence words and tells some events in confused order • the introduction is weak • provides very few descriptive details • shows little personal involvement • sentences are mostly the same • frequent errors make it hard to understand

Your Turn

Reflect and Set Goals After students have evaluated their own friendly letters, tell them to reflect on their progress as writers. Encourage them to consider areas where they feel they have shown improvement and to think about what areas need further improvement. Have them set writing goals to prepare for their conference with the teacher.

Conference with Students

Use the Rubric and the Anchor Papers provided online in Writer's Workspace as you evaluate student writing. The anchor papers provide samples of papers that score from 1 to 4. These papers reflect the criteria described in the Rubric. Anchor papers offer a standard against which to judge writing.

Review with individual students the writing goals they have set. Discuss ways to achieve these goals and suggest any further areas of improvement students may need to target.

NARRATIVE TEXT Personal Narrative

Writing Process Lesson 2

Birds and More Birds
by Sarah H.

I stood shivering. I was silent except for the chatter of my teeth. It was late March just before dawn with temperatures around freezing. "What am I doing standing in a field watching birds?" I muttered to myself. My older sister planned this trip months ago, and I was flattered that she asked me to go with her. Now I was having second thoughts.

Earlier, we met the park ranger at 5:00 am and he gave a short presentation about sandhill cranes. These amazing birds migrate thousand of miles from the southwest to central Canada and beyond. Some even fly to eastern Siberia. On this cold March day, the ranger said there were close to 250,000 cranes along the Platte River. The river and surrounding corn fields are important sources of food during the long migration of these birds.

"Let's go see some birds!" the ranger said.

Then our small group started out. We left the warmth of the center and headed for the viewing blind. As we trudged across the field, the sound of boots crunching the frozen corn husks echoed in the dark. I was cold but also very curious.

Soon the first rays of sunlight pierced the horizon, and the fields and river came alive. Thousands of sandhill cranes began

Expert Model PDF Online

OBJECTIVES

CCSS Orient the reader by establishing a situation and introducing a narrator and/or characters; organize an event sequence that unfolds naturally. **W.4.3a**

ACADEMIC LANGUAGE

personal narrative, first person, purpose, audience, topic, sequence

Read Like a Writer

Point out that all people have special events and experiences in their lives that they want to remember or share with others. When you write about these personal experiences, you are using a form of writing known as a personal narrative. Read and discuss the features of a personal narrative.

Provide copies of the Expert Model "Birds and More Birds" and the features of a Personal Narrative found online in the Writer's Workspace.

Features of a Personal Narrative

→ It tells a true story from the writer's life.

→ It uses *I* and *me* and is told from the first-person point of view.

→ It expresses the writer's thoughts and feelings.

→ It develops the experience with narrative techniques such as dialogue and description.

→ It begins with an interesting lead and gives a sense of closure at the end.

Discuss the Expert Model

Use the questions below to prompt discussion of the features of personal narratives.

→ Who tells the story? (The words *I* and *my* show that the writer tells her own story.)

→ What personal feelings does the writer express about this experience? (At first, she wondered why she was there. By the end she will never forget the experience.)

→ What descriptive details does the writer provide? (the sounds of the bird calls, flapping of wings, light at dawn, very cold)

→ How does the writer begin her story? (She describes how cold she was and sets the scene for the reader.)

Go Digital

Writer's Workspace

PREWRITE

Discuss and Plan

Purpose Discuss with students the purpose for writing a personal narrative. They can share thoughts and feelings about an experience that really happened to them. Personal narratives can also entertain the reader.

Audience Have students think about who will read their personal narratives, such as friends, family members, and classmates. Ask: *What do you want your readers to remember about your story?*

Teach the Minilesson

Sequence of Events Explain that writers often tell the events in a story in the order they happened. This sequence of events helps readers understand what happened and why. Words and phrases such as *earlier, later, first,* and *last* can help establish the order of events.

Distribute copies of the Model Sequence Chart found online in the Writer's Workspace. Point out that the events in Sarah's personal narrative unfold naturally, as they really happened. She organizes the events in order by telling what happened first, next, and last.

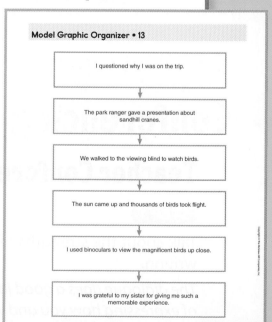

Your Turn

Choose Your Topic Have students work in pairs or small groups to brainstorm experiences in which they learned something new and interesting. Remind them to focus on a single event. Ask questions to prompt thinking. Have students record their topics in their Writer's Notebooks.

→ What interesting places have you visited?

→ What are some challenging or interesting experiences you have had?

→ Why was this experience interesting to you? How did you feel about it?

→ What happened first? What happened next? How did it end?

Plan Provide copies of the blank Sequence Chart found online in Writer's Workspace. Ask students to put the important events in order, or sequence. The beginning should set the scene and tell readers what they need to know to understand the experience.

ENGLISH LANGUAGE LEARNERS

Beginning

Demonstrate Comprehension Have students draw pictures of the events from their personal narrative.

Intermediate

Explain Have partners make a written list of the details described in the sample personal narrative.

Advanced/High

Expand Have partners write simple sentences responding to the questions about the sample personal narrative.

MODEL SEQUENCE CHART

Model Graphic Organizer • 13

I questioned why I was on the trip.

↓

The park ranger gave a presentation about sandhill cranes.

↓

We walked to the viewing blind to watch birds.

↓

The sun came up and thousands of birds took flight.

↓

I used binoculars to view the magnificent birds up close.

↓

I was grateful to my sister for giving me such a memorable experience.

NARRATIVE TEXT Personal Narrative

DRAFT

OBJECTIVES

CCSS Use dialogue and description to develop experiences and events or show the responses of characters to situations. **W.4.3b**

CCSS Use a variety of transitional words and phrases to manage the sequence of events. **W.4.3c**

ACADEMIC LANGUAGE

draft, dialogue, conclusion, revise, peer review, sequence words

Discuss the Student Model

Review the features of personal narratives. Provide copies of the Student Model found online in Writer's Workspace.

Teach the Minilesson

Dialogue To make their narratives more interesting, writers often use dialogue. Explain that dialogue can help advance the story the writer is telling. It also reveals the thoughts and feelings of someone in the narrative.

Discuss with students how the following dialogue reveals the characters' thoughts and feelings.

> "But she's my best friend!" cried Megan.
>
> "Not after she told *everyone* what happened to you," remarked Carey.
>
> "I am so embarrassed. How could she do this to me?" Megan moaned.

Invite students to share dialogue from stories they have read.

Your Turn

Write a Draft Have students review the Sequence Charts they prepared in Prewrite. Remind them to use dialogue.

Go Digital

Writer's Workspace

Conferencing Routines

Teacher Conferences

STEP 1

Talk about the strengths of the writing.

The dialogue does a good job of expressing how you and your friend felt about the experience.

STEP 2

Focus on how a writer uses a writing trait.

The sequence words you used help me understand what happened and when.

STEP 3

Make concrete suggestions for revision.

Your lead would be more interesting if you added more details to tell what it was like to be in such a strange place.

REVISE

Discuss the Revised Model

Distribute copies of the Revised Student Model found online in Writer's Workspace. Read the model aloud and have students note the revisions that Jason made. Use the specific revisions to show how adding details, reviewing word choice, and combining sentences to improve flow all help to make the personal narrative more engaging.

Teach the Minilesson

Transitions Remind students that readers need to be able to easily follow the sequence of events in a narrative. Writers can use transitional words and phrases to help readers recognize sequence. Explain that transitional words such as *first, next, finally,* and *suddenly* can help readers identify shifts in time. These kinds of transitions are also called sequence words.

Have students find an example of a revision in the Revised Student Model that shows where the writer added a sequence word. Discuss how this revision helps manage the sequence of events in the narrative.

Your Turn

COLLABORATE

Revise Have students use the peer review routine and questions to review their partners' drafts. Then have students select suggestions from the peer review to incorporate into their revisions. Provide the Revise and Edit Checklist from Writer's Workspace to guide them as they revise.

REVISED STUDENT MODEL

Revised Student Model • Personal Narrative • 16

Stomping in the Swamp
by Jason C.

Our trip to the swamp was like going to a different world. On the bus, the air-conditioning was quiet. It made the air so cold. But after we got off the bus. Sounds of birds and bugs filled the humid air. Sweat poured down my face and trickled down my back. It was one of the hotest days of the year and there was no breeze at all in the swamp.

I'm not looking forward to this hike, my friend Charles complained.

"I am!" I replied. "This is going to be the most exiting field trip ever!"

"We'll see. Right now that cool bus is very appealing," sighed Charles.

We met the park ranger just past the parking lot at the head of the trail. He told us that the thick, green leaves and muddy water around us hid storks, turtles, and otters. He explained that we needed to stay on the trail so that we did not disturb the habitat of any of these animals.

I wanted to see as many animals as I could, but I was really looking forward to seeing an alligator. I had my camera ready to snap a shot of this reptile.

The ranger leads us along the path. At first it was very dark. After a while, our eyes got used to the dim light. When we crossed over a creaky wood bridge, we saw some beavers swim

Peer Conferences

Review with students the routine for peer review of writing: Listen carefully as the writer reads his or her work aloud. Begin by telling what you liked about the writing. Then ask a question that will help the writer think more about the writing. Finally, make a suggestion that will make the writing stronger.

Use these questions for peer review.

- ☑ Does the writing have a lead that captures your attention?
- ☑ Is there a strong conclusion?
- ☑ Are events told in the order they happened?
- ☑ Are descriptive details included to help you picture events?

NARRATIVE TEXT Personal Narrative

PROOFREAD/EDIT AND PUBLISH

EDITED STUDENT MODEL

Edited Student Model • Personal Narrative • 17

Stomping in the Swamp
by Jason C.

¶Our trip to the swamp was like going to a different world. On the bus, the air-conditioning was quiet. It made the air so cold. But after we got off the bus, sounds of birds and bugs filled the humid air. Sweat poured down my face and trickled down my back. It was one of the hottest days of the year and there was no breeze at all in the swamp.

"I'm not looking forward to this hike," my friend Charles complained.

"I am!" I replied. "This is going to be the most exciting field trip ever!"

"We'll see. Right now that cool bus is very appealing," sighed Charles.

We met the park ranger just past the parking lot at the head of the trail. He told us that the thick, green leaves and muddy water around us hid storks, turtles, and otters. He explained that we needed to stay on the trail so that we did not disturb the habitat of any of these animals.

I wanted to see as many animals as I could, but I was really looking forward to seeing an alligator. I had my camera ready to snap a shot of this prehistoric-looking reptile.

The ranger lead us along the path. At first it was very dark. After a while, our eyes got used to the dim light. When we crossed over a creaky wood bridge, we saw some beavers swim

Discuss the Edited Model

Provide copies of the Edited Student Model found online in the Writer's Workspace. Read the model aloud and have students note the editing changes that Jason made. Use the specific edits to show how editing for complete sentences, spelling, verb tenses, punctuation, and subject-verb agreement improves the personal narrative.

Your Turn

Edit Have students use the edit questions on the Revise and Edit Checklist to guide them as they review and edit their drafts on their own. Remind them to read for one type of error at a time.

Publish

For the final presentation of their personal narratives, have students choose a format for publishing. Students may want to consider:

Print Publishing	Digital Publishing
Personal Book	Writer's Workspace
Journal Entry	Class Blog
Collaborative Class Book	Class Zine

Whether students handwrite or use a word-processing program, they should be sure to use standard margins and format their final drafts so that it is easy for readers to follow the flow of the text. Make sure students demonstrate sufficient keyboarding skills to type at least a page of their narrative in a single sitting.

Explain to students that adding visual and multimedia elements can strengthen their writing and presentation, making them more engaging for their readers and audience. Allow time for students to design and include illustrations, photos, maps, videos, audio, and other visual or multimedia elements that will enhance their personal narratives. Encourage students to collaborate and help each other with multimedia additions.

Go Digital

Writer's Workspace

EVALUATE

Discuss Rubrics

Guide students as they use the Student Rubric found online in Writer's Workspace. Help them understand that using a rubric helps them identify and focus on areas that might need further work. Work with the class to review the bulleted points on the rubric.

→ **Focus and Coherence** Does the personal narrative tell about an important event in the writer's life in an interesting way?

→ **Organization** Are events told in an order that makes sense? Is there a beginning, middle, and end?

→ **Ideas and Support** Are ideas developed carefully so readers understand the importance of the event?

→ **Word Choice** Are descriptive details used? Do sequence words show the order of events? Is the dialogue realistic?

→ **Voice/Sentence Fluency** Does the writing sound like a real person wrote it? Does it include a variety of sentence types?

→ **Conventions** Are errors in grammar, spelling, punctuation, and capitalization corrected?

Writing Rubric • 19

	Personal Narrative Rubric
4 Excellent	• gives a lively, interesting, and detailed description of a personal experience • uses sequence words to tell events in the order they happened • the strong beginning tells when and where the story happened • uses rich descriptive details • realistic dialogue adds to the story • has a strong personal message • has a variety of sentences that flow • is free or almost free of all errors
3 Good	• tells about a personal experience with details • uses some sequence words and presents events in the correct order • the beginning gives some details about when and where the story happened • a few descriptive details • includes some dialogue • makes an effort to share a personal message • has a variety or sentences • has a few errors but is easy to read
2 Fair	• tries to describe a personal experience but lacks details • does not use sequence words and tells some events out of order • the beginning does not provide enough detail to understand the story • very few descriptive details • dialogue is distracting and doesn't seem real • show little personal involvement • sentences are all the same • frequent errors make it hard to understand

Your Turn

Reflect and Set Goals After students have evaluated their own personal narratives, tell them to reflect on their progress as writers. Encourage them to consider areas where they feel they have shown improvement, and to think about what areas need further improvement. Have them set writing goals to prepare for their conference with the teacher.

Conference with Students

Use the Rubric and the Anchor Papers provided online in Writer's Workspace as you evaluate student writing. The anchor papers provide samples of papers that score from 1 to 4. These papers reflect the criteria described in the Rubric. Anchor papers offer a standard against which to judge writing.

Review with individual students the writing goals they have set. Discuss ways to achieve these goals and suggest any further areas of improvement students may need to target.

READING Extended Complex Text

Close Reading Routine

Read the Text *What does the author tell us?*

Assign the Reading

Depending on the needs of your students, you can

→ ask students to read the text silently

→ read the text together with students

→ read the text aloud

Take Notes

Students generate questions and take notes about aspects of the text that might be confusing for them. Encourage students to note

→ difficult vocabulary words or phrases

→ details that are not clear

→ information that they do not understand

Students complete a graphic organizer to take notes on important information from the text.

Reread the Text *What does the text mean?*

Ask Text-Dependent Questions/Generate Questions

Students reread and discuss and take notes on important shorter passages from the text. Students should

→ generate questions about the text

→ work with partners or small groups to answer questions using text evidence

Write About the Text *Think about what the author wrote.*

Students write a response to the text, using evidence from the text to support their ideas or arguments.

Use the Literature Anthology

Getting Ready

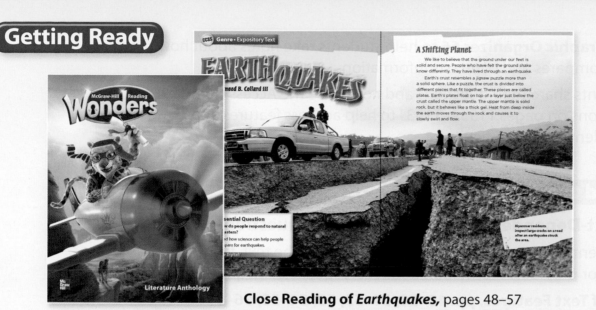

Close Reading of *Earthquakes*, pages 48–57

Use the suggestions in the chart to assign reading of the text and to chunk the text into shorter passages for rereading.

ESSENTIAL QUESTION *How do people respond to natural disasters?*

COLLABORATE

Ask students to discuss what they have learned about the different ways in which people respond to natural disasters.

Suggested Pacing

Days 1–2	**Read** pp. 48–53 pp. 54–57
Days 3–7	**Reread** pp. 48–50 pp. 51–52 p. 53 pp. 54–55 pp. 56–57
Days 8–10	**Write About the Text**

Read the Text   *What does the author tell us?*

Assign the Reading

Ask students to read the text independently. You may want to read pages 48–53 together with students due to the domain-specific vocabulary used in the text.

Take Notes

As students read, ask them to generate questions and other notes on features of the text they find difficult to understand. For this selection, students may note:

→ information and details that are unclear

→ words they do not know

→ lack of knowledge about the content

Model for students how to take notes.

Think Aloud I don't understand some of the words, such as *plates* and *upper mantle*. The photograph doesn't help me picture what the author is describing in the text. I wonder what these words mean.

> p. 49
> Earth's plates?
> Upper mantle?

Assign **Graphic Organizer 66** to help students take notes about how the author compares and contrasts information.

As students share their questions and notes, use the Access Complex Text suggestions on pages T153A–T153J to help address features about the text that students found difficult.

Reread the Text   *What does the text mean?*

Ask Text-Dependent Questions/Generate Questions

Ask students to reread the shorter passages from the text, focusing on **how** the author provides information about earthquakes. Ask questions about

→ **Use of Text Features, pp. 48–50, 51–52, 53, 54–55, 56–57**

→ How is information provided in visual features such as photographs, captions, and diagrams?

→ How does the information support the main text?

→ **Text Structure, pp. 48–50, 51–52, 53, 54–55, 56–57**

→ How does the author organize information?

→ **Firsthand and Secondhand Accounts, pp. 51–52**

→ What is the impact of using firsthand accounts? How is it different than the impact of using secondhand accounts?

→ **Word Choice, pp. 54–55**

→ When does the author use figurative language? Why does he do that?

Use the prompts on Teacher Edition pages T153A–T153J for suggested text-dependent questions. Remind students that they are to look back into the text to cite evidence to support their answers.

Model citing text evidence as needed.

Why is the way a city is built important if an earthquake happens?

Think Aloud   On page 56, I read that many countries have special building laws that require buildings to be strong and flexible. This keeps the buildings from collapsing during an earthquake. The author explains that many people were killed in the 2010 Haiti earthquake because of collapsing buildings.

As they reread each section, students should continue to generate their own questions about the text. As each student shares a question, ask all students to go back into the text to find text evidence to answer the question. Encourage students to

→ point out the exact place within the text they found evidence

→ reread and paraphrase the section of the text that they think supports their answer

→ discuss how well the cited evidence answers the question

→ identify when an answer to a question cannot be found in the text

Write About the Text   *Think about what the author wrote.*

Essential Question

Have students respond in writing to the Essential Question using evidence from the text.

How do people respond to natural disasters?

Students should use their notes and graphic organizers to cite evidence from the text to support their answer.

Model how to use notes to respond to the Essential Question:

Think Aloud The notes I took while reading pages 56 and 57 can help me answer the question. I noted that cities in many countries have laws that require buildings to be strong and flexible so they won't collapse during an earthquake. I can include that fact in my writing. I also took notes about what people can do to stay safe during an earthquake. Knowing what to do ahead of time helps people respond correctly during a natural disaster, so I can include some of this information as well. I'll look through the rest of my notes to find more text evidence to support my answer.

Students can work with a partner and use their notes and graphic organizer to locate evidence that can be used to answer the question. Encourage students to discuss the strength of the evidence cited and give arguments about what may be strong or weak about a particular citation.

READING Extended Complex Text

Use Your Own Text

Classroom Library

Classroom Library lessons available online.

or Choose from your own Trade Books

The Skirt
Genre Realistic Fiction

Lexile 540
TextEvaluator™ 27

The Accidental Hero
Genre Fiction

Lexile 780
TextEvaluator™ 50

America's Champion Swimmer: Gertrude Ederle
Genre Biography

Lexile 580
TextEvaluator™ 38

Happy Birthday, Martin Luther King
Genre Biography

Lexile 800
TextEvaluator™ 9

→ Use this model with a text of your own choice. Go online for title-specific classroom library book lessons.

→ Assign reading of the text. You may wish to do this by section or chapters.

→ Chunk the text into shorter important passages for rereading.

→ Present an Essential Question. You may want to use the Unit Big Idea.

Read the Text *What does the author tell us?*

Assign the Reading

Ask students to read the assigned sections of the text independently. For sections that are more difficult for students, you may wish to read the text aloud or ask students to read with a partner.

Take Notes

As students read, ask them to take notes on difficult parts of the text. Model how to take notes on

→ identifying details or parts that are unclear

→ words they do not know

→ information they feel is important

→ ways in which information or events are connected

→ the genre of the text

You may wish to have students complete a graphic organizer, chosen from within the unit, to take notes on important information as they read. The graphic organizer can help them summarize the text.

Help students access the complex features of the text. Scaffold instruction on the following features as necessary:

- → Purpose
- → Genre
- → Specific Vocabulary
- → Sentence Structure

- → Connection of Ideas
- → Organization
- → Prior Knowledge

Reread the Text *What does the text mean?*

Ask Text-Dependent Questions/Generate Questions

 Ask students to reread the shorter passages from the text, focusing on how the author provides information or develops the characters, setting, and plot. Focus questions on the following:

Literature Selections	**Informational Text**
Character, Setting, and Plot Development	Main Idea and Supporting Key Details
Word Choice	Word Choice
Genre	Text Structure
Point of View	Text Features
	Genre

Have students discuss questions they generated. As each student shares a question, ask all students to go back into the text to find text evidence to answer the question. Encourage students to

- → point out the exact place within the text they found the evidence
- → reread and paraphrase the section of the text that they think supports their answer
- → discuss how well the cited evidence answers the question
- → identify when an answer to a question cannot be found in the text

Write About the Text *Think about what the author wrote.*

Essential Question

Have students respond in writing to the Essential Question, considering the complete text. Students can work with a partner and use their notes and graphic organizers to locate evidence that can be used to answer the question.

 **SCOPE & SEQUENCE**

READING PROCESS	K	1	2	3	4	5	6
Concepts About Print/Print Awareness							
Recognize own name							
Understand directionality (top to bottom; tracking print from left to right; return sweep, page by page)	✔						
Locate printed word on page	✔						
Develop print awareness (concept of letter, word, sentence)	✔						
Identify separate sounds in a spoken sentence	✔						
Understand that written words are represented in written language by a specific sequence of letters	✔						
Distinguish between letters, words, and sentences	✔						
Identify and distinguish paragraphs							
Match print to speech (one-to-one correspondence)	✔						
Name uppercase and lowercase letters	✔						
Understand book handling (holding a book right-side-up, turning its pages)	✔						
Identify parts of a book (front cover, back cover, title page, table of contents); recognize that parts of a book contain information	✔						
Phonological Awareness							
Recognize and understand alliteration							
Segment sentences into correct number of words							
Identify, blend, segment syllables in words		✔					
Recognize and generate rhyming words	✔	✔					
Identify, blend, segment onset and rime	✔	✔					
Phonemic Awareness							
Count phonemes	✔	✔					
Isolate initial, medial, and final sounds	✔	✔					
Blend spoken phonemes to form words	✔	✔					
Segment spoken words into phonemes	✔	✔					
Distinguish between long- and short-vowel sounds	✔	✔					
Manipulate phonemes (addition, deletion, substitution)	✔	✔					
Phonics and Decoding /Word Recognition							
Understand the alphabetic principle	✔	✔					
Sound/letter correspondence	✔	✔	✔	✔			
Blend sounds into words, including VC, CVC, CVCe, CVVC words	✔	✔	✔	✔			
Blend common word families	✔	✔	✔	✔			

KEY	✔ = Assessed Skill
	Tinted panels show skills, strategies, and other teaching opportunities.

	K	1	2	3	4	5	6
Initial consonant blends		✔	✔	✔			
Final consonant blends		✔	✔	✔			
Initial and medial short vowels	✔	✔	✔	✔	✔	✔	✔
Decode one-syllable words in isolation and in context	✔	✔	✔	✔			
Decode multisyllabic words in isolation and in context using common syllabication patterns		✔	✔	✔	✔	✔	✔
Distinguish between similarly spelled words	✔	✔	✔	✔	✔	✔	✔
Monitor accuracy of decoding							
Identify and read common high-frequency words, irregularly spelled words	✔	✔	✔	✔			
Identify and read compound words, contractions		✔	✔	✔	✔	✔	✔
Use knowledge of spelling patterns to identify syllables		✔	✔	✔	✔	✔	✔
Regular and irregular plurals	✔	✔	✔	✔	✔	✔	✔
Long vowels (silent *e*, vowel teams)	✔	✔	✔	✔	✔	✔	✔
Vowel digraphs (variant vowels)		✔	✔	✔	✔	✔	✔
r-Controlled vowels		✔	✔	✔	✔	✔	✔
Hard/soft consonants		✔	✔	✔	✔	✔	✔
Initial consonant digraphs		✔	✔	✔	✔	✔	
Medial and final consonant digraphs		✔	✔	✔	✔	✔	
Vowel diphthongs		✔	✔	✔	✔	✔	✔
Identify and distinguish letter-sounds (initial, medial, final)	✔	✔	✔				
Silent letters		✔	✔	✔	✔	✔	✔
Schwa words				✔	✔	✔	✔
Inflectional endings		✔	✔	✔	✔	✔	✔
Triple-consonant clusters		✔	✔	✔	✔	✔	
Unfamiliar and complex word families				✔	✔	✔	✔
Structural Analysis/Word Analysis							
Common spelling patterns (word families)		✔	✔	✔	✔	✔	✔
Common syllable patterns		✔	✔	✔	✔	✔	✔
Inflectional endings		✔	✔	✔	✔	✔	✔
Contractions		✔	✔	✔	✔	✔	✔
Compound words		✔	✔	✔	✔	✔	✔
Prefixes and suffixes		✔	✔	✔	✔	✔	✔
Root or base words			✔	✔	✔	✔	✔
Comparatives and superlatives			✔	✔	✔	✔	✔
Greek and Latin roots			✔	✔	✔	✔	✔
Fluency							
Apply letter/sound knowledge to decode phonetically regular words accurately	✔	✔	✔	✔	✔	✔	✔
Recognize high-frequency and familiar words	✔	✔	✔	✔	✔	✔	✔
Read regularly on independent and instructional levels							
Read orally with fluency from familiar texts (choral, echo, partner, Reader's Theater)							
Use appropriate rate, expression, intonation, and phrasing		✔	✔	✔	✔	✔	✔
Read with automaticity (accurately and effortlessly)		✔	✔	✔	✔	✔	✔
Use punctuation cues in reading		✔	✔	✔	✔	✔	✔

	K	1	2	3	4	5	6
Adjust reading rate to purpose, text difficulty, form, and style							
Repeated readings							
Timed readings		✔	✔	✔	✔	✔	✔
Read with purpose and understanding		✔	✔	✔	✔	✔	✔
Read orally with accuracy		✔	✔	✔	✔	✔	✔
Use context to confirm or self-correct word recognition		✔	✔	✔	✔	✔	✔

READING LITERATURE

Comprehension Strategies and Skills

	K	1	2	3	4	5	6
Read literature from a broad range of genres, cultures, and periods		✔	✔	✔	✔	✔	✔
Access complex text		✔	✔	✔	✔	✔	✔
Build background							
Preview and predict							
Establish and adjust purpose for reading							
Evaluate citing evidence from the text							
Ask and answer questions	✔	✔	✔	✔	✔	✔	✔
Inferences and conclusions, citing evidence from the text	✔	✔	✔	✔	✔	✔	✔
Monitor/adjust comprehension including reread, reading rate, paraphrase							
Recount/Retell	✔	✔					
Summarize			✔	✔	✔	✔	✔
Story structure (beginning, middle, end)	✔	✔	✔	✔	✔	✔	✔
Visualize							
Make connections between and across texts		✔	✔	✔	✔	✔	✔
Point of view		✔	✔	✔	✔	✔	✔
Author's purpose							
Cause and effect	✔	✔	✔	✔	✔	✔	✔
Compare and contrast (including character, setting, plot, topics)	✔	✔	✔	✔	✔	✔	✔
Classify and categorize		✔	✔				
Literature vs informational text	✔	✔	✔				
Illustrations, using	✔	✔	✔	✔			
Theme, central message, moral, lesson		✔	✔	✔	✔	✔	✔
Predictions, making/confirming	✔	✔	✔				
Problem and solution (problem/resolution)		✔	✔	✔	✔	✔	✔
Sequence of events	✔	✔	✔	✔	✔	✔	✔

Literary Elements

	K	1	2	3	4	5	6
Character	✔	✔	✔	✔	✔	✔	✔
Plot development/Events	✔	✔	✔	✔	✔	✔	✔
Setting	✔	✔	✔	✔	✔	✔	✔
Stanza				✔	✔	✔	✔
Alliteration						✔	✔
Assonance						✔	✔
Dialogue							
Foreshadowing						✔	✔

KEY	✔ = Assessed Skill
	Tinted panels show skills, strategies, and other teaching opportunities.

	K	1	2	3	4	5	6
Flashback						✔	✔
Descriptive and figurative language		✔	✔	✔	✔	✔	✔
Imagery					✔	✔	✔
Meter					✔	✔	✔
Onomatopoeia							
Repetition		✔	✔	✔	✔	✔	✔
Rhyme/rhyme schemes		✔	✔	✔	✔	✔	✔
Rhythm		✔	✔				
Sensory language							
Symbolism							

Write About Reading/Literary Response Discussions

	K	1	2	3	4	5	6
Reflect and respond to text citing text evidence		✔	✔	✔	✔	✔	✔
Connect and compare text characters, events, ideas to self, to other texts, to world							
Connect literary texts to other curriculum areas							
Identify cultural and historical elements of text							
Evaluate author's techniques, craft							
Analytical writing							
Interpret text ideas through writing, discussion, media, research							
Book report or review							
Locate, use, explain information from text features		✔	✔	✔	✔	✔	✔
Organize information to show understanding of main idea through charts, mapping							
Cite text evidence	✔	✔	✔	✔	✔	✔	✔
Author's purpose/ Illustrator's purpose							

READING INFORMATIONAL TEXT

Comprehension Strategies and Skills

	K	1	2	3	4	5	6
Read informational text from a broad range of topics and cultures	✔	✔	✔	✔	✔	✔	✔
Access complex text		✔	✔	✔	✔	✔	✔
Build background							
Preview and predict	✔	✔	✔				
Establish and adjust purpose for reading							
Evaluate citing evidence from the text							
Ask and answer questions	✔	✔	✔	✔	✔	✔	✔
Inferences and conclusions, citing evidence from the text	✔	✔	✔	✔	✔	✔	✔
Monitor and adjust comprehension including reread, adjust reading rate, paraphrase							
Recount/Retell	✔	✔					
Summarize				✔	✔	✔	✔
Text structure	✔	✔	✔	✔	✔	✔	✔
Identify text features		✔	✔	✔	✔	✔	✔
Make connections between and across texts	✔	✔	✔	✔	✔	✔	✔
Author's point of view					✔	✔	✔
Author's purpose		✔	✔				
Cause and effect	✔	✔	✔	✔	✔	✔	✔

	K	1	2	3	4	5	6
Compare and contrast	✔	✔	✔	✔	✔	✔	✔
Classify and categorize		✔	✔				
Illustrations and photographs, using	✔	✔	✔	✔			
Instructions/directions (written and oral)		✔	✔	✔	✔	✔	✔
Main idea and key details	✔	✔	✔	✔	✔	✔	✔
Persuasion, reasons and evidence to support points/persuasive techniques						✔	✔
Predictions, making/confirming	✔	✔					
Problem and solution		✔	✔	✔	✔	✔	✔
Sequence, chronological order of events, time order, steps in a process	✔	✔	✔	✔	✔	✔	✔
Writing About Reading/Expository Critique Discussions							
Reflect and respond to text citing text evidence		✔	✔	✔	✔	✔	✔
Connect and compare text characters, events, ideas to self, to other texts, to world							
Connect texts to other curriculum areas							
Identify cultural and historical elements of text							
Evaluate author's techniques, craft							
Analytical writing							
Read to understand and perform tasks and activities							
Interpret text ideas through writing, discussion, media, research							
Locate, use, explain information from text features		✔	✔	✔	✔	✔	✔
Organize information to show understanding of main idea through charts, mapping							
Cite text evidence		✔	✔	✔	✔	✔	✔
Author's purpose/Illustrator's purpose							
Text Features							
Recognize and identify text and organizational features of nonfiction texts		✔	✔	✔	✔	✔	✔
Captions and labels, headings, subheadings, endnotes, key words, bold print	✔	✔	✔	✔	✔	✔	✔
Graphics, including photographs, illustrations, maps, charts, diagrams, graphs, time lines	✔	✔	✔	✔	✔	✔	✔
Self-Selected Reading/Independent Reading							
Use personal criteria to choose own reading including favorite authors, genres, recommendations from others; set up a reading log							
Read a range of literature and informational text for tasks as well as for enjoyment; participate in literature circles							
Produce evidence of reading by retelling, summarizing, or paraphrasing							
Media Literacy							
Summarize the message or content from media message, citing text evidence							
Use graphics, illustrations to analyze and interpret information	✔	✔	✔	✔	✔	✔	✔
Identify structural features of popular media and use the features to obtain information, including digital sources				✔	✔	✔	✔
Identify reasons and evidence in visuals and media message							
Analyze media source: recognize effects of media in one's mood and emotion							
Make informed judgments about print and digital media							
Critique persuasive techniques							

KEY ✔ = Assessed Skill
Tinted panels show skills, strategies, and other teaching opportunities.

WRITING	K	1	2	3	4	5	6
Writing Process							
Plan/prewrite							
Draft							
Revise							
Edit/proofread							
Publish and present including using technology							
Teacher and peer feedback							
Writing Traits							
Conventions		✔	✔	✔	✔	✔	✔
Ideas		✔	✔	✔	✔	✔	✔
Organization		✔	✔	✔	✔	✔	✔
Sentence fluency		✔	✔	✔	✔	✔	✔
Voice		✔	✔	✔	✔	✔	✔
Word choice		✔	✔	✔	✔	✔	✔
Writer's Craft							
Good topic, focus on and develop topic, topic sentence			✔	✔	✔	✔	✔
Paragraph(s); sentence structure			✔	✔	✔	✔	✔
Main idea and supporting key details			✔	✔	✔	✔	✔
Unimportant details							
Relevant supporting evidence			✔	✔	✔	✔	✔
Strong opening, strong conclusion			✔	✔	✔	✔	✔
Beginning, middle, end; sequence		✔	✔	✔	✔	✔	✔
Precise words, strong words, vary words			✔	✔	✔	✔	✔
Figurative and sensory language, descriptive details							
Informal/formal language							
Mood/style/tone							
Dialogue				✔	✔	✔	✔
Transition words, transitions to multiple paragraphs				✔	✔	✔	✔
Select focus and organization			✔	✔	✔	✔	✔
Points and counterpoints/Opposing claims and counterarguments							
Use reference materials (online and print dictionary, thesaurus, encyclopedia)							
Writing Applications							
Writing about text	✔	✔	✔	✔	✔	✔	✔
Personal and fictional narrative (also biographical and autobiographical)	✔	✔	✔	✔	✔	✔	✔
Variety of expressive forms including poetry	✔	✔	✔	✔	✔	✔	✔
Informative/explanatory texts	✔	✔	✔	✔	✔	✔	✔
Description	✔	✔	✔	✔			
Procedural texts			✔	✔	✔	✔	✔
Opinion pieces or arguments	✔	✔	✔	✔	✔	✔	✔
Communications including technical documents			✔	✔	✔	✔	✔
Research report	✔	✔	✔	✔	✔	✔	✔
Responses to literature/reflection				✔	✔	✔	✔

	K	1	2	3	4	5	6
Analytical writing							
Letters		✔	✔	✔	✔	✔	✔
Write daily and over short and extended time frames; set up writer's notebooks							
Penmanship/Handwriting							
Write legibly in manuscript using correct formation, directionality, and spacing							
Write legibly in cursive using correct formation, directionality, and spacing							

SPEAKING AND LISTENING

Speaking	K	1	2	3	4	5	6
Use repetition, rhyme, and rhythm in oral texts							
Participate in classroom activities and discussions							
Collaborative conversation with peers and adults in small and large groups using formal English when appropriate							
Differentiate between formal and informal English							
Follow agreed upon rules for discussion							
Build on others' talk in conversation, adding new ideas							
Come to discussion prepared							
Describe familiar people, places, and things and add drawings as desired							
Paraphrase portions of text read alone or information presented							
Apply comprehension strategies and skills in speaking activities							
Use literal and nonliteral meanings							
Ask and answer questions about text read aloud and about media							
Stay on topic when speaking							
Use language appropriate to situation, purpose, and audience							
Use nonverbal communications such as eye contact, gestures, and props							
Use verbal communication in effective ways and improve expression in conventional language							
Retell a story, presentation, or spoken message by summarizing							
Oral presentations: focus, organizational structure, audience, purpose							
Give and follow directions							
Consider audience when speaking or preparing a presentation							
Recite poems, rhymes, songs							
Use complete, coherent sentences							
Organize presentations							
Deliver presentations (narrative, summaries, research, persuasive); add visuals							
Speak audibly (accuracy, expression, volume, pitch, rate, phrasing, modulation, enunciation)							
Create audio recordings of poems, stories, presentations							
Listening							
Identify musical elements in language							
Determine the purpose for listening							
Understand, follow, restate, and give oral directions							
Develop oral language and concepts							
Listen openly, responsively, attentively, and critically							

KEY	✔ = Assessed Skill
	Tinted panels show skills, strategies, and other teaching opportunities.

	K	1	2	3	4	5	6
Listen to identify the points a speaker makes							
Listen responsively to oral presentations (determine main idea and key details)							
Ask and answer relevant questions (for clarification to follow-up on ideas)							
Identify reasons and evidence presented by speaker							
Recall and interpret speakers' verbal/nonverbal messages, purposes, perspectives							

LANGUAGE

Vocabulary Acquisition and Use

	K	1	2	3	4	5	6
Develop oral vocabulary and choose words for effect							
Use academic language		✔	✔	✔	✔	✔	✔
Identify persons, places, things, actions		✔	✔	✔			
Classify, sort, and categorize words	✔	✔	✔	✔	✔	✔	✔
Determine or clarify the meaning of unknown words; use word walls		✔	✔	✔	✔	✔	✔
Synonyms, antonyms, and opposites		✔	✔	✔	✔	✔	✔
Use context clues such as word, sentence, paragraph, definition, example, restatement, description, comparison, cause and effect		✔	✔	✔	✔	✔	✔
Use word identification strategies		✔	✔	✔	✔	✔	✔
Unfamiliar words		✔	✔	✔	✔	✔	✔
Multiple-meaning words		✔	✔	✔	✔	✔	✔
Use print and online dictionary to locate meanings, pronunciation, derivatives, parts of speech		✔	✔	✔	✔	✔	✔
Compound words		✔	✔	✔	✔	✔	✔
Words ending in -er and -est		✔	✔	✔	✔	✔	
Root words (base words)		✔	✔	✔	✔	✔	✔
Prefixes and suffixes		✔	✔	✔	✔	✔	✔
Greek and Latin affixes and roots			✔	✔	✔	✔	✔
Denotation and connotation					✔	✔	✔
Word families		✔	✔	✔	✔	✔	✔
Inflectional endings		✔	✔	✔	✔	✔	✔
Use a print and online thesaurus			✔	✔	✔	✔	✔
Use print and online reference sources for word meaning (dictionary, glossaries)		✔	✔	✔	✔	✔	✔
Homographs				✔	✔	✔	✔
Homophones			✔	✔	✔	✔	✔
Contractions		✔	✔	✔			
Figurative language such as metaphors, similes, personification			✔	✔	✔	✔	✔
Idioms, adages, proverbs, literal and nonliteral language			✔	✔	✔	✔	✔
Analogies							
Listen to, read, discuss familiar and unfamiliar challenging text							
Identify real-life connections between words and their use							
Use acquired words and phrases to convey precise ideas							
Use vocabulary to express spatial and temporal relationships							
Identify shades of meaning in related words	✔	✔	✔	✔	✔	✔	✔
Word origins					✔	✔	✔	✔
Morphology				✔	✔	✔	✔

	K	1	2	3	4	5	6
Knowledge of Language							
Choose words, phrases, and sentences for effect							
Choose punctuation effectively							
Formal and informal language for style and tone including dialects							
Conventions of Standard English/Grammar, Mechanics, and Usage							
Sentence concepts: statements, questions, exclamations, commands		✔	✔	✔	✔	✔	✔
Complete and incomplete sentences; sentence fragments; word order		✔	✔	✔	✔	✔	✔
Compound sentences, complex sentences				✔	✔	✔	✔
Combining sentences			✔	✔	✔	✔	✔
Nouns including common, proper, singular, plural, irregular plurals, possessives, abstract, concrete, collective		✔	✔	✔	✔	✔	✔
Verbs including action, helping, linking, irregular		✔	✔	✔	✔	✔	✔
Verb tenses including past, present, future, perfect, and progressive		✔	✔	✔	✔	✔	✔
Pronouns including possessive, subject and object, pronoun-verb agreement, indefinite, intensive, reciprocal; correct unclear pronouns		✔	✔	✔	✔	✔	✔
Adjectives including articles, demonstrative, proper, adjectives that compare		✔	✔	✔	✔	✔	✔
Adverbs including telling how, when, where, comparative, superlative, irregular		✔	✔	✔	✔	✔	✔
Subject, predicate; subject-verb agreement		✔	✔	✔	✔	✔	
Contractions		✔	✔	✔	✔	✔	
Conjunctions				✔	✔	✔	✔
Commas			✔	✔	✔	✔	✔
Colons, semicolons, dashes, hyphens						✔	✔
Question words							
Quotation marks			✔	✔	✔	✔	✔
Prepositions and prepositional phrases, appositives		✔	✔	✔	✔	✔	✔
Independent and dependent clauses						✔	✔
Italics/underlining for emphasis and titles							
Negatives, correcting double negatives					✔	✔	✔
Abbreviations			✔	✔	✔	✔	✔
Use correct capitalization in sentences, proper nouns, titles, abbreviations		✔	✔	✔	✔	✔	✔
Use correct punctuation		✔	✔	✔	✔	✔	✔
Antecedents				✔	✔	✔	✔
Homophones and words often confused			✔	✔	✔	✔	✔
Apostrophes				✔	✔	✔	✔
Spelling							
Write irregular, high-frequency words	✔	✔	✔				
ABC order	✔	✔					
Write letters	✔	✔					
Words with short vowels	✔	✔	✔	✔	✔	✔	✔
Words with long vowels	✔	✔	✔	✔	✔	✔	✔
Words with digraphs, blends, consonant clusters, double consonants		✔	✔	✔	✔	✔	
Words with vowel digraphs and ambiguous vowels			✔	✔	✔	✔	✔
Words with diphthongs		✔	✔	✔	✔	✔	✔

KEY	✔ = Assessed Skill Tinted panels show skills, strategies, and other teaching opportunities.

	K	1	2	3	4	5	6
Words with r-controlled vowels		✔	✔	✔	✔	✔	✔
Use conventional spelling		✔	✔	✔	✔	✔	✔
Schwa words				✔	✔	✔	✔
Words with silent letters				✔	✔	✔	✔
Words with hard and soft letters				✔	✔	✔	✔
Inflectional endings including plural, past tense, drop final e and double consonant when adding -ed and -ing, changing y to i		✔	✔	✔	✔	✔	✔
Compound words		✔	✔	✔	✔	✔	✔
Homonyms/homophones			✔	✔	✔	✔	✔
Prefixes and suffixes		✔	✔	✔	✔	✔	✔
Root and base words (also spell derivatives)				✔	✔	✔	✔
Syllables: patterns, rules, accented, stressed, closed, open				✔	✔	✔	✔
Words with Greek and Latin roots						✔	✔
Words from mythology						✔	✔
Words with spelling patterns, word families		✔	✔	✔	✔	✔	✔

RESEARCH AND INQUIRY

Study Skills

	K	1	2	3	4	5	6
Directions: read, write, give, follow (includes technical directions)			✔	✔	✔	✔	✔
Evaluate directions for sequence and completeness				✔	✔	✔	✔
Use library/media center							
Use parts of a book to locate information							
Interpret information from graphic aids		✔	✔	✔	✔	✔	✔
Use graphic organizers to organize information and comprehend text		✔	✔	✔	✔	✔	✔
Use functional, everyday documents				✔	✔	✔	✔
Apply study strategies: skimming and scanning, note-taking, outlining							

Research Process

	K	1	2	3	4	5	6
Generate and revise topics and questions for research				✔	✔	✔	✔
Narrow focus of research, set research goals				✔	✔	✔	✔
Find and locate information using print and digital resources		✔	✔	✔	✔	✔	✔
Record information systematically (note-taking, outlining, using technology)				✔	✔	✔	✔
Develop a systematic research plan				✔	✔	✔	✔
Evaluate reliability, credibility, usefulness of sources and information						✔	✔
Use primary sources to obtain information					✔	✔	✔
Organize, synthesize, evaluate, and draw conclusions from information							
Cite and list sources of information (record basic bibliographic data)					✔	✔	✔
Demonstrate basic keyboarding skills							
Participate in and present shared research							

Technology

	K	1	2	3	4	5	6
Use computer, Internet, and other technology resources to access information							
Use text and organizational features of electronic resources such as search engines, keywords, e-mail, hyperlinks, URLs, Web pages, databases, graphics							
Use digital tools to present and publish in a variety of media formats							

INDEX

A

B

C

F

G

H

Haiku, 2: T268–T269, T274–T275

Higher-level thinking. *See* Comprehension skills; Comprehension strategies; Text connections.

Historical fiction. *See under* Genre: fiction.

Homographs. *See* Vocabulary: homographs.

Homophones. *See* Phonics/Word Study: homophones.

Hyperbole, 5: T86–T87, T89E

I

Idioms. *See under* Vocabulary: figurative language.

Illustrations/photographs, using, 1: T25B, T89D, T153B, T217B, 217C, T217Q, **2:** T25B, T25F, T25L, T89G, T153B, T153D, T153L, T153M, T153N, T153Q, T217B, **3:** T23, T25B, T25N, T89B, T153B, **4:** T86–T87, T89B, T153B, T153C, T153F, T209, T217B, **5:** T25B, T89B, T153B, T153C, T153N, **6:** T89B, T153A, T153B, T153J, T217B

Illustrators and photographers,

Alarcão, Renato, **2:** T89Q

Andrews, Benny, **3:** T153S

Auch, Herm, **1:** T25Q

Auch, Mary Jane, **1:** T25Q

Bishop, Nic, **2:** T217Q

Carpenter, Nancy, **5:** T89Q

Drummond, Allan, **6:** T153S

Erwin, Steve, **1:** T217Q

Gallagher, S. Saelig, **5:** T25Q

Garth, Williams, **3:** T25Q

Minor, Wendell, **2:** T153Q

Nelson, Kadir, **3:** T217U

Parra, John, **3:** T89M

Pinkney, Jerry, **4:** T153Q

Rodanas, Kristina, **6:** T89O

Schanzer, Rosalyn, **5:** T153Q

Spector, Joel, **6:** T25M

Smith, Elwood, **4:** T25M

Teague, Mark, **4:** T89U

Whatley, Bruce, **2:** T25O

Imagery, 6: T278–T279, T281B, T281C

Independent reading. *See* Reading independently.

Inferences, drawing, 1: S12–S14, S25, T25F, T153H, **2:** T25F, T25I, T153E, T153L, T217H, **3:** T25C, T25E, T25I, T25N, T153N, T217H, **4:** T25I, T25K, T89L, T217E, **5:** T25D, T25G, T25J, T89O, T153D, T153J, T217H, T217M, **6:** T25F, T89K

Inflectional endings. *See* Spelling: inflectional endings.

Information and Media Literacy. *See* Computer Literacy; Informational text; Media Literacy; Research and Inquiry; Technology.

Informational text. *See* Genre: informational text.

Integrate knowledge and ideas, 1: S35, T28–T29, T92–T93, T156–T157, T220–T221, T284–T285, **2:** T28–T29, T92–T93, T156–T157, T220–T221, T284–T285, **3:** T28–T29, T92–T93, T156–T157, T220–T221, T284–T285, **4:** T28–T29, T92–T93, T156–T157, T220–T221, T284–T285, **5:** T28–T29, T92–T93, T156–T157, T220–T221, T284–T285, **6:** T28–T29, T92–T93, T156–T157, T220–T221, T284–T285

Internet. *See* Computer Literacy.

Interview, 1: S35, T28, **3:** T28, **4:** T183, **6:** T284

J

Journal writing. *See* Writer's Notebooks.

K

Key details. *See* Comprehension Skills: Main idea and key details.

L

Language arts, 1: T30–T39, T94–T103, T158–T167, T222–T231, T286–T295, **2:** T30–T39, T94–T103, T158–T167, T222–T231, T286–T295, **3:** T30–T39, T94–T103, T158–T167, T222–T231, T286–T295, **4:** T30–T39, T94–T103, T158–T167, T222–T231, T286–T295, **5:** T30–T39, T94–T103, T158–T167, T222–T231, T286–T295, **6:** T30–T39, T94–T103, T158–T167, T222–T231, T286–T295

Latin roots. *See under* Vocabulary: base words/root words.

Legend. *See under* Genre: fiction.

Lesson Plans, 1: T6–T7, T70–T71, T134–T135, T198–T199, T262–T263, T324–T325, **2:** T6–T7, T70–T71, T134–T135, T198–T199, T262–T263, T324–T325, **3:** T6–T7, T70–T71, T134–T135, T198–T199, T262–T263, T324–T325, **4:** T6–T7, T70–T71, T134–T135, T198–T199, T262–T263, T324–T325, **5:** T6–T7, T70–T71, T134–T135, T198–T199, T262–T263, T324–T325, **6:** T6–T7, T70–T71, T134–T135, T198–T199, T262–T263, T324–T325

Letters,

expository, **5:** T344–T349

friendly, **1:** T344–T349

Level Up, 1: T41, T49, T59, T105, T113, T123, T169, T177, T187, T233, T241, T251, T297, T305, T315, T336–T339, **2:** T41, T49, T59, T105, T113, T123, T169, T177, T187, T233, T241, T251, T297, T305, T315, T336–T339, **3:** T41, T49, T59, T105, T113, T123, T169, T177, T187, T233, T241, T251, T297, T305, T315, T336–T339, **4:** T41, T49, T59, T105, T113, T123, T169, T177, T187, T233, T241, T251, T297, T305, T315, T336–T339, **5:** T41, T49, T59, T105, T113, T123, T169, T177, T187, T233, T241, T251, T297, T305, T315, T336–T339, **6:** T41, T49, T59, T105, T113, T123, T169, T177, T187, T233, T241, T251, T297, T305, T315, T336–T339

Leveled Reader Lessons. *See under* Approaching Level Options; Beyond Level Options; English Language Learners; On Level Options.

Library or media center, using. *See under* Study skills. *See also* Theme projects.

Listening,

develop skills in speaking/listening, **1:** S6, S20, T28, T92, T138, T156, T204–T205, T220, T268–T269, T284, **2:** T28, T92, T138, T156, T204–T205, T220, T268–T269, T284, **3:** T28, T92, T138, T156, T204–T205, T220, T268–T269, T284, **4:** T28, T92, T138, T156, T204–T205, T220, T268–T269, T284, **5:** T28, T92, T138, T156, T204–T205, T220, T268–T269, T284, **6:** T28, T92, T138, T156, T204–T205, T220, T268–T269, T284

for a purpose, **1:** T12–T13, T76–T77, T140–T141, T204–T205, T268–T269, **2:** T12–T13, T76–T77, T140–T141, T204–T205, T268–T269, **3:** T12–T13, T76–T77, T140–T141, T204–T205, T268–T269, **4:** T12–T13, T76–T77, T140–T141, T204–T205, T268–T269, **5:** T12–T13, T76–T77, T140–T141, T204–T205, T268–T269, **6:** T12–T13, T76–T77, T140–T141, T204–T205, T268–T269

M

N

O

Q

genre, **1:** S11–S12, T12, T22–T23, T25J, T25S, T40, T41, T48, T49, T52, T53, T59, T76, T86–T87, T89A, T89D, T104, T112, T116, T122, T233, T241, T245, T251, **2:** T12, T22–T23, T25C, T25E, T25Q, T28, T40, T41, T48, T49, T52, T53, T59, T76, T81–T83, T86–T87, T89C, T89I, T104, T105, T112, T113, T116, T117, T122, T123, T217S, T233, T241, T245, T251, T268, T274–T275, T281A, T281C, T297, T305, T309, T315, **3:** T12, T22–T23, T25D, T40, T41, T48, T49, T52, T53, T58, T59, T76, T86–T87, T89A, T89D, T89E, T104, T112, T116, T120, **4:** T76, T81, T86–T87, T89D, T104, T111, T112, T115, T116, T119, T120–T121, T122, T140, T150–T151, T153A, T153F, T168, T169, T176, T177, T180, T181, T187, T217Q, T233, T241, T245, T251, T268, T274–T275, T279, T296, T297, T304, T305, T308, T309, T314, T315, **5:** T12, T22–T23, T25M, T40–T41, T48–T49, T52–T53, T56–T57, T58–T59, T76, T80–T81, T86–T87, T89A, T89L, T89M, T104–T105, T112–T113, T116–T117, T120–T121, T122–T123, T217U, T217V, T233, T241, T245, T251, **6:** T12–T13, T22–T23, T25A, T25G–T25H, T40–T41, T48–T49, T52–T53, T58–T59, T76, T86–T87, T89L, T104, T112, T116, T120, T153U, T169, T177, T181, T187, T233, T241, T245, T251, T268, T274–T275, T281B

character, **2:** T28, T89

plot, **2:** T28, T89V

setting, **2:** T28

theme, **2:** T20–T21, T29, T47, T51, T55, T59, T93

integrate ideas. *See also* Integrate knowledge and ideas.

characters, **2:** T217S, **3:** T40, T52, T58, **6:** T76, T104, T110, T111, T112, T113, T115, T116, T119

key details, **2:** T89C, T110, T111, T115, T119, **4:** T89G, T89V, T153J, T276–T277, T302, T303, T307, T310, T311, T313, **5:** T210, **6:** T89P, T110–T111, T115, T119, T121, T276–T277, T281C, T303, T307, T311, T313

narrator, **3:** T20–T21, T25E, T25G, T25K, T40–T41, T47, T51, T52, T55–T56, T58, T84–T85, T89C, T89G, T89J, T95, T104, T110–T111, T115, T119

point of view, **3:** T20–T21, T25C, T25E, T25G, T25K, T29, T40–T41, T47, T48, T49, T51, T52–T53, T55, T56–T59, T84–T85, T89B, T89C, T89G, T89J, T89N, T93, T104, T110–T11, T112–T113, T115–T116, T119, T120–T121

point of view, **1:** S13–S14, **4:** T84–T85, T89C, T89E, T89H, T89I, T89K, T89N, T89O, T89R, T89U, T93, T104–T105, T110, T111, T112–T113, T115, T116–T119, T120–T123, T148–T149, T153A–T153R, T157, T168, T169, T174, T175, T176, T177, T179, T180, T181, T183, T186, T187

character, **4:** T140, T148–T149, T150, T151, T153B, T153R, T174, T175, T179, T180

first person, **1:** S13–S14, T89C, T89K, **2:** T276, T302, T303, **3:** T20–T21, T40, T55, T84–T85, T89C, T89G, T89J, **4:** T84–T85, T89C, T89I, T89K, T89N, T89U, T148, T153C, T153I, T153M, T153R, T174, T175, T176, T179, T183, T186, **6:** T89O

narrator, **4:** T84–T85, T89C

third person, **1:** S13–S14, T89K, T89M, **2:** T276, T296, T302, T303, T304, T308, T314, **3:** T20–T21, T25C, T25G, T25K, T47, T48, T51, T52, T55, T57, T58, T84–T85, T104, T111, T115, T116, T122, **4:** T84–T85, T89H, T89O, T89R, T89U, T148–T149, T153C, T153I, T153M, T153R, T168, T174, T175, T176, T179, T180, T183, **5:** T105, T113, T117, **6:** T25F

theme, **1:** S13–S14, **2:** T111, T115, T119, **4:** T276–T277, T281A–T281D, T297, T302, T303, T305, T307, T308, T309, T310, T311, T313, T315, **6:** T20–T21, T25D, T25H, T25L, T29, T46–T47, T51, T52–T53, T55, T56–T59, T80–T81, T84–T85, T89A–T89P, T93, T104–T105, T110–T111, T112–T113, T115, T116, T117, T118, T119, T121, T123, T276–T277, T281A–T281D, T281E, T285, T297, T302, T303, T304, T307, T311, T313

Reading rate. *See* Fluency: rate.

Realistic fiction. *See under* Genre: fiction.

Reference and Research. *See* Computer Literacy; Research and Inquiry; Study skills; Text features; Theme projects; Vocabulary.

Reference materials,

dictionary, **1:** S27, T216, T230–T231, **2:** T24, T38–T39, **3:** T166–T167, **4:** T24, T280, T284, T295

glossary, **1:** S27, **5:** T88, T89, T101, T103, T125, **6:** T214, T216

thesaurus, **1:** S16, T24, T38–T39, T102–T103, T295 **2:** T166–T167, **3:** T152, T167, T230, **4:** T38, T152, T167, T231

Repetition, 4: T270, T278–T279, T297, T305, T309, T313, T315

Reread for comprehension, 1: T21, T46, T83, T119, T140–T141, T144–T145,

T146–T147, T149, T153A–T153L, T175, T179, T183, T204–T205, T208, T210–T211, T213, T217A–T217T, T239, T243, T247, T249, T268–T269, T272, T274–T275, T303, T307, T311, **2:** T16, T19, T21, T25, T80, T82–T83, T85, T89C, T89G, T89N, T89P, T111, T144, T147, T149, T175, T211, T213, T270, T272, T275, T277, T281, **3:** T19, T21, T25C, T25J, T25M, T80, T83, T85, T87, T89F, T89I, T89L, T89P, T89R, T140–T141, T144–T145, T146–T147, T149, T153A–T153T, T175, T179, T183, T185, T204–T205, T208, T210–T211, T213, T217A–T217V, T239, T243, T247, T268–T269, T272, T274–T275, T281A–T281D, T303, T307, T311, **4:** T16, T19, T21, T23, T25H, T25K, T25P, T80, T85, T89H–T89I, T89K, T89M, T89S, T89X, T210–T211, T213, T217E, **5:** T16, T19, T21, T25E, T25F, T25I, T25T, T59, T80, T83, T85, T89F, T89O, T89T, T144, T147, T149, T153D, T153G, T153O, T153T, T175, T179, T183, T208, **6:** T12–T13, T16, T18–T19, T21, T25C, T25I–T25K, T46, T47, T51, T55, T57, T76–T77, T80, T82–T83, T85, T89A–T89P, T89R, T111, T115, T119, T121, T144, T146–T147, T149, T153V, T208, T268–T269, T272, T275

Research and Inquiry, 1: S35, T28, T92, T156, T220, T284, T330–T333, **2:** T28, T92, T156, T181, T220, T245, T284, T330–T333, **3:** T28, T92, T156, T181, T183, T220, T245, T284, T330–T333, **4:** T28, T92, T156, T182, T220, T284, T330–T333, **5:** T28, T92, T156, T220, T245, T247, T284, T309, T330–T333, **6:** T28, T92, T153T, T156, T182, T183, T220, T284, T330–T333

citing and recording sources, **1:** T156, T220, T284, **2:** T28, T92, T220, T284, **3:** T28, T92, T156, T284, T330, **4:** T28, T220, **5:** T156, T220, T284, T330, **6:** T156, T220

creating presentation, **1:** T28, T92, T156, T220, T284, T331, **2:** T28, T92, T156, T220, T284, T331, **3:** T28, T92, T156, T220, T284, T331, **4:** T28, T92, T156, T220, T284, T331, **5:** T28, T92, T156, T220, T284, T331, **6:** T28, T92, T156, T220, T284, T331

evaluating sources, **1:** T92, T156, T220, **2:** T28, T92, T156, T220, T284, T330, T332, **3:** T28, T92, T156, T332, **4:** T28, T92, T220, T284, T332, **5:** T28, T330, T332, T352, **6:** T28, T156, T220, T330, T332

finding information, **1:** T28, T92, T156, T220, T284, T332, **2:** T28, T92, T156, T220, T284, T330, **3:** T28, T92, T156, T220, T284, T332, **4:** T28, T92, T220, T284, T332, **5:** T28, T92, T156, T220, T284, T330, T332, **6:** T28, T92, T156, T220, T332

S

T108, T125, T172, T189, T236, T253, T300, T317, **3:** T44, T61, T108, T125, T172, T189, T236, T253, T300, T317, **4:** T44, T61, T108, T125, T172, T189, T236, T253, T300, T317, **5:** T44, T61, T108, T125, T172, T236, T253, T300, T317, **6:** T44, T61, T108, T172, T189, T236, T253, T300, T317

homographs, **5:** T88, T89J, T89R, T103, T109, T112, T114, T118, T121, T122, T125, T217B, **6:** T38

multiple-meaning words, **1:** T152–T153, T153E, T153L, T185, T189, **2:** T38, **4:** T229, **5:** T118, T153K, T217B

posttest, **1:** T37, T101, T165, T229, T293, **6:** T293

prefixes,

number, **6:** T27, T43

pronunciation and meaning,
   1: T153G, T217T, **2:** T24, T25B, T39, T216, T217C, T282, **3:** T24, T217K, **4:** T229, T238, T299, **5:** T103, T155, **6:** T26, T90, T106–T107, T125, T216, T282

related words, **1:** T10, T38–T39, T102–T103, T138, T166–T167, T295, **2:** T74, T102–T103, T166–T167, T230–T231, T237, T294–T295, **3:** T10, T38–T39, T45, T102, T103, T166–T167, T202, T230–T231, **4:** T10, T38–T39, T45, T102–T103, T166–T167, T230–T231, T266, T294–T295, **5:** T38–T39, T102–T103, T166–T167, T230–T231, **6:** T38–T39, T102–T103, T166–T167, T230–T231

review, **1:** T39, T50, T103, T114, T167, T178, T231, T242, T295, T306, **2:** T39, T44, T50, T54, T60, T103, T108, T114, T118, T124, T167, T172, T178, T182, T188, T231, T236, T242, T246, T252, T295, T300, T306, T310, T316, **3:** T39, T44, T50, T54, T60, T103, T108, T114, T118, T124, T167, T172, T178, T182, T188, T231, T236, T242, T246, T252, T295, T300, T306, T310, T316, **4:** T39, T44, T50, T54, T60, T103, T108, T114, T118, T124, T167, T172, T178, T182, T188, T231, T236, T242, T246, T252, T295, T300, T306, T310, T316, **5:** T39, T44, T50, T54, T60, T103, T108, T114, T118, T124, T167, T172, T178, T182, T188, T231, T236, T242, T246, T252, T295, T300, T306, T310, T316, **6:** T39, T44, T50, T54, T60, T103, T108, T114, T118, T124, T167, T172, T178, T182, T188, T231, T236, T242, T246, T252, T295, T300, T306, T310, T316

strategies, **1:** T103, T152, T153G, T217S, T280–T281, T281A, **2:** T152, T231, T249, T280–T281, **3:** T152, T217L, T217V, T280–T281,

4: T89S, T152–T153, T216–T217, T280–T281, T281C, T281D, **5:** T103, T216–T217, T280–T281, **6:** T89G, T89P, T103, T152–T153, T280–T281,

synonyms, **1:** S15, S16, T24–T25, T25R, T38–T39, T48, T102–T103, T165, T167, T231, T295, **2:** T14–T15, T79, T89R, T101, T103, T142–T143, T167, T189, T229, T231, T252, T271, T295, T316 **3:** T39, T45, T60, T103, T143, T152–T153, T153H, T153T, T166–T167, T173, T178, T180, T182, T185, T188, T189, T206–T207, T230–T231, T252, T281F, T295, **4:** T39, T45, T60, T103, T143, T152–T153, T153K, T153R, T167, T173, T178, T180, T182, T185, T187, T189, T229, T231, T252, T270–T271, T294–T295, **5:** T37, T39, T45, T101, T102–T103, T124, T167, T188, T207, T217N, T231, T252, T295, **6:** T38–T39, T78–T79, T103, T109, T165, T167, T217E, T231, T252, T271, T295, T316

unfamiliar words, **1:** S28, T24–T25, T39, T153G, T216, T217S, T231, T280, T281A, T306, **2:** T25A, T39, T45, T61, T103, T118, T125, T152–T153, T153I, T153O, T167, T237, T242, T246, T253, **3:** T38–T39, T54, T88, T125, T152, T166–T167, T173, T189, T216, T217K, T217M, T231, T237, T249, T253, T280, T281C, T281E, T295, T301, T306, **4:** T18, T24–T25, T25G, T39, T45, T61, T152, T167, T173, T178, T214–T217, T231, T237–T238, T253, T310, **5:** T25U, T152, T153I, T155, T167, T173, T216, T231, T281E, **6:** T12, T25C, T152, T153K, T153W, T167, T217E, T217M

vocabulary words, **1:** T14–T15, T38–T39, T102–T103, T142, T166–T167, T230–T231, T294–T295, **2:** T14–T15, T38–T39, T102–T103, T142–T143, T166–T167, T230–T231, T294–T295, **3:** T14–T15, T38–T39, T102–T103, T142–T143, T166–T167, T230–T231, T294–T295, **4:** T14–T15, T38–T39, T102–T103, T142–T143, T166–T167, T230–T231, T294–T295, **5:** T14–T15, T38–T39, T44, T102–T103, T142–T143, T230–T231, T294–T295, **6:** T14–T15, T38–T39, T102–T103, T142–T143, T166–T167, T230–T231, T294–T295.

See also **Approaching Level Options: vocabulary; Beyond Level Options: vocabulary; On Level Options: vocabulary; Vocabulary: content.**

word parts, **1:** T281A, **2:** T42, T106, T170, T216, T217R, T218, T237, T282, T292–T293, T298–T299, T318, **3:** T250, T253, T281C–T281D,

4: T25G, T154, T170, **5:** T170, T298, **6:** T42, T107, T170, T282, T298

word squares, **1:** T39, T103, T167, T231, T295, **2:** T39, T103, T167, T231, T295, **3:** T39, T103, T167, T231, T295, **4:** T39, T103, T167, T231, T295, **5:** T39, T103, T167, T231, T295, **6:** T39, T103, T167, T231, T295

word webs, **1:** T39, T167, T231, T252, T289, **2:** T103, T231

W

Word study. *See* Phonics/Word Study.

Write About Reading, 1: S36, T20, T25R, T25T, T25U, T29, T41, T49, T53, T59, T89L, T89N–T89O, T93, T105, T113, T117, T123, T148, T153L, T157, T169, T177, T181, T187, T212, T217R, T217U, T221, T233, T241, T245, T251, T276, T285, T297, T305, T309, T315, **2:** T20, T25P, T29, T41, T49, T53, T59, T84, T89R, T89U, T93, T105, T113, T117, T123, T148, T153R, T153U, T157, T169, T177, T181, T187, T212, T217R, T276, T281D, T285, T297, T305, T309, T315, **3:** T20, T25R, T29, T41, T49, T53, T59, T84, T89N, T89Q, T93, T105, T113, T117, T123, T148, T153T, T153V, T153W, T157, T177, T181, T187, T212, T217V, T221, T233, T241, T245, T251, T276, T285, T297, T305, T309, T315, **4:** T20, T25N, T25Q, T29, T41, T49, T53, T59, T84, T89V, T89X, T89Y, T93, T105, T113, T117, T123, T148, T153R, T153U, T157, T169, T177, T181, T187, T212, T217P, T217R, T217S, T221, T233, T245, T251, T276, T281D, T285, T297, T305, T309, T315, **5:** T20, T25R, T29, T41, T49, T53, T59, T84, T89R, T89T, T89U, T93, T105, T113, T117, T123, T148, T153R, T153T, T153U, T157, T169, T177, T181, T187, T212, T217T, T217W, T221, T233, T241, T245, T251, T276, T285, T297, T305, T309, T315, **6:** T20, T25N, T25P, T25Q, T29, T41, T49, T53, T59, T84, T89P, T89R, T89S, T93, T105, T113, T117, T123, T148, T153T, T153V, T153W, T157, T169, T177, T187, T212, T217L, T217N, T221, T233, T241, T245, T251, T276, T281D, T285, T297, T305, T309, T315

Write to Sources. *See* Write About Reading.

Writer's Craft. *See also* Writing traits.

capitalization, **2:** T29, T34, T35, T63, **6:** T99

character development, **4:** T94–T95, T96–T97

conventions, **1:** T349, T355, **2:** T349, T355, **3:** T349, T355, **4:** T349, T355, **5:** T349, T355, **6:** T349, T355

Common Core State Standards Correlations

English Language Arts

College and Career Readiness Anchor Standards for READING

The K-5 standards on the following pages define what students should understand and be able to do by the end of each grade. They correspond to the College and Career Readiness (CCR) anchor standards below by number. The CCR and grade-specific standards are necessary complements—the former providing broad standards, the latter providing additional specificity—that together define the skills and understandings that all students must demonstrate.

Key Ideas and Details

1. Read closely to determine what the text says explicitly and to make logical inferences from it; cite specific textual evidence when writing or speaking to support conclusions drawn from the text.

2. Determine central ideas or themes of a text and analyze their development; summarize the key supporting details and ideas.

3. Analyze how and why individuals, events, and ideas develop and interact over the course of a text.

Craft and Structure

4. Interpret words and phrases as they are used in a text, including determining technical, connotative, and figurative meanings, and analyze how specific word choices shape meaning or tone.

5. Analyze the structure of texts, including how specific sentences, paragraphs, and larger portions of the text (e.g., a section, chapter, scene, or stanza) relate to each other and the whole.

6. Assess how point of view or purpose shapes the content and style of a text.

Integration of Knowledge and Ideas

7. Integrate and evaluate content presented in diverse media and formats, including visually and quantitatively, as well as in words.

8. Delineate and evaluate the argument and specific claims in a text, including the validity of the reasoning as well as the relevance and sufficiency of the evidence.

9. Analyze how two or more texts address a number of similar themes or topics in order to build knowledge or to compare the approaches the authors take.

Range of Reading and Level of Text Complexity

10. Read and comprehend complex literary and informational texts independently and proficiently.

CCSS Common Core State Standards
English Language Arts
Grade 4

Each standard is coded in the following manner:

Strand	Grade Level	Standard
RL	4	1

Reading Standards for Literature

Key Ideas and Details	*McGraw-Hill Reading Wonders*
RL.4.1 Refer to details and examples in a text when explaining what the text says explicitly and when drawing inferences from the text.	**READING/WRITING WORKSHOP:** Unit 1: 26, 27, 40, 41 Unit 2: 98, 99, 112, 113 Unit 3: 170, 171, 184, 185 Unit 4: 256, 257, 270, 271 Unit 5: 314, 315, 328, 329 Unit 6: 386, 387, 400, 401 **YOUR TURN PRACTICE BOOK:** 3–4, 53–54, 103–104, 153–154, 203–204, 253–254 **READING WORKSTATION ACTIVITY CARDS:** 12 **TEACHER'S EDITION:** Unit 1: T25B, T25F, T25L, T25P, T80, T82 Unit 2: T18, T25F, T25I, T25J, T25L, T25P Unit 3: T25L, T25O, T25P, T25R, T81, T82, T89D Unit 4: T76, T80, T82, T89B, T89D, T89G, T89L, T89S Unit 5: T89B, T89H, T89K, T89O, T217V, T217W Unit 6: T18, T25F, T25K, T82, T89K, T278 www.connected.mcgraw-hill.com: **RESOURCES** **Student Resources:** Comprehension Interactive Games and Activities **Teacher Resources:** Interactive Read Aloud Images
RL.4.2 Determine a theme of a story, drama, or poem from details in the text; summarize the text.	**READING/WRITING WORKSHOP:** Unit 2: 94–97, 99, 108–111, 113 Unit 4: 294–297, 299 Unit 6: 382–385, 387, 438–441, 443 **LITERATURE ANTHOLOGY:** Unit 2: 90–105, 108–125, 172–175 Unit 4: 356–359, 360–361 Unit 6: 458–471, 534–537, 538–539 **LEVELED READERS:** Unit 2, Week 1: *The Cockroach and the Mouse* (A), *The Badger and the Fan* (O, ELL), *The Wings of the Butterfly* (B) Unit 2, Week 2: *Saving the Green Bird* (A), *The Prince Who Could Fly* (O, ELL), *Behind the Secret Trapdoor* (B) Unit 6, Week 1: *The Visit* (A), *Our Teacher, the Hero* (O, ELL), *Continuing On* (B) **YOUR TURN PRACTICE BOOK:** 53–55, 63–65, 253–255 **READING WORKSTATION ACTIVITY CARDS:** 4 **TEACHER'S EDITION:** Unit 1: T25R, T51, T76, T84, T89L Unit 2: T12, T20, T25C, T25H, T25K, T25M, T25P, T28, T46, T47, T51, T55, T76, T84, T89C, T89F, T89I, T89M, T89O, T89R, T110, T111, T115, T119 Unit 3: T12, T25R, T76 Unit 4: T76, T89Q, T276, T281B, T303, T307 Unit 5: T12, T16, T20, T25O, T25R Unit 6: T20, T25D, T25H, T276, T281C, T303, T307 www.connected.mcgraw-hill.com: **RESOURCES** **Student Resources:** Comprehension Interactive Games and Activities **Teacher Resources:** Graphic Organizers, Interactive Read Aloud Images, Skills Review

Reading Standards for Literature

Key Ideas and Details	McGraw-Hill Reading Wonders
RL.4.3 Describe in depth a character, setting, or event in a story or drama, drawing on specific details in the text (e.g., a character's thoughts, words, or actions).	**READING/WRITING WORKSHOP:** Unit 1: 22–25, 27, 36–39, 41 **Unit 5:** 310–313, 315, 324–327, 329 **LITERATURE ANTHOLOGY:** Unit 1: 10–27, 32–43 **Unit 5:** 362–379, 384–401 **LEVELED READERS:** Unit 1, Week 1: *Clever Puss* (A), *Jack and the Extreme Stalk* (O, ELL), *Charming Ella* (B) **Unit 1, Week 2:** *The Dream Team* (A), *Rosa's Garden* (O, ELL), *Saving Grasshopper* (B) **Unit 5, Week 1:** *Saving Stolen Treasure* (A), *The Perfect Present* (O, ELL), *First Edition* (B) **Unit 5, Week 2:** *The Adventures of Sal Fink* (A), *The Great Man of Nebraska* (O, ELL), *The Tale of John Henry* (B) **YOUR TURN PRACTICE BOOK:** 2–5, 13–15, 23–25, 203–205, 213–215 **READING WORKSTATION ACTIVITY CARDS:** 1, 2, 3 **TEACHER'S EDITION:** Unit 1: T12, T20, T25I, T25M, T25O, T25R, T46, T47, T51, T55, T76, T81, T84, T85, T89A, T89C, T89E, T89G, T89I, T104, T110, T111, T112, T115, T116 **Unit 2:** T28, T89D, T89H, T89J, T92 **Unit 3:** T12, T18, T82, T86 **Unit 4:** T89M, T89Q **Unit 5:** T12, T18, T20, T25C, T25F, T25G, T25H, T25I, T25J, T25K, T25N, T76, T80, T82, T84, T89C, T89F, T89G, T89H, T89I, T89K, T89N, T89O **Unit 6:** T12, T76 **www.connected.mcgraw-hill.com: RESOURCES** **Student Resources:** Comprehension Interactive Games and Activities **Teacher Resources:** Graphic Organizers, Skills Review

Craft and Structure	McGraw-Hill Reading Wonders
RL.4.4 Determine the meaning of words and phrases as they are used in a text, including those that allude to significant characters found in mythology (e.g., Herculean).	**READING/WRITING WORKSHOP:** Unit 1: 22–25 **Unit 2:** 94–97 **Unit 5:** 324–327 **READING WORKSTATION ACTIVITY CARDS:** 13 **TEACHER'S EDITION:** Unit 1: T24, T25E, T25N, T25R, T88, T89F, T120, T145 **Unit 3:** T24, T25E, T25G, T25I, T25R, T81, T88, T89E, T89N **Unit 4:** T88, T89C, T89H, T89P, T89V, T145, T217R **Unit 5:** T25U, T88, T89E, T89J, T89K, T217W **Unit 6:** T25C, T88, T89K, T154, T171 **www.connected.mcgraw-hill.com: RESOURCES** **Student Resources:** Comprehension Interactive Games and Activities, Vocabulary Interactive Games and Activities **Teacher Resources:** Graphic Organizers
RL.4.5 Explain major differences between poems, drama, and prose, and refer to the structural elements of poems (e.g., verse, rhythm, meter) and drama (e.g., casts of characters, settings, descriptions, dialogue, stage directions) when writing or speaking about a text.	**READING/WRITING WORKSHOP:** Unit 1: 42 **Unit 2:** 114, 154 **Unit 4:** 298 **Unit 6:** 442 **LITERATURE ANTHOLOGY:** Unit 2: 108–125, 172–175, 176–177 **Unit 4:** 356–359 **LEVELED READERS:** Unit 2, Week 2: *Saving the Green Bird* (A), *The Prince Who Could Fly* (O, ELL), *Behind the Secret Trapdoor* (B) **YOUR TURN PRACTICE BOOK:** 6, 16, 63–65 **READING WORKSTATION ACTIVITY CARDS:** 25, 27, 28 **TEACHER'S EDITION:** Unit 1: T25J, T25T, T86 **Unit 2:** T12, T22, T76, T81, T82, T86, T89C, T89I, T89T, T89U, T89V, T268, T274, T278, T281C **Unit 3:** T22, T25D, T86 **Unit 4:** T76, T140, T150, T274, T278, T281A, T281C, T281E **Unit 5:** T22, T76 **Unit 6:** T268, T274, T281B **www.connected.mcgraw-hill.com: RESOURCES** **Student Resources:** Comprehension Interactive Games and Activities **Teacher Resources:** Genre Study Reproducibles, Graphic Organizers
RL.4.6 Compare and contrast the point of view from which different stories are narrated, including the difference between first- and third-person narrations.	**READING/WRITING WORKSHOP:** Unit 2: 150–153, 155 **Unit 3:** 166–169, 171, 180–183, 185 **Unit 4:** 252–255, 257, 266–269, 271 **LITERATURE ANTHOLOGY:** Unit 3: 178–195, 198–211 **Unit 4:** 288–309, 314–331 **LEVELED READERS:** Unit 3, Week 1: *A New Bear in the Forest* (A), *Not From Around Here* (O, ELL), *Cara and the Sky Kingdom* (B) **Unit 3, Week 2:** *Playground Buddy* (A), *Brick by Brick* (O, ELL), *Standing Guard* (B) **Unit 4, Week 2:** *Floozle Dreams* (A), *The Wolves of Yellowstone* (O, ELL), *Krillville* (B) **Unit 4, Week 3:** *Ron's Radio* (A), *The Freedom Machine* (O, ELL), *A Better Way* (B) **YOUR TURN PRACTICE BOOK:** 103–105, 113–115, 163–165, 183–185 **READING WORKSTATION ACTIVITY CARDS:** 5 **TEACHER'S EDITION:** Unit 1: T89K **Unit 2:** T276, T281E, T281F **Unit 3:** T20, T29, T47, T51, T55, T84, T89N **Unit 4:** T84, T89O, T89R, T89U, T89V, T111, T115, T119, T148, T174, T175, T179, T183 **www.connected.mcgraw-hill.com: RESOURCES** **Student Resources:** Comprehension Interactive Games and Activities

Reading Standards for Literature

Integration of Knowledge and Ideas		*McGraw-Hill Reading Wonders*
RL.4.7	Make connections between the text of a story or drama and a visual or oral presentation of the text, identifying where each version reflects specific descriptions and directions in the text.	**YOUR TURN PRACTICE BOOK:** 6, 106, 166 **READING WORKSTATION ACTIVITY CARDS:** 14 **TEACHER'S EDITION: Unit 1:** T22, T25B, T40, T58, T89D **Unit 2:** T25B, T25G, T89G, T89Q **Unit 3:** T22, T23, T25N, T89B **Unit 4:** T86, T89B, T89F, T89U, T153B, T153C, T153F **Unit 5:** T89C, T89E **Unit 6:** T89B www.connected.mcgraw-hill.com: **RESOURCES** **Student Resources:** Comprehension Interactive Games and Activities, Music/Fine Arts Activities **Teacher Resources:** Interactive Read Aloud Images, Music/Fine Arts Activities
RL.4.8	(Not applicable to literature)	(Not applicable to literature)
RL.4.9	Compare and contrast the treatment of similar themes and topics (e.g., opposition of good and evil) and patterns of events (e.g., the quest) in stories, myths, and traditional literature from different cultures.	**LITERATURE ANTHOLOGY: Unit 4:** 352–355 **READING WORKSTATION ACTIVITY CARDS:** 15 **TEACHER'S EDITION: Unit 1:** T25T, T25V, T29, T93 **Unit 2:** T17, T20, T25R, T29, T55, T74, T89V, T93, T217S, T217T **Unit 3:** T17, T25S, T25T, T29 **Unit 4:** T93, T157, T217T **Unit 5:** T25T, T25V, T29, T93, T217X **Unit 6:** T29, T153X, T281F, T217N www.connected.mcgraw-hill.com: **RESOURCES** **Student Resources:** Comprehension Interactive Games and Activities

Range of Reading and Level of Text Complexity		*McGraw-Hill Reading Wonders*
RL.4.10	By the end of the year, read and comprehend literature, including stories, dramas, and poetry, in the grades 4–5 text complexity band proficiently, with scaffolding as needed at the high end of the range.	**READING/WRITING WORKSHOP:** These units reflect the range of text complexity found throughout the book. **Unit 2:** 108–111, 150–153 **Unit 6:** 438–441 **LITERATURE ANTHOLOGY:** These units reflect the range of text complexity found throughout the book. **Unit 2:** 90–95, 108–125, 172–175 **Unit 4:** 288–309, 314–331, 356–359 **Unit 5:** 362–367, 406–423 **Unit 6:** 534–537 **LEVELED READERS: Unit 2, Week 2:** *Saving the Green Bird* (A), *The Prince Who Could Fly* (O, ELL), *Behind the Secret Trapdoor* (B) **Unit 3, Week 1:** *A New Bear in the Forest* (A), *Not From Around Here* (O, ELL), *Cara and the Sky Kingdom* (B) **Unit 4, Week 3:** *Ron's Radio* (A), *The Freedom Machine* (O, ELL), *A Better Way* (B) **Unit 6, Week 1:** *The Visit* (A), *Our Teacher, the Hero* (O, ELL), *Continuing On* (B) **READING WORKSTATION ACTIVITY CARDS:** 22, 25, 27, 28 **TEACHER'S EDITION: Unit 1:** T22, T25A, T25S, T47, T51, T55, T86 **Unit 2:** T47, T51, T55, T86, T89A, T89S, T120, T274, T281A, T281E **Unit 3:** T51, T86, T89A, T111, T115, T119 **Unit 4:** T153A, T175, T179, T183, T217Q, T274, T281A, T281E **Unit 5:** T16, T22, T25A, T25S, T80, T86, T89A, T217U **Unit 6:** T22, T25A, T86, T89A, T153U, T217M, T274, T281A, T281E www.connected.mcgraw-hill.com: **RESOURCES** **Student Resources:** Comprehension Interactive Games and Activities

Reading Standards for Informational Text

Key Ideas and Details		McGraw-Hill Reading Wonders
RI.4.1	Refer to details and examples in a text when explaining what the text says explicitly and when drawing inferences from the text.	**READING/WRITING WORKSHOP:** Unit 1: 54, 55, 68, 69, 82, 83 **Unit 2:** 126, 127, 140, 141 **Unit 3:** 198, 199, 212, 213, 226, 227 **Unit 4:** 242, 243, 284, 285 **Unit 5:** 342, 343, 356, 357, 370, 371 **Unit 6:** 414, 415, 428, 429 **LEVELED READERS:** Unit 3, Week 3: *Jacob Riis: Champion of the Poor* (A, O, ELL, B) **YOUR TURN PRACTICE BOOK:** 123–125 **READING WORKSTATION ACTIVITY CARDS:** 12 **TEACHER'S EDITION:** Unit 1: T890, T144, T146, T153F, T153H, T153J **Unit 2:** T153R, T153U, T217H, T217R **Unit 3:** T204, T209, T212, T217H, T217V **Unit 4:** T12, T18, T25F, T25H, T25I, T25N, T25P, T25Q, T89X, T89Y **Unit 5:** T89T, T89U, T153B, T153D, T153G, T153J, T153T **Unit 6:** T153D, T153G, T153P, T217C, T217H www.connected.mcgraw-hill.com: **RESOURCES** **Student Resources:** Comprehension Interactive Games and Activities **Teacher Resources:** Interactive Read Aloud Images
RI.4.2	Determine the main idea of a text and explain how it is supported by key details; summarize the text.	**READING/WRITING WORKSHOP:** Unit 1: 78–81, 83 **Unit 2:** 122–125, 127, 136–139, 141 **Unit 6:** 396–399, 401, 410–413, 415, 424–427, 429 **LITERATURE ANTHOLOGY:** Unit 1: 84–87 **Unit 2:** 130–147, 152–169 **Unit 6:** 476–491, 496–515, 520–531 **LEVELED READERS:** Unit 2, Week 3: *Saving San Francisco Bay* (A, O, ELL, B) **Unit 2, Week 4:** *Extreme Animals* (A, O, ELL, B) **Unit 6, Week 3:** *Planet Power* (A, O, ELL, B) **Unit 6, Week 4:** *The Bike Company* (A, O, ELL, B) **YOUR TURN PRACTICE BOOK:** 73–75, 83–85, 273–275, 283–285 **READING WORKSTATION ACTIVITY CARDS:** 6 **TEACHER'S EDITION:** Unit 1: T140, T148, T153L **Unit 2:** T140, T146, T148, T153C, T153D, T153F, T153G, T153H, T153J, T153K, T153N, T153O, T153P, T208, T210, T212, T217C, T217D, T217E, T217G, T217I, T217J, T217K, T217L, T217N, T217M, T217O **Unit 3:** T140, T153R **Unit 4:** T25J, T25L **Unit 5:** T140, T144, T153E, T153J, T153K, T153R **Unit 6:** T148, T153C, T153E, T153I, T153L www.connected.mcgraw-hill.com: **RESOURCES** **Student Resources:** Comprehension Interactive Games and Activities **Teacher Resources:** Graphic Organizers, Interactive Read Aloud Images, Skills Review
RI.4.3	Explain events, procedures, ideas, or concepts in a historical, scientific, or technical text, including what happened and why, based on specific information in the text.	**READING/WRITING WORKSHOP:** Unit 4: 238–241, 243, 280–283, 285 **Unit 5:** 338–341, 343, 352–355, 357 **LITERATURE ANTHOLOGY:** Unit 4: 270–283, 336–351 **Unit 5:** 428–447 **LEVELED READERS:** Unit 4, Week 1: *A Day in the Senate* (A, O, ELL, B) **Unit 4, Week 4:** *Stargazing* (A, O, ELL, B) **Unit 5, Week 4:** *Secrets of the Ice* (A, O, ELL, B) **YOUR TURN PRACTICE BOOK:** 153–155, 183–185, 233–235 **READING WORKSTATION ACTIVITY CARDS:** 7, 8, 9, 10, 17 **TEACHER'S EDITION:** Unit 1: T217E, T217G **Unit 2:** T212, T217I, T217K **Unit 3:** T146, T153C, T210, T217C, T217K **Unit 4:** T18, T204, T212, T217E, T217F, T217G, T217H, T217J, T217K, T217L **Unit 5:** T146, T148, T153F, T153H, T153M, T153U, T210, T212, T217C, T217F, T217I, T217K, T217Q **Unit 6:** T140, T146, T210 www.connected.mcgraw-hill.com: **RESOURCES** **Student Resources:** Comprehension Interactive Games and Activities **Teacher Resources:** Graphic Organizers, Skills Review
Craft and Structure		***McGraw-Hill Reading Wonders***
RI.4.4	Determine the meaning of general academic and domain-specific words or phrases in a text relevant to a grade 4 topic or subject area.	**READING/WRITING WORKSHOP:** Unit 1: 50–53, 64–67 **Unit 2:** 122–125, 136–139 **Unit 4:** 280–283 **Unit 5:** 338–341 **Unit 6:** 410–413, 424–427 **READING WORKSTATION ACTIVITY CARDS:** 21 **TEACHER'S EDITION:** Unit 1: T152, T153E, T216, T217H, T280 **Unit 2:** T152, T153I, T153O, T216, T217N **Unit 4:** T216, T217E, T217P **Unit 5:** T152, T153G, T153I, T153K, T216, T217H, T217I **Unit 6:** T152, T153G, T153K, T217E www.connected.mcgraw-hill.com: **RESOURCES** **Student Resources:** Comprehension Interactive Games and Activities, Vocabulary Interactive Games and Activities **Teacher Resources:** Graphic Organizers

Reading Standards for Informational Text

Craft and Structure		McGraw-Hill Reading Wonders
RI.4.5	Describe the overall structure (e.g., chronology, comparison, cause/effect, problem/solution) of events, ideas, concepts, or information in a text or part of a text.	**READING/WRITING WORKSHOP:** Unit 1: 50–53, 55, 64–67, 69 **Unit 5:** 338–341, 343, 366–369, 371 **LITERATURE ANTHOLOGY:** Unit 1: 48–59, 62–79 **Unit 5:** 406–423, 452–455 **LEVELED READERS:** Unit 1, Week 3: *Changing Landscapes* (A, O, ELL, B) **Unit 1, Week 4:** *George's Giant Wheel* (A, O, ELL, B) **Unit 5, Week 3:** *The Inventive Lewis Latimer* (A, O, ELL, B) **YOUR TURN PRACTICE BOOK:** 23–25, 33–35, 223–225 **READING WORKSTATION ACTIVITY CARDS:** 7, 8, 9, 10 **TEACHER'S EDITION:** Unit 1: T148, T153C, T153G, T153I, T174, T175, T179, T183, T212, T217E, T217G, T217I, T217K, T217L, T217O **Unit 2:** T153E, T153M **Unit 3:** T153M **Unit 4:** T20, T25C, T212, T217F, T217H, T217J **Unit 5:** T148, T153F, T153H, T153M, T212, T217C, T217E, T217F, T217G, T217I, T217K, T217L, T217Q www.connected.mcgraw-hill.com: **RESOURCES** **Student Resources:** Comprehension Interactive Games and Activities **Teacher Resources:** Graphic Organizers, Skills Review
RI.4.6	Compare and contrast a firsthand and secondhand account of the same event or topic; describe the differences in focus and the information provided.	**LITERATURE ANTHOLOGY:** Unit 3: 216–235 **LEVELED READERS:** Unit 3, Week 3: *Jacob Riis: Champion of the Poor* (A, O, ELL, B) **YOUR TURN PRACTICE BOOK:** 123–125 **READING WORKSTATION ACTIVITY CARDS:** 11, 18 **TEACHER'S EDITION:** Unit 1: T153D **Unit 3:** T153V, T153W, T153X, T174, T217C, T217F, T217I, T217O, T217R www.connected.mcgraw-hill.com: **RESOURCES** **Student Resources:** Comprehension Interactive Games and Activities

Integration of Knowledge and Ideas		McGraw-Hill Reading Wonders
RI.4.7	Interpret information presented visually, orally, or quantitatively (e.g., in charts, graphs, diagrams, time lines, animations, or interactive elements on Web pages) and explain how the information contributes to an understanding of the text in which it appears.	**READING/WRITING WORKSHOP:** Unit 1: 50–53, 64–67, 78–81 **Unit 2:** 122–125, 136–139 **Unit 3:** 194–197, 208–211, 222–225 **Unit 4:** 280–283 **Unit 5:** 338–341, 352–355, 366–369 **Unit 6:** 410–413 **LITERATURE ANTHOLOGY:** Unit 1: 48–59, 84–87, 88–89 **Unit 2:** 148–151, 152–169 Unit 3: 212–215, 236–239, 264–267 **Unit 4:** 284–287, 310–313, 336 351 **Unit 5:** 402–405, 424–427, 428–447, 452–455, 456–457 **Unit 6:** 472–475, 492–495, 496–515, 520–531 **LEVELED READERS:** Unit 1, Week 3: *Changing Landscapes* (A, O, ELL, B) **Unit 4, Week 1:** *A Day in the Senate* (A, O, ELL, B) **Unit 5, Week 4:** *Secrets of the Ice* (A, O, ELL, B) **Unit 6, Week 3:** *Planet Power* (A, O, ELL, B) **YOUR TURN PRACTICE BOOK:** 23–25, 153–155, 233–235, 273–275 **READING WORKSTATION ACTIVITY CARDS:** 16, 23 **TEACHER'S EDITION:** Unit 1: T10, T74, T138, T150, T151, T153B, T328–T329 **Unit 2:** T153B, T157, T202, T214, T217B, T328–T329 **Unit 3:** T10, T74, T138, T150, T153J, T328–T329 **Unit 4:** T217B, T217D, T217M, T217O, T328–T329 **Unit 5:** T150, T153B, T153C, T153N, T153Q, T153U, T328–T329 **Unit 6:** T10, T74, T138, T153J, T217B, T266 www.connected.mcgraw-hill.com: **RESOURCES** **Student Resources:** Comprehension Interactive Games and Activities, Music/Fine Arts Activities **Teacher Resources:** Graphic Organizers, Interactive Read Aloud Images, Music/Fine Arts Activities
RI.4.8	Explain how an author uses reasons and evidence to support particular points in a text.	**READING/WRITING WORKSHOP:** Unit 3: 194–197, 199, 208–211, 213, 222–225, 227 **LITERATURE ANTHOLOGY:** Unit 3: 240–261, 264–267 **LEVELED READERS:** Unit 3, Week 4: *Nellie Bly: Reporter for the Underdog* (A, O, ELL, B) **YOUR TURN PRACTICE BOOK:** 133–135 **READING WORKSTATION ACTIVITY CARDS:** 11, 19 **TEACHER'S EDITION:** Unit 2: T153K, T153R **Unit 3:** T148, T153C, T153E, T153G, T153I, T153K, T153O, T153Q, T157, T174, T175, T179, T183, T212, T214, T217C, T217E, T217G, T217J, T217K, T217Q, T217R, T239, T243, T247 **Unit 4:** T17, T22, T208 **Unit 5:** T145, T153R www.connected.mcgraw-hill.com: **RESOURCES** **Student Resources:** Comprehension Interactive Games and Activities **Teacher Resources:** Graphic Organizers, Skills Review

Reading Standards for Informational Text

Integration of Knowledge and Ideas | *McGraw-Hill Reading Wonders*

RI.4.9 | Integrate information from two texts on the same topic in order to write or speak about the subject knowledgeably. | **READING WORKSTATION ACTIVITY CARDS:** 20
TEACHER'S EDITION: Unit 1: T89P, T105, T113, T117, T123, T153M, T153N, T157, T217V, T221 **Unit 2:** T153T, T153V, T157, T209, T221 **Unit 3:** T89P, T89R, T93, T153V, T153X, T157, T217W, T217X, T221 **Unit 4:** T25P, T25R, T29, T89X, T89Z, T153T, T153V, T221 **Unit 5:** T89T, T89V, T153T, T153V, T157, T221 **Unit 6:** T25R, T89T, T157, T221

www.connected.mcgraw-hill.com: RESOURCES
Student Resources: Comprehension Interactive Games and Activities

Range of Reading and Level of Text Complexity | *McGraw-Hill Reading Wonders*

RI.4.10 | By the end of year, read and comprehend informational texts, including history/social studies, science, and technical texts, in the grades 4–5 text complexity band proficiently, with scaffolding as needed at the high end of the range. | **READING/WRITING WORKSHOP:** These units reflect the range of text complexity found throughout the book.
Unit 1: 40–53 **Unit 2:** 136–139 **Unit 3:** 194–197 **Unit 4:** 280–283 **Unit 5:** 338–341 **Unit 6:** 410–413
LITERATURE ANTHOLOGY: These units reflect the range of text complexity found throughout the book.
Unit 1: 48–59 **Unit 2:** 152–169 **Unit 3:** 216–235 **Unit 4:** 270–283 **Unit 5:** 406–423 **Unit 6:** 520–531
LEVELED READERS: Unit 2, Week 4: *Extreme Animals* (A, O, ELL, B) **Unit 3, Week 4:** *Nellie Bly: Reporter for the Underdog* (A, O, ELL, B) **Unit 4, Week 1:** *A Day in the Senate* (A, O, ELL, B) **Unit 6, Week 4:** *The Bike Company* (A, O, ELL, B)
READING WORKSTATION ACTIVITY CARDS: 22, 26
TEACHER'S EDITION: Unit 1: T89M, T150, T153A, T153M, T214, T217A, T278, T281A, T281E **Unit 2:** T150, T153A, T153S, T175, T179, T183, T214, T217A **Unit 3:** T89O, T150, T153A, T153U, T175, T179, T214, T217A, T217W, T248, T278, T281A, T281E **Unit 4:** T22, T25A, T250, T47, T51, T55, T89W, T153S, T208, T214, T217A **Unit 5:** T153A, T153S, T208, T214, T217A, T278, T281A, T281E **Unit 6:** T250, T89Q, T150, T153A, T214, T217A

www.connected.mcgraw-hill.com: RESOURCES
Student Resources: Comprehension Interactive Games and Activities

Reading Standards: Foundational Skills

There are no standards for Print Concepts (1) or Phonological Awareness (2) in Foundational Skills for Grade 4.

Phonics and Word Recognition		McGraw-Hill Reading Wonders
RF.4.3	Know and apply grade-level phonics and word analysis skills in decoding words.	
RF.4.3a	Use combined knowledge of all letter-sound correspondences, syllabication patterns, and morphology (e.g., roots and affixes) to read accurately unfamiliar multisyllabic words in context and out of context.	**READING/WRITING WORKSHOP:** Unit 1: 85 Unit 2: 143 **YOUR TURN PRACTICE BOOK:** 8, 18, 28, 38, 47, 48, 78, 87, 88, 108, 148, 168, 198, 208, 228, 258, 268, 298 **PHONICS/WORD STUDY WORKSTATION ACTIVITY CARDS:** 5, 8, 16, 18, 23, 27, 30 **TEACHER'S EDITION:** Unit 1: T26, T27, T42, T43, T90, T91 Unit 2: T43, T90, T106, T107, T154, T155, T170, T171 Unit 3: T217L, T218, T219, T234, T235 Unit 4: T107, T154, T155, T170, T171, T218, T219 Unit 5: T27, T90, T91, T152, T153G, T154, T155, T218 Unit 6: T26, T42, T43, T90, T106, T282 www.connected.mcgraw-hill.com: **RESOURCES** **Student Resources:** Word Study Interactive Games and Activities **Teacher Resources:** Decodable Passages

Fluency		McGraw-Hill Reading Wonders
RF.4.4	Read with sufficient accuracy and fluency to support comprehension.	
RF.4.4a	Read on-level text with purpose and understanding.	**READING WORKSTATION ACTIVITY CARDS:** 2, 7, 10, 14, 18, 22, 27, 29, 30 **TEACHER'S EDITION:** Unit 1: T44, T108, T172, T236, T326–T327 Unit 2: T44, T91, T108, T172, T236, T326–T327 Unit 3: T27, T44, T108, T172, T219, T236, T326–T327 Unit 4: T27, T44, T108, T155, T172, T236, T326–T327 Unit 5: T27, T91, T326–T327 Unit 6: T26, T44, T90, T108, T326–T327 www.connected.mcgraw-hill.com: **RESOURCES** **Student Resources:** Fluency Interactive Games and Activities
RF.4.4b	Read on-level prose and poetry orally with accuracy, appropriate rate, and expression on successive readings.	**READING WORKSTATION ACTIVITY CARDS:** 3, 8, 12, 13, 15, 20, 26, 28, 29, 30 **YOUR TURN PRACTICE BOOK:** 3–5, 63–65, 133–135, 173–175, 213–215, 263–265 **TEACHER'S EDITION:** Unit 1: T27, T46, T91, T105, T110, T113, T117, T123, T219, T238, T326–T327 Unit 2: T27, T46, T91, T110, T155, T174, T219, T238, T282, T302, T326–T327 Unit 3: T27, T46, T91, T110, T155, T174, T219, T238, T326–T327 Unit 4: T27, T46, T91, T110, T155, T174, T218, T238, T282, T302, T326–T327 Unit 5: T27, T155, T219, T326–T327 Unit 6: T26, T41, T90, T282, T302, T326–T327 www.connected.mcgraw-hill.com: **RESOURCES** **Student Resources:** Fluency Interactive Games and Activities
RF.4.4c	Use context to confirm or self-correct word recognition and understanding, rereading as necessary.	**READING/WRITING WORKSHOP:** Unit 1: 29, 57, 71 Unit 2: 115, 129 Unit 3: 173, 187 Unit 4: 273, 287 Unit 5: 359 **YOUR TURN PRACTICE BOOK:** 7, 27, 37, 67, 77, 107, 117, 177, 187, 237 **READING WORKSTATION ACTIVITY CARDS:** 3, 8, 13, 18, 23, 28 **TEACHER'S EDITION:** Unit 1: T155, T174 Unit 2: T155, T174 Unit 3: T155, T174 Unit 4: T218, T238 Unit 5: T155, T174 Unit 6: T46, T218, T238 www.connected.mcgraw-hill.com: **RESOURCES** **Student Resources:** Fluency Interactive Games and Activities

CORRELATIONS

College and Career Readiness Anchor Standards for WRITING

The K-5 standards on the following pages define what students should understand and be able to do by the end of each grade. They correspond to the College and Career Readiness (CCR) anchor standards below by number. The CCR and grade-specific standards are necessary complements—the former providing broad standards, the latter providing additional specificity—that together define the skills and understandings that all students must demonstrate.

Text Types and Purposes

1. Write arguments to support claims in an analysis of substantive topics or texts, using valid reasoning and relevant and sufficient evidence.

2. Write informative/explanatory texts to examine and convey complex ideas and information clearly and accurately through the effective selection, organization, and analysis of content.

3. Write narratives to develop real or imagined experiences or events using effective techniques, well-chosen details, and well-structured event sequences.

Production and Distribution of Writing

4. Produce clear and coherent writing in which the development, organization, and style are appropriate to task, purpose, and audience.

5. Develop and strengthen writing as needed by planning, revising, editing, rewriting, or trying a new approach.

6. Use technology, including the Internet, to produce and publish writing and to interact and collaborate with others.

Research to Build and Present Knowledge

7. Conduct short as well as more sustained research projects based on focused questions, demonstrating understanding of the subject under investigation.

8. Gather relevant information from multiple print and digital sources, assess the credibility and accuracy of each source, and integrate information while avoiding plagiarism.

9. Draw evidence from literacy or informational texts to support analysis, reflection, and research.

Range of Writing

10. Write routinely over extended time frames (time for research, reflection, and revision) and shorter time frames (a single sitting or a day or two) for a range of tasks, purposes, and audiences.

CCSS Common Core State Standards
English Language Arts

Grade 4

Each standard is coded in the following manner:

Strand	Grade Level	Standard
W	4	1

Writing Standards

Text Types and Purposes	*McGraw-Hill Reading Wonders*
W.4.1	Write opinion pieces on topics or texts, supporting a point of view with reasons and information.
W.4.1a	Introduce a topic or text clearly, state an opinion, and create an organizational structure in which related ideas are grouped to support the writer's purpose.	**READING/WRITING WORKSHOP:** Unit 3: 230–231 Unit 5: 318–319 **YOUR TURN PRACTICE BOOK:** 150, 210 **WRITING WORKSTATION ACTIVITY CARDS:** 3, 7 **TEACHER'S EDITION:** Unit 3: T344, T346, T350, T352 Unit 4: T30, T32–T33 Unit 5: T30, T32, T33, T62 Unit 6: T344, T346, T350, T352 www.connected.mcgraw-hill.com: **RESOURCES** **Student Resources:** Writer's Workspace
W.4.1b	Provide reasons that are supported by facts and details.	**READING/WRITING WORKSHOP:** Unit 3: 202–203 **YOUR TURN PRACTICE BOOK:** 30, 130 **WRITING WORKSTATION ACTIVITY CARDS:** 3, 9, 23, 26 **TEACHER'S EDITION:** Unit 1: T93 Unit 2: T29, T93, T221 Unit 3: T93, T158, T160–T161, T190, T344, T352 Unit 6: T93, T344, T346, T350, T352 www.connected.mcgraw-hill.com: **RESOURCES** **Student Resources:** Writer's Workspace
W.4.1c	Link opinion and reasons using words and phrases (e.g., *for instance, in order to, in addition*).	**READING/WRITING WORKSHOP:** Unit 5: 346–347 Unit 6: 418–419 **YOUR TURN PRACTICE BOOK:** 230, 280 **WRITING WORKSTATION ACTIVITY CARDS:** 13 **TEACHER'S EDITION:** Unit 3: T350, T352 Unit 5: T93, T95, T96, T97, T158 Unit 6: T158, T160, T161, T350, T352 www.connected.mcgraw-hill.com: **RESOURCES** **Student Resources:** Writer's Workspace
W.4.1d	Provide a concluding statement or section related to the opinion presented.	**READING/WRITING WORKSHOP:** Unit 3: 216–217 **WRITING WORKSTATION ACTIVITY CARDS:** 10 **TEACHER'S EDITION:** Unit 3: T222, T224–T225, T346, T350 Unit 6: T346 www.connected.mcgraw-hill.com: **RESOURCES** **Student Resources:** Writer's Workspace
W.4.2	Write informative/explanatory texts to examine a topic and convey ideas and information clearly.
W.4.2a	Introduce a topic clearly and group related information in paragraphs and sections; include formatting (e.g., headings), illustrations, and multimedia when useful to aiding comprehension.	**READING/WRITING WORKSHOP:** Unit 2: 144–145 Unit 4: 246–247 **YOUR TURN PRACTICE BOOK:** 90, 160 **WRITING WORKSTATION ACTIVITY CARDS:** 6, 11 **TEACHER'S EDITION:** Unit 2: T157, T222, T224–T225, T346, T348, T350, T352, T354 Unit 4: T30, T32–T33, T62, T221 Unit 5: T221, T348 www.connected.mcgraw-hill.com: **RESOURCES** **Student Resources:** Writer's Workspace

Writing Standards

	Text Types and Purposes	*McGraw-Hill Reading Wonders*
W.4.2b	Develop the topic with facts, definitions, concrete details, quotations, or other information and examples related to the topic.	**READING/WRITING WORKSHOP: Unit 1:** 58–59 **Unit 2:** 130–131 **Unit 3:** 202–203 **YOUR TURN PRACTICE BOOK:** 30, 80, 160 **WRITING WORKSTATION ACTIVITY CARDS:** 6, 11 **TEACHER'S EDITION: Unit 1:** T29, T158, T160–T161, T190 **Unit 2:** T158, T161, T160, T190, T344, T352 **Unit 5:** T346 www.connected.mcgraw-hill.com: **RESOURCES** **Student Resources:** Writer's Workspace
W.4.2c	Link ideas within categories of information using words and phrases (e.g., *another, for example, also, because*).	**READING/WRITING WORKSHOP: Unit 6:** 418–419 **YOUR TURN PRACTICE BOOK:** 280 **WRITING WORKSTATION ACTIVITY CARDS:** 6, 19 **TEACHER'S EDITION: Unit 1:** T157 **Unit 2:** T344, T350 **Unit 5:** T158, T160–T161, T190, T344, T350, T352 **Unit 6:** T94, T96–T97 www.connected.mcgraw-hill.com: **RESOURCES** **Student Resources:** Writer's Workspace
W.4.2d	Use precise language and domain-specific vocabulary to inform about or explain the topic.	**READING/WRITING WORKSHOP: Unit 2:** 158–159 **Unit 6:** 390–391 **YOUR TURN PRACTICE BOOK:** 100, 260 **WRITING WORKSTATION ACTIVITY CARDS:** 1, 14, 15, 18, 27 **TEACHER'S EDITION: Unit 1:** T156 **Unit 2:** T286, T288, T346 **Unit 4:** T222, T224–T225 **Unit 5:** T222, T224–T225, T344 **Unit 6:** T222, T224–T225 www.connected.mcgraw-hill.com: **RESOURCES** **Student Resources:** Writer's Workspace
W.4.2e	Provide a concluding statement or section related to the information or explanation presented.	**READING/WRITING WORKSHOP: Unit 5:** 374–375 **YOUR TURN PRACTICE BOOK:** 250 **WRITING WORKSTATION ACTIVITY CARDS:** 10 **TEACHER'S EDITION: Unit 1:** T84, T221 **Unit 2:** T346 **Unit 3:** T222, T224–T225 **Unit 5:** T221, T286, T288–T289, T344, T346 www.connected.mcgraw-hill.com: **RESOURCES** **Student Resources:** Writer's Workspace
W.4.3	Write narratives to develop real or imagined experiences or events using effective technique, descriptive details, and clear event sequences.	
W.4.3a	Orient the reader by establishing a situation and introducing a narrator and/or characters; organize an event sequence that unfolds naturally.	**READING/WRITING WORKSHOP: Unit 2:** 102–103 **Unit 4:** 274–275 **YOUR TURN PRACTICE BOOK:** 60, 180 **WRITING WORKSTATION ACTIVITY CARDS:** 2, 5, 7, 8 **TEACHER'S EDITION: Unit 1:** T94, T222, T224–T225, T254, T344, T346, T350 **Unit 2:** T30, T32–T33, T62 **Unit 4:** T158, T160–T161, T190, T344 www.connected.mcgraw-hill.com: **RESOURCES** **Student Resources:** Writer's Workspace
W.4.3b	Use dialogue and description to develop experiences and events or show the responses of characters to situations.	**READING/WRITING WORKSHOP: Unit 1:** 30–31 **Unit 4:** 260–261 **YOUR TURN PRACTICE BOOK:** 10, 170 **WRITING WORKSTATION ACTIVITY CARDS:** 4 **TEACHER'S EDITION: Unit 1:** T94, T96–T97, T126, T352 **Unit 2:** T94, T96–T97, T126 **Unit 4:** T94, T96–T97, T126, T158, T160–T161, T344, T346 **Unit 6:** T30, T32–T33 www.connected.mcgraw-hill.com: **RESOURCES** **Student Resources:** Writer's Workspace
W.4.3c	Use a variety of transitional words and phrases to manage the sequence of events.	**READING/WRITING WORKSHOP: Unit 1:** 72–73 **Unit 3:** 174–175 **YOUR TURN PRACTICE BOOK:** 40, 110 **WRITING WORKSTATION ACTIVITY CARDS:** 19, 25 **TEACHER'S EDITION: Unit 1:** T222, T224–T225, T254, T344, T352 **Unit 3:** T30, T32–T33, T62 **Unit 4:** T344 **Unit 6:** T94, T96–97, T126 www.connected.mcgraw-hill.com: **RESOURCES** **Student Resources:** Writer's Workspace

Writing Standards

Text Types and Purposes		McGraw-Hill Reading Wonders
W.4.3d	Use concrete words and phrases and sensory details to convey experiences and events precisely.	**READING/WRITING WORKSHOP:** Unit 1: 30–31, 44–45 **Unit 3:** 188–189 **Unit 4:** 302–303 **Unit 6:** 446–447 **YOUR TURN PRACTICE BOOK:** 10, 20, 120, 200, 300 **WRITING WORKSTATION ACTIVITY CARDS:** 2, 16, 17 **TEACHER'S EDITION:** Unit 1: T30, T32–T33, T62, T346 **Unit 2:** T94, T96–T97 **Unit 3:** T94, T96–T97, T126 **Unit 4:** T222, T224–T225, T254, T286, T288–T289, T350, T352 **Unit 6:** T30, T32–T33, T286, T288–T289 www.connected.mcgraw-hill.com: **RESOURCES** **Student Resources:** Writer's Workspace
W.4.3e	Provide a conclusion that follows from the narrated experiences or events.	**READING/WRITING WORKSHOP:** Unit 3: 216–217 **YOUR TURN PRACTICE BOOK:** 140 **TEACHER'S EDITION:** Unit 1: T222, T224–T225, T346 **Unit 3:** T222, T224–T225, T254 **Unit 4:** T158, T160–T161, T344 www.connected.mcgraw-hill.com: **RESOURCES** **Student Resources:** Writer's Workspace

Production and Distribution of Writing		McGraw-Hill Reading Wonders
W.4.4	Produce clear and coherent writing in which the development and organization are appropriate to task, purpose, and audience. (Grade-specific expectations for writing types are defined in standards 1–3 above.)	**READING/WRITING WORKSHOP:** Unit 2: 116–117 **Unit 3:** 230–231 **Unit 5:** 360–361 **Unit 6:** 404–405 **YOUR TURN PRACTICE BOOK:** 70, 150, 240, 270 **WRITING WORKSTATION ACTIVITY CARDS:** 20, 21, 22 **TEACHER'S EDITION:** Unit 1: T32–T33, T96–T97, T160–T161, T224–T225 **Unit 2:** T32–T33, T96–T97, T160–T161, T224–T225, T254 **Unit 3:** T32–T33, T96–T97, T160–T161, T224–T225 **Unit 4:** T32–T33, T96–T97, T160–T161, T224–T225, T350, T352 **Unit 5:** T32–T33, T96–T97, T160–T161, T224–T225 **Unit 6:** T32–T33, T96–T97, T160–T161, T224–T225 www.connected.mcgraw-hill.com: **RESOURCES** **Student Resources:** Writer's Workspace
W.4.5	With guidance and support from peers and adults, develop and strengthen writing as needed by planning, revising, and editing.	**READING/WRITING WORKSHOP:** Unit 1: 31, 45, 59, 73, 87 **Unit 2:** 103, 117, 131, 145, 159 **Unit 3:** 175, 189, 203, 217, 231 **Unit 4:** 247, 261, 275, 289, 303 **Unit 5:** 319, 333, 347, 361, 375 **Unit 6:** 391, 405, 419, 433, 447 **TEACHER'S EDITION:** Unit 1: T32–T33, T96–T97, T160–T161, T224–T225, T344–T349, T350–T355 **Unit 2:** T32–T33, T96–T97, T160–T161, T224–T225, T344–T349 **Unit 3:** T32–T33, T96–T97, T160–T161, T220, T224–T225, T350–T355 **Unit 4:** T32–T33, T96–T97, T156, T160–T161, T224–T225, T344–T349, T350–T355 **Unit 5:** T32–T33, T96–T97, T156, T160–T161, T224–T225 **Unit 6:** T32–T33, T96–T97, T160–T161, T224–T225, T344–T349, T350–T355 www.connected.mcgraw-hill.com: **RESOURCES** **Student Resources:** Writer's Workspace
W.4.6	With some guidance and support from adults, use technology, including the Internet, to produce and publish writing as well as to interact and collaborate with others; demonstrate sufficient command of keyboarding skills to type a minimum of one page in a single sitting.	**TEACHER'S EDITION:** Unit 1: T332, T348, T354 **Unit 2:** T332, T348, T354 **Unit 3:** T156, T332, T348, T354 **Unit 4:** T156, T332, T348, T354 **Unit 5:** T156, T332, T348, T354 **Unit 6:** T156, T332, T348, T354 www.connected.mcgraw-hill.com: **RESOURCES** **Student Resources:** Writer's Workspace

Writing Standards

Research to Build and Present Knowledge		McGraw-Hill Reading Wonders
W.4.7	Conduct short research projects that build knowledge through investigation of different aspects of a topic.	**TEACHER'S EDITION:** Unit 1: T28, T92, T156, T220, T328–T329, T330–T333 Unit 2: T28, T92, T156, T220, T330–T333 Unit 3: T28, T92, T156, T220, T328–T329, T330–T333 Unit 4: T28, T92, T156, T220, T328–T329, T330–T333 Unit 5: T28, T92, T156, T220, T328–T329, T330–T333 Unit 6: T28, T92, T156, T220, T328–T329, T330–T333 www.connected.mcgraw-hill.com: **RESOURCES** **Student Resources:** Research and Inquiry, Writer's Workspace **Teacher Resources:** Graphic Organizers, Research and Inquiry
W.4.8	Recall relevant information from experiences or gather relevant information from print and digital sources; take notes and categorize information, and provide a list of sources.	**TEACHER'S EDITION:** Unit 1: T28, T92, T156, T220, T330–T333 Unit 2: T28, T92, T156, T220, T328–T329, T330–T333 Unit 3: T28, T92, T156, T220, T330–T333 Unit 4: T28, T92, T156, T220, T330–T333 Unit 5: T28, T92, T156, T220, T330–T333, T350, T352 Unit 6: T28, T92, T156, T220, T330–T333 www.connected.mcgraw-hill.com: **RESOURCES** **Student Resources:** Research and Inquiry, Writer's Workspace **Teacher Resources:** Graphic Organizers, Research and Inquiry
W.4.9	Draw evidence from literary or informational texts to support analysis, reflection, and research.	
W.4.9a	Apply *grade 4 Reading standard*s to literature (e.g., "Describe in depth a character, setting, or event in a story or drama, drawing on specific details in the text [e.g., a character's thoughts, words, or actions].").	**YOUR TURN PRACTICE BOOK:** 9, 19, 59, 69, 109, 119, 169, 179, 209, 219, 259, 269 **WRITING WORKSTATION ACTIVITY CARDS:** 26 **TEACHER'S EDITION:** Unit 1: T29, T93 Unit 2: T28, T29, T92, T93 Unit 3: T29, T93 Unit 4: T93, T157 Unit 5: T29, T93 Unit 6: T29, T93 www.connected.mcgraw-hill.com: **RESOURCES** **Student Resources:** Writer's Workspace
W.4.9b	Apply *grade 4 Reading standard*s to informational texts (e.g., "Explain how an author uses reasons and evidence to support particular points in a text").	**YOUR TURN PRACTICE BOOK:** 29, 39, 49, 79, 89, 129, 139, 159, 189, 229, 239, 249, 279, 289 **WRITING WORKSTATION ACTIVITY CARDS:** 26 **TEACHER'S EDITION:** Unit 1: T157, T221, T285 Unit 2: T157, T220, T221 Unit 3: T157, T221 Unit 4: T29, T221 Unit 5: T157, T221, T285 www.connected.mcgraw-hill.com: **RESOURCES** **Student Resources:** Writer's Workspace
Range of Writing		**McGraw-Hill Reading Wonders**
W.4.10	Write routinely over extended time frames (time for research, reflection, and revision) and shorter time frames (a single sitting or a day or two) for a range of discipline-specific tasks, purposes, and audiences.	**READING/WRITING WORKSHOP:** Unit 1: 72–73 Unit 2: 116–117 Unit 3: 216–217 Unit 4: 246–247 Unit 5: 318–319 Unit 6: 446–447 **WRITING WORKSTATION ACTIVITY CARDS:** 20, 21, 22, 23, 24, 25, 26, 27, 28, 29 **TEACHER'S EDITION:** Unit 1: T25R, T25T, T29, T30, T89N, T94, T157, T158, T222, T286, T344–T349, T350–T355 Unit 2: T25P, T29, T30, T89R, T94, T153R, T158, T222, T286, T344–T349, T350–T355 Unit 3: T25R, T30, T89N, T94, T158, T222, T344–T349, T350–T355 Unit 4: T25N, T30, T89V, T94, T153R, T158, T217P, T222, T286, T344–T349, T350–T355 Unit 5: T25R, T28, T89R, T220, T286, T344–T349, T350–T355 Unit 6: T25N, T30, T94, T153T, T158, T222, T344–T349, T350–T355 www.connected.mcgraw-hill.com: **RESOURCES** **Student Resources:** Research and Inquiry, Writer's Workspace **Teacher Resources:** Research and Inquiry

College and Career Readiness Anchor Standards for
SPEAKING AND LISTENING

The K-5 standards on the following pages define what students should understand and be able to do by the end of each grade. They correspond to the College and Career Readiness (CCR) anchor standards below by number. The CCR and grade-specific standards are necessary complements—the former providing broad standards, the latter providing additional specificity—that together define the skills and understandings that all students must demonstrate.

Comprehension and Collaboration
1. Prepare for and participate effectively in a range of conversations and collaborations with diverse partners, building on others' ideas and expressing their own clearly and persuasively.
2. Integrate and evaluate information presented in diverse media and formats, including visually, quantitatively, and orally.
3. Evaluate a speaker's point of view, reasoning, and use of evidence and rhetoric.

Presentation of Knowledge and Ideas
4. Present information, findings, and supporting evidence such that listeners can follow the line of reasoning and the organization, development, and style are appropriate to task, purpose, and audience.
5. Make strategic use of digital media and visual displays of data to express information and enhance understanding of presentations.
6. Adapt speech to a variety of contexts and communicative tasks, demonstrating command of formal English when indicated or appropriate.

CCSS Common Core State Standards
English Language Arts
Grade 4

Each standard is coded in the following manner:

Strand	Grade Level	Standard
SL	4	1

Speaking and Listening Standards

Comprehension and Collaboration	McGraw-Hill Reading Wonders
SL.4.1 Engage effectively in a range of collaborative discussions (one-on-one, in groups, and teacher-led) with diverse partners on *grade 4 topics and texts*, building on others' ideas and expressing their own clearly.	
SL.4.1a Come to discussions prepared, having read or studied required material; explicitly draw on that preparation and other information known about the topic to explore ideas under discussion.	**READING/WRITING WORKSHOP: Unit 1:** 26, 27, 40, 41, 54, 55, 68, 69, 82, 83 **Unit 2:** 98, 99, 112, 113, 126, 127, 140, 141 **Unit 3:** 170, 171, 184, 185, 198, 199, 212, 213, 226, 227 **Unit 4:** 242, 243, 256, 257, 270, 271, 284, 285 **Unit 5:** 314, 315, 328, 329, 342, 343, 356, 357, 370, 371 **Unit 6:** 386, 387, 400, 401, 414, 415, 428, 429 **READING WORKSTATION ACTIVITY CARDS:** 24 **TEACHER'S EDITION: Unit 1:** T29, T93, T157, T221, T285 **Unit 2:** T29, T93, T157, T221, T285 **Unit 3:** T22, T28, T29, T93, T157, T221 **Unit 4:** T29, T93, T157, T221 **Unit 5:** T29, T93, T157, T221, T266, T285 **Unit 6:** T29, T93, T157, T221, T285 www.connected.mcgraw-hill.com: **RESOURCES** **Teacher Resources:** Build Background Videos
SL.4.1b Follow agreed-upon rules for discussions and carry out assigned roles.	**READING WORKSTATION ACTIVITY CARDS:** 24 **TEACHER'S EDITION: Unit 1:** T10, T138 **Unit 2:** T10, T202 **Unit 3:** T10, T74, T202, T266 **Unit 4:** T10, T138, T266 **Unit 5:** T10, T138 **Unit 6:** T10, T266 www.connected.mcgraw-hill.com: **RESOURCES** **Teacher Resources:** Build Background Videos
SL.4.1c Pose and respond to specific questions to clarify or follow up on information, and make comments that contribute to the discussion and link to the remarks of others.	**READING/WRITING WORKSHOP: Unit 1:** 18–19, 32–33, 46–47, 59–60, 74–75 **Unit 2:** 90–91, 104–105, 118–119, 132–133, 146–147 **Unit 3:** 162–163, 176–177, 190–191, 204–205, 218–219 **Unit 4:** 234–235, 248–249, 262–263, 276–277 **Unit 5:** 306–307, 320–321, 334–335, 348–349, 362–363 **Unit 6:** 378–379, 392–393, 406–407, 420–421, 434–435 **READING WORKSTATION ACTIVITY CARDS:** 24 **TEACHER'S EDITION: Unit 1:** T28, T74, T92, T202, T332 **Unit 2:** T266, T332 **Unit 3:** T138, T332 **Unit 4:** T74, T138, T202, T332 **Unit 5:** T74, T332 **Unit 6:** T74, T138, T202, T332 www.connected.mcgraw-hill.com: **RESOURCES** **Student Resources:** Research and Inquiry **Teacher Resources:** Build Background Videos, Research and Inquiry
SL.4.1d Review the key ideas expressed and explain their own ideas and understanding in light of the discussion.	**READING WORKSTATION ACTIVITY CARDS:** 24 **TEACHER'S EDITION: Unit 1:** T28, T29, T93, T138, T157 **Unit 2:** T29, T74, T138, T157, T221 **Unit 3:** T29, T93, T157, T221 **Unit 4:** T29, T93, T157, T221 **Unit 5:** T29, T93, T157, T202, T221 **Unit 6:** T29, T93, T157, T221 www.connected.mcgraw-hill.com: **RESOURCES** **Teacher Resources:** Build Background Videos

Speaking and Listening Standards

Comprehension and Collaboration		*McGraw-Hill Reading Wonders*
SL.4.2	Paraphrase portions of a text read aloud or information presented in diverse media and formats, including visually, quantitatively, and orally.	**TEACHER'S EDITION:** Unit 1: T10, T12, T16, T74, T92, T104, T112, T116, T122, T140, T168, T176, T208 **Unit 2:** T10, T12, T76, T140, T202, T204 **Unit 3:** T12, T74, T76, T138, T150, T202, T204 **Unit 4:** T10, T12, T74, T76, T140, T202, T204 **Unit 5:** T10, T12, T76, T140, T150, T204 **Unit 6:** T10, T74, T138, T202 www.connected.mcgraw-hill.com: **RESOURCES** **Student Resources:** Music/Fine Arts Activities **Teacher Resources:** Interactive Read Aloud Images, Music/Fine Arts Activities
SL.4.3	Identify the reasons and evidence a speaker provides to support particular points.	**TEACHER'S EDITION:** Unit 1: T29, T93, T157, T221 **Unit 2:** T29, T93, T157, T221 **Unit 3:** T29, T93, T157, T221 **Unit 4:** T29, T93, T157, T221 **Unit 5:** T29, T93, T157, T221 **Unit 6:** T29, T93, T157, T221 www.connected.mcgraw-hill.com: **RESOURCES** **Student Resources:** Research and Inquiry **Teacher Resources:** Research and Inquiry

Presentation of Knowledge and Ideas		*McGraw-Hill Reading Wonders*
SL.4.4	Report on a topic or text, tell a story, or recount an experience in an organized manner, using appropriate facts and relevant, descriptive details to support main ideas or themes; speak clearly at an understandable pace.	**TEACHER'S EDITION:** Unit 1: T28, T29, T92, T156, T220, T284, T332, T334–T335 **Unit 2:** T28, T156, T284, T332, T334–T335 **Unit 3:** T28, T92, T221, T332, T334–T335 **Unit 4:** T28, T92, T156, T220, T332, T334–T335 **Unit 5:** T28, T92, T220, T332, T334–T335 **Unit 6:** T28, T156, T220, T284, T332, T334–T335 www.connected.mcgraw-hill.com: **RESOURCES** **Student Resources:** Research and Inquiry **Teacher Resources:** Research and Inquiry
SL.4.5	Add audio recordings and visual displays to presentations when appropriate to enhance the development of main ideas or themes.	**TEACHER'S EDITION:** Unit 1: T156, T220, T284, T332, T334–T335 **Unit 2:** T156, T220, T284, T332, T334–T335 **Unit 3:** T92, T156, T332, T334–T335 **Unit 4:** T92, T156, T220, T332, T334–T335 **Unit 5:** T28, T92, T220, T332, T334–T335 **Unit 6:** T28, T220, T332, T334–T335 www.connected.mcgraw-hill.com: **RESOURCES** **Student Resources:** Research and Inquiry **Teacher Resources:** Research and Inquiry
SL.4.6	Differentiate between contexts that call for formal English (e.g., presenting ideas) and situations where informal discourse is appropriate (e.g., small-group discussion); use formal English when appropriate to task and situation. (See grade 4 Language standards 1 for specific expectations.)	**TEACHER'S EDITION:** Unit 1: T28, T220 **Unit 2:** T28 **Unit 4:** T92 **Unit 5:** T92 www.connected.mcgraw-hill.com: **RESOURCES** **Student Resources:** Research and Inquiry **Teacher Resources:** Research and Inquiry

College and Career Readiness Anchor Standards for LANGUAGE

The K-5 standards on the following pages define what students should understand and be able to do by the end of each grade. They correspond to the College and Career Readiness (CCR) anchor standards below by number. The CCR and grade-specific standards are necessary complements—the former providing broad standards, the latter providing additional specificity—that together define the skills and understandings that all students must demonstrate.

Conventions of English

1. Demonstrate command of the conventions of standard English grammar and usage when writing or speaking.

2. Demonstrate command of the conventions of standard English capitalization, punctuation, and spelling when writing.

Knowledge of Language

3. Apply knowledge of language to understand how language functions in different contexts, to make effective choices for meaning or style, and to comprehend more fully when reading and listening.

Vocabulary Acquisition and Use

4. Determine or clarify the meaning of unknown and multiple-meaning words and phrases by using context clues, analyzing meaningful word parts, and consulting general and specialized reference materials, as appropriate.

5. Demonstrate understanding of figurative language, word relationships, and nuances in word meanings.

6. Acquire and use accurately a range of general academic and domain-specific words and phrases sufficient for reading, writing, speaking, and listening at the college and career readiness level; demonstrate independence in gathering vocabulary knowledge when encountering an unknown term important to comprehension or expression.

CCSS Common Core State Standards
English Language Arts
Grade 4

Each standard is coded in the following manner:

Strand	Grade Level	Standard
L	4	1

Language Standards

Conventions of English		McGraw-Hill Reading Wonders
L.4.1	Demonstrate command of the conventions of standard English grammar and usage when writing or speaking.	
L.4.1a	Use relative pronouns (*who, whose, whom, which, that*) and relative adverbs (*where, when, why*).	**READING/WRITING WORKSHOP:** Grammar Handbook: 463–465, 468–469 **TEACHER'S EDITION: Unit 1:** T225, T226 **Unit 4:** T29, T34 **Unit 6:** T32, T33, T34, T63 www.connected.mcgraw-hill.com: **RESOURCES** **Student Resources:** Grammar Interactive Games and Activities, Music/Fine Arts Activities **Teacher Resources:** Music/Fine Arts Activities
L.4.1b	Form and use the progressive (e.g., *I was walking; I am walking; I will be walking*) verb tenses.	**READING/WRITING WORKSHOP:** Grammar Handbook: 458 **TEACHER'S EDITION: Unit 3:** T93, T96, T97, T98, T127 www.connected.mcgraw-hill.com: **RESOURCES** **Student Resources:** Grammar Interactive Games and Activities, Music/Fine Arts Activities **Teacher Resources:** Music/Fine Arts Activities
L.4.1c	Use modal auxiliaries (e.g., *can, may, must*) to convey various conditions.	**READING/WRITING WORKSHOP:** Grammar Handbook: 460–461 **TEACHER'S EDITION: Unit 3:** T157, T160, T161, T162, T191 www.connected.mcgraw-hill.com: **RESOURCES** **Student Resources:** Grammar Interactive Games and Activities, Music/Fine Arts Activities **Teacher Resources:** Music/Fine Arts Activities
L.4.1d	Order adjectives within sentences according to conventional patterns (e.g., a *small red bag* rather than a *red small bag*).	**READING/WRITING WORKSHOP:** Grammar Handbook: 466–467 **TEACHER'S EDITION: Unit 5:** T29, T32, T33, T34, T63 www.connected.mcgraw-hill.com: **RESOURCES** **Student Resources:** Grammar Interactive Games and Activities, Music/Fine Arts Activities **Teacher Resources:** Music/Fine Arts Activities
L.4.1e	Form and use prepositional phrases.	**READING/WRITING WORKSHOP:** Grammar Handbook: 471 **TEACHER'S EDITION: Unit 6:** T224, T225, T226, T255, T290, T319 www.connected.mcgraw-hill.com: **RESOURCES** **Student Resources:** Grammar Interactive Games and Activities, Music/Fine Arts Activities **Teacher Resources:** Music/Fine Arts Activities
L.4.1f	Produce complete sentences, recognizing and correcting inappropriate fragments and run-ons.	**READING/WRITING WORKSHOP:** Grammar Handbook: 450–451 **YOUR TURN PRACTICE BOOK:** 50 **TEACHER'S EDITION: Unit 1:** T29, T32, T34, T63, T93, T96, T98, T127, T160, T162, T191, T224, T225, T288, T289, T290, T291, T319 www.connected.mcgraw-hill.com: **RESOURCES** **Student Resources:** Grammar Interactive Games and Activities, Music/Fine Arts Activities **Teacher Resources:** Music/Fine Arts Activities

Language Standards

Conventions of English		McGraw-Hill Reading Wonders
L.4.1g	Correctly use frequently confused words (e.g., *to, too, two; there, their*).	**PHONICS/WORD STUDY WORKSTATION ACTIVITY CARDS:** 13, 14 **TEACHER'S EDITION:** Unit 4: T226, T282, T290, T299, T319 Unit 5: T219, T235 www.connected.mcgraw-hill.com: **RESOURCES** **Student Resources:** Grammar Interactive Games and Activities, Music/Fine Arts Activities **Teacher Resources:** Music/Fine Arts Activities
L.4.2	Demonstrate command of the conventions of standard English capitalization, punctuation, and spelling when writing.	
L.4.2a	Use correct capitalization.	**READING/WRITING WORKSHOP:** Grammar Handbook: 474–476 **TEACHER'S EDITION:** Unit 1: T35 Unit 2: T29, T32, T33, T34 Unit 3: T34 Unit 6: T98 www.connected.mcgraw-hill.com: **RESOURCES** **Student Resources:** Grammar Interactive Games and Activities, Music/Fine Arts Activities **Teacher Resources:** Music/Fine Arts Activities
L.4.2b	Use commas and quotation marks to mark direct speech and quotations from a text.	**READING/WRITING WORKSHOP:** Grammar Handbook: 479, 480 **TEACHER'S EDITION:** Unit 1: T226 Unit 4: T162 Unit 5: T32, T33, T34 Unit 6: T98, T226 www.connected.mcgraw-hill.com: **RESOURCES** **Student Resources:** Grammar Interactive Games and Activities, Music/Fine Arts Activities **Teacher Resources:** Music/Fine Arts Activities
L.4.2c	Use a comma before a coordinating conjunction in a compound sentence.	**READING/WRITING WORKSHOP:** Grammar Handbook: 479 **TEACHER'S EDITION:** Unit 1: T161, T162, T191, T225, T226, T255 Unit 5: T226, T290 Unit 6: T98 www.connected.mcgraw-hill.com: **RESOURCES** **Student Resources:** Grammar Interactive Games and Activities, Music/Fine Arts Activities **Teacher Resources:** Music/Fine Arts Activities
L.4.2d	Spell grade-appropriate words correctly, consulting references as needed.	**TEACHER'S EDITION:** Unit 1: T36, T62, T100, T126, T164, T190, T228, T254 Unit 2: T36, T62, T100, T126, T164, T190, T228, T254 Unit 3: T36, T62, T100, T126, T164, T190, T228, T254 Unit 4: T36, T62, T100, T126, T164, T190, T228, T254 Unit 5: T36, T62, T100, T126, T164, T190, T228, T254 Unit 6: T36, T62, T100, T126, T164, T190, T228, T254 www.connected.mcgraw-hill.com: **RESOURCES** **Student Resources:** Grammar Interactive Games and Activities, Music/Fine Arts Activities **Teacher Resources:** Music/Fine Arts Activities

Knowledge of Language		McGraw-Hill Reading Wonders
L.4.3	Use knowledge of language and its conventions when writing, speaking, reading, or listening.	
L.4.3a	Choose words and phrases to convey ideas precisely.	**READING/WRITING WORKSHOP:** Unit 1: 30–31, 44–45 Unit 2: 158–159 Unit 3: 188–189 Unit 4: 302–303 Unit 6: 390–391, 446–447 **YOUR TURN PRACTICE BOOK:** 10, 20, 100, 120, 200, 260, 300 **TEACHER'S EDITION:** Unit 1: T30, T61, T94, T125, T156, T189 Unit 2: T61, T94, T125, T189 Unit 3: T61, T94, T118, T125, T189, T253 Unit 4: T61, T92, T125, T156, T189, T222, T253 Unit 5: T28, T61, T125, T189, T253 Unit 6: T61, T92, T125, T189 www.connected.mcgraw-hill.com: **RESOURCES** **Student Resources:** Writer's Workspace
L.4.3b	Choose punctuation for effect.	**READING/WRITING WORKSHOP:** Grammar Handbook: 477 **TEACHER'S EDITION:** Unit 1: T34, T63 Unit 2: T94 Unit 6: T92 www.connected.mcgraw-hill.com: **RESOURCES** **Student Resources:** Writer's Workspace
L.4.3c	Differentiate between contexts that call for formal English (e.g., presenting ideas) and situations where informal discourse is appropriate (e.g., small-group discussion).	**TEACHER'S EDITION:** Unit 2: T28, T92, T94 Unit 3: T28, T220 Unit 4: T156 Unit 5: T156, T222, T224–T225 www.connected.mcgraw-hill.com: **RESOURCES** **Student Resources:** Writer's Workspace

Language Standards

Vocabulary Acquisition and Use		McGraw-Hill Reading Wonders
L.4.4	Determine or clarify the meaning of unknown and multiple-meaning words and phrases based on grade 4 reading and content, choosing flexibly from a range of strategies.	
L.4.4a	Use context (e.g., definitions, examples, or restatements in text) as a clue to the meaning of a word or phrase.	**READING/WRITING WORKSHOP:** Unit 1: 29, 57, 71 **Unit 2:** 115, 129 **Unit 3:** 173, 187 **Unit 4:** 273, 287 **Unit 5:** 359 **YOUR TURN PRACTICE BOOK:** 7, 27, 37, 67, 77, 107, 117, 177, 187, 237 **PHONICS/WORD STUDY WORKSTATION ACTIVITY CARDS:** 1, 3, 4, 7 **TEACHER'S EDITION:** Unit 1: T38, T54, T152, T153E, T166, T173, T178, T182, T189, T216, T217H, T230, T237, T242, T246, T253 **Unit 2:** T25P, T38, T88, T152, T153R, T166, T173, T178, T182, T189 **Unit 3:** T24, T25E, T25G, T25I, T25R, T38, T45, T50, T54, T61, T88, T89E, T102, T109, T114, T118, T125, T166 **Unit 4:** T38, T102, T153R, T166, T216, T217E, T217P, T230, T237, T242, T246, T253 **Unit 5:** T25U, T88, T89E, T89J, T153K, T216, T217H **Unit 6:** T88, T102, T109, T114, T118, T125 www.connected.mcgraw-hill.com: **RESOURCES** **Student Resources:** Vocabulary Interactive Games and Activities
L.4.4b	Use common, grade-appropriate Greek and Latin affixes and roots as clues to the meaning of a word (e.g., *telegraph*, *photograph*, *autograph*).	**READING/WRITING WORKSHOP:** Unit 3: 215, 229 **Unit 4:** 245 **Unit 5:** 345 **Unit 6:** 417 **YOUR TURN PRACTICE BOOK:** 137, 147, 157, 227, 277 **PHONICS/WORD STUDY WORKSTATION ACTIVITY CARDS:** 10, 11, 15 **TEACHER'S EDITION:** Unit 2: T26, T216, T217N, T217R, T219, T237, T242, T246, T253 Unit 3: T166, T216, T217L, T230, T237, T242, T246, T253 **Unit 4:** T38, T45, T50, T54, T61, T166, T219, T230, T235 **Unit 5:** T27, T152, T153G, T153R, T155, T166, T209 **Unit 6:** T91, T107, T152, T153G, T219, T230 www.connected.mcgraw-hill.com: **RESOURCES** **Student Resources:** Vocabulary Interactive Games and Activities
L.4.4c	Consult reference materials (e.g., dictionaries, glossaries, thesauruses), both print and digital, to find the pronunciation and determine or clarify the precise meaning of key words and phrases.	**READING/WRITING WORKSHOP:** Unit 6: 424–427 **TEACHER'S EDITION:** Unit 1: T24, T153G, T216, T217T **Unit 2:** T24, T25B, T216 **Unit 3:** T24, T152, T217K **Unit 4:** T24, T92, T152, T280, T284 **Unit 5:** T88, T152 **Unit 6:** T25B, T92, T214, T216 www.connected.mcgraw-hill.com: **RESOURCES** **Student Resources:** Vocabulary Interactive Games and Activities
L.4.5	Demonstrate understanding of figurative language, word relationships, and nuances in word meanings.	
L.4.5a	Explain the meaning of simple similes and metaphors (e.g., *as pretty as a picture*) in context.	**READING/WRITING WORKSHOP:** Unit 2: 157 **Unit 5:** 317 **Unit 6:** 445 **YOUR TURN PRACTICE BOOK:** 97, 207, 297 **PHONICS/WORD STUDY WORKSTATION ACTIVITY CARDS:** 9 **LITERATURE ANTHOLOGY:** Unit 2: 172–175, 176–177 **Unit 6:** 534–537, 538–539 **TEACHER'S EDITION:** Unit 2: T25F, T153L, T280, T281B, T281C **Unit 3:** T25K, T89I, T217F **Unit 4:** T153K, T153N **Unit 5:** T24, T25D, T25E, T25L, T25Q, T25R, T153L, T217O **Unit 6:** T25C, T89J, T280, T294 www.connected.mcgraw-hill.com: **RESOURCES** **Student Resources:** Vocabulary Interactive Games and Activities
L.4.5b	Recognize and explain the meaning of common idioms, adages, and proverbs.	**READING/WRITING WORKSHOP:** Unit 1: 43 **Unit 4:** 259 **Unit 5:** 373 **Unit 6:** 431 **LITERATURE ANTHOLOGY:** Unit 1: 37, 43 **YOUR TURN PRACTICE BOOK:** 17, 167, 247, 287 **PHONICS/WORD STUDY WORKSTATION ACTIVITY CARDS:** 2 **TEACHER'S EDITION:** Unit 1: T25H, T88, T89F, T102, T109, T114, T118, T125, T166 **Unit 2:** T25R, T28 **Unit 4:** T25F, T88, T89, T89H, T89P, T89V, T102, T109, T114, T118, T125 **Unit 5:** T89D, T153L, T280, T294, T301, T306, T310 **Unit 6:** T166, T216, T217G, T230 www.connected.mcgraw-hill.com: **RESOURCES** **Student Resources:** Vocabulary Interactive Games and Activities

Language Standards

Vocabulary Acquisition and Use		McGraw-Hill Reading Wonders
L.4.5c	Demonstrate understanding of words by relating them to their opposites (antonyms) and to words with similar but not identical meanings (synonyms).	**READING/WRITING WORKSHOP:** Unit 1: 29 Unit 2: 115 Unit 3: 201 Unit 4: 273 Unit 5: 359 **YOUR TURN PRACTICE BOOK:** 7, 67, 127, 177, 237 **PHONICS/WORD STUDY WORKSTATION ACTIVITY CARDS:** 1, 7 **TEACHER'S EDITION:** Unit 1: T24, T38, T45, T50, T54, T61, T102, T109, T237 Unit 2: T88, T89K, T89R, T102, T109, T114, T118, T125, T166, T237 Unit 3: T45, T152, T153H, T153T, T166, T173, T178, T182, T189, T230 Unit 4: T38, T45, T152, T153K, T166, T173, T178, T182, T189 Unit 5: T216, T217H, T217T, T230, T237, T242, T246, T253 Unit 6: T173 **www.connected.mcgraw-hill.com: RESOURCES** **Student Resources:** Vocabulary Interactive Games and Activities
L.4.6	Acquire and use accurately grade-appropriate general academic and domain-specific words and phrases, including those that signal precise actions, emotions, or states of being (e.g., *quizzed*, *whined*, *stammered*) and that are basic to a particular topic (e.g., *wildlife*, *conservation*, and *endangered* when discussing animal preservation).	**READING/WRITING WORKSHOP:** Unit 1: 20–21, 34–35, 48–49, 61–62, 76–77 Unit 2: 92–93, 106–107, 120–121, 134–135, 148–149 Unit 3: 164–165, 178–179, 192–193, 206–207, 220–221 Unit 4: 236–237, 250–251, 264–265, 278–279, Unit 5: 308–309, 322–323, 336–337, 350–351, 364–365 Unit 6: 380–381, 394–395, 408–409, 422–423, 436–437 **YOUR TURN PRACTICE BOOK:** 1, 11, 51, 61, 101, 111, 151, 161, 201, 211, 251, 261 **TEACHER'S EDITION:** Unit 1: T14, T38, T44, T45, T50, T54, T60, T173, T178, T182, T188, T206, T230, T236 Unit 2: T38, T44, T45, T50, T54, T60, T78, T102, T108, T109, T114, T118, T124, T142, T166, T172, T173, T178 Unit 3: T14, T38, T44, T50, T54, T60, T78, T102, T108, T109, T236, T237, T242, T246, T252 Unit 4: T114, T118, T124, T142, T172, T173, T178, T182, T188, T206, T236, T237 Unit 5: T14, T44, T45, T50, T54, T60, T78, T142, T206 Unit 6: T14, T44, T45, T50, T60, T78, T108, T142, T172, T178, T182 **www.connected.mcgraw-hill.com: RESOURCES** **Student Resources:** Vocabulary Interactive Games and Activities **Teacher Resources:** Build Background Videos, Graphic Organizers

CCSS Language Progressive Skills

Below are the grade 3 Language standards indicated by CCSS to be particularly likely to require continued attention in grade 4 as they are applied to increasingly sophisticated writing and speaking.

Language Progressive Skills

Standard		McGraw-Hill Reading Wonders
L.3.1f	Ensure subject-verb and pronoun-antecedent agreement.	**READING/WRITING WORKSHOP:** Grammar Handbook: 459, 463 **TEACHER'S EDITION:** Unit 2: T319 Unit 3: T98, T127, T162, T226, T255 Unit 4: T34, T63, T98, T162, T191, T255 www.connected.mcgraw-hill.com: **RESOURCES** **Student Resources:** Grammar Interactive Games and Activities, Music/Fine Arts Activities **Teacher Resources:** Music/Fine Arts Activities
L.3.3a	Choose words and phrases for effect.	**READING/WRITING WORKSHOP:** Unit 1: 30–31, 44–45 Unit 2: 158–159 Unit 3: 188–189 Unit 4: 302–303 Unit 6: 390–391, 446–447 **YOUR TURN PRACTICE BOOK:** 10, 20, 100, 120, 200, 260, 300 **TEACHER'S EDITION:** Unit 4: T92, T156, T222 Unit 5: T28 Unit 6: T92 www.connected.mcgraw-hill.com: **RESOURCES** **Student Resources:** Grammar Interactive Games and Activities, Music/Fine Arts Activities **Teacher Resources:** Music/Fine Arts Activities

Language Progressive Skills

Below are the grade 3 Language standards indicated by CCSS to be particularly likely to require continued attention in grade 4 as they are applied to increasingly sophisticated writing and speaking.

Language Progressive Skills	
Standard	McGraw-Hill Reading Wonders
L.3.1f Ensure subject-verb and pronoun-antecedent agreement.	**READING/WRITING WORKSHOP:** Grammar Handbook 459–463 **TEACHER'S EDITION:** Unit 2: T319; Unit 3: T95, T123, T163, T228, T295; Unit 4: T7K, T61, T95, T107, T191, T255 **www.connected.mcgraw-hill.com: RESOURCES** **Student Resources:** Grammar Interactive Games and Activities, Music/Fine Arts Activities **Teacher Resources:** Music/Fine Arts Activities
L.3.3a Choose words and phrases for effect.	**READING/WRITING WORKSHOP:** Unit 1: 11–17, 44–45; Unit 2: 103–109; Unit 3: 188–150; Unit 4: 302–303; Unit 6: 390–391, 446–447 **YOUR TURN PRACTICE BOOK:** 19, 20, 160, 170, 200, 300–300 **TEACHER'S EDITION:** Unit 1: T92, T156, T222; Unit 5: T78; Unit 6: T7V **www.connected.mcgraw-hill.com: RESOURCES** **Student Resources:** Grammar Interactive Games and Activities, Music/Fine Arts Activities **Teacher Resources:** Music/Fine Arts Activities